PEOPLE AND POLITICS

Willy Brandt

People and Politics
The Years 1960-1975

Translated from the German
by J. Maxwell Brownjohn

COLLINS
St James's Place, London   1978

William Collins Sons & Co. Ltd
London · Glasgow · Sydney · Auckland
Toronto · Johannesburg

Originally published in German under
the title *BEGEGNUNGEN UND EINSICHTEN*
Copyright © 1976 by Willy Brandt
First published by Hoffmann & Campe Verlag, Hamburg 1976

© In the English translation by William Collins
Sons & Co. Ltd London and Little, Brown & Company
New York 1978

ISBN 0 00 216501 5

Set in Garamond

Made and Printed in Great Britain by
William Collins Sons & Co. Ltd Glasgow

Contents

Foreword		11
1	The Wall	13
2	The End of the Adenauer Era	42
3	John F. Kennedy	70
4	Minor Steps	94
5	Conversations with de Gaulle	114
6	The Grand Coalition	138
7	Federal Foreign Minister	151
8	Ostpolitik	166
9	1968	198
10	The Palais Schaumburg	223
11	European Unification	239
12	Washington	278
13	Moscow	323
14	Erfurt, Kassel and Berlin	366
15	Warsaw and other Landmarks	398
16	A Change of Direction?	429
17	Crises and Opportunities	451
18	Outlook	494
Index		505

Illustrations

Chancellor Adenauer and Burgomaster
Brandt   *between pages* 152-3
With President de Gaulle
With Edward Heath
Tel Aviv, 1973
With President Kaunda
At the memorial in the Warsaw ghetto
With President Pompidou   *opposite page* 320
Walking with Indira Gandhi
Fishing off Florida   321
Leningrad, July 1975   336
Tête-à-tête with the Shah
     With Mr Brezhnev   337
     Conversation with Kissinger and Schmidt

Illustrations

Abbreviations

ABDA	American-British-Dutch-Australian Command
ABM	Anti-ballistic missile
ADA	Americans for Democratic Action
BND	Federal (West) German Intelligence Service
CDU	Christian Democratic Union Party
CIA	Central Intelligence Agency (USA)
CMEA	Council for Mutual Economic Aid (Comecon)
CPSU	Communist Party of the Soviet Union
CSCE	Conference on Security and Cooperation in Europe
CSSR	Czechoslovak Socialist Republic
CSU	Christian Social Union (Bavarian sister party of the CDU)
DDP	German Democratic Party
DDR	German Democratic Republic (East Germany)
DGB	(West) German Trade Union Congress
DKP	German Communist Party (newly founded in West Germany 1968)
DM	Deutsche Mark
DNVP	German National People's Party
DP	German Party
DPA	(West) German News Agency
DVP	German People's Party
ECE	Economic Commission for Europe (UN)
EDC	European Defence Community
EEC	European Economic Community (Common Market)
EFTA	European Free Trade Area
EKD	Evangelical Church of Germany
ERP	European Recovery Plan (Marshall Plan)

FDGB	Free (East) German Trade Union Congress
FDP	Free Democratic Party
FDR	Federal German Republic (West Germany)
FRG	*ditto*
GDR	German Democratic Republic (East Germany)
ICBM	Intercontinental ballistic missile
KPD	German Communist Party (original)
LCY	League of Communists of Yugoslavia
MBFR	Mutually Balanced Force Reductions
MLF	Multilateral Force
MIRV	Multiple independently targeted re-entry vehicle
NATO	North Atlantic Treaty Organization
NPD	National Democratic Party (of Germany)
OECD	Organization for Economic Cooperation and Development
OPEC	Organization of Petroleum Exporting Countries
PCI	Italian Communist Party
PCP	Portuguese Communist Party
PLO	Palestine Liberation Organization
PSP	Portuguese Socialist Party
SALT	Strategic Arms Limitation Talks
SDS	Socialist German Student Federation
SED	Socialist Unity Party (East German ruling party)
SPD	Social Democratic Party
UN	United Nations
UNESCO	United Nations Educational, Scientific and Cultural Organization
UNICEF	United Nations International Children's Emergency Fund
WEU	Western European Union

Foreword

After resigning the office of Federal Chancellor in spring 1974 I was asked if the time had not come to assemble my personal recollections. It seemed appropriate to draw up a preliminary account of the years during which I bore political responsibility as Mayor of Berlin, head of government of the German Federal Republic and Chairman of the German Social Democratic Party.

In working on this book I have concentrated largely on attempting to trace lines of thought and action directed towards problems insoluble by one country alone but crucial to the fate of its citizens. The following account may convey the impression that I had to concern myself almost exclusively with foreign policy. This is not so, but the circumstances and history of the Federal Republic invest its foreign relations with special importance. I did my best to allow for this.

The changes induced by a policy may be slow or swift. In either event, the ideas of those involved are affected by extraneous circumstances. Sometimes, therefore, my record of personal and political experiences will mirror developments at various stages and from the aspect of more than one participant or observer. This will illuminate the stratified and complex nature of a policy, its variations and transformations. The reader will also discover that many things – particularly in my own attitude – remain unaltered.

It will become apparent that numerous passages are based on notes as well as memory. I have been at pains to avoid damaging my country's interests and hampering the future development of a policy of practical co-operation. In other words, I have told the truth without being indiscreet.

This book, which will be followed by a second volume dealing with my early years, is not simply a translation of the German edition which appeared in early summer 1976. Many aspects of the German political scene are of minor interest to the foreign reader. A few terms and concepts required explanation, just as some events and developments had to be more closely defined. I have also tried, wherever possible, to lay additional stress on matters of special interest to the British and American public.

The present account is not my final word. I hope to be able to contribute still further to the attainment of the objectives that have always been my concern: peaceful co-operation and a proper blend of freedom and justice.

Bonn, autumn 1977   Willy Brandt

I

The Wall

13 August 1961, the day on which the building of the 'Wall' was decreed, was a hot summer Sunday. Unable to spend their holidays outside the city, many of my fellow-citizens had been looking forward to a carefree swim in one of the lakes on the city's outskirts – perhaps to a few hours' reading. They were startled to hear the early morning news: Berlin had been divided and sealed off. 13 August became a day of horror, alarm and bewilderment.

News of the closure – the physical wall was not actually erected until three days later, under the supervision of armed contingents – reached me as I was travelling by train from Nuremberg to Kiel. I had addressed a big party gathering at Nuremberg the day before and planned to launch the election campaign proper at Kiel that Sunday. Just five weeks separated us from the Bundestag elections, in which my political associates had nominated me as their candidate for the Chancellorship.

It was dawn when a railway official knocked at the door of my compartment. He informed me that a complete closure of the Eastern Sector had begun, and that I was requested to return to Berlin by the fastest possible route. Accompanied by a small party of colleagues, I left the train at Hanover at about 5 a.m., caught the early morning flight to Berlin and drove at once from Tempelhof Airport to the sector boundary, first Potsdamer Platz and then the Brandenburg Gate. I surveyed the barriers that had been hauled into place in the past few hours and were now being reinforced with a truly German attention to detail. Concrete posts had been sunk in the streets and were being draped with barbed wire. I saw some of the strong military units – East German, not Russian – whose instructions were to seal the border. I looked into the vacant eyes of uniformed compatriots doing their duty on the other side. Above all, I saw concern and despair written on the faces of my fellow-citizens of West Berlin.

Like any responsible person in an emergency, I felt it incumbent on me to act rather than look on helplessly. It was hard to remain calm and composed. We had been obliged to keep our heads in many an earlier Berlin crisis. Though not a direct military threat, this was the gravest challenge since the Blockade of 1948. Then, it had been we who were segregated from the outside world by force; this time, a régime was segregating itself and its citizens from us. Even so, the feverish work on the barricades and the heavily armed border guards presented a menacing picture. According to our interpretation of the city's 'Four-Power status', East German forces had no business in the territory of East Berlin. Were we to swallow this crude violation of the law governing and pertaining to Germany? Were we to tolerate what was being done to our compatriots, the citizens of East Berlin and the 'Zone'? Would the Allies sit back and accept this new development? Would we again be 'fobbed off' – as more than one person phrased it that Sunday morning – with feeble protests?

At the Rathaus – Berlin's city hall – I conducted a special session of the Senate, as our municipal government was called in line with the Hanseatic tradition set by Lübeck, Hamburg and Bremen (because we were only half a city but a whole *Land* within the meaning of the Basic Law, Germany's post-war constitution). Later that morning I drove to the Allied Kommandantura building for the first and only time in my years as Mayor, my normal practice being to meet the Western Commandants at their residences, at my office in the Rathaus or in a private setting. I was surprised to find the Kommandantura still adorned with a picture of General Kotikov, the last Soviet Commandant, whom the Kremlin had ordered to vacate the building over thirteen years before. The Allies had left his photograph where it was – not, presumably, as a token of respect but in pedantic observance of the city's Four-Power status, which remained valid there. They even reserved a place at the conference table for his notional successor.

The three Western Allies – or, as we used to call them in Berlin, our Protecting Powers – were confronted by grave problems on this 13 August. The Russians had transferred all essential areas of control over East Berlin to the government of the GDR. The latter sent in troops, assumed unilateral control of internal means of communication and controlled passenger traffic. Such inhabitants of West Berlin as were, in the usual arbitrary manner, termed 'peace-loving' received permission to cross the border for a further ten-day period. Thereafter, and until the signing of the passes agreement at the end of 1963, border traffic was abruptly and totally suspended for Berliners – though not for West

Germans, who could still visit the GDR provided they paid the stipulated toll.

The Interior Minister of the GDR issued regulations affecting the Allies themselves. Though not in principle denied access to the eastern part of the city – provocation was not carried to those lengths – the Americans, British and French were restricted to specified crossing-points. Within a few days, the only one left available to them was the Friedrichstrasse access which gained worldwide notoriety as 'Checkpoint Charlie'. The truly novel and dramatic feature of the situation – a development of fundamental importance – was that the Western Powers were complying not with Russian but with 'East German' orders. To put it more bluntly, the mighty United States was letting itself be pushed around, in contemporary parlance, by a 'satellite' of the other super-power.

The Allied Commandants and their civilian deputies, who were foreign office personnel, felt just as disconcerted and disoriented that 13 August as did we, their German partners in Berlin. They gave us an attentive hearing but could not so much as lodge a protest with the Soviet Commandant at Karlshorst in default of instructions from their various capitals – it was Sunday! Scanning the troubled faces of my American friends, I could imagine what had happened. They had alerted the Pentagon, the State Department and the White House, only to be told that ungovernable reactions must be avoided at all costs. Besides, West Berlin was under no immediate threat . . . The Russians kept order in their German domain, as one US Senator put it. They employed brutal methods, to be sure, but one could understand their desire to halt the unceasing flow of refugees that threatened to bleed the 'Zone' to death, economically and intellectually.

The Commandants did not, of course, disguise their sympathy for our citizens. They had grown close to 'their' Berliners and had come to identify themselves with the city's problems, but they were expressly advised that 'trouble' was undesirable and strictly forbidden to act on their own initiative. Negotiations would have to be preceded by con-sultations between Washington, London and Paris. If any reference was made to Bonn in this context, it could only have been peripheral.

The President of the United States was on his yacht, but his day of rest did not go undisturbed. He must have been primarily interested in knowing whether any Allied rights in West Berlin had been directly infringed. This was not the case. On the other hand, Allied rights pertaining to Berlin as a whole had been almost contemptuously brushed aside.

We were later able to glean from the memoirs of Kennedy's

associates that Khrushchev's ultimatum and the possibility of a nuclear crisis preyed more heavily on the President than any other problem because events in Berlin seemed to threaten a war capable of destroying civilization – 'and he thought about little else that summer' (Arthur Schlesinger Jr). At the beginning of August, the President remarked to one of his aides that Khrushchev would probably have to undertake some action (in the GDR) in order to regain control of the situation. He went on: 'I can set the alliance in motion if he (Khrushchev) does something against West Berlin, but not if he starts something in East Berlin.' Since a few crossing-points still remained open, the tendency in Washington on that grim August Sunday was to believe that the Russians and their East German allies meant to curb the flow of refugees rather than stem it altogether – in retrospect, an incomprehensible miscalculation. This, to quote one witness, 'would scarcely have been a reason for marching into the Eastern Sector, thereby provoking a counter-blow and risking war'.

I was equally destitute of proposals for any real counter-measures at the morning meeting on 13 August in the Allied Kommandantura, but I did urge that a protest be lodged, not only in Moscow but in the capitals of the other Warsaw Pact countries in whose name a statement justifying the closure had just been issued. (The central organ of the SED announced on Sunday morning that the closure of East Berlin accorded with a decision reached some days earlier by the Warsaw Pact governments, though this official 'blessing' did not necessarily imply that the operation had been unopposed.) 'At least send some patrols to the sector border immediately,' I said, 'to combat the sense of insecurity and show the West Berliners that they are not in jeopardy.'

Twenty hours elapsed before the military patrols I had requested appeared on the city's internal border.

Forty hours elapsed before a legal protest was dispatched to the Soviet Commandant.

Seventy-two hours elapsed before a protest – couched in terms that were little more than routine – was lodged in Moscow.

On the evening of 13 August our Berlin Chamber of Deputies met in special session. My task was to voice the outrage of our fellow-citizens but restrain them and counsel prudence. It was not the first or last time this duty fell to me, and I did not always find it easy to perform. Seldom if ever during my mayoral term had the meaning of impotent fury been more gallingly apparent to me. Separation from those across the Wall was not just a political problem to be dismissed as a remote abstraction – it affected millions of people. Ties were being sundered between countless individuals who loved, needed and depended on each other, between us and many friends on the other side, fellow social democrats who had boldly stood their ground. (Our party was not banned in East Berlin and led a legal but shadowy existence there, as opposed to the 'Zone', where its amalgamation with the communist KPD into the SED, or German Socialist Unity Party, had been universally enforced in 1946.) I did not pay many visits to East Berlin during the years between the Blockade and the Wall but had occasionally called on my political associates there. They, in turn, had still been able to participate regularly in our discussions in West Berlin.

World War II had reduced Berlin to a sea of rubble. Rebuilding had proceeded considerably faster in the western sectors than in the eastern part of the city. West Berlin, with its two-and-a-quarter million inhabitants, had again become Germany's largest industrial city after weathering a period of severe unemployment. It was also making strides as a scientific and cultural centre, and its artistic achievements enjoyed widespread esteem. One noticeable concomitant of all these things was a certain insularity bred by the absence of a territorial hinterland and restricted communication with West Germany. Doubts about the future were offset by a substantial dose of local pride. Irrespective of social status, the Berliners were touchingly devoted to their little homeland.

How, I wondered, would the people of Berlin withstand the shock and strain? We had assured them, repeatedly and in good faith, that we would not allow access to be barred. Now the bar had fallen and we were helpless. It must have seemed painfully obvious to many people, just as it did to me, that Berlin's claim to be the German capital-in-retirement had been shaken. The rupture was a deep one indeed, and not for me alone, and it prompted consideration of how our people (and a divided Europe) would fare against such a background.

My sole contact with the Bonn authorities that 13 August was a telephone call from the Federal Foreign Minister, Heinrich von Brentano. He stated that we must co-operate closely from now on. That was all. Adenauer said nothing. A US observer in Washington noted ironically that Bonn was dominated by a twofold fear: that the Americans might turn soft – or stand firm.

The events of 13 August 1961 were not a bolt from the blue. How much did the Allies know? Who had discovered what in advance? Common enough at the time, these questions later became more frequent. It has sometimes been surmised that I had received forewarnings of some kind because only this would account for my public pronouncements

P.P.—B

in the days immediately preceding. On 11 August, before travelling to Nuremberg, I had called on the Federal Foreign Minister in Bonn and urgently stressed the danger of rigorous closures, pointing out that self-preservation alone would probably impel the GDR authorities to seek approval of drastic expedients from their Soviet masters. Speaking in the Marktplatz at Nuremberg on the afternoon of 12 August, I reported that the number of people deserting the East in a single 24-hour period had exceeded 2500 for the first time – and emphasized the gravity of the situation. I added that it was not, as everyone knew, my habit to cry wolf. To quote: 'We all know our compatriots in the Zone fear that their escape route may be cut off, that they may be left on their own and locked in.'

Had I genuinely known what would happen, I should never have retired to my sleeper in the Kiel express but flown back to Berlin at once. I had discerned only the basic situation, not the timing and actual course of events. I had a more immediate sense of mounting drama than others who were remote from the scene. In other words, I reproached myself afterwards for being lulled by the thought that it was still far from certain *when* anything would happen.

I cannot judge whether any realistic inferences could have been drawn from intelligence reports. No hints were conveyed to me by the German or Allied intelligence services, and it genuinely seems that preparations for the closure were camouflaged with total success. BND and CIA, British Secret Service and French – all the Western intelligence networks appear to have been deceived. This remains a noteworthy circumstance. West Berlin was regarded, probably with justification, as a high-yield intelligence centre. It is quite possible, of course, that interesting reports petered out within the networks because the political and military authorities were, as we shall see, prepared for another type of crisis.

It is possible that many people regarded what actually happened in Berlin as a lesser evil. Be that as it may, the patent ineffectiveness of the intelligence services – or so it seemed to me – was highlighted by Walter Ulbricht's brazen assertion at a press conference on 15 June that nobody intended to erect any wall ... Rumours were also rife that the Western Powers had received intimations via their military missions at the Soviet Headquarters in Potsdam that certain measures were imminent which did not, however, affect Allied interests. This was officially denied, though not in such a way as to dispel all doubt.

Others alleged that John McCloy, US High Commissioner during the early years of the Federal Republic, was warned at the end of July while visiting the Black Sea resort of Sochi to negotiate problems of disarmament with Nikita Khrushchev on his President's behalf. When I raised this with McCloy a few months later, he formally and credibly assured me that he had received no such hint. Stung by a Kennedy speech, Khrushchev had given vent to generalized threats which were more indicative of a readiness to engage in military confrontation.

Probably more important than the question of the intelligence services' effectiveness is the simple fact that the Allies had been tremulously awaiting a phoney crisis. So had the Federal Government. To be more explicit: what we in Berlin regarded as a cruel blow may almost have come as a relief to others. The separate peace treaty with the GDR, so often threatened by the Russians, had not been concluded, nor had the presence of the Allied garrisons been called in question. Above all, war did not seem imminent. Things had been different early that summer.

In May, Secretary of Defence McNamara had reported to the President that existing plans would, in the event of military confrontation, entail an almost immediate transition to nuclear war. Because he regarded this as a lethal limitation in the most literal sense, Kennedy commissioned plans for a non-nuclear response when conferring with the Secretary of State, the Secretary of Defence and General Taylor, head of the Joint Chiefs of Staff, at Hyannis Port early in July.

Prior to these consultations, various scenarios had been submitted to the President by his experts, who included Dr Kissinger. The sole outcome of Kennedy's political planning assignment was an inconclusive meeting of Western Foreign Ministers in Paris at the beginning of August. Many people must later have wondered if it would not have been wise to invite the Russians to a Four-Power conference, as London had – without opposition from Bonn – suggested.

When it was all over, commentators had little difficulty in rationally dovetailing the Wall's traumatic construction into the pattern of contemporary history and in perceiving the logic of a development that had begun much earlier. They saw the Wall as confirming a delimitation of the interests reserved by the victorious powers at the end of the war; as setting the seal on an administrative separation of East from West to which Berlin had, in all essential respects, been subject since 1948; and as a consequence of the fact that two states had grown up on German soil.

At the time, however, it was asking too much of people merely to register outrage and calmly regard the closure as a function of world events. Fury and despair were the only natural response to the bisection of a metropolitan organism inhabited by millions and the thousandfold severance of family ties. Our compatriots in the other part of Germany realized only too clearly that they had lost a potential haven, for escape via West Berlin had not been unduly difficult. To many of them, the possibility of occasional meetings in our city with friends and relations from the West had meant even more.

The shock travelled westwards, too. Despite Bonn's manifest paralysis, Germans in the Federal Republic wondered how this major Berlin crisis would end – the third since the 1948 Blockade and the Khrushchev ultimatum of 1958. Would the Allies continue to give West Berlin their full support? Would they be able to ensure that Four-Power responsibility for Germany as a whole – that of the three Western Powers and the Soviet Union – remained inviolate? Beyond the borders of Germany as well, people wondered anxiously if complications would arise which might lead to open conflict between the super-powers.

The latter danger had almost receded, but this was far from fully apparent on 13 August. Certainty always comes with hindsight. To the mayor of a divided city which had remained united in the minds of its citizens, few things could have seemed graver than the events of 13 August and all the attendant human tragedies that defied statistical definition. As a German politician with European responsibilities, I was compelled to question the significance of this drastic rupture, above and beyond its immediate injustices.

I said later that in August 1961 a curtain was drawn aside to reveal an empty stage. To put it more bluntly, we lost certain illusions that had outlived the hopes underlying them – illusions that clung to something which no longer existed in fact. Ulbricht had been allowed to take a swipe at the Western super-power, and the United States merely winced with annoyance. My political deliberations in the years that followed were substantially influenced by this day's experience, and it was against this background that my so-called Ostpolitik – the beginning of détente – took shape. I do not mean the determination to reach an understanding: that I never lacked, even when we had to defend ourselves during the Cold War, nor – particularly during the most 'militant' years – did I ever view the Berlin problem except in terms of its effect on the securing of peace. My new and inescapable realization was that traditional patterns of Western policy had proved ineffective, if not downright unrealistic.

The beginning of June 1961 had witnessed a meeting in Vienna between Nikita S. Khrushchev, the rugged Kremlin overlord, and John F. Kennedy, youthful President of the United States. The Soviet leader gave notice of his decision to conclude a separate peace treaty with the GDR by the year's end and – something which had long been mooted – confer free-city status on West Berlin. This would have meant not only the end of Quadripartite responsibility for Germany as a whole but the termination of Allied rights in Berlin (although Khrushchev was, he cautiously added, prepared to accept the presence of Western troops under certain conditions). The Soviet leader's threats could hardly have been more blatant. If the United States wanted war, he said, that was its own affair. Kennedy's parting remark to his opposite number was that it was going to be a 'cold winter'. He had informed Khrushchev in the course of their hard-hitting discussions that he refused to accept any ultimatum – he had not become President in order to lead his country into isolation. The United States had fought its way to Berlin and its continuing presence in the city was based on treaty rights. If it suffered itself to be 'dismissed' from Berlin, its undertakings and obligations would be regarded as scraps of paper. The abandonment of West Berlin would mean the abandonment of Western Europe, which was indispensable to the security of America. The supposition is that Kennedy did not discuss East Berlin in Vienna. Back in Washington, he reported to the nation that 'our most sombre talks were on the subject of Germany and Berlin'. At the same time he made it clear that the Americans were not seeking to change the existing situation. The Western Powers could not, however, renounce their obligations to the people of West Berlin.

This clarified something which many people had consistently ignored: that when the Americans said Berlin they meant West Berlin, Allied rights, and our protection. At the NATO meeting in Oslo in April 1961, three basic essentials had been formulated: an Allied military presence, free access, and viability for West Berlin. We did not regard these formulations as wholly satisfactory. Did right of free access apply to the Allies alone, or was it at last, after all the restrictions and harassment to which we had been subjected since the end of the Blockade, to become a reality for Germans too? Were the Allies sufficiently aware that West Berlin's viability would be guaranteed only if the city retained its organic links with the West German economic system and with the Federal Republic? Finally, did the three 'essentials' mean that the Russians could do as they pleased in, and with, East Berlin?

My friends and I speculated that we might be faced with a substantial worsening of the present position, a *status quo minus*, if efforts were limited to a defence of the *status quo*. I hazarded the possibility of expanding and, at the same time, modifying this theme. Why, if suitable guarantees were given, should negotiations not be instituted regarding free-city status for the whole of Berlin? I said I knew that such a solution had been contemplated on the Russian side in recent years – a senior Foreign Office official had drawn my attention to this – but that it had been vigorously opposed by the GDR authorities. Early in July I got Berlin's plenipotentiary in Bonn to ask the Federal Government whether it might not be advisable to propose Berlin's reunification to the Russians rather than narrow the scope for debate still further. Our suggestion fell on stony ground. Bonn replied that we must cling to the *status quo* and be extremely chary of new proposals.

This was easily said and spared mental exertion, as I realized a second time when I sought to bring pressure to bear on the Western Foreign Ministers' Conference in Paris at the beginning of August. An official Berlin representative in Bonn was instructed to raise the question of how the Allies proposed to react if East Berlin were sealed off. He never got further than the German delegation, where it was intimated to him that the Allies must not be distracted from the real subject under review. This was the threat of a separate peace treaty with the GDR, from which would flow the consequences we feared for Berlin – additional confirmation of my belief that the West was concentrating on the wrong crisis.

During the summer of 1961 I also queried in public – not for the first time – whether there was not a great deal to be said for accepting the Russian peace conference proposal instead of blocking discussion of the German question from the Western side or simply leaving it in the air. I thought that Khrushchev should be taken at his word and his demands met with something which would find support among all the countries ranged against Hitler Germany during the war.

The settlement of Germany's fate could not, I said, be left to the Soviet Union alone. Discounting us Germans, who were primarily affected, it concerned every country that had helped to defeat the Third Reich. Any peace treaty should be regarded as a matter for all the victorious powers. Furthermore, the rights of the United States in Berlin and Germany were just as legitimate as those of the Soviet Union. In making these remarks, which I delivered at a Bonn press conference, I felt certain that the US Government could be sold on such a procedure. Kennedy clearly indicated this in a broadcast to the nation at the end of July. He declared that the United States had no intention of leaving it to others to 'choose and monopolize the forum and the framework of discussion'. He was also prepared to allow Berlin and the German people as a whole to vote on the presence of American troops. Bonn considered all this too risky. Adenauer, with whom I discussed the matter more than once, had himself (in 1960) raised the idea of a referendum in West Berlin. I could not reconcile myself to limiting the issue to the Allied presence. My concern was to see membership of the Federation confirmed and dispel any impression that the vested rights of the Western Powers could be abrogated. Adenauer, in his turn, opposed my favourable approach to the idea of a peace treaty conference.

John F. Kennedy's Berlin speech was the fruit of thorough and painstaking preparation. Dean Acheson, who had served President Truman as Secretary of State and was now charged with elaborating a strategy for Berlin in consultation with the Allies, had warned of an impending crisis in a report submitted at the beginning of the year. He recommended massive nuclear deterrence and a substantially larger military budget (consequent on a big increase in Soviet arms expenditure). He saw little scope for negotiation. Kennedy resolved on a middle course: military reinforcement (though less drastic than proposed), a more flexible deterrent (designed to leave more time and space between non-war and a nuclear holocaust), and a basic readiness to negotiate. The President also rejected Acheson's suggestion that a state of national emergency be proclaimed. At the same time he declared:

> We cannot and will not permit the Communists to drive us out of Berlin gradually or by force. The fulfilment of our pledge to that city is essential to the morale and security of West Germany, to the unity of Western Europe, to the faith of the entire free world . . . We will at all times be ready to talk, if talk will help. But we must also be ready to resist with force, if force is used upon us.

This 'middle course' was in line with the attitude I considered proper and necessary, though Khrushchev described Kennedy's words (to John McCloy) as 'belligerent' and 'hysterical' and threatened to step up the pressure.

In reality, the Kremlin leaders had nonetheless modified their programme after Khrushchev's Vienna meeting with the President. Although Moscow repeated the demand for a peace treaty at the beginning of August, it added that there was no intention of infringing the legitimate rights of the Western Powers, and that no blockade of West Berlin was planned.

One of President Kennedy's advisers called the building of the Wall 'a crisis within a crisis'. He regarded the tragedy as one more stage in the great dispute over Berlin and Germany. Kennedy probably shared this view. The Russians began by describing the Wall as 'a protective measure against subversive activities and the slave trade'. It was later upgraded, with unparalleled propagandist effrontery, into the 'Peace Wall'. Setting aside such cosmetic inanities, one is left with the concept of 'protection'. Loathsome though it seemed to us, the Russians may well have regarded the Wall as a rearguard position from which to defend the GDR and an important item of Soviet property – in other words, a brutally extorted chance to consolidate the East German communist state, which had to be safeguarded against the loss of its major capital: large numbers of able-bodied workers. Over 3 million Germans had fled to West Germany from the Soviet-occupied zone. In 1961 the figures rose alarmingly: 20,000 in June, 30,000 in July, and nearly 1500 a day during the first ten days of August. They included numerous academics, skilled workers and young people. No feat of the imagination is required to grasp why Ulbricht must repeatedly and urgently have demanded the adoption of a form of 'protective custody' for his citizens.

This achieved a substantial measure of what Khrushchev's ultimatum had been designed to effect at the end of 1958. Confusion on the German side and a certain loss of faith in the Allies were, from the Soviet angle, a welcome bonus.

In fact, the Western Powers took a long time to realize what the limited crisis meant in comparison with their fears of the foregoing months. Even the central government offices in the various capitals remained unmanned on Sunday 13 August. No special crisis team assembled at the White House. Kennedy spent his weekend sailing and Adenauer was preoccupied with the election campaign. Adenauer did not visit Berlin for ten days, a fact which my ever critical fellow-citizens resented. The excuse was that an earlier visit by the Federal Chancellor might have precipitated disturbances in the 'Zone'. At the end of August, Adenauer himself offered the startling theory that Khrushchev had had the Wall constructed for the electoral benefit of my party.

What appeared to us in the West, and especially in Berlin, to be a new and major crisis may have been seen by the Soviet leadership as an escape from another and even greater crisis: the one triggered by Khrushchev himself in the late autumn of 1958. At that time the Kremlin demanded that West Berlin be transformed into a 'free' city within six months – free not only from close ties with the Federal Republic but also from the garrisons of the Western Protecting Powers. (We christened this status not *frei* but *Vogelfrei*, or 'outlawed'.) It also threatened to conclude a separate peace treaty with the GDR if no peace treaty with both the German states came into being. Although this ultimatum aroused deep alarm and concern in the West, it also engendered a hardening of attitudes. Khrushchev later defused his threat. Voluminous exchanges of notes and public speeches ensued on the Four-Power Foreign Ministers' Conference in summer 1959. At Geneva, representatives of the two German states participated for the first time – at separate tables.

By the late summer of 1961 it had to be acknowledged that the closure of East Berlin to the West was a reality: the form of coexistence that had evolved in Berlin was no more. The Russians and the GDR accepted the political and psychological débâcle of the Wall's construction because they attached greater importance to an ability to consolidate the GDR behind it. Nobody can now deny that this opportunity has been exploited.

But what could we have done? I often asked myself in later years why our demands had to take so maladroit, not to say impotent, a form. We issued appeals to boycott the Leipzig Fair and helped to paralyse inter-German sport for a time, but our sole achievement was a feeble continuation of policy by non-political means which were never more than half-hearted. When considering the possibility of suspending inter-zonal trade, the Berlin Task Force in Washington – representatives of the three Western Powers and the German Embassy – rejected even this measure as 'too drastic'. I clearly recall John F. Kennedy irritably remarking not long afterwards that nobody – neither the German Federal Government nor the Mayor of Berlin – had advised him to remove the Wall by force. That was enough. Arthur Schlesinger is correct in reporting of a conversation with me that nobody recommended direct counter-measures on 13 August because the risk of a military confrontation was considered too great, and that I declined to reinterpret my attitude after the event. Such acknowledgements are not enough, however.

To restate the position clearly: while not imposing its demands in full, the Soviet Union had defied the major power in the Western world and effectively humiliated it. The Western Powers, with the United States at their head, were compelled to tolerate measures formally enacted in the name of a 'satellite régime'.

There were good reasons for contending that the Soviet decision to allow the GDR to assume control of East Berlin had created a vacuum in terms of international law. It followed that it would have been legally tenable to replenish that vacuum by invoking the hard-worked concept of Quadripartite status. In practice, this would have entailed a decision on the part of the Western Powers to occupy East Berlin militarily. I said at the time that, however logical this might be, it was certainly impracticable. The Allies could nonetheless have sought by means of vigorous diplomatic moves, coupled with a show of military strength on the sector boundary, to compel the Russians to acknowledge and avow their own responsibility for East Berlin. The Soviet leadership still attached importance to the exercise of a victorious power's rights in and over Germany, and a simultaneous invitation to negotiate might have made it easier for Khrushchev to reconsider the problems of status. This was the line I urged in those days – though not, I must admit, with anything like enough force and clarity.

There are not the smallest grounds for boasting of Federal German ingenuity or Bonn's resolute attitude. Foreign Minister Heinrich von Brentano had, as I have said, stressed the need for close co-operation in a telephone call on the evening of 13 August. On 14 August Konrad Adenauer opened the 'hot' phase of the election campaign with some remarks calculated to discredit my career. Berlin was, for all that, visited by a party of senior Bonn parliamentarians the same day. We drove to the Brandenburg Gate. GDR soldiers had dragged barriers across our side of what we and the world had long regarded – since 17 June 1953, since Hitler's brown-shirted torchlight parade on 30 January 1933, or even since Napoleon's entry into the Prussian capital – as perhaps the most outstanding symbol of German history. We stared across. Members of the 'People's Police' were bringing up water-cannon and dispersing East Berlin citizens who were watching us and timidly trying to wave. Suddenly a young man broke away and ran towards us past the barriers. I shall never forget the scene or the look on his face, which was a mixture of joyous excitement and cool determination. He had spotted his fleeting opportunity in a flash – no soldier would have dared to fire in the direction of the President of the Bundestag and the Governing Mayor – and used us to cover his escape. His gamble paid off. We didn't reproach him for taking it when we spoke to him afterwards. His own words were recorded as follows: 'I'd been trying to get across for hours. When Brandt arrived the People's Police were all eyes. That's when I spotted my chance and ran for it.'

Bonn officialdom seemed far removed from all this. On 16 August Adenauer received Soviet Ambassador Smirnov, and it was announced that they had agreed 'not to enlarge the present object of contention'. Smirnov informed Adenauer that Soviet measures were not directed against the Federal Republic. Adenauer replied that the Federal Government would take no steps which might impair relations with the Soviet Union and aggravate the international situation. The Federal Chancellor also remarked to journalists a few weeks later that he might be meeting Khrushchev. The latter had told Ambassador Kroll at the beginning of September that he would gladly see Adenauer and expound his policy to him. This showed that the old Chancellor had greater flexibility than many people credited him with.

I do not condemn the widespread attempts that were made to play the situation down. Reviewing the course of events, however, one cannot help wondering whether the days between 13 and 16 August – between the erection of temporary barriers and the building of the Wall itself – were used as they ought to have been: whether a change for the better might not, after all, have been effected by combining imagination and goodwill, flexibility and firmness. I cannot tell whether such a change would have been achieved. I only know that it was never seriously attempted.

It should be remembered that, for three whole days, nothing was done which might have prompted the Russians to reconsider their decisions. Many people, having recovered from their initial shock, began to question their attitudes to German reunification, a policy whose validity had never been challenged. If Berlin's capital-in-retirement status had become so problematic, what were the prospects for Germany as a whole?

The three Western Powers had repeatedly declared themselves amenable to the reunification of what was left of Germany on terms approved by the Federal Government, basing their attitude on agreements and legal titles from which Berlin's Quadripartite status derived. The actual course of developments had long since widely diverged from the concept of a city under joint responsibility. In reality, what was termed joint administration (the final decision rested with the various Sector Commandants) had only existed during the first three post-war years. As early as 1948, the authority of the *Stadtverordneten-versammlung* [city parliament] – elected two years earlier under Four-Power supervision – was restricted to the Western sectors. It was ousted from its original seat in the Eastern sector and a separate administration established for the Russian-occupied part of the city. During the disturbances of June 1953, which shook the entire fabric of the GDR, the sector border was closed, albeit only temporarily, from the Soviet side. Even at this stage there was a firm assertion of the Russian principle 'We decide what happens here – unilaterally, if we so wish.'

All the controlling powers favoured a united Germany with Berlin as its capital – according to their official pronouncements. In reality, conflicting interests declared themselves soon after the end of hostilities. The Cold War rent Europe asunder and ossified the division of Germany, which was partly anticipated, partly reproduced, in Berlin. Looking back, I can think of three sets of circumstances that might have opened up different perspectives for Germany and Berlin, and thus for Europe.

In the first place, the Allied Control Commission should during the early post-war months have agreed to set up German central administrative bodies covering major subsections of government. This plan was vetoed by France, though French fears of a united Germany were not wholly unwelcome to the other victorious powers. The Russians took advantage of the respite to concentrate on their own sphere of control. The Americans and British were afraid, in any case, that central administrative departments based in Berlin might be sucked into the communist vortex.

A second possibility is that in spring 1949, when the *Grundgesetz* or Basic Law designed to convert the Western zones into the Federal Republic was under discussion, an attempt might have been made to start negotiations in which Moscow, too, seemed interested because it had no wish to see West Germany become a member of the North Atlantic Alliance, then in process of formation. This was proposed by Ernst Reuter, my pugnacious predecessor as Mayor of Berlin. Such negotiations would not, however, have been justified unless the Russians had approved a currency reform and refrained from unsettling or fettering the economy. Postponement of the 1948 currency reform would doubtless have plunged Germany into an unholy economic and, thus, political mess.

A third opportunity: though we did not know it at the time, the German question provoked controversy among the Soviet leaders after Stalin's death. They even discussed proposals to abandon the GDR as an independent political structure and relegate the ruling communists there, in company with their West German colleagues, to the role of an opposition party. Winston Churchill may have received firm indications of these debates at an early stage, but they did not come to our ears until after the downfall of Lavrenti Beria, the secret service chief, and the neutralization of the so-called Herrnstadt Group in East Berlin, an SED group centred on the editor of *Neues Deutschland*, the party newspaper.

Stalin's successors were evidently under the impression that the economic strength of Russia and Eastern Europe was being overtaxed. Vladimir Semyonov, hitherto adviser to the Soviet Control Commission but appointed 'High Commissioner' at the end of May and to that extent placed on a par with the representatives of the Western Powers, was dispatched to East Berlin with fresh instructions. There was talk, after a Politburo meeting attended by him, of having to accept the role of an opposition party, if not actual illegality. Some members of the

Politburo were beginning to call for Ulbricht's dismissal on the grounds that his policy had alienated the Party from the masses. Instability and rivalry within the SED leadership meant more in the months preceding the June disturbances than anyone could then have been aware.

Ulbricht managed to consolidate his position after 17 June, and the Soviet Politburo decided against a change of course in its German policy. Beria's fall at the end of June was the first definite indication of this. At the next Plenum of the Central Committee, Ulbricht accused Beria of having wanted to 'sell out' the GDR in negotiations with the West, and Khrushchev denounced the secret service chief in similar terms.

Churchill had explained to Adenauer, who visited him in mid-May, why he took the signs of a change in the Soviet Union seriously and believed that the Russians' desire for security should be accommodated. In the interests of a general European peace settlement, he said, a reunited Germany would also have to make sacrifices in regard to its eastern frontiers. Churchill's illness, American scepticism and Adenauer's mistrust prevented the Soviet Union from being invited to negotiations on Germany. Serious analysts have come to the conclusion that a unique opportunity was lost here.

Even discounting such considerations, it would have been right – as I realistically believed, even then – to pursue the Russian proposals of spring 1952, which spoke of a united, non-aligned Germany whose government would be the product of free elections. The German policy laid down by Konrad Adenauer made no allowance for any testing of this offer to negotiate – not even so as to counter subsequent accusations that a potential avenue had been left unexplored. The first Federal Chancellor, with the American fear of German and European un-certainties at his back, had no wish to be delayed in his progress towards military links with Western Europe and the Atlantic Powers.

I wondered then, not for the first or last time, whether the two super-powers might not, with adamantine consistency, have been pursuing the same principle in Europe since 1945: that, whatever happened, they would respect the spheres of influence broadly agreed at Yalta. This would have presupposed a division of Germany and the Continent. Nothing since Stalin's offensive policy in Berlin has, in fact, managed to shake this principle – neither the remilitarization of both parts of Germany, which stemmed logically from such a policy, nor attempts to modify internal power structures in the countries of Western or Eastern Europe. The Western Powers, with America in the van, stood idly by while various forms of insurrection in East Germany (1953), Poland

and Hungary (1956) and Czechoslovakia (1968) were quelled, crushed and smothered. The Russians, in their turn, accepted the suppression of the communists in Greece (1946) and tolerated Tito's withdrawal from the Soviet camp (1948), though with much gnashing of teeth because Yugoslavia lay at the intersection of the two spheres of influence. Finally, they have done little to support the communist parties of Italy or even France in their efforts to gain power.

Here we encounter the underlying pattern of a power strategy in Europe which, for all its complexity of detail, appears to have survived almost unaltered since 1945. Events in Germany must likewise be viewed against this background. The basic principle governing the tacit arrangement between Moscow and Washington remained in force during the construction of the Wall and thereafter.

The week following 13 August was one of the most strenuous in my life. It was my task, once again, to allay fears, curb rash reactions and restore confidence. On the afternoon of 16 August we summoned our fellow-citizens to join in a mass protest. The space in front of the Schöneberger Rathaus was packed with people – 250,000 or more. The workers had come straight from their factories, the office workers from their offices, the students from their lecture-rooms. More people thronged the side-streets. The atmosphere was fraught with anger and resentment. I received an enthusiastic welcome and was frequently interrupted by rapturous applause. There were banners proclaiming that paper protests were not enough – words must be backed by deeds. There were also shouts of 'Where's Adenauer?' and 'What are the Americans doing?' It was an extremely volatile situation. The possibility of incidents was real enough, especially since one midday paper had splashed a story that the Americans knew everything in advance. The anger of the disillusioned Berliners might easily have turned against the Protecting Powers. I would not wish the difficulties of such a situation on any responsible public speaker. Equal damage may be done by one word too many or one too few, for either can strike the spark that will ignite an uncontrollable blaze. How to speak and what to say when one knows full well that one's audience can only be told a fraction of what it wants to hear?

My message on 16 August was clear: 'This city wants peace but will not capitulate. There can be no city in the world with a greater desire for tranquillity and security, but peace has never yet been preserved by weakness.' Confident of my Berliners' approval, I announced that I had dispatched an urgent letter to President Kennedy. My communication had been cabled to him a few hours before. When I had visited Kennedy in Washington in February, he told me to contact him direct whenever I deemed it useful or important. A telephone call on 13 August itself had not been feasible. The text of my letter was first divulged to a journalist in Bonn. I was thereupon asked publicly whether I was authorized – in terms of protocol, as it were – to address myself to the President of the United States direct. The Federal Foreign Minister reproached me in a lengthy missive for having subjected the Western Powers to 'intense pressure'.

In fact, my letter of 16 August to John F. Kennedy not only spoke of a grave upheaval but pointed out that the Western Powers – despite their invocation of Four-Power status – were in process of being ousted from areas of joint responsibility. A crisis of confidence loomed. Any further drift towards the 'free city' scheme could be expected to trigger an exodus of refugees from West Berlin. I had few suggestions to offer at the time, but I did urge, first, that the US garrison be reinforced; secondly, that Three-Power responsibility for West Berlin be firmly stressed; and, thirdly, that it be definitely indicated that the German question must not be regarded as closed while a peace settlement was still outstanding. Fourth and last, I asked the President to bring the Berlin problem before the United Nations.

I do not expect such steps to produce any significant material change in the present situation and cannot help but reflect bitterly on the statements which repudiated negotiations with the Soviet Union on the grounds that one should not negotiate under duress. We now have a state of consummate blackmail, and I am already told that it will be impossible to turn negotiations down. It is doubly important in such a situation at least to show political initiative, even if the scope for an active initiative is so limited. After accepting a Soviet démarche which is illegal and has been termed illegal, and in view of the many tragedies that are today being enacted in East Berlin and the Soviet Zone of Germany, none of us will be exempt from the risks attendant on ultimate determination . . . I deem the situation grave enough to write to you, Mr President, with the total candour possible only between friends who trust each other fully.

Discounting the petty reaction from Bonn, I received a threefold response to my letter. Kennedy informed me that he would be sending Vice-President Johnson to Berlin in a few days' time. He also sent

word that he was transferring an additional combat group to West
Berlin. Finally, he transmitted a formal written reply via Lyndon B.
Johnson.

It was important, he wrote, to remain in close touch at this time. The
actions of the Soviet Government 'and their puppets in East Berlin'
had aroused disgust in America. This operation showed what the
Soviet Government meant by freedom for a city and freedom for a
people, and demonstrated the transparency of Soviet pretexts. The
Americans realized that this move came as a hard blow to the people of
West Berlin, but there were (as I myself had said) no steps that could
bring about any significant material change in the present situation.
War was out of the question and most of the proposed measures were
trivial in relation to what had happened.

An immediate appeal to the United Nations seemed to offer little
prospect of success but merited further consideration. The best
immediate answer was to reinforce the Western garrisons, and not
merely in a symbolic sense. At the same time, the agreed reinforcement
of Western military strength should be speeded up. Kennedy approved
of the referendum idea which I had raised under these circumstances.
He did not concur with my proposal to reassert the Three-Power status
of West Berlin because it might further weaken Four-Power rights in
respect of Berlin as a whole. (Latent in this are the seeds of what is, to
Berlin experts, a quasi-theological problem almost inexplicable to
outsiders.)

President Kennedy went on to say that West Berlin was more
important than ever. The ties between the city and the free world
were more than rhetorical. The citizens of West Berlin were not only
an outpost of freedom but an important part of the free world and all
its undertakings. We were partners in this dual task, and he was firmly
convinced that we should be able to depend on each other in future as
we had done hitherto. These words do not support the contention that
Kennedy replied adversely to my urgent appeal. Just as erroneous was
the sporadic rumour that I had criticized Kennedy for leaving us in the
lurch.

On 18 August I attended a special Bundestag (Lower House) debate
on the Wall, which resembled a set exercise more than anything else.
On Saturday 19 August Lyndon B. Johnson flew into Berlin with the
Texan unpretentiousness and common touch of a man who, as leader of
the Democrats in the US Senate, had long been the President's real
parliamentary partner. His companions included General Clay, who
accompanied Ambassador Bohlen and was particularly welcome
in Berlin. The Berliners had regarded Lucius Clay as one of their own

ever since the Blockade. It was known of Charles Bohlen that he, George Kennan and Llewellyn Thompson had made up the brilliant 'triple constellation' of US Eastern diplomacy during the post-war period. I had known the Vice-President since my first trip to America early in 1954.

The streets and squares were lined with people. They gave Johnson a tempestuous welcome which made it clear to him that they regarded his visit as a token of support and encouragement. To the alarm of his security men, this public enthusiasm moved him to indulge in some American-style campaigning. He shook thousands of hands, a gesture which was enthusiastically received. Johnson did not eschew strong words. He recalled President Roosevelt, with whose work he had been so closely associated as a young politician, and quoted the famous phrase from the Inaugural Address of 1933: '. . . the only thing we have to fear is fear itself.'

The most important part of Kennedy's verbal reply confirmed that an American combat group would move up the Autobahn to Berlin next day. Although it numbered only 1500 men, their reassignment – in response to the East's stereotyped demand for an Allied withdrawal – was an act of exceptional significance. The President had issued the order personally, and the Vice-President satisfied himself of its implementation on the spot. It was a memorable moment when Johnson and I welcomed the armoured column – which no attempt had been made to stop – at the city limits.

Conversation with our distinguished visitors became somewhat strained when it turned to that part of Kennedy's reply which dealt with my critical remarks about Four-Power status and Three-Power responsibility. I naturally had not the slightest objection to demanding the re-establishment of Four-Power status for the whole of Berlin, reminding the Russians of their obligations and leaving the door ajar to a reasonable future. What I did firmly oppose was the extension of this principle to West Berlin alone. The demand for a Soviet garrison in our part of the city, which would almost logically have stemmed from this, had already been made from time to time. Seemingly abstract but terribly concrete in reality, these associated factors were hard for our visitors to grasp. My own concern under present circumstances was that the Western Powers should refuse to cede any of their responsibility for West Berlin and not prevent us from drawing as close as possible to the Federal Republic.

On 20 August the Vice-President and I toured Berlin in an open car and visited the refugees encamped at Marienfelde. It was moving to meet these people who had abandoned their homes at the eleventh hour. Lyndon B. Johnson exhibited all his robust vitality, all his rather folksy and sometimes rather unsophisticated humour. He more than once made a point of taking me up on a phrase in my letter to Kennedy. 'You called for deeds, not words,' he told me. 'Well, now I want to see some action.' (As, for instance, when we had to procure some shoes from a store on Saturday night, long after closing time, because he liked my own so much – and he needed two pairs of each because his feet differed in size. As, for instance, when an assortment of electric razors had to be obtained on Sunday as gifts for friends. As, for instance, when he visited the china factory – also shut, of course – on the afternoon of the same Sunday: we had presented him with a service but he promptly ordered a bigger one for formal occasions. As, for instance, when a director of the factory called at the Berlin Hilton that evening to take an order for a sizeable number of small ashtrays. Johnson's disarming explanation: 'They look like a dollar and cost me only 25 cents.')

The night at the Hilton dragged on, and conversation centred less on politics than an outsider might, given the circumstances, have supposed. There was only just time to freshen up and change afterwards. The plane to Washington left Tegel at 5 a.m.

The President appointed Lucius D. Clay his personal representative in Berlin after Johnson's visit. Clay's reputation in the States was more than that of an exceptionally able soldier. Respected for his political influence as well, he paved the way – if my information is correct – for Eisenhower's presidential candidacy in 1952 and organized its financial backing. He dissociated himself from McCarthy's right-wing radicalism despite his ingrained conservatism and used his authority as the hero of the Berlin Blockade to warn his fellow-countrymen against relapsing into isolationism. In October 1950 he brought us our own Liberty Bell. My friends and I never omitted to call on General Clay and bring him news of 'his' city when we visited New York. In May 1959, ten years after the lifting of the Blockade, he and his British and French colleagues had been rapturously received. As I said at the time, never had representatives of victorious powers and occupation authorities been so fêted as by us in Berlin.

So Clay, whom a French ambassador referred to in his memoirs as 'American omnipotence personified', returned to us during the latter half of September 1961. We flew in from Frankfurt by the same commercial flight. The General can hardly have relished the prospect of his new assignment. Immediately after the Wall he would probably have been accepted as a sort of super-commandant. Now, a few weeks later, he wielded the same moral authority but was not equipped with the requisite powers. His appointment by the US President did not affect the status of the three Allied Commandants or the chains of command linking them with their capitals. Clay's inadequately defined role soon proved a handicap. He quickly sensed a lack of understanding in Washington too. In any case, he was powerless to change the political climate.

Thus the range of functions which he could perform or influence remained far more limited than he had come to expect. He devoted himself, *inter alia*, to stimulating Berlin's economy, and his proposals for investment in the city were well-gauged. His only dramatic moment came with the decision to order tanks to Checkpoint Charlie at the end of October. What occasioned this confrontation was the Americans' justifiable wish to see their right of unrestricted access to the Eastern Sector clearly confirmed in respect of civilians as well because it might become a precedent governing the corridors to West Germany. Allan Lightner, the US Minister, tested this freedom of passage, first on his own and later with an armed escort. When the GDR persisted in maintaining the right of supervision delegated to them by the Russians, General Clay ordained a 'minor escalation'. Ten Patton tanks rolled up to the foreigners' checkpoint in Friedrichstrasse, that is to say, Checkpoint Charlie, escorted by a couple of helicopters, some military police and an infantry unit. On a number of occasions, non-uniformed Americans insisted on driving through unchecked. After a few days Soviet tanks took station less than two hundred yards away on the other side of the border. This was precisely what the Americans (and I, in principle) wanted. The Russians were meant to show the flag. The deployment of their armoured vehicles confirmed that they still had the 'last word' in the Eastern Sector. To that extent the test was passed and the Allied legal position maintained – but nothing more.

Clay and I often discussed the precariousness of the situation in private. We also acquired common experience of the bitter reality of the tensions surrounding Berlin. While flying us to Bremen to attend the traditional *Schaffermahlzeit*, a commercial banquet, early in 1962, our special US plane was buzzed by Soviet fighters.

The General was not exempt from offence and disappointment. Shortly after his arrival in autumn 1961 he had talked to some journalists at his house. This interview gave rise to a grotesque misinterpretation: he – a conservative who remained unruffled even when labelled a Cold War warrior – had to swallow imputations of 'untrustworthiness'. Certain newspapers questioned whether he fully supported the German approach to reunification and might not, after all, be toying with the idea of recognizing the GDR. In fact, he had wondered aloud whether the Germans could not make a greater contribution to their own unity. This was not an uncommon line of thought among Americans and one I had encountered more than once – as, for example, in conversation with Secretary of State Dean Rusk. Clay had further remarked that it was for the Federal Republic to determine the extent of the risks to be taken in Berlin. All this amounted to was an understandable demand that Bonn share the Allied dangers there. Although strong language was often on tap in the Federal capital, there was an aversion to direct and full commitment. Reactions of this kind showed that, where reunification and Berlin were concerned, the gulf between emotionalism and reality, word and deed, was threatening to become a national trauma.

Clay relinquished his special mission in May 1962. Enthusiastically acclaimed for the last time at our traditional May Day rally, he assured the people of Berlin that he would always be one of them. Our farewell tribute to him was a grant of honorary citizenship – a distinction conferred on no non-German since Tsar Nicholas.

Barely two months after the building of the Wall I flew to New York for a few days to deliver a speech and receive an award. On the evening of 6 October I addressed an influential group of businessmen. Next morning – it happened to be the day on which my third son Matthias was born – President Kennedy telephoned me and discussed the situation at length. He told me he wanted an agreement that would genuinely improve Berlin's position. The American and German governments ought, he said, to be more frank with one another. He seemed to be growing increasingly irritated by Bonn's negative attitude – towards negotiations or even soundings, towards discussion of the eastern border question, towards acknowledgement of the second state that had now been established on German soil – and by the persistent mistrust of Adenauer and his entourage. In a remark aimed mainly at the French, he added that we should gird ourselves, not just talk.

After this American trip, which, though brief and limited to New York, left me time for some useful informative discussions, I drafted a memorandum for Chancellor Adenauer and brought it to the notice of the party chairmen in the Bundestag. I pointed out, with justification, that we were expected to share more fully in the risks of the Berlin crisis. I was further at pains to stress the importance of the three 'essentials'. Where overland communication was concerned, an attempt should be made to improve the present position. Berlin's attachment to the Federal Republic was also a consequence of self-determination on the part of its citizens. Under the aegis of Three-Power responsibility, West Berlin must be enabled to play its part as a *Land* of the German Federal Republic more fully than heretofore. I also canvassed the advisability of appealing to the United Nations Commission on Human Rights and seeking the establishment of a special UN authority in Berlin.

The crisis that had been so sorely accentuated by the building of the Wall dragged on. Although Khrushchev tacitly allowed his peremptory threats after 13 August to lapse into oblivion, the danger could have flared up again at any moment. The twin stimulus-words 'free city' figured repeatedly in contentious statements issued by East Berlin and Moscow.

To the people of Berlin, the Wall itself was more than a mere stimulus-word, more than the symbol of a latent material and moral crisis threatening the GDR's existence: they regarded it as a provocation and an acute threat. We had extreme difficulty in controlling the angry demonstrations that marked the first anniversary of 13 August. A few days later, on 17 August 1962, an eighteen-year-old building worker named Peter Fechter bled to death near Checkpoint Charlie while a crowd looked on, unable and forbidden to help. He had tried to scale the Wall with a companion (who succeeded) and was shot several times. Many had suffered a similar fate before him, but not within sight of so many West Berliners. The People's Police took their time about removing his body, and angry spectators on our side of the Wall refused to accept a US lieutenant's statement to the effect that it was not his problem. This incident hit the Berliners hard and exacerbated their sense of outrage. Many voiced their disillusionment at the Americans' inability to help a young man who was bleeding to death.

Righteous indignation was commingled with disorder and demagogy. Young people talked of blasting holes in the Wall. One cheap rag accused us of treachery on the grounds that we were employing the police to protect it. I was summoned to the Rathaus by phone one evening because an impromptu demonstration was expected. Addressing the youngsters over the loud-hailer of a police car, I told them that the Wall was harder than the heads that wanted to batter it down, and that indulging in escapades would not help our compatriots on the other side. We had to convince students and other young people that the problem of the Wall could not be solved with plastic explosives. By dint of much talking in factories and offices, my colleagues and I strove to show the people of Berlin what was possible and what was not. The borders whose inviolability was later stipulated on paper were, in fact, respected by the competent Allied and German authorities even then, but it was not good form to say so aloud. Things were left vague and allowed to drift.

We had just weathered the Peter Fechter crisis when alarming reports reached us of troop concentrations in the GDR. The Allies informed me of the disturbing situation at their operations centre in the Olympic Stadium. A surprise attack on West Berlin could not be ruled out. It was possible that our opponents in the East were toying with the dangerous idea that such an operation, if carried out with sufficient speed, might be devoid of military repercussions and could force us to negotiate on the basis of newly accomplished facts. I did not doubt that the Allied forces would offer more than symbolic resistance despite their inferior numbers and fire-power, and that the people of West Berlin, in so far as they were able to do anything at all, would not remain mere onlookers. The essential thing in such an eventuality would be to survive the first 24 hours so that decisions could be taken in the Allied capitals and the UN Security Council convened.

The Berliners were quite as unaware of this danger as the citizens of the Federal Republic and Allied countries. It would have been pointless to alarm them. The 'secret Berlin crisis' had to be dealt with behind the public's back, as it were, though I did advise my closest associates at the Rathaus – not purely in jest – to have some stout shoes ready because we might have a long walk ahead of us. One afternoon I drove home for a serious chat with my fourteen-year-old son Peter. It was possible, I told him, that his father would be away for some time. If so, he would become the man of the family and must help his mother as best he could . . .

During those weeks the super-powers were drifting towards another and graver crisis which carried them to the brink of nuclear confrontation. The Americans were well aware that Soviet missiles had been installed in Cuba. I was not, but my American partners associated Moscow's Cuban manœuvre with news of Soviet troop movements in the GDR. I assume they considered it improbable that the Russians would simultaneously bring matters to a head at two widely separated points. It was not by chance, however, that Secretary of Defence McNamara made a lightning tour of US bases in the Federal Republic at this period. Presidential Assistant McGeorge Bundy of the National Security Council visited Berlin to deliver an address in which he warned against the illusion that the United States had resolved not to use nuclear weapons in the event of a military conflict. This was no coincidence either.

I tried at the time, in both Berlin and America, to emphasize the perils of miscalculation. If a move were made against Berlin, I said, we would be unable to mollify our compatriots in the 'Zone' . . . Although this was condemned as playing with fire by some who were ignorant of the facts, we had good reason to supplement the weightier admonitions of a world power with a warning of our own. It may well have found its intended mark. A revolt similar to that of June 1953 would hardly have been in the interests of the Soviet Union.

During my subsequent visit to the White House on 5 October 1962, the President took no trouble to conceal his exasperation at the criticism levelled at him in Germany. He was tired of hearing nothing from Bonn but niggling remarks and negative reactions to American proposals. The Germans should be good enough to do more than state what they disapproved of – they should say what they themselves wanted. 'I don't want to be hustled after a spell of inactivity,' he declared.

Discussion in the preceding months had centred mainly on the possibility of defusing the Berlin situation by means of an international access authority. Consultation with the Russians produced a scheme for a thirteen-member monstrosity including one representative each from the two German states and the two halves of Berlin. Though not over-impressed by the idea of such a cumbersome and unwieldy body, I did – in view of the uncertainty and ambiguity which had ruled our lives for so many years – approve the basic principle that access routes be regulated by guarantee. After initially rejecting the proposal out of hand, Bonn insisted that the authority's German representatives should have no voting rights on the grounds that this would tend towards recognition of the 'Zone'. The Americans, on the other hand, proceeded upon the realistic assumption that the GDR authorities – originally under Soviet orders – had for years exercised *de facto* control over civilian passenger and goods traffic to and from Berlin. It was not, therefore, a question of making Ulbricht any new offers or breaking new ground, merely of binding him to regulations that were already contractually established.

I explained my views on this matter to Kennedy during our talk in October, at which I also discussed the advisability of holding a referendum in West Berlin. I had told the Assembly of the Western European Union in Paris in December 1961 that I would not hesitate to call one if it became desirable for the people of Berlin to express their wishes publicly. Before visiting Washington I had also discussed the subject with Secretary of State Rusk in New York, likewise with Konrad Adenauer when I visited him at Cadenabbia in September. As already mentioned, the Chancellor had earlier proposed a vote on whether we wished to keep the Allies in Berlin. I considered the question wrongly formulated, preferring it to stress our membership of the Federation. Kennedy was somewhat hesitant and asked us not to rush things. He was, however, receptive to my suggestion that we should try and make the Wall more 'permeable' and seek to ameliorate the situation on a humanitarian level, for instance by reuniting divided families.

What mattered was to make it clear, not only to our friends but to the Russians and our East German opposite numbers, that we would not simply come to terms with the terrible *fait accompli* of closure and the Wall. Then as always, I refused to let our policy congeal into a purely defensive posture. We had to try and progress – draw the correct inferences from cruel realities. In spite of everything, we had to resist discouragement.

The Bundestag elections of 17 September 1961 resulted in a still substantial majority for the CDU/CSU. My colleagues and I had been well aware that we stood no chance of winning, but we did chalk up some sizeable electoral gains. I was only able to take a limited part in the campaign proper. My post was in Berlin, where my mornings were devoted to mayoral duties. The election campaign did not begin for me until the afternoon or evening, and I always flew home for the night in a small British charter plane. The city saw me almost every day, so I hardly missed a single major sitting or private discussion. I also cultivated the closest possible contacts with my fellow-citizens. They were exciting, challenging days and weeks. It was our duty to convey confidence, warn against resignation and acts of imprudence, and publicize new plans for the development of our city – *inter alia* in reply to Khrushchev, who had informed me through visitors that the problem of West Berlin would 'resolve itself', that its inhabitants would clear out and economic life collapse . . . He proved wrong.

It was not just a question of money and administrative planning. Neither of these could dispel the human tragedies that were becoming commonplace. Divided families stood weeping at the barriers. People in houses overlooking the sector boundaries jumped from upstairs windows – until they were bricked up – or slid down ropes. Daring schemes, many of them carried out by students, enabled refugees to escape through sewers, through tunnels, with the aid of forged permits and fake uniforms, in hijacked locomotives, river-steamers, or cars which either charged the barriers or smuggled their clandestine cargoes through. There has long been room for a comprehensive documentary account of the courage and cunning, bravery and endurance shown during those weeks and months, not only on the Western side but also by the citizens of East Berlin and the 'Zone'. Many escape stories resembled scenarios for tragic, adventurous and dramatic films, often with a dash of deliberate or unintentional comedy. The Wall was surmounted by a resort to veritable circus acts, feats of athletic or artistic prowess.

My fellow-countrymen displayed qualities of moral courage, wit and imagination, which did not match their international image. This was what so endeared the Berliners during those dark days. Never since the Blockade had I felt so deeply attached to this 'special breed'. What united me with the city was the challenge it posed day by day: it was Europe's major trouble-spot, a focus of international interest and tension, a fount of opportunities, exploited and neglected. Berlin might have been described as Germany's city of destiny. What bound me to its citizens was their display of strength in impotence, greatness in adversity. Their spirit of resistance reminded me of my adopted Norwegian homeland, whose population was little greater than that of the whole of Berlin. The big-city counterpart of Norway's sturdy rustic independence and sober cosmopolitanism was realism and an urbane generosity of spirit. In both places I encountered solidarity, a marked awareness of the basic values of human existence and an open-mindedness that transcended nationalism.

The Berliners' anti-communism was not their way of compensating for the resistance they had neglected to offer the Nazis. So far from being a displacement activity, it manifested their utter repudiation of all totalitarian attempts to destroy freedom and the democratic system. Their opposition to Soviet policy never aspired to be anti-Russian. In this, too, the people of Berlin had respected the legacy of Ernst Reuter – the heritage which I had assumed and sought to preserve through thick and thin.

On 6 December 1961, before resigning my new-won parliamentary seat, I addressed the Bundestag as spokesman of my party. I said that we must stop turning our backs on our fellow-countrymen in the GDR. The present reunification policy had failed. I quoted from Kennedy's interview with Alexei Adzhubei, editor of *Izvestia* and Khrushchev's son-in-law, in which the President had declared that German reunification was clearly impossible without the concurrence of the Soviet Union. The present crisis merely overlaid 'the task of entering into a new relationship with the Great Power in the East'. This, in a nutshell, defined our crucial task in foreign policy during the years to come.

2

The End of the Adenauer Era

My own party and the FDP, or Free Democrats, increased their vote by roughly 2 millions apiece in the Bundestag elections of September 1961. This meant that the Social Democrats had boosted their electoral support from 31.8 to 36.3 per cent and their Bundestag representation from 169 to 190, or almost 40 per cent of all seats – the best performance recorded by the German Social Democrats since the National Assembly elections of 1919. Quite contrary to many summer forecasts, which predicted a two-thirds majority, the CDU/CSU share of the vote fell from 50.1 to 45.2 per cent. The FDP fared exceptionally well, in relative terms, with over 12 per cent of all votes cast.

The main immediate consequence was that the CDU and CSU no longer commanded an absolute majority. The formation of the new Federal Government required another coalition. Adenauer's authority had been dented and the end of the era associated with his name was beginning to loom. It was hardly surprising that his retirement should have become a topic of discussion and covert negotiation – he was, after all, 85 years old. In summer 1959 he had flirted with the idea of getting himself elected Federal President in succession to Theodor Heuss. His fleeting inclination towards such a candidacy was prompted by the illusion that, if reinterpreted with sufficient vigour, the Basic Law would permit a strengthening of the President's powers. It is probable that Adenauer decided to retain the Chancellorship mainly because he had no wish to see Ludwig Erhard succeed him.

His manœuvres in the matter of the Presidency had diminished the Chancellor's standing. Leading Christian Democrats were trying to pave the way for a post-election removal of the 'Old Man'. Strauss, too, was obviously hoping to succeed Erhard as Chancellor after a transitional period. The Free Democrats had stated during the campaign that they would not participate in any new government headed by Adenauer, but this decision was later modified.

Some uncertainty reigned in Bonn on the evening of election day and during the small hours of 18 September. It did not afflict Adenauer, who had retired to bed early in his usual way. Almost before the rest of the world was awake, he faced the press. Blandly, he informed friend and foe that he would continue as Chancellor in coalition with the Free Democrats.

The Free Democratic Party bears only limited comparison to, say, the Liberal Party of Great Britain. It is one (but not the sole) heir to the German liberalism which seemed to offer Germany a chance of democratic development during the revolution of 1848. The monarchic dynasties and feudal structures of the German States then proved too strong for it. German liberalism never really recovered from this blow. It remained the political philosophy of the progressive middle class but never became a determinant of industrial society as it has, for instance, in Britain and the United States. Bismarck split the forces of liberalism. The national-liberal wing adapted itself to his conservative régime while a more left-wing liberal minority expended its strength in opposition. Although both bodies of opinion acquired considerable influence immediately after World War I, they were virtually extinct by the time the Weimar Republic fell.

Both traditions converged in the Free Democratic Party founded after World War II. Traces of bourgeois liberalism had survived, mainly in South Germany and the Hanseatic cities. In other parts of the country, conservative and nationalist influences predominated. Although the new party duly joined Adenauer's government when the Federal Republic was established, some of its younger and more lively spirits rebelled as the years went by. Foremost among these was Walter Scheel, later to become Federal President. Dissatisfaction and protest centred primarily on Adenauer's autocratic methods, but there were also misgivings about the influence of the Churches, and the Catholic Church in particular, as exerted through the parties styling themselves 'Christian'. The rebels pressed for liberal measures designed to emancipate the citizen from state tutelage, which they considered reprehensible, and became receptive to modern social welfare legislation. In foreign policy they drew closer to the Social Democratic position. They took the problem of German unity seriously and aspired to a progressive rather than a rigidly conservative Europe. The FDP began by sharing the historical fate of German liberalism and was more than once threatened with disintegration. During the 1956 crisis

Adenauer detached the party's conservative wing, which was later absorbed into the CDU. By so doing, the Chancellor quite involuntarily paved the way for a change of generations in the FDP leadership. The younger elements, who now commanded a majority, formed an alliance with Adenauer's successor. In 1966, however, when Erhard not only became entangled in the first recession crisis but lost control over divergent groups inside the CDU, the FDP brought him down. Throughout those galling years in opposition, while the CDU and SPD were governing jointly, Walter Scheel adapted his little party to a progressive programme of reform and created the prerequisites for a coalition with the Social Democrats. The two parties were found to possess historical ties because the ideas of 1848 lived on in both. For the first time since the tragic Weimar interlude, the heirs to the liberal-social tradition became a decisive force in German history.

I and some of my associates discreetly aired the possibility of an all-party government or 'cabinet of national concentration'. In company with Ollenhauer, Erler and Wehner, I explained our motives during a discussion with Bundestag President Eugen Gerstenmaier. He was receptive to the idea, being himself a candidate for office in such a government. The Federal Republic was confronted by problems of such magnitude that its destinies might best have been guided for a limited period by all the democratic parties working in harness. What primarily concerned us, with the Wall preying on all our minds, was the controversy over the so-called German question. Many of us were even then tormented by the question of how the interests of the German Federal Republic could be effectively maintained – particularly if no further progress towards reunification were made – in view of far-reaching changes in the international situation. We were conscious of the need to place our relations with the Soviet Union and other East European countries on a new footing. Domestically, too, there existed an accumulation of problems whose solution might have been furthered by their temporary removal from the arena of violent political controversy and an attempt to tackle them jointly. I make no secret of the additional motive that influenced but did not dominate our thinking: to us Social Democrats, the formation of a broad-based government seemed during those years to be the only means of proving our administrative competence – other than at *Land* level – and of demolishing the prejudices that had grown up against the democratic Left in Germany over a period of decades.

A coalition with the FDP would also have been feasible, numerically speaking, but the Free Democrats had committed themselves over our heads. Although I had a private meeting with FDP leader Erich Mende at the home of a Ruhr industrialist, it produced no more than a friendly but noncommittal exchange of views and a tentative exploration of future intentions. Wolfgang Döring, the energetic leader of the FDP's 'Young Turks', confirmed to me that a coalition between our two parties was still inconceivable under present circumstances. Apart from his friend Walter Scheel, Döring might have been the person to bring the Free and Social Democrats together a few years earlier. To me, this self-willed man seemed to personify a generation purged by war. His forthrightness was reminiscent of the verve of certain young politicians in the United States, perhaps because that was where Döring underwent his formative post-war experiences. I was saddened by his tragic death in mid-January 1963 – the result of a heart attack.

The President of the Bundestag, at whose apartment we discussed the outlines of an all-party government, was not alone in his party. Personal reservations notwithstanding, I also expounded our views to Defence Minister and Bavarian CSU Chairman Strauss, emphasizing both to him and to others that a greater measure of co-operation must be achieved, if only in the field of foreign policy, between all parties represented in the Bundestag. Among those who strongly urged the formation of a broad-based government behind the scenes was Professor Wilhelm Grewe, the German Ambassador in Washington, who drew attention to the dangers in respect of foreign policy.

Within our own party, we had prepared the ground for this essay in greater solidarity with some care. In 1959, for instance, I drew up a list of topics on which we were in basic agreement with the other parties. The support these common positions received in the Bundestag was not over-welcome to the government parties, and least of all to their leader Konrad Adenauer, because they were seeking points of difference rather than a consensus. For understandable reasons of electoral psychology, the Federal Chancellor emphasized his critical detachment. Only his coalition was to rate as 'fit to govern'.

I met Adenauer a few days after the elections. This conversation was apostrophized as a 'secret meeting', but there were no secrets that should or could have been exchanged. On 25 September the talks were resumed in company with a few colleagues from the inner leadership of the SPD. The Old Man had no time for an all-party government but did not immediately make this clear. For him, contact with the Social Democrats had the tactical advantage of disconcerting the Free Democrats and forcing down their price in the coalition negotiations.

As foreseen, the Union (CDU/CSU) parties and the Free Democrats agreed to re-elect Adenauer Chancellor. The coalition partners had swiftly reached an accord on foreign policy, which remained essentially unchanged.

I had not, of course, seriously ventured to hope that the autumn 1961 elections would leave my party the strongest in the Bundestag – the CDU/CSU lead was too great for that – but I was a trifle disappointed when the first results reached me on the evening of election day while I was flying from Berlin to Bonn, once again in a small British charter plane. The faces that greeted me at the '*Baracke*' (hut), our party headquarters in Bonn, were not universally cheerful. It had turned out, I was told by my party chairman, who certainly meant no offence, that other people couldn't perform miracles either. Given the relative stability of domestic political forces in Western Europe, our gain of four and a half per cent was a thoroughly creditable achievement. It was repeated in 1965, 1969 and 1972. My party did not lose strength during the years in which I led it to the polls.

Our prospects of acquiring new political weight in the Federal Republic were regarded with scepticism by friends at home and abroad. During a visit to Copenhagen in summer 1959, my friend Jens Otto Krag – then Danish Foreign Minister – told me that he could not see how we German Social Democrats had any chance of ousting Adenauer and Erhard under conditions of almost continuous economic growth. For all its social inequalities, the 'economic miracle' was indeed a potent card in the government's hand. The same went for our newly acquired friendship with the Western Powers. Finally, the whole scene was dominated by the father figure – or, rather, patriarchal presence – of Konrad Adenauer.

Our Social Democratic achievements in the cities and *Länder* could not be ignored. However, three conditions required fulfilment before we could be regarded as 'government material' by a majority of our fellow-citizens. We had to jettison ideological ballast, hammer out a modern economic policy and, at the same time, make it plain that national security and inter-allied relations would be safe in our hands.

In 1959 we replaced traditional socialist doctrines with newly defined basic principles and confirmed the SPD's development into a national rather than a class-based party. Ideas of a planned economy were contrasted with the sensible rule of thumb 'competition where possible, planning where necessary'. In foreign policy we adhered to the European, internationalist, peace-keeping tradition, but drew an even sharper distinction between ourselves and the communists.

Early in summer 1960 the executive organs of my party nominated me a candidate for the Chancellorship. What probably clinched matters was the worldwide attention I had attracted as Mayor of Berlin and the fact that, in German politics, a man of 46 rated as positively young. Another major factor was, no doubt, that we had anticipated the national party idea in Berlin from the domestic standpoint and, in foreign policy, pursued a course which the public deemed realistic.

My nomination was confirmed late in 1960 and I submitted a programme of reform which concentrated on the country's neglected social problems: not just the expansion of social security but education and research, environment and infrastructure. I was quite wrongly represented as saying that we did not propose to do anything different (from the CDU). My actual words were 'not everything differently but many things better'. Among other things, this meant a new climate of candour and objectivity as opposed to intrigue and malice. Our nation had deserved more love and less cunning. Mind should rule over money, not money over mind. Spiritual and moral values had suffered from an exclusive devotion to material reconstruction. 'The elimination of injustices at home and a desire for détente abroad are twin aspects of an integrated policy, a policy *for* Germany and *with* the peoples of the world.'

As I have already recounted, dramatic events in Berlin subsequent to 13 August prevented me from taking more than a sporadic lead in the election campaign proper. I did, however, tour wide areas of the Federal Republic in a carefully planned pre-election campaign. Some commentators called this form of electioneering an 'Americanization' of political propaganda. My colleagues Klaus Schütz and Alex Möller, the 'Comrade Managing Director' from Karlsruhe, had indeed observed American campaign methods at first hand. Many things we found useful, others not. We 'Germanized' certain American techniques, as it were, and the other parties were quick to follow suit. We had to break with traditions, some ideological and some not. In fact, we flung the windows wide and established contact with classes that had been wholly out of touch with the SPD. In many areas the Governing Mayor of Berlin was probably the first Social Democrat the citizens had ever listened to.

On the darker side, our campaign suffered from the defamatory tactics which many Union strategists felt unable to forgo. Attempts were made in pamphlets, leaflets and newspaper articles to demolish the SPD candidate psychologically. My absence abroad during the Nazi period and my adoption of Norwegian nationality, the Nazis having revoked my citizenship, were distorted into an abandonment of my own people. It was alleged that I had written and fought 'against

Germany'. The fact that I was a left-wing socialist in my youth and had defended the cause of the Spanish Republic was used to insinuate that I might be a crypto-communist. Disparaging remarks were made about my origins and the decision not to reassume my original name. It was disputed that I had passed my school-leaving examination in Lübeck and alleged that my reasons for fleeing the city were not political at all. It was small consolation that this 'right-wing' barrage of mud derived vigorous encouragement, both then and in later years, from sources in East Berlin.

It cost me a great deal of time and energy, then and afterwards, to resist these vile attacks. Summonses were taken out, temporary injunctions obtained, virulent pamphlets confiscated and, ultimately, a few satisfactory judgements given in my favour. My political associates were undeceived. Most newspaper, radio and television commentators dissociated themselves from such violations of political and human decency – indeed, firmly repudiated them. Being thin-skinned by nature, I was wounded nonetheless. My opponents were sometimes successful to the extent that they kept me from my work for days on end. I was often depressed and occasionally felt like writing a satirical parody of Ernst von Salomon's anti-denazification novel *Der Fragebogen* (The Questionnaire): Why *weren't* you a National Socialist? Why *weren't* you in favour of Hitler's war? Why *didn't* you get yourself killed?

Although these were not official campaigns run by the Union parties, they involved more than mere pockets of lingering Nazi sentiment. Finance was undoubtedly provided by people who had not fared badly under Hitler and were now back on top. Many of Adenauer's supporters dissociated themselves from these calumnies. Others wallowed, albeit covertly, in the political pornography which they themselves had produced. The leader of the Bavarian CSU, Franz Josef Strauss, did not bother with camouflage, nor did he confine himself to promoting a campaign by others. His Ash Wednesday speech at Vilshofen contained the words: 'We are entitled to ask Herr Brandt: What were you doing abroad for twelve years? We know what *we* were doing in Germany!' Did he really know? Did he want to know?

I asked Adenauer at the Palais Schaumburg in spring 1961 whether we really wanted our battle for the voters' confidence to be waged on this abject level. His surprising response: 'But Herr Brandt, I don't know what you're driving at. If I had anything against you, I'd tell you.' This did not inhibit him from giving his supporters free rein. On the very morrow of 13 August, the day of the Wall, he himself gave vent to slogans which encouraged his paladins in their unbridled attacks. Adenauer's disingenuous reaction proved, in fact, that he was far from fastidious in his dealings with people. On the other hand, it was pointed out to me by friends who knew him better than I did that he would have shown greater restraint had he not recognized in me a political opponent who could be dangerous to his party.

Adenauer was the very opposite of an emotional man. He was almost immune to disillusionment because he took human failings for granted and knew how to exploit them. His relations with the truth were fickle and his chosen methods not invariably in the best of taste, as witness the following minor incident. After Adenauer had visited Berlin in 1957, my immediate predecessor Otto Suhr and I – then President of Berlin's Chamber of Deputies – escorted the Federal Chancellor from the Schöneberger Rathaus to Tempelhof Airport. I got in beside the chauffeur as we drove off. Adenauer, who had not noticed, assumed that I must be a plainclothesman. The car had scarcely left the Rathaus square when Adenauer began talking vehemently to Suhr, whose health was failing fast: 'I know you're a sick man, Herr Suhr, but you must do your utmost to get better. You're indispensable here. What's more, you know I have confidence in you.' Suhr: 'Very good of you to say so, Herr Bundeskanzler, but Willy Brandt will take over my job when I'm past it.' Adenauer: 'I'm not so sure about that. I'll tell you what he wants – he wants you out of the way.' Suhr knew I was in the car and conversation lapsed. Then Adenauer noticed that I was sitting up front. Disarmingly unabashed, he said: 'Ah, there *is* the Herr Präsident. So tell me, Herr Brandt, what are you really interested in? I'm interested in gardening and rose-growing, as you know.' I half turned. 'Personally, Herr Bundeskanzler, I'm interested in political biographies.' Adenauer: 'What do you mean by that?' Silence reigned till we said goodbye at the plane.

Adenauer thought more subtly than he spoke. He had an uncommon capacity for simplification. This was no real advantage in foreign policy or socio-political contexts. In domestic political debate, however, this double-edged talent for simplification proved a great asset. Adenauer seldom refused a fight and usually went looking for one because he needed confrontation in order to discipline his party-political cohorts.

Konrad Adenauer's most decisive advantage may, perhaps, have been his very age. He entered German politics as a patriarchal figure. Few 73-year-olds would have possessed the stamina to take on the strenuous daily duties of a party leader who was soon to become head of government as well. By the time he assumed political responsibility in Bonn, the provisional capital, he could look back with cool detachment on the fortunes of at least two generations. This in itself guaranteed him the trust of many of his compatriots. In their eyes he lent continuity to a historical thread which seemed to have been snapped by two world wars, a revolution and a barbarous dictatorship. Adenauer never accepted these profound and, on the face of it, irreparable breaks in his fellow-countrymen's progress through the twentieth century. For better or worse, he saw the Federal Republic as a polity in line of succession from its precursors: the Empire, the Weimar Republic and the Third Reich. His political beliefs were rooted in strata still deeper than the superficial overlay of Bismarck's Prussian-dominated Reich. He was a Catholic and a Rhinelander – more precisely, a citizen of Cologne, that southern Hanseatic city in which the traditions of municipal independence and ecclesiastical supremacy met and mingled. The Rhineland had passed under Prussian sovereignty after Napoleonic emancipation and the Congress of Vienna. The Rhinelanders felt thoroughly German but regarded the régime from the Protestant north-east as alien. Their middle class never became entirely reconciled to Prussian 'occupation'. The citizens of Cologne tended to look westwards and southwards. They felt an affinity with the Dutch and Flemings and their cultural climate was substantially influenced by France. Contact with the South German States remained close.

Adenauer's background was humble and his childhood spent in frugal and straitened circumstances. His legal qualifications, which he acquired by dint of sheer hard work, equipped him for a routine career in the civil service. Being thoroughly alive to the fact of his social advancement, however, he soon became assimilated into Cologne's upper middle class, whose Protestant elements were financially predominant. Yet he never lost his unerring common touch. It was this combination of popular appeal and friends in high places which elevated him to mayoral office in 1917, during World War I. His power base was the Centre Party, a political group born of Catholic resistance to Bismarck. This had undergone its ordeal by fire during the so-called 'Kulturkampf', when the German clergy refused to surrender control over major areas of ecclesiastical administration to the state and the Vatican stressed Catholic dissociation from all secular systems and the Protestant Churches by proclaiming the dogma of infallibility. The Centre Party remained in opposition even when this conflict was resolved. It commanded strong support among Catholics and embraced some sections of the Catholic working class. Thanks to the influence of a small band of socially responsible bishops and theologians, it showed itself receptive to reformist ideas and sometimes came close to social democracy, from which it was, at the same time, divorced by the allegedly trenchant antithesis between Christian and Marxist ideology.

As Mayor of Cologne, Adenauer became one of the Centre Party's leading lights. He was later accused of having flirted with post-war separatists who wanted to detach the Rhineland from Germany and, if possible, unite it with France. Adenauer did, in fact, engage in a number of rather obscure discussions while French troops were occupying the Rhineland provinces. He thought it sensible to separate the Rhineland from Prussia but did not wish to detach it from the 'Reich'. These plans, which may not have been wholly mistaken, came to nothing. By virtue of his office, Adenauer still belonged to the so-called Herrenhaus or Prussian First Chamber, which later became the Staatsrat, or body representing the provinces in matters concerning state legislation and administration. He thus attended regular meetings in Berlin but did not disguise his dislike of these trips to the east. To him the Reich capital remained an alien and even hostile place – a Babylon amid the heathen steppes. He also mistrusted the stability and solidity of the Republic, even though members of his own party played a major role in forming its governments and often led them. He was more than once mooted as a candidate for the Chancellorship but consistently steered clear of such discussions, feeling that his time had yet to come. By so doing he may have helped to subject the Centre Party to the growing influence of hidebound nationalists who gave ground to the DNVP (German National People's Party) and National Socialists when they were abandoned by President Hindenburg. It was von Papen, a man of the Centre, who eventually ushered Hitler into power.

The National Socialists sent Adenauer into retirement under humiliating conditions. He watched the progress of the Third Reich with abhorrence and scepticism. Apart from a brief spell in detention towards the end of the war, he was left almost unmolested. Although members of the conservative resistance movement sometimes got in touch with him, he took no active part in their conspiracies. His mordant realism was, he felt, ultimately vindicated when Hitler's dictatorship had to be destroyed by total defeat rather than removed by a *coup d'état*.

Promptly reinstated in his former post by the Allies, Adenauer was soon dislodged by a British general. Some critics thought this accounted for his subsequent opposition to Britain's membership of the European Community, but they were undoubtedly oversimplifying. His pro-French attitude went deeper than that. In Robert Schuman (as in Alcide de Gasperi of Italy) Adenauer discovered a like-minded adherent of European Catholicism, though his denominational ties were not as narrow as of old. Catholic and Protestant Christians alike had learnt that no established tradition was safe from the totalitarian ideology of

Nazism. Both communities had sought to avert total disaster by compromising with tyranny, just as both had suffered persecution and
made sacrifices. It was only logical that, in the ruins of fortified
Germany, men from the ambit of both Churches should have resolved
to assume joint political responsibility. In many parts of Germany,
both east and west, the rudiments of a Christian Democratic Party
began to take shape. With the professionalism of an old hand, Adenauer
secured himself a key position in the British-occupied zone. His claim
to leadership was not undisputed. Certain of the younger men would
have preferred their new party to establish itself somewhat to the left
of Adenauer. He himself thought it better to aim at the politically
homeless middle class. He was undeterred by the perils of monopolizing Christian sentiment on behalf of a single party and tacitly
branding other parties, and the Social Democrats in particular, as
'non-Christian'. This ran counter to the views of that great Social
Democrat Kurt Schumacher, who was striving, after a decade's imprisonment by the Nazis, to throw wide the doors of the classical
working-class party. Schumacher welcomed all citizens committed to
the aims of social democracy regardless of whether they were guided
by Marxist social analysis, philosophical idealism or the spirit of the
Sermon on the Mount. Far from fearing a cleavage between ideological
camps, Adenauer deliberately sought confrontation. He therefore
decided, when the Federal Republic came into being, that the Germans
would be ill served by a broad coalition. It did not worry him that the
parliamentary balance during the Chancellorship election was such as to
assure him of office by only one vote (his own). His strategy was in
some ways comparable to that of General de Gaulle. He wanted to see
the political landscape clearly divided between Left and Right, and he
almost succeeded. Only the diminutive Free Democratic Party managed
to escape polarization.

Adenauer's scheme of things possessed advantages which corresponded in some important respects to the aims of Schumacher, his
Social Democrat opponent. Communists and right-wing extremist
groups were driven far out on to the fringes of society and the Federal
German middle class acquired an unprecedented sense of identity. At
the same time, the Social Democratic opposition gradually increased its
electoral strength. Adenauer had not foreseen that it would pick up
more and more middle-class as well as working-class votes. Presumably
believing that a conservative middle-class party would always manage
to cement its majority, especially under the 'Christian' banner, the first
Chancellor proceeded to assert this claim with chill determination. He
did not, for example, shrink from alarming many of his compatriots by

maliciously asserting that a Social Democratic victory at the polls would spell the downfall of Germany. Fortunately, this statement was taken with a pinch of salt. His demagogy was strangely at odds with his cool and objective conduct of affairs. His language was homely and inelegant but had the advantage of being intelligible to the people at large. Adenauer's lack of rhetorical skill tended to be an asset. Germans accustomed to the booming bombast of Nazism found his somewhat subdued tone a guarantee of staunch reliability. They were further reassured because the Christian Democrats managed for so long to conceal the essential conservatism of their policies at a time when everyone was talking of 'root-and-branch renovation'. Some thought was, it is true, devoted to a few basic reforms such as equal co-determination by labour and capital in the coal and steel industries, and the principles of the constitution afforded scope for far-reaching changes (they did, in fact, help to mould the social climate). It was taken for granted that rapid economic reconstruction would entail the reappearance of old structures likely to impose rigid restrictions on social progress. Adenauer accepted this. After 1945, national efforts had been focused on sheer survival. It was forgotten that the coming decades would confront Germans with demands for which no answer could be found in the philosophy of the nineteenth century.

Adenauer's Europeanism was sustained by pre-Bismarckian experience. In so far as he thought in historical terms, he saw the destruction of the German nation-state as a chance to establish a European federation akin to the ideas of Metternich. Most Germans in the Federal Republic were prepared to follow his lead. Excessive nationalism had become a nightmare to them. Besides, their panic fear of the communist menace and the oppressive power of the Soviet empire prompted them to seek protection in a West European community and an Atlantic alliance. Moves towards European unity and the Federal Republic's accession to the Atlantic Pact were, in effect, dictated by an almost ineluctable train of logic. What was more, many Germans regarded 'the West' as an emotional surrogate for the nation they had lost.

There was a failure to realize that this would not solve the problems of national identity. The traditional nation-states of Western Europe not only continued to exist but were far less eager than the Federal Republic to abdicate their so-called sovereignty in favour of European institutions, nor was it possible to sever all ties with the seventeen million Germans in the other, communist-ruled, state across the Elbe. Adenauer regularly paid lip-service to the goal of reunification. Under Kurt Schumacher and his successors, the Social Democrats took their duty to national solidarity more seriously. Schumacher himself was largely guided by a fear that the brutal partition of Germany might some day promote a resurgence of nationalism. Anxious to prevent right-wing extremists from monopolizing the nationalist cause, he strove to bring such sentiments under the aegis of the Left, and his oratory sometimes verged on radical nationalism. The Social Democrats repeatedly warned Adenauer to take advantage of any opportunity for talks on reunification, determined that the Federal Republic should commit no sin of omission in the sight of history. At the same time, they played their part in the development of Europe. Kurt Schumacher probably underestimated his compatriots' realism. They showed no inclination to gamble with new imponderables for the sake of national unity.

Whether it would have been possible to pursue a course other than the one adopted by Adenauer must remain an open question, but he cannot be acquitted of having shirked all genuine debate on the subject. No one man could simultaneously have wanted an Atlantic alliance, a European federation and the restoration of the German nation-state. Opting for 'the West' meant abandoning reunification until further notice, and the German people were entitled to be faced with this choice. Rhetorical demands for reunification created a kind of national living lie for which Adenauer's party paid the penalty, long after his death, by losing control in Bonn. There was an imperceptible change of roles. The Social Democrats steadfastly continued to develop the European Community and support the Atlantic Alliance. Their so-called *Ostpolitik* was a way of facing up to the realities which had bred a second world war in Central and Eastern Europe and, thus, of gaining scope for understanding and co-operation with the countries o Eastern Europe and the other German state. To that extent, they have not only lent substance to Adenauer's plans but rendered them honest.

After finally renouncing the Chancellorship, Adenauer discreetly intimated that he accepted the changed face of reality and conveyed as much to me in private conversation. He had neither the energy nor the authority to change his party's course. On the threshold of death he more than once succumbed to the profound pessimism which his generation had inherited from its historical experience. While still in power he translated his fear of the future and his mistrust of man's moral exertions into mocking scepticism. Although dry humour undoubtedly constituted an engaging aspect of his character, it was not lost on any of his supporters or opponents that he amused himself primarily at the expense of others whose weakness and impotence he exploited without scruple. He could never have been called a lover of his fellow-men. Only a small circle of friends and relations experienced the kindness of which he was also capable.

Konrad Adenauer lived and governed like a nineteenth-century patriarch. That was his strength. It endeared him to a majority of his compatriots, who were heartened by his vitality and austere presence. Mingled with their respect was a strong dose of nostalgia – a yearning to turn the clock back. Adenauer jutted into our era like an ancient monument, yet he had a thorough grasp of some of the twentieth century's fundamental problems – indeed, his instinct was surer than that of many younger contemporaries who all too readily yielded to the whims of the moment. That was why, although essentially conservative, he also managed to pave his party's way towards a modern social policy. The first workers' co-determination scheme and an appreciable measure of social security would never have been introduced without his help. In this respect he rates comparison with Bismarck. The founder of the 1871 Reich likewise showed a tendency to make popular concessions in the field of social legislation, though as a means of denying the masses a share in political responsibility. Unlike Bismarck, of course, Adenauer was a European and a democrat, even if his vision of democracy contained authoritarian features. He may well have eased the Germans' transition from dictatorship to liberal democracy, but he also neglected, from the birth of the Second Republic onwards, to promote the formation of democratic sentiment.

A great man? I am sparing with this historical predicate because supposed greatness is all too readily associated, especially in the German view of history, with a glorification of authority. The Old Man displayed great qualities. He could also be extremely small-minded. All in all, he was an outstanding figure who performed a significant function in German and European history and left his mark on the Federal Republic's first fifteen years of existence.

Strange to say, my personal relations with Adenauer were passable despite my criticism of his obvious shortcomings and his own effronteries to me. Although he rarely visited Berlin, he was always accessible to its mayor. He did not show himself ungenerous in the matter of Federal finance for Berlin. There is no doubt that he also regarded money as a means of evading awkward political questions. This is not, however, to deny the stirrings of sympathy repeatedly felt by a former Mayor of Cologne who had always believed – with little exaggeration – that money was there to be raised and spent. He was impressed by West Berlin's town planning and transportation schemes, and said so. The Federal Minister of Finance was more than once outmanœuvred with Adenauer's help. On the mayor-to-mayor level, as it were, we exchanged many a candid word – indeed, many a token of mutual trust. Adenauer sometimes voiced extreme criticism of respected figures at home and abroad, notably those of his own party associates whom he considered boring or over-zealous, nor did he hesitate to advise me of changes in his cabinet long before any rumours appeared in the press.

His relations with Berlin and what he called the 'East' were, as I have already indicated, difficult. Robert Tillmanns, the Protestant Christian Democrat from Berlin, used to tell a story which he had doubtless heard from the Old Man himself. When Adenauer was President of the Prussian Council of State prior to 1933 and often travelled by rail from Cologne to Berlin, he always had the uneasy feeling – once across the Elbe – that he was 'almost in Asia'. He may also have regarded Berlin as an 'un-Christian, heathen' city and felt little desire to see it a capital again. Besides, he must surely have been aware that there were few votes to be garnered by him in Central Germany's cradle of social democracy.

Adenauer took a regrettably oversimplified view of the political landscape of Eastern Europe and was somewhat blunt in his verdicts on the leaders of communist countries. When I first visited him at his Rhöndorf home, Yugoslavia was on the verge of establishing full diplomatic relations with the GDR. Adenauer: 'You know all about the East,' – because I came from Berlin! – 'so what do you make of Herr Tito?' I essayed a qualified reply but did not get far. 'No, I'll tell you what I think: he's a common-or-garden bandit.'

Adenauer's instinctive and almost indiscriminate anti-communism went hand in hand with a tendency to underestimate the Soviet Union and its resources. He thought it only a matter of time before overwhelming US superiority contained the Russians and rolled them back, coincidentally writing finis to the GDR's communist régime. The Cold War had to be endured because it would end in favour of the West.

At the same time, Adenauer had a swift and intuitive grasp of many international configurations and often commented on them with dry humour. During my visit to his holiday retreat at Cadenabbia in autumn 1962 I was accompanied by Senator Klaus Schütz, later Mayor of Berlin. Adenauer had also invited Felix von Eckardt, the long-time chief press officer at Bonn and former head of the German UN 'observer' team who was now Federal Plenipotentiary in Berlin. Our discussions that day centred on the question of whether and how to normalize relations with the GDR. We debated whether it might be useful to develop the Fiduciary Authority for Inter-zonal Trade headed by Dr Kurt Leopold, which had existed since the Occupation and served as a commercial link between the two states. That would indeed have been an interesting approach to direct inter-governmental relations. Felix von Eckardt produced some informative reports on discussions with intermediaries from the other side. Adenauer was uninterested in the details, but at table he summarized all there was to say, from his point of view, in the inimitable words: *'Prost* to Leopold and the Chinese!' I also noted the following preprandial remark: 'Things haven't gone as we thought they would in 1948.' The Federal Chancellor did not, however, reach any decision on the matter.

The Berlin Wall had glaringly revealed the limitations of Adenauer's German policy and that of the Western Powers as well. The Chancellor's attitude towards ensuing negotiations between the Americans and the Soviet Union was not only sceptical but thoroughly mistrustful. His suspicious tendencies were such that he described two senior US officers to me as 'unreliable types' and declared that General Clay thought so too. It so happened that Clay was visiting Germany privately in his capacity as a member of the General Motors board. I called on him at the Hotel Petersburg and was able to dispel this dangerous misunderstanding at once.

Adenauer even complained to his immediate circle about John McCloy because he recommended recognition of the Oder-Neisse frontier and had allegedly hinted that relations with the GDR merited reconsideration as well. In general, Adenauer favoured a reliance on de Gaulle's reputedly inflexible approach to the Berlin question. He missed the long-standing support of his friend John Foster Dulles, although the latter had, during his final months in office, favoured a realistic review of outworn attitudes which conflicted with Bonn's scheme of things.

Adenauer's relationship with President de Gaulle had become steadily closer since autumn 1958. It soon took on a warm and even friendly character. Unfortunately, this major improvement in the Franco-German partnership was not kept well enough in balance with the rapport between Germany and other members of the Western Alliance. Relations with London and Washington turned cool. In January 1963 Adenauer and de Gaulle concluded the Franco-German Treaty of Co-operation, which I regarded as a major element in our own conception of our European role and later sought, as Federal Chancellor, to invest with new weight. Quite contrary to Adenauer's intentions, the Bundestag prefaced it with a pro-Atlantic preamble. This preamble diminished the treaty's importance in de Gaulle's eyes, though the French President bore a large measure of responsibility for its insertion:

a few days before signing the Elysée treaty, he had vetoed Britain's admission to the European Economic Community.

I discussed Britain and Europe quite frankly with Adenauer while visiting him at Cadenabbia on that fine autumn day in 1962. I argued that Europe had already been split once, and once too often. We could not afford another division on our own side of the Iron Curtain, and Britain's worldwide experience would contribute a great deal to the Community. I appealed to him to use his authority to overcome Franco-British rivalry in the European interest. His frank response: 'I won't do that, Herr Brandt. Look, what *is* Europe? . . . First and foremost, France and us. And things are going well. If the British make a third, there's no certainty that they'll continue to do so. With a threesome, you always have to allow for the possibility that two will gang up, and I'm afraid we'll be the odd man out.'

Quite obviously, I was disappointed by this information. It revealed Adenauer to be a thoroughgoing product of the nineteenth century. At the same time, I was amused by the peasant cunning of his terse and oversimplified analysis. Something else seemed clear as well: the elderly Chancellor was dominated by a kind of apprehensive patriotism. He was, in fact, worried about 'what will become of Germany' (to quote his heartfelt remark to Premier Bech of Luxemburg at Claridge's in London). He was always a little wary of his compatriots and their propensity for folly.

The final chapter of the Adenauer era really opened with the *Spiegel* affair in autumn 1962. The noted but not universally esteemed Hamburg weekly fell prey to a police operation which touched on the very essence of press freedom. It was occasioned by the so-called 'Fallex' report. This disclosed certain weaknesses in our defence system – weaknesses which were all too apparent and needed no 'breach of security' to point them out. The *Spiegel*'s editorial offices were ransacked in the course of a secret raid and its editor, Rudolf Augstein, was arrested in Hamburg. Adenauer talked recklessly of an 'abyss of treason'. The Old Man seemed to think, partly as a result of misleading hints from his intelligence services, that Augstein might be a Soviet agent. All these grave allegations misfired, but it became clear within a few days that the CSU boss and Defence Minister, Strauss, had been involved in the operation, which many construed as an act of vengeance.

Thanks to vigorous pressure from my friends in the Bundestag and committed members of the public, the *Spiegel* affair became a full-scale government crisis. The liberal Minister of Justice resigned (later to join our SPD ranks). F. J. Strauss's position in the Defence Ministry became untenable after he had lied to parliament, and Adenauer was forced to dismiss him.

The cleft was deeper than we realized. For all his characteristic realism, Konrad Adenauer had entirely misjudged the forces by which political, intellectual and social reality are moulded. He failed to grasp that government authority had been publicly and irreparably discredited. Already out of tune with the conservative CDU leadership, intellectuals protested on a broad front against the abuse of power which Strauss had come to symbolize. Over and above their flat rejection of the arrogance displayed by the 'party of government', writers, journalists, artists and academics began to develop an active commitment to social democracy. At the same time, however, there were sporadic tendencies towards total protest – towards a rejection of parliamentary democracy. An extra-parliamentary opposition began to stir. The upsurge of the youthful elements who believed our 'system' incapable of genuine self-reformation also dated from this occurrence, which was a moral petition in bankruptcy by those who had ruled the destinies of the Federal Republic during its first two decades. Whether the Social Democrats would (or could) assume their share of responsibility became the really vital question confronting our democracy. The *Spiegel* crisis thus became a sort of qualifying examination, not only for those affected, who had sometimes used 'Bonn' as a convenient scapegoat, but also for us.

The feasibility of a Grand Coalition first received serious consideration at Bonn in December 1962. Adenauer and Ollenhauer met on 3 December, but even their preliminary talks broke down – officially because my party refused to accept the plurality voting system demanded by the CDU/CSU but really because Adenauer still felt capable of sustaining his more convenient alliance with the Free Democrats. Adenauer's fifth cabinet was installed on 14 December, but his grip on the leadership had begun to slacken.

In mid-July 1963 I delivered a speech at the Evangelische Akademie in Tutzing for which I had chosen the title '*Denk ich an Deutschland*' ('Thinking of Germany'). I took as my starting-point the fears expressed by the international press that the Federal Republic had acquired greater significance than its allies intended. There had been a similar debate in earlier years, when controversy surrounded the question of rearmament. The problem had then been reduced to the briefest of formulas: the Federal Republic should be strong enough to hold the Soviet Union in check but – simultaneously and preferably – weaker than Luxemburg. This debate showed that the veneer of trust remained thin and that the Federal Republic was in many quarters viewed with critical detachment rather than friendly understanding – a state of affairs widely unperceived by our citizens.

I asked our friends in the outside world not to forget that one-third of our people had no conscious recollection of the Hitler years, and that this proportion was steadily growing. I could refer without an inferiority complex to the then Federal Chancellor's prestige abroad, but I knew that it would be one of our major tasks in the years ahead to widen and deepen this basis of trust in the world at large. We had achieved a great deal in the Federal Republic, but it was not enough to think in economic orders of magnitude. The country's internal structure was askew. There had been a failure to explain to people that their personal welfare must inevitably suffer if communal responsibilities were neglected. There had been a failure to define these communal responsibilities clearly and tackle them with vigour.

Turning to German foreign policy, I said that the real test was yet to come: 'We are neither the weight that tips the scales, nor an American antipole, nor a Cold War spearhead. The Federal Republic has its own part to play in the Concert of the West and its own contribution to make in accordance with a responsibility of which it cannot be deprived.'

In thinking 'of Germany' I was not merely taking my cue from Heinrich Heine's famous lines but making an unintentional allusion to Adenauer's cry from the heart. In retrospect I seem almost to have heralded his departure from government with a critical résumé. One day, I said, it would probably be deemed a major achievement on Chancellor Adenauer's part that he substantially helped to prevent our nation from tearing itself apart over questions relating to the dark days before 1945; that with his help much time had been gained in which bygone evils could fade. But this success had been achieved by a largely opportunist attitude. It was not the product of a full national debate about ourselves and our past. In default of German self-purification, our nation would lack the strength to confront its past with objective rigour and compassionate sincerity . . .

A nation must look upon its history, peaks and troughs included, as an indivisible burden that cannot be evaded and must be borne. Adenauer succeeded by dint of personal authority and acquired prestige in winning the confidence of the outside world. He was less successful in transmitting this confidence to our people. On the contrary, he spoke anxiously of the time when his hand would no longer hold the reins.

On 15 October 1963, after fourteen years of reconstruction and a decade of undisputed leadership, Konrad Adenauer's Chancellorship came to an end. He had bidden farewell to Berlin a few days earlier. At my instance, he was awarded honorary citizenship. I pointed out during the investiture that I regarded this award as a matter of political style: 'Honouring a person entails honesty. We must not now act as if there has been no tension between Bonn and Berlin, no opposition between Adenauer and Reuter, no conflict between Adenauer and Brandt. That there has been, and a thing or two besides, and we do not gloss it over. But none of this alters the fact that the German capital is honouring the man who stood at the helm of free Germany for fourteen years, and that even his political opponents are paying tribute to that man.'

I listened to Adenauer's speech of thanks with considerable pleasure. His relaxed manner and the artful simplicity with which he fielded my carefully chosen remarks were a demonstration of the gifts that had enabled him to dominate the political stage of his native Cologne and eventually of the German Federal Republic. Allusions had been made to conflicts, he said: 'I know nothing of conflicts any more.' But his attitude throughout life had been that anyone 'who has never had a conflict, ladies and gentlemen, isn't worth much . . . Conflicts must be fought to a finish. When they are, they belong to the past . . . Why should they trouble us further in our common task?' Adenauer also made one of his somewhat rare and doubtless slightly insincere avowals of faith in Berlin's future as a capital city. Whether or not with deliberate intent, he did so rather perfunctorily.

So now this incomparable personality – Wehner likened Adenauer to 'political bedrock' – had suddenly ceased to be the decisive and formative figure in the young German state. Everyone knew that the day must come. The Old Man had truly grown old in harness. Many of his party associates seemed faintly relieved to be rid of him at last (although he retained the party chairmanship until March 1966). His political opponents felt no inclination to cast stones at him on his departure from office. I recall his 90th birthday in January 1966, which he celebrated with a large party of guests at Godesberg's La Redoute. I can still see him standing there, poker-backed and speaking without notes as he took us back in time to the last century. It was true – he spoke of 1888 and told how he had witnessed Kaiser Wilhelm's visit to Cologne as a schoolboy . . .

Adenauer set himself at the head of the Christian Democratic Union and made it an umbrella movement in the dual sense. The CDU accommodated those elements in the political spectrum of the Weimar Republic that had transferred their allegiance from the Catholic centre, via the right-wing liberal DVP (German People's Party; some supporters of the erstwhile 'left'-leaning DDP or German Democratic Party included), to the DNVP or German National People's Party. Smaller parties were absorbed by the CDU. But Adenauer, who had never personally made concessions to the Nazis, applied no strict criteria to fellow-travellers and supporters of National Socialism. They remained unscathed, especially the bureaucrats among them, and found it easy enough to reoccupy their former niches in industry or carve out new ones. Adenauer reserved the arbitrary right to decide who was, and who was not, a Nazi. One example of this was his toleration of State Secretary Hans Globke, who admittedly became an indispensable administrative aide. The stigma that had clung to Globke since his commentary on the Nuremberg Laws was not expunged by his tenure of a highly responsible post. Other forms of service could have been found for him and his like.

Our Christian Democratic parties are complicated organisms. Originally weak in terms of grass roots organization, they rather resembled electoral clubs centred on influential figures in the municipalities and *Länder* and designed to secure majorities and political office for representatives of their own colour. Competition with the Social Democrats gradually developed them into modern parties with subscribing members and a hard core of local and regional associations. However, the self-styled 'Christian' parties have continued to present a variegated appearance and cannot be understood without reference to their historical and regional characteristics. The following is a simplified account of their main constituents. One of the latter was a legacy from the Catholic Centre Parties mentioned above, principally those of the Rhineland and Westphalia, which displayed elements of a modern social policy. The Bavarian counterpart was more conservative. Protestant influence stemmed from a strong base in the nationalistic middle and lower middle class but was sporadically tinged with liberal traditions. Co-operation between Catholics and Protestants in the anti-Hitler resistance movement, which strongly influenced sentiment in the immediate post-war period, never entirely waned, but the spirit of conservatism has predominated over the decades.

There still exists a small 'left-wing' group sustained primarily by Catholic members of the working class. Although this has sometimes stood out in sharp relief against the party majority while in opposition, it has seldom affected the climate or decisions of the party as a whole. The broad centre of the CDU/CSU is moderately conservative and tries to combine European with traditional nationalist ideas. Although it sometimes shows itself receptive to liberal ideas and social progress, the forces of inertia predominate.

Finally, one can speak of a powerful right wing personified by the Bavarian leader Franz Josef Strauss. In Bavaria the party styles itself the Christian Social Union (hence 'CSU') but is more conservative than its sister-party elsewhere in Germany. The CSU may fairly be said to have militantly reactionary and nationalistic leanings. This right wing, which also possesses influential allies and numerous supporters in the north and west of the Federal Republic, has consistently aroused the fiercest opposition among liberal intellectuals. Although Strauss and his backers have never won a majority in the party as a whole, they are powerful enough to exert an appreciable influence on CDU/CSU policy. Again, even though Strauss has never been a candidate for the Chancellorship, he has often wielded sufficient authority to impose his will on the Union. He continues to be a fierce opponent of social liberalization, industrial democracy and, last but not least, our policy of détente. Whether by design or not, his populist presentation of national-ism has secured him the backing of groups which either hanker after the Third Reich or aspire to emulate it in some modified form.

This process of accumulation was Adenauer's paramount achieve-ment in the field of national politics. For the CDU, it naturally carried a penalty. The evil spirit of yesteryear still marched in the ranks of many groups that attached themselves to it, so the cardinal need to tackle the 'recent past' became obscured. The past was 'surmounted' by the passage of time. Younger age-groups were following on. A coalition of grandparents and grandchildren seemed to be prevailing over the generation that had been rent and riven by the Third Reich. Perhaps the risk was a necessary one. I will not pass judgement on it. I myself became familiar with the problems of integration in another way.

But this contribution to the shaping of our political geography strikes me as more important than the superficial linking of Adenauer's name with the amazing economic resurgence known as the 'German miracle'. On this score greater tribute should be paid to Ludwig Erhard, to the trade unions, to the extreme diligence of factory and office workers, to the constructive enthusiasm of millions of refugees, to the Marshall Plan and the discernment of our conquerors, to the strange metamorphosis of destruction and dismantlement into scope for modernization, and to many other factors. It is possible that all of this presupposed psychological dependence on some figure who could wield a fortifying and reassuring influence after the profound mental confusion to which our fellow-countrymen had been subjected, after their drastic disenchantment and unremitting fear – after the most radical hiatus in their history.

The Old Man certainly never exaggerated his respect for parliament.

I recall a visit to the Chancellor's private residence at Rhöndorf in autumn 1958 (he had a cold). 'Have you heard?' he said. 'When de Gaulle enters the National Assembly, everyone has to stand up.' (De Gaulle was head of government at the time, not President.) Brentano, who was also present, ventured an interpolation: 'He's a little bit envious, wouldn't you say?' Once during a visit to Berlin, as we were walking downstairs from my office in the Schöneberger Rathaus, he reverted to an earlier conversation: 'We were speaking of the Bundestag, Herr Brandt. I'll tell you what to do with the Bundestag – perhaps you'll think it over some time. You have to pay the gentlemen well, let them travel a lot and give them plenty of time off.'

Perhaps Adenauer sensed more clearly than some of his opponents that – at least for the present – most Germans had been purged of nationalism and might be ripe for a European nexus. Apart from his doubts about the chances of reunification, this was probably the intuitive origin of the foreign policy that so swiftly harnessed our young republic to the West.

There is, however, absolutely no sign that Adenauer and his opponents – mainly but not exclusively Social Democrats – ever disputed the relative merits of orientation towards West or East. Schumacher was a resolute anti-communist, Reuter defended Berlin, and the SPD had always espoused European unity. The question was not whether, but how. The first Chancellor's opponents wanted more fully to explore the possibility that assured democracy and friendship with the West might yet permit a compromise with the East which would enable the division of Germany to be surmounted.

It may be said that Adenauer was quicker than others to recognize the permanence of the demarcation agreed on by the Russians and Americans at the end of the war. This did not, for all that, deter the Chancellor from continuing to speak of reunification and even from expressing his hope that the East Prussians, as well as the Pomeranians and Silesians, would return to their homelands. It may equally be said that Adenauer substantially helped to crystallize the *status quo*. He undoubtedly attached more importance to securing the latter than to the possibility of change. Opportunities which presented themselves were left unexploited or even unexplored. Although Adenauer acted consistently from his own point of view, the implied reproach cannot be dismissed. Overall political performance, both positive and negative, is based on consistency.

It would be wrong to suppose that Adenauer regarded the Federal Republic's foreign policy objectives as fulfilled by the irrevocable link with Europe and America. To him, *Ostpolitik* existed less as a formula

than as an outline for a new developmental phase towards which he
groped his way far earlier than the public suspected.

His party associates were startled, if not shocked, when he followed
up his retirement from the Chancellorship at the CDU Conference
of March 1966 by unexpectedly classifying the Soviet Union (with reference to its soothing influence on the clash between India and Pakistan)
as one of the countries which 'want peace'. This surprisingly positive
change of tack was not unheralded. Adenauer's memoirs tell us how
profoundly he had been impressed by his visit to Moscow and his talks
with Khrushchev. This meeting had little influence on his actual
policies, however, and he never brought himself to draw the conclusions which a revised attitude towards Eastern Europe and the
Soviet Union would have entailed. Adenauer never became an advocate
of détente, even in retirement. As late as 1967 he christened the Nuclear
Non-Proliferation Treaty a 'Morgenthau Plan squared'.

He did, nevertheless, fully grasp the need to submit our position to
critical appraisal and look for new openings, even if he always publicly
sacrificed that need to his demagogic invocations of the 'Red peril' and
innuendoes against political opponents at home. On 17 June 1963, while
we were talking in my Berlin office, Adenauer suddenly gave the
conversation an unexpected twist. 'Tell me, Herr Brandt,' he said
abruptly, 'what do you think of the Hallstein Doctrine?' (This prescribed the severance of diplomatic relations with countries recognizing
the GDR as a sovereign state.) Justifiably reluctant to commit myself
on the spot, I simply said, 'Herr Bundeskanzler, how am I meant to
take your question?' Adenauer: 'Well, you know – you have to give
certain things away as long as you get something in return.'

I said I would call on him in Bonn in a few days' time because I
wanted more information about his ideas before considering what joint
action our two parties might be able to undertake. I arranged to meet
him at the Palais Schaumburg the very next day, but Adenauer had
clearly lost all inclination to pursue the subject which he himself had
broached. Whether or not his advisers had warned him off, he sought
refuge in trivia. To put it another way, he lacked the strength, not the
discernment, to throw his weight behind a revision of the German
policy established during his years in office even though he considered
its revision necessary.

We now know that he was far from regarding his own rigid norms
as sacrosanct, and that he tentatively juggled – at least from time to
time – with various solutions of the 'German question'. As early as
March 1958 he proposed in the Bundestag a ten-year guarantee of the
status quo balanced by a settlement covering the Soviet-occupied zone

which corresponded to the four victorious powers' treaty in respect of Austria. (The Chancellor privately remarked to his friend Heinrich Krone that, if the scheme came off, the whole of Berlin could ultimately be incorporated in the GDR.) That same spring, he canvassed the idea of a kind of 'Austrian solution' (neutralization of the 'Zone'), first to Ambassador Smirnov and a second time during Deputy Premier Mikoyan's visit to Bonn at the end of April.

Moscow showed no tendency to accept an altered situation which would have diminished the Soviet Union's influence in Central Europe. Instead, Nikita Khrushchev resolved on an offensive. On 10 November 1958 at the Moscow Palace of Sport, he delivered the blustering speech that heralded the Berlin ultimatum formulated seventeen days later in notes to the three Western Powers. He had previously sent Ambassador Smirnov to Adenauer to inform him – whatever he meant by it – that Soviet measures were not aimed at impairing relations with the Federal Republic.

There appears to have been a growing realization in Adenauer's entourage that the grim prospect of dramatic developments in and over Berlin precluded an attitude of pure inertia. In the course of secret deliberations never expressly approved by the Federal Chancellor, even in private, tests were run on some more constructive proposals culminating in the so-called 'Globke Plan' of early 1959. By November 1960 there existed an amplified version which outlined the following solution. The two German states were provisionally to retain their status as sovereign entities and establish diplomatic relations. After five years, the question of reunification would be settled by a referendum. It would thereafter be decided whether a reunified Germany should join NATO or the Warsaw Pact. That part of Germany which thereby severed its links with one or other of the alliances would be demilitarized. Free-city status was proposed for Berlin, and the settlement was not to affect the eastern territories under Polish administration.

To the best of my knowledge, this plan was never discussed with the Western Powers, still less with any representatives of the Soviet Union. Adenauer remarked to Kennedy during a visit to Washington in November 1961 that he was counting on a new status for Berlin (this was after the Wall!) and that no concessions must be made to the Russians on the German question. Speaking to Heinrich Krone on 7 December 1961, however, he said that for the 'rest of his life, he considered it of paramount importance . . . to set our relations with Russia tolerably straight.'

In the spring of 1962, American proposals for talks between

Kennedy's Secretary of State, Dean Rusk, and his Soviet opposite number, Andrei Gromyko, became known in consequence of Bonn indiscretions for which Brentano himself has sometimes been blamed. (Whatever the truth, the position of Grewe, our not over-popular ambassador in Washington, became untenable and he was replaced.) The American scheme envisaged an international access authority for Berlin. NATO and the Warsaw Pact were to exchange non-aggression declarations guaranteeing the existing frontiers. It was further proposed to agree on the non-transference of atomic weapons to either German partner. The German Federal Republic and the GDR were to set up joint technical commissions. Finally, the status and development of Germany and Berlin would be supervised by a standing conference of the deputy foreign ministers of the four victorious powers.

In summer 1962 Adenauer submitted his offer of a 'truce' in Germany. Though not precisely defined, this may have been largely identical in substance with the 'Globke Plan': the 'German question' was, in a sense, to hang fire for ten years. In July 1962 the Federal Chancellor told the Soviet Ambassador that a 'people's peace' (whatever that meant) could be concluded on the basis of the *status quo* provided conditions in the 'Zone' were ameliorated in the interests of greater freedom. The Chancellor retrospectively confirmed this plan in 1963, stating that he had proposed the holding of a referendum on reunification after ten years if the prerequisites for a free vote had since been created in the 'Zone'. (The Soviet Foreign Ministry disputed these conditions.)

It did indeed betoken a growth of understanding when Adenauer announced to the Bundestag on 9 October 1962: 'I again declare that the Federal Government is ready to discuss a great many things if our brothers in the 'Zone' can dispose their lives as they wish. To us, considerations of humanity play an even greater role here than national considerations.' This formulation became a sort of key to the crucial question of our attitude to national unity, but it went unanswered and had no effect on the attitude of the Federal Republic itself. Although Adenauer spoke of a 'standstill agreement' during his Washington visit in November 1962, the Americans seem to have either misunderstood or rejected the suggestion. In any case, relations between Adenauer and the young American President were temporarily cooling off. Kennedy conferred with the British Prime Minister, Harold Macmillan, in Bermuda at the end of 1962. As a solution to the problem of nuclear arms for Great Britain and the countries of Western Europe, the ghost-fleet known as MLF (Multilateral Force) was devised. Macmillan had earlier – if French records are correct – turned down de Gaulle's proposal for a joint nuclear force. Paris reacted irritably to the Bermuda decisions, and Adenauer, who had covertly mistrusted the Americans for some time, sought even closer links with de Gaulle's France. In this connection, the Franco-German friendship treaty was upgraded several notches. Largely owing to Foreign Minister Schröder's influence, Bonn nonetheless accepted the scheme – in which Kennedy soon lost interest – for a nuclear-armed fleet.

Bonn's mood did not improve when, after the treaty of friendship had been concluded with Paris, Kennedy wrote Adenauer a letter containing the barbed remark that the Federal Republic must make up its mind whether to go with France or the United States. US-German relations were further strained by Bonn's sour attitude to the nuclear test-ban treaty signed in Moscow on 5 August, which many analysts of East-West relations rightly identified as the prologue to a strategy of détente. Khrushchev had meanwhile shown repeated signs of interest in a visit to Bonn. Heinrich Krone, probably Adenauer's most faithful chronicler, notes that the Federal Chancellor did not respond at this stage because he no longer felt fully competent to act.

He made no visible or audible response, either, during the presentation of honorary Berlin citizenship a few days before his retirement, when I spoke of our duty to persuade Russia to adopt a different German policy. Quoting the key phrase from the communiqué released by Adenauer and Kennedy on the eve of the American President's visit to Germany – 'strategy of peace' – I added that, although different methods might be necessary in future, we must never lose sight of the objective . . . Later, when Adenauer had left office and I had yet to become Foreign Minister of the Grand Coalition, he remarked in the course of conversation: 'We handled the Russians badly. The gentlemen of the Foreign Office did the wrong thing. Just think how they treated the [first Soviet] ambassador!'

Trying to summarize the various facets of Adenauer's *Ostpolitik*, one might say that they often displayed the necessary toughness but were amply distinguished by obstinacy, timidity – and sporadic flashes of insight. This implies that it is possible to draw up a list of neglected opportunities. Against this, there is the Federal Republic's incorporation in the burgeoning European Community and the Western Alliance. Many citizens of the Federal Republic additionally construed this process as a moral and spiritual decision in favour of the Western way of life and ideals of existence.

The term 'citizen' touches some common chord. Adenauer did not stand for the middle class which was said to be at last fulfilling the ideals of democratic revolution after a lapse of more than a century, but he did, despite his relatively humble origins, represent the upper-middle-class type. Middle-class social responsibility was not at variance with the patrician concept of authority which the first Federal Chancellor had adopted.

Adenauer ruled the German Federal Republic like a mayor armed with far-reaching powers. His hatred of dictatorship and blatant assaults on freedom impressed me as heartfelt and staunchly middle class. His imperious manner was the distillation of a long and arduous life. Not a word of my televised tribute on the night of 19 April 1967 stemmed from a purely conventional respect for the dead:

He made the free part of Germany an ally of the West, lent powerful impulses to West European unity and, last but not least, devoted himself to Franco-German reconciliation. He has bequeathed us the task of bringing the divided German people together in the process of European development . . . Konrad Adenauer personified the continuity of peaceful thinking in Germany through four political epochs. His personal authority and the pugnacious verve that accompanied him into the latter years of his life evoked enthusiastic assent or firm rejection. Even his political opponents of yesterday are conscious that Germany is poorer for the loss of a man who set standards.

The lifetime's achievements of this man were great enough for the international wielders of power and responsibility to gather at his grave as they did on the death of Churchill, Kennedy or de Gaulle. He himself would hardly have thought this possible when he took the oath as Federal Chancellor in 1949. He could not have guessed that the pomp which attended his funeral would be the new German democracy's first major solo performance on the world stage. As a pragmatist, he would probably have smiled to see the touchingly maladroit way in which President Lübke made sure that Lyndon B. Johnson and Charles de Gaulle held hands for an official photo. As a lover of cynical little jokes, he would not have been offended that advantage was taken of the occasion to hold brisk *ad hoc* conferences which rapidly earned it the name of a 'working funeral'.

3

John F. Kennedy

My personal and political ties with the United States, which became more and more manifold as the years went by, were strengthened by contact with a man who exemplified the qualities of modern America with uncommon vividness and clarity: John F. Kennedy. I am as unconcerned with hero-worship as with harsh retrospective criticism, both of which now seem to govern popular assessments of a statesman whose fate it was to assume responsibility for his nation at the age of 43. It was hardly surprising that I experienced a sense of partnership at our very first meeting. I was only a few years older. We both belonged to the generation that had entered political life during World War II, though by very different routes. Above and beyond the defence of traditional values, we were prepared to contemplate 'new horizons' in the development of our peoples. We strove to remain receptive to the intellectual stimuli and currents of our time. We could laugh together – and this was not unimportant – at the same remarks and jokes.

I was fascinated by the man who had written a book about the cardinal need for courage in politics and had opened it with a fine definition by Ernest Hemingway which characterized himself: courage is 'grace under pressure'. I was equally impressed by his plea for the necessity of compromise, which he openly defended, only to add: 'We can compromise our political positions, but not ourselves. We can resolve the clash of interests without conceding our ideals. And even the necessity for the right kind of compromise does not eliminate the need for those idealists and reformers who keep our compromises moving ahead . . .' This blend of loyalty to principle and sceptical discrimination corresponded to the attitude on which, in my judgement as well as his, a political existence should be founded.

John Fitzgerald Kennedy was certainly not as liberal, still less 'socialistic', as many Europeans (and Latin Americans) supposed or many of his fellow-countrymen suspected. If we must label him, he may in many respects be classified as an ultra-modern conservative who was unusually receptive to new lines of questioning, remarkably free from prejudice, and endowed with a felicitous combination of political acumen and intellect, personal authority and mental drive.

The effect of this combination was accentuated by the aristocratic glamour of his appearance, which was, in turn, slightly diminished by an impression of youthful light-heartedness. Many people innocently regarded the young President as a sort of elective monarch. To me, of course, he was first and foremost a staple ingredient of the international scene, crucial to the East-West conflict and important to Atlantic and US-German relations. Although I could not devote equal attention to his strenuous political endeavours at home, I was able to sense that he had, as it were, raised his aerial to pick up storm warnings and signals relating to the future needs of modern industrial society. This also went for the field of tension which has, over the years, engendered a world-wide North-South conflict of ever more discernible and threatening proportions. Kennedy was ahead of his time in both respects.

He was even more alive to the problems of East-West relations, the perils of the arms race and nuclear escalation in particular, and thus to the objective need for US relations with the other super-power to be reorganized – in other words, based as far as possible on businesslike, if not relaxed, co-operation. A decade-and-a-half later, it is possible to contend that President Kennedy might well have bequeathed us something more than the Cold War had prescribed in advance, and that his much lauded courage in taking the ultimate gamble was qualified by an adherence to outmoded patterns of thought. Be that as it may, he had a better and more intimate understanding than any other contemporary statesman of how to outline the route to organized world peace, win the hearts of people throughout the globe, and sow the seeds of hope. The 'new frontiers' that were intended to characterize his domestic programme transmitted themselves to us as a peace-keeping system to be maintained by novel means.

Kennedy's typical combination of firmness and flexibility may never have been more clearly comprehended than during his triumphal visit to Berlin on 26 June 1963. Never in the city's history, I suppose, has a visitor been greeted with such genuine rejoicing. Enthusiasm blazed up almost too fiercely for my taste when Kennedy, speaking in well-turned phrases, appealed to the harassed city's spirit of resistance. Any notes of compromise and conciliation were drowned by the thunder of applause. It was hard not to be swept along. The elegance and intelligence of Kennedy's language were admirable.

By the time we drove through the streets in an open car, it is probable that even Konrad Adenauer was reconciled to the President's Berlin visit, which had encountered a few reservations in Bonn and scattered resistance in Washington. The Federal Chancellor stood on my left, protocol having placed me, as host, in the centre. John F. Kennedy stood on my right, and it was to him that so many thousands of hands shot out. The arrangements had been laborious enough. The administrative details had occupied a long evening at the Pacelli-Allee residence of General James Polk (the US Commandant), where we discussed them with Kenneth O'Donnell, Kennedy's human appointments book, and his cheerfully astute press officer Pierre Salinger. Salinger belonged to the nucleus of intellectuals whom Kennedy had gathered about him (in addition to the 'Irish Mafia' which controlled his organization). Prominent among them were the likeable and egregious Theodore Sorensen, who had consulted me in Bonn about the line to be taken by the President's speech, the brilliant historian Arthur Schlesinger Jr, the cool but committed analyst McGeorge Bundy (of the National Security Council), and Richard Goodwin, Kennedy's 'chief of staff'. The team also included Henry Kissinger (briefly) and many others. Kennedy had been adept in recruiting people and gaining their loyalty.

In Berlin, John F. Kennedy received the fervent acclamation he was so seldom unanimously accorded at home. Security men had to put up with the fact that crowds repeatedly broke through the cordon and tossed flowers into the car. The Berliners fêted him as something more than a powerful friend and guarantor of their freedom. Their homage contained an element of gratitude towards a former enemy who was demonstrating to the Germans that the West's foremost power had made its peace with them – that they had rejoined the family of nations.

The first item on the programme – rather a superfluous one by current Bonn standards – was a visit to the conference of the Bau, Steine, Erden industrial trade union, which was meeting under the chairmanship of Georg Leber, subsequently Minister of Transport and Defence. Also present were George Meany, the tough AFL/CIO President, and Ludwig Rosenberg, President of the DGB (*Deutscher Gewerkschaftsbund* or Federation of German Trade Unions). Kennedy was at pains to emphasize the achievements of labour and the role of the trade unions during his visit to Germany, which could do him no harm at home. The American trade unions had been good friends to us in the Federal Republic and Berlin during the difficult post-war years.

We made two stops at the sector border, where we saw a depressing sight. An additional barrier had been erected for the occasion on the other side of Checkpoint Charlie. A few East Berliners could just be glimpsed in the far distance, waving timidly. At the Brandenburg Gate, the view had been obscured by red bunting. As we lingered on the wooden platform, gazing across, Kennedy asked where the Hotel Adlon had stood. He had followed up a visit to his father, then US Ambassador in London, by spending a few days there just before the outbreak of war. He also toured the devastated remains of the capital as an International News Service reporter during the Potsdam Conference in summer 1945.

A seething mass awaited us outside the Schöneberger Rathaus in Rudolph-Wilde-Platz, since renamed Kennedy-Platz. Kennedy projected himself into the minds of his audience with uncommon skill. The crowd roared its approval when he declared that he was a Berliner – he had rehearsed the German sentence during a breather in my office. The public expected more than it could be given, but the President not only extolled the city's spirit of resistance and the superiority of the West (which Khrushchev proposed to 'bury'); he drew attention to the prospects for a just peace. I contrived, as on other occasions, to subdue the crowd's emotions with a few incisive gestures. It was an unprecedented demonstration, both in size and fervour – the biggest welcome Kennedy had ever received, so Salinger announced on his behalf. Schoolchildren were excused classes and well over a million people turned out. The security men had a hard time. Police cordons were repeatedly broken, and it was not always easy to intercept the bunches of flowers that came the President's way. But, for all the passions it inflamed, the huge demonstration in front of the Rathaus passed off without incident.

Kennedy's hours in Berlin were the undoubted high-spot of his trip to Germany. Despite his faint air of exhaustion when saying goodbye at Tegel airfield that evening, he did not disguise how much he had enjoyed the day's experiences. He would, he said, leave his successor at the White House a brief note to be opened in time of discouragement: 'Go to Germany, go to Berlin!' Jacqueline Kennedy and his mother, Rose Kennedy, told me after the President's death that he had more than once watched the documentary film of his visit to the Federal Republic and Berlin.

Although his relations with Bonn officialdom were not trouble-free, as I have said, the spontaneous welcome given him by people at every stage in his German tour – in Cologne, Bonn and Frankfurt – could not fail to move this cool and detached but far from unemotional man. He sensed that he was getting his message across to the Germans too. They seemed to understand that this young statesman was opening up new political dimensions. Like his fellow-countrymen, they listened with fervent eagerness to his appeal to the unexpended spiritual and moral forces that counselled a farewell to smug complacency, called for self-sacrifice, inspired pride and awakened a realization that it is not enough to ask what 'your country can do for you, but what you can do for your country'.

Kennedy had a lively urge for self-assertion, and he sometimes expressed himself in an imperious way. He also showed, however, that he was thinking beyond the Cold War and planned an advance to 'new frontiers' in foreign as well as domestic policy. Some have said that he brought the United States to a zenith of 'imperial' self-esteem, and they may be right. His Presidency is not without reason held responsible for the transition to the second stage of America's involvement in South-East Asia. I nonetheless doubt whether – despite the temptations of the 'domino theory', which he did not strictly disavow – he would ever have got himself as deeply and inextricably entangled as his successor, Lyndon B. Johnson. It became evident, particularly in East-West relations, that he did not regard foreign policy simply as an extension of military strategy. To him, power-political responsibility entailed a combination of firmness, moderation and the spirit of compromise.

Frankfurt's Church of St Paul, that symbol of our abortive democratic revolution of 1848, is an anchorage-point in US-German relations because many refugees sought a new home in America after the liberal uprising was quelled. Shrewdly advised, Kennedy chose the Church of St Paul for the central speech of his German visit. It was here that he called for an Atlantic partnership – a totality of independent parts in which burdens and decisions would be shared. The United States was risking its cities to defend ours because it needed our freedom to protect its own. Kennedy further called for the development of a democratic European community but left it to the Europeans to choose their own roads to unity, for it was 'the Europeans who are building Europe'. Nobody had ever before heard an American declare himself so clearly in favour of the laboriously developing unification of the Continent. At the same time, his candour was designed to accommodate de Gaulle. Here, too, Kennedy was striving to open a door.

Look to the future – that was the lesson of his visit. I saw Kennedy three times in Bonn before he came to Berlin. Just after 8 a.m. on 25 June 1963 I met him for breakfast and a private talk at the residence of the US Ambassador. Unlike me, he was in top gear at that early hour. He was also clearly accustomed to an ample breakfast and chided me because, in accordance with my usual habit, I had tea and little else. We discussed the possibility of fresh co-operation in the coming years. Kennedy surmised that Harold Wilson would soon be Prime Minister of Great Britain and that I and my friends stood a fair chance in Germany. Together with the Scandinavians, we could initiate a whole range of sensible policies. With his concurrence, Hubert Humphrey and Walter Reuther were maintaining contact with the circle of politicians and trade unionists which had for years been meeting at Tage Erlander's (Swedish Social Democrat, premier 1946–69) home in Harpsund. Italy, said Kennedy, remained a difficult area, and the French socialists worried him because of their popular front tendencies.

Turning to Bonn, he declared that Adenauer's mistrust astonished him. He reverted to it at lunch next day in Berlin's Brandenburghalle. Having presented the city's leading political figures to him in the Senate Chamber, I was detained for a few minutes by a conversation with one of my associates. Kennedy and Adenauer sat down together in an adjacent room. The Old Man put these minutes to strange use by striving to persuade our guest that the German Social Democrats were unreliable types from the Western point of view. Kennedy confided this episode to me with a touch of glee which in no way conflicted with his respect for the Chancellor.

At the beginning of June 1963, or shortly before Kennedy's German visit, I spent a few days in the United States (though not in Washington). In New York I dined with Adlai Stevenson, who was then representing his country at the United Nations as an ambassador with cabinet rank. He had a rather reserved attitude to the problems of Germany and was insufficiently well-informed about Berlin, but he impressed me, as ever, by his brilliant intellect. Recalling him later, I said that his influence on American policy would be enduring. The moral categories of his practical thinking were inseparable from the international debate on human coexistence. Pursuing the question of coexistence, which has become a fundamental thread in my own fabric of ideas, I quoted his dictum: 'Coexistence is not a form of passive acceptance of things as they are.'

I was invited to Harvard to receive an honorary degree in company with Secretary of State Dean Rusk, UN Secretary-General Sithu U Thant and my old friend George Kennan, the leading expert on Russia and Germany. On 10 June, while I was staying in New York, Kennedy delivered his speech on peace, 'the most important topic on earth', at the American University in Washington. Its theme was that total war had become senseless and that the Cold War was obsolete. What had to be created was not 'a *Pax Americana* imposed on the world by American weapons of war', not 'the peace of the grave or the security of the slave' (as Arthur Schlesinger Jr expressed it): 'Not merely peace for Americans but peace . . . in all time . . . the rational end of rational men.' He hoped that the Soviet leaders would adopt a more enlightened attitude and believed that they could be helped to do so. America must manage its own affairs in such a way that the Russians deemed it in their own interests to make progress towards a genuine peace. The President pleaded for increased contacts and better understanding, likewise for a new effort to reach agreement on a nuclear test ban. 'History teaches us,' he declared, 'that enmities between nations . . . do not last for ever . . . So let us persevere. Peace need not be impracticable, and war need not be inevitable.'

This was something new. The speech issued a summons. Commenting from America, I said that it disclosed a new, comprehensive and realistic attempt to modify the East-West relationship. It carried particular weight with us because we saw it as a logical extension of the speech he had made at Philadelphia a year earlier, in April 1962, in which he had voiced his country's hopes for a united Europe within the framework of an Atlantic partnership. He contrasted 'interdependence' with the American 'independence' that had been proclaimed at Philadelphia in 1776. He also showed in the same speech that a close connection existed between the establishment of a US-European partnership and a new social order.

What impressed me even more than Kennedy's fascinating power of words was his determination to think creatively – to think ahead, as it were. Many ideas which I myself had noted – and sometimes voiced – tended in a similar direction. I felt emboldened to explore 'new frontiers' in a divided world at my own post of responsibility.

Some months after Kennedy's German visit I voiced my agreement and support for the President's main points in a speech at Nuremberg's Amerikahaus. The supervision and limitation of armaments was only another aspect of the same security policy. We had to make it clear beyond all doubt that Germany was interested in détente, not in the maintenance of tension. The communist peril still existed, but it was not what it had been a few years previously. The East-West conflict still existed, but it was becoming partially overlaid by the South-North conflict between affluent and impoverished nations. 'I consider it pernicious to insinuate that the American President is seeking agreements with the Soviet Union at the expense of the Federal Republic and the Europeans. Kennedy has stressed the contrary . . . They (the Americans) naturally have as little desire to see a vacuum in Central Europe as we do . . . They naturally realize as well as we do that détente may only remain a temporary process.' I added that, whether as a whole or in part, Europe must not lapse into a relationship of inferior status, and that to talk of Europe as a world power would be wholly in keeping with this idea. There was no need for the Federal Republic to be one day compelled to choose between friendship with France or the United States. We must not fall prey to morbid mistrust. German-American friendship remained one of our cornerstones amid the turbulence of international politics.

Experience of American solidarity during the painful post-war history of Berlin – from the Blockade, via Khrushchev's ultimatum, to John F. Kennedy's triumphal visit to my city – had confirmed what I expounded for my own and others' benefit in war-time discussions and public pronouncements: that a democratic Germany and a free Europe could only live in clear accord with the United States because the two continents were linked by vital interests.

It had become apparent in each of the Berlin crises that the United States could not be regarded as an alien power on our continent. Conservative isolationist forces had succeeded in forcing America to abnegate its international responsibilities after World War I. This could not be allowed to happen again. Joint US responsibility for the fate of Germany and Berlin had become inalienable under the laws of conquest and occupation, and the US presence, legitimized by international law, became more consolidated the more ruthlessly an aggressive policy on the part of the Russians and their German allies sought to oust US troops from Berlin, if not from Germany and Western Europe as a whole. In reality, America had spoken and acted since 1945 as a quasi-European power. It also showed itself determined to organize US-European relations within the Atlantic partnership of which Kennedy spoke. It was a long time – not until the Conference on Security and Co-operation in Europe – before an East-West consensus accepted the American (and Canadian) presence in Western Europe as a matter of course.

For me, close links with the United States – which by no means militated against the goal of a European Union – were a basic requirement of German policy. President Eisenhower, first head of the US Military Government in Germany and four years later appointed to command the Atlantic Pact forces, could be regarded as a personified guarantee of the fateful but constructive link between American and German developments. He received me at the White House twice, once in February 1958 and again in 1959.

Eisenhower had just recovered from the effects of a stroke when I first visited him. He greeted me cordially and, in simple words, emphasized his commitment to the people of Berlin. In spring 1945, when US troops could easily have pushed on to the German capital but were held in check on political instructions, he is said to have remarked –

rather casually – that it wasn't too important who held Berlin. If so, he had long since seen his mistake and was at pains to shroud the recollection during our talk.

The detailed aspect of our problems interested him little, but he fully grasped the importance of Berlin as a fundamental problem in its own right. It was easy to recognize the experienced military leader accustomed to making decisions and delegating responsibility for their execution. Eisenhower managed with some success (at least in foreign policy) to adapt a supreme commander's thought-patterns to his style of political leadership. Although it could not be said that any lively exchange of ideas emerged from our talk, reassurance about Berlin's position was my principal concern. Despite a certain lack of mental affinity between us, I was impressed by the serenity and lucidity apparent in the gestures and demeanour of the man who had been acclaimed as the strategist of victory in Europe.

In December 1958, shortly after the Khrushchev ultimatum, I visited Paris to submit my report and recommendations to the Foreign Ministers of the Western Powers. It had long become routine for them and the Foreign Minister of the Federal Republic to meet on the eve of NATO conferences and reach agreement on problems concerning Germany and Berlin. I shall never forget how John Foster Dulles, already a dying man, walked round the table after I had spoken, shook my hand and said, 'We won't let you down.'

By the time I visited Washington in February 1959, illness had left an even clearer imprint on his face. He was not long back from his last visit to Bonn, during which he had given Adenauer some innocuous reason for his declining strength. This he later corrected in moving terms when told that he was suffering from cancer. A year earlier we had had an exhaustive discussion at Blair House, the Presidential guesthouse. His sister Eleanor Dulles, a special assistant at the State Department's Office of German Affairs, was also present. 'You've infiltrated us very neatly,' the Secretary of State told her with a smile. Eleanor Dulles had indeed become an ardent and persuasive champion of our cause, and had no difficulty in buttonholing her boss and brother on problems connected with Berlin. She earned our gratitude not only by her political concern but by her eminently practical support for projects such as the Congress Hall, the American Memorial Library, the Student Village and, finally, a substantial part of the Free University Clinic. Some colleagues (at the US Embassy in Bonn, for example) seemed to consider her zeal excessive. Personally, I appreciated her loyalty and was sorry when she – in company with several other old friends – found it hard to understand the courses we later sought from, and for, Berlin.

Her brother, John Foster Dulles, had become a quasi-symbolic figure in the West's prosecution of the Cold War. His watchwords 'brinkmanship' and 'roll-back' (of communism) bred misgiving and misinterpretation. The real man was more complex. At home in the mighty financial world of Wall Street before entering politics, he was undoubtedly permeated by a spirit of stern puritanical moralism. Critics justly pointed to his missionary and ideological rigidity, but there was more to the man than that. Beneath his often harsh phraseology lay an icy realism that extended to the German question as well. In 1959 he told me quite coolly that our routine demands for free elections would get us nowhere. When I broached the possibility of special status for Germany, he rose and said, without asperity but in chill tones, 'We and the Russians may disagree about a thousand things, but there's no difference of opinion between us on one point: we shall never permit a reunited and rearmed Germany to roam around in the no-man's-land between East and West.'

For six long years Dulles remained the most influential member of the Eisenhower administration, if also the most enigmatic and controversial. He became celebrated – though not popular – for his fervent belief in the need to meet the challenge of the age head on, both in Washington and during his frequent trips abroad. He was not a sectarian zealot, as many have supposed, but guided in the main by a dispassionate sense of power and balanced conservatism which encouraged him to hope for radical changes in the domain of his country's foremost rival. Towards the end of his time in office he formed the conclusion – unwelcome to his friend Adenauer – that talks with the Soviet Union were unavoidable and that a preliminary move should be made in that direction. Thus, his hard-line doctrine mellowed into the beginnings of a flexible policy.

Dulles's verdict on the future of Germany lingered with me. I sometimes bit my tongue when political opponents, Adenauer included, gave the impression that they could hold the Americans to their promises of reunification. If anyone was the official voice of America at that time, it was Dulles. He made it drastically clear that, for all his fundamental anti-communism, neither he nor the United States would take a gamble on Germany's account. It became evident, long before the Wall, that Moscow and Washington subscribed to a sort of tacit agreement on the non-violation of European spheres of influence. It was not surprising, therefore, that Dulles took the relatively 'soft' line of tactical adjustment to the Berlin ultimatum at the end of 1958. His comment on the Soviet demand for control of access routes was that it could be got round (as it actually was) with the formula 'identification but not control'. He did not consider the obstruction of civilian passenger and goods traffic a central problem because Allied interests were not directly affected. His verbal approach to free elections, too, ceased to imply that they were a key to the solution of the German question, nor was he shocked when Macmillan raised the possibility of force reductions.

Dulles was admitted to hospital and underwent surgery a few days after my 1959 visit. Widespread admiration was aroused by the fortitude with which he bore his sufferings. Although unable to share his moralistic stringency, I could not but respect the man himself and the iron determination that possessed him.

It was during my visit in February 1958 that I first met John F. Kennedy at a working lunch with some Senators on Capitol Hill. His name had meant something to me since 1956, when he offered himself as a vice-presidential candidate. Although we had no private conversation, my attention was captured by the young politician's elegant appearance, clean-cut features and coolly appraising eyes. He had recently betrayed reservations about the official approach to Germany, arguing that Adenauer's time was up and German rearmament should not be rushed. There was no indication that two years later, after winning a succession of primaries, he would assert his claim to national leadership.

I first saw Kennedy at the White House on 13 March 1961, just two months after the inaugural address in which he had, in the now classic phrase, summoned his nation to 'new frontiers' of responsibility. Coming straight to the point, the young President referred to my assertion at a televised press conference the night before that repeated protestations of American friendship and loyalty were superfluous. He was grateful, he said. Arthur Schlesinger records that the President sometimes mockingly likened the Germans to the woman who nightly asks her husband, 'Do you love me too?', is dissatisfied with his assurances, asks him, 'Do you *really* love me?' – and then employs a private eye to tail him. In fact, this behaviour imposed a needless strain on relations between Bonn and Washington. The Americans did not have to fear any needless mistrust from me, so our conversation got off to a good start.

Kennedy, who was noted for his thorough pre-talk briefings and knew just what questions to ask, differed from his predecessor and successor, Eisenhower and Johnson, in having a detailed knowledge of the problems connected with Germany and Berlin. He fired off a series of questions and gave me a chance to speak frankly about the points I had intended to raise. Apart from Berlin, he was interested in the

'Zone'. How were our relations with Eastern Europe shaping? Couldn't the Federal Republic do something to improve relations with Poland? What was my opinion of developments in Western Europe? How would the EEC develop as presently constituted and in its relations with Great Britain? (US policy was at that time far from the realization so firmly espoused by Kennedy at Philadelphia in 1962 and at Frankfurt's Church of St Paul in 1963: that there must be a free Europe capable of speaking with one voice.) George Ball, who played an important part in moulding US foreign policy as Undersecretary of State, advised against an enlarged EEC and thought that consultations between the Common Market and Free Trade Area should be conducted within the OECD framework.

The outcome of World War II had bound Western Europe closely to the United States. These ties were reinforced by US economic aid and by NATO, the Western defensive alliance. But the circumstances prevailing when the war ended and the Cold War began did not remain static. Rapid economic recovery strengthened Europe's self-awareness and the threat from the East lost immediacy as time went by. The German Federal Republic became a major industrial power with growing political influence. The French had difficulty in renewing their claims to great-power status and found little support for their aspirations to leadership in Europe. The British regarded West European unification with favour but had yet to see themselves as part of that process, preferring instead to rely on their imperial traditions and a special relationship with the United States.

My Washington interview with Kennedy on 13 March barely touched on the problems that were to acquire such cardinal importance after the Bermuda Conference late in 1962 and the hardening of de Gaulle's attitude. The President was in process of forming a general picture. He asked me if foreign policy would play a part in our election campaign and inquired about the problems of conventional and nuclear weapons within the Alliance. He also pointed to the growing importance of overseas aid. (By harnessing the enthusiasm of his young compatriots and the organizing abilities of his brother-in-law, Sargent Shriver, Kennedy planned to build up the Peace Corps, which achieved much that was good but in general failed to fulfil the idealistic expectations it aroused.) The President explored other aspects of the German election campaign that coming autumn. He smiled when I spoke of neglected social responsibilities and said, 'That sounds familiar'.

Knowing that I was to address the ADA (Americans for Democratic Action) that evening, through the good offices of Victor Reuther, brother of Walter Reuther, the automobile workers' leader, Kennedy said I would feel at home in such friendly company. We had, in fact, long maintained ties of friendship with this organization, whose liberal and in many respects social democratic membership is drawn largely from the Democratic Party. The function I was to attend had been instituted in memory of Franklin D. Roosevelt. That evening, Hubert Humphrey made a point of wearing his campaign badge from the previous year's election, in which – partly because of his hopeless financial inferiority – he had been worsted by Kennedy. I remained in close touch with the ADA for many years, likewise with Hubert Humphrey himself, whose unflagging optimism had won him the sobriquet 'the happy warrior'.

In 1964 I attended another ADA dinner at which I spoke after Martin Luther King. The leader of Black America possessed personal magnetism, but I first experienced his incomparable skill as a public speaker in autumn 1964, when he helped to inaugurate Berlin's new philharmonic hall at the suggestion of our friend Nicolas Nabokov and preached from the open-air stage one Sunday afternoon. Moral force transcended the language barrier, and even our own people were carried away by his noble and impassioned oratory.

King was undoubtedly the figure whom America's black citizens needed to prepare them for civil and social emancipation under Kennedy's and Johnson's civil rights legislation – and would long have continued to need had he not succumbed to an assassin. He combined passion, rationality and the strength of a living and effective Christianity in an almost magical way. Like many of my compatriots, I watched televised excerpts from his great 'I have a dream' speech, followed by clips from his last great sermon. Hearing him proclaim that he had seen 'the Promised Land', one sensed that he was prepared for his own death.

I also met Dean Rusk during this first Washington encounter with the Kennedy Administration. To the surprise of many of his friends, who considered Adlai Stevenson the better candidate, Kennedy had imported him into the State Department from the Rockefeller Foundation. Anxious to retain personal control of foreign policy, the President had looked around for a loyal and efficient administrator who would ensure that his decisions were punctiliously carried out. Rusk had written his own testimonial in the form of a treatise on the nature of the Presidency. We had many searching discussions over the years, more particularly after I became his opposite number at the Federal Foreign Office. Neither his modesty nor his unshakable and almost 'oriental' equanamity prevented him from championing a cause with unremitting vigour and determination. Reasons of state may often have prompted him to conceal his personal opinions, but this well-developed sense of duty was far from being the 'sepulchral chill' of which some people accused him. On the contrary, he had a Southerner's friendly manner and was cordial and relaxed – often high-spirited – in private. However tough our joint dealings, his humanity was always apparent despite the bias imposed upon him by his country's hopeless involvement in Vietnam. He has never brought himself to revise his position publicly and describe the war in Vietnam as the catastrophe it was. This inflexibility, which was based on personal conviction, is part of his nature. He remained loyal to the President he served, even beyond the grave, and has never disclaimed one iota of the responsibility he shouldered under Kennedy and Johnson.

Reverting to our first talk, Rusk asked me – *inter alia* – what approach I favoured in Laos, which was then in danger of being overrun by native communist insurgents. He saw a connection between the fate of this small Far Eastern country and Berlin. I was reluctant to commit myself. I can only say that in 1961 – and even in 1962 – it was far from clear to me that the Americans were girding themselves for a massive and protracted intervention in Indo-China.

Half-unconsciously, both then and later, I strove to dismiss this problem. My prime realization was that Berlin's existence depended on the American commitment there and that nothing could replace the close US-German relationship. It was also my long-standing contention that the credibility of American guarantees in our own part of the world would inevitably suffer if it were shattered elsewhere. Like others, I was not uninfluenced by the 'domino theory' – that strategic concept which Johnson, in particular, so fatally allowed to govern US policy in Asia. I accepted – to a certain extent – the theory that America bore a global responsibility and must thus, as Kennedy's inaugural address implied, perform the functions of a world policeman.

Whether during talks at the Pentagon (with Secretary of Defence Robert McNamara and Paul Nitze, then Assistant Secretary, later Secretary, of the Navy), in conversation with the diplomat Charles Bohlen (already preoccupied with growing nationalist tendencies in the communist domain), or at a reception given for me at Fort Meyers by my friend Barksdale Hamlett (formerly US Commandant in Berlin, later Vice Chief of Staff at the Pentagon) – I everywhere noticed the mood of reorientation that characterized the early days of the Kennedy era. With a sigh of relief, people hailed the intellectual and moral vigour that was sweeping away the staleness of Eisenhower's latter years.

I also noticed, in the meetings with Kennedy that followed my first visit to his country, how the burdens of office left their mark on his face (and the faces of his subordinates). One observer of the Washington scene was probably right in saying that the leadership of a world power resembles a daily examination in survival or extinction, and I understood the melancholy of a remark Kennedy made shortly before his death: 'Life is unfair.' Strain and disappointment had long since etched themselves into his face.

While visiting the States in 1961 I was subjected to malicious attacks at home during the run-up to the German election campaign. The Bonn administration itself showed little restraint, which made the impeccable behaviour of German representatives abroad doubly gratifying. This applied not only to our ambassador in Washington but also to Consul-General Federer in New York, both of whom made it abundantly clear that I represented the interests of my city and our country. General Steinhoff, who was then heading the German Military Mission in Washington, made a point of meeting me together with his officers. This was ill received by the heads of the Bonn Defence Ministry.

The occasion of my next transatlantic flight was an invitation from Harvard University to give two lectures dealing with problems of East-West relations. As usual, I took advantage of the visit to fulfil an exacting programme. The year before I had been talked into attending the great St Patrick's Day Parade on Fifth Avenue (they even knotted a green tie round my neck). Representatives of the German associations thereupon extracted a promise from me to attend the next Steuben Parade, the German-American equivalent, threatening to invite the Mayor of Dublin instead if I refused. I turned up with Governor Rockefeller, Mayor Robert Wagner Jr (whose late father, a prominent Senator, had still spoken German), and Senator Jacob Javits. All three were well aware that citizens of German descent packed an electoral punch, but I was surprised to see some black youngsters marching blithely behind the banner of the German-founded bakery workers' union. The 'United Bavarians of Greater New York' gave me a more cordial welcome than many who shared their blood at home. Beside me stood General Clay, who was also hailed as a Berliner in New York. It was a stirring scene, but full of comedy. It became apparent to me that, under the impact of two world wars, the German-American parade had inevitably degenerated into an impersonal and rather trite display of folklore. This did not worry my American friends.

The General Assembly was in session at the UN building. Although besieged by colleagues from all over the world, Dean Rusk found time to receive me in one of the Waldorf Astoria suites where I quite often stayed and worked in later years. I conveyed my doubts about the wisdom of the Western tactic which Bonn had exalted into a doctrine: that questions relating to Germany and Berlin should as far as possible be isolated from the United Nations.

My schedule was carefully planned and supervised, not only by the consulate-general but by the head of a public relations firm, Roy Blumenthal, who had realized soon after the war that Germany would not be permanently engulfed in a slough of defeat and guilt. Very discreetly, he began to establish valuable contacts. It was he who helped to pave the way for a dialogue between Adenauer and Ben-Gurion. Many of my own contacts stem from him, notably among the prominent Jewish citizens of New York. I also have him to thank for an intimate knowledge of economic and political conditions in the States, but most of all for a friendship rare in its warmth, loyalty and readiness to help. Blumenthal best exemplifies, perhaps, the often significant political assistance rendered me by 'unofficial' sources – by people without official titles, posts and functions. I have always thought it worthwhile to sidestep protocol and seek out those – whether journalists, scientists or industrialists – who serve a cause with the lack of inhibition that springs from an independent outlook.

Part of my hectic stay in New York was devoted to revising the lectures I had been invited to give by Harvard's Graduate School of Public Administration and its Dean, Don Price. I had entitled my remarks 'The Ordeal of Coexistence'. Speaking in German, I implied that coexistence was not so much an ordeal as a compulsion to be venturesome.

Coexistence, I declared, was neither an invention nor a monopoly of the Russians. The difference between the communists' plans and our own stemmed from our wholly dissimilar views of the nature of our divisive conflict. The Soviet leaders' interests were patent but their theory was erroneous because conflict between states with differing social and economic systems was not inevitable.

Khrushchev's peaceful coexistence is not a quest for permanent stability. The Russians proceed upon the assumption that history is logically developing in their favour. Peaceful coexistence is intended to speed up this process. It is not a lull in the battle but a new means of extending their spheres of power and influence without having to risk a nuclear war . . . One thing strikes me as certain: the possibility of genuine coexistence in our world depends on the Russians' real interests, not on their theoretical principles.

Our political strategy had to presuppose that the ordeal of co-existence could be survived only if we were free from a diffuse fear of communist superiority, but free as well from a naively optimistic unconcern based on the comfortable conviction that the better cause automatically prevails. The fulfilment of genuine coexistence was confronting democracy with the greatest test which history had ever summoned it to pass. 'We shall not only have to avert disaster and assert ourselves in the face of Soviet pressure. This defensive task must not hypnotize us and claim our whole attention, for the East-West conflict is not the sole and, in essence, not even the most important problem to be solved if we wish to win the future.'

On 4 October, after my sojourns in Boston and the friendly university city of Cambridge with its handsome old buildings and tranquil avenues, I had my first meeting with the President's brother in Washington. The super-powers were now on the threshold of the Cuban crisis. I was alarmed by signs that a dangerous confrontation was imminent – the most dangerous since 1945. The Russians had announced their mutual assistance pact with Fidel Castro at the end of August. In mid-September the President told a press conference that the United States would not tolerate the introduction of offensive weapons into Cuba. By the end of September, rumours of substantial Soviet shipments were stronger than ever. Although I had taken note of this, my attention was focused on Berlin. This, I feared when I came to America, was where tensions would crystallize. Cuba I regarded as a pressure-point. I did not foresee that the dispute over Soviet shipments would bring our world to the brink of disaster.

This impression (which many Americans shared) was not corrected when I lunched with General Taylor, Paul Nitze and others as a guest of Attorney-General Robert Kennedy. I had become well acquainted with 'Bobby', that exceptionally dynamic man, when he and his wife Ethel visited Berlin early in 1962. For him, this was the culmination of a world tour which he subsequently described in a book. His visit to Berlin, he wrote, had impressed him more than anything else. The Berliners certainly made their presence felt: over one hundred thousand of them congregated outside the Schöneberger Rathaus.

It was a chill, raw day when Robert Kennedy arrived in Berlin. I can see him now, hatless (of course) and trembling with cold in a shabby overcoat. His language, which was firm and resolute, matched the general mood. When propaganda balloons drifted across from the Russian sector, he remarked, 'The communists let their balloons through, but not their people!' At the same time, he successfully eschewed exaggeration. He had discarded an over-impassioned and aggressive draft on the grounds that it would help no one to whip up emotions. Together with Arthur Schlesinger, he worked out some new passages which laid greater emphasis on the constructive elements in his thinking. He addressed the students of the Free University. He debated with Berlin citizens in the morning and shop stewards in the afternoon, and did not shrink from telling them, half seriously and half in jest, that they must wean themselves from the suspicion that the United States had written off its solemn obligations if a senior American official failed to visit Berlin once a month to reaffirm them. As for reunification, they must put their faith in the historical process. He visited the Wall, but he also visited the place of execution at Plötzensee where the rebels of 20 July 1944 had been put to death after an abortive coup by the German Resistance which might have ended the *danse macabre* of Hitlerism and World War II before its terrible culmination.

When inscribing the Golden Book, he declared that our task was to improve Berlin's status by means of negotiation. My own words on the same occasion were: 'We are not interested in remaining a bone of contention, but we are very much interested in becoming a place whose preservation is of interest to all parties.' We wondered if ten years would have to elapse before serious negotiations were conducted to this end, and whether better results might have been obtained ten years earlier.

I also met Edward, the President's second brother, while the Attorney-General was visiting Berlin. We gathered at the city's guest-house to celebrate the birthday of 'Ted', who sang some folksongs with a friend of his. I soon saw him again in Boston, where he was competing – as the President's successor, so to speak – to become one of the two Senators for Massachusetts. I have no hesitation in adding that I viewed the political aggrandizement of a single family with some uneasiness. (I also met Edward's rival at the home of the German Consul-General. He was the son of the same Henry Cabot Lodge who had once lost his Senatorial seat to John F. Kennedy and briefly became US Ambassador in Bonn after holding various other important posts.)

I have never forgotten 'Bobby's' comment on a toast I proposed at the guest-house to the 'President, government and people of the United States': 'That's us three. My brother's the President – the government, that's me, and you,' he said laughingly, pointing at Ted, ' – you're the people.' Edward Kennedy and I walked side by side in the procession held to mark Harvard's annual celebrations early in the summer of 1963. We often saw each other in the years that followed.

and he was one of the last foreign guests whom I entertained as Federal Chancellor in 1974.

When the President received me in the Oval Study the day after my second lecture at Harvard, he began by gesturing to copies of the text which had been politely left in readiness. Gently rocking to and fro in his chair, he spoke of various passages which seemed to confirm or develop his own ideas. Then, as I have already recounted, conversation centred on Berlin.

After this official exchange, the President invited me for a stroll in the garden because he did not wish his remarks to be recorded and transmitted to Bonn by our ambassador. For a start, he acquainted me with his impression that some sections of Bonn officialdom were playing along with his domestic political opponents. He confined himself to general allusions and did not expect an answer. (Bonn was disquieted by the exchange of letters initiated by Kennedy and Khrushchev in September 1961 and followed by bilateral soundings. Foreign Minister Schröder intervened at the end of the year with a request that these be limited to Berlin. The Americans, who wished to extend their scope, were contemplating a security plan for Central Europe, nor was discussion of Berlin limited to the access authority project alone. Consideration was belatedly given to the status of Berlin as a whole. The Americans even explored the plan – favourably debated by ourselves but not taken seriously – to transfer UN Headquarters to Berlin. Beyond this, Adenauer suspected the two super-powers of aiming at a tacit agreement not to use nuclear weapons against one another. He publicly warned against the putative dangers of US-Soviet bilateralism. In May 1962 he took advantage of a Berlin visit to reject the plan for an access control authority as impracticable and demand that talks be broken off. He used the same occasion to describe British membership of the EEC as not necessarily welcome. There had been a commotion in April when journalists in Bonn were apprised of the information and directives given the German Ambassador regarding short-term consultations with our government: preliminary moves towards an agreement on the non-diffusion of atomic weapons, the proposal for an exchange of non-aggression declarations between NATO and the Warsaw Pact, and the suggested establishment of committees composed of representatives from both German states.)

The President's next question was: 'Shall we be faced with reunification for as long as you and I bear political responsibility?' I replied that I doubted if this was a problem confined to the generation now at the helm. New generations were following on, and these would presumably be less inhibited than the people of my own generation, who were living with the immediate legacy of Hitler's war, in demanding that Germans, too, should have the right to achieve national unity.

Later in our walk, Kennedy said very gravely that he was not sure if it would be possible to avoid a clash with the Soviet Union. The situation that had arisen in and over Cuba was causing him great concern. He alluded briefly to the build-up of strategic weapons on the island, but left it at that. (Although the Americans were aware of the ships and their suspect cargoes, it was not until 9 October, or four days after our talk, that the President ordered an aerial reconnaissance by U-2 aircraft. On 15 October he had the evidence in his hands.) Theodore Sorensen's memoirs make it clear that the President long suspected that the installation of a Russian offensive base in Cuba might be a feint to divert attention from Berlin. If asked at the time, I myself would probably have concurred with this theory.

My thoughts on the homeward flight were far more preoccupied with the tribulations of Berlin than with Kennedy's words of warning about Cuba. It is not for me to present yet another account of the dramatic controversy that raged in Washington, but waves of mounting tension spilled over into Europe as well. On 17 October the American President received the Soviet Foreign Minister. Their main topic of conversation was, in fact, Berlin. After the US mid-term elections (in November), said Gromyko, Moscow would put its separate peace treaty with the GDR into effect. Soviet aid to Cuba was simply a contribution to the island's defence and the development of its peaceful economy. Kennedy limited himself to repeating the text of his September admonition. The Soviet Foreign Minister gave absolutely no hint that the missiles on Cuba could threaten the United States, and the President conveyed no sign that he was already in possession of evidence to that effect.

On Monday, 22 October 1962, while my wife and I were attending a film première at the Kongresshalle, I was informed that the US Minister (and Assistant Chief of Mission) Allan Lightner, wished to speak to me that same night. I invited him to my home on the Schlachtensee. There Lightner told me that the President had reached an important decision regarding Cuba and would announce it personally at midnight Central European Time. Together, we listened to Kennedy broadcasting over the American Forces Network. He had definite evidence, he said, that offensive missile bases were under preparation in Cuba. The armed forces of the United States had been mobilized (which meant, among other things, that units of the Strategic Air Command were now at operational altitude). Kennedy's speech twice referred to Berlin as a scene of possible retaliation and a place where

American undertakings still held good. Washington did, in fact, assume that military action against the missile bases on Castro's island would be countered by a blockade of Berlin.

Before the American diplomat left me – I had met him casually in Stockholm during the war and renewed our acquaintance in Berlin shortly thereafter – he inquired if I had any communication for the President. I asked him to convey the following brief message: I was grateful to the President for so clearly underscoring US commitments in Berlin. For the rest, he must tread the path he had resolved to take – we were ready to share the consequences. My remarks were forwarded at once, with the result that they reached his White House desk before those of most foreign governments.

Kennedy's reply was brought to me at the Rathaus next day. The dispute over Cuba would probably have significant repercussions on Berlin: 'That is precisely what makes your clear and unequivocal attitude so gratifying.' Contrary to our expectations, Berlin was subjected to no additional pressure. Without surrendering to a false sense of security, therefore, we could watch the dramatic unfolding of the American blockade and, as far as anything could be gleaned from hints, follow the dialogue between Moscow and Washington. Slowly, we began to hope that good sense would prevail, thanks above all to Kennedy's clear-sighted moderation and steady nerves. The peace that reigned in and around Berlin was an encouraging sign. The Russians were evidently unprepared to raise the stakes with a second confrontation in Europe which might easily have got out of control. We breathed a sigh of relief when, on the morning of Sunday 28 October, after 13 harrowing days, Khrushchev announced the withdrawal of Soviet missiles in his third letter to Kennedy.

It soon became apparent that this nuclear confrontation was a watershed in the East-West conflict. John F. Kennedy and Nikita Khrushchev had both looked into the abyss. Where 'our' side was concerned, what clinched matters was that the supreme leader of the Western world had not wavered; he had not tried to force his adversary to his knees but skirted the extremes of humiliation and annihilation.

Addressing a German-US conference in Berlin on 19 November 1962, with the Cuba crisis and my own experiences in mind, I declared that there was no all-or-nothing policy and pleaded for a Western initiative on Berlin: 'The aim should be to develop Berlin in a state of relative détente.'

A year later, on the afternoon of Friday, 22 November 1963, my wife and I returned to Berlin from Africa. At about 7.30 p.m. a journalist friend called to say that an attempt had been made on

Kennedy's life in Dallas, and that he might already be dead. Switching on the news, we soon heard these sad tidings confirmed. I drove to see General James Polk, the US Commandant, and express my condolences. After that, the television studio. Then to the Rathaus.

That same November night, unsummoned by officialdom or a political party but responding to a student initiative, tens of thousands of my fellow-citizens assembled in the Rathaus square, most of them young and many carrying torches. Speaking extempore, I said:

> The Americans have lost the President of whom it was believed by so many that he would be able to lead us firmly along the road to a just peace and a better life in this world. But we in Berlin grieve because we have lost our best friend . . . I myself am profoundly moved and shocked tonight because I feel that I have lost someone – as, indeed, I have – with whom I was privileged to consort in trust and friendship.

Many flowers were deposited on the Rathaus steps next day. That evening the people of Berlin put candles in their windows as they had long done on special occasions, notably to symbolize the unity of divided families on Christmas Eve. Our sorrow in the West was matched in the East. Concern and dismay could be observed throughout the globe. Seldom before, in a torn and divided world, had a political leader so ably succeeded in kindling people's hopes for a brighter future. The citizens of East and West, not only in our own partitioned land but in the communist-dominated world, together with those of the young and non-aligned nations, shared our feeling that John F. Kennedy was a man with a deep and genuine commitment to world peace – a man to be trusted.

As I said in my television address on 23 November, 'The world is a poorer place. But the goals this man set for humanity cannot be gunned down, and we cannot better express our attachment to him and the American people than by pursuing them further: a better peace in genuine safety for mankind; more justice and liberty for human beings wherever they live.'

On 24 November I flew to America to pay my last respects to President Kennedy. I met Jean Monnet on the plane from New York to Washington, which was also carrying Prince Bernhard of the Netherlands and other mourners. Many of them recalled the atmosphere that had succeeded the Reichstag fire. I was greeted at the airport by Klaus Schütz, who had just concluded an official visit, accompanied by three Berlin schoolchildren who had seen the President at the White

House some days earlier. Schütz was greatly concerned. Watching television a few hours before, he had witnessed the shooting of Lee Harvey Oswald by bar-owner Jack Ruby while remanded in custody. Schütz: 'Anything can happen in this place. Better get out of here as soon as possible . . .'

While I was attending the funeral ceremony as a 'friend of the family', the square in front of the Rathaus in Berlin was renamed Kennedy-Platz. That afternoon the new President, Lyndon B. Johnson, who had been hurriedly sworn in, received foreign guests at the State Department. I was talking to King Baudouin when the head of protocol came with a message from Jacqueline Kennedy inviting me to call at the White House. After greeting me, Robert Kennedy left me alone with the President's widow. I found her no less courageous than she had seemed to the entire world when tragedy struck at Dallas. Bobby saw me to the car. I guessed that he was afraid I might ask who had really killed his brother.

The findings of the Warren Commission did not, in fact, convince me, and my doubts have not diminished with the passage of time. The neurotic Oswald definitely opened fire, but his motives remain obscure. So does the question of whether he acted alone and on his own initiative.

That evening at the Swedish Embassy, Senator Hubert Humphrey gave me a lively explanation of why Lyndon B. Johnson – whose Vice-President he was destined to become in 1965 – would make a good President. In the fields of domestic and social policy, he proved right. However, Johnson never managed to supplant Kennedy in the popular imagination although he sometimes strove, desperately but only half-consciously, to do so. He laboured under the lingering superiority of his younger partner, whose personal impact still defies analysis.

Why did so many people in so many countries mourn Kennedy's passing? Why do so many humble Italian or Latin American homes display pictures showing him with the 'good Pope', John XXIII?

His intelligence, his youth, his personal appearance, his rhetorical verve, his drive and self-assurance, his delight in things cultural, the fascination inspired by his boldly innovative approach and courageous advance into uncharted intellectual, political and social territory – these things account for a great deal, but not for the magic of the man who so easily evoked a hero-worship and romanticization against which his ready wit and spirit of irony provided no defence. The regal atmosphere of the White House, a would-be commingling of intellectual brilliance and aesthetic charm, was relaxed but not without its perils.

It would be unfair to regard John F. Kennedy solely as a practitioner of foreign relations. His domestic programme, on which he had embarked with such high hopes, soon fell foul of a Congress that watched him more jealously than any US President before Richard Nixon. Lyndon Johnson was able to reap the fruits of much that had been sown under Kennedy, and he added to that inheritance with his own brand of hectic energy. There is no doubt, however, that it was his forerunner who prepared the break-through to equal rights for citizens black and white, thereby seeking to heal America's deepest national trauma. It was Kennedy – more a liberal conservative by nature and background – who strove to resuscitate Roosevelt's policy in favour of the poor and underprivileged. Speaking to Germans in a context of some importance, I once employed an English word which Kennedy did not invent but used with a special emphasis: compassion. I translated it not as sympathy, not merely kindness to one's neighbour, but as heartfelt human fellowship. The public sensed this quality in John F. Kennedy (and later in his brother Robert), and it redounded to them in death like a mighty wave. It was compassion that endeared the President to people and moved them without militating against their desire to see a resplendent hero in the classic mould reborn in our own day. At all events, it was his courage – his grace under pressure – that won the admiration of his contemporaries.

4

Minor Steps

The Wall was a dire reality. When complete, it formed a demarcation system of concrete slabs, steel mesh, barbed wire, observation towers, pill-boxes, dog-runs, trenches and detector-fences. Zigzagging round street corners, skirting houses and surmounting every obstacle, it wound through Berlin for kilometre after kilometre. Seldom had a neighbour, policy, rival creed or social order been insulated against its supposed adversary with more loathsome perfectionism.

But reiterated demands that the Wall should go were powerless to abolish it. However frequently lamented, the partitioning of Berlin, Germany and Europe was not abandoned. We in Berlin were compelled to accept that the Wall could not be eliminated by an isolated campaign. Two world powers faced each other across our city, and it had been borne in on us that they were capable of compromise as well as confrontation. However one viewed its historical background, the partitioning of Germany was an established factor in the complex system of demarcation and deterrence which both menaced and consolidated the equilibrium that was currently entering common parlance under the neutral designation 'East-West relations'. Respect for spheres of influence seemed to accord with a tacit agreement which held as good for Dulles and Kennedy – so all experience indicated – as for Khrushchev and his successors.

It would have been tempting to sit back and accept this state of affairs, but history is a dynamic process in which nothing resists change. What mattered was to help mould that change without being precipitate. It was this realization which prompted me to declare, in my address commemorating the 150th anniversary of Lincoln's birth in February 1959, that no isolated or sudden solution was possible and that we should hope for gradual changes, 'for gradual solutions resulting from dogged argument'.

Disregarding the broader perspectives, however, our problem in Berlin was simply to combat human hardship. For many families, arbitrary separation was an almost unendurable source of sorrow. Married couples could not meet, children were denied their mothers, engaged couples could not marry. Elderly people found it particularly hard to be cut off from their friends and relations. Many were thrown into prison for braving the Wall and the barbed wire in an attempt to cross one of the internal borders. Young people were arrested for aiding fugitives. Our own circle of friends included a medical student sentenced by a GDR court for the 'crime' of abetting an escape. He told us after his release that the East German State Security Service possessed a detailed layout of our apartment and had even described the position of individual pieces of furniture. This was only one of several indications that the GDR's secret service had its eye on me.

The Churches were sometimes able to help in cases of special hardship. I also kept in touch with representatives of the International Committee of the Red Cross, which occasionally managed to secure exit permits for the old and sick. Although we bombarded East Berlin with proposals designed to render the Wall slightly more 'permeable' or 'transparent', they long went unanswered. Stubbornly intent on preserving its supposed interests, the GDR Government rejected every compromise and any reasonable settlement.

Not until late in 1963 did word filter through to us – via journalists – that the other side might be willing to talk. More detailed information was passed to our commercial department at the Rathaus by Dr Schiebold, a businessman experienced in trading with the GDR. We assumed that those who had approached him hoped to secure commercial advantages from an arrangement governing visits. We also found it significant that passenger traffic between member-states of the Warsaw Pact was becoming easier at this time. Hitherto, countries in the Soviet bloc had been as strictly segregated as if they required protection against their direst foes – and even now, three decades after the war's end, the dismantling of these barriers is far from complete.

But even the GDR, which aspired to recognition by the neutral and Western world, was labouring under the Wall's disastrous symbolism. The leaders of the Soviet Union must have been just as unhappy with this steel and concrete admission of their German satellite's material and ideological vulnerability. For them too, the Wall represented a psychological burden. Day after day, sightseers from all over the world thronged the observation platforms that had been erected at prominent points along its extent. The authorities in East Berlin and Moscow found it expedient to make at least one humanitarian gesture. East Berlin was being subjected to some pressure by a 'public opinion' which manifested itself in Party and factory debates – sometimes even in readers' letters to the SED press. This may have been another factor, though not the decisive one.

On 5 December 1963 I received a letter from Alexander Abusch, Deputy-Chairman of the Council of Ministers of the GDR. It embodied a limited and temporary offer to grant travel permits. I acted without delay. The Berlin Senate conferred the same day. The Federal Government and the Allies were informed at once. Natural and necessary as this was, Bonn could not be prevented from committing an indiscretion which might have hindered the opening of talks. The procedure to be adopted was agreed at a meeting next day.

The head of the Fiduciary Authority whose position derived from two forms of warrant, one of them issued by the Governing Mayor, had been regularly dispatched to East Berlin whenever it became necessary to discuss the obstruction of access routes to Berlin. However, the GDR Government was unwilling to accept him as a negotiator in the matter of passenger traffic and wanted to deal with the Senate direct. The purpose of this East Berlin tactic was to draw nearer the 'free city' objective, which made it doubly important for us to ensure that the proceedings were not construed as negotiations between two independent states.

We had to prevent this without blighting the talks – something which sounds easier a dozen years after the event than it actually was. In retrospect, some may complain that we too often allowed ourselves to be delayed by GDR ploys. After a lot of preliminary exchanges, formal talks began in East Berlin on 12 December. I made it clear, at the same time, that no irrelevant political considerations must be linked with our endeavours to relieve human hardship.

By 17 December, seven meetings lasting a total of 30 hours had taken place. The East Berlin authorities wished to restrict potential visitors from West Berlin to an absolute minimum and proposed that they be limited to relatives of the first and second degree. In fact, this qualification was considerably relaxed. The GDR even agreed to waive the law punishing 'desertion of the Republic'. What its leaders wanted – and this proved our main difficulty – was to extract an agreement carrying the flavour of international law. We, in our turn, had to insist on an administrative arrangement which would not confirm, however indirectly, the proposition that West Berlin was a separate political entity.

East Berlin made a remarkable number of concessions. The acrobatic formulas devised to protect each side's interests must appear not only incomprehensible but positively absurd to the outsider. We had to insist that the offices where permits were to be obtained should not act as GDR authorities exercising 'sovereign functions' on the soil of West Berlin, so the East Berlin clerical staff were listed as post office personnel. On our side, responsibility for the permit offices – one in each of our twelve precincts – was vested in the *Land* postal authority. The first passes agreement was signed on 17 December and came into force next day (my 50th birthday). It was scheduled to expire on 5 January, or eighteen days later.

I still find it miraculous that such intricate problems should have been so speedily resolved in the face of so many bureaucratic shifts and evasions. There was a bolder display of improvisation than is normal in the sphere of German officialdom. After a break of 28 months, the way was clear for a great and moving reunion on the other side of Berlin – a referendum conducted with hearts as well as feet. We recorded approximately 1.2 million visits to East Berlin during this period. Many relatives and friends flocked in from the 'Zone' as well, so it would not be an exaggeration to say that 4 million people were granted an opportunity to see each other once more.

Limited though it was, the respite we had obtained was almost universally welcomed by the people of Berlin. Their satisfaction was strongly and favourably echoed in the Federal Republic and abroad. Even at this stage, however, we discerned covert rather than open criticism among those who saw the new development as a blow to their hopes or even feared that it might jeopardize their characterization of Berlin as an 'open wound'. I had to emphasize more than once that there were no plans to introduce a 'new' policy. Addressing the Chamber of Deputies, I added that policies existed to help people and that it had never been laid down 'that liberal or Western or German policy had necessarily to consist of wanting all or nothing'. I took care to point out that our demand for freedom of movement remained unaltered and that the 'permits' were not of our devising.

The permit operation of Christmas 1963 did not, of course, pass off without a hitch. Many people had to wait for hours at the few crossing-points, nor were there sufficient offices where permits could be applied for and collected. The second passes agreement covered the periods round All Souls' Day and Christmas 1964, Easter and Whitsun 1965, by which time we had managed to improve some aspects of our organization. Would-be visitors were again numerous. We had set up a bureau dealing with urgent family matters where people could apply to pay visits outside the agreed times. Thirty-six thousand availed themselves of this opportunity in the course of a single year. The

P.P.–G

permits also gave married couples who were still separated a chance to reunite their families from the East Berlin end. The third agreement related to Christmas and New Year 1965–6, the fourth to Easter and Whitsun 1966.

The other side now declined to accept that the agreements should contain a clause setting out our divergent political and legal positions, and we failed to reach a satisfactory compromise. No passes agreements were fixed for Christmas 1966 or the holiday periods in succeeding years, though this was unconnected with the transference of my duties from Berlin to Bonn. Not until the Quadripartite Agreement on Berlin came into force in 1972 did new travel facilities open up for West Berliners – non-relatives included – and, in addition to East Berlin, for the GDR itself.

Looking back on our hard-fought permit negotiations, I am still enraged by the pseudo-legal quibbles and ideologically camouflaged jealousies that hampered our work from the Bonn end. I seldom referred to them in public for fear of prejudicing our cause, and then only by implication, but I did not disguise from my political associates that I had exercised the utmost self-restraint 'precisely because our concern was to gain a success for human beings, not to gather the political fuel that so often lay in our path; that we left lying there.' We would not be hampered by pettifogging considerations, I told the Party Conference at Karlsruhe in November 1964, and the whole of politics could go hang unless its purpose was to make people's lives easier instead of harder: 'What is good for the people in our divided land is good for the nation as well.'

I should have liked, more vehemently than the situation allowed, to confront my critics in the Federal Republic with the fact that we in Berlin – unlike them in their West German haven – were obliged to *live* with the Wall. I should have liked to draw their attention more explicitly to the warring emotions of a Berlin mayor who had to muster the police to 'protect' the Wall from the wrath of student demonstrators eager to charge that hated obstacle. Only as the years went by did people seem to grasp that minor steps were better than no steps at all. Furthermore, the realization later dawned that it is sometimes possible to let conflicting legal positions rest.

Summarizing my early Berlin experiences at Harvard University in autumn 1962, I said, 'Berlin has taught me that we need have no fear of communism.' Realistic self-assurance on the part of the West and an awareness of the specific superiority of its image of man absolved us from any fear of contact with its political and ideological opponent. On the contrary, we must seek it. I was slightly more explicit in an amplified version of my Harvard lectures intended for publication in Germany. Underscoring the need for reunification, I stressed that no unauthorized persons should be allowed to usurp 'the banner of national unity'. The German theme must be viewed in the context of coexistence. I outlined a few principles:

First, nobody need credit me with believing that Germany's task was to extract national advantage from the conflicts of the 1960s or 1970s. Any such notion was foolish.

Second, I by no means believed that we Germans and our 'German question' were the weight that would tip the scales of the future. The German question was not the key to an understanding of the world-wide conflict between East and West. We could, however, regard it as a kind of proving-ground on which to test the super-powers' willing-ness and ability to resolve knotty international problems under the auspices of reason and an acceptable idea of coexistence. Although not the cause of all the world's existing tensions, the German question contributed to those tensions and was one of their regional – and, for those affected, particularly distressing – consequences.

Third, my native land was not a world power. To strive to reconcile human and national interests was to act in the spirit of Ernst Reuter. If a choice became unavoidable, greater weight should be given to human interests than national.

Fourth, what was attainable in the case of France should not, in the long term, be impossible in that of Poland. A genuine frontier settle-ment might entail sacrifices but must be sustained by the concurrence of both peoples.

Fifth, nothing could affect the now established interdependence between the German question and the problems of European and worldwide security.

My phrasing had to remain cautious, tentative and a trifle nebulous. Its political substance can only be seen in the context of a few essays and initiatives made behind the East-West diplomatic scenes – pre-liminary moves which could not be publicized at the time.

The tactics and strategy of Kennedy's policy were known to me from my time in Washington. Contact with Paris had familiarized me with de Gaulle's ideas and I was directly involved in consultations between the West German social democrats. On the other hand, I was nowhere near as isolated from the East as it may have appeared. There had always been a kind of 'secondary level' in the polyphonic East-West dialogue.

In early summer 1960 – prior to the Wall and on the eve of the

Four-Power summit conference which was so brusquely discontinued because of the U-2 incident, Eisenhower's apology notwithstanding – a Soviet delegation was visiting Austria for bilateral talks. On the periphery of these talks, Gromyko handed the Austrian Foreign Minister, Bruno Kreisky, a document in Russian (with an unofficial German translation) and left him free to make what use of it he chose.

Kreisky notified Egon Bahr, who was visiting Vienna in mid-July. The Soviet memorandum was officially handed to State Secretary Globke, who was in Vienna the same day, for transmission to Adenauer and me.

According to Egon Bahr's notes, the document began by expressing a wish to apprise the Austrian Foreign Minister of the Soviet attitude towards the questions of a German peace treaty and Berlin. The absence of a peace treaty jeopardized the interests of the peoples of Europe. Because no unified German State could be expected to emerge in the near future, the countries involved in the war against Hitler Germany had no choice but to conclude a peace treaty with both the German states together or each of them separately. Despite the Soviet Union's patient attitude, no agreement with the West had been reached. The Soviet Union would not permit this question to remain open. The unsolved Berlin problem was of benefit to neither side. If no German peace treaty came into being and the question of West Berlin were not settled on that basis, the Soviet Union would be forced to conclude a peace treaty with the GDR to which other European countries would doubtless subscribe.

Such a treaty, the memorandum went on, would also solve the 'West Berlin question' because the rights accruing to the victorious powers from Germany's unconditional surrender would thereby lose their validity. This applied in particular to the right of communication between West Berlin and the outside world – by land, water and air. In the above eventuality, full control would pass to the GDR and the use of these routes would require its consent. Nobody would go to war on account of such a development, neither the Federal Republic nor America, Great Britain nor France. The Soviet Union further reiterated its pledge of support for the GDR.

Thus far, the document anticipated the statements with which Nikita Khrushchev confronted President Kennedy at their meeting in Vienna nine months later, but it also embodied shades of meaning worthy of closer study.

The memorandum turned to the Berlin Senate, which must, it said, be interested in ensuring that the question of West Berlin's status was settled, not unilaterally but in harmony with the aims of all concerned and without unnecessarily aggravating the situation. Leading politicians in West Berlin were still far removed from such an attitude. The Governing Mayor was mistaken if – as his speeches implied – he placed his main dependence on the strength of the West. Until now, nobody had yet advanced a better solution to the Berlin problem than a status providing for non-interference under the most effective possible Four-Power guarantees, the latter ultimately secured by the United Nations. The GDR would 'faithfully' undertake to observe any such settlement.

The Austrian Foreign Minister was requested 'to bring these remarks to Herr Brandt's notice' because it was to be assumed that he had an eye to the future and was seeking an escape from the present impasse. Egon Bahr formed the impression that the Soviet phrasing did not preclude our links with West Germany and hinted at the possibility that their extent would depend on Berlin itself. Bruno Kreisky commented that the text contained little that was new but did embody certain political and practical leads which it would be sensible to explore. Although unwilling to act as a mediator, he said he might question the Russians on one or two points of detail in his own name. Kreisky's feeling was that Khrushchev intended to wait until spring, in other words, until after the inauguration of the new American President.

The course of events confirmed this. John F. Kennedy and the Western Alliance succeeded, thanks to their steadfast attitude, in deterring Khrushchev from an assault on Allied rights in West Berlin because this might have entailed a war unwanted even by the Kremlin's overlord. I doubt if a personal talk between Khrushchev and myself – something hinted at by the Soviet memorandum – would have changed the pattern of developments. It remains debatable whether we, in Berlin as well as Bonn, took all these pointers seriously enough and whether the way might have been paved to an earlier and perhaps more favourable agreement on Berlin. It might even have been possible, under certain circumstances, to negotiate an acceptable status for the whole of Berlin prior to 13 August 1961. Although neglected opportunities belong to the marginal notes of history, personal responsibility dictates that even these belated questions should not be evaded . . .

It is worthwhile touching on the history of two unexploited chances to confer with Khrushchev. Early in 1959, when he was still State Secretary at the Austrian Foreign Ministry, my friend Bruno Kreisky had given a lecture advocating consideration of a special statute embracing the whole of Berlin (that is to say, not West Berlin alone), the stationing of UN troops in the city (contingents from the four victorious powers and two neutral countries), and the guaranteeing of corridors to the Federal Republic. Assuming that Kreisky's remarks were 'inspired' by me, the Russians instructed their ambassador in Vienna to ask Kreisky to transmit an immediate and confidential invitation to me to meet Khrushchev. I declared myself willing in principle but pointed out that I should first have to notify the Protecting Powers and the Federal Chancellor.

Adenauer left me free to accept the invitation or decline it as I thought fit. The Berlin Senate were little disposed to pin any hopes on such an encounter. What was more, many people suspected that Adenauer's cautious approval was a political trap. In fact, Kreisky had always been encouraged in his contacts by State Secretary Globke and Adenauer himself, and no contacts existed which might have been concealed from the Federal Government. My good friend from the days of exile in Sweden was a stickler for political honesty. There is no doubt that he increasingly succeeded in regaining for Vienna something of the diplomatic glamour of years gone by. Thanks to an indiscretion, however, garbled and distorted reports of the Soviet démarche were made public. This did not enhance the prospects of a meeting with Khrushchev. More important still, the Americans – if their attitude was correctly represented by their envoy in Berlin – were far from enthusiastic. I duly declined, equipped with a legitimate pretext by the Russians' major breach of diplomatic convention.

It is not uninteresting to note that, more or less coincidentally with their Vienna memorandum, the Russians submitted counter-proposals to de Gaulle in Paris. As late as autumn 1960, Khrushchev mentioned his message to me to Hans Kroll, the German Ambassador in Moscow, and regretted that he had left the drafting of the document to 'diplomats' incapable of 'using clear and intelligible language'.

Two-and-a-half years later, in January 1963, the Soviet leader travelled to East Berlin to attend an SED party conference. He notified me through a Soviet Embassy official and two consuls-general – the Austrian and the Swedish – that he was available for discussion. Once again, acceptance of the invitation struck me as more beneficial than rejection. I telephoned Adenauer and again received no definite advice. The old Chancellor left the decision to me and said that such an exchange would do neither good nor harm. Rainer Barzel, who was briefly serving as Minister for All-German Affairs, called me from Bonn soon afterwards and vigorously assailed the projected interview, and the Federal Foreign Office doubtless shared this view. My consultations with the Allies produced no clear picture. I wanted to telephone Kennedy and obtain his concurrence but was dissuaded by the State Department representative.

My CDU colleague, Deputy-Mayor Franz Amrehn, imposed a thorough-going veto. Though only half-heartedly supported by some of his party associates, he made it clear to me at an extraordinary session of the Senate that his party would desert the Senatorial coalition if I agreed to meet Khrushchev: Berlin could not, Amrehn declared, conduct a foreign policy of its own. This was not in dispute. Amrehn's forebodings could have been quashed by objective argument. On the other hand, I could not meet the world's second most powerful man with the Senate divided on this very issue and at this very juncture.

Again, my sole course was to decline at the last minute. I found it hard. Khrushchev must have taken my refusal as an affront. Ambassador Abrassimov later gave me a vivid description of the total dismay that overcame his erstwhile master when the news was communicated to him. Khrushchev, caught in the act of changing, almost dropped his trousers with surprise when the newly appointed ambassador delivered my reply. He could not understand my change of mind. Abrassimov added that it had been a missed opportunity because Khrushchev 'wanted to give me something' at the time.

Whatever that may have meant, I doubt if it will ever emerge whether the missed opportunity was genuine or not. I nonetheless believe, in retrospect, that I should have done better to pursue a different course. Whatever one's opinion of Khrushchev – and he apostrophized me unflatteringly in more speeches than one – it was foolish to neglect the chance of a talk and reject it in a seemingly offensive manner.

I had one more indirect contact with Khrushchev in summer 1964, when his son-in-law, A. I. Adzhubei, then editor of *Izvestia*, was touring the Federal Republic. I met him on 27 July at the Berlin guesthouse in Bonn. Our conversation was rich in substance and extremely pleasant in tone. Adzhubei's mission was to prepare the ground for a visit by his father-in-law to the Federal Republic. Professor Ludwig Erhard, by then Federal Chancellor, alluded to the proposed visit in the Bundestag on 14 October. The same day, Khrushchev was relieved of his duties and retired in semi-disgrace.

Yet the de-Stalinizer, partial reformer and unpredictable power-politician remained unscathed. Unlike his predecessor Malenkov, he escaped banishment to Siberia after being stripped of power. This too betrayed a change which demonstrated that even an empire as cumbersome as the Soviet Union is subject to the process of transformation, however slow its pace. Whatever the real cause of Khrushchev's downfall – whether he was too erratic and autocratic for his partners in the Politburo, whether he was indicted for the failure of his somewhat grandiose agricultural policy, whether the effects of the Cuba crisis persisted, or whether his colleagues viewed the progress of de-Stalinization with misgiving and feared for the internal stability of the régime – German policy seems to have helped seal his fate just as it did Beria's ten years earlier. Nobody wishing to form an accurate assessment of internal developments in Moscow should overlook the connection between the German question and problems of Soviet leadership.

It was not until May 1966 that the opportunity for an exchange of views with the Soviet Government finally arose, though in a way which I myself would not have thought feasible only six months before. I met Pyotr Abrassimov, Soviet Ambassador to the GDR, over morning drinks at the Dahlem residence of Sven Backlund, the shrewd and circumspect Swedish Consul-General who later became his country's ambassador in Brussels and Bonn.

Simple as it may sound today, arrangements for this two-and-a-half-hour meeting entailed several months of discreet diplomatic activity. Both sides finally agreed that the Swedish diplomat should be asked to set the meeting up, so it was arranged in January that Abrassimov and I should each accept an invitation to celebrate Sweden's National Day on 6 June.

In mid-April the Russians in Berlin urgently inquired whether it might not be possible for us to meet before 6 June, preferably in private and without publicity. We duly met on hospitable Swedish territory a month ahead of time. But oh, the problems that had to be sorted out – not to mention all the preparatory talks – before this semi-private conversation could take place! There were at least seven hurdles to surmount:

First, I was at pains to establish that the initiative emanated from the Soviet side. For his part, Abrassimov strove to create the impression that we were meeting at my request. Experience has repeatedly taught me that, however disconcerting one finds this Russian exercise, it must always be allowed for.

The second point to establish was the capacity in which we would be meeting. No misunderstanding could prevail in my own case: as long-time Chairman of the SPD, I would be there in a dual role. As for Abrassimov (a member of the Central Committee of the CPSU), I had to ensure – so as to avoid awkward questions of status – that he did not attend as Soviet Ambassador to the GDR Government but as one of the four persons who continued to wield responsibility for Berlin and the whole of Germany in their residual function as High Commissioners.

Next came the question of who should attend with whom. Abrassimov had asked me to come alone, saying that he would only be accompanied by a colleague-cum-interpreter. In the event, he turned up with one of his aides plus a highly efficient interpreter, but I had no cause to feel isolated. My friend and host Sven Backlund remained present throughout the talk, Abrassimov having genially intimated that the Swede was at liberty to hear anything he had to say to me.

My fourth concern was to safeguard the proceedings against misinterpretation. I personally informed Foreign Minister Schröder and his State Secretary, Karl Carstens, both of whom left me free to arrange matters as I thought fit.

Fifth, the Allies in Berlin had to be initiated into the secret. For once, the information could be restricted to a very small circle. The French and British had no misgivings. The Americans, who were cautious but not averse, wanted the 'private' nature of the meeting to be emphasized. Like me, they presupposed that I would make no pledges or agreements affecting the Allies. They also shared my unwillingness to enter into discussions that might result in an additional Soviet presence in West Berlin.

Sixth, I spoke to the Swedish Foreign Minister, Torsten Nilsson, while visiting Stockholm on another matter at the beginning of May. Although Backlund enjoyed his Foreign Minister's confidence, I did not want him to bear the brunt of any complications arising from the arrangement on his premises.

Last of all, there was the problem of secrecy. This entailed agreement on the press release that would be issued in the event of a leak. Astonishingly enough, my first meeting with Abrassimov passed unnoticed, and no such laborious precautions had to be taken in respect of our four subsequent encounters in Berlin during 1966.

Abrassimov opened the discussion on Sunday, 8 May. Speaking with a mixture of Bolshevist self-assurance and remoteness from the West, he talked of our respective ways of life and invoked the tribulations suffered by the peoples of the Soviet Union during World War II. In trying to unravel a few threads of the argument, we swiftly came to the German question. I explained how mistaken it was to conceive of the German Federal Republic as a great power capable of constituting a military threat. However understandable this misconception might be from the standpoint of many of our contemporaries, the Soviet leaders – of all people – must know better. Besides, the Soviet Union was ill advised to concentrate exclusively on the smaller part of Germany and neglect the opportunities that might stem from practical co-operation with the larger.

Although I regarded the unsolved German question as part of an international complex and did not myself believe in isolated solutions, I could not renounce my people's claim to the right of national unity, including the right to dwell under one political roof. It was asking a great deal of us to confirm a demarcation of frontiers in the East exceeding that which had been envisaged in the Potsdam Agreement while simultaneously – and again in conflict with the Potsdam Agreement – accepting our division into two states. West Berlin was, I said, dependent on its ties and connections with the Federal Republic.

Abrassimov had at the outset described any questioning of the eastern frontiers as a symptom of aggression. On German unity, he espoused the current position of his government: the Soviet Union was in favour of unity, not against it, but both Germanys must reach agreement on the subject and the social achievements of the East must be preserved. It was wholly false to regard the GDR as a satellite state. As for West Berlin, Bonn should not behave as if it belonged to the Federal Republic. Bundestag sessions in Berlin – of which the last had been convened at the Kongresshalle in April 1965 – were a provocation. Berlin meetings of the various parliamentary parties were equally unacceptable.

On 4 April, three days before the Bundestag met in plenary session in Berlin, I had been refused access at Horst on the northern transit route after visiting my mother in Lübeck. (Perhaps I should have tried a sit-in rather than switch to a plane!) The Russians had indeed protested – deafeningly – against this Bundestag session by making nuisance flights with their military aircraft. Supersonic fighters were repeatedly sent over on later occasions, too, as a visible and audible show of strength. Many people, especially the old and sick, found the supersonic bangs a strain on their nerves. I told Abrassimov it could hardly be in the Soviet interest that my four-year-old son should identify everything Russian as 'boom-boom'. The ambassador replied that note had been taken of my words of condolence when two Soviet pilots crashed into the Havel on a low-level flight the year before. Whether influenced by the above arguments or feeling that a display of goodwill was in order, Abrassimov promised to look into the matter. The nerve-shattering aerial demonstrations were, in fact, discontinued after a few days.

It was further discussed whether Berlin should be included in cultural exchanges with the Soviet Union – as happened soon afterwards – and how an expansion of trade could be brought about. Abrassimov said that my public references to 'minor steps' had been favourably received by his own side.

I received plenty of hints that the Soviet Union no longer viewed the Social Democrats with extreme hostility and might even wish them success. In this context, the Russians betrayed an exceptional ignorance of our circumstances. I took care to avoid being played off against the Federal Government and declined to accept any postulates of 'common interest'. Abrassimov inveighed against the banning of the KPD (Communist Party of Germany). Did the Federal Republic want to be on a par with Spain and Portugal in this respect? I explained to him that, while we had considered the Adenauer government's bill banning the KPD to be politically injudicious, we were as much bound by the rulings of the Federal Constitutional Court as anyone else.

The ambassador asked if I would visit him in East Berlin. Although I did not refuse, I drew his attention to the fact that West Berliners were forbidden to enter the other part of the city and told him I wanted no visitor's permit of a kind denied to others. Before we said goodbye, Abrassimov mentioned that I was welcome to visit Moscow whenever it suited me.

Preceded by yet another laborious exchange of queries (though each party knew the other would come), our next meeting took place on 6 June, as planned, at the Swedish National Day reception in Pücklerstrasse, Dahlem. This was the opposite of a secret assignation. Everyone was at liberty to note that we engaged in over an hour's concentrated but relaxed discussion in the garden of Backlund's house.

The ambassador made various approaches to the question of when I would call on him and whether I would visit Moscow. What about a trip to his holiday home outside Berlin? If I couldn't find the time myself, would my wife pay a visit with our Swedish friends? An early visit to Moscow would be beneficial – but again, perhaps my wife would like to come in advance. Having recently been in Prague, why shouldn't she do some theatre- and concert-going in Moscow as well? I countered by hoping that Helmut Schmidt would be well received during his forthcoming trip to Moscow.

On 29 September of the same year, 1966, a Russian orchestra performed before an enthusiastic audience at Berlin's philharmonic hall. Afterwards, Nabokov gave a dinner at the Hotel Zellermayer. It had again been carefully arranged that Abrassimov and I should attend. The ensuing reception was not publicized – there was no need – but the press got to know of it a few days later and accused me, quite unjustly, of clandestine goings-on.

The evening reception took an entertaining turn and the atmosphere might even have been described as cordial, thanks not least to the presence of numerous Soviet artists. Even before we sat down to dine, Abrassimov remarked that we must meet again soon, either on his territory in East Berlin or on mine in the West. I told him that I would accept an invitation but that transit must be arranged in a form acceptable to myself.

It was brought home to me that evening how emotionally charged the Russian aversion to China can be. The explosion came when our friend Nabokov inquired, undiplomatically but without malicious intent, whether we proposed to drink the health of Chairman Mao. Abrassimov flared up at this. Why not drink to Hitler while we were about it? Didn't we realize that what was being advertised on Mao's authority as cultural revolution amounted to cultural barbarism?

The customary Russian alternation of speeches and toasts prompted Abrassimov to address me by my first name as the night wore on. Egon Bahr tried with little success to steer the conversation into more serious channels. He made a short, sharp speech designed to convince our fellow-guests that it was not just the Germans who were feared in Russia – from dire experience – but that there were good reasons to fear the Russians in Germany. Although his words made little impression under the circumstances, they were not taken amiss.

The new Soviet Ambassador in Bonn, Semyon Tsarapkin, had recently paid me an introductory call in my capacity as party chairman. I found him quite congenial too, but he argued far more vigorously than his colleague in East Berlin. Tsarapkin's not unmerited nickname was 'Pincers'. The ambassador's powerful jaws sometimes snapped shut with a force suggestive of the intention to pulverize his words. Then, as on many subsequent occasions, we discussed the German question and our differences of attitude.

On 12 October 1966 I visited Abrassimov by appointment at the Soviet Embassy in Unter den Linden. Our transit had been carefully arranged. My wife and I crossed the border at Checkpoint Charlie, which was normally reserved for foreigners, so we did not have to stop or produce any papers. I caught a fleeting glimpse of GDR border guards standing rigidly at attention. On arrival at the embassy we were conducted to Abrassimov's private quarters. The Backlunds had also been invited. So, to our delight, had the great 'cellist Mstislav (Slava) Rostropovitch, fresh from a triumphant performance in Berlin the night before. Abrassimov summoned him to produce his instrument after dinner. I found it rather inappropriate that such an inspired musician should be called on to garnish our discussions with Bach and Handel.

We later became close friends. Rostropovitch performed in Bonn when I was Federal Chancellor. In summer 1968, during my spell at the Foreign Ministry, we met in Scotland to receive honorary degrees from St Andrews University. Being uncertain how a German and a

Russian would get on, the organizers did their best to keep us apart before the ceremony. Our hosts were duly astonished, when I went to the robing room to don my gown, to see us hug each other like a couple of old friends.

While Rostropovitch and the ladies were being shown a film that night at the Soviet Embassy, Abrassimov and I conversed until half past midnight. Sven Backlund, never a man to overdramatize, declared shortly afterwards that our meeting might well acquire 'historic' significance. What he meant, first and foremost, was that the ambassador had listened intently and made no demur when I expounded the technique of 'bracketing off' controversial questions so as to further a solution of this practical problem or that – a technique, if one will, of 'negative compromise' which can reveal positive openings as though by mirror-image. To be more explicit, one party reiterated that he could not depart from the principle of national unity, even if a solution in terms of political reunification were not currently feasible, while the other laid stress on his government's obligations towards the GDR. My own conclusion: we had to live with both attitudes and concentrate on matters capable of solution in the shorter term – for instance trade, culture and the alleviation of human hardship.

Abrassimov asked me for an assessment of the situation in the Federal Republic. He also broached the possibility of talks between the CPSU and SPD. I was not amenable to this and stressed that my own concern was for better relations between our countries and peoples, not between two disparate parties. There was more talk of trade and a renewed inquiry as to when I intended to visit Moscow. I replied that this might be possible towards the end of January.

An equally full discussion took place when I returned Abrassimov's hospitality at the Senate guest-house on 22 November. The Backlunds were again present. Of my own associates, Klaus Schütz and Egon Bahr both attended. The atmosphere at table was rather subdued, and Abrassimov did nothing to brighten it. His after-dinner speech embodied another reference to inter-party co-operation. He also hinted at the existence of compromising documents relating to Kurt Georg Kiesinger, who was then being mooted as Chancellor of a grand coalition. These were, in fact, GDR publications which contained nothing new and had to do with Kiesinger's work for the old Foreign Office.

None of this helped, nor was it particularly tactful. Afterwards, in my office, the ambassador applied himself to proposals which were equally remote from Federal German reality. I read him some extracts from the already published eight-point paper setting out our Social

Democratic provisos for talks on a coalition. Naturally enough, Abrassimov paid special attention to our outline of the need for a new policy towards the East. I urgently requested him to advise the SED leaders to facilitate the signing of a new passes agreement imbued with symbolic effect. Whether or not he forwarded my recommendation, nothing came of it.

My contact with Abrassimov, who was reappointed to his ambassadorial post in East Berlin in March 1975, after some years in Paris and the International Section of the Central Committee of the CPSU, never entirely ceased. We had a long talk in Paris during the summer of 1968 and exchanged intermittent greetings thereafter.

My dialogue with this tough but not inflexible diplomat may well have helped in some small measure to alleviate the pressure on Berlin. It could, however, do little to promote even the most tentative relationship between East Berlin and Bonn. Any moves in that direction seemed doomed to peter out in a maze of hostility and prejudice.

It did not escape the close attention of observers in East Berlin, as in Moscow, that the SPD was gaining strength with every election and that the day could not be far distant when it would assume joint responsibility for the administration of the German Federal Republic. The party's positions on foreign and German policy were constantly and critically re-examined by its executive bodies and local organizations alike. Rather than take refuge in exalted dreams of reality, we wanted to get a grip on that reality by means which included the necessary revision of outmoded ideas. To me, the precondition of every constructive move was, and continued to be, that we should seek the closest possible dialogue and an ever deeper accord with our Atlantic partners and our friends in Europe. Being Mayor of Berlin as well as Chairman of the Social Democratic Party, I had many practical opportunities to seek an understanding with the men and the political forces that dominated the capitals of the West.

My line of reasoning at the SPD's Karlsruhe conference late in 1964 was still clearly dictated by the hope that it might be possible to pave the way for a peace treaty and thereby open the road to German reunification. Our ideas on the German peace treaty must, I said, be crystallized and clarified in advance with our allies. To this end, we should mobilize the ambassadorial steering group in Washington composed of representatives from the three Western Powers and the Federal Republic. Then, when the opportunity arose, serious discussions should be initiated with the Soviet Union. Some may object that a peace treaty seemed virtually out of the question at the time, and that it might under certain circumstances have been undesirable because it would have included provisions likely to give the Germans a new Versailles complex. This may be so, but we in Berlin had the Wall looming over us. We had to search for ways of dissolving an encrusted situation.

I was also able to state at the Karlsruhe conference that, but for the responsible attitude of my party, several major decisions could never have been taken. This was not merely a reference to the 'consolidation' of the Franco-German treaty and the passes agreements in Berlin, but rather to the establishment of German missions in East European countries. In the guise of trade missions, these had begun to operate in Poland, Hungary and Rumania in 1963 and in Bulgaria during 1964. My friends and I welcomed this move and advocated that relations with our East European neighbours be normalized as far as possible. We further supported ratification of the nuclear test-ban treaty which the Americans and Russians had signed in August 1963. This had met with considerable opposition. Foreign Minister Schröder spoke to me at the time about the 'madmen' who were making life difficult for him, and he was not referring to members of the SPD.

After exploring new avenues at the Karlsruhe conference, I detailed our German policy at Dortmund early in June 1966. Turning to the three points then at issue, I declared that they were insufficient to constitute a policy: references to 'Four-Power responsibility' should not serve as a pretext for doing nothing; the 'claim to sole representation' must not entail that the representatives of Communist Germany should determine, even indirectly, where the German Federal Republic had to haul down its flag; and, finally, we must not convert the thesis of 'non-recognition' into a strait-jacket for ourselves. Too many people behaved as if we still owned the territories east of the Oder and Neisse.

Like Adenauer, I proceeded on the assumption that the Soviet Union, too, was interested in the maintenance of peace. I called for a conference between the NATO states and those of the Warsaw Pact. There was, I emphasized, no road to Germany which bypassed Europe. As to our relations with the GDR, communist plans for a confederation would benefit nobody who aspired to German unity in freedom. It was something quite else to contemplate 'a qualified, controlled and temporary coexistence of the two territories' if the way were paved by international decisions and public opinion left free to develop in the other part of Germany. This would be a *modus vivendi* sustained by a dogged determination to solve further problems in a positive manner.

At the time of this party conference in Dortmund there were some grounds for hoping that a first-ever public debate would be conducted with representatives of the ruling SED. The communist side withdrew from this battle of words, but it is worth noting that a public encounter of this kind, summarized by the catch-phrase 'exchange of speakers', seemed imminent during the first half of 1966.

It began with an open letter sent by Ulbricht on 7 February and published in *Neues Deutschland*, his principal newspaper, on 11 February. The writing of the letter was no novelty, this being a time-worn technique often employed by the SED leadership. What was new was that we formally took it up and expressed interest in an exchange of views on the 'German question'.

After lengthy negotiations, it was agreed that two public debates be held, the first of them at Karl-Marx-Stadt (Chemnitz) on 14 July. After some procedural difficulties, the Bundestag had arranged for members of the SED leadership to be granted safe conduct. It required the co-operation of the CDU/CSU bloc to ensure, from the legal aspect, that their visit would not be curtailed by the courts. The SED leaders were dissatisfied with this and used procedural problems as a pretext for withdrawing from the scheme. They further buttressed their refusal by arguing that they declined to concede the sole representation claim – which was not, in fact, under current discussion. Presumably, they had begun to fear that our public appearance in the GDR might evoke some uncontrollable response. I also gained the impression that their Soviet advisers took a jaundiced view of the 'exchange of speakers' project and had finally recommended its rejection. Being acquainted with the East German atmosphere, they probably feared an SED fiasco and may also have wondered if 'the Germans' would really confine themselves to wrangling in public – they might have opened their mouths wider still.

It was clear to me that we had, at Chemnitz, encountered representatives of a régime on which time had not failed to leave its mark. True, the SED state had remained a dictatorship dependent on Soviet military strength, but we could not act as if no developments had occurred 'over there'. 1961 and the construction of the Wall had meant a profound upheaval, not only for us, and Berlin in particular, but for our compatriots in the GDR as well. It had thrown them back on their own resources and banished hope of assistance from the West. It had also helped in some respects to consolidate the régime. The GDR's economy had made notable strides and many of its inhabitants felt proud of successes achieved under difficult circumstances, external and domestic. We could not deplore this. Moreover, I thought I perceived a transition from satellite to partner in the GDR's relations with the Soviet Union.

We were prepared for something more than a rhetorical argument: 'An exchange of blows – yes, as far as necessary, but objectivity for the sake of practical advances, be they never so small – yes, as far as possible.' On 14 July 1966, when we should really have been in Chemnitz, Erler, Wehner and I spoke on television and radio (it was Fritz Erler's last public appearance). I appealed to my fellow-countrymen as follows:

We are witnessing a shift in power blocs coupled with new developments between East and West. Western and Eastern Europe are outgrowing their rigid alignments. This process must not pass Germany by. We must not remain excluded, nor must we exclude ourselves. Germany, too, must strive to relax its state of internal cramp. That is what matters. For the sake of human beings, not of argument, we ask: Can something be done – and if so what – to make people's lives easier despite everything and keep the unity of our divided nation alive? Every step on this road to relaxation and détente is a German contribution to the better securing of peace. That is what I call a peace policy – in, of and for Germany.

5

Conversations with de Gaulle

Many of my friends express surprise when they learn that I was for a long time more conversant with France and the French language than with the English-speaking world. I had only one opportunity to spend a few days in England before World War II. France I often visited during my years as an exile, sometimes for months on end. Most of the people I met there were companions in misfortune from Germany, but I also had access to everyday life in France. To a young man from Hanseatic Lübeck, notwithstanding a measure of familiarity with the history of its revolutions and 'left-wing' literature, France had at first seemed very remote. Although there were many gaps in my outsider's picture of its national characteristics, on-the-spot experience of the country bred a high regard for its culture as manifested in real life – and this despite the limitations imposed on a young and impoverished expatriate.

The France to which I remained close, even when many external ties were sundered, was the Free France of the Resistance. I had no difficulty in rediscovering that bridge of mutual confidence after the war. Membership of the Resistance also formed the basis of my relations with General de Gaulle. I first met the General in June 1959 as a guest of the city of Paris, which cordially welcomed the Mayor of Berlin through its Président du Conseil Municipal, Dr Pierre Devraigne. A special note was struck by the ceremony at the Tomb of the Unknown Soldier. On arrival, I had recalled my visits to Paris before the war. I stressed that I was also there to say that, in company with many of my fellow-countrymen, I had not forgotten the havoc wrought in France and its capital by an infamous German régime. 'We have striven,' I said, 'to wash away the disgrace.'

De Gaulle had by then been back in office for a year. The National Assembly had elected him premier on 1 June 1958 and the new constitution had come into force at the beginning of 1959, when he assumed the Presidency of the Republic. This inaugurated a political era which has left an enduring mark on modern France. All controversy apart, the French can surely consider themselves fortunate to have been able to fall back on a political leader with sufficient authority to prevent the dying embers of their colonial past from kindling the holocaust of a civil war. After the turmoil of the Fourth Republic, most Frenchmen regarded Gaullist rule as a guarantee of relative stability – even if relief was succeeded by growing concern lest the patriarchal and authoritarian features of Gaullism prove too obstructive to the development of a modern industrial society. De Gaulle left a deep imprint on the rest of Europe as well. However one views them, his independent efforts to establish a dialogue with the Warsaw Pact and his rigid attitude towards European unification were of signal importance. The least that can be said is that, but for de Gaulle, events in Europe would have taken a different turn.

The style that reigned during my visits to the Elysée remained almost unaltered for a decade-and-a-half and was perpetuated under President Pompidou. As I myself had frequent occasion to note in later years, the Federal Chancellor was accorded picturesque military honours. Protocol was strictly observed. I often reflected on the wide gulf between French etiquette and Bonn's lack of outward ceremony. Nobody was kept waiting in a Parisian reception room. I shall never forget de Gaulle's friendly habit of greeting me in German and saying a few words in my language when I took my leave. Each of us conversed in his mother-tongue, de Gaulle's interpreter being present to make notes. Occasionally, when we wanted to make doubly sure of some point, he was requested to translate a particular word or passage. In June 1959 de Gaulle's style of conversation took me aback. I was surprised and secretly a little amused when he questioned me in the manner of a C-in-C eliciting information from one of his divisional commanders:

What can the Mayor tell me about conditions in Berlin?

How are things in the Federal Republic?

What about the situation in Prussia?

After taking a few moments to grasp that 'Prussia' meant the GDR, I made a qualified rejoinder whose sole effect was to prompt de Gaulle to speak, on another occasion, of 'Prussia and Saxony'. This terminology was dictated by his notion of historical continuity. Social systems and the development of political blocs meant nothing to him; nations, peoples and traditional nation-states meant everything. He invariably referred to the Soviet Union as 'Russia'.

Finally he asked, 'What is the SPD up to?' I had expected this fourth question least of all. The President limited his comments on my brief account to remarking that, in his view, Berlin's mayor was one of the European figures of whom more would be heard in future. He reverted to this a year later, as I recorded in the following note: 'He referred to remarks which he had made to me in 1959 on the role of various figures in the future development of Europe.'

My attitude to de Gaulle was twofold and has, in certain respects, remained so. To me he was a symbolic personification of the French Resistance. I had followed his career with sympathy and admiration from the collapse of 1940 – when, from a prison camp, I heard him proudly proclaim that France would soldier on – to his march through Paris in 1944. Who could have failed to respect the way in which his steadfast faith and iron determination secured an honorary place for France at the great powers' table? He also regarded me as a man of the Resistance – not to carry the comparison further – so it was quite natural that I, like his own companions of darker days, tended to address him as General rather than President when we were alone together or conversing informally.

On the other hand, I was not uninfluenced by the disparaging reports that had filtered through from Anglo-American sources, even during the war, and painted his sense of mission in ironic colours. His ideas on many subjects were far removed indeed from those of a social democrat, especially one of Scandinavian complexion. Moreover, even discounting the anti-German sentiments of the early post-war years, his approach to European development and international co-operation often seemed old-fashioned and rigid. It was false to dismiss him as a reactionary, however, and still is. His mind compounded pre-revolutionary tradition with ideas that reached into the future. Besides, who else could have taken it upon himself or mustered the authority to end the war in Algeria before still more mischief was done? Who, again, would dismiss the enduring effects of de Gaulle's insistence on European autonomy – despite his frequent tendency to confuse Europe with France – or his eye for all-European perspectives?

The French Foreign Minister of the day was Maurice Couve de Murville, formerly ambassador in Washington and Bonn. I had got to know him quite well during his time in Bonn, and we often met during his ten years at the Quai d'Orsay. We spoke English and got on well together, although it should be said that he seldom strayed one milli-metre from the General's current guide-line. He was a brilliant power-technician, an elegant man endowed with the keen intelligence so often encountered among the Protestant élite of the French aristocracy. Usually rather reserved, Couve could be humorous in private conversation. I still chuckle when I recall his anecdote about the Indonesian dictator Sukarno, who spotted some paragons of feminine beauty on an old tapestry at the Quai d'Orsay and delightedly exclaimed, 'Finally – women!'

As long as conversation did not actually centre on my desire for stronger links with the Federation, I could almost always count on Couve's support over Berlin. De Gaulle's attitude to my city was just as unwavering. This dependability proved itself on many occasions, notably the Geneva Conference of 1959, which gave me scope for some intensive discussions on the side-lines.

In September 1962 the French President undertook the state visit to Germany which earned him such wild acclaim. (Adenauer, who found this almost too much of a good thing, urged us not to forget that de Gaulle had another side to him. He also commented to me on the Germans' tendency to lose their sense of proportion. He found it undignified that the Bavarians should have presented our guest with a picture of Napoleon entering Munich!) De Gaulle told me that the tour had become 'more emotional' than he expected, but he too must have grasped the reasons for this jubilation. To the majority of Germans, reconciliation with France was an emotional need and a rational requirement. Enthusiasm for Europe was then at its peak among the young (and not so young). In addition, the Germans' exalted friend gave them a chance to disburden their souls of a national complex – perhaps a sense of guilt – and drown it in cheers. He was the first prominent foreigner to make a post-war reference to the great German nation. It impressed people that a man of his stature should pay such a tribute. Say what one will, de Gaulle's visit was a major emotional landmark in post-war history. It was also regarded by many of my fellow-countrymen as a step on the road to Europe, be it only de Gaulle's '*Europe des patries*'.

After a dinner given by de Gaulle at La Redoute in Bad Godesberg, he invited me to talk *à deux*. He thanked me for welcoming his visit in a parliamentary statement made that afternoon and went on to stress that France would continue to support a firm stance on the Berlin question. With the Americans, there was always a risk that they would accept sham compromises. The West had ample means of responding to Soviet pressure in Berlin with counter-pressure elsewhere. My attitude was appreciated in France.

Berlin was not included in the General's itinerary. He always politely evaded my invitations to visit the city. The first time, in 1959, I was told that he hesitated to come because he did not possess the same resources as the Americans. In 1963 he told me that it had seemed impracticable to pay a visit in the preceding year – and anyway, he had not been invited by the Federal Government. It was, he said, improbable that his next visit would take in Berlin either. Besides, the American President had just completed his trip to the Federal Republic and Berlin, and Kennedy – as I myself must know – was animated by considerations different from his own. It was simply a question of opportunity. Visiting Paris in 1965, I reminded the General that he would always be welcome in Berlin. Expediency might, in the not too distant future, prescribe that things be said from Berlin which would be of significance to Europe as a whole.

Instead of contradicting me, de Gaulle employed a recapitulation which I recorded in my notes, especially as I had heard it before: he could not come under present circumstances 'so as not to recognize the Wall'. This was a peculiar statement and made little sense. I found it more understandable when he volunteered a critical comparison of the visits of President Kennedy and Queen Elizabeth. He did not repeat his hint that the Federal Government had not proposed a visit to Berlin.

In April 1963 a series of cultural functions took me back to Paris. (I had been informed that de Gaulle wanted to see me on this occasion but was absent from the capital and would grant me an interview at a place still to be determined.) Opening a Watteau exhibition at the Louvre in company with André Malraux, I had a chance to study the language and the nervously sensitive gestures of that extraordinary man, who sees world history as a vision of ancient cultures, exalted ideas and the emanations of a few great men.

I also met members of the official and unofficial opposition such as the socialist ex-premier Guy Mollet, who had broken with de Gaulle in profound disappointment, and my paternal friend, Jean Monnet, out of favour with the President because of his championship of European integration. The ties between us were not dependent on the approval or disapproval of French officialdom. I revered Monnet as one of the architects of our new Europe and admired the tenacity with which he pursued his aims. Like many preachers of other gospels, he often appeared to repeat the same – largely reasonable – arguments and deliver the same speeches. It does not detract from his importance that he sought the right opening in the wrong place, namely by integrating the coal (and steel) industry when coal seemed to have lost its prime importance. The fact remains that he activated the mechanisms which Europe needed, if only to develop into an economic community. His error lay in believing that economic integration automatically leads to political integration. This, as we were all to learn, requires an independent effort of the political will, but Monnet taught us what would continue to apply to the building of Europe: that reason can be set to work by force of conviction.

I saw the President before my Paris schedule began. Our talk, which lasted 70 minutes instead of the scheduled 45, naturally concentrated on problems affecting Berlin. Apart from a greater French contribution to the cultural life of my city, I said, my main desire was for French support in at least mitigating the inhumane consequences of the Wall and the division of Germany. The East was always equipped with a series of offensive positions. The West's political freedom of movement was restricted. Over and above the assertion of Western rights in Berlin, however, there must be a constant quest for ways and means of improving the human condition. Even if little were achieved, the people on the other side of the Wall would feel that they were not forgotten.

De Gaulle declared that everything from Berlin, particularly in the cultural and intellectual sphere, received his sympathetic attention. The French position on Berlin was clear beyond doubt. It was France's policy to surrender nothing that the free world possessed. In so far as possible, the inhabitants of East Berlin and the 'Zone' should be urged not to despair. If there were any ways of bringing relief and encouragement to the people in the East, whether through the International Red Cross or by some other means, he would be receptive to them. If I had any practical suggestions to make in the future course of developments, I must not hesitate to communicate them. The President also referred to his fears of an exodus of citizens from West Berlin during the past year. He carefully noted the figures I gave him relating to increased production and the influx of labour from West Germany.

The General expressed dissatisfaction with the talks between the Americans and the Russians because there was always a chance that they would endanger Western positions. One had to be especially wary of the United Nations, mainly on account of the neutral countries which tended to adopt an attitude convenient to the Soviet Union. The logical conclusion: no change in the status of Berlin. That status could endure for another eighteen years, he said – then we should see where the Russians stood. The people of West Berlin need have no doubts about France. She was not alone, however, nor did she represent the strongest Western Power.

The nub of our discussion concerned de Gaulle's attitude towards the Atlantic Alliance and the Franco-German treaty signed by himself and Konrad Adenauer in January 1963. I introduced the subject by observing that, while I could not speak for the German Government, I could do so for nearly 40 per cent of the German electorate. All or almost all responsible circles in the Federal Republic were agreed on the cardinal importance of Franco-German reconciliation and co-operation. I was aware of the General's historic role but wished to say, quite frankly, that the German people should not be embroiled in needless disputes. This applied particularly to Germany's relations with the United States, which had played such a crucial part in its post-war development and was continuing to do so. Later in our talk I forecast that the January treaty would be ratified by large majorities in the Bundesrat and Bundestag. De Gaulle must not misunderstand if it were made clear, either through a preamble or in some other way, that nothing should be allowed to impair the Federal Republic's links with the Atlantic Alliance in general and the United States in particular, nor its obligations under the EEC treaties signed in Rome.

On the subject of the Alliance and Europe, de Gaulle denied that France wanted any breach with the Atlantic Alliance or the US because she was just as threatened as Germany. Peace and the *status quo* could only be preserved with American assistance, and it would be childish to think otherwise. (Three years were to pass before France withdrew from an integrated NATO, but de Gaulle had already withdrawn the French Mediterranean Fleet from NATO command in spring 1959 after Eisenhower rejected his request for greater inter-Allied consultation. Speaking to Adenauer at Rambouillet in summer 1960, he said that France's position in NATO could not last long 'in its present form'. After the Nassau Agreement of December 1962, under which Kennedy made available Polaris missiles to Macmillan, de Gaulle described the US President's Atlantic idea as an ideological façade for American supremacy. He did not consider Britain truly European and terminated British attempts to negotiate admission to the EEC by casting his veto a week before concluding the Franco-German treaty.)

If we wanted Europe, de Gaulle went on, it had to be just that. Otherwise it would be merely America plus individual countries such as Germany, France and Britain – a vague and incoherent structure. We should negotiate with the Americans as Europe, and that would be possible only if there were a lasting settlement between Germany and France. If not, no enduring community could be summoned into being. 'Europe has yet to be created because Germany and France were against it until now. Now the time has come, but Europe is not a matter for technocrats.'

Turning to the Franco-German treaty, de Gaulle expressed some annoyance at the German reaction because France's approach to the treaty had also entailed a surmounting of the past. I replied that the younger generation regarded the idea of a new conflict with France as absurd. It did, however, approach the problems of its native land with fewer prejudices and more self-assurance than those who had required forgiveness for so many things in the past. The new generation would not renounce its concern for those Germans who were segregated from the Federal Republic.

De Gaulle said that he fully sympathized with this attitude. For the rest, either there would be war – and a future which no one could foresee – or the Soviet Union would be faced with new problems. Both as a doctrine and a régime, communism had already become harder to uphold and less cogent than in Stalin's day, not only in its own land but in the countries of Eastern Europe – 'including Prussia and Saxony'. The General ended by sending cordial and confident greetings to the people of Berlin, coupled with his best wishes. Berlin's role was an important one, and the Governing Mayor had a major share in it.

I have indicated that I was not too happy with the preparation and parliamentary handling of the Franco-German Treaty of Co-operation. Opportunities for close Franco-German co-operation remained un-exploited, particularly in regard to the growth of European unity, because the Federal Republic's tentative behaviour could not fail to annoy the French President. At the same time, US-German relations would have fared better had the need for close co-operation between France and the Federal Republic been soberly advocated instead of nervously glossed over in a manner that aroused doubts about the *bona fides* of German foreign policy. A bolder and more imaginative policy might also have precluded any need for the preamble drafted by my Social Democrat associates in concert with the Free Democrats and the 'Atlanticists' of the CDU. It fell to me to report on the treaty's provisions to the Bundesrat, but I spoke again during the ratification debate. I pointed out that our special relationship with the United States had never yet brought us into serious conflict with France or Britain. It had never faced us with a choice. From Berlin's point of view, I could only hope and expect that this treaty, which was designed to seal Franco-German reconciliation, not initiate it, would never bring the Federal Republic, including the *Land* of Berlin, into dispute with our other friends.

Turning to Adenauer, I went on:

I doubt, Herr Bundeskanzler, if there is anyone in this chamber who does not feel an exceptional measure of admiration for President de Gaulle . . . He possesses the courage and strength to entertain new plans, whether or not they are always right. But it will most certainly be impossible, according to the spirit of the treaty under consideration, to pursue those plans against the wishes of the German Federal Republic . . . I say this quite frankly, Herr Bundeskanzler: because nations are concerned, and because reconciliation has reached a stage at which our young people can no longer conceive of the insanities perpetrated in both countries by earlier generations – that is why no one opposes the ratification of this treaty. It is, therefore, a regard for the relationship between peoples, not for that between governments.

My contacts with leading French socialists during these years were not as active as they should have been. I did not meet François Mitterand, that ambitious yet sensitive and widely gifted man who drew over 45 per cent of votes as the presidential candidate of the Left late in 1965, until several years later, when he was already heading a reconstituted socialist party. Rich in political experience garnered from membership of several governments under the Fourth Republic, he devoted all his energies to transforming the French socialists into a new source of national leadership, not merely to restoring their former political importance. I was impressed by his efforts.

Guy Mollet, Mayor of Arras and long-time secretary-general of the SFIO, the traditional French socialist party, had retired from the forefront of politics in the mid-1960s. I cherished a high regard for him despite his occasional lapses into pedantry, but I doubt if he ever really forgave me my links with de Gaulle. I maintained friendly contacts with Gaston Defferre, Mayor of Marseilles and leader of the socialists in the National Assembly. I also called on him at his Paris apartment in March 1964, when – first mooted for discussion by Jean-Jacques Servan-Schreiber as 'Monsieur X' – he was working on his presidential candidacy.

When de Gaulle visited Bonn in summer 1964, we spoke together after dinner at the Palais Schaumburg. He had been interested to note my recent remarks to the Foreign Policy Association in New York – deliberately made on the eve of a visit to Washington:

We still have no constructive Atlantic partnership. Instead we see the signs of crisis in NATO . . . Instead of a free Europe speaking with one voice, we hear again and again the discord of a strength-sapping rivalry . . . In my opinion it is neither sensible nor fair to hold General de Gaulle responsible for all the difficulties we in the West face. Some decisions by the French President certainly are not easy to understand. But I did not come to the United States in order to complain about him. Rather there is ample reason to recognize the fact that in his own way de Gaulle is thinking the unthinkable with audacity and determination, and that he has begun to draw certain conclusions as a result . . . The balance of terror maintained by the two super-powers provides the opportunity to set rigid positions in motion. The French President takes advantage of this in his own way. And indeed, sometimes I ask myself as a German: Why only he?

My 'Why only he?' not only met with ill-informed criticism but drew anxious queries even from close political associates. I did not find them hard to dispose of. In an address to the German Foreign Policy Association in June 1964, even before the next round of consultations in Bonn, I spoke of the experience I had gained from this controversy and reminded my audience of the commonplace that some political realities can be embraced neither by a simple *pro* nor by a straightforward *contra*. Correct as it might be to say that movement was not good in itself, the same went for immobility – 'especially when an ice-field breaks up and the floes begin to move'. Not only the French, I argued, but the British and others – including, naturally, the Americans –were exploiting this relative freedom of movement after their own fashion. 'And what are we doing?' I demanded. The Federal Republic must not create the impression that it had no interests or will of its own. It, too, was confronted by the problem of how to exploit opportunities for movement, and this explained the respectful or friendly admonition underlying the question 'Why only he?'

I thus assumed a qualified stance between the 'Atlanticist' and 'European' camps into which opinion at Bonn was divided. In my view this confrontation was unreal and doctrinaire because it did justice neither to Washington's position nor to that of Paris. The 'Europeans', or, as they liked to call themselves, the 'German Gaullists', failed to grasp that the General would not pursue their dreams of a European nuclear deterrent (he firmly rejected German participation). They also overlooked the fact that he was engaged in devising a policy of détente which could never have been supported by the Union's right wing and was really, in many respects, paving the way for our subsequent *Ostpolitik*. The 'Atlanticists', for their part, chased after the illusion of a 'special relationship' between the Federal Republic and the United States for which America, too, lacked what they conceived to be the prerequisites. They refused to acknowledge that some of the political planners and strategists in Washington – probably including President Johnson – paid no more than lip-service to European unity. It was far from certain that they genuinely wished Europe to develop an independent will and a dynamism born of union (if only in a *Europe des patries*).

The harshest criticism then merited by Bonn's Western policy was that it lacked imagination. Only this can account for the perplexity with which the Bonn cabinet greeted de Gaulle's visionary ideas during the consultations at the Palais Schaumburg in summer 1964. The President had prepared himself for these talks with especial care and came to Bonn accompanied by the key political members of his cabinet. He expounded his ideas boldly and unreservedly. Federal Chancellor Erhard did not react and Gerhard Schröder requested that a start be made on the agenda. Of course a German government could not unconditionally pursue de Gaulle's ideas – of course it could not allow him, any more than Washington, to compel the Federal Republic to choose between France and the United States – but the German reply need not have been silence. It was appropriate neither to the subject nor to the man. His productive suggestions deserved a response.

It was probably because I aspired to a more discriminating analysis of the General's attitudes and ideas that, even under these circumstances, he sought a dialogue with the SPD Chairman and Mayor of Berlin. I attribute his candour to the same considerations.

I revisited Paris at the beginning of June 1965, during the campaign for the Bundestag elections, partly to address the Western European Union Assembly. Once again, my interview with de Gaulle opened with Berlin. He suggested that we get down to '*affaires*' right away, so I communicated my anxiety at the state of Franco-German relations.

De Gaulle owned to the impression that he had been in agreement with Adenauer on the elements of a common policy. The preamble added to the treaty had largely robbed it of value by making joint action dependent on others. The treaty had become more of a sentimental than a political matter. His assessment of the two-year-old accord could thus be called negative rather than critical, but he drew no inferences that might have called its existence in question. The press should take a more moderate line, he said, as was largely the case in Paris.

I submitted that differences of opinion, for instance over defence planning, should be openly discussed and closer co-operation sought in practical spheres such as research projects and military equipment. The President replied that such openings had seldom if ever been exploited on the German side. Arms contracts had almost always been placed in the United States.

Concerning the Alliance, he spoke of his fears that the Europeans might fall prey to a misconceived American strategy. Preparations were being made to defend the West with conventional and so-called tactical atomic weapons (through the 'strategy of flexible deterrence' developed under Kennedy by General Taylor, which France was seeking to counter with the *force de frappe* scheme that had originated even prior to de Gaulle). The sufferers, continued de Gaulle, would be both parts of Germany and probably France as well. The really essential thing was America's determination to launch an all-out counter-strike with nuclear weapons. We should, however, proceed on the assumption that neither the Soviet Union nor the United States was disposed to make war. I conceded that the problems of defence planning needed clarification. Where Germany's relationship to key factors abroad was concerned, I spoke in Paris as I did in Washington. German policy could not, in my view, treat the two factors as interchangeable. Until the international situation underwent some fundamental change, US guarantees and commitments would remain indispensable.

De Gaulle rejected any imputations of foolishness. Of course he too believed that the Atlantic Alliance must remain in being. Details of organization would need to be discussed, but the Defence Ministers would hardly be conferring in Paris at that moment if he were fundamentally opposed to NATO.

I wondered aloud if General de Gaulle suspected us Germans of relishing the role of a US 'satellite'. This was incorrect. He should accurately assess Germany's post-war development and do nothing to help restrict its freedom of decision more than circumstances already did. De Gaulle replied that he thoroughly appreciated Germany's position and my own suggestions. (The French transcript, which was brought to the notice of our ambassador, displayed a more negative tendency. It recorded the President's belief that American 'predominance' should be overcome.)

On the current state of European co-operation and its future prospects, de Gaulle pronounced it ridiculous to try and ignore the real existence of the European nations. It was, however, quite possible that moves might be made towards the establishment of a confederation. Apart from the six existing EEC countries, he named Britain, the Scandinavian states and Spain as possible partners.

Referring to a speech made by the President at Strasbourg, I stressed that I myself would favour a federative line. However, even limited political co-operation would be a step forward. Should not consideration be given to possible arrangements between the EEC and EFTA plus Britain (the European free-trade zone outside the EEC)? Lodged at this stage, a British application for membership might conceivably impose additional strains on the relationship between Paris and Bonn. Would it not be better to adapt oneself to a long-term process during which the various countries could find the place that suited them? De Gaulle said he fully concurred with this line of thought.

The General passed a few comments on changes in the communist world. I gave an account of the moves currently being made by Germany, for example Erhard's 'peace note' to the East European states and Schröder's contacts with Rumania and other countries behind the Iron Curtain. I also drew attention to my own proposals for an *Ostpolitik*. Our policy towards Eastern Europe was not that of an American spearhead, nor must it be so fashioned that the Soviet Union felt needlessly provoked. I intimated that the General needed co-operation with Germany if his policy were not to fail and stated my belief that France could not pursue a fruitful policy of détente in isolation. The success or failure of Europe's East-West policy depended on Franco-German solidarity.

De Gaulle waxed faintly sarcastic about German problems. In the Dulles era, he said, Western policy had been to conquer the Soviet Union and then solve the German question. There now seemed to be a belief in Germany that the German question would be solved if the Western Powers submitted an occasional petition to Moscow. France supported reunification even though her experience of a united Germany was not unduly favourable. It must, however, be realized on the German side that reunification stood no chance unless the frontiers with Czechoslovakia and Poland were recognized – nor, if we wanted a united Germany, should we press for nuclear weapons. (Such statements would greatly have dismayed the self-styled 'German Gaullists', had they taken note of them, but they shunned any sober analysis of French policy. 'German Gaullism' did not base itself on de Gaulle, least of all when he devoted his energies to an accommodation with the East.)

I replied that the German question was part of a historical process. Any frontier settlement must take account of the relevant legal, human and psychological problems, and the first category bore upon France's ties under the German treaty. We were prepared for wide-ranging economic co-operation with Eastern Europe. The crucial point was whether national reunification should be weighed against other factors

or whether we were merely being confronted with 'advance concessions'. I still hoped that some modifications could be obtained in
respect of boundaries. The General had, I argued, mentioned German
rearmament in connection with a peace settlement. My response to that,
based on my personal view of German affairs, was that a reunified
Germany would naturally have to accept the negotiated conditions
governing a European security system. On the other hand, it was
essential for the Federal Republic to have a joint say in the nuclear
defence of the Alliance and satisfy itself that it was not denied information of major importance to non-military production.

De Gaulle made fun of the expression 'joint say', which he repeated
a few times in German. Did I seriously believe that one nuclear power
would really allow others a 'joint say'? There was fundamental agreement in both East and West that nuclear weapons should be withheld
from Germany. I asked why, if the Russians were as apprehensive on
this score as I supposed, their anxiety was not used as a bargaining
counter. Why was no attempt being made to make political progress,
however modest?

We also discussed a 'Europeanization' of the German question.
De Gaulle said that his sole aim – for instance at a press conference on
4 February – had been to acquaint the other side with the crucial issues
that should be covered by any peace settlement, but he still remained
doubtful whether the Germans were really interested. If need be,
France could live with a partitioned Germany. (Contemporary historians divided de Gaulle's Eastern policy into two distinct periods,
pre- and post-1964. A 'hard' line had, they claimed, been succeeded by
an essay in co-operation with the Soviet Union, also with Poland and
Rumania. I did not regard this as a new departure. The *détente-entente-
coopération* triad had been current even prior to 1964.)

The General commented on certain developments in Asia and Latin
America. France had resolved on an independent appraisal of international events; the Federal Republic was evidently unwilling to follow
suit. His example: France resisted when the Russians exerted pressure
on Berlin; she had decided to recognize Peking after grave differences
arose between Russia and China. I did not follow up this allusion or its
inherent note of irony. De Gaulle was naturally aware that Erhard had
allowed Johnson to dissuade him from pursuing negotiations with
Peking during his Christmas visit to the United States. However, one
was not impressed by every comment on the subject heard in the
President's entourage, for instance that 'difficulties between China and
the United States need not be disadvantageous to Europe'. At the end
of the interview de Gaulle commented very favourably – in German –

on my 'minor steps' policy.

Couve told me next day that his government had at first viewed that policy with reserve. It had, however, been established that the legal position remained unimpaired, so it was in the general interest that the policy be prosecuted with success. At the same time, he drew attention to something which seemed to him to exemplify a difference of position in the two capitals: Paris considered it senseless, if not futile, to aim at a form of insulation between the East European countries and Moscow. Although this view entirely accorded with my own, it was not shared by everyone in the government camp at Bonn, where many traces of an old and appalling '*Polen-Verachtung*' (contempt for the Poles) lingered on.

When I pointed out to the Foreign Minister that the EEC and EFTA would be faced with certain inevitabilities in 1967 (when the ten-year term of the free-trade zone expired), he expounded what he called the French Government's increasingly pragmatic attitude. In so doing, he hinted that the door would not remain for ever barred to Britain. This was not, incidentally, the only occasion on which Couve, who could certainly not be classified as 'left-wing', spoke of his belief that we should have to master our fear of economic planning.

After my stay in Paris I drove home via Verdun. There I paid another visit with my son Lars and one of his school-friends. I wanted to show them the battlefields where World War I had turned into the species of mass murder known as a war of attrition. Few things could more vividly have illustrated the perils of European self-destruction than the sight of those interminable cemeteries. This brief encounter with the tragic past restored my sense of proportion and demonstrated our task in Europe more clearly than any words could have done.

My first trip abroad after becoming Foreign Minister in December 1966 took me to a meeting of the NATO Council in Paris. Consultations between the Foreign Ministers of the Atlantic Alliance were overshadowed by France's decision to withdraw from an integrated defence system and request the Americans to vacate their military installations on French territory. NATO Headquarters had, as a result, to be transferred from France to Belgium.

I regretted de Gaulle's decisions, with their inherent assumption that the Federal Republic was neither willing nor able to associate itself with them. Their immediate consequence, for which preparations had been made by the previous Federal Government, was that we concluded an agreement with Paris on the stationing of French troops in Germany. This entailed laborious negotiations affecting the so-called 'general treaty' of 1955, which had conferred sovereignty on our country.

Agreement on each party's defensive aims was tacitly assumed.

But dissatisfaction with France's go-it-alone defence policy could not be the sole determinant of our attitude. We had to make a serious effort – Federal Chancellor Kiesinger and I were at one on this point – to disencumber and revitalize Franco-German relations.

De Gaulle and his associates had of course noted, prior to my visit, the Franco-German emphasis clearly discernible in the Grand Coalition's policy statement. Kiesinger had declared, with my concurrence, that the facts of European geography and the historical balance-sheet of our continent did, under present circumstances, disclose an unusually large measure of harmony between the interests of our two peoples and countries. The co-operation we desired was directed against no other people or country. It was indispensable if Europe was to become a jointly responsible partner. The Europe that spoke 'with one voice' – as American statesmen demanded – presupposed a steady convergence in the policies of Germany and France. Franco-German co-operation in as many areas as possible would be of the utmost value in improving relations with our East European neighbours. For all these reasons, the Federal Republic wished to make the fullest and most practical use of the opportunities for policy co-ordination afforded by the treaty of January 1963.

Bonn did, however, take advantage of the same occasion to point out that the two nations' special circumstances would continue to yield differences of interest and opinion in many fields. Friendship did not connote a neglect of one's own interests or a lack of candour towards others. We bluntly told our French neighbours that we disagreed with them on the subject of an enlarged EEC. We were just as explicit that the American alliance was vital to European security and that Europe could only exist in open transatlantic co-operation, not with its back to America.

On 13 December I paid a call on Couve de Murville. I enlarged on our policy statement and its foreign and domestic policy aspects. We discussed the French military presence in Germany. I welcomed the reaching of a settlement satisfactory to both parties. Couve stressed the importance of this agreement. He then spoke of Kosygin's recent visit to Paris. The Soviet Premier's main arguments still centred on European questions and on what the Russians called 'European security', which they equated with the problem of Germany's future. They inevitably raised the question of recognition for the 'Zone', as they always did, and Couve doubted if anything would change this. He had also gained the impression that the Russians were waiting with interest to see what line the new German Government would take.

Though never explicitly mentioned, this had become quite apparent. The Russians had repeatedly stressed that their relations with the Federal Republic were satisfactory, though he discounted the speeches made for propaganda purposes. They had also persevered in their proposal for an all-European conference.

The French replied that they did not in principle oppose this idea. Differences of opinion persisted on account of the GDR. No reference was made on the Russian side to France's relations with the East European countries, nor did the French broach this subject themselves. The Russians seldom mentioned it in any case, Couve said. He himself had told them that France had always advocated improved relations between the Federal Republic and all Central and East European governments, not merely the Soviet Union. He added that the French Government was in favour of formal relations between Germany and those countries. The Russians had apparently raised no objection.

Two days later President de Gaulle granted me a private interview. I conveyed the Federal Chancellor's respects and drew attention to the policy guide-lines that had been laid before the Bundestag. We were serious in our attempt to give fresh substance to the Franco-German treaty despite past disappointments. This followed from the definition of our own interests.

General de Gaulle welcomed my appointment as Foreign Minister and did not disguise his satisfaction at having to deal with a new Federal Chancellor in Herr Kiesinger. He did not, of course, harbour any animosity towards Ludwig Erhard, whom he respected and with whom he had always co-operated whenever possible. He had been very interested – indeed, very heartened – by our policy statement.

So what remained to be done? Something had already been achieved in the establishment of personal contacts between the two governments. France considered these extremely important, and they would continue. Personal contacts apart, however, how could we act together? Our intentions did not differ widely on this point. France was sensible of the German desire for reunification and Germany knew that France, so far from demurring, shared that desire – not only from a feeling of friendship for Germany but because reunification alone could set a seal on World War II and its consequences. France was, therefore, wholeheartedly in favour of reunification. Both sides naturally knew that this goal would not be easy to attain, but it was not impossible. It would have been impossible, under Cold War conditions, because it would have entailed a war against Russia. Nobody had wanted that, not even Germany – nor had America. It followed that there had been no position of strength from which to effect reunification. Another way would now have to be found: 'As you know, France recommends the path of European détente. In the French view, nothing can happen – especially in the matter of reunification – without the prior development of a complete change in the relations now prevailing between the countries of Europe.'

The President continued: 'What is to be done, and how is it to be done? Germany has seen what France is doing to effect a détente with the Soviet Union.' In the French view, Russia had not and would not go further than the Yalta agreement allowed. She would attack neither Germany nor France nor America, because everything argued against such an intention.

'China,' said the President, 'is Russia's main worry – one that has become greater than her concern over Germany. Besides, the Russians have to develop their own country, and for that they need the assistance of the West. Communism as an ideology has, after all, substantially declined. Of course there exists in Russia a very strong, vigorous, technocratic and totalitarian régime. But this régime has ceased to be communism, nor does it any longer exert much attraction, particularly on Western Europe. There are a few communist parties in the West, but these are less ideologically communist than communist in terms of working-class demands. In any case, Russia has changed and is bound to change. She is peaceable, albeit in her own way. France is trying to take advantage of this. She is entering into contact with Russia, striving for détente and even, perhaps, for practical co-operation. It is, above all, the best policy for Western Europe and, in my view, the best policy for Germany as well.

'This path is not easy, not comfortable, not pleasant for Germany. But it is not fruitless either – nor futile. In fact, a start has already been made. I believe that the Russians will not reject it. I asked Kosygin, "If Herr Brandt comes to Moscow" – and I am sure you will – "will the Russians give him a good reception?" Kosygin replied, "Well, yes – perhaps."

'In this connection,' de Gaulle went on, 'everything still remains to be done. If Germany so desires, France will help her along this path – as she has already begun to – particularly in Moscow. France will do nothing detrimental to Germany in pursuing a policy of détente. It goes without saying that Kosygin, Brezhnev and Podgorny pestered me to recognize two German states during my stay in Russia. I flatly refused, declaring that there were not two German states; there was one German people. The GDR was an artificial construction devoid of deeper reality. France duly declined to recognize it as a state and would not do so in future. You are conversant with the French approach to the frontier question. France will not change her mind over the question of German boundaries in the East and South. France is Germany's friend but can be so only if Germany is not imperialistic. She cannot be Germany's friend if Germany aspires to regain what she lost in war after attacking Poland and Czechoslovakia. France cannot permit any union with Austria either. She could not feel sure of Germany otherwise – indeed, Germany could not feel sure of herself if she took that road again. Nor will Germany have any chance whatever of shifting her frontiers eastwards, because the Russia of today is not comparable with the Russia of yore.

'As for practical relations with the inhabitants of the Soviet Zone, fundamental truth reposes in the fact that there is only *one* German nation. Whenever the Federal Republic seeks to improve practical contacts – in economic, scientific and technical matters as well as by exchanges of individuals, tourist traffic and family visits – France considers this satisfactory to all parties, and especially to the Germans themselves, as a means of maintaining contact with the Germans who are kept artificially segregated from their fellow-countrymen. This is France's policy . . .

'The prime essential, however, is that each country should have a policy of its own. France must have a French policy, and she has. Germany must have a German policy, and it is up to Germany to create one. A French or German or British policy which was an American policy would not be a good policy. France is in no way opposed to America. On the contrary, she is America's friend, but nothing can be worse for Europeans than an American hegemony which enfeebles Europe and prevents the Europeans from being themselves. Such a hegemony also hinders agreement with the East – in fact it hinders absolutely everything. The Americans are Americans, not Europeans. I am far from angry with the Americans on that score. I realize that the Alliance with the United States was concluded at a time of acute danger. That Alliance was justified, although I declined integration even then. The Alliance is still justified today, though to a smaller extent, because one must always be careful. But the situation has changed, and American hegemony – dependence on the United States – is a bad policy for France. It inhibits faith in self and inhibits others from faith in the countries of Europe. It has to be realized that France exists, and Germany, and Britain.'

I listened intently to these remarks. Then I gave de Gaulle a few pointers to our political problems at home, the economic and financial matters that were engaging our attention, and the scattered electoral successes of the extreme right-wing NPD, which had caused some dismay abroad. I said we would cope with these problems. Germany's friends need have no fear.

Turning to the Soviet Union, I said that things were naturally harder for Germany than France. The Soviet leaders at present refused to discuss our national problem, whose solution de Gaulle had years ago described as a historical necessity because no nation could remain divided for ever. I had informed the Soviet Government that points for discussion existed despite such difficulties. These lay in the field of bilateral relations and problems of security. For example, the Russians were now clearly interested in an exchange of declarations renouncing the use of force as well as similar exchanges between Germany and Eastern Europe. It might be possible to incorporate the problems of a divided Germany in these declarations. Ever mistrustful on this point, the Russians had demanded what was to become of the GDR. Did we mean to ignore it when, under our scheme of things, declarations were to be exchanged with the Soviet Union, Poland and Czechoslovakia? The Federal Republic now said that, although it did not recognize the GDR as a second German state, it proposed to renounce the use of force in settling this question: the problem could thus be included in a declaration renouncing the use of force.

I went on to say that, like de Gaulle, I assumed the unlikelihood of a Russian attack under present and foreseeable circumstances, my one reservation being that we had no idea who would rule the Soviet Union in years to come. The Germans were, perhaps, more preoccupied with this question because Soviet divisions occupied German soil and the chances of miscalculation were imponderable. In general, however, I concurred with the President and believed that one should realistically and perseveringly encourage those Soviet leaders who wanted détente. We should probably be establishing diplomatic relations with some of the East European countries in the months ahead. Our policy statement had gone as far to meet Czechoslovakia and Poland as present circumstances permitted. We were dealing with creatures of flesh and blood, so necessities and possibilities had to be weighed. Prague had correctly interpreted the German statement: that which Hitler had imposed by force and with the help of three heads of government from three outside countries could no longer be valid. In regard to the frontier question, the Federal Government could not officially do more to accommodate Poland at present than evince an understanding of the Polish desire to live within secure frontiers. De Gaulle had also mentioned Austria. I told him that no responsible person in Germany contemplated an *Anschluss*. The situation after World War I had been different and could not recur.

In reply, de Gaulle said that he flatly regarded the so-called neo-Nazis as a marginal phenomenon – they were not the German people. All countries, France included, had vociferous totalitarian groups of their own. He considered the matter unimportant. It had been different with Hitler, who was cause and effect combined. Germany was then undergoing a severe economic crisis; it had experienced inflation and possessed a strong and menacing communist party. The power relationship between Germany and her foreign neighbours had also presented quite another picture because France, Britain and Russia were very weak. Hitler thus had numerous opportunities which simply did not exist today.

'What you say about the Soviet Union,' de Gaulle went on, 'impresses me as very sensible. It implies that the Federal Government, without abandoning future reunification, means to negotiate important matters with the Soviet Union in the interim, notably détente and a new Russo-German relationship. I consider your policy towards Czechoslovakia sound. As regards Poland, the Federal Government is not very definite but merely states that these matters will require future discussion. I doubt if this will alter the situation. In view of all that became clear to me during my visit to Russia, I am bound to emphasize that the Russians and Poles have not forgotten, and cannot forget, the war. They naturally exaggerate this problem and represent it as *the* great question – which, in reality, it is not. The fact remains that the war took place, with all its atrocities in those countries. Independent of the communist régime, these peoples feel an undercurrent of disquiet about Germany which has yet to subside. This disquiet is not, therefore, mere propaganda policy but possesses a genuine psychological basis. One must not lose sight of these facts, and one must act accordingly. Thus a new policy is first and foremost a psychological operation, because the psychological attitude of these countries towards Germany must be changed. Once their psychology changes, so will their policies.

'My contacts with the Russians – with Kosygin, Gromyko and Co. – have made me realize that it will one day be possible to achieve a fitting and, particularly for Germany, acceptable European settlement. I might almost say that the Russians told me as much themselves. It will take time and require a complete change of circumstances. I am convinced that the Russians will ultimately accept such an accommodation, though I am naturally ignorant of its precise form. The Russians will, of course, pose certain conditions, but they do not reject the idea that there must one day be a reunited Germany. Everything else is tactics, in other words, politics.'

We devoted little time to the EEC and its possible lines of development. This was one of the subjects scheduled for official discussion in Paris in the middle of January. De Gaulle remarked that Mr Wilson would doubtless apply for membership but that he would do so *à l'anglaise*, by simultaneously combining his 'candidacy' with so many provisos that the vote would go against him.

The General's response when I asked what we could tell the public about our conversation was that it had been very cordial. Both he 'and, I am sure, the whole of France' considered the Federal Government's attitude, as manifested in its policy statement, to be extremely sound and satisfactory.

It came as no surprise to me, after this concentrated discussion with the President, that the new Federal Government managed to establish a very close understanding with France in matters affecting policy towards the East. We found ourselves confronted by the question – and posed it ourselves – of why the Franco-German treaty should not enable us to attain a far more comprehensive political accord. As Foreign Minister, I swiftly concluded that the consultations envisaged by the treaty could take a more effective form. My fear was that a major enterprise might degenerate into pure routine.

My place in the cabinet hierarchy forbade me to partner the President in discussions while Foreign Minister of the Grand Coalition. My immediate opposite number in the semi-annual 'major' consultations – New Year in Paris, mid-year in Bonn – was the French Foreign Minister or, on specifically bilateral matters, the Prime Minister. It was customary at these 'major' consultations, of which five took place before de Gaulle's retirement, that Pompidou and I be invited to attend a concluding talk between the President and the Federal Chancellor. Apart from this, of course, there were many opportunities for conversation at table and after dinner. De Gaulle always treated me in a very cordial manner.

During meal-time conversations – even when the cuisine falls short of the Elysée standards of those days – one inevitably devotes more attention to one's table-companions than to the topics discussed. I remember that de Gaulle disliked English being spoken at Franco-German gatherings. Noticing at one meal that Schiller and Giscard were breaking his unwritten rule for convenience's sake, he said to Pompidou, 'Now you can hear what will happen to language in Europe if we don't watch out.' On another occasion early in 1969, after the Presidential change-over in Washington, he asked if I shared his opinion that Nixon had demonstrated the ability of men between fifty and sixty to change. I readily agreed with him. Neither of us guessed what lay ahead.

I was particularly impressed by the masterly way in which de Gaulle summarized our deliberations at full meetings attended by members of both cabinets, seldom employing even a sketchy written draft. This could not, however, disguise the comparative frequency with which the treaty's consultative bodies ticked over idly – and I do not deny that routine can have its beneficial side. After Michel Debré had become Foreign Minister in 1968, I once ventured to suggest at a meeting in Brussels that we might invest our consultations with greater flexibility. The French response came as something of a shock: my suggestion for changes in form was assumed to conceal a desire for changes in substance. On the other hand, I secretly learnt to admire the perseverance with which our French partners brought their interests into play, not only in arms and prestige projects but in information techniques within their own government. On the few occasions when we sought our own national advantage, they evinced a somewhat exaggerated disappointment.

De Gaulle visited Bonn in September 1968, later than usual, after a trying few months. Caught in Rumania when the student revolts came to a head, he had returned home on 19 May. One event still cloaked in mystery is his helicopter flight to Baden-Baden on 29 May to visit General Massu, the Algerian veteran whom I had known in Berlin when he became French Commander-in-Chief in Germany. The next day de Gaulle was back in Paris. There were big conservative counter-demonstrations, and new elections were announced. Having saved the régime by his *sang-froid*, Pompidou surrendered the premiership to Couve (not because this placed him 'in reserve', as de Gaulle put it, but more because the General no longer wanted him). The Gaullist arch-loyalist, Michel Debré, Pompidou's predecessor, had meanwhile taken Couve's place at the Foreign Office. I got on well with this ardent but inhibited patriot.

I was in no doubt that de Gaulle had called the spring 1969 referendum – which was limited to a few essentially secondary issues such as decentralization and Senate reform, and accompanied by the announcement that he would go if there were no majority – in the realization that it was time for him to depart. Afterwards, it will be remembered, he drove without a farewell word to Colombey-les-deux-Eglises.

It was obvious that the outcome of the referendum would have important repercussions, not only on the French political scene but on

Europe at large. De Gaulle's historic achievements were manifest. On his retirement, I recalled that our last two meetings – September 1968 in Bonn and March 1969 in Paris – had carried a certain flavour of resignation, strongly critical in undertone in Bonn but more conciliatory in Paris. (The after-effects of the French crisis were unmistakable, and were probably compounded with disappointment over Soviet intervention in Prague.) The helm had finally been relinquished by one of the last statesmen born in the previous century. He had reminded us that we were a great nation but frustrated our European resolve. There was nothing really surprising in this, given that he made no secret of his ideas.

Speaking in Munich, I once more emphasized that the General had begun by salvaging his nation's self-respect and then proclaimed its attitude to self. His European policy had met with opposition. 'It is not, however, paradoxical to number de Gaulle among the great Europeans. His view of things was sometimes trammelled by the past, but it sometimes spanned vast distances and expanded into visions of the future which not everyone was capable of following. His contribution to the political thinking of our time is the tangible utopia of a Europe permanently at peace.'

One might have guessed that the General would not long survive his departure from power – it was hard to conceive of him as an old and slowly declining man. I was deeply affected by the news of his death in November 1970, but an attack of influenza prevented me from attending the funeral ceremony in Paris. 'In General de Gaulle,' I said in a memorial tribute, 'the last giant of the war and post-war years has passed away. He outlived Roosevelt, Stalin and Churchill and remained active long after their deaths. In so doing, he built a bridge between the past, which he never disavowed, and our present-day world . . . He always saw himself as a representative of our continent, whose international status, influence and independence he sought to extend. Even if we go further than many of his ideas, we concur in those aims.' In Paris on 25 January 1971, I said: 'On my way here this morning, not far from the battlefields of ill-starred wars, I visited the grave of the man who had a greater awareness than most statesmen of the bitter experiences in our common history and was able, probably for that very reason, to help mould the development of our peoples' mutual understanding into friendship.' Instead of travelling to this Franco-German conference by air in the usual way, I had taken the night train. In the half-light of a gloomy winter's morning I stood beside the plain and unadorned grave at Colombey-les-deux-Eglises in token of my respect for the dead.

6

The Grand Coalition

Great changes had overtaken the Bonn scene and the political climate of the Federal Republic. Adenauer had been succeeded by Erhard and the Social Democrats were gaining strength. Although the Federal Republic had suffered no hard knocks, a number of major problems remained unsolved.

Theodor Heuss, the Federal President of the Republic's first decade, was laid to rest in Stuttgart shortly before Christmas 1963. I had been close to him, and he had always treated me with a kind of paternal trust. The same period deprived us of Erich Ollenhauer, our SPD chairman. I was confidentially informed the same evening that I should have to take over the office of party chairman (as Ollenhauer himself had intended). An extraordinary party conference held at Bad Godesberg on 15 February elected me chairman of the German Social Democratic Party by 320 votes to 14 and, at the same time, appointed me to lead the party in the forthcoming parliamentary elections.

I had not forgotten my experience of the perils of internal dissension. Both before and after World War II, the socialist parties of Europe had provided an alarming illustration of how political strength can be dissipated by the factionalism which some would number among the original sins of the Left. The maintenance of productive unity was the basic chord to be struck for my party's benefit. The reinforcement of democratic freedom, of social security and spiritual foundations – that was to be its main political emphasis at home. Where foreign and German policy were concerned, I developed the line I had tried to set forth on my nomination for the Chancellorship in 1960. We had no need of a Great Wall of China policy in our exchanges with the communists, communist governments included. I made it plain at the same time that, as things stood, any meaningful German foreign policy would be futile without the strength of the West. On the other hand, military security was 'not an end in itself but the base from which, in company with others, we propose to develop the strategy of peace'. Our goal, I said, was clear: Europe and the United States must become equal partners, and it was time to think of Europe as a whole. 'This Central European nation of ours cannot live in perpetual fear of its Eastern neighbours, in enmity or even hatred.'

As party chairman, I now had to visit Bonn almost weekly, sometimes for several days at a time. My colleagues helped me, of course, and many meetings, especially those of the party presidium, were held in Berlin. I also had to conduct a series of official discussions in the Federal capital. I usually attended the meetings of the Bundesrat, over which I had to preside during my first year as '*Landeschef*'. In addition, I was president of the *Städtetag*, or council of German municipalities, between 1958 and 1963.

It would, however, be a mistake to think that the city in my charge ceased to be of prime concern to me during these years. Exacting though they were, I performed my duties at the city hall with pleasure. Routine matters apart, it was my daily task to ward off threats of an acute or insidious nature, to represent local interests in Bonn and with the Allies, and to help reinforce West Berlin's economic foundations and will to prevail. I had to safeguard employment and solicit investment, stem any drift in the labour force and attract workers from West Germany, stimulate cultural activity and create model municipal institutions.

My duties in Berlin far exceeded the scope of local government. The mayor of Berlin heads a large municipal administration, but he also, like his counterparts in Hamburg and Bremen, fulfils prime ministerial functions. He is involved, and was so particularly at that time, in fundamental questions of foreign policy. It was one of my most important tasks to show the Americans that their commitment to Berlin paid. I found the close conjunction of 'high-' and 'low-'level politics fascinating. Local government can give much pleasure and satisfaction to those involved because it enables them to take part in limited projects whose planning and implementation brings them into close contact with their fellow-citizens.

Our basis of trust in the city grew stronger during my years in office as Mayor and President of the Chamber of Deputies. In the 1958 elections my party won back the absolute majority it had lost in 1950 and failed to regain in 1954. I continued to co-operate with the CDU, so work in the Senate relied on a grand coalition. This was terminated by the Berlin elections of 17 February 1963, in which the SPD won 62 per cent of the vote. I was returned as member for my own constituency, Wedding, with over three-quarters of the poll. Wedding had been a communist stronghold in Weimar days. The communist SED now had to be content with a vote of less than 2 per cent.

Not wanting to form a monochrome municipal government, I invited the Free Democrats, with their three Senatorial seats, to take part. Although co-operation with the CDU presented little difficulty where purely municipal problems were concerned, Federal controversies imposed a strain on our relations because of my increasing involvement in the leadership of my party. Incomprehensible as it may seem, Khrushchev's invitation to me in the middle of the election campaign was the real cause of the breach I have already described.

I discovered at the party's Karlsruhe conference in November 1964 that it can be even harder to assemble a government team in opposition than to form an actual government. Some people are more eager for nomination than for the potentially onerous responsibilities of office. We nonetheless succeeded in clearly defining our foreign and domestic objectives. I was able to draw on the results of our past preoccupation with neglected social responsibilities. Greater effort would have to be devoted to education and vocational training, to research, public health, transportation and local government. We spoke of the need to plot an accurate course for the decade ahead. We proposed, in defiance of Bonn's prevailing practice, to rely on specialist advice. We defined our views on democratic government and clearly stated our intention of democratizing the relevant areas of society. We also pointed out that a new balance must be sought between the material and spiritual elements in politics.

For the election campaign of 1965, I coined the phrase to which I reverted after my election to the Chancellorship in autumn 1969: peace within and without, peace in Germany and for Germany. My response to the ubiquitous purveyors of hot air was: 'The day will never dawn when we win World War II after the event.'

The non-German reader may find this statement somewhat puzzling, but many of my compatriots fully grasped its significance. In 1945, when Germany lay in ruins, they had accepted the material – and moral – totality of defeat. Since then, rapid reconstruction and the triumphs of the so-called economic miracle had caused many of them to forget the material and moral abyss into which the Nazi dictatorship and World War II had plunged our own nation and the whole of Europe. The burden of 'collective guilt' was rejected, and rightly so. People pointed to the millions of innocent lives that had been claimed from the Germans themselves and recalled the bloody suppression of the naive anti-Hitler resistance movement, but not everyone had absorbed the first President's reference to collective shame. Personally, I preferred to speak of collective responsibility, meaning that the price of war and dictatorship was a bitter one. Although people tended to thrust this fact out of their minds, the realities were plain enough. They included the loss of one-third of the territory enclosed by Germany's 1937 frontiers, the flight and expulsion of millions of our compatriots, and the partition of our country.

Many citizens of the Federal Republic were being seduced into a belief that the resurgence of the western part of their nation would some day enable partition and possibly, too, the loss of the eastern territories to be abolished by a wave of the wand. They wanted to postpone paying the bill for as long as possible in the hope that it would sooner or later be torn up under the stress of relations between the victorious powers. There were good and objective grounds for refusing to approve partition in terms of international law because it had suspended the Germans' right of self-determination, but it was wrong to misuse this proviso in order to foster the dangerous notion that history could be rewritten. The growth of nationalist revisionism along the 'seam' between East and West would have created an explosive situation. Thus, 'recognition' of the altered circumstances bequeathed us by World War II fulfilled an international as well as a moral requirement. Anyone who denied this was, in effect, seeking to persuade the Germans that Hitler and World War II had never happened and entering a plea that history should be rewritten. To encourage such an attitude was to behave as if the Germans had really won the war after all.

The 1965 election results consolidated our party's position. Its proportion of the poll rose from 36.2 to 39.3 per cent and its parliamentary representation from 190 seats to 202. With thirteen million votes – nearly fourteen, including Berlin – the SPD could claim a substantial measure of support. Although not a bad result, it impressed me personally as more of a defeat. I had been hoping for a vote in excess of 40 per cent, but that was not the main thing. What really depressed me was the despicable way in which this campaign, too, had been waged by so many of those involved. It had availed little that Erhard discussed the question of fair tactics with me in advance. Even his own adherence to them was only partial, though our relations in the coming years remained cordial and correct. He certainly acknowledged the possibility that alternatives can present themselves within a democracy.

I could not disguise my disappointment, neither from myself nor from those around me, when the elections were over and the results on record. I felt it wrong to expect my friends to back me indefinitely, especially in areas where our support was weak. This was what underlay my personal decision, made without consulting my colleagues on the party executive, to cancel my availability as a candidate for the Chancellorship. I discussed it with nobody on election night itself, which I divided between party headquarters and the Berlin Building, and announced it at a Bonn press conference.

This gave birth to a legend which has been perpetuated by many subsequent publications. It seems that I planned to quit German politics and retire to Norway on the advice of my wife. Rut certainly telephoned me on election night and advised me to come 'home', in other words, re-devote myself to my work in Berlin, but there was no question of my resigning the party chairmanship, which I would in any case have retained until the next SPD conference. As in 1961, I took the logical step of declining my seat in the Bundestag.

I spent an October holiday at Ste Maxime with my sons, Peter and Lars, but was slow to recover my spirits. Many such bouts of depression are probably attributable to the sheer fatigue induced in modern politicians by the rigours of electioneering or crises of responsibility. I sometimes see us as the victims of merciless exploitation by ourselves and others.

However, all I usually needed was a short spell devoted to catching up on my sleep. A few days' concentration on personal matters was worth a great deal, above all the chance to be alone for a while, to read and go for walks. Thus it was in autumn 1965. I was welcomed back to Berlin – almost too heartily, like a prodigal son – and did my best to speed up plans for the city's economic and cultural development.

I did not neglect my chairman's duties or my international contacts. The party conference held in Dortmund at the beginning of June 1966 was notable for its resolute and constructive tone. This carried over into the North Rhine–Westphalia Landtag elections, in which the Social Democrats gained a handsome victory by winning 99 out of 200 seats. The party conference gave me an overwhelming vote of confidence: I was re-elected by 324 votes to 2. Some impressions left by the foregoing election campaign were worthy of further thought. The passage of time and the rise of a new generation called for a clearer definition of the Federal Republic's attitude to itself and its role in the world. In this connection, I had noted during my numerous visits to the Ruhr that the incorporation of the working class into our democratic system was far from complete. There was a widespread sense of exclusion from political activity. On the other hand, I also noted the spontaneous support bestowed on us by the German intelligentsia – by writers, scientists, artists and other representatives of intellectual life.

Sad to say, insufficient advantage was taken of the opportunity to make a clean breast of Germany's recent past and define our role in the post-war world. Instead of gaining depth and substance, the consensus between the major parties remained superficial. Although no one outside a few small fringe-groups would have denied abhorrence of Nazi crimes, little attempt was made to trace the responsibility for this descent into barbarism. The aim – as I have already mentioned in connection with Adenauer – was to let time perform the task of dissociation. Whether because of genuine inability or a bad conscience, parents and teachers were slow to assist the younger generation in understanding and analysing what had happened prior to 1945. There was a danger that pent-up curiosity would erupt and further the trend towards extenuation.

Germany's role in the world had been predetermined by changes in the international power structure. Although it was uncertain whether people would remain aware of Germany's central responsibility for the war, a relapse into territorial aggrandizement could be ruled out. The German débâcle had been too absolute and the map of the world had changed too greatly.

The condition of the Federal Republic was characterized by mounting problems of public finance, by a coal crisis in the Ruhr and other structural weaknesses. Relative equilibrium reigned between the major political forces. 'We have grown stronger,' I said, 'but not strong enough; too big to be able to stand aside, not strong enough to set a course. The others no longer can, we cannot yet – that is the present position.'

On 1 December 1966 the Erhard government was succeeded by the Grand Coalition. My own job in the new cabinet was that of Foreign Minister. I also became Vice-Chancellor. Submitting his policy statement to the Bundestag, Kurt Georg Kiesinger rightly declared that the formation of his cabinet had been preceded by 'a long, smouldering crisis whose origins can be traced back for years'. The government was not the product of a brilliant electoral victory 'but of a crisis followed with deep concern by our people'.

Some may call it ironical that Ludwig Erhard should have foundered on the very rock – that of economics – whose avoidance had earned him such acclaim as a successful helmsman, not only within his own party but far beyond its confines. The Federal Republic was in the throes of a recession which had not been occasioned by worldwide economic trends. Members of the government openly declared that beneficial effects were awaited from a rise in unemployment. The public finances were in bad shape and the Federal Bank was submitting government policy to close scrutiny. The extreme right-wing NPD had made dangerous inroads into CDU and SPD support in the Landtag elections. Here and there in the outside world, people were beginning to ask if this augured a long-dreaded relapse into extreme nationalism.

In foreign policy, the 'mighty midget' known as the Federal Republic conveyed a helpless impression. Almost naively preoccupied with the maintenance of good relations with the United States and President Johnson, Erhard lacked all sense of the need for a careful adjustment with our partners in Western Europe. He made pledges to Washington which could not be kept, for instance when negotiating the apportionment of expenditure on US forces in our country.

Erhard was compelled to modify his own undertakings during a visit to the White House in autumn 1966. De Gaulle, who had watched his treaty with Adenauer waste away, was meanwhile making efforts to revive France's friendship with the Soviet Union. Dependent on the goodwill of America *and* France, the Federal Republic saw its relations with both partners vitiated by clumsiness and lack of imagination.

Erhard, who was never a true party man and had not even belonged to the Christian Democratic Union in the first place, quickly lost ground inside the Union and its Bavarian sister-party when the Social Democrats won a near majority in the North Rhine–Westphalia elections of summer 1966.

Now that he had been deserted by his '*Fortune*' (a current Bonn revival of Frederick the Great's favourite word), the old-fashioned late-comer's personal associates were quicker than most to forget his past services.

Ludwig Erhard probably showed the right instinct when he urged that economic forces should be allowed to develop as freely as possible during the Federal Republic's early years. He was less well advised when he converted this into an ideology. It was his good fortune that things could not fail to improve after such a calamitous war.

All forms of planning were anathematized in Erhard's day, even though agriculture, housing and other sectors were not, of course, really governed by the laws of the free market economy. Urgent problems of social equality were neglected or simply forgotten during the early years of reconstruction. Erhard had little experience of international affairs. It would not be unfair to call him an apolitical politician. His dream of a well adjusted 'national community', which he entitled the 'aligned society', remained nebulous and ill-defined. Adenauer's spiteful comment on Erhard and his ideas was 'Try nailing a blancmange to the wall!' The old Chancellor made it his last major political objective at home to bar Erhard's route to the Palais Schaumburg. His party thought otherwise. It settled on the 'miracle-worker' as a recipe for success, only to abandon him without scruple when the plums stopped falling into his lap.

In summer 1959 we had all gone for a boat trip on the Tegernsee. Adenauer had got himself nominated for the Federal Presidency and then thought better of it. Erhard found it hard to suppress his resentment of the man who was making every effort to keep him from the Chancellorship. 'You've no idea how he's treated me,' was how he put it. It escaped him that what really went against the Old Man's grain was the sort of naivety which he, in his artless indignation, had just displayed. He made a similar impression on me. Once during talks in Berlin, for instance, he seriously intimated that the GDR could in due course be 'bought' from the Russians.

Erhard seemed clumsily insensible of what lay in store for him when his administration withered and disintegrated in the autumn of 1966. Our relations during my years as Foreign Minister and Federal Chancellor were all that they should have been in a democracy. I was able to assist him on a few of his trips abroad. He felt less well treated by certain members of his own party. His letters to me more than once stated that personal respect should not be impaired by differing political views.

Following upon the downfall of the Erhard government, the Grand Coalition was far from a natural solution. There was a strong groundswell of Union opinion in favour of reviving the CDU/CSU/FDP coalition. Even after Kiesinger was nominated for the Chancellorship, this question remained temporarily unresolved. A few Social Democrats were strongly inclined to explore the possibility of an alliance with the FDP, even though any such coalition could only have counted on a wafer-thin majority. Leading members of our party were determined on the 'grand solution'. I only decided in favour of coalition with the CDU/CSU in the course of negotiations. A broad-based government would, I believed, make it easier to solve the problems of recession and pave the way for reforms.

The coalition talks culminated on 24 November. Once we and the CDU/CSU had agreed in principle to form a government, I had to decide on the form my own participation would take. During preliminary discussions conducted first by Wehner and Kiesinger and then, in private, by Kiesinger and myself, consideration was given to my own proposal that I might take on the Ministry of Research in addition to the Vice-Chancellorship. I would have been stimulated by a post which seemed to present so many opportunities of helping to shape the future.

It would also have left me freer than the Foreign Ministry to continue my chairmanship of the SPD, which was hardly a part-time job. At a meeting of the party's small negotiating committee, I once more questioned whether it might not be better for me, as party chairman, to retain my post in Berlin and remain outside the cabinet. I asked my colleagues to weigh this carefully. I was not in the best of health, having suffered an attack during October which temporarily affected my breathing, and my wife was not overjoyed at the prospect of moving to Bonn.

My colleagues insisted on my joining the cabinet as Foreign Minister and Vice-Chancellor. For understandable reasons, Helmut Schmidt decided to forgo a place in the cabinet. The Union had a claim on the Ministry of Defence (which went to Gerhard Schröder). With me at the Foreign Office, it was only reasonable that Schmidt should give precedence to leading the party in parliament. The organization of parliamentary leadership and control acquires special importance in any 'grand coalition'. In Rainer Barzel, Schmidt found a partner with whom he soon managed to establish a businesslike relationship.

Serious misgivings were expressed, not least inside my own party, about the Union candidate for the Chancellorship, Kurt Georg Kiesinger. His rejection was also urged in CDU circles. Many people were reluctant to see the government of a democratic German state headed by a man who had identified himself, albeit only formally, with the Third Reich. An erstwhile but not an active member of the Nazi Party, Kiesinger had worked for the press department of the Foreign Office during the war.

Kiesinger the sometime *Mitläufer* (nominal Nazi Party member) and Brandt the anti-Nazi *émigré* could be regarded as authentic personal representatives of Germany as it actually was. Numerous votes were withheld from Kiesinger in the Chancellorship election, just as enthusiasm for the Grand Coalition remained limited.

In December 1966 I wrote a letter to the members of my party expressing appreciation of the confidence shown by all those who had urged us to try and form a government under SPD leadership. They could rest assured that it was not lack of courage which had deterred us from such an endeavour. 'A calculated risk might have been justified, but we could not commit our party or our nation to an adventure.'

The new government's programme was a fair compromise. All the essential points previously outlined in our eight-point paper were taken into account. We saw economic growth and the reorganization of public finances as the foundations of domestic social advancement. This was the basis of a continuous policy at home and towards the outside world. On the subject of foreign policy, we had stated that relations with Washington and Paris must be put in order and our aspirations to a share in the nuclear arsenal abandoned for the sake of Allied stability and détente. The new government must take steps to normalize our relations with the countries of Eastern Europe and secure a reconciliation with our neighbours in the East. It must define our internal scope for dealings with the rulers of East Berlin and exploit it to the full.

My response to anyone who asks what the Grand Coalition achieved in 1967–68 is not merely that, many inadequacies and much opposition notwithstanding, the Federal Republic's foreign policy became less rigid. Most important of all, the recession was swiftly overcome and the threat of mass unemployment averted. Prospects for overall economic planning were also explored, but these soon proved to have been overrated. The public finances were put in order and our currency remained stable.

The dreaded 'social demolition job' which many expected from the Grand Coalition did not take place. On the contrary, the welfare state was consolidated and in some areas extended. A start was made on adapting to the need for a structural policy in coal and transportation. No transition was possible to a second phase in domestic policy whose programme would have included the modernization – and, in my view, democratization – of political institutions, industrial activity and educational establishments. It was only logical, therefore, that I embarked on my own Chancellorship under the auspices of domestic reform.

But for us Social Democrats there were other and, from the historical aspect, doubtless more important arguments in favour of the Grand Coalition – notably that it gave us a chance to prove ourselves in central government. People were accustomed to seeing the SPD in charge of big cities and a number of regional administrations, but it had been excluded from the responsibilities of central government since 1930. Curiously enough, many people regarded its participation in the Federal Government as a sensational new departure. Had it not been for this trial run in alliance with the Federal Republic's 'traditional' ruling party and a good cabinet team, therefore, the SPD's assumption of leadership in 1969 would scarcely have been possible.

My work centred largely on foreign affairs. The direction of foreign policy gave me pleasure, even if it made me more remote from the

ordinary citizen than my duties as Mayor of Berlin. Heading the
Foreign Office did not, however, absolve me from general cabinet
work. Special responsibility devolves on the Vice-Chancellor when two
major parties govern in harness. I had, for instance, to ensure that
Social Democrats in the government adopted a co-ordinated approach
to important questions. My obligations as party chairman could not be
neglected either, and inevitably involved me in meetings, private
planning sessions, public statements, regional conferences and election
campaigns.

Co-operation between the Grand Coalition partners did not for long
remain as smooth and effective as we had hoped (or as it had originally
promised to be). Once the Union began to recover from its autumn
1966 shock, there was a widespread tendency to readopt old attitudes
and look upon partnership with the Social Democrats as a tiresome
obligation, nothing more. Both the major parties had one eye on the
next parliamentary elections, so there was great difficulty in co-
ordinating a team whose leading figures alternately conferred as
partners in government and members of rival parliamentary parties.
Far too often, controversial issues had to be bypassed or shelved.

Foreign policy seemed to command a particularly wide measure of
agreement at first. After some time, however, right-wing sections of
the Union, and above all the CSU, bestirred themselves to contrast their
illusory or nationalistic demands with the policy of diplomatic détente
and psychological relaxation which I, in line with our government
policy statemen', was trying to evolve. Problems of foreign policy
were converted into blunt instruments for use in political skirmishes at
home. Exception was taken, for instance, to my discriminating and
fundamentally favourable attitude to proposals for a nuclear non-
proliferation treaty. Strauss talked of our being threatened by a 'new
Versailles of cosmic dimensions' – a phrase devoid of substance when
measured against reality. Kiesinger himself wavered between fears of
'nuclear complicity' between the super-powers and the realization that
our national interests prescribed a wary but constructive acceptance of
this scheme.

I got on best with Chancellor Kiesinger on the relatively few
occasions when we had a chance to talk alone. The Swabian politician
had distinguished himself during the first two Federal parliaments as a
pugnacious and sometimes demagogic debater, mainly in the field of
foreign policy. He went to Stuttgart as premier late in 1958, after being
denied ministerial rank and parliamentary leadership under Adenauer.
His style of government was markedly egocentric, and his monologues

disrupted the timetable of many a cabinet meeting. He was also moody and thin-skinned. Once, when he had delayed the start of yet another cabinet meeting by complaining about unfavourable or hostile press comment, I politely – and with the blithe approval of my cabinet colleagues – advised him not to read so many newspapers.

In general, however, Kiesinger was not unpleasant to work with. He was a knowledgeable and intellectually stimulating man. Discounting his interest in foreign affairs, he could put on a scintillating display of legal knowledge and experience derived from an education commonly described as tending towards the Baroque. When Carlo Schmid and he discussed political philosophy or lamented the decline of political ethics over the cabinet table, their platonic dialogues made quite agreeable listening even though they consumed the time which in Bonn can seldom – unfortunately – be spared.

We agreed that our relations with France and America must be restored to a firm footing. Although Kiesinger wanted to normalize relations with our Eastern neighbours, we differed in our choice of realistic ways and means to this end – and not only because he found it harder to free himself from the formulas and ideological restrictions of the early post-war years.

There is no doubt that Kiesinger wanted the Grand Coalition to succeed. He would have been only too happy if it had developed the strength to apply itself more resolutely to major tasks of modernization in fields such as education and structural policy. This was hampered less by the inevitable rivalry between the two main parties than by conflicting tendencies inside the CDU/CSU.

Kiesinger seemed increasingly torn between the two wings of his party as time went by. Our relationship suffered in consequence. Apart from this, any Foreign Minister is almost bound to have trouble with a head of government who takes a keen personal interest in foreign affairs.

Bonn's technique of kindling suspicion with reports from obscure sources was more than merely irksome. These interruptions, coupled with much unjustifiable interference from the Chancellery, sometimes prompted me to wonder if it would not be better to resign. I stayed because I could not be the one to bring the Grand Coalition down. We had to persevere until the programme's main points had been implemented. I did not resign even when the cabinet overrode my advice in spring 1969 and broke off relations with Cambodia because the Phnom Penh government had found it necessary to recognize East Berlin. (True, we did not shut up shop entirely but maintained a non-ambassadorial presence – 'Cambodeering', as it was then called.) All in all, no petty disagreements could mar the enthusiasm and pleasure with which I worked at the Foreign Office. My years there were a productive spell in office. They enabled me to do something useful, not only for my own country but for our European partners and the Atlantic Alliance.

7

Federal Foreign Minister

Addressing the assembled staff on taking up my appointment at the Foreign Office, I said that no one with a sense of history would readily forget what it meant that a man of my beliefs should have become Germany's Foreign Minister. Discounting a few months in 1920, no Social Democrat had ever presided over the old Wilhelmstrasse. The sole precursors whom a man of my own political complexion, experience and objectives could have wished to invoke were Walther Rathenau, a left-wing liberal of upper middle-class Jewish origins, and – in many respects – Gustav Stresemann, the liberal conservative, both of whom pioneered a realistic foreign policy on behalf of the first German republic.

What fascinated me about Rathenau, whose murder provided an early foretaste of the first republic's tragic fate, was that his undoubtedly upper middle-class but liberal cast of mind forged a path to democracy and social responsibility. I also appreciated his recognition of the historical need for a harmonious compromise between Germany's policies towards West and East.

My youthful attitude to Stresemann was detached. Unfair as it may have been, I judged him not only by the patriotic pose typical of his German People's Party but by the bourgeois constraint with which he, as party leader, seemed to approach social problems. I may also have underrated the heartfelt realism of his self-sacrificial peace policy and the courage demanded of him by nationalistic hatred. In a speech commemorating the 90th anniversary of his birth on 10 May 1968, I essayed a fair historical assessment of him. Although he realized that economic co-operation would not as yet bring European political fusion in its train, Gustav Stresemann desired European unity. He had inferred from the course of the passive resistance campaign in the Ruhr that Germany would gain nothing from violence, obstructionism and nationalistic fervour. 'The only hope, albeit a very bold one, was to make friends with our foes. There began a policy of common sense, not of fanfares, a policy of quiet and dogged endeavour. It had to prevail over cheap, easy, foolish emotions. It became a policy of practical success which human passions tore to shreds, scorned, mocked, doubted, disavowed and finally – so far as its internal effects were concerned – killed.' It was also Stresemann who had said that some negotiations must be conducted even if one fears them to be hopeless.

I set out four directional aids for the benefit of myself and my assistants. The first was the active safeguarding of peace – a common denominator of our endeavours on behalf of Europe and in the world at large. As our policy statement had implied, the desire for peace and understanding was the alpha and omega and basis of our foreign policy.

Second came the interpretation of our specific interests, which I discussed quite frankly when my first official engagement abroad took me to Paris. Visiting Washington two months later, in February 1967, I added that we espoused our interests confidently but without arrogance.

In the third place, I insisted on boldly bracketing off the past and rebutting a few of the arguments with which many people sought to preserve a false continuity by including the Hitler era. Anyone who thought it possible to manage without this definite dividing-line would come to grief. No reservations, no whitewash: 'Neo-Nazism and nationalism are a betrayal of our country and nation.'

Last of all, I attacked the credulous assumption that legal formulas could help us, if not to win the war after the event, at least to escape its consequences. We had to overcome the all-or-nothing attitude which even Bismarck had condemned.

The officials in Koblenzer Strasse and their Social Democratic Foreign Minister embarked on a joint experiment. It did not go unrewarded. My experience of the Foreign Ministry was thoroughly satisfactory, but a department of this type is always in danger of self-isolation. I did not find it easy to overcome the influence of social ideals which had little connection with reality. Economic and cultural matters had long been classed as secondary or tertiary.

The role of ambassadors, especially in countries whose political leaders often meet in person or simply converse by phone, has radically altered, though they still perform many important functions. It must also be acknowledged that modern telecommunications are conducive to feverish superficiality. The days when policy was shaped by careful analysis and unhurried correspondence, instead of at hectic con-

Bi-partisan Berlin
policy: Chancellor
Adenauer and
Burgomaster Brandt

Dialogue with
President de Gaulle

1973 in Tel Aviv with Golda Meir, President Katzir and Foreign Minister Eban

Conversation with Edward Heath

With President Kaunda

At the memorial in the Warsaw ghetto

ferences thronged with agitated aides, did have their advantages. The statesman of our own day must steer a sensible middle course between the classic and modern diplomatic styles or risk becoming a slave of his own machine.

To revert to my inaugural staff meeting, I made a point of stating that I would always approve of departmental loyalty provided it did not conflict with my view of current requirements. Something of the old Wilhelmstrasse tradition lingered on, of course, inherited from a Berlin Foreign Office whose diplomatic *esprit de corps* had not only existed since Bismarck's day but survived the Nazi period with changes that were not invariably for the worse. However, there was also a younger tradition shaped by the resistance of some Foreign Office personnel to Hitler's dictatorship. I was fortunate enough to work with efficient subordinates, some of them first-class. I seldom had cause to complain of disloyalty and demonstrated my confidence by eschewing the introduction of too many outsiders.

I had meant to concentrate on 'inside duties', putting in a lot of desk work and travelling little, but this stationary existence remained a pious hope. I must have spent a third of my time on the move. I sometimes wonder – and this applied in part to my term as Chancellor – if these trips bore a sensible relationship to the results obtained. Personal contact between leading politicians can often be beneficial, of course, because they genuinely do represent an international version of the extended family. I nevertheless fear that modern methods of travel provide an over-simple expedient, especially as more and more of the time gained by soaring across countries and continents is consumed by a bustle and activity which leaves one shorter of time than ever. Visits by heads of government and Foreign Ministers should be tailored to a pattern that dispenses with unnecessary ceremonial and reduces official banquets – which are a health hazard anyway! – to a minimum.

It also remains to be asked whether the politicians of our time are menaced with asphyxia by a superabundance of information. The speed with which teleprinters operate is an invitation to fire off reports of excessive frequency and length. Compared with their forerunners, senior officials are positively deluged with informative and analytical material culled not only from newspapers and periodicals but from research institute reports and literature devoted to foreign affairs, economic policy and matters of general interest. Good synopses are hard to produce. Do we, thanks to this flood of information, know more than we did fifty years ago? I am not so sure.

For all that, I naturally read as much as possible while in office, and not official documents only. I made it a daily rule to dip into a book which had no direct bearing on my work. Rather than base my memoranda on ghost-written drafts, I preferred in important cases to formulate them myself.

In my time, as always, the foreign policy of Federal Germany was first and foremost a Western policy concerned with our status in the Atlantic Alliance and the various European communities, and with our role as a major exporting nation which has to tend its interests throughout the world. I once said of our Eastern policy – and not for the mere fun of juggling with words – that it, too, was rooted in the West.

This presupposed a mutually trustful relationship with the members of the Atlantic Alliance and the United States in particular. Our policy statement declared that we had laid too much stress on our own worries in the past and overlooked the fact that America had problems too. Consideration was to be given to how we, in company with our European partners, could assume a greater responsibility for world peace. These key-words were carefully noted, and not only in Washington. The NATO conference of December 1966 was the first I attended as Foreign Minister and the last to be held in Paris before NATO headquarters moved to Brussels. The new German delegation was welcomed with much cordiality and some curiosity.

It should not be supposed that a great deal of 'consultation' took place at these conferences. The delegations of the fifteen member-countries are not large. Each minister is accompanied by two or three aides apart from the NATO ambassador. However, if the Ministers of Defence and Finance attend in addition to the Foreign Minister, numbers are appreciably swelled not only by their aides but by members of the Secretariat-General and the Military Committee as well. Certainly during my years in office, most of the time was taken up with ministerial statements made in alphabetical order of countries. It was not unusual for the bulk of these speeches to be released to the press correspondents of the country in question, and some of my colleagues were not averse to representing their country's contribution as the focal point of conference activity. All that any interested party had to do was spread out the press reports from participating countries side by side in order to gain, if not an altogether accurate picture, at least a comprehensive survey of the relevant NATO meeting. To that extent, the intelligence services were deprived of a job.

The second time-consuming part of a NATO conference was (and still is) devoted to producing the final communiqué. The Secretary-General submits a preliminary draft and senior officials work on it in consultation with their ministers. It was (and still is) far from rare for the final editing at the conference table to take several hours. Sometimes occasioned by understandable national interests or tiresome considerations of prestige, this haggling over a single sentence may also mask the clarification of some important element in common policy. Better results can often be obtained from private discussions on the periphery of such conferences, either held by prior arrangement or – time-table permitting – set up on the spot.

The subject that concerned this particular conference was paraphrased as 'the reform of the Alliance'. Its purpose was to define the twin functions of 'defence' and 'détente' as the new task facing us in international relations. These key-words were reiterated in Luxemburg in June 1967 and at the Brussels conference in December of the same year. Military strength and political solidarity were to be adequately maintained for the deterrence of aggression and other attempts to exert pressure, likewise for the protection of any member-country compelled to defend its territory. At the same time, efforts would be made to promote a more stable East–West relationship in Europe so as to facilitate the resolution of basic political conflicts. There was discussion of realistic proposals conducive to détente, and talk of 'general' disarmament was abandoned in favour of reciprocal arms supervision and limitation.

It had become an established rule that the Foreign Ministers of the United States, Britain, France and the Federal Republic should meet for dinner on the eve of NATO conferences to co-ordinate their views on Berlin and questions affecting Germany. At the 'German dinner' in the Icelandic capital I enlarged on one or two basic ideas which were later reflected in the Quadripartite Agreement on Berlin and in agreements between the two German states. I also informed my colleagues that Ambassador Abrassimov, whom I had met shortly before, had reacted favourably to the proposal for a lump-sum payment in respect of the use of access routes to Berlin. Dean Rusk commented that, if this came off, it would be a major step forward . . .

In April 1969 the ministerial conference in Washington was highlighted by the twentieth anniversary of the Alliance. I had visited Canada on my way to the US capital. President Nixon and I spoke at a public gathering in the Labor Department auditorium which was also attended by the co-founders of the Alliance: Henri Spaak of Belgium, Dirk Stikker of Holland and Halvard Lange of Norway. As chairman by rotation, I emphasized three facts about NATO: first, it had prevented armed conflicts between its members (a statement I would some years later have qualified in view of the Cyprus crisis and the dispute between Britain and Iceland); secondly, it had proved itself a defensive alliance which presented no threat to any country or people; and, last but not least, it had gained its principal objective, which was to keep the peace in our part of the world. 'The peoples of the West and East want security. They still vie for security today. To find security together would accord with the real aim of the Atlantic Alliance.'

The US Government was currently suggesting that the Alliance should apply itself to questions other than those of security in the narrow sense. Modern social problems, including environmental protection, were recommended for joint discussion. Working parties were formed to map out and survey these fields of inquiry. Experience showed, however, as it had in the past, that NATO did not offer a suitable framework for such endeavours. No amount of verbal effort could make it function as a federation.

Nixon, as host, invited us to attend a ministerial meeting accompanied by one aide only. He briefed us on the development of strategic nuclear weapons in language expressive of consternation at the level of Soviet progress. Seven years earlier, during the Cuban crisis, the ratio of US nuclear weapons to Soviet had been ten-to-one. That stage had long been superseded, and parity was forecast in another seven years' time. Nixon also informed us about the prelude to the negotiations that had been initiated under his predecessor and were later to enter the political vocabulary as SALT (Strategic Arms Limitation Talks).

At the same Washington conference, the President observed that it had been fashionable a year or two earlier to bewail the critical state of the Alliance and predict its speedy end. Since then, the subject had lapsed. Allied solidarity was essential to the success of a policy aimed at reducing tension and realistically safeguarding peace. Nixon further declared – and Kissinger's handwriting was clearly discernible here – that we were moving towards an age of negotiation, hence the importance of attending 'properly' to our relations with the Warsaw Pact countries. The West must not, he said, be drawn into a selective détente which would leave the Soviet Union more or less free to determine where it considered détente appropriate or a continuation of the Cold War expedient.

On this occasion, either despite the Czech crisis or on that very account, I recommended that we critically examine the idea of a European security conference rather than abandon it to communist propaganda. Pietro Nenni, the elderly Italian socialist leader who was then his country's Foreign Minister, went so far as to propose that the West should itself take the lead in calling for a security conference. Although exposed to a great deal of natural scepticism because of his close but temporary collaboration with the communists, Nenni impressed one with his quiet resolve. He was an indefatigable champion of peace and an unflinching upholder of Western values.

Our bilateral exchanges with the United States had quickly re-assumed the character of a friendly dialogue based on mutual trust. While discussing the non-proliferation treaty, our experts had taxed the patience of the competent authorities in Washington. This was one of the main themes of Kissinger's visit in August 1967, on which I accompanied him. Both during my first ministerial visit in February 1967 and subsequently, I played my part in helping to dispose of the tiresome 'offset' problem. The Americans, notably some influential US Senators, insisted on parity of foreign exchange expenditure in respect of the cost of stationing troops on our soil. Georg Ferdinand Duckwitz had been instrumental in settling this question (with Britain as well) before joining me as State Secretary. His American partner was John McCloy, a wielder of great financial and political influence, whose friendship for 'his' Federal Republic continued unabated. Soon concluded on a two-yearly basis, the offset agreements encountered the problems inevitably attendant on any balance of payments adjustment. They were further bedevilled by the fact that the Americans wanted to sell us more arms than we could use. The situation was eased by our investing in special medium-term US Government securities and instructing the Federal Bank to announce that it would convert dollar reserves into gold. By 1969 nobody could continue to disregard the soundness of our currency.

I travelled to America by ship on only one occasion, in February 1969, and then only because my doctor had advised me to do so after an attack of pleurisy. The *Cristoforo Colombo* had a stormy passage, but my week in the Atlantic was restful in a way I had long forgotten. No newspapers, no daily documents, no appointments, just some very brief informative cables from Bonn which the ship's radio-room picked up for me once or twice a day. There was plenty of time to read and gather my thoughts while walking on deck, so I had at least one opportunity to form a personal impression of the ocean which has been called the inland sea or Mediterranean of the Western world and its alliance.

In New York I took advantage of a speaking engagement to tell the Americans that we should jointly strive to maintain the foundations of our mutual trust. These remarks were also intended to set the tone for Nixon's forthcoming visit to Bonn and Berlin, which was only a few days off.

Partnership with our French neighbours remained the key to European unification – more concretely, to the cardinal problem of how to bring the dispute over British entry to a favourable conclusion. We were still a long way from the understanding reached by Pompidou and myself at the end of 1969, and even further from the British referendum of early summer 1975. Precious time was lost, both before and afterwards.

In the EEC, the Luxemburg compromise had not exactly overcome the paralysis induced by France's opposition to the possibility of majority votes (envisaged by the Treaty). It had since become prescriptive that no member-government could be overruled in defiance of its vital interests. When I first headed the German delegation at the April 1967 meeting of the Council of Ministers in Brussels, I promised that the Federal Government would do its utmost to implement the aims of the EEC Treaty. We must progress from the customs and agricultural union to an economic union proper (something which still remains a pipe-dream eight years later). The EEC nevertheless contributed to the successful conclusion of the international agreement on tariff reductions in 1967. It also proved capable of concerted action in solving current international monetary problems, though these were only a pale reflection of what lay ahead.

The ministerial meetings in Brussels soon became routine to me in the best and worst sense of the word. The negotiating climate was impaired by its bleak architectural setting. There was no lack of cordiality between the delegates, but I was shocked by their ponderous working methods. The intimacy appropriate to a 'council' was totally absent. The chamber regularly held at least 150 and more often 200 persons (ten to twenty per delegation plus the Commissioners, their staffs and the Secretariat), which made it more like a medium-sized popular assembly. This plethora of delegates simply proved how hard the various governments found it to reach internal agreement on a summary of their European responsibilities. What was more, the Treaty of Rome was only imperfectly and imprecisely fulfilled in that the powers of the Council of Ministers and the Commission were (and are) staked out with insufficient clarity. Many other shortcomings apart, this has led to the growth of a double bureaucracy.

As a modest step forward, we urged that the three communities (European Coal and Steel, EEC and Euratom) be brought together and their organs merged in the European Community. This was confirmed at a summit conference held in Rome at the end of May 1967 in solemn commemoration of the treaties concluded there ten years earlier. De Gaulle attended in person, but the negotiations yielded little. Hypercritical observers claimed that the only real outcome was Professor Hallstein's resignation as President of the EEC Commission. (De Gaulle found Hallstein suspect because of his outspoken and sometimes excessive advocacy of the supranational principle.)

Rome also produced no move towards agreement with the French on the question of how to treat the British, who were now – this time led by a Labour government – preparing a new application for admission to the EEC. Harold Wilson and his Foreign Minister, George Brown, had tested the water during a tour of the member-countries' capitals at the beginning of the year. They visited Bonn in February 1967. Wilson argued so fiercely that Kiesinger felt cornered. Brown had one of his temperamental altercations, this time with Strauss, who harboured an extreme mistrust of British motives.

The British took heart from what was said to them in Rome and the capitals of the Netherlands, Belgium and Luxemburg. There was a widespread tendency to believe, wrongly, that strong words from Bonn would bring Paris to heel. On the contrary, we had to eschew the temptation to confront France as a united five-member bloc. True, representatives of the Five once or twice met for breakfast at the *Hotel Amigo* in Brussels (a Spanish prison in the Duke of Alba's day), but I was careful to avoid any entrenchment of our conflicting positions.

De Gaulle was unimpressed by the new London overture and our sympathetic reception of it. Paris also criticized Britain's choice of method when submitting its application to the Community in summer 1967. The occasion was a Hague meeting of the Foreign Ministers of the Western European Union – in those days an institutional bridge between the Six and Great Britain – which took place under my chairmanship. Having naturally informed me in advance, George Brown read out a lengthy and well-worded statement which culminated in an expression of readiness to join and conveyed his country's faith in the potential of an enlarged Community.

The French President stood pat. The British were too close to the Americans for his taste. He doubted if they were willing or able to fit into a Continental community and was probably afraid that Britain might contest the role of spokesman or leader which he conceived to be a French prerogative. At the end of the preceding round of negotiations for entry, which de Gaulle terminated at his press conference in January 1963, Couve de Murville is reputed to have turned to the senior British negotiator, Edward Heath, and remarked with a shrug that the General considered Britain an island. Heath retorted that it had been one when negotiations began. On the other hand, I did hear de Gaulle say that he did not exclude the possibility that Great Britain might one day moor her ship to the Continental quay.

The Federal Government's course was no longer governed by the reservations so clearly expressed by Adenauer. Erhard saw things differently. I, like my party, had always been in favour of British membership and refused to be dissuaded by America's attitude towards the Community, which was equivocal: outwardly encouraging, inwardly somewhat tentative or temporizing.

I expected political and economic benefits to accrue from Britain's entry, nor had my faith been shaken by Jean Monnet, who declared when he first visited me in Berlin in 1963 that British entry – which he so vigorously supported later on – was far too premature.

During the early months of 1967, at the very outset of my tenure of the Foreign Ministry, I advocated the admission of new members to EEC governments, before the Council of Europe in Strasbourg, and in Scandinavia. It required no mental effort to grasp that the dispute over expanded membership was prejudicial to the existing Community and obstructive of its development. I fully understood the nature of French misgivings. Criticism of the traditional British 'special relationship' with the United States was mingled with fears of an Anglo-German get-together inside the EEC, doubts about the efficiency of British industry and a sceptical view of Whitehall's attitude towards strengthening the Community's authority. At the same time, France's own position in regard to the renunciation of sovereign rights was far from consistent.

The EEC countries made no progress towards a unified foreign policy during these years. Experience showed that it had been wrong to expect an automatic transition from economic to political integration. It also taught us, as I publicly stated, that the sensible course in inter-governmental co-operation was to aim for the possible. Limited political co-operation would not be easy, I surmised, but it was attainable and could count for a great deal. (It has, in fact, shaped well since 1970–71.)

Also latent in my commitment to British entry was the hope that the Community would benefit from Britain's worldwide experience and tradition of parliamentary democracy. I was prompted by the feeling that Britain's steadfast resistance in World War II, her sacrifices and sufferings, should not be consigned to oblivion. As a European, I rather disconcertedly wondered why the British had to hammer on our door at all. Hadn't they already demonstrated their membership in Europe's darkest hour?

I still consider it a mistake to have kept Britain waiting so long. Of course, it may also be asked why the British themselves took so long to join. The likelihood is that their economic crisis would have been mitigated by an earlier link with the Community. By the time they secured admission, their problems were accumulating fast. On the other hand, and with all due respect, I found that the British are not easy partners. The loss of their role as a world power came hard to them.

Even as open-minded and widely travelled a man as the then leader of the Labour Party, Hugh Gaitskell, found it quite natural to introduce me to a London gathering in 1962 as 'our friend from overseas'. He had sharply rejected British entry at a Labour Party Conference not long before. My friend Per Haekkerup, the Danish Foreign Minister, who had been a guest at Brighton, told me that he felt throughout Gaitskell's speech as if the doors at the back of the hall might open at any moment and Queen Victoria come striding in. In December 1967, when I paid a ministerial call on George Brown, who had opposed his friend Gaitskell at Brighton and was now Foreign Minister, I was greeted by the perplexing and disillusioning plea: 'Willy, you must get us in so we can take the lead.'

Despite his insularity, which was nonetheless of imperial dimensions, Hugh Gaitskell possessed uncommon intellectual and political gifts.

Gaitskell and I met quite frequently at international functions. He visited us even before my mayoral term in Berlin, and I first came to London as his guest in the spring of 1958. In company with Denis Healey and other associates, he called for closer co-operation between Europe's two largest social democratic parties. In spring 1962 some friends in Parliament arranged a meeting for me at Friends House. Gaitskell led off, Wilson wound up. It was a noisy occasion. I was heckled by communists for being a fascist and by sundry fascists for being a Red. John B. Hynd, the post-war Labour government's 'Minister for Germany', later reported in a small book about me that the hecklers' real targets were Gaitskell and Wilson. Pamphlets proved, he said, that the demonstration had been instigated by East Berlin.

It was agreed with Gaitskell on the same occasion that Harold Wilson, as Shadow Foreign Minister, would visit Berlin with a sizeable delegation of Labour MPs. They arrived at the end of June 1962, the largest party of MPs ever to travel abroad as a single group. Wilson told me later that this trip had been highly instrumental in getting him elected Gaitskell's successor (and subsequently appointed Prime Minister). It enabled him to form closer contacts with fellow-members of his parliamentary party who had hitherto treated him with reserve.

The network of contacts and friendships that linked me with the island became stronger and more close-knit as the years went by. Political interests and personal sympathies corresponded and complemented each other across the frontiers of ideology and – something that still counts for more in Britain than elsewhere – across the barrier of 'class'. Edward Heath, the Conservative leader, demonstrated in our work together after his election victory in June 1970 (the biggest surprise since Truman's re-election) that it was indeed possible to be a Briton and a staunch European at one and the same time. I naturally had fewer dealings during my years as Chancellor with Harold Wilson, who became Prime Minister in October 1964 and returned to office in 1974. I nevertheless came to know and respect him as a man who not only acted on Bismarck's dictum that politics is the art of the possible, but did so with vigorous pragmatism and a well-developed feeling for the art of the opportune. This facility enabled him to represent the Labour Party to the British public as the 'natural' party of government – in itself no mean feat.

The British application for membership with which the Irish, Danes and Norwegians (and, in a 'special letter' the Swedes) associated themselves, was submitted to the Commission in summer 1967 with a request that it report on the problems arising therefrom. When the report was presented in September, the economic problems were described as soluble. It was, however, stipulated that applicants would have to assume the responsibilities undertaken by existing member-countries and concur in the general aims of the Community. Before the Council of Ministers could consider its verdict at the end of the year, de Gaulle once again anticipated the French decision at a press conference in late November: France, he bluntly declared, would not assent.

The outlook was bleak when the Council of Ministers assembled in the Belgian capital shortly before Christmas. Addressing the Bundestag a few days earlier, I had said that, although we did not speak in terms of claims to authority, demonstrations or threats, we must urgently recommend our French neighbours not to make things difficult for themselves and others. We argued vigorously with Couve de Murville, both formally and in private. Despite his unyielding attitude, he strove to maintain a friendly tone and hinted at the very limited room for manœuvre available to him. Once it had been ascertained that all the member-countries except France were in favour of starting entry negotiations, but that none was opposed in principle to the Community's enlargement, the applications stayed on the agenda. No actual progress was made, but further discussion of the entry question remained at least technically feasible.

A few days before the December 1967 meeting of the Council of Ministers, I spent a weekend in England. Harold Wilson had invited me to a gathering of party leaders at Chequers. I spent the eve of the meeting with George Brown at Dorneywood, a handsome country house at the Foreign Minister's disposal. I have already described his unceremonious attempt to enlist my services. The Foreign Minister of the United Kingdom had little time for diplomatic niceties. This was part of his charm, and it enabled him to treat me with a warmth which I gladly reciprocated. His conception of Britain's role in the unification of Europe was coloured by intense national pride. As he wrote in his memoirs, *In My Way*: 'We *have* a role: our role is to lead Europe.' It was typical of his endearing and somewhat eccentric personality that he liked to deliver late-night harangues about religious matters (which I did not regard as such). Shadow-boxing, as it were, he did battle on behalf of Catholicism, which he considered the one and only road to salvation.

The talks at Chequers, the Prime Minister's country residence, and elsewhere, disclosed that our British friends were purely concerned to know whether negotiations for entry would be opened at once. Intermediate solutions did not interest them. They were rather displeased with us, and took a jaundiced view of our close ties with France, which we valued for all our differences of opinion. We tried as far as possible to play the honest broker without falling between two stools.

The disagreements with France that had arisen during the debate on enlarging the Community were not easily overcome. In mid-February 1968, when we visited Paris for the regular Franco-German consultations, it was stated that both governments were fundamentally in favour of enlargement. It was first proposed, 'with a view to admission', that an agreement on trade policy should be examined, but London showed no enthusiasm for such an arrangement. Equally abortive was a proposal that British admission to Euratom be given priority, thus securing the technological co-operation which London had offered.

Failure also attended suggestions from the Benelux countries that co-operation with Britain – with or without France – should be speeded up in fields extraneous to the Rome treaties. In autumn 1968 the Council of Ministers discussed a series of interim measures, and I recommended that Britain should as far as possible be included in our political consultations. My proposals were simultaneously aimed at promoting the Community's internal development. In the event, stagnation persisted.

The Republic of Ireland had joined the United Kingdom in applying for membership. The economic destinies of the smaller of the British Isles, which I was regrettably unable to visit as Foreign Minister or Chancellor, were (and still are) dependent on those of Britain. Although London called the tune, Dublin had a wholly Irish interest in the Continental link: in the long term, membership of the Community offered the Irish Republic greater room for manœuvre because numerous dependences on Europe, while not replacing the original dependence on Britain, could supplement it in a flexible manner. Dublin may also have hoped for psychological relief from the oppressive problem of Northern Ireland under the illusion that a wider partnership would end the smouldering civil war in which tragic social conflict masquerades as a stale and outworn religious controversy. Although Ireland has enriched the European Community, the North still suffers from the creeping contagion which I regard as one of our waning century's most terrible absurdities.

The question had yet to arise whether Greece and Spain should become members of the Community and how quickly Portugal could be introduced into its ranks. All three countries were problem children of the Alliance and of democratic Europe. In view of Germany's own experiences, I did not think it right to sit in moral judgement, but we could not remain indifferent to the fate of these nations. We had to show solidarity wherever possible. I was never in any doubt that dictatorships hamper Western co-operation and do not belong in the European Community.

We were also worried by internal developments in Italy. I recall a confidential talk with Pietro Nenni at Strasbourg in 1968, while we were both Foreign Ministers. He communicated his fears of a lurch to the right and his forebodings that 'the Greek example' might infect his native land. Italy did, in fact, enter the danger zone at least once. There are numerous historical and social reasons why Italy obliges the countries and societies of Western Europe to pose fundamental questions about the vitality and viability of the democracies. Examining that turbulent country, I always seem to discern reflections of what is perhaps our century's most thorny problem: the extent to which our society is capable of democratic reform. It can hardly be coincidental that we meet this challenge on the soil of so ancient and sensitive a culture.

Quite a different problem arose for our southern neighbours, Austria and Switzerland, who were interested in beneficial arrangements with the EEC. This was a matter whose vital importance to Austria, in particular, I repeatedly impressed on our EEC partners. In the north, Denmark and Norway had co-ordinated their applications for membership with that of Britain and the Swedes had inserted a foot in the door by means of their 'special letter'.

Scandinavia's European links were of special concern to me, and not only because my years there had left an enduring mark. They also preoccupied me because of my belief that these countries have much to contribute to European co-operation. With its humanitarian tradition and practical democracy, intellectual breadth and pioneering work in the field of social progress and equality, the north has a role to play in Europe. Nevertheless, opposing tendencies soon made themselves felt. Stronger in Norway than Denmark, these stemmed – discounting superficialities – from the fear that European integration would rob small nations of their identity. The Danes, for example, were afraid that the loveliest parts of their country would be bought up by wealthy Hamburg businessmen in quest of holiday homes (though they took measures to protect themselves against this hazard). The Norwegians were haunted by a pietistic tee-totaller's nightmare that the Common Market might oblige them to become regular wine-drinkers and that their girls would be carried off by swarthy southerners.

I will not embark on a straightforward enumeration of all my trips abroad as Foreign Minister. No Foreign Minister can confine himself to focal points of activity. Even if he is unable to devote equally close attention to all areas, he has to maintain contact with a multiplicity of countries. This entails telegrams, memoranda, files, interviews with ambassadors and opposite numbers, and foreign travel. I had shown my face in numerous parts of the world even when I was Mayor of Berlin. It was essential to keep in personal touch with the Protecting Powers and exert an influence on public opinion in other countries. Not a week went by in the city itself without our receiving courtesy calls from foreign visitors of varying prominence. As party chairman, I was additionally responsible for cultivating our European and world-wide links with other social democratic parties.

It was also in my capacity as leader of the German Social Democrats that I frequently had to apply myself to the problems of the so-called Third World (and the Fourth). There was symbolic significance in what I said beside the grave of August Bebel in Zurich on 13 August 1963, not only 50 years after the death of the great German labour leader whose successor in office I was, but 50 years after my own birth. I declared that the political map of the world had been redrawn after World War II. Side by side with the East–West conflict, there was latent antagonism between the northern and southern hemispheres. We could already discern evidence that the clock of history did not stand still in the communist-ruled part of the world either. The hitherto undreamed-of potentials of science and technology should be used to abolish hunger, disease and ignorance throughout the world. We must leave the old behind and construct 'a system devoid of poverty and fear, a system superior to all gainsayers of freedom'.

8

Ostpolitik

No one could fail to acknowledge that one of the Grand Coalition's principal aims was to improve relations with the 'East' and place them on as normal a footing as possible. Its success was only partial. Foreign resistance and domestic opposition proved stronger than we could initially have foreseen. Despite this, 1967 and 1968 witnessed the development of a new policy which I managed to bring to provisional fruition as Chancellor, and which, over and above its importance to the German Federal Republic, had European and worldwide repercussions.

It goes without saying that my so-called *Ostpolitik* was not first devised in 1966. The Adenauer and Erhard governments had both, in their own way, striven to ease our relations with the Soviet Union and Eastern Europe. In June 1961 the Bundestag had unanimously passed a resolution calling for moves to this end. My own ideas and recommendations had taken shape over a period of many years, and my party's proposals were available during the formation of the Kiesinger-Brandt government.

In offering to exchange renunciation-of-force declarations with the Soviet Union, Poland, Czechoslovakia and, in principle, other interested countries, we did not merely reiterate the 'peace note' of March 1966 but went beyond it. Kiesinger's government policy statement in December contained no precise reference to Poland's western border but expressed an understanding of the Polish people's desire 'to live at last in a national territory with secured frontiers'. Its reference to the Munich *Diktat* of 1938, which had doomed the Czechoslovak Republic to destruction, was unequivocal: the Munich Agreement, which had 'come into being under the threat of force', was 'no longer valid'. We also made it clear that we did not mean to exclude the other German state from our renunciation-of-force policy and were prepared 'to embody the outstanding problem of German partition in this offer'.

The German Democratic Republic was not, however, mentioned by name, nor was there any immediate or universal realization that we would consider negotiating fundamentals with the GDR. Rather, interest at first centred on the settlement of practical problems and on the 'unclenching' of the relationship between the two parts of Germany.

In examining the motives that impelled us to redirect the Federal Republic's German policy, one should bear in mind that only shades of opinion separated the coalition partners and members of the Union itself. As it turned out, many politicians in the Union parties wanted to take the plunge without getting their feet wet. It should in fairness be said, however, that there was a genuine desire – at least where Kiesinger and I were concerned – to contribute towards overcoming dangerous tensions in the East–West relationship and their attendant military confrontation.

Whatever the meaning of the word détente – and its introduction into the field of international debate was not our doing – it pointed to a common interest: a desire for survival in the nuclear age. There had long been indications that the United States and the Soviet Union aspired to a new relationship. The need for an accommodation had been dramatically highlighted by the Cuban crisis. Prevailing assessments of Richard Nixon as a politician gave no hint that détente would assume so definite a shape during his Presidency. He was observing a precept that had become more and more discernible under President Johnson, despite or precisely because of America's growing involvement in the Vietnam War. French policy, with its different emphasis, sounded yet another warning note. We could not become the last of the Cold War warriors, the opponents of change and thus, perhaps, the world's leading trouble-makers (and whipping-boys). It could not be our concern alone to help maintain peace and serve the vital interests of our people, for whom a war fought with nuclear weapons would spell certain destruction. Beyond that, but on this side of the lethal borderline, we had a duty to preserve our country from isolation.

Associated with this was the hope that a détente in East–West relations and changes in the European landscape resulting from co-operation might possibly create a new framework for the solution of the 'German question', if only by mitigating the hardships and burdens arising from partition. There was never any real dispute inside the Grand Coalition government that the German question must be kept open.

Above and beyond the German question, we felt it impossible to persevere in a simple acceptance of prevailing conditions in Europe.

What really mattered was to create a climate in which the *status quo* could be changed – in other words, improved – by peaceful means. I was unjustly accused, both then and later, of 'bowing to realities'. I was, and still am, of the opinion that realities can be influenced for the better only if they are taken into account.

I must once more emphasize that it was evident, for all their continuing rivalry, that the super-powers would reach a new form of accommodation. Their quest for co-operation had been perceptible even before the Cuban crisis and survived the protracted struggle in Vietnam. It was almost unaffected by the Czech crisis of 1968 – however one evaluates that fact – and persisted in the face of conflict in the Middle East. It led, by way of the test-ban and non-proliferation agreements, to the treaties relating to limitation of strategic nuclear weapons. Despite competing aspirations and opposing social systems, objective communities of interest became manifest in a joint approach to new scientific discoveries. The super-powers must nonetheless stand accused of devoting far too little attention to the worldwide problems that have become the prime movers of our time: the scientific and technological revolution on the one hand, and the population explosion and world hunger on the other. Even the medium-term problems of oil and raw materials were long neglected, and the industrialized nations of the West and East showed little sense of joint responsibility.

I suggested at an earlier stage that the two super-powers may since 1945 have consistently pursued the principle of respecting spheres of influence roughed out between them prior to the end of World War II. This is not to deny that Washington would have rejoiced if the countries of Eastern Europe had remained exempt from régimes of a definitely communist character, or that Moscow would have exploited opportunities to wield greater influence in Western Europe if these had presented little risk. Nevertheless, Washington and Moscow were both unwilling to court the dangers associated with German reunification. The progress of efforts to limit and reduce tension remained almost unaffected by events in Czechoslovakia during 1968 – a fact which deserves particular emphasis.

An essential ingredient of our *Ostpolitik* was that we applied ourselves to our own affairs in a new and more positive manner instead of relying solely on others to speak for us. This meant that, while remaining in touch with our allies and retaining their confidence, we became the advocate of our own interests *vis-à-vis* the governments of Eastern Europe. By so doing we strengthened our voice inside the bodies devoted to West European, Atlantic and international co-operation. The Federal Republic became more independent – more adult, so to speak. A contributory factor was that our allies came to regard us as a country with definite frontiers which no longer burdened the European Community with problems whose solution would have entailed a fundamental change in the international and European *status quo*. I do not disguise that I was also motivated from the outset by concrete economic considerations. Even as Foreign Minister, I told the Bundestag that our policy must be focused on the problems of existence in an immediate sense as well: we had to safeguard employment and open up new fields of economic opportunity.

The initial failure of our political approaches to the Soviet Union is sometimes blamed, far too simply, on an attempt to reach accommodations with the other Warsaw Pact countries over the Soviet Union's head. This is not so. What is true is that we underestimated the influence of the GDR when we persisted in refusing to treat it as a country of equal standing. Any attempt to isolate the Soviet super-power would have been foolish. Equally, I never subscribed to the pseudo-Bismarckian notion that we could dismiss the intrinsic importance of the individual East and South European countries in favour of an interplay of German and Russian interests. To repeat: we did not leave the Soviet Union in the dark about our relations with their Pact partners, and we were just as explicit to the latter about the importance that would attach to an easing of relations with Moscow, not only for us but for Europe as a whole. (I need hardly add that we also kept Washington fully informed – like London and Paris – via our embassies and the Bonn 'Group of Four' in which Federal German officials regularly conferred with representatives of the Three Powers. Additional consultations took place with the State Department, and Secretary of State Dean Rusk assured me that he had the fullest confidence in our endeavours.) There were good reasons why the Soviet Union took precedence in the foreign policy section of our government statement of December 1966. We also made it clear that we made not the slightest concession to the obvious and much-canvassed theory that it would be profitable to exploit the Russo-Chinese dispute. Not one of our *démarches* in Eastern and Southern Europe took the Soviet authorities by surprise. At no time did we try to conduct an *Ostpolitik* behind the Soviet Union's back. Our sense of priorities prohibited any such lack of realism.

Despite this, it was only a few weeks before our Soviet collocutors, who had evinced friendly interest immediately after the new government took office and made its policy statement of December 1966, switched to an attitude of chill reserve. The probability is that Moscow was swayed by regard for the GDR leaders. Ulbricht and his team, with their natural hostility to the Social Democrats and particular prejudice against the Grand Coalition, lived in dread of being isolated by our Eastern policy. They not only undertook political action and agitation against us as best they could but evolved their counterpart to the Hallstein Doctrine. With the co-operation of the Warsaw régime and, to some extent, of the then rulers of Prague, sundry provisos for negotiations with the Federal Republic were extracted from the resolution passed by the Warsaw Pact countries in July 1966: acceptance of the Oder–Neisse Line, formal recognition of the GDR, a formal declaration that the Munich Agreement was invalid 'from the outset', and adoption of the formula that West Berlin was an 'independent political entity'. The Federal Republic's renunciation of nuclear weapons was also mentioned in this context. On the other hand, the Warsaw Pact's Bucharest declaration of July 1966 suggested that military pacts be dissolved – a suspect proposal which sank from view in the next few years, not least, one assumes, because of the Czech crisis.

Although Soviet policy adopted a hard line towards us, it could not prevent our establishment of diplomatic relations with Rumania at the end of January 1967. The initiative came from Bucharest, and we had no reason to spurn it. We also gained the impression that the authorities in Budapest, and possibly in Sofia too, were toying with the idea of discussing an exchange of ambassadors. Rumania remained an isolated case for the moment, but there was an improvement in economic and, to a lesser extent, cultural relations with the other countries of the Eastern bloc. In summer 1967 Prague consented to an exchange of trade missions with consular powers, an agreement whose negotiation I had entrusted to Egon Bahr. Diplomatic relations were re-established with communist but non-aligned Yugoslavia in January 1968, after a lapse of ten years. 1968 also witnessed the beginning of a dialogue with Poland, initially in the form of public declarations. Even the Kremlin leaders were content that our intergovernmental exchanges should not remain bogged down in polemics.

A meagre interim result? I did not find it so. The most cogent and immediate effect of our policy was observable in the West and the Third World. We won approval, improved the international climate and enhanced the importance of Federal German policy. The Federal Republic lost its reputation as a trouble-maker. Our honest endeavours had an undoubted effect on the peoples of Eastern Europe. They not only dispelled prejudices but exerted some influence on those in political authority.

The new Soviet Ambassador, Semyon K. Tsarapkin, had called on me at my Bonn party office in autumn 1966, before I became Foreign Minister. 'The facts of life' – we spoke English together – seemed to have become one of his favourite verbal props. Like other and more influential exponents of Marxism-Leninism, he found it quite impossible to grasp that facts not only become modified in the historical process but are open to various interpretations as well. I mentioned that I had just finished the second part of Ilya Ehrenburg's memoirs, in which he recounts how he visited Albert Einstein at Princeton shortly after the end of the war. The scholar asked the writer if he was quite positive that twice two made four – personally, he sometimes had his doubts. My Russian visitor was taken aback. What did I mean? How could two people have a serious discussion if doubts were cast on the product of two and two? I did not pursue the subject, being reluctant to overtax the ambassador's sagacity and sense of humour.

Our next conversation took place just after the government change-over. A few days later Tsarapkin called at my office and I was able to give him a definite answer to one of his main points: we did not aspire to possess any atom bombs or wield national control over nuclear weapons. On the frontier question, I referred him to our policy statement. The ambassador's principal emphasis was on matters relating to the GDR. Its recognition was, he said, indispensable to peace in Europe and inseparable from better relations with the Soviet Union. I replied that this was a point on which we unfortunately differed, but that the Federal Republic intended to do everything possible to ease relations with the other part of Germany instead of letting them petrify still further. Since Moscow and Bonn were clearly unable, or temporarily so, to agree on the German question, the logical course was to apply ourselves to other spheres of common interest. I was here referring not only to trade and culture but to an outspoken political exchange of views. When Tsarapkin inquired the nature of the matters to be discussed, I said that I was thinking mainly of security problems. I was, for example, interested in certain elements of the Bucharest declaration and would welcome enlightenment on their precise meaning.

Having spent the turn of the year in Moscow, Tsarapkin obviously came back armed with instructions to keep his distance – indeed, I recall him behaving almost as if he were Ulbricht's ambassador at a reception given by my party executive for a group of Soviet journalists. Representatives of the Warsaw Pact countries had already met in

Warsaw during February to criticize Rumania for stepping out of line. Mutual assistance pacts with the GDR were agreed and concluded in the ensuing months by Warsaw, Prague, Budapest and Sofia. Poland, the CSSR and the GDR drew closer to form what was known as the Iron Triangle. A Polish study made it clear that the Warsaw authorities had played a leading role in this process. It was intended to show us 'that any attempt to evade the major problems affecting relations between the German Federal Republic and the socialist countries of Europe, and any policy aimed at isolating the GDR, was doomed to failure'.

In April, the communist parties of Eastern and Western Europe – Rumania excepted – held a conference at Karlsbad. Abuse was heaped on the Federal Republic, and campaigns against 'West German militarists and revanchists' served as grist to the communist mill. If only for form's sake, the Soviet Union nevertheless began to discuss the renunciation-of-force theme raised by our policy statement.

Soviet diplomats had betrayed a certain interest in this subject, both before and immediately after the formation of the new government. They had asked, off the record, how we proposed to fit the GDR into a renunciation-of-force context. As I have already pointed out, the Grand Coalition government had signified its willingness to include the outstanding problem of German partition in its offer. Kiesinger and I later agreed – as I publicly stated at the NATO conference of June 1968 and elsewhere – that this should be associated with a willingness to exchange declarations on a bilateral basis. The exchange of written positions between us and the Soviet Union had begun early in February. Draft renunciation-of-force declarations were handed to the Soviet Ambassador by State Secretary Schütz. They contained only one paragraph outlining the obligation of both countries to formulate their policies in accordance with the principles of the UN Charter and, above all, to renounce the use of force in pursuing their aims as regards the German question.

Unofficial talks conducted during the spring and summer made it clear that an agreement on the somewhat abstract renunciation-of-force principle was not going to be enough. We had let it be known, independently of this, that we were prepared to embark on a review of all the material problems affecting our relations. In autumn 1967 Tsarapkin handed me two memoranda setting forth what his government regarded as the obstacles to an exchange of renunciation-of-force declarations. In the Soviet view – or deliberate contention – the German Federal Republic's policy was aggressive and revanchist. The Soviet drafts were correspondingly biased and abounding in mistrust. Instead of allowing the conversational thread to snap, I stated during the Bundestag defence debate on 7 December 1967 that I intended to pursue a confidential exchange of views with patience and goodwill. I announced our readiness to carry out balanced arms reductions and was careful to add that I had encountered favourable interest on the Soviet side, not merely suspicion and polemical insinuations.

Despite this, those who dominated the Soviet leadership continued to favour a hard line, hammering away at the subject of militarism and neo-Nazism.

Our relations with Rumania were normalized in the second month of the new government's existence. The Rumanian Foreign Minister, Corneliu Manescu, travelled to Bonn, and the establishment of diplomatic relations was agreed on 31 January 1967. I found Manescu pleasant to deal with and, during my return visit in August, a charming host. Tall, genial and handsome, he spoke with appealing candour and had a fondness for graphic metaphors drawn from rural life. The atmosphere after the official dinner at his cheerful modern residence was relaxed, and I also had the pleasure of meeting his elegant wife, who edited a leading Rumanian periodical. I met Manescu again the following year in New York, where he was presiding over the UN General Assembly.

This was the first time I had had dealings with a fellow Foreign Minister from the Eastern bloc. Manescu was an open-minded man, and represented his country's interests with little sign of constraint. Economic co-operation with the Federal Republic was successful – we already ranked second among Rumania's trading partners – and the Rumanians made no secret of their efforts to develop this co-operation in so far as it was feasible for us and beneficial to themselves. They were naturally at pains, despite their boldly independent attitude, to avoid unnecessary clashes with 'Big Brother'. Manescu was not exactly overjoyed, therefore, when Chancellor Kiesinger thought it necessary to combine his Bundestag statement on the establishment of diplomatic relations with a declaration to the effect that our claim to sole German representation still stood. Modifying this, I said: 'Our aim is not to annex anything, but to relax and objectify the situation on German soil. However, time cannot paralyse nor claims to authority stifle our peaceful desire to dwell together as a nation in a political community.'

I had been alive to Rumania's special role – in foreign policy, but certainly not at home, where even modest essays in liberalization had ground to a halt – well before the Rumanian Central Committee passed its April 1964 resolution on an 'own road to socialism'. Evangelos

Averoff, the Greek Foreign Minister, had informed me of Rumania's endeavours as early as my visit to Athens in autumn 1960. More plainly than any other source of information had so far conveyed, he intimated that Bucharest thought it could afford to exploit Soviet–Chinese antagonism. In July 1965, Nicolae Ceauşescu was elected to succeed Gheorghiu-Dej as Party leader at the age of 47. He then got himself elected President. Ceauşescu, who has demonstrated a consistent mastery of the political machine, possesses certain autocratic traits. Rather short and stocky, he gives a somewhat diffident impression at first, although he has overcome a minor speech defect with great self-discipline. Long years in prison have undoubtedly left their mark on him. He knows French but prefers to use his mother-tongue. His basic political formula may be defined as apparat-plus-nationalism. We met for a long talk when I paid my return visit to Rumania at the beginning of August 1967, accompanied by my son Lars.

Ceauşescu was staying at his spacious and well-guarded villa on the Black Sea. He not only laid emphasis on new forms of co-operation but waxed eloquent in encouraging me to develop our *Ostpolitik* still further on the assumption that the concept of national unity would gain the upper hand in Germany too. The historical process would, he said, be helped rather than hindered by the recognition of a second German state. Our talks conveyed his strong sense of Rumanian nationhood and his efforts to pursue an independent policy, for which Rumania required partners. He vigorously rejected all that fostered subordination to super-powers, reinforced their influence or augmented the power-potential of the opposing blocs. In the Rumanian view, European security was a long-term problem whose solution had to be approached by way of bilateral talks. Ceauşescu opposed a security conference at the present juncture because it would lead to a hardening of alignments, though such a conference might prove useful later on. He was allergic to anything that might promote renewed subordination.

Ceausescu treated time as imperiously as he instructed his Foreign Minister to provide us with food. Our memorable conversation ended after seven hours. (Also memorable were some brief encounters on the beach at Mamaia, where visitors from the Federal Republic and the GDR had a chance to talk together. Greeted by members of both groups, I thought how absurd it was that relatives from Leipzig and Cologne should have to travel to the Black Sea in order to meet!) Prominent among my fleeting impressions of the country were its relics of the Roman period. At Constanza, history seemed to have prescribed that Rumania should never entirely surrender her inherent links with

Southern and Western Europe. The Latin derivation of the language is so perceptible that I could at least partially follow the meaning of speeches in Rumanian.

My meeting with Premier Ion Gheorghe Maurer was remarkably informal. Maurer had enjoyed Ceauşescu's confidence ever since the latter's persecution in the days of the Iron Guard régime, when he had defended the young politician in the dictatorship's courts. Somewhat liberal by communist standards, Maurer peppered his conversation with anecdotes and personalities. Other guests had been invited to lunch at one o'clock. One-thirty passed, two o'clock came and went, three o'clock drew near. I gave several pointed glances at my watch. Maurer beckoned an aide, whispered some instructions and turned to me. 'I just quoted Napoleon,' he said with a chuckle. 'I gave orders for the lady to undress.' Maurer was also responsible for the following *bon mot*: Which is the most neutral country in the world? Czechoslovakia, because it doesn't even intervene in its own internal affairs.

For all his rather robust humour, Maurer was a competent political advocate. During his return visit to Bonn in 1970 he warned us not to be gulled by the super-powers and, above all, not to neglect our relations with Rumania. The normalization of relations between our two countries was formally confirmed by the state visits of Presidents Heinemann and Ceauşescu to Bucharest and Bonn respectively.

Diplomatic relations with Yugoslavia had been broken off at the end of 1957, when Belgrade recognized the GDR. Our actual relations suffered little damage, certainly where trade and tourism were concerned. A renewed exchange of ambassadors could not fail to be in our best interests, there being no logical reason why we should penalize ourselves while leaving Belgrade in full enjoyment of trade and tourism. Contacts were established in 1967 with the help of a Paris-based Yugoslav journalist whom I had got to know well during my Berlin days. Relations between Bonn and Belgrade were resumed by the year's end.

In June 1968 my wife and I paid an official visit to Yugoslavia. Unlike an earlier, private visit in summer 1955, this was no routine occasion. We realized, I said in Belgrade, 'how much wrong had been done to the peoples of Yugoslavia in the abused name of Germany'. Irrespective of differing social systems and despite our security-policy status, we had a large number of common interests. On major questions of European policy, our aims coincided. Quoting the Yugoslav formula of active coexistence, I said that I was largely in favour of it.

From Belgrade we flew to Pula and made the crossing to Brioni by boat. I admired the spacious grounds, which reminded me of romantic picture-book illustrations of Venetian gardens. Our host maintained a game reserve and a sizeable zoo. His excellent house wine was grown on a neighbouring island. All in all, majestic would have been a pale word to apply to the style of the establishment, its lavish amenities and numerous staff. We were lodged in a guest-house normally used by Party and government representatives (in 1973, during my time as Chancellor, our quarters were a palatial villa reserved for state visitors). Tito's personal appearance matched the environment he had created for himself – in fact many people found him less like a revolutionary leader than a ruler who contrived to personify the old era and the new. This mixture of styles had transmitted itself to his staff, of whom one – a vine-dresser – amiably inquired during a visit by Haile Selassie how 'the Comrade Emperor' was today. Tito's manner towards his aides struck me as direct and open. He treated me in a wholly relaxed and cordial fashion, reminiscing about his days in Germany as a journeyman metal-worker employed by firms such as Daimler-Mannheim. He spoke fluent German, having learnt it partly in Wilhelminian Germany but more particularly in the Austro-Hungarian army, in which he had served as a sergeant until captured by the Russians. He also made occasional forays into English.

The conversational atmosphere was relaxed and cheerful. Tito devoted himself to bilateral and international manners. He apologized for broaching a number of 'ticklish' subjects but said it was good that we had made a fresh start. We must proceed by stages, beginning with economic affairs. He was particularly concerned to increase his exports of agricultural products. According to him, problems with the EEC were imposing a stronger Eastern bias on Yugoslavia's trade relations. The Soviet Union was at present her principal trading partner, and the long-term nature of such agreements invested this trade with a gratifying element of stability. On the other hand, the success of Yugoslav economic reforms was heavily dependent on increased trade with the West. Yugoslavia wanted a trade agreement with the EEC. I affirmed our readiness to help.

Tito raised three subjects which had already been discussed in Belgrade and which recurred in subsequent conversations with him: some measure of compensation for National Socialist acts of violence, Yugoslav migrant workers in the Federal Republic, and the activities of 'fascist elements' in Yugoslav expatriate circles. By these Tito meant the right-wing Croatian Ustaše, who stirred up trouble abroad and had assassinated several Yugoslav diplomats in the Federal Republic. We were endeavouring to keep this problem under control, partly by means of co-operation between the security authorities in both countries.

Yugoslav workers were popular in the Federal Republic. Tito deplored the fact that so many 'specialists' worked for us because they were really needed in their own country. He was naturally aware, however, that remittances from his fellow-countrymen – plus tourism – represented a welcome source of foreign currency. In a later talk, Tito urged a better appreciation of opportunities for industrial co-operation in Yugoslavia itself. We ought to invest in his country rather than employ its migrant workers. Still on this subject, we discussed the terms that might be offered to foreign firms in Yugoslavia. It is true, discounting isolated cases, that we have made things rather too easy for ourselves by indiscriminately applying foreign labour to capital instead of devoting greater thought to how capital and technology can be applied to human resources.

When Tito broached the subject of reparations, I pointed to the legal and political difficulties they raised for us – *inter alia* because of the London Debt Agreement. Nevertheless, it could not be denied that Yugoslavia was owed compensation by West Germany under decisions taken by the victorious powers. I therefore recommended that we work towards an 'indirect solution' beneficial to the Yugoslav economy. Subsequent critics have refused to acknowledge that I had reached prior agreement on this subject with Kiesinger.

At the time, Tito showed little appreciation of my remarks. Yugoslav honour was at stake, he said. The matter must therefore be settled, though not necessarily at once. It was 1973–4 before the question was resolved.

We naturally discussed Czechoslovakia, where Dubček and his associates had embarked on their great and courageous experiment. Tito, who opined that the new régime's main difficulties lay in the economic sphere, seemed quite unaware that intervention was imminent. Although he welcomed my announcement of a NATO initiative in the matter of force reductions, he had always opposed any moves towards détente or disarmament which, being effected through the two blocs, would only reinforce their importance. The non-aligned nations had a right to be heard, and no peace settlement could come into being without their participation. On the subject of non-proliferation, Tito stressed his great concern at the attitude of the Chinese. So far from subscribing to the treaty, they would continue to develop their nuclear weapons. In Vietnam, they would doubtless fight to the last Vietnamese.

No amount of respect for Tito's statesmanlike achievements could win my comprehension or approval of the severity with which he disciplined politicians, many of very senior rank, whose socialist or communist loyalties were beyond doubt. Shortly after I had visited him as Foreign Minister, Nikezić was elected Party leader of Serbia. Following the Croatian example, he took advantage of the scope afforded by Serbian national sentiment to evolve methods which were reviled as liberalism, or rather, 'putrid anarcho-liberalism'. In 1972 he was forced to resign. Mirko Tepavać, the newly appointed Foreign Minister who visited me in Bonn in summer 1969, was relieved of his duties in the same connection. When I 'inquired' after the two men during my 1973 visit, I was told that they had not been expelled from the Party and would keep their membership books. They were nonetheless expelled in 1974. In 1975 I was informed that their living conditions were adequate, and personal messages I sent them were reciprocated. (I had similar experiences in other countries. My opposite number at the Portuguese Foreign Office was Franco Nogueira – the charming reactionary, as I called him. Hearing that he had been arrested when I visited Lisbon in 1974, I was able to help him by interceding with the army on his behalf.)

At the expense of anticipating slightly, I think it appropriate to outline the course of one subsequent meeting with Tito. When I paid him an official visit as Federal Chancellor in April 1973, again on the island of Brioni, the most urgent problem was that of mounting tension in the Middle East. Tito stressed the growing precariousness of the armistice and said that a new war could break out at almost any moment – an impression he had gained from his talks with Sadat. (I shall revert to this ominous part of our conversation when dealing with the Middle East crisis of late autumn 1973.) After this alarming prologue, during which Tito urged me to impress the gravity of the situation on Nixon in particular, our *tour d'horizon* touched on the problems of Asia. Tito feared a growth of confrontation in the Far East. He was extremely worried about Cambodia and said that the Chinese would never consent to its surrender. The Americans were at present bombing the Plaine des Jarres – they would be better advised to drop their bombs in the sea if they had too many. George Kennan (formerly President Kennedy's ambassador in Belgrade) had visited him only the day before and expressed grave concern about the internal condition of his country. The United States would probably refrain from sending more troops to the Far East, but the situation in that part of the world was bleak and had not substantially improved since the Paris peace agreements. The civil war in South Vietnam would continue.

We then turned to Africa, and I drew attention to the role of the oil-producing countries. Events in the area of the Persian Gulf were materially contributing to the instability of the international monetary system. Tito spoke of preparations for a new conference of non-aligned countries in Algiers.

I asked Tito if he regarded Albania, which had totally isolated itself from Eastern Europe and sought to rely on the far-off Chinese, as a non-aligned country. Tito said no, it leaned too heavily on China. 'The Albanians attack us – recently, however, not as much as they did . . . We maintain normal relations with China. China used to attack us fiercely. For a long time it attacked the Soviet Union indirectly via us, then it attacked us direct. Now China is attacking the Soviet Union direct. We have no strongly defined political relations with China.' (Things were different a few years later.) On the other hand, Tito continued, Yugoslavia maintained good relations with the Soviet Union.

For Yugoslavia, the uppermost question was that of security. 'We demand that there be no regional discrimination in Europe. Complete equality for all is the main theme of our attitude towards the Helsinki Conference.' I reported that now we had concluded treaties with the Soviet Union and Poland, the Czech treaty would probably materialize as well. I had actually come quite close to a solution with Brezhnev at our Crimea meeting in 1971, but the legal experts had made the situation more complicated than it really was. I shared Tito's opinion that there must be no regional discrimination in Europe.

Tito replied that we were in broad agreement on problems of security. He felt bound to add that the present negotiations would never have come about if our courageous policy had not resolved points at issue between us and the Soviet Union and Poland. But the said complex of problems relating to security and European co-existence could not be solved at a single conference and would probably have to be dealt with by separate commissions in the future. As to timing, he favoured a gradual approach. An ill-prepared summit meeting would be politically detrimental.

I took the opportunity of presenting petitions from the German PEN Centre on behalf of persecuted Yugoslav writers. They came, I said, from people like Heinrich Böll, who were friends of mine and meant no harm. Tito: 'Their good intentions are relative . . . Our courts have to treat all people alike, whether they're writers or ordinary workers.' I was dissatisfied with this reply. I could not understand why a man like Milovan Djilas (to name only one), who had belonged to the Marshal's intimate circle, was imprisoned for years before at least being allowed to pursue his literary labours. Ever since my days in

Berlin – and I am not now speaking of a particular country or point of the compass – I have made it my business to 'inquire' after the fate of those who have been disciplined and persecuted. This form of intervention, which I consider totally divorced from interference, has proved its worth on numerous occasions. However, the fact that I was *able* to help now and then – though far from invariably, alas – has never consoled me against the depressing necessity of so often *having* to help. No favourable effect can blind one to an adverse cause.

On the question of reparations, Tito said he found it extremely distasteful to raise the subject, but I knew that it was presenting him with problems in his own country. Couldn't we adopt an indirect approach? 'We both have difficulties with this problem,' I replied. 'Half the people in my country were born after the war. For many of them, this is simply past history. Far be it from me to run away from history, but what matters is to guard against setbacks to a policy which is fundamentally acknowledged to be correct. As Federal Chancellor, I have adjusted our relations with our Eastern neighbours. I have accepted the Oder–Neisse frontier. The incorporation of large numbers of people from these areas has brought burdens in its train.' I would not, I said, be justified in accepting a liability amounting to thousands of millions of marks. I also had to bear in mind the possibility of meeting demands from other quarters. On the other hand, I did not wish our communiqué merely to reaffirm the existence of outstanding questions requiring further negotiation. It would be better to issue a guide-line, for instance to the effect that both sides had undertaken to endow their economic co-operation with greater scope and thereby liquidate the liabilities of the past.

Tito wanted to discuss the matter again next day, and his aides were also of the opinion that this item on the agenda should be disposed of. I then proposed a formula which was echoed by the final communiqué: 'Both sides formed the belief that relations have reached a stage at which long-term co-operation in the economic sphere can be substituted for previously proposed solutions to outstanding problems from the past.' This was later christened the Brioni Formula. Our financial advisers had agreed that a credit of DM300 million should be advanced, followed by another of DM700 million, with interest payable as for development aid.

It was a full year before the experts reached a settlement on the above lines. Coupled with a Polish agreement which was still under discussion at the time, this wrote finis to the story of financial compensation – or so I continue to hope. As a rider to this statement, I must emphasize my full awareness that no material effort could ever erase the sufferings and crimes wrought by war and the Nazi dictatorship. I considered our country and nation to be bound by a historic duty and responsibility which could not be shrugged off as the rulers of the other German state were seeking to do. Although the German Federal Republic has done a great deal under the heading of 'compensation', this must not diminish our moral vigilance. To me, the recognition of realities entailed, first and last, sufficient courage to acknowledge our own history and its consequences.

This applied above all to our relations with Poland. No country had suffered more grievously from Hitler's war and the destructive attentions of his totalitarian government, party and military machine. Never had – or have – our relations with any country apart from Israel been as fraught with painful memories and emotional prejudice. This was brought home to me with full force and ferocity in the course of negotiations and discussions preparatory to the signing of the Warsaw treaty, but much water had flowed under the bridge since the years of the Grand Coalition. The dialogue opened tentatively with an exchange of speeches. The soil in which reconciliation could flourish required careful spadework. This necessitated a willingness to live with the forcible, inequitable and morally unjustified territorial corrections of 1945, be it only from a realization that demands for change would create more injustice and threaten the already precarious peace of Europe. Reason dictated that an enforced revision of the historical process whereby millions of Germans had lost their homeland was out of the question, and that there was no hope of achieving it by peaceful means.

It was now beyond doubt that the Poles wanted guaranteed confirmation of their frontiers before they would agree to normalize relations with the German Federal Republic. The backing of their East European neighbours was important to them in this respect, but Western politicians – indeed, our best friends – were also growing more and more insistent, both publicly and in private, on the need for responsible figures in the Federal Republic to take a courageous decision. I will not disguise that, partly out of respect for the feelings of our displaced fellow-countrymen, I clung to my reservations for a long time.

On 1 October 1965 the Public Relations Chamber of the Evangelical Church in Germany (EKD) submitted a memorandum on the frontier question and German–Polish relations which was supported by the EKD Council. This initiated a process of psychological relaxation. In March 1968 a memorandum from German Catholic intellectuals (the

'Bensberg Circle') made urgent reference to our 'liability' and to the growing numbers of Polish citizens who had been born in the territories east of the Oder–Neisse line and could now, in their turn, claim the right to live there.

This exchange between the Churches and their members preceded any dialogue between politicians. One or two talks with Polish journalists bore fruit as well. I also took public note of some remarks by the Polish Foreign Minister, Adam Rapacki, whose plans for détente in Europe and the dissolution of allied blocs had met with opposition in the West and criticism, if not downright suspicion, on the part of the Kremlin. Infinite patience was needed to break down the ingrained prejudices on both sides. In 1956–7, after the Polish 'spring in October' which brought Gomulka to power, the German Federal Republic could probably have established diplomatic relations without any provision in respect of the frontier question. All Bonn then wanted, prior to the Hallstein Doctrine and in fear of its own daring, was a trade mission. During this period, a leading Polish journalist visited me in Berlin. I had not forgotten his remark: 'What do a hundred kilometres matter? What we want to know is something else. How will Germany develop – what sort of Germany will we have to deal with?' I regarded this as confirmation of my own attitude at the end of the war. Although convinced that the old frontiers could not be restored, I also opposed the inordinacy of Russian and Polish ideas. Ernst Reuter reinforced our view that Poland would have to be accommodated.

Even the first programme I had to advocate as a candidate for the Chancellorship in 1961 stated that a future Social Democratic government, though unable to pre-empt a peace treaty, could tread the path of peaceful co-operation with all the peoples of Eastern Europe and, more particularly, with our Polish neighbours. I reverted to the subject in greater detail at the Dortmund party conference in June 1966. Being frank with our people meant an even more explicit admission that a peace settlement, when it came, would demand sacrifices. These sacrifices would be construed by the world as the price, in terms of international law, of the war which Hitler had launched and lost: 'Many people behave as if we possess the areas east of the Oder–Neisse. In this sense, we do not even possess what lies between us and the Oder and Neisse. Many people behave as if friendly countries were committed to us by something more than legal provisos. Some of them, as we all know, are not even committed by those. But I would add something else. There were, and are, good reasons for our carefully considered statements, and I will tell you why: nobody does well to promise more than he can grant.' Admittedly, the going was harder now. From 1965 onwards Warsaw demanded recognition not only of the Oder–Neisse frontier but of the GDR as well, a further sign that time had worked against rather than for us and that the influence of the GDR was growing.

Long before I became Federal Foreign Minister, I was convinced that reconciliation with the Poles carried the same historical importance as Franco-German understanding. A politician must know when the time is ripe. Addressing the SPD's Nuremberg conference on 18 March 1968, I said we knew that even recognition of the Oder–Neisse line would not now result in the establishment of diplomatic relations with Poland. Nobody could be so rash as to contemplate another expulsion when forty per cent of those who lived in the former German territories had been born there. 'The German nation needs reconciliation with Poland even without knowing when it will derive national unity from a peace treaty. What follows from this? What follows is recognition or observance of the Oder–Neisse line pending a settlement by peace treaty.' That was the crucial sentence, and the party conference adopted a resolution to that effect.

Reports of a rumpus inside the coalition flew thick and fast. I was accused of not clearing my statement with the Federal Chancellor in advance – nor had I. I telephoned Kiesinger from Nuremberg, and we talked with asperity. His objections related to tactics rather than substance. First and foremost, he had the Union refugee leaders breathing down his neck. For public consumption, I stated that 'The Chancellor does not determine the guide-lines of the party conference, but this subject has been independently discussed with him.'

In mid-May my Nuremberg pronouncement drew a response from Wladyslaw Gomulka – restrained rather than rapturous, of course, but essentially favourable. For the first time in years the Polish side was showing a readiness to talk. I was greatly heartened to conclude from a spate of reports and correspondence that my words had been correctly interpreted by many Polish citizens.

I could go no further, having exhausted my room for manœuvre within the Grand Coalition. The establishment of relations had to be postponed in the hope of new majorities in the Bundestag. Later, when our *Ostpolitik* got under way, circumstances demanded that the Moscow treaty should take precedence over the Warsaw treaty. I travelled to the Polish capital to sign the latter in December 1970. The normalization of relations continued, as it still does, to be a feat of patience.

Circumstances had favoured the normalization of our relations with Czechoslovakia in 1968. Exploratory soundings suggested that the factitious legal dispute over the Munich Agreement could easily have been disposed of. The Prague crisis, which frustrated this in addition to all else, belongs in another context, likewise the role played by the SED leaders immediately prior to 21 August 1968.

Many of us in the Federal Republic, not to mention our friends outside Germany, were unaware how great an influence the GDR leaders contrived to wield, both inside the Eastern bloc and at its Muscovite seat of power. Theirs had ceased to be a strength born of weakness, as in earlier years. The GDR's status in the Warsaw Pact bloc was no longer that of a partner whose sole claim to Soviet support consisted in its exposed position. Sad to relate, the Berlin Wall had been a consolidating factor. Although approval of the régime remained limited, untested and questionable, people were adjusting themselves to the prospect of its long duration. Nobody dared to hope for any rapid changes. Thanks to hard work and despite inadequate planning, an impressive edifice took shape. Economically, the GDR assumed first place among the allies of the Soviet Union. It also became one of the world's top ten trading nations.

Against this, the SED régime was not exactly popular with its bloc partners. Ulbricht rated as a persistent bore and his aides enjoyed the dubious reputation of being the know-alls of the communist world. German pedantry (Eastern version) reigned supreme. It can truly be said that the German bent for thoroughness received a special imprint in the GDR, becoming more Russian than the Russians (just as many of our compatriots had tried to be more Nazi than the veteran Nazis after 1933 and many West Germans more American than the Americans after 1945). My party's attitude was, and continued to be when the Grand Coalition was formed, that there was no question of formally recognizing the GDR and, thus, the partition of Germany. Having referred at the Dortmund party conference in 1966 to 'settled co-existence' between two German states, but without legal recognition, I began to dismantle some of the quasi-legal impediments. 'Sole representation' I interpreted in accordance with the duty laid upon us by the Basic Law. We did not aspire to wield sovereignty over areas beyond the jurisdiction of the Basic Law. Discounting the fact of partition, non-recognition was likewise to be construed in a way which forbade us to recognize the SED régime as democratically legitimized.

The CDU/CSU found it very hard to throw off the political postures and juridical formulas of past years and adapt itself to the changed situation. This was characterized by an ever more definite acceptance of the GDR as a separate state. There was no power, still less political configuration, which might in the foreseeable future have helped us to restore national unity. The mere parroting of reunification slogans did not inhibit us from making that specific contribution to a settlement with the East which was becoming more and more essential in our own and the general interest.

Addressing the Bundestag in autumn 1967, Kiesinger said: 'We naturally acknowledge that something has taken shape over there – a phenomenon with which I have entered into correspondence.' Although the euphemism 'phenomenon' was not very encouraging, the exchange of letters was a step forward. (In the very early years of the Federal Republic, incidentally, there had been an observance of the sensible rule that letters which were not anonymous should be read and, if possible, answered. Heuss had done this with letters from President Pieck and Reuter with similar communications from Mayor Ebert of East Berlin.)

In April 1967 the Federal Government submitted a series of proposals for the expansion of inter-German contacts in scientific and cultural spheres and for concrete agreements to this end as a move towards détente. Herbert Wehner, the Minister of All-German Affairs, was the Federal Chancellor's principal adviser in this field. On behalf of the SPD, we sent these government proposals to the delegates of the 7th SED Conference with an accompanying text – a final fanfare to the abortive 'exchange of speakers'. On 10 May Stoph wrote to Kiesinger in his capacity as premier, or Chairman of the Council of Ministers, suggesting a meeting. He did not go into the Bonn proposals but wanted to negotiate the establishment of normal relations. Kiesinger replied in June, suggesting in his turn that representatives be nominated to conduct actual negotiations. In September Stoph sent a draft treaty. Shortly afterwards the East Berlin government obtained authorization from the *Volkskammer* [GDR parliament] to appoint a representative. Nothing more happened. East Berlin jibbed. Some people later asserted that we had no intention of concluding a treaty valid under international law. This is incorrect.

Ulbricht's intransigent attitude, as manifested by the rejection of Bonn's offers to talk, was far from popular in some sections of the communist camp. Widely differing views were expressed there, for instance at the Bucharest conference of the Warsaw Pact countries in July 1966. Although there was a noticeable restriction of phraseology to our detriment at the Karlsbad conference of East and West European communist parties in April 1967, the Budapest conference of the Warsaw Pact countries in March 1969 revived the Bucharest approach. The delegates avoided polemics and added a few new notes to the security conference theme. The German communist leaders belonged to the most reactionary wing of the communist bloc, but this did not alter the fact that international recognition of the GDR could not be delayed much longer. Although the Western Powers would have been prepared to respect our wishes for some time to come, the GDR's admission to international organizations could scarcely be prevented. It would have succeeded in joining the World Health Organization as early as 1968 if we had not built up a tactical position which enabled us to parry this move for the time being.

I was compelled to state openly at the Nuremberg party conference in 1968 that the reunification of our country did not figure in the current international agenda. It followed that we must do everything conceivable to regulate the coexistence and co-operation of the two parts of Germany in the interests of people and of peace. I insisted, as I did in my own government policy statement of the following year, that we could not regard the GDR as a foreign country.

I had pointed out at the NATO Council meeting in June 1968 that it was probably no coincidence that Moscow had sanctioned the renewed obstruction of Berlin traffic. The Soviet Union wanted to cement the European *status quo* by adopting a rigid counter-stance. Anyone would understand how depressing we Germans found this anachronistic situation. We could travel to the North Cape, to Sicily or Anatolia, with an identity card alone – not even a passport. We could travel to Belgrade and Tokyo without a visa. But on the way to and from Berlin, from Germany to Germany, we were expected to produce a passport *and* a visa, not to mention the tolls and charges imposed on passenger and goods traffic. This was a blow aimed at the policy of détente by the rulers of East Berlin. They wanted isolation and tension – partly, no doubt, because of developments in the so-called socialist camp. Any final solution of the German problem would be the outcome of a lengthy process. That was why both parts of Germany had to strive for the interim solution afforded by settled and peaceful coexistence. The Federal Government had offered to discuss this with East Berlin, so far without receiving an answer. The Federal Government was prepared to affirm the renunciation-of-force principle in respect of the direct relationship between the two parts of Germany and apply it to the problems arising therefrom.

Our allies fully grasped that this heralded a policy which was prepared to abandon old positions – but only given a Western consensus and the other side's willingness to talk. This was why I deliberately associated the 'German question' with an all-European peace settlement at the NATO meeting at Reykjavik in June 1969. We did not, I said, make our policy of détente dependent on progress in the German question. Lasting peace in Europe presupposed a balanced security system. We knew that the construction of perfect models was of only limited utility. All of us agreed that our first endeavour should be to reach partial East–West agreements which could in themselves constitute an important step towards security in Europe. On the basis of our proposed bilateral renunciation-of-force declarations, we should try to achieve a balanced reduction of forces in East and West. The GDR could not be excluded from such considerations.

I had thus indicated the Federal Government's attitude to the disarmament and security conference questions. The idea of a European security conference was something of a Soviet diplomatic chestnut, having first been mooted for international discussion in 1954. Ten years later the cry was taken up by Adam Rapacki, the Polish Foreign Minister. Although Moscow's attitude was not always unequivocal, neither then nor subsequently, the idea took on clearer outlines at the Party leaders' conferences at Bucharest in 1966 and Budapest in 1969, and prior conditions were eventually dropped. In March 1969 I delivered a favourable response in the Bundestag. Speaking in Washington in April of the same year, I said that the scheme for an all-European conference should be carefully prepared, not left to hang fire on principle. We could not dispense with the participation of the United States and Canada. I received brickbats from the East and a mixed reception in the West when I said that the Federal Republic's presence at a European security conference would serve no purpose unless relations between the two parts of Germany were regularized beforehand. The Federal Republic had a small lever here. I did not overrate its importance, but it existed. My argument was that, if one partner fails to turn up for a wedding, the other gets little out of it. Our allies accepted this attitude. They adopted our demands and later linked them with the conclusion of a quadripartite agreement on Berlin.

It remains for me to record that the European Security Conference was decided upon by the Council of Ministers of the Atlantic Alliance, not by Brandt and Brezhnev at Oreanda. Early in 1975, under the heading of 'Brandt's dangerous activities', Franz Josef Strauss disseminated the myth that in early autumn 1969, unbeknown to the then Federal Chancellor and contrary to his wishes, I authorized a favourable response to the Finnish Government's suggestion that a European security conference be held in Helsinki. In reality, the cautious but not hostile Foreign Office reply was naturally approved by the Chancellor, as press reports stated at the time. Although I saw no point in holding a European security conference before our relations with the GDR were regularized, I was anxious not to abandon the theme of peace to the communists. I wanted the Federal Republic to play a positive and active role, as it did. European security, arms limitation and nuclear non-proliferation were inherently related. All three problems were greeted with mistrust by our partners in the Grand Coalition, especially the right wing. There were signs in all three areas of a stagnation which showed that the government alliance was beginning to flag. It became clear that the three tasks – and the accommodation I was seeking with the countries of Eastern Europe – would have to be shouldered by a future Federal Government.

The 'Reykjavik signal', which I was largely instrumental in drafting, formed paragraph 7 of the declaration annexed to the communiqué issued by the NATO Ministerial Council meeting of 24 and 25 June 1968. It ran as follows:

In particular, Ministers agreed that it was desirable that a process leading to mutual force reductions should be initiated. To that end they decided to make all necessary preparations for discussions on this subject with the Soviet Union and other countries of Eastern Europe, and they call on them to join in this search for progress towards peace.

Preparations for MBFR were initially frustrated by Soviet military intervention in Prague because it appeared to rob the subject of all topical relevance. The debate was resumed in 1971, after Brezhnev's cautiously favourable response to the 'signal' in a speech at Tiflis. Although the Russians rejected NATO's proposal to allow Manlio Brosio, the Italian Secretary-General of the Atlantic Alliance, to study the problem, they eventually sat down to talk in Vienna at about the time the European Security Conference opened in Helsinki. MBFR will probably be numbered among the perennials of the conference world. Patience and perseverance may, however, obtain results by slow degrees.

There was a close inherent connection with the problem of the nuclear non-proliferation treaty. During the plenary session of the United Nations in autumn 1966, representatives of the United States and the Soviet Union had agreed on a basic formula. Secretary of State Dean Rusk handed me the draft of the first article in Paris in December 1966.

The Grand Coalition government's attitude was based on four considerations: first, our own security must be safeguarded; secondly, there must be a guaranteed transition to further progress in arms control; thirdly, the treaty must have no adverse effects on European unification; and, fourthly, we wanted an assurance of non-discrimination in regard to the peaceful use of nuclear energy. I additionally summarized my own arguments under three headings: first, I did not want national access to nuclear weapons, and the bulk of my fellow-countrymen agreed that we had no need of them; secondly, Europe must not be defenceless in the face of a continuing threat; and, thirdly, we must have a say in matters that affected, or might affect, our interests.

If these principles remained inviolate, the non-proliferation treaty could only benefit, not harm us. This was the attitude underlying my September 1968 speech at the conference of 'nuclear have-nots' in Geneva's Palais des Nations.

I said that the countries which did not possess nuclear weapons wanted to know how they could achieve greater security. Without faith in certain basic rules of international coexistence, there could be no control over the destructive forces latent in nuclear energy. Signatures were worth nothing unless they reposed on a minimum of good faith. Those who possessed power, especially nuclear power, did not necessarily have morality or wisdom on their side. The greatest dangers to mankind stemmed from great powers, not small. (I am bound to add, at this distance in time, that small countries have a tendency to nudge super-powers into confrontations.) 'There must also be a definition of the obligations to which the nuclear-armed powers should submit.'

I naturally referred to the shock caused by the Prague tragedy, which was perceptible in the big conference hall itself but more particularly in the corridors outside and in numerous private conversations. Everyone knew, I said, that threats of force and the fear of force were not abstract questions. Everyone knew that nations feared for their independence and that there was deep concern over the future of mankind. Those norms of international coexistence which seemed to have grown up in the years following World War II, though not without relapses, were once more in the balance: sovereignty, territorial integrity, non-violence, national self-determination, human rights. Every nation must be able to tread its own path, however, 'for only then will countries join in best serving humanity, which still has so many and such great unsolved problems'.

Security guarantees, disarmament and prospects for the peaceful use of nuclear energy could not be discussed with any hope of success unless a common resolve and joint proposals adjusted the criteria governing the system of which the community of nations stood in such urgent need. To confine the renunciation of force selectively to certain countries was therefore unwarrantable. Referring to ourselves, I added:

'We concede the right of intervention to no one!' Forty-two years ago, I reminded the delegates, Gustav Stresemann had led Germany into the League of Nations on this very spot. By alluding to his speech of the time, I brought home the frightful price that the nations of Europe had had to pay because his and Briand's warnings had been ignored. We had learnt from the past. I could assert that the Federal Republic was pursuing a policy designed to substitute a European peace settlement for the balance of terror – there was no reasonable alternative. We should not respond, even to shows of strength by others, in such a way as to increase tension still further.

Our dialogue with the Soviet Union had ground to a halt in 1967 and was still making no headway. Then, at the end of June 1968, Gromyko announced before the Supreme Soviet that the Soviet Union was prepared to resume an exchange of views with us. A week later Ambassador Tsarapkin (who called on me several times during 1968) delivered a contentious aide-mémoire which referred – to crown everything – to the obsolete 'enemy state articles' of the UN Charter. The Russians published the text of their communication, so we had to deliver a counterblast. Presumably, Moscow's attitude was at this time dominated by the mounting crisis over Czechoslovakia.

The immediate item on my time-table for autumn 1968 was a meeting with the NATO Foreign Ministers, notably those of our American, British and French partners, during the UN's October session in New York. My friend Otto Leichter, who represented the German Press Agency at the UN, arranged a meeting on 8 October between myself and the Soviet Foreign Minister, Andrei Gromyko. Also present were his deputy, the veteran German expert Vladimir S. Semyonov, Egon Bahr, and one official from each side.

I found Andrei Gromyko very much more affable than the picture one had formed of the acid 'Mr Nyet' over the years. He was friendly, relaxed, composed – almost Anglo-Saxon in his reserve. His political know-how, acquired as the 'senior' Foreign Minister and perhaps the most experienced diplomat on the international scene, was perceptible in an unobtrusive way. His memory was reputed to be phenomenal. His disciplined self-assurance also conveyed, no doubt, that he had climbed a long way up the Kremlin ladder.

Andrei A. Gromyko was nearly sixty when we first met and had occupied senior diplomatic posts for 30 years. Head of the North America Section of the Soviet Foreign Ministry in 1939, he was posted to the Soviet Embassy in Washington in the same year and took over as ambassador in 1943. In 1946 he was appointed permanent Soviet representative at the United Nations (where his intransigence gave rise to the catch-phrase 'veni, vidi, veto'). He returned to the Foreign Ministry in 1948, became First Deputy Minister in 1949, held the London ambassadorship in 1952–3, resumed the post of First Deputy Minister, and has been Soviet Foreign Minister ever since 1957. Gromyko has survived every vicissitude from Stalin's day to Brezhnev's and risen from executive to decision-making status in the field of Soviet foreign policy. Full membership of the Politburo has finally confirmed his place in the Soviet empire's inner circle of leaders.

What mainly characterizes the career of this man, who was born in a White Russian village, trained as an agrarian economist and lectured in economics before World War II, is his sheer durability rather than his personal advancement itself. People found it easy to believe the Soviet diplomats who described him as a hard, self-disciplined worker, and his staying-power was obvious to all who had regular dealings with him. He never tired, whenever he thought it expedient, of repeating the same thing over and over again in his deep bass voice. Interested observers could not make up their minds whether he derived his strength from a conservative faith in communism or a belief that nothing could halt Russia's transformation from a world power into a super-power. For all the obstinacy he displayed as a negotiator, he also possessed an ability to listen and, if need be, take account of altered circumstances.

Under Khrushchev, Gromyko helped first to foment the Berlin crisis of the late 1950s and then to defuse it as unobtrusively as possible. The same applied, at a somewhat higher level, to the Cuban crisis of 1962. In the Middle East he saw Soviet influence over the Arab states begin to waver but simultaneously contrived to build up a substantial measure of power in the region. I would surmise that Henry Kissinger came to respect him as a doughty opponent, not only in this field but in East–West negotiations proper, especially those concerned with the limitation of strategic weapons. This certainly went for Egon Bahr, who was present at our first meeting in New York and negotiated the German–Soviet treaty with him in Moscow in 1970. Gromyko was not wholly inflexible, but the Berlin question filled him with a mistrust that was to cause much needless aggravation in years to come.

I opened our New York discussion in October 1968 by stating that there were many problems outstanding between our two countries which recent developments had done nothing to diminish. I hoped the Soviet Government had grasped that the Federal Government was trying to improve bilateral relations. Gromyko's speech to the General Assembly on 3 October had raised a question: in which areas did

Moscow now mean to improve co-operation? I set out our attitude to the renunciation of force, referring to our note of 9 April 1968. Although written and verbal pronouncements from Soviet sources disclosed an intention to pursue our exchange of ideas, this would be meaningful only if there were a growing readiness to understand the other side's position. In contrast to other Soviet pronouncements, I had detected positive endeavours of this nature on the part of Ambassador Abrassimov. To us, renunciation of force meant that no changes in the *status quo* should be made without the consent of the peoples and governments affected. This was in the interests of a European security system and European co-operation.

Gromyko emphasized that bilateral questions were closely linked with questions of security. Several groups of related problems affecting allies of the Soviet Union had therefore to be dealt with. His government cherished a desire for better relations but was doubtful if the Federal Government shared it. The Soviet Government had inquired into the criteria governing German policy towards the USSR. Statements made by us from time to time did not accord with the sum of measures taken in Europe and elsewhere by the Federal Government. He was bound to say, regretfully, that the Federal Government's political practice should be regarded as the sole criterion. The Soviet people did not look upon the West German population as an eternal foe, but there were enduring memories of what Germans had done to the people of the Soviet Union during World War II. Radical change, for which the Soviet Union was prepared, demanded that the Federal Republic should actually embark on a policy aimed at détente and the solution of European problems.

Particularizing, the Soviet Foreign Minister said: 'The question of the frontiers that came into being after World War II is the question of war and peace.' Frontier problems could not be divorced from those of bilateral relations and European security. The Federal Government did not actually recognize the above frontiers. Doubts about West German policy were not, therefore, confined to the Soviet Union and its allies. Our 'notoriously hostile attitude' towards the GDR took no account of the actual existence of another German state, and this was bound to produce increased tension. Federal German claims to West Berlin would continue to provoke disputes or crises. The Soviet Government would permit no change in the status of Berlin. Gromyko did not understand the German attitude to the Munich Agreement. The Soviet Government did not hold us responsible for that agreement, but governmental continuity existed.

On the renunciation of force, Gromyko said that this 'unfinished business' must be pursued further. His government was prepared to intensify negotiations, but their success would depend on our side's acceptance of a connection with the European security problems to which he had referred. Existing German proposals left these problems out and were a shell devoid of material content.

I denied that we had a smaller interest in improving relations. However much I sympathized with those who remembered times not long past, I must draw attention to the younger generation in Germany. They had no wish to be burdened with their fathers' mistakes, and the Soviet Union would be well advised to recognize this fact. For the rest, we entertained no hostility towards the GDR, as the Federal Government's series of practical proposals had demonstrated. It was my impression that the Soviet Government had performed a fundamental *volte-face* in its policy towards Germany since proposing a peace treaty in 1959. The possibility of coexistence by all Germans had then been left open. I was not now speaking of reunification, but no solution of major political problems was feasible unless it granted the Germans some prospect of coexistence and normalization.

I rejected the charge that the Federal Government was putting forward unjustified claims to Berlin. We did not want to change its status either. However, the city's viability depended on its links with the Federal Republic. Account must be taken of this as of many other realities, distasteful or not. The city of Berlin would be able to play a different role if relations between the Federal Republic and the GDR improved. Turning to the Munich Agreement, I said that the Federal Government had been hoping a few months earlier to reach a solution with the government of the CSSR and clear up some thorny legal problems (the nationality and property of Sudeten Germans). Where renunciation of force was concerned, we were at the outset of a debate which thoroughly deserved to be invested with substance, though this presupposed genuine negotiations and not a mere acceptance of Soviet views. On the subject of the non-proliferation treaty: by invoking the so-called enemy state articles of the UN Charter when the problem of admission was being discussed, the Soviet Union had given the impression that it claimed the right to intervene in the internal affairs of the Federal Republic. That had not been helpful.

Gromyko only had time to take up my concluding points. Where the articles of the UN Charter were concerned, he said, it would be better to proceed to questions with a closer bearing on reality. The fuss over these articles was unjustified. On the renunciation of force, he hoped that the shell of the German proposals could be invested with content. The Soviet Government would await our suggestions. Talks on this subject should be continued. Finally, Gromyko and I agreed that our conversation could be described as 'good and useful'.

In 1969 the German–Soviet climate seemed to improve. In February Tsarapkin visited me and was conciliatory on the subject of the enemy state articles. In March (shortly after the Federal Assembly) he called on me to deliver a lengthy account of the incidents on the Ussuri. I also received confidential reports that Moscow was extremely worried about relations with China and could be expected to adopt a less hostile attitude towards us. In May, after the Warsaw Pact countries had met at Budapest, Tsarapkin paid me yet another visit. He was obviously concerned to present the conference in the friendliest possible light. On the frontier question, reference had been made to 'major conditions for the guaranteeing of European security'. The ambassador stressed that the security conference itself was subject to no preconditions. I grasped this important shade of meaning. It was possible that the Moscow authorities had read an article by me in the April 1969 issue of *Foreign Affairs*. In this I had stated that, although everything was open to discussion, we were not prepared to accept any preconditions for negotiations. Tsarapkin said that the subjects raised in Budapest were not preconditions but topics for diplomatic debate. Armed with this key, we were able to open the connecting-door to the subject of Berlin. During his German visit early in 1969, we had persuaded President Nixon that he ought to give a sign. This he did in a constructively worded speech at the Siemens works in Berlin. On 10 June Gromyko reacted in the Supreme Soviet: West Berlin could be discussed with the Western Powers if the latter so desired. Western memoranda on the subject were delivered in Moscow at the beginning of August.

The not over-restful summer of 1969 was followed by an exceptionally strenuous autumn. I had another Bundestag election campaign to conduct and a series of meetings with fellow social democrats. On 22 September 1969 I met the Soviet Foreign Minister for a second time in New York. We could both point to progress and tokens of goodwill. My one-hour talk with Gromyko was again arranged by Otto Leichter and took place, as before, at the Soviet Mission to the United Nations. Gromyko brought along Ambassador Falin of the Soviet Foreign Ministry, whom I was soon to know better. I was accompanied by State Secretary Duckwitz, our UN Ambassador Egon Bahr, and the latter's deputy. Gromyko opened by asking: 'How are things going in Europe, in the direction of war or somewhere else?' Where Germany was concerned, I replied, the path would be one of peace. The marks Gromyko had awarded us in his otherwise very interesting speech during the general debate were surely not good enough.

Gromyko retorted that the marks he had given us were not as bad as all that; both sides should learn to exploit the openings that presented themselves. I welcomed the fact that his remarks were directed at both sides. A few minor advances had been made since our previous year's conversation in New York, even if there had been little movement on major and fundamental points. This brought us straight back to the renunciation-of-force issue. I confirmed receipt of the latest Soviet note and regretted that our reply to the paper delivered by Abrassimov in mid-January had not followed until early in July. I appreciated the fact that this delay had not resulted in a polemic from the Soviet side. The Soviet proposal now to hand, namely, that negotiations on the renunciation of force should take place in Moscow, would have to be formally answered by the post-election Federal Government. I had no doubt that the new government would concur; at all events, that would be my own recommendation. Although fundamental problems still remained unsolved, it was advisable to embark on serious discussions.

Gromyko replied that election campaigns often revealed sore points, but 'certain circles' were well aware that Soviet foreign policy reposed on definite principles of a fundamental nature. These entailed that the Soviet Union was interested in improving bilateral relations with the German Federal Republic, but only on the assumption – which many overlooked – that its policy developed a more realistic shape. 'If the Federal Government is sensible, success will follow. We await your communication.' I replied: 'We have gathered that the Soviet Union is in favour of practical measures.' Signs of this were already apparent. Trade was shaping well, talks were in progress on the purchase of natural gas, a Soviet proposal to exchange technological know-how had aroused our interest, and fresh negotiations on air traffic would be held before long.

Gromyko then asked why the Federal Republic was not adopting a 'constructive' attitude towards the scheme for a European security conference. Nobody was against the development of better relations between us and the GDR, but the differing views on this subject were well known. Was I seeking to make a conference conditional on a change of policy by the GDR? That would be unsound. On the contrary, a conference might actively promote better relations between the two German states. I made it clear that we neither wanted nor imposed any preconditions. 'All we say is that the elimination of difficulties on German soil – travel restrictions, for example – would facilitate the holding of a conference.' Gromyko replied that, notwithstanding the importance of relations between us and the GDR, the conference faced other problems, for instance those of security. It should not be asked whether security came before disarmament or disarmament before security, or 90 per cent of existing agreements would never have been concluded. It was interesting in this respect that I posed no preconditions for the conference, 'which everyone needs'.

On the subject of non-proliferation, Gromyko referred to the dialogue which our parliamentary chairman, Helmut Schmidt, had recently conducted in Moscow. What was the prevailing climate of opinion in West Germany? I replied that the treaty had played no role in the early stages of the election campaign. It was to be assumed that the new Federal Government would reach a decision with comparative speed, though clarification might be required on a few points which had less immediate connection with the text of the treaty than with the setting in which it was placed. I had, I said, been gratified to learn from Helmut Schmidt that the Soviet Union was prepared to discuss such matters.

Gromyko replied that, in so far as I was referring to alleged obstacles to the peaceful use of nuclear energy, he could categorically state that the Soviet Union would create no such impediments. I said I appreciated this, but there were other problems associated with the inspection to which non-nuclear countries were to be unilaterally subject at their own expense. Gromyko said that the importance of inspection should not be exaggerated. These questions could be settled in Vienna (head-quarters of the international supervisory authority). For the rest, his general comment on disarmament problems was that every proposal by the Soviet Union was regrettably and almost automatically greeted with disfavour by Bonn before being checked for ulterior motives.

I observed that the dissipation of mutual mistrust was a laborious process. We ourselves had formed the impression that we were not always correctly understood in Soviet quarters. NATO's proposal for a balanced reduction of forces in Europe was mainly attributable to German efforts. This proposal had unfortunately come to grief 'because of other developments' (an allusion to the crisis in Czechoslovakia), but the Federal Government had made further suggestions. Only a few days ago, for example, it had proposed total disarmament in the B- and C-weapon categories. German mistrust was an indisputable fact. I recommended that our proposals should not be left to wither, even if we were only a small country compared to the Soviet Union.

Gromyko drew attention to the proposals which he had recently advanced in the UN General Assembly. Even though the Federal

Republic was not a member of the United Nations, its co-operation could be useful. The Soviet Union had made proposals addressed to 'all countries'. I said we would revert to them. In conclusion, the Soviet Foreign Minister remarked that personal exchanges were always better than written, but all forms of contact must be utilized.

From some aspects, this conversation provided a bridge to those areas of *Ostpolitik* which were to open up during my early years as Chancellor.

9

1968

In West and East alike, the year 1968 brought upheavals whose effects were long-lasting even though the traces of change seemed to vanish swiftly and the established orders to reassert their authority with remarkable ease.

The 'Prague spring' was a dramatic efflorescence of hopes which were, in terms of superficial logic, doomed to failure from the outset. I dispute that this is really so. I am certain that the yearning for freedom continues to exert an influence on the state socialism of Eastern Europe, as on Western communist parties, in the form of changes which could never be entirely reversed and are still operative in visible or latent realities even as I commit these thoughts to paper. Hardly less interesting are its repercussions in social democratic and liberal quarters.

The youthful storm in the West, whose high-water mark was the May 1968 movement in France, has not simply ebbed and been forgotten either. It introduced our societies to a process of manifold change which penetrated the most varied domains and even left its mark on conservative schools of thought.

Internal unrest and active rebellion developed independently in East and West. Although they followed courses which had little in common, they were not unrelated. One could, in fact, call them emotionally and spiritually synchronized. It was not immaterial to the dissidents of Eastern Europe and Czechoslovakia in particular that, even before 1968, young people in the West were fiercely protesting in a way which the silent majorities and minorities on the other side of the 'Curtain' could not but regard as confirmation (and sometimes as an abuse) of freedom. For rebellious youngsters at universities and schools in West European countries, related dreams and objectives became crystallized in the 'socialism with a human face' which gave promise of fulfilment in Prague. Nearly all the groups whose routes converged into a 'movement' felt in some way committed to socialism, and they wanted an expansion of freedom, not its extinction. They sensed a need to seek the freedom of the many in new and more equitable systems.

These challenges and their shock-effects disrupted the political routine of various countries in a way which was sometimes repellent but often salutary. They intensified the emotional and intellectual participation of young people in public debate. I was sometimes appalled by the quasi-religious fervour which proliferated in the guise of infinite reason, but the impulses towards liberty and justice stirred me and revived memories of my own early endeavours. At the same time, I had long grown out of the unrealistic romanticism which so readily degenerates into dogmatism and hypocrisy. In my experience, an intense desire for change does not fare badly when tempered with a dash of scepticism.

No comprehensive account or penetrating analysis of the protest movement and the 'revolutionary' year 1968 has yet been produced. What is certain, however, is that – except for a few days in Paris – the working class remained almost universally aloof from disturbances and essays in revolt. Indeed, they quite often greeted them with hostility. Nowhere did the leaders and agitators of the protest movements manage to infiltrate the 'masses' for any length of time, far less carry them along. Students and schoolchildren had the stage to themselves. Their spokesmen and protagonists came largely from the middle class, and it was not uncommon for revolutionary activities to be subsidized by parental affluence. This was not necessarily a suspect phenomenon, nor do we have to look far to find historical precedents for it. It is nonetheless clear that the very gulf between young student activists and the working classes (not only the working class in the old sense) led to an arrogant intensification of extremist attitudes on the part of the spurned suitors: if the 'masses' failed to realize where their duty and earthly bliss lay, they had to be coerced into that realization by a 'revolutionary change of circumstances'. In a minority of cases, Leninist élitism and anarchist propaganda actively commingled. In a few others, protest was transmuted into terrorism.

It was hypothesized at the time that advocacy of socialist and radical reformist ideas had passed from the workers to the intellectuals, a subject on which much has since been written. There is, however, a widespread failure to recognize that no country in the world can point to a socialist movement which has *not* been decisively influenced by 'intellectuals'. It is equally true that the old pattern of working class and 'new middle class' does less than justice to the continuing socio-logical and technological transformation of society. The students tended to overestimate their specific role and may well do so again. One certainly cannot underestimate the growing – and quantitative – importance of the scientific and technical, administrative, educative and artistic professions. My own belief is that movements dedicated to social and democratic progress must continue to be rooted in the broad working masses, but that professional groups with an 'intellectual' background will play a part which the pioneers of the old labour movement could never have foreseen.

Where the protest movement was concerned, America held yet another long lead over Western Europe. The 'free speech' movement which originated in the late 1950s at Berkeley, California, was an early reaction to the university overcrowding that conflicted, both formally and inherently, with the ossified structures of the teaching system and the academic bureaucracy. The students saw their universities as mirrors reflecting the problems of society. The deep-seated disorders and senseless built-in obsolescence of life in our technicized world were indeed a summons to ponder whether 'everything' should be 'different': whether the dictates of industrial labour should be changed, whether society was really doomed to an inequitable distribution of opportunities and worldly goods. Smallish groups underwent a rapid transition from cultural radicalism to socio-political extremism. In the course of this transformation, pre-eminent importance attached to a growing sense of responsibility for what was happening abroad and particularly in the 'Third' or underprivileged world. The increasing poverty there was felt to be a sharp indictment of the social, political and moral structure of the West. The heroes of the poor nations' struggle for the right to exist became symbols which appealed not only to the intellect but also to sentiments not far removed from romantic emotionalism.

Nowhere did the 'system' put itself more terribly in the wrong, in the eyes of young people, than Vietnam. Intervention in South-East Asia seemed to imply that the United States, once a refuge for the poor, oppressed and hopeless, was setting out on a road that would lead, via its own idea of a democratic world mission and concrete great-power interests, to a repetition of all the original sins of imperialism. Had Europe been less deeply permeated by American influence, the American Vietnam protest movement might not have transmitted itself to Germany, France and Italy with such explosive fervour. This was not merely a result of the US military presence on European soil. Our partial 'Americanization' forbade the misfortunes of our most powerful partner to be greeted with indifference.

Protest at our German universities was summoned forth by problems

similar to the ones that precipitated the American free speech movement at Berkeley. Those receiving a university education in the Federal
Republic had far more than doubled in number since 1950. The same
went for England. In Italy and France the number had quadrupled,
and the situation in Japan was no different. Although conditions of
study had drastically altered everywhere, both outwardly and intellectually, university structures remained exempt from change for far too
long. The opportune moment for reform had been missed. Berlin was
the only place where it seemed that the system's incrustations might be
dissolved by its own discernment. I greatly regretted it when the Free
University, which largely owed its existence to American aid, failed
utterly in its initial attempts at peaceful change – not that this was an
argument against reform. Apart from its many youthful idealists, the
Free University attracted eccentric groups inspired by dreams of
revolution. These fostered a mood of permanent protest and feverish
activism. In addition to a fairly peaceable 'subculture' (or counter-
culture), militant sects took shape and swiftly transmitted their influence
to West German universities. Unrest first came to a head in June 1967,
when a student was shot by a policeman during a demonstration against
the Shah's visit to Berlin. At Easter 1968 the student leader Rudi
Dutschke was gravely wounded by a would-be assassin. These incidents had a crucial effect on the course of developments.

Dutschke gave my eldest son Peter his first interview (for a school
newspaper). Peter, who had joined a socialist youth group at the age of
fourteen, subsequently established links with organizations of a more
radical nature. For him and his younger brother, Lars, 'Vietnam'
became a fundamental element of criticism. Peter was arrested during
the Easter disturbances of 1968 and fined for a demonstration offence.
His younger brother had little taste for the activities of sectarian
groups, preferring to follow the critical impulses of cultural radicalism.
It was important to me to be confronted by the ideas and emotions of
the younger generation inside my own family circle. Although we
should have discussed matters more often and more fully, I do not think
I ever became insensitive to the questions and problems or the world of
ideas and emotions that preoccupied my sons, their friends and contemporaries. March 1968 was to bring me an experience of a different
kind.

At the start of the SPD conference at Nuremberg, groups drawn
from the extraparliamentary opposition (plus the hooligans who never
let such an opportunity slip) formed a human barrier outside the
Meistersingerhalle in an attempt to bar our path. I and Herbert Wehner
were subjected to some rough handling. I was unperturbed by these

scenes. My reaction was one of anger mingled with a quest for understanding, and I made it abundantly clear what I thought of physical violence. Almost overnight and unperceived by many, I said, a species of new International had come into being. Until recently we had been worrying about youthful indifference and career-mindedness. If young people were now aiming at a target that transcended the bounds of reason, we must do something more imaginative than invoke the authority of the state. All the signs were that this crisis did not derive from any external hazard or any acute threat to the country's economic existence. It was something still impalpable and imponderable.

That which was sometimes regarded as a troublesome disorder, having now become widely perceptible, was often, in reality, more of a reaction to the disorder in our society. That which had for so long been called order was felt to be humanly inappropriate and accused of being the true disorder. It could be said that youthful critics very often posed the right questions. That was something in itself, even if the right answers were seldom forthcoming (a fact for which theoretical grounds were adduced).

Twice during the second half of 1968 I claimed the attention of international gatherings in an attempt to encourage reasonable responses to the rebellion of the young. Young people did not understand, I said in my speech at the Geneva conference of non-nuclear countries, why we, their elders, failed to deal with the problems of our science-dominated age – why we reconciled ourselves to the lamentable state of our international system. Our impotence was becoming the trauma of the younger generation. I reverted to this subject in Paris at the autumn session of the UNESCO General Conference. Young people did not, I said, measure the present by the past – in other words, see our present situation as the product of a murderous world war – but by what it could be. They were also in revolt against alienating and soul-destroying phenomena. Latent in many noisy protests was the question 'Freedom for what?' I went on: 'Has it not been forcibly impressed upon us that material betterment and technical perfection represent no ultimate goal? Is it not clear that political decision-making processes are becoming more and more obscure and, consequently, less intelligible? Are we not confronted by the fear that man could be planned amiss, that he could become degraded into a manipulable robot?'

Nowhere was the radical theme as keenly formulated as in France, and nowhere was the student movement more aggressive than in Paris, where academic disorganization was particularly far advanced. Quite apart from this, France had barely recovered from her own colonial disaster, the war in Algeria. The taut authority of the Gaullist régime was a positive incitement to opposition and rebellion. The young were not prepared to bow to rulers for whom, to put it mildly, the demands of the state consistently took precedence over those of democracy.

May in Paris began with a 'happening' on a grand scale. The authorities were compelled to ban a lecture at Nanterre (part of the Sorbonne) on the grounds that it was pornographic. The students responded with protests and demonstrations. Instead of quenching the flames, tough police intervention rapidly bred the solidarity needed to transform a spark of defiance into an extensive conflagration. Rebellion spread to the residential area on the Left Bank and barricades were erected in the Latin Quarter.

Although I was in Provence at this time, my visit remained peculiarly untouched by events. On 10 May I had spoken at Mainz on the 90th anniversary of Gustav Stresemann's birth. Afterwards we drove to Besançon, where we spent the night. Edgar Faure, one of the most distinguished politicians of the Third and Fourth Republics, happened to be there on a visit to his constituency. Learning of my presence, he asked me to breakfast with him next morning. As far as I recall, our talk contained not a single presentiment of the dramatic days to come. That evening I was due in Dijon to receive a traditional Burgundian honour: membership of the 'Confrérie des Chevaliers du Tastevin', or grand order of viticulturalists. My colleague Couve de Murville, who had also travelled to Dijon, enlivened the ceremony with a good-humoured and exhilarating speech. Some French friends told me they had never seen him so cheerful and relaxed. Did he, too, have no inkling of what lay in store for Paris?

The same day, Premier Pompidou hurried back from a state visit to Afghanistan, little suspecting that the events of the coming weeks would cost him his job and that Couve would become his successor. The university had been reopened, but operational bases were set up in the Sorbonne and at the Odéon. Workers launched their first sympathy strikes. Withdrawals of labour spread, and it looked as if the student rebels would succeed in carrying the workers with them. Millions demonstrated with sit-in strikes and demanded wage increases against the wishes of the communist-led (and largest) trade union, the CGT. Memories of the 1936 general strike revived and talk of a new Popular Front was rife. Observers later referred, not without reason, to the 'almost-revolution'. It was a situation in which anything seemed possible.

President de Gaulle cut short his state visit to Rumania on 19 May. Students now controlled the Latin Quarter and chaos was spreading throughout Paris. There is no doubt that de Gaulle made his mysterious flight to General Massu in Baden-Baden to satisfy himself of the army's loyalty in case it became necessary to combat the insurrection with extreme force. It was communists who saved the régime, however, not soldiers. The CGT rejected all links with the rebellious students and disclaimed any intention of toppling the government. The French Communist Party declared that no revolutionary situation existed. Then came the announcement of fresh elections. The President-General banished Pompidou to the wilderness from which he so triumphantly returned a year later, and Couve de Murville became premier. The student movement dissolved, but illusory hopes were not all that died with its passing: what had manifested itself during these weeks was an impetus of which our society stood in urgent need. The activists congregated into groups, cliques, sects and miniature parties which provided a breeding-ground for squabbles as well as utopias. One of the most able of the young demagogues, who had probably been the driving-force behind the revolt at Nanterre, was Daniel Cohn-Bendit, with whom I had a few distant encounters in the Federal Republic.

In autumn 1968 Cohn-Bendit led the riotous demonstrations at the Frankfurt Book Fair against Leopold Senghor, the President of Senegal, who was awarded the German Book Trade's Peace Prize as a poet of 'négritude' and politician of consequence. The scenes I witnessed outside the Church of St Paul were degrading and demeaning to our helpless police force. The demonstrators also succeeded in barring access to the *Frankfurter Hof*, the hotel where a banquet was to be given in our guest's honour. The motorcade in which I, Senghor and the premier of Hesse were travelling was diverted to the outskirts of the city. After debating the problem, we resolved to make another attempt to reach the hotel. The police forced a passage for us, but it rained cobblestones. My after-dinner speech turned into an angry summation. I later told the Bundestag that I had no wish to be Foreign Minister of the German Federal Republic if our country's hospitality could no longer be guaranteed. 'I have seen *one* German republic come to grief. We will not and shall not repeat that experience. We know where intolerance, hatred and violence lead . . .'

I last heard of Cohn-Bendit in September 1975, when he and a few hundred young people were organizing a demonstration against a meeting of Frankfurt Social Democrats at which I appeared with Mario Soares, the leader of the Portuguese Socialists. The movement that had once flared into such potent life had dwindled to a wretched handful of purblind fanatics.

It turned out, in practice, that the self-appointed extremist avant-garde of the student movement was all on its own, both in Germany and elsewhere. Its vigour would never have sufficed to carry the mass of students along, either in the Federal Republic or in France, had not the oppressive state of society supplied it with topics which gained an increasing hold on the minds of wide sections of the younger generation. Nothing else can account for the simultaneity of the disturbances (despite their secondary ignition by the media). In Rome, unrest had been emanating from the university since spring 1966 (and was viewed with detachment, there too, by the national communist party); in spring 1968 the Italian capital rang with calls for the 'overthrow of capitalism'. In Madrid and other Spanish cities, demonstrations had grown in frequency and violence – and with reason – since 1965; May 1968 brought clashes between students and police. The old unrest in the Basque region and Catalonia intensified. Although motives for rebellion against an authoritarian but far from powerful régime were not far to seek in Spain, it was not altogether self-evident that serious signs of protest should declare themselves even in Sweden, that most socially equitable of democracies: in Stockholm, students tried to force their way into the parliament building.

The problems of the young Scandinavians were not, one suspects, too far removed from those of their German contemporaries. In both countries, fundamental criticism was levelled at the long unmodified conventions governing assessment of social and international conditions. In both countries, too, reasonable expectations often turned into pipe-dreams and sane hopes into a utopian craving for salvation. There was a widespread refusal to acknowledge that social and political tensions cannot be dispelled with a wave of the wand. In so far as these young people would accept a commitment to one of the parties of the Federal German 'system', their interest centred mainly on the Social Democrats. It hit them all the harder that this very party should have entered into a coalition with a conservative bloc and subscribed to compromises which they found hard to understand. My friends and I were determined to integrate these youthful forces into our society, our state and party. Total success eluded us, it is true, but we did persuade the majority to co-operate. Although we did so at the expense of introducing a not always salutary turbulence into the SPD, one should try to picture what would have become of the German Federal Republic if we had failed to make the experiment. We should certainly have experienced a tension capable of plunging us into a constitutional crisis. The fact that this integrative process could not be fulfilled inside the Grand Coalition, and that it might have promoted an extraparliamentary alignment among the young activists, was very clear to me when I decided in favour of a coalition with the Free Democrats on election night in November 1969.

If I tried to bestow sympathetic attention on the young, it by no means implied that I would unresistingly have yielded to exorbitant demands. We sought to display our own kind of authority by speaking out in favour of reason. I was also at pains to draw clear distinctions by not speaking of *the* students or merely of *the* left-wing students when referring to extremist minorities. The better to track down the reality of the younger generation, its expectations, dreams, criticisms and categories of thought, I arranged an SPD congress at Bad Godesberg in January 1969 under the title 'The Younger Generation and the Future of Democracy'. The gathering suffered from internal disruption. I did not consider it a success, but it did give me a chance to reflect publicly on the questions that faced us:

Young people expect forward thinking instead of tactical manœuvres, moral courage instead of opportunism, a bold acceptance of the arduous instead of appeals to convenience. Political power and its manipulation must be transparent. Political authority must always be rationally justified afresh. Political commitment does not exhaust itself in great and thrilling alternatives.

I spoke of the unsolved problems that were accumulating – world hunger, for example. I also questioned whether the traditional organization of parliamentary democracy could cope with the political tasks of the future; whether the instrumentation now available to politics was sufficient to control the process that would decisively help to fashion our society in the coming decade. On the other hand:

Nobody whose path through life has been hard, like mine, can dwell on the future alone; he must also look back on the terrible experiences he has undergone. He must speak of them, not to impose something on you but to introduce something into our debate which it is not proper to forget. Experience has taught me this: you cannot drop out. You cannot drop out of history; you cannot drop out of your environment; you cannot disown your family, your education or the tradition in which you have grown up, neither in good times nor bad. In 1930 and 1931, as a sixteen- and seventeen-year-old, I chanted: *Republik, das sei nicht viel, Sozialismus sei das Ziel* [or, loosely, 'The Republic, that's pretty tame; let socialism be our aim']. Yet the

Weimar Republic was quite something compared with what preceded it and, above all, what came after it.

I still find it remarkable that the problems which so fiercely impinged on the West were not brought up short by the barrier between us and the countries of Eastern Europe. In Belgrade, students protested not only at inadequate university teaching but also against restrictions on academic freedom. Disturbances were recorded in Warsaw, Budapest and even Sofia, where rumour has it that little ever happens. In Moscow itself, students ventured a few demonstrations which, though tentative, must have required true courage. This confirmed that the sentiments, ideas and problems of the younger generation transcended national boundaries.

But these phenomena were entirely overshadowed by the tragic events in Prague, which represented perhaps the grimmest milestone in the post-war history of the East European peoples and were simultaneously a summons to self-appraisal whose influence has persisted through the years. Here, too, the clock of history could not be put back. The brutal reversal of a development did not connote a restoration of the past. Prague, too, has left a profound mark on the world.

During the night of 20–21 August 1968, while travelling by coaster from Hammerfest to Trondheim, I received an alarming report from my Bonn office that Warsaw Pact forces had begun their march into Czechoslovakia. Early in the morning I left the ship at Harstad in the Lofoten Islands and flew by air-taxi to Bodø, where I was collected by a slow air force prop-driven plane which did not get me to Bonn until late that afternoon. I made a sharply worded statement on television, drove to see the Federal Chancellor and conferred with my party presidium.

Czechoslovakia had found it harder than other East European countries to emerge from the rigours of a Stalinist régime which had nowhere been guilty of more frightful excesses than in that unhappy land. It had been seized and enslaved by Hitler. After the collapse of the Third Reich (and the forcible expulsion of German citizens), hopes momentarily arose that Czechoslovakia could again become a democracy – possibly, even, the 'Switzerland' of Eastern Europe. Any such expectations were swiftly dashed by the mysterious death of Foreign Minister Masaryk, son of the country's founder, and all illusions were finally dispelled by the purges that followed. Antonin Novotný, Party leader and head of government, was deeply implicated in these Stalinist crimes. His overthrow early in 1968 came as no surprise. Groups of intellectuals had shown persistent recalcitrance in the preceding years. A measure of liberalization had been in progress for five years, and potent influences had emanated from the Writers' Union Congress that spring. There were open stirrings of discontent in Slovakia, which had always felt itself to be a rather underprivileged component of the state. Among the Party's general membership, a growing anti-Stalinist bloc worked doggedly – behind the scenes, as it were – to tilt the balance of power. Even so, a change of leadership would scarcely have been possible without Moscow's approval. (There were no public or dramatic demonstrations, as in the 'Polish spring' of 1956.) A simplified description of what happened inside the Prague leadership at the beginning of 1968 would be that the 'liberals' and Slovaks formed a new majority. It seems probable that Moscow sanctioned their desire for changes in government and Party institutions.

The General Secretariat of the Czechoslovak Communist Party settled on Alexander Dubček, an outwardly unimpressive member of the 'apparatus' but one who well knew how to articulate the popular demand for reform. Thus it was that his name came to be linked with the moving attempt to create 'socialism with a human face'. The Prague experiment was designed to produce liberal structures in community life and working conditions. Above all, it aspired to broaden the frontiers of the mind. The Czechs hoped to realize more freedom than the 'bourgeois' democracies of the West, not less.

Their hopes were far-reaching. They not only tried to formulate a new synthesis of socialism and democracy but rhapsodized about 'a humanist alternative to modern civilization'. At the same time, consideration was given to practical reforms which would modify the country's economic structure. Ota Šik, the deputy-premier responsible for the economic management of the new régime, realized that greater personal freedom could pave the way for increased productivity. To orthodox communists, these were alarming views. To the people, they were glad tidings which were greeted initially with caution but soon with tumultuous enthusiasm. The police apparatus was rigorously examined and Stalinist injustice – where possible – put right. Legal security was guaranteed. Journalists and artists were given back the freedoms without which they cannot properly exist. Freedom of debate was assured. It was planned to grant trade unions a certain degree of autonomy. Experts of greater competence were drafted into economic management. Discrimination against the Slovaks was abolished.

Contrary to the charges levelled against them, however, the reformers did not question the Party's monopoly. They did not contemplate abandoning their 'achievements' (communist-style). They were determined to fulfil their obligations under the Warsaw Pact. The reform-communists' courage in exposing a socialist republic to ordeal by freedom won the support of a broad majority of the population, who were simultaneously confirmed in their sense of national identity.

Czechoslovakia's East European neighbours, notably the Hungarians but others as well, observed the Prague experiment with sympathetic interest. Belgrade considered the CSSR to be on the right track. Support in several Western communist parties, above all the Italian, was manifest from the outset. Leading circles in several Warsaw Pact countries were deeply suspicious, however, and the GDR set the tone in this respect.

Czechoslovakia was the only country in the communist bloc of which I had first-hand knowledge. I spent Christmas and New Year 1936 with some German friends in Prague and attended a clandestine conference at Mährisch-Ostrau. In summer 1947, before the communist take-over and after the SPD's second post-war conference at Nuremberg, I spent a few more days in the country, which was just beginning to recover from the effects of the war and its chaotic aftermath. My contacts with friends in the CSSR had never been entirely severed – yet another reason why I followed these exciting developments with special interest. In my judgement, Czechoslovakia's continuing membership of the Eastern Alliance was the only thing that could prevent a repetition of the Budapest tragedy of autumn 1956, and I said so publicly. At the same time, I wondered how far reform-communism would be able to progress and whether it would ultimately be possible for a communist régime to become gradually transmuted into a democratic socialist system. Past experience counselled scepticism.

I received many personal letters couched in moving language. My name occasionally appeared on placards at peaceful demonstrations. The social democratic example and our delineation of all-European potentialities undoubtedly claimed attention on the other side of the Czech borders, which were now reopened to tourist traffic. For many German expellees, this was a first-ever opportunity to revisit their former homeland and the scenes of their childhood. We had agreed on an exchange of trade missions in summer 1967, during the Novotný régime. These were installed in Prague and Frankfurt and invested with consular powers. We did not force the pace. I insisted on an attitude of extreme restraint to avoid giving anyone the impression that the Federal Republic was exerting even an indirect influence on the course of events. In summer, when the situation became more acute, I telephoned Defence Minister Schröder from Brussels requesting him to switch routine army manœuvres from the German-Czech frontier area.

P.P.–O

The June manœuvres of the Warsaw Pact forces in Czechoslovakia had not escaped our notice, but we did not want to furnish a pretext for cheap propaganda.

I had said at the SPD's Nuremberg conference in March 1968 that nothing would be more inopportune at this juncture than to utter a yell of triumph. 'We have even less reason to do so because developments there are attributable solely to those who are, with courage and discernment, doing what they hold to be right. But we are following this process interestedly and open-mindedly, regardless of the fact that it has yet to diminish the obstacles that separate us in foreign policy.'

It could not by then be ignored that the authorities in Moscow and East Berlin, and probably, too, in Poland, were observing the progress of the Prague reforms with mounting suspicion. A summit conference was convened at Dresden on 26 March, the Rumanians being conspicuous by their absence. Dubček clearly had a hard time of it. He defended his policy to Brezhnev and Kosygin, Gomulka and Cyrankiewicz from Warsaw, Kádár and Premier Fock from Budapest, Zhivkov of Bulgaria, and Ulbricht and Stoph of the GDR. (The initiative for the meeting was attributed to Ulbricht.) Dubček appears in some degree to have succeeded in allaying his colleagues' suspicions. The final communiqué expressed confidence that 'the proletariat and all working people of Czechoslovakia, under the leadership of the Communist Party of Czechoslovakia, would ensure the further progress of socialist construction in the country'. Naturally, these words contained a hidden warning. From what we heard, the Czechoslovak spokesman had urged that no ammunition be supplied to 'the opponents of détente' at a time when Foreign Minister Brandt was 'setting limits' on revanchism.

Others took an entirely different view. In Moscow and East Berlin – and not there alone – it was feared that Czech relaxation might spread to the neighbouring countries. That spring, Polish students had demonstrated against the constraints of the Gomulka régime, under which all recollections of the 'spring in October' had become a distant dream. Signs of intellectual unrest were detectable in the GDR. There were reports of ferment in the Ukraine, too. Czech representatives visiting Moscow at the beginning of May were subjected to harsh criticism based, *inter alia*, on the so-called West German threat.

Commenting on developments during visits to Vienna and Belgrade at the beginning of June, I said we sympathized with the CSSR's need to fulfil its obligations as an ally. However, just as the Federal Republic did not necessarily espouse the views of all its allies on any particular point, so it seemed incomprehensible that the members of the Warsaw Pact should adopt a specific attitude towards the Federal Republic and

comrades in Prague and expressed a confidence in Dubček which they have never since retracted. The French Communist Party failed to hammer out a similarly unequivocal approach. Instead, their leader, Waldeck Rochet, proposed an all-European conference of communist parties which, if it had been convened without delay, might well have played an interesting role.

Prague was granted only a brief respite. At the end of July a high-ranking Soviet delegation led by Brezhnev negotiated at Cierna, a Slovakian township on the Ukrainian border, with Party Secretary Dubček, the new President, General Svoboda (a rather unpolitical soldier who had been victimized under the Novotný régime), Premier Černik, and Parliamentary President Smrkovsky. Svoboda declared on television that the Czechs knew they could exist only 'as a firm component of the socialist community'. The Moscow delegation trundled back over the Soviet frontier in its special train – ostensibly to report to the waiting representatives of Poland and the GDR. Premier Stoph, it was said, had repeatedly tried to urge a 'hard line' on Brezhnev in Ulbricht's name. The Cierna conference was swiftly followed on 3 August by another at Bratislava which Rumania again declined to attend. The final communiqué was signed in the mirrored chamber of the city hall where Napoleon and the Austrian Emperor made peace in 1805. It stated that 'each fraternal party' could, in the creative solution of problems relating to further socialist development, 'take account of national peculiarities and conditions'. This implied that the Czech communists were guaranteed the freedom to pursue their 'own road'. Had this really been so, one would happily have accepted the branding of Federal Germany, Israel and America as 'imperialist aggressors'.

The citizens of Bratislava seemed to breathe again. Jubilant crowds cheered Dubček as he drove through the streets in the same car as Brezhnev. A reporter noted that one of the spectators eventually urged his neighbours to cheer Brezhnev too, which they prudently did. Ulbricht, on the other hand, was greeted with boos and hisses. A deceptive calm prevailed. It was not until 1975 that the world learned the text of the final warning dispatched to Prague by the Soviet Politburo on 17 August. It expressed the conviction that the Presidium of the Central Committee of the Czechoslovak Communist Party understood 'our fears and our disquiet' and would take the requisite steps forthwith. The Soviet leaders charged Dubček and his friends with breaking their pledges and failing to combat the 'antisocialist attitude' of the mass media and various clubs and groups: 'Unfortunately, the situation is not improving.'

The signs are that Moscow's course was already set by this time.

Ulbricht had visited Karlsbad to pontificate a little while earlier. Kádár and Ceauşescu came to moderate but not to encourage. Tito told me later that he had been in Moscow not long before, and that Brezhnev had asked him to help to find a way out. 'I travelled to Czechoslovakia and gave the comrades some advice. By the time I returned, the Russians had already marched in. They never told me they intended to do so.'

The course of the tragedy need not be described in every detail here. Josef Smrkovsky wrote an unadorned but enthralling account of it shortly before his death in 1974, telling how he, Dubček, Černik and three other companions were arrested on the morning of 21 August and carted away like criminals. (They were flown to the Warsaw Pact staff headquarters at Liegnitz and from there to the Transcarpathian Ukraine, whence they were transferred to the environs of Moscow.) On 23 August President Svoboda flew to Moscow on his own initiative, accompanied by a party which included Gustav Husak, who was then a deputy-premier but held no Party post. Svoboda, who went so far as to say that survival meant little to a man of his years, refused to negotiate unless the abductees were present, declaring that he proposed to take them home with him as free men. He succeeded on both counts. After humiliating Dubček and his friends during the initial phase of the talks, which lasted for days, the Soviet authorities switched to a policy of heavily loaded compromise.

When the Czech politicians flew home on 27 August, they were hopeful that their policy of reform would retain some latitude and that the withdrawal of Russian troops could be seriously negotiated. They duly sought to restrain civil resistance, which was now widespread and became even more intense when the unpublished portions of the Moscow 'compromise' leaked out. The National Assembly returned an unequivocal negative. Weeks elapsed before opposition waned, but it was only months before the reformers were ousted and disciplined. (Tens of thousands of Party members were expelled and even more had their membership suspended. For many of them, this meant the loss of their jobs as well.)

There are grounds for supposing that the Soviet Politburo's drastic step was resisted to the last. The voting was probably six to five. It later seemed that Brezhnev, who may well have cast the deciding vote, was unhappy about the decision of August 1968. When the Ukrainian Party leader, Pyotr Shelest, was dismissed, he, too, was charged with presenting an inaccurate account of developments in Czechoslovakia.

It may be deduced from this that the risk of 'infection' among party leaders in the Ukraine and the Baltic area (apart from those of Poland and the GDR) was taken very seriously. There were also strategic fears of a military and political nature. A minority of the Politburo probably thought they could be handled without open intervention, and fears of repercussions on the international communist movement doubtless played a part as well.

Be that as it may, military intervention was justified not by the thesis of limited sovereignty but by the argument that 'the imperialists' had launched a campaign of 'ideological subversion'. East Berlin alleged that 'Zionist forces in Prague' and social democrats were responsible for popularizing the slogan of democratic socialism. The belief that we ourselves had ventured too far and were partly to blame found adherents in the West, too, and notably in France. Early that September I visited Paris in an attempt – which was only moderately successful – to talk de Gaulle's new Foreign Minister, Michel Debré, out of his rather irrational ideas on the subject. Debré was the author of the unfortunate phrase 'historical road accident'.

Some serious critics have opined, in retrospect, that 'half-measures' in our *Ostpolitik* fostered the development that culminated on 21 August 1968 or influenced it in an adverse way. I consider this verdict wholly unfair. Evidence that the spectre of joint Federal German responsibility continued to haunt some minds in the West comes from an American study which declared that West Germany's increasing economic and financial presence in Eastern Europe, and particularly in Czechoslovakia, seemed (together with a number of other decisive factors such as general Soviet mistrust of any form of liberalization) 'to have played a certain role in Moscow's decision to use military force against the Dubček government in August 1968. The Soviet pretext that West Germany and other countries had introduced NATO weapons into Czechoslovakia in order to pave the way for a counter-revolution there was clearly pure invention. There is, however, something in the argument that the Soviet Union was disturbed by the general effects of Bonn's *Ostpolitik* on the Warsaw Pact countries.'

The true picture was this: on 21 August a Czech envoy sat, thunderstruck, in our Foreign Ministry. Having come to sound out the future course of treaty negotiations, which had gone well, he learned from us what was happening in Prague.

I had more than once said in the preceding weeks that military intervention could not, unfortunately, be ruled out. I always added, however, that I considered this improbable because the Russians would give the subject mature consideration in the light of their own interests. Tito, who thought likewise, angrily referred to 21 August as an invasion. The Italian Communist Party, and to some degree the French and other Western communists, voiced their indignation in even stronger terms. They were under no illusion as to the true culprits. The only references to German part-responsibility bore upon Ulbricht and his régime, who had sent field-grey troops to subjugate a peaceful country. 'To insinuate,' I said, 'that we intervened or planned to intervene in the affairs of the CSSR is to slander the government of the German Federal Republic, in which we Social Democrats play an authoritative role, and to deceive the world. It was others who intervened, not the Federal Republic.' All we had done was announce our willingness to co-operate on a good-neighbourly basis. We had thrust ourselves on no one and shown an understanding of the Prague government's interest in adhering to the Warsaw Pact. 'It was and is correct to say that we avoided provocation and urged common sense and self-discipline.' Such was our restraint, in fact, that our response to inquiries about whether we would support the re-establishment of the Czech Social Democratic Party had been a friendly but firm recommendation to avoid complicating matters, and the foundation committees had discontinued their work in July.

On the GDR's part in the intervention, I expressed 'a sincere apology to our Czechoslovak neighbours'. They must not bear a grudge against the German people because some of its sons had again been stationed on their soil as occupying troops. 'We would have given a great deal to save our people this.' Meanwhile, the 'New Germany' tirelessly pictured the counter-revolutionary perils that would have stemmed from the acceptance of demands from West German Social Democrats . . .

In a moving letter addressed to the Federal Assembly of the CSSR and the Slovak National Council in autumn 1974, Alexander Dubček described the victimization to which he had been subjected and defended his policy against distortion. I reproduce without comment what he said about the German Federal Republic and my party:

It is true that our plan of action had drawn attention to the need to support progressive and anti-fascist forces (non-communist included). I do not disguise that we were thinking of social democracy and, in particular, of Willy Brandt's strivings toward a new line in domestic and foreign policy. This clearly displeased the current party leadership of the GDR . . . It is a fact that the policy implemented by Willy Brandt represents the most significant force and best safeguard against revanchism and fascism in the Federal Republic. Developments have fully borne this out.

Dubček went on to insist in unmistakable terms that the so-called 'Brezhnev Doctrine' – or thesis of limited sovereignty *vis-à-vis* the Soviet Union – set harsh and inhuman bounds on the process of détente because it rigorously curtailed the internal development of the 'socialist' countries. It availed little that Leonid Brezhnev himself denied the existence of the doctrine that still encumbers his name. What weighs more heavily is that 'socialist internationalism' has effectively been construed and utilized as a right of intervention. Thus it was in East Berlin in 1953, in Budapest in 1956, and finally in Prague. Titoism set an example which has never been followed. Yugoslavia won her independence in 1948 because the Soviet Union balked at open hostilities with the partisan Marshal – and probably at the then imponderable risk of an American reaction. The case of Czechoslovakia revealed, yet again, that 'observance of spheres of influence' had become a dominant factor in the super-powers' policy towards Europe. Washington uttered numerous regretful comments, of course, but they were doubtless in only partial accord with prior communications which the majority of the Soviet leaders had reason to interpret as helpful.

In the days following the intervention, many people asked if NATO couldn't 'do something'. This question, which I even heard from the lips of a despairing communist, never arose for the Western Alliance itself. There was a momentary fear that the invasion might have unforeseen military consequences. The Rumanian leaders made no secret of their understandable concern, and Yugoslav mobilization was not attributable to any expectations of a surprise attack from Austria or Italy. We had, once again, to acknowledge our limited ability to influence events. We knew that there was no alternative save one created by a long and patient peace-seeking process during which doctrines and spheres of influence would lose their importance.

Gritting my teeth, I clung to the realization that we had, even now, to maintain a course aimed at reducing tension – partly, if it ever became possible, in order to prevent tragedies like the one in Prague. This attitude was never in dispute between me and Kiesinger. NATO deliberated on the subject of reinforcements and took one or two practical steps. Relative military strength had altered less than many assumed at the time. The two super-powers pursued their own interests but did not break off talks. We were indeed confronted by a highly contradictory process.

I found it illuminating when President Pompidou stated during one of our Franco-German consultative discussions (end-January 1970) that those engaged in a dialogue with the East must recognize the Soviet Union's fear lest too much openness and communication between a communist and a Western country should bring about the fall of the former's régime. This, he said, had been clearly demonstrated by the Soviet intervention in Czechoslovakia. The Soviet Union had not acted out of purely military considerations. Ulbricht and his cadres were bound to fear a similar result if contacts between the Federal Republic and the GDR became too close. It was also pointless, Pompidou went on, to ignore the Soviet Union's genuine fear of German reunification.

I soon came to the conclusion – and my view was essentially shared by our allies – that Prague had to be seen as a tragic hiatus but not a historic turning-point in the relations between East and West. A renewed hardening of bloc alignments could not be ruled out, but we should not accept this as the end of our *Ostpolitik*. Most of our Czech friends thought we were right.

I devoted much attention after summer 1968 to the effects of the Prague tragedy on the communist world. It was indisputable that no event in Eastern Europe – not even Budapest – had more profoundly stirred the left-wing intellectuals of the West. It even shook those who had consistently propagandized on the Soviet Union's behalf and made the communist cause their own. Many of them, like Louis Aragon of France or Ernst Fischer of Austria, never recovered from the shock of Prague and never forgave the Soviet Union for intervening.

To those who still preserved illusions, Prague was more than a hiatus. The invasion of Czechoslovakia supplied the radical anti-Soviet Left with its strongest arguments. It compelled other more reflective spirits to debate once more whether their cause might not be better served by the parties of democratic socialism. Even the communist parties which, though critical, did not withdraw their allegiance from Moscow found it hard enough to cope with the Prague complex. In reality, there was only one way to overcome the trauma. This was to face the facts, and it has provided a point of departure for something new whose existence is beginning to gain recognition in East and West alike: a communist plurality.

Addressing members of our Frankfurt party in autumn 1968, I remarked that it was many years since any event beyond our borders had so passionately involved us as the Czech conflict. 'We in the Federal Republic have witnessed a rare phenomenon,' I said. 'Alexander Dubček is the first communist to have become genuinely popular in Germany.' I went on to reaffirm that 'What invested developments in

Czechoslovakia with the character of a historic experiment was the attempt to reconcile humanity and communism, democracy and socialism in the Eastern mould; to promote consumer-oriented production and personal initiative in a system which is supranationally state-controlled, to establish relative freedom of the press, of culture and science, and to restore personal freedom of movement.' There was no reason either to plume ourselves on what had happened to the Czechs or to put on mourning. We must not act as if the historical process had been terminated by the occupation.

Events had shown, I continued, that the leaders of the Soviet super-power would find it hard to cope with the fact that 'intellectual currents in the last third of our century are transcending national boundaries'. Communist societies, too, were having to grapple with new lines of inquiry. This had nothing to do with a transition to democracy in the Western mould, but that was not what mattered in the present context. The striving for national identity and for forms of human coexistence objectively attainable by means of science, technology and economic activity, would persist. Discussion was also being devoted – as witness the SED's positively hysterical campaign against 'social democratism' – to attitudes which approximated to those of social democracy. This development could not be permanently held in check by the conflict with Soviet Russia's claim to hegemony, which would continue to be disputed even in the communist world. To the extent that the process of differentiation in international communism continued, non-ruling and ruling communist parties would acquire a certain measure of autonomy.

I pursued these ideas further at the NATO Council meeting in April 1969. 'The changes inside the communist world will continue,' I said. 'Counter-measures will delay them but cannot hold them permanently in check. We cannot, however, expect this to be a continuous process. We must allow for interruptions and retrogressive developments, and cannot rule out the possibility of critical complications involving the West.' In fact, the invasion of Czechoslovakia did not even gain the approval of all the communist parties in power. Disregarding China and Albania, the Hungarians had serious misgivings and the Rumanians – not to mention the Yugoslavs – were totally opposed. Most of the Western communist parties dissented, though many of them soon moderated their criticism. In Western Europe, sounds of approval were to be heard only from the Luxemburg and Cypriot parties, likewise from the loyalists of Federal Germany and West Berlin.

The Italian communist leader, Luigi Longo, who had strongly identified himself with the Prague reform process, declared that efforts to create 'a developed socialist democracy' held great significance for the whole of Europe. On the day of the intervention he restated his support for Prague, and that autumn he publicly assailed theoretical justifications of the invasion by *Pravda* and the SED press. Those who took up the demand for reform, he said, must no longer be branded as deliberate or unwitting agents of imperialism. 'Such a course promotes the internal rigidification of life in these countries.' Longo and his associates were pursuing the line recommended by their late party leader, Palmiro Togliatti, who died in 1964. His political 'testament' called for a detached attitude towards Moscow and criticized the suppression of democratic and political freedom he had experienced there. He also opposed uniform guide-lines for communist parties in individual countries and declared that their unity must find fulfilment in a variety of concrete political positions.

My friend Leo Bauer had known Luigi Longo for many years, having occupied the same French internment camp at the beginning of the war. Ulbricht, who was sent away with a flea in his ear when he warned his Italian colleague against Bauer, found it necessary to state that the German had cured the Italian's boils. Leo Bauer became a communist Landtag representative in Hesse after the war, then moved to East Berlin as editor of the so-called *Deutschlandsender*. At the time of the show-trials in Prague and Budapest he was arrested and charged with having worked for the American secret service. He escaped the death penalty after being brutally interrogated, but was sentenced to a long term of imprisonment in Siberia. Some years later he returned to the Federal Republic with his health gravely impaired – ironically enough, in company with the prisoners of war whose release Adenauer had procured in Moscow in 1955. During the post-1965 years he was one of my closest and most valued assistants.

Right-wing circles in the Federal Republic cobbled together the myth that, under cover of the Grand Coalition, close ties had developed between the SPD and PCI. Suspect corroboration from the intelligence services was adduced to support this theory, but their reports were neither accurate nor imbued with political discernment. It was, for example, alleged that I had met Longo several times in Rome. The fact was that I exchanged no more than a single sentence with him when visiting Rome with Kiesinger early in 1968. The Italian President was holding a banquet at the Quirinale, and one of the guests was the general secretary of the PCI. To my regret, I was only able to greet him – and others – in passing. I did not attend the banquet, so a malicious observer might just as well have said that I left Kiesinger alone with Longo. Meanwhile, Franz Josef Strauss not only wrote but encouraged others to write that the foundations of our new *Ostpolitik* had been discussed and worked out by prominent members of the SPD and representatives of the Italian Communist Party behind the backs of our CDU/CSU partners in the Grand Coalition.

What was the truth of the matter? After preparatory talks with Sergio Segre of the international section of the PCI executive, Bauer had fixed a meeting in Rome for late November 1967. This was attended by Egon Franke in his capacity as a member of the SPD presidium and, on the Italian side, by Longo, the future Party leader Enrico Berlinguer, Deputy Carlo Galluzzi, and Lama, the trade union leader. They took an unprejudiced view of our policy – indeed, they had defended it at the previous Karlsbad conference against Ulbricht's absurd contention that the Federal Government in which we shared was 'worse than all its predecessors'. We were interested in knowing how international and inter-communist developments looked through the eyes of the Italian communist leaders, and found it illuminating in this respect that they should set store by their deputies' attendance at the EEC Parliament. We were also interested in the extent to which they already stressed their independent line, rejected subordination to an international headquarters or 'supreme' party, and approved of political pluralism.

In March 1968 Egon Bahr and Berlinguer met in Munich for a discussion which was also subsequently hyperbolized into a 'secret meeting'. Thereafter and at longish intervals, informative exchanges were held in Rome, and occasionally Bonn, in which I took no personal part but always showed an interest. I particularly recall hearing Leo Bauer's account of the PCI conference at Bologna, which he had just attended as an observer, during a brief visit to Rome early in February 1969. Longo had again proclaimed his support of the Czech model and declared that he wanted 'a socialism qualitatively different from that which has been implemented hitherto'. He had also devoted no time to the once obligatory tirade against 'Bonn revanchism'.

Enrico Berlinguer, the new General Secretary – a Sardinian aristocrat of Catalonian descent – adopted a more cautious tone when addressing the Moscow conference of communist parties in spring 1969, no doubt in deference to the orthodox reactionaries in his own party. He did not, for all that, hesitate to take a stand against the Prague intervention and in favour of party independence. To the surprise of those who attended, *Pravda* did not gloss over his criticism or that of others. The French contented themselves with making critical remarks behind closed doors. Brezhnev did not exempt the SPD from attack, and Ulbricht was pretty well isolated.

I have since devoted some thought, and not without reason, to the question of how a large communist party like the PCI will develop. Although distinct from the rest, it is not unique. Developments in other parts of the world make it seem more and more doubtful that one can still talk of 'world communism'. The rift between the Peking and Moscow authorities went deep, and there was no indication that it could be healed in the foreseeable future. On the contrary, other parts of Asia such as Vietnam and North Korea were also developing communist leaderships which aspired to independence from the Soviet Union and even from China as well. In a number of countries – India and Sri Lanka, for example – communist factions became parties in their own right and feuded fiercely among themselves.

Even before entering government, I had alluded in spring 1966 to the possible development, alongside the twin centres of Moscow and Peking, of a third ideological force linked with the pre-Leninist positions of the European Left – I might equally have said, born of dissociation from dogmatic Soviet attitudes. However, my initial tendency was to relate this hypothetical development too closely to the Yugoslav model. Wherever, as in Italy, France and Japan, communist parties have gained mass support in democratic countries during the post-war period, those parties have sooner or later embarked on an often long and painful process of adaptation to their democratic environment coupled with gradual dissociation from the dogma of Party dictatorship and slavish adherence to the Soviet line. I do not believe that 'Euro-communism' has proved an illuminating catchword because differences between one country and another are too readily obscured by reductions to a common denominator. It has not, however, been uninteresting to detect the noises made in recent years by communist leaders in Rome or, for that matter, Madrid. Despite justified scepticism, they have seemed to hint at something that will lead to more than a superficial acceptance of parliamentary democracy and formal support for European unification. This process will probably have a divisive effect. We may also assume that it will, in the course of time, exert an influence on the ideas of rising generations in the communist-ruled countries.

None of my friends bestowed more fervent attention on these problems than Leo Bauer, whose experience of our age had been grievous enough in all conscience. He died in October 1972 from the effects of the illness he had brought home with him from Siberia.

It was no coincidence that my funeral address for Leo Bauer contained a first reference to the key-word 'compassion', which had, in another way, defined the quality of the Kennedy brothers.

10

The Palais Schaumburg

Nearly forty years had passed since Hermann Müller, the last socialist Chancellor, resigned the post in March 1930. They were years during which my party was shattered by a reign of terror, many of its members suffered unutterable torments and not a few met a violent end; years during which, after the terror ended and a new organization had been built, it assumed local and regional responsibility, resisted the onslaught of a new dictatorship, played a decisive part in shaping the Federal Republic and was finally entrusted with the burdens of office. It was not surprising that the result of the Bundestag elections of September 1969 and my own election as Federal Chancellor in October were noted with interest by the outside world. Both events have been described as the beginning of a new phase in the history of the Federal Republic. Political leadership passed smoothly from one major party to the other: our political system had stood the test.

Our success, which was anything but a foregone conclusion, came late in the day. On election night itself, preliminary results suggested that the CDU/CSU would just obtain an absolute majority of seats. The atmosphere at party headquarters was subdued. People could be heard grumbling that the SPD had paid a high price – perhaps too high – for the Grand Coalition. In our then headquarters, which were affectionately known as 'the Hut' (*die Baracke*), disappointment and resentment mingled with the depressive exhaustion that almost inevitably results from weeks of strenuous electioneering. I myself had often been afflicted with the same grinding fatigue. That night I remained wide awake. We appeared to have missed the electoral target. Although it was clear that we had definitely broken the 40-per-cent barrier at last, our strength seemed insufficient to form a government. Kiesinger's camp had grounds for feeling confident of victory. President Nixon telephoned from Washington to congratulate the Chancellor.

Towards 10 p.m., a clearer picture emerged: the Union parties were not, after all, going to obtain a majority of seats. The final results confirmed this. The Union remained the strongest party bloc (with 46.1 of second votes, or 1.5 per cent less than in 1965). The FDP, then in the throes of transition to a reformed social liberalism, was badly mauled (its share of the poll dwindled from 9.5 to 5.8 per cent). The extreme right-wing NPD failed to clear the 5-per-cent hurdle.

My own party increased its share of the poll by 3.4 per cent to 42.7. Like others, I calculated that the SPD and FDP could between them muster twelve more seats than the Union parties (222 for the SPD, 30 for the FDP). Although this was only five seats more than the absolute majority required to elect a Chancellor, I resolved to run the risk even if the 'small' SPD/FDP coalition failed to last the entire legislative period. There could be no return to the Grand Coalition: the CDU/CSU and SPD had diverged too widely in their basic objectives. A continuation of the alliance would have been greeted with particular disfavour by the young people who were pinning their hopes on my party, and would have prompted them to turn, by way of fringe groups, into radical opponents of our democratic system. Finally, the SPD had no wish to be shunted back into the opposition siding for an indefinite period.

The CDU declined to acknowledge this reality. Kiesinger felt that he had gained a major personal triumph. Meanwhile, the CDU leaders began to woo representatives of the FDP with extreme vigour. Not only were they prepared to assign them half a dozen seats in the Federal Government; they also intimated that good behaviour on the Federal level might be rewarded with long-term participation in the *Land* governments. When things failed to work out, Kiesinger rather blatantly displayed his annoyance – and his misjudgement of the actual position – by threatening that the FDP would be 'kicked out' of the regional parliaments.

I left no one in any doubt that I wanted to become Chancellor. I had talked to Walter Scheel, leader of the FDP, a few times before the election, and we had agreed to examine the possibility of a coalition seriously. If the election result permitted, we did not wish to let such a solution slip because of offers from third parties. There was nothing new about the idea of co-operating with the FDP. We had already explored it in 1966, and the changes in the party that had become manifest since Scheel assumed the leadership (in autumn 1968) commended its renewed consideration to many of my fellow-Social Democrats. The coalition talks were harmonious. When they were over I took a short 'working holiday'. On 21 October the Bundestag elected me Chancellor by 251 votes to 235 – two more than the absolute majority I needed. Although I had taken the result for granted and was already engrossed in thoughts of the task ahead, I was not indifferent to the delight and satisfaction with which my friends and supporters surged around me. I needed their good wishes – many of the rosy hopes I had heard expressed were rather disquieting. To me, what mattered most of all was that the many friends and associates who had helped me bear the burdens of hard-fought electoral battles should regard my election to the Chancellorship as a victory of their own and a boost to their own self-confidence. This applied equally to my youthful critics, who, despite numerous and persistent reservations, had lent me vigorous and spirited support.

Immediately after my election I met the members of my parliamentary party and thanked them for having accompanied me along a road which had not been invariably easy. The general atmosphere was grave rather than exuberant. As one correspondent reported of the Chancellorship election, 'No signs of noisy triumph could be detected . . .' Being preoccupied with my impending duties, I felt anything but exultant. A television interviewer asked me a few weeks later if, when moving into the Palais Schaumburg, I had sensed the proximity of history – the 'hem of the mantle of history' to which Bismarck once alluded. I replied that I had got over the feeling in the interval between the parliamentary election and my own. I had given clear consideration to the demands of the job during that time. Two or three weeks had elapsed before I sensed the real significance of the task and all that its fulfilment entailed.

Interviewed by foreign journalists at the same period, I confessed to a feeling that Hitler had finally lost the war. 'I see myself as the Chancellor of a liberated, not a defeated, Germany. Our partners in the world will be dealing with a loyal government but not always an easy one.' During my Stockholm and early Berlin days, when my influence on the course of events was small, one or two friends predicted that I would some day head a government. I preferred not to listen. Now that they had been proved right, I hoped to assist my native land along the road to liberal and social democracy – to kindle a spirit of regeneration. It was my firm intention to promote European co-operation and understanding, and I was well aware, without overrating them, that our efforts would have worldwide significance. My government policy statement concluded by expressing our wish to be a good-neighbourly people, both at home and in our relations with the outside world.

As in 1954, 1959 and 1964, the President of the Bundestag had summoned the Federal Assembly to convene in Berlin. The Russians launched a lively diplomatic campaign aimed at persuading us to change the venue. Shortly before Christmas 1968 they conveyed a protest to the Western Powers, whose official position – as confirmed to us during Nixon's visit at the end of February – was that the decision rested with us. Off the record, of course, one heard Allied hints that the Russians should not be unnecessarily provoked. The latter, who were using fewer threats than previously in their dealings with the Federal Government, placed their main emphasis on offers of improved relations.

Under prevailing circumstances, my own attitude differed somewhat from that of Kiesinger and Wehner in that I favoured Berlin as a venue but did not in principle reject talks on compensation if enough could be extracted from them. This was the gist of a telex message I sent in response to a letter from Ulbricht: '. . . There can be no discussions between the SPD and yourself relating to the Federal Assembly and its meeting-place.' As for problems relating specifically to Berlin and discrimination against the people of West Berlin in particular, the Governing Mayor had already consulted the Council of Ministers of the GDR. I added that Mayor Schütz's endeavours enjoyed our full support.

The Berlin talks proved unproductive and foundered on the rigid conditions imposed by the GDR authorities. The GDR had proclaimed a transit ban on members of the Federal Assembly. In addition, Warsaw Pact manœuvres near Berlin were scheduled for the beginning of March. On 28 February Moscow sent a note to the GDR demanding that steps be taken against the allegedly military activities of West Berlin industry. East Berlin imposed strict checks on traffic. During the first week of March, vehicles using the Autobahnen were greatly impeded. Access was almost daily barred for hours on end, though interruptions were less severe than in 1965, when the Bundestag held its last plenary session in Berlin.

Considerations of balance and the SPD's important bearing on the substance of German democracy prescribed that we should now select a man from our own ranks for the country's highest office. The CDU/CSU decided that the ex-Foreign Minister and current Minister of Defence, Gerhard Schröder, should enter the lists.

My concern was to put forward a candidate who stood a good chance of winning the Free Democrats' votes as well as our own. We settled on Justice Minister Gustav Heinemann, who had been Interior Minister in Adenauer's first cabinet and had resigned at the prospect of re-armament. Heinemann, a prominent and worthy spokesman on behalf of German Protestantism, had tried to form a party of his own before joining the SPD in 1957. He was accounted a symbol of liberal constitutionalism and, as such, won the sympathies of our restive and uneasy younger generation.

After the Social Democratic members of the Federal Assembly had voted among themselves I drove to the Hilton to submit our proposal to Walter Scheel and some of his associates. Scheel jokingly remarked that we had made it very difficult for them not to support our candidate. Our FDP colleagues did not, for all that, find the choice an easy one. Whatever their underlying motives, Scheel deployed great powers of persuasion in getting his electors to vote as unanimously as possible for Heinemann. A preliminary secret ballot of the FDP group yielded 57 votes for Heinemann and 23 for Schröder (with two abstentions and one absence). A second ballot made it 78 to 5.

The Federal Assembly itself, which convened in one of the exhibition halls at the Berlin Funkturm, was a tense affair. Gustav Heinemann was elected Federal President on the third ballot by 512 votes to 506.

We improvised a brief victory celebration in the exhibition grounds and invited those of our FDP colleagues who were available, congratulating them with good-natured mockery on their 'social integration'. Joy was great but far from unconfined – that would not have suited our new head of state. Even so, there was a feeling that power had 'changed hands', a phrase of Heinemann's which rankled with the future Opposition. The day closed with a round-table discussion at the *Hotel Schweizerhof*. Günter Grass, the theologian Helmut Gollwitzer and other friends had a rather pensive conversation with Heinemann in which thought was devoted to the forms and foundations of a new style, a regenerated substance and different spirit in German politics.

My relationship with Federal President Heinemann in subsequent years was co-operative and sustained by mutual trust. However, I was more than once at a loss to answer his urgent and impatient inquiries as to what he could do in addition to his predominantly ceremonial duties. He did, in fact, accomplish a great deal, above all by his simple and sincere example. Gustav Heinemann saw himself as a citizen President and contributed greatly to the internal equilibrium of our country's classes and groups. He promoted public awareness of the links between our own democracy and the emancipatory movements in German history. His trips to former occupied countries – to Denmark, Norway, Holland and Belgium – made a deep impression. They demonstrated a common desire to face up to the facts of history and the need for reconciliation.

Six months later, on the morrow of the Bundestag election, I called on the Federal President in accordance with the procedure governing the formation of a cabinet. Later at the Berlin Building, Scheel and I had a preliminary talk about the new Federal Government we hoped to form jointly.

The very next day we met to discuss coalition plans at my official residence. We began, rather exuberantly, with a game of football which was dominated by the Interior Minister of North Rhine-Westphalia, Willi Weyer (later president of the German Athletics Association). After technical problems had been delegated to experts from both parties, these discussions produced a series of concrete agreements which I worked into my government policy statement. We did not have to dwell long on questions of personnel.

I regarded collaboration with the Free Democrats not as a mere marriage of convenience but as a 'social-liberal' alliance that would provide the right basis – and not just in foreign policy – for tackling some of the problems to be solved by the Federal Republic in the 1970s. Social democracy and liberalism had diverged widely in the time of Bismarck, although the early labour movement was inseparable from the liberal spirit of 1848 and both movements had many early points of contact. They had co-operated with the Catholic Centre Party in founding the Weimar Republic after World War I. Under the Federal Republic, the FDP had begun by adopting a position to the right of the Christian Democrats, but repeated electoral setbacks were creating fresh opportunities for a revival of socially committed liberalism – hence the possibility of a collaboration transcending mere tactics.

The parliamentary basis of our social-liberal alliance was weak. I should perhaps have paid more attention to the 'right flank' of the FDP, as Agriculture Minister Ertl sometimes suggested. Walter Scheel's position became precarious in early summer 1970 when his party only just passed the electoral five-per-cent mark in the largest Federal *Land*. Some people speculated that the FDP might not survive at all, and the critical situation became universally apparent when FDP ex-chairman Erich Mende and two fellow-parliamentarians went over to the Opposition in autumn of the same year. This gave the coalition a margin of only six seats in the Bundestag, and even this very slender majority vanished in spring 1972 when more FDP representatives, this time joined by some from the SPD, changed sides under circumstances that provoked universal disquiet.

The composition of my cabinet had not presented any great difficulty. In contrast to earlier years, the Federal Ministers were sworn in on the day of the Chancellorship election, and four days later I presented our government policy statement. As far as possible, Social Democrat ministers from the Grand Coalition cabinet were reappointed. The ministries were reduced in number, a popular but slightly overrated step. What was more important and remained more difficult was the appropriate relationship of ministries to each other and the Chancellery. Every Federal Minister was assigned a Parliamentary State Secretary, a practice introduced in some departments under the Grand Coalition.

I had settled the composition of the Chancellery on the afternoon of election day itself. I tried to run the Chancellery, and more particularly the cabinet, in as collaborative a manner as possible. It has never been my habit to seek unqualified approval or expect discussions to confirm me in a preconceived opinion. Although I seldom recall interrupting a member of the cabinet and did not apply the rules of procedure in a strict and formalistic way, cabinet meetings rarely became digressive under my chairmanship. The counting of heads was very infrequent. It had been my belief and practice, both as mayor and as chairman of my party, that the attainment of an executive consensus nearly always produces better results than a formal vote. I took more than usual care to preserve human solidarity when real differences of opinion arose. Not all who share political responsibility can be friends, but a good personal atmosphere fosters practical co-operation.

One of my difficulties, particularly in the handling of delicate problems associated with foreign policy and security, stemmed from the occasional need to withhold full and immediate information from all but the colleagues directly concerned. Thanks to these differences in 'information status' and the fact that knowledge, while not necessarily connoting power, has a bearing on prestige, the uninitiated acquire a distasteful sense of being second-class cabinet members. I tried to keep this differentiation within bounds. More worrying were the vanities and jealousies which sometimes frustrated my efforts at teamwork. They had little to do with the coalition or our political partners. I was sometimes more disappointed by the inability or reluctance of members of my own party to fall into line and keep the work of government free from emotional ballast than by the little games in which our FDP colleagues also indulged from time to time. In the cramped and loquacious confines of Bonn, every rumour, every petty squabble and complaint, becomes amplified a thousandfold. To those in a teacup, the storm inside it is still a storm. It was a senior American politician who confided to me that, in many respects, Washington is an outsize version of Bonn.

I did not at that time devote much thought to whether the modern industrial nations would remain governable in the traditional manner, nor were my subsequent conclusions as pessimistic as those reflected in the utterances of contemporary statesmen or political analysts. It is nonetheless true that the sheer number and magnitude of the problems requiring solution exert a pressure undreamed of by those who designed our parliamentary and administrative machinery, and that our democratic institutions were fashioned under quite different and far less complex circumstances. It is also true that we are faced with an ever-growing mass of bureaucratic decisions – though with prior decisions of an almost immutable nature – and that it seems fair to ask whether we are not increasingly succumbing to forms of technocratic domination. At least in the short term, this line of questioning is even more applicable to countries under communist rule.

There is no rational purpose to be served by shirking the realization that those who govern the Western democracies are becoming increasingly exposed to pressure of circumstances and mass sentiment, and that they find it hard to cope with them. Unlike certain pessimists, however, I conclude that we should be fully capable of adapting our democratic institutions to altered circumstances. This will, of course, entail a far swifter response to new and relevant scientific discoveries, quite apart from a readiness to take a stratified view of democracy and ensure that it is broadly based.

My original allocation of time as Federal Chancellor proved a mirage. I had hoped it would be possible to steer clear of routine for at least a couple of days each week, but the appointments book turned out to be more of a terror now than it had been at the Foreign Office. Even at weekends there was insufficient time to work out a new problem at my leisure or – just as important – to read books which had little direct bearing on my work. I was particularly overburdened by the Landtag and municipal elections, which succeeded one another with little respite and entailed a sort of election campaign in perpetuity. I often said jokingly that we were trying, in an excess of German zeal, to make up for what we had missed during twelve years of dictatorship.

It is impossible to describe a Federal Chancellor's 'typical' working day – there is no such thing. One day may be almost entirely given up to budgetary consultations, to parliament, to the party executive, to an election campaign or a foreign visitor. Another day may bring the Chancellor a steady stream of callers – if he is not already occupied with small group discussions, cabinet committees, representatives of various associations, senior members of his own party or parliamentary group, press conferences and interviews. But every day requires him, more or less intensively, to confer with his immediate associates and study press synopses, ambassadorial cables, memoranda and important correspondence. I devoted much time to working on the text of speeches, statements, articles and written interviews. However good the preparatory drafts which my abundance of public utterances rendered indispensable, I insisted on polishing them myself. Anyone who imagines that I accepted ghost-written drafts without clarifying their substance, emendations, amplifications and reformulations, even in routine matters, is mistaken. Apart from this, most people have a false idea of this amplificatory and collaborative technique. There were no protracted, meditative or convoluted discussions in which hazy 'visions' took shape over bottles of red wine – pressure of work ruled this out. I did, however, encourage my aides to devote disciplined mental effort to the guide-lines imposed by my political objectives, and I only wish there had been more time for the productive discussions known elsewhere as 'brain-storming'.

Another misconception which has been nurtured into a sort of legend is that I took far less interest in domestic than foreign policy and consequently spent too little time on the former. In reality, I always devoted by far the greater part of my time to domestic political issues in the wider sense. This applied even to the year 1970, with its strong emphasis on foreign policy. It is true, on the other hand, that domestic undertakings did not always receive sufficient preparation and were not co-ordinated with sufficient accuracy. I also failed to evaluate new problems as quickly as practical politics required. Finally, we may also have failed in our duty to render problems of social and economic policy sufficiently intelligible and attractive to the general public. A whiff of tedium clings to these topics, as every journalist knows, whereas they are really abrim with tension and excitement. We may not have conveyed that it is these very problems which demand commitment and richly repay an investment of enthusiasm and imagination. But that, I suspect, requires a lengthy educative process.

My policy statement of 28 October 1969 embarked in this direction. 'Continuity and renewal' were to be interpreted as non-conflicting concepts, just as preservation implied change. 'We are determined to safeguard the security of the Federal Republic of Germany and the cohesion of the German nation, to preserve peace and join in working for a European peace settlement, to extend the liberties and welfare of our people and develop our country in such a way that its status will be recognized and secured in the world of tomorrow.'

One sentence which aroused much subsequent controversy stated our determination to 'venture more democracy'. It was indeed our aim to illuminate the workings of government and be more receptive to critical demands for information. 'We are not at the end of our democracy; we are at its beginning.' A provocative statement, true, but quite intentional. I wanted my government to show from the first that its utterances were not meant to ingratiate. We were seeking the partnership of social groups, the advice of the Churches, the commitment of the young. Our policy statement duly announced some far-reaching domestic reforms. We had recognized that security could only be guaranteed by mobility and renewal. Many citizens found this hard to understand, especially when viewed against the backcloth of our country's disastrous history in the first half of the century. Our more reactionary opponents exploited this by trying to convey the impression that a Federal Government led by Social Democrats would make Germany less secure, and in many cases they produced a genuine sense of insecurity bordering on panic.

Being hard put to it to submit convincing alternatives, however, our parliamentary opponents usually came off badly. Their star began to regain the ascendant only when the drive and enthusiasm with which we had pursued our policy of reform was checked by our own shortcomings and, more particularly, by worldwide economic developments, while a peculiar and almost indefinable psychological shift concealed the realization that security and change go hand in hand. German history discloses that we have a stronger tendency than others to respond to major (or supposedly major) problems by retrogressing instead of boldly advancing.

Having already essayed a full account of our programme, our work and the obstacles we encountered in a book published a few months after my resignation (*Über den Tag hinaus*, summer 1974), I shall here confine myself to a few pointers. One of them is that we intended no break with the market economy system. On the contrary, we wanted competition to develop where it had previously been subject to unnecessary restrictions.

Our most visible and impressive achievements were in the field of social policy. War victims' pensions were increased and 'dynamized', in other words, geared to wage-levels. I had long found it shameful that victims of the war, of all people, should have to demonstrate in support of their demands for an income adjusted to national economic growth. As announced in our government programme, statutory old-age pension rights were made available to groups which had hitherto been excluded. The flexible retirement age was adopted early in the autumn of 1972, before the premature dissolution of the Bundestag. Where health insurance was concerned, increased benefits were secured for salaried employees, the continuation of wage payments for workers incapacitated by illness having already been introduced by the Grand Coalition. We also gave an undertaking – which we kept –

to devote special attention to those fellow-citizens 'who, despite a boom and full employment, are compelled to live in the shadows'.

Another major field of reformist activity centred on the need to adapt obsolete criteria governing penal and civil law to changed circumstances. This applied mainly to legislation affecting marriage and the family.

Pride of place among our reforms had been assigned to educational planning, which was to be directed at the central objective of the Basic Law: that all citizens should have an equal chance to develop their personalities. I stated quite clearly that this requirement had not been met. An amendment to the Basic Law had provided the Federal Government with a constitutional basis for joint educational planning with the *Länder*. Taking our stand on this, we produced an overall plan which – for all its inadequacies – contributed to a significant development of the educational system.

The well-nigh explosive rise in educational expenditure not only helped to solve old problems but created new ones. Grave miscalculations arose, primarily in the field of public health.

It became fashionable to bemoan the consequences of reformist euphoria, and it is true that the word reform had tripped rather too easily off the tongues of many of our supporters. Many of them undoubtedly thought that a new age had dawned in which everything conducive to a more humane society could be accomplished. It is equally true, however, that our general line was bound to provoke opposition in reactionary quarters. Setbacks occurred, both avoidable and unavoidable, but I am convinced that we took the proper course in 1969 when we set to work to clear the log-jam of reforms and develop our country as justly and humanely as possible. For all the recent talk of a changed climate of opinion, the majority of our countrymen want the development of our liberal and social system to continue.

I would nonetheless concede, with critical hindsight, that many aspects of our programme were prepared with insufficient care. Focal points were not always clearly enough discernible amid the rival interests of competing groups and departments. The daily work of government, with its inevitable compromises, was too often indiscriminately evaluated. So were our changes of direction, whether or not they cost money. The interdependence of projected reforms on the one hand and economic and financial policy on the other may not have been explained with sufficient clarity. There was a disquieting tendency for public expenditure to rise – as it has throughout the world – but not that proportion of it devoted to investment. Despite this, we largely fulfilled the declared aims of our policy statement. In many areas, notwithstanding a curtailed legislative period, we actually accomplished more than we had set out to do.

This was one of the factors that prompted me to suggest a quantified overall scheme for social policy at the SPD's Saarbrücken conference in spring 1970. I wanted to place our reform policy on a firmer footing and discover a solid centre midway between the orientation of our fundamental values and the daily business of government and parliament. I was further concerned to bring home the cost of a reform policy – the simple realization that a finite public share of the national product cannot be used several times over, and that one must know exactly what consequences will flow from what redistribution of, or increase in, taxation.

The Saarbrücken conference exposed us to harsh criticism from some of the young Social Democrats. They pressed for a 'more socialist' policy, but most of their spokesmen remained bogged down in verbal radicalism.

In relation to my experience of such party conferences and further debates, as well as to numerous conversations with fellow socialists from other parts of the world, I often asked myself how democratic socialism should now be defined. I find it easy enough to say what I have long ceased to mean by it. I do not equate it with the socialization or nationalization of large firms or branches of industry. This policy, which has hitherto resulted in the mere imposition of state ownership, was the one adopted by critical socialists after World War II. The German social democrats would also have followed this path if they had wielded sufficient influence. Although we have since learnt that public ownership (in varying forms) may be imperative, we believe that transfers of title are a matter of expediency, not dogma, and that ideas of blind and inhuman economic growth should be treated with caution.

The Scandinavian social democrats, whom we in Germany and our friends in Austria and other countries have emulated to this extent, have followed up the first and second phases of their endeavours – equal civil rights and social security for the broad mass of the population – by preparing for a third phase which can only be described as a campaign for social democracy. This entails broad democratic participation coupled with co-determination in employment, economic activity and other relevant social spheres. The aim is to transform more and more people into responsible decision-makers and attach a new value to individual freedom and responsibility.

My party suffered a number of reverses in the Landtag elections – no rare affliction for a ruling party to undergo in mid-term. Its self-presentation and self-confidence were often inadequate, and it also suffered from an occasional tendency to overreach itself. The incessant hammering of the Opposition, which had exceptional difficulty in accepting its new role, was not devoid of effect either. The Union parties barred access to the renovation they needed by deluding themselves that they were born to govern, as it were, and had been ousted from their right of primogeniture. This benefited neither them nor us, and their partial successes at the polls did not prove otherwise.

In October 1971 Rainer Barzel became chairman of the CDU in addition to leading it in parliament. He had first caught my attention when heading the 'Save Freedom' committee at the beginning of the 1960s. There was something of the zealot about his activities in those days. In the years that followed I came to know him as an astute and intelligent politician endowed with considerable debating skill. I also gained the impression that he would cling to a middle-ground position favouring social equality and the suppression of nationalism even if the bulk of his party failed to approve. Although I cannot pretend that the road which brought us closer was an easy one, the relationship we developed over the years was governed by mutual respect and, I hope, beneficial to the interests of the country at large.

Controversy was not restricted to our line in foreign policy, even though disputes over Eastern and foreign policy evoked great public interest and commitment. The permanent hostility which so sorely tried the nerves of both parliamentary blocs stemmed from the out-and-out opposition of the Union parties, who felt it incumbent on them, whatever the time or place, to conjure up visions of industrial and financial ruin. They had no qualms about blaming the government for difficulties imposed on the Federal Republic by economic developments in the outside world. A more sophisticated controversy centred on our differing interpretations of what modern democracy means: an organizational principle essentially restricted to the politico-national domain, or a vision of mature and articulate citizenship requiring fulfilment by its rational application to the major sectors of economic and social life. We made an approach, albeit far too gingerly, to novel fields of inquiry dealing with the quality of economic growth, and many of our supporters began to see more clearly that living standards and the quality of life are not identical.

To me, reform was always associated with hope – and this at a time when many younger people viewed the future with concern and alarm: alarm at the destructive power of military establishments, concern about the bases of existence in a threatened environment, concern for the Third World, fear of manipulation allied with a mistrust engendered by lack of veracity.

In foreign policy, my government programme proceeded from this simple realization: that only peace can render our world secure, and that peace can become diffused only if underpinned by security. Cognizant of its special responsibilities in Europe but mindful of its limitations, the Federal Government would make every effort to attain this goal. We stressed the importance of our partnership with the developing countries, of moves towards disarmament and arms limitation, of external cultural policy, and of our intention to collaborate more effectively in the United Nations and other international bodies.

We emphasized that our policies would be in harmony with the North Atlantic Alliance, which had proved its worth in twenty years of existence and would continue to guarantee our security in future. Its firm solidarity was a *sine qua non* of our collective efforts to achieve détente in Europe.

Just as the Western Alliance was defensive, so was our contribution thereto. The Bundeswehr was unsuited to offensive purposes by training and organization, arms and equipment. The Federal Government would make no bones about the defensive principle underlying its defence policy.

We underlined our close relations with the United States and affirmed our belief in the binding nature of US obligations towards Europe, the Federal Republic and West Berlin. Our common interests required no additional assurances or repeated declarations. They could well sustain an independent German policy in a more active partnership.

On West European unification, we said that special importance attached to the forthcoming conference of the Six at The Hague (scheduled for early December). The European concert of nations must include the British if Europe were not to harm itself. It was time to initiate the process. In this context, we meant to work towards a situation in which the Community would develop new forms of economic co-operation with those European countries which were unwilling or unable to join it. We would promote the development of closer political co-operation in Europe with the aim of 'evolving a collective attitude in international affairs, step by step'.

Our national interest, we went on, did not permit us to stand between East and West. Our country needed co-operation and agreement with the West and an understanding with the East. 'Against this background, I strongly emphasize that the German people need peace, in the full sense of that word, with the peoples of the Soviet Union and of the European East as well.'

Internal German policy was allotted a section of its own:

This government works on the assumption that the questions which have arisen for the German people out of World War II and from the national treachery committed by the Hitler régime can find their ultimate answers only in a European peace settlement. However, no one can dissuade us from our conviction that the Germans have no less a right to self-determination than any other people. The object of our practical political endeavours in the years immediately ahead will be to preserve the unity of the nation by easing the relationship between the two parts of Germany out of its present rigid state. The Germans are linked not only by reason of their language and their history, with all its splendour and misery; we are all at home in Germany. We also have common tasks and a common responsibility: to ensure peace among ourselves and in Europe. Twenty years after the establishment of the Federal Republic of Germany and the GDR, we must prevent any further alienation of the two parts of the German nation – that is, try to arrive at a regular *modus vivendi* and from there progress to co-operation. This is not just a German interest; it is of importance to peace in Europe and East–West relations as well.

We soon showed that the new government meant business. On 24 October 1969, even before our policy statement, we implemented a long debated decision: the Deutsche Mark was revalued upwards by 8.5 per cent. The German export industry survived this operation unscathed. In November we signed the non-proliferation treaty, thereby consummating yet another long delayed decision. Early in December the heads of state and government of the Six attended a summit conference in the Dutch capital. President Pompidou and I finally succeeded in establishing the conditions under which Britain and other countries could enter the European Community. Contrary to some reports, the French head of state expressly assured us of his confidence in our approaches to the East. At the NATO Council of Ministers meeting in Brussels in mid-December, the British Foreign Minister, Michael Stewart, left us in no doubt of his government's support. His American colleague, William Rogers, was emphatic that relations between the United States and the Federal Republic had improved. His government hoped that our efforts towards constructive talks with the Soviet Union and the countries of Eastern Europe would meet with a favourable response. Still in December, negotiations were started with Moscow and Warsaw. We also embarked boldly on preparations for talks with East Berlin.

Bonn was subject to no psychological law which prescribed that a government's fate and achievements be determined by the 'first hundred days'. It must, however, have been clearly apparent that a new chapter in German politics was beginning. We worked hard, but I was not sufficiently aware that the days of our first spirited onset would be succeeded by long periods in which the prime need was for perseverance, tenacity and an unflinching pursuit of our self-imposed aims.

11

European Unification

Brief as it still is, the history of the European Community is the sum of its crises. It might also be described as a process of development *in* crises and *through* them. In reality, debate on the need for European integration suffered not only from the often emotional claims advanced to justify this major objective of post-war policy but also from the dull monotony with which national prejudice and recalcitrance appeared to gain the upper hand. It was easy to soar above national egocentricities on wings of rhetoric, but this achieved little more than a Europe of declamations. What really counted were the interests that merited serious consideration: concern over employment levels and balances of trade, over the weal or woe of whole sectors of industry, over the prosperity of ever-plaintive farmers (on both sides of the Rhine, and not always plaintive without reason) – the list is interminable. To the man in the street, EEC co-ordination generally represented a ceaseless erosion of advantages or squabble over prerogatives. The European thrust of the early post-war period was swiftly blunted by these un-fortunate impressions. It is also true that the Brussels technocrats, who should have kept the machinery of our common institutions running in top gear, not only devised sensible rules but cultivated bureaucratic excrescences. The grand design was in danger of drowning in a sea of tedium. On the other hand, people sometimes overlooked the fact that Community normalization was bound to take on an element of habit and routine. The knitting together of national interests required patience. What mattered was to prevent a relapse into conflicts pre-judicial to internal equilibrium. This meant keeping the Community in motion because every standstill threatened to become a setback. Europe could not be integrated in a series of dramatic bursts. Whenever political energies needed mustering, however, traditions and real or imaginary national peculiarities and reservations crowded into the foreground. The adjustment of interests and prejudices is never a process calculated to arouse enthusiasm. Even so, there are worse places than our workaday Europe and its existence cannot be ignored.

Nationalism has been called the twin of democracy, and it is certainly true that both great impulses emanated from the French Revolution. The concept of nationhood had existed prior to this historic upheaval. It was linked with the concept of monarchy but underpinned by collective experience of a common tongue, a common culture, a religious tradition and a historical idea. The pre-Revolutionary nation-state attained its most pronounced form in France and Great Britain. The nation did not, as it were, pass into public ownership until society was reoriented by the French Revolution. But this early popular nationalism was allied with a claim to universality. Although nationhood construed as an experience and possession of the masses first evolved in France, which was strongly influenced by the American War of Independence, the intention was that all peoples should attain it. When invading Germany, with its dynastic dissensions, its temporal and spiritual principalities, its royal and ducal relics of a crumbling empire, the Jacobin armies and their Napoleonic successors saw themselves as agents of social and national emancipation – which they were. German Jacobins, who may be regarded as the earliest German democrats, fervently identified themselves with the French cause. So did the patriots of Italy and the intellectual avant-garde of the Slav peoples. There was a current saying that every civilized man had two countries, his own and France.

As everyone knows, the French Revolution degenerated under Robespierre into a reign of terror (even the sympathetic Jefferson turned from it in disgust) and paved the way for Bonaparte's dictatorship. In Germany, Spain and – above all – Russia, the Emperor of the French encountered nationalist resistance from patriots who rebelled against foreign domination and rallied round their monarchs. Although the demand for social reform was at least partially adopted, those manifestations of nationalism may be said to have been overwhelmingly conservative in character. They were compounded with something other than an experience of social protest as formulated in France, namely, with the discovery of 'the people', its language, legends and myths, its music, poetry and ethos. Such was the gospel of romanticism, which gained a profound hold on the world of German literature. Goethe was responsive to its call, as were those of his numerous contemporaries and successors who hearkened to, and wrote for, the people. This concentration on the people was also universalist in character. No one perceived this more clearly, perhaps, than the theologian Johann Herder, who alerted the Slav peoples east of Germany to their literature and ancient culture.

The wars of liberation against Napoleon were instinct with a desire to combine awareness of national existence with the concept of nationhood and social and democratic reforms. This dream foundered on the grim and galling reality of what was wrought by the Congress of Vienna and the 'Holy Alliance' between the rulers of Europe – a restoration which assured Europe of peace for almost fifty years but stifled the democratic and social desire for an emancipated existence. The spirit of rebellion flared up again and again, particularly in France. The middle class, which gained strength as industrialization commenced and trade expanded, took over the democratic legacy of 1789 and the national ethos as well. Its liberalism was, in fact, interwoven with nationalism. The intellectual avant-garde devoutly hoped that the liberation of every nation would bring peaceful coexistence to all.

Meanwhile, the interests of the dynastic states continued to operate. National egoisms were aggravated by industrial expansion and the growth of the middle class. Great Britain and France were already translating their dreams of national greatness into colonial empires expressive of a desire to rule or at least share the world. The peoples of Europe were still awaiting internal liberation, democratic and social reform. In 1848 the hour seemed to have struck, in Germany as elsewhere. Allied for the first time with sections of the new working class, middle-class liberals hoped that their revolution would compel the establishment of a national and democratic state. The German princes, together with the king in Prussia and the emperor in Vienna, seemed prepared to yield, but this dream, too, evaporated. The rebels had been bought off with vague promises. The monarchs graciously consented to grant constitutions but did not surrender control over the absolute powers of government. German unity was frustrated by the self-interest of the two great powers, Prussia and Austria.

Soon afterwards France experienced a resurgence of Bonapartism under Napoleon III. The relationship between the people and their self-anointed semi-dictator displayed many pre-fascist characteristics, if so they may be called. Nationalism became more pronounced under the new Bonaparte and tension between the countries of Europe increased. In Prussia Bismarck decided to solve the problem of German unity by force, not only without the Austrians but in spite of them. He used the brief war of 1866 as a brutal means of excluding the emperor in Vienna and the German citizens of the Danubian monarchy from membership of the German nation-to-be. The clash with France in 1870 became a national war and gave birth to the Second or 'Lesser' German Reich. Bismarck granted it a quasi-democratic constitution which imposed definite restrictions on the popular will. This Prussian-style nation-state never entirely lost its artificial character. It was created from above and lacked democratic legitimation.

The very artificiality of this structure may have accounted for its reliance on psychological exaggeration. German nationalism was beginning to run riot, encouraged by the country's rapid accretion of industrial and military strength. Many of its citizens now devoted themselves to noisy and arrogant demonstrations expressive of an underlying inferiority complex. They also turned their thoughts to the Germans who had been excluded from the 'Kleindeutscher Reichs-verband', in other words, the Germans of Austria. There was a deluge of Pan-German propaganda which went much further still, befogging the public with visions of a Greater Germanic Empire. Across the frontier, French nationalism was for ever being rekindled by shameful memories of defeat in 1871, which had also shattered a social utopia by bringing down the Paris Commune.

Meanwhile, the idea of nationhood was transmitted with growing urgency from Western to Eastern Europe. The peoples of the Danubian monarchy were becoming conscious of their own historical destiny. The very least they demanded was equality with Hungary, which had survived as a kingdom within the framework of the Austro-Hungarian federation. Was not Bohemia entitled to similar status? In the south-east, Slovenes, Serbs and Croats bickered fiercely both inside and outside the confines of the Danubian monarchy. In the east, the Poles rebelled against the partition of their country by Austria, Prussia and despotic Russia.

Bismarck employed an intricate system of treaties and secret agree-ments to keep his new great power in a state of peaceful equilibrium, though this balance required continual and skilful diplomatic adjust-ment. Doubtless aware of the dangers besetting his work, he strove to urge moderation on the Germans and restrained the belated desire for colonies which was bringing them into direct competition with the French and British. Economic rivalry engendered an unprecedented level of prosperity but one from which the broad masses derived scant benefit. This bred envy, especially among the Germans, who persuaded themselves that the malice of their neighbours, and notably of their 'hereditary foes' the French, had for too long barred their admission to the community of great and equal nations.

When Bismarck resigned in 1890, it was only a matter of time before the European boiler burst under the combined pressure of imperial megalomania, economic expansion, social unrest and nationalistic delusions. Every colonial incident was a potential prelude to disaster. The tragedy opened at Sarajevo in summer 1914, when Serbian nationalists assassinated the Austrian heir to the throne. Crucial diplomatic blunders on the part of Bismarck's successors were substantially responsible for the chain reaction which caused the European peace-keeping system to collapse like a house of cards. The British Foreign Secretary, Sir Edward (later Viscount) Grey, remarked that Europe had slid into war. This was doubtless true, but everyone – British, French, Germans, Austrians and Russians – had helped to dismantle the barriers that might have halted the plunge.

During that exultant outburst of collective dementia in August 1914, World War I seemed to be the culmination of European nationalism. It also seemed, with its murderous static warfare, millions of dead, mass starvation and universal impoverishment, to herald the death of such emotions. Not so. The unjust and, worse still, injudicious peace of Versailles proved an almost daily irritant to the Germans on whom it had been imposed and whose pride was already wounded by defeat. The conservative upper crust of society – landowning noblemen and captains of industry – could not reconcile themselves to the loss of so many of their privileges and mourned the institutions of the 'good old' or dynastic days. Apart from this, the revolution of 1918 had been a half-hearted affair which damaged the old power structures without demolishing them. The property-owning middle class flinched at the total revolution which seemed to be spreading from communist Russia. Inflation and recession not only wiped out established fortunes but destroyed the savings of ordinary people. A harsh and inexorable spirit of revenge, particularly in France, undermined the democratic and conciliatory governments of the Weimar Republic. Humiliated and bewildered, the Germans looked around for scapegoats. A minority turned to the communists in a superstitious belief that poverty could be banished by taking a leaf out of the Russian book. Another minority, which ultimately became a near-majority, sought deliverance in the irrational promises and anathemas of an Austrian agitator named Hitler, who blamed everything on capitalists, communists, social democrats, liberals and Jews – especially Jews, whom he regarded as the ringleaders of an international conspiracy. The masses came to share his mania. In Nazism – and, less extremely, in Italian fascism – nationalism attained a new and orgiastic pitch. Even more than in the years preceding 1914, collective exaggeration of national Messianism testified to underlying weakness.

Clashes with the youthful nation-states of Eastern Europe were not only inevitable but intentional. We all know what happened, just as we all know of the fresh hope that stirred so tentatively after 1945 – the hope that World War II and the crimes of the Third Reich had cauterized the cancer once and for all. The nationalisms of Eastern Europe – of which it cannot be said for certain that their brief history has allowed them to 'mature' fully – were brought under Soviet control when the continent was partitioned. Whether this will always remain so may reasonably be doubted because history seldom writes finis to anything.

The West witnessed a reawakening of the ancient dream of European unity, a distant vision which had continually fired the best minds in Europe. Though dispelled again and again, it survived in the internationalism of the labour movement, whose social democrats were natural Europeans from the very first. Meanwhile, responsibility for the fortunes of France, West Germany and Italy was initially entrusted to conservative politicians in the Catholic mould. Robert Schuman, Alcide de Gasperi and Konrad Adenauer translated Jean Monnet's ideas into reality and set to work to create the basis of a political union or federation, first through joint supervision of the coal and steel industries and later by means of an economic community. The French proposal that America's demand for the rearming of the Federal Republic within the framework of the Western Alliance should be countered by the establishment of a European defence association might possibly have shortened the road to political unity. This plan was thwarted by the opposition of conservative and communist deputies in the French National Assembly, but also by the abstention of the British, who at first opposed all forms of integration under Churchill's ageing leadership.

It turned out that national egoisms had yet to be wholly overcome. The road to European union has proved rough and arduous, yet the Treaty of Rome laid the foundations of a union which could and had to be developed further. As fears of political and military pressure from the Soviet Union waned, so progress became slower. It has taken people time to bow to the realization that Europe can and must be more than a mere bulwark against the communist menace, in other words, a product of peace and constructive co-operation.

Having assumed responsibility for the government of the German Federal Republic, I found myself confronted by one of the incessant crises referred to above – and not the easiest of them. Nothing was stirring in Brussels. Feelings of disgruntlement, disquiet and plain indifference were rife in the countries of Western Europe, which needed and wanted to unite but seemed incapable of doing so. Realism prompted one to ask whether what had been accomplished would grind to a halt unless there were a break-through to fresh ground.

The enlargement of the Community was still an open question. The British had shown no interest in a trading arrangement and were insisting on entry negotiations. France's tentative – indeed, negative – attitude was vitiating relations between the six founder-members of the Community. Tension between Paris and London was such that the French Foreign Minister's seat on the Council of the Western European Union – the Six plus Great Britain – remained unoccupied. The customs union had come into being despite a multitude of problems, and the three executives of the EEC, the European Coal and Steel Community and Euratom had been merged. Treaty provisions stated that the EEC would enter upon its final phase of development from January 1970 onwards, but the effects of the mounting crisis in the monetary system could no longer be ignored. More important things apart, what was to become of the common agricultural market, which, as an item of advance integration, was tied to a single unit of account?

To my satisfaction, the French proposed a European Community summit conference. (My aversion to the 'summit' cliché failed to dislodge it from the political vocabulary; the thing itself I thoroughly approved of.) The heads of government could not, of course, usurp the place of established Community institutions. Their aim had to be something more than a mere upgrading of the (necessary) Brussels routine. It was clear that the malaise in Brussels could not be overcome or the meeting between the heads of government prove successful unless Bonn and Paris found the strength and ability to evolve common answers. I had satisfied myself by direct correspondence with President Pompidou and through our respective ambassadors that we stood a genuine chance of substantially developing the Community and, at the same time, of taking the crucial step towards its enlargement. The formula for British entry – and this was the focus of interest – remained open. Pompidou and I did not agree upon it until the evening of the first day.

The conference took place at The Hague on 1 and 2 December 1969 in the 600-year-old Ridderzaal, part of the architectural complex occupied by both chambers of the Dutch parliament. Premier de Jong, an elegant-looking man who had been a submarine commander during the war, played host and chaired the talks with great skill. I was flanked at the conference table by Walter Scheel, a newcomer to the Foreign Ministers' club, and Katharina Focke, whose adamantine faith in Europe so often put us all to shame.

'The nations of Europe are expecting and insisting that statesmen should match the logic of history with the will to succeed.' As I said on 1 December, 'Europe has need of our success.' The German Bundestag and public opinion in my country expected me not to return without some concrete agreements on the subject of enlargement. Experience had shown, I said, that further delay might paralyse the Community. All our interests would be served if the Community expanded at a time when we were striving for closer co-operation between West and East. The Community must develop beyond the Six if it wanted to assert its place beside the super-powers, scientifically and technologically, and fulfil its international responsibilities. 'Anyone who fears,' I added, 'that the economic weight of the German Federal Republic may upset the Community's internal balance should favour enlargement for that reason too.' The contacts that had preceded the conference encouraged me to hope that the heads of government present were fundamentally agreed on enlargement. I proposed that countries desirous of membership be informed that negotiations could commence in spring 1970. We must not concentrate on Britain to the exclusion of other would-be members. The best interests of Europe dictated that our future relations with other countries, notably the members of EFTA, should also receive due attention.

Agreement was actually reached on the evening of the first day, during a conversation I had with Pompidou at the dinner given by Queen Juliana. The President wanted to satisfy himself that Franco-German co-operation would not in my view suffer from the Community's enlargement. More particularly, he wanted safeguards in respect of agricultural finance – a subject of great political importance to himself. I reassured him, but insisted that the agricultural regulations be revised so as to abolish the financing of surpluses. On the question of entry, I did not stipulate that an exact date be set for the start of negotiations. Pompidou, who had no wish to seem over-compliant in Paris, gave his consent to 'preparatory' talks between the Six and also to the formula that negotiations with Britain and other applicants could begin 'in the course of the year'.

The second complex of questions dealt with the intrinsic development of the Common Market. This presented more practical difficulties, although the magnitude of the obstacles had yet to dawn on us. The Council of Ministers was appointed to collaborate with the Commission in producing, by the end of 1970, a graduated plan for the development of economic and monetary union. A committee chaired by the Luxemburg head of government had already done some valuable groundwork. We were determined to make concerted and realistic progress towards economic and monetary union. Structural disparities between member-countries and divergences in economic aims and practices were real problems which only perseverance and co-operation could resolve. We emphasized that our goal was not an inflationary community, hence our desire that, during the preliminary phase, harmonization of aims should go hand in hand with the effective co-ordination of short-term economic policy.

In this context – encouraged by Jean Monnet and urged to exercise the utmost caution by my financial experts – I made an important offer: the Federal Government, which had never shown a lack of solidarity in regard to monetary policy, would fully co-operate in establishing a European reserve fund. Once the prerequisites were fulfilled, we intended to join others in setting up such an instrument of common policy and in determining its procedures. We would then be prepared to transfer a certain proportion of our currency reserves to the reserve fund, to be jointly administered with the reserves which our partners would also deposit in proportion to their resources.

My third request at The Hague was that a fresh attempt be made to co-operate in the field of foreign policy. There had been no progress since 1962. Our exchange of views, in which Great Britain had shared as a member of the WEU, had not taken us far. To resume it would not be enough. I proposed that the Foreign Ministers be instructed to work out a draft accord on the gradual development of political co-operation, tacitly presupposing the admission of new member-countries. This met with general approval. Consultations between the six – later nine – Foreign Ministers got off to a promising start in autumn 1970, though it still remains doubtful whether their formal statement of views on the situation in the Middle East was the right curtain-raiser.

The British approach to entry negotiations was of crucial importance to European development. I was curious to know what I should hear on the subject from Prime Minister Harold Wilson when I visited London early in March 1970. During an after-dinner speech there, I expressed my hope that the conference at The Hague had been a breakthrough for common sense. I was convinced of the vital importance of British collaboration inside the European Community.

Wilson and I talked at 10 Downing Street, first alone and then with our aides. He said that his government was entering into negotiations with the firm intention of bringing them to a successful conclusion. We should regard the recently published White Paper on the cost of membership – which had conveyed a largely unfavourable impression – as a 'tactical but honest' document. The difficulty was that the disadvantages were more or less quantifiable, whereas the benefits –

especially the dynamic effect of entry – defied quantification. No less than his successor, Edward Heath, the Prime Minister evinced keen interest in the political co-operation agreed upon at The Hague. Great Britain wished to be involved in this, if possible before the start of entry negotiations. Things having gone better since the December summit than I expected, I was able to inform Wilson that negotiations for entry would be instituted in the middle of the year. Although the details would first have to be worked out with Britain, a common date of entry would be fixed for all new members.

Our hosts had gone to great trouble to endow my visit with a ceremonial flavour. Wilson held a reception attended mainly by representatives of the London cultural scene, together with a number of Britons who had served in Berlin, and Harold Macmillan conferred an honorary degree on me in the Sheldonian Theatre at Oxford. I did not have to give a speech, much to my relief, but was obliged to read my words of thanks in Latin. The occasion enabled me to see how much had stuck after my years of study at the Johanneum in Lübeck (my comprehension was not total!). I was also welcomed in the Royal Gallery at Westminster by the Lord Chancellor and Mr Speaker, and addressed members of both Houses.

A few months later, in June 1970, the Conservatives took over from the Labour Government. Harold Wilson retained the leadership of his party, led it to victory at the polls early in 1974, and became Prime Minister once more. Shortly after leaving office he published a comprehensive and almost pedantic account of his official activities between 1964 and 1970. What surprised me was that, Commonwealth ties apart, he dealt with international affairs as if Britain were still a world power. Although I greatly respected Britain's efforts to tread the post-imperial path, I also considered it a blessing that the Federal Republic did not have to slough off any far-flung ambitions.

I and many of my friends were disappointed that the Labour Party had renewed its stand against the Community while in opposition, but I refrained from any form of interference and firmly emphasized that each country must decide the question of membership for itself. A substantial number of Labour politicians – led by the admirable Roy Jenkins – steadfastly clung to their pro-European resolve and, as it turned out, proved right in the end. Once again, it was not our business to judge whether our Labour friends were well advised to depart from British tradition and hold a referendum on the result of fresh negotiations. We could only point out, with due candour, that fresh negotiations could affect neither the Community treaties nor the substance of what had already been accomplished.

I had known Edward Heath, the new head of government, for years. He had visited me in Berlin and Bonn just as I had visited him in London, and each of us regarded the other as a worthy European partner. The fact that I now had to deal with a Conservative colleague in London was not in any way disruptive, either of bilateral co-operation or of our consultations on European topics. I never felt Edward Heath's reputed lack of personal warmth. Uncomplicated and characterized by mutual trust, our talks might almost have been described, without triteness, as friendly. Jean Monnet once said that the Pompidou-Heath-Brandt constellation could have been a good thing for Europe. He did not, of course, foresee that all of us – and Edward Heath in particular – would be prevented by economic and monetary problems from carrying out the wide-ranging programme agreed with our partners at the Paris summit conference in autumn 1972. By spring 1974, though for very different reasons, all our three countries were under different leadership.

When Heath visited Bonn in April 1971, I reaffirmed that the Federal Government would do everything in its power to guide the entry negotiations to a successful outcome. In private, however, I pointed out to the Prime Minister that some sectors of British public opinion took an unrealistic view of the Brussels entry negotiations. A BBC interviewer had, for instance, asked me a few days earlier why the Federal Republic did not exert 'more pressure' on France. I replied that I did not believe in pressure. At the same time, we had to make it consistently clear that unsuccessful negotiations would not only have adverse effects on Western Europe but might poison the existing Community. Nevertheless, nothing had occurred to change my belief that Pompidou desired a favourable outcome. I inferred from one of the President's letters that he himself was somewhat more flexible than the pronouncements of his representatives in the Council of Ministers suggested.

Heath said he had always been opposed to the formation of an anti-French Fronde. He had taken this view even when negotiations failed in 1963, and he still adhered to it. We discussed the expediency of direct talks between Heath and Pompidou. The Prime Minister, who drew encouragement from my visit and arranged a meeting with the French President immediately thereafter, wanted to know how my other partners would react to this idea and how I myself had managed to reach agreement with Pompidou at The Hague. Had I encountered any particular fears of Britain in France? I replied that one or two orthodox Gaullists 'like my friend Debré' looked upon Great Britain as an outpost of the United States. Pompidou adopted a more balanced attitude, but there were certain imponderables like the language problem, which should not be underestimated. Heath appreciated this. He stressed that Britain had accepted the Community in its final shape. All that now remained was to agree on intermediate steps, but it seemed hard to impress this on the French.

Foremost among Britain's practical problems was that of sugar from the Caribbean area – one good reason for me to include Jamaica in the itinerary of my forthcoming trip to America. Then there was the question of dairy products from New Zealand – a point on which I assured the New Zealand premier of my support when he visited Bonn. Another problem was the staggering of British financial contributions to the Community. The sterling problem (sterling's reserve currency status) could not be solved in a hurry, Heath insisted. The British were prepared to accept the regulations laid down by the Common Market treaties. Replying, I said that, for all the importance of sugar, cheese and finance, we should constantly underscore the major political need for unification and point out the dangers that would arise in the event of failure. Heath declared that public opinion in his country was sceptical. It did, however, contain a substantial 'grey area' in which pro-Market attitudes would gain the upper hand if it became evident that success was feasible. The dangers of ultimate failure were great indeed, not least from the aspect of East–West relations.

In October 1971 the British House of Commons voted for entry by a clear majority. The treaties were signed while I was visiting London in April 1972. Heath wanted as many as possible of his senior and junior ministers to familiarize themselves with the problems and procedures of the Community. That was why he had doubts about the appointment of Ministers for Europe, an idea which Pompidou and I were then considering.

Where the substance of foreign policy was concerned, London and Bonn adopted a very similar stance. Heath backed our policy towards the East, and our governments worked closely together in NATO.

Invited to Windsor Castle in the spring of 1972, my wife and I were impressed by a small but carefully selected exhibition designed to illustrate the House of Windsor's German connections. (One item we saw was a letter from Wilhelm II to his grandmother, Queen Victoria.) It was pleasant to accompany Queen Elizabeth on an evening tour of the castle and hear her discourse on her ancestors and the history of her country. A relaxed atmosphere prevailed in the royal family, even during meals with official guests. The Queen, whom I had more than once met in London since our first encounter during her visit to Berlin in 1965, chatted with an affability which was somewhat austere but far from strained. She showed herself well informed and asked some shrewd questions. Prince Philip, a jovial character, made it clear that his interests ranged far beyond sporting activities. He spoke eagerly of various topical questions – divorced from day-to-day politics – to which he had applied himself. One such problem was that of environmental protection, which we discussed in depth.

Like Norway and Denmark, Great Britain had renewed its experience of the unifying effects of a royal house during World War II. I would not wish to give the impression that my years in Scandinavia have converted me to monarchy – certainly not where Germany is concerned – but I fully appreciate that a modern society can derive benefit from traditional ties. I have never forgotten how Haakon VII squashed some angry conservative objectors after summoning his first socialist prime minister to form a government: 'Gentlemen, I am also king of the communists.'

Edward Heath and I met twice more during 1972, not only at the Paris summit conference in October but earlier on the occasion of the Munich Olympic Games. Heath visited me beside the Starnberger See on the very day when the attack on the Israeli team had reduced us all to a state of grim suspense. Although it was not easy to concentrate on political topics under these distressing circumstances, we weighed the chances of the expansionary process that was to be accelerated by a meeting between heads of state and government.

While Heath was revisiting Bonn early in March 1973, our fears were aroused by a strong speculative movement into dollars. The looming monetary crisis compelled him to return to London prematurely. This was a stage at which bold action might perhaps have imparted a decisive fillip to European monetary union. I let it be known that we were ready to pay a high price – in other words, extensive support for Britain in particular – if a European solution could be found. The first prerequisite would have been a universal freeing of exchange rates. Like us, Heath saw a chance to emerge from the crisis by means of a major forward step. We conferred with our experts late that evening at Schloss Gymnich and next afternoon in my office. That was as far as we got. On the British side, political determination failed to overcome the ifs and buts of the experts. Our own experts, and above all the gentlemen of the Bundesbank, probably heaved a sigh of relief as well. They regarded the risks as great, although they were prepared to go a long way, where sums, interest rates and time-scales were concerned, to render possible a support operation of unprecedented scope. This would have meant pooling our reserves and agreeing on the parity of sterling. Like Italy, Britain remained outside the West European currency 'snake', from which France also withdrew for eighteen months at the beginning of 1974.

In October, when I visited him at Chequers, the Prime Minister discussed his preliminary experience of the European Community. He regretted the absence of a 'cabinet' on which problems could converge and from which initiatives could flow. In the public mind, Brussels signified nothing but conflict and controversy. Was the existing machinery good enough? Were consultations at Foreign Minister level sufficient, or should we aim higher in order to combat adverse developments? Would I object if he stated publicly that occasional meetings between heads of government were desirable? I agreed, naturally, this being a point to which Jean Monnet and I had devoted thorough consideration. He proposed quarterly 'summit conferences'. I favoured the formulas 'twice a year or more often' and 'presidential meetings'.

During this same weekend at Chequers, Heath and I received the alarming news that a new war had broken out in the Middle East. We discussed its provisional outcome when I visited London for a party leaders' conference one month later. During December we conferred with other heads of government in Copenhagen. A few months later, Labour was back in office.

In November 1970, one year after I had assumed the Chancellorship, I was able to tell the Bundestag – which was largely united on this score – that we had substantially helped to overcome years of stagnation in European policy. Thanks to German initiatives, things were again on the move. In demanding that more be done to promote European integration, my government was preaching to the converted.

No discussion of Europe can fail to revert to the Bonn–Paris relationship. During the years under review, this meant co-operation between Pompidou and Brandt. Georges Pompidou, whom I had met while Mayor of Berlin, had been close to de Gaulle almost throughout the post-war period. He worked in the provisional head of government's office immediately after the Liberation and was appointed premier in 1962. Counting three summit conferences, we met on fourteen occasions during his years as President and mine as Federal Chancellor. We spent many hours in conversation and periodically exchanged confidential letters. Pompidou and I had three private talks on the occasion of Franco-German consultations. He generally rounded these off by calling in his prime minister, with whom I discussed bilateral matters at a separate meeting. We adopted our predecessors' habit of concluding the second day of consultations with a full meeting at which we ourselves and our departmental ministers presented a résumé of the proceedings. Pompidou used an interpreter, but he understood German quite well. He sometimes delivered his after-dinner speeches – or parts of them – in German, as when my wife accompanied me to Paris early in 1971. We did more than establish the requisite practical working relationship. Our private talks were characterized by a candour and mutual understanding which remained intact even when differences of interest and opinion reared their heads.

A true son of Auvergne in the rural heartland of France, Georges Pompidou was shrewd and circumspect but not without mental agility – conservative, but not blind to the needs of the future. His deep regional roots underpinned a brilliant education which reflected the proud traditions of the French bourgeoisie and was all the more impressive because he never ostentatiously flaunted it. A sober and rational cast of mind did not prevent him from overcoming his initial reserve and forging friendships.

Pompidou's personal relations with de Gaulle did not remain un-clouded. His office displayed a picture of the General – dating from the end of the war – and he often mentioned the name of his great pre-decessor, particularly in our latter conversations. During my first visit to Paris as Chancellor, however, when I innocently suggested that we might send de Gaulle a joint greeting (we were seated over our after-dinner coffee with a few others), my proposal was received in such silence that I felt guilty of a *faux pas*. Pompidou never got over the fact that the General had withheld his support when he became the victim of a malicious and slanderous campaign a few weeks before being elected President. I avoided drawing any premature conclusions from this. President Pompidou always considered himself – especially in foreign policy – to be the executor of de Gaulle's political estate.

Given the snail's pace of European unification, it was inevitable that the same subjects should recur. When he visited Bonn in July 1970, Pompidou emphasized that France and Germany must keep in close touch during negotiations with Britain. (Introductory talks on entry negotiations had just taken place in Luxembourg.) The overriding problem, he said, was monetary and financial. Britain's troubles were far from over – in fact they might be only just beginning. Six months later Pompidou opined that, where Community obligations were con-cerned, the British were at a 'humorous' stage. (They wanted to start with a contribution of 3 per cent, whereas the Dutch contribution in the old Community amounted to 10 per cent.) I commented that the British were demanding too much and the French conceding too little. Pompidou replied that he was confident of British entry. Traditional insular reactions were involved, of course, as – at the moment – were certain tactical considerations. However, the British had discovered that they could not destroy the Community and that membership was consequently in their interests. My own view was that we should not carry the dispute over figures too far. 'So many unknown factors will become operative in the next five to eight years – we can't form any estimates of them at this stage.'

Despite everything, the conditions under which Britain could enter the Common Market were agreed at Brussels in June 1971, aided by the direct contacts between Heath and Pompidou which I had recommended to both men in the spring and of which they both kept me faithfully informed. In view of this, I could only smile at reports that a new *entente cordiale* had dawned. I welcomed Franco-British co-operation in the interests of Europe as a whole. Next time we met, Pompidou reported that Heath wanted his country to devote itself unreservedly to Europe. This had been apparent from their discussions, he said. Once Britain entered the Common Market, everything would go more quickly. This would mark the beginning of a process which should be viewed from the aspect of 'finality' – in other words, from that of European political integration. The British would then have to venture a mutation of their traditional policy: they would have to give their links with Europe precedence over existing ties with the Commonwealth and the United States.

During the Paris consultations in January 1971, I referred to conjectures in the French press that 'certain persons in the Federal Government' wanted discussion of economic and monetary union to aim so high that it would inevitably fail and leave us a 'free hand in the East'. In reality, *Ostpolitik* was one of our reasons for wanting progress in the West. I pointed out that we and our partners had agreed at The Hague to invest the European Community with a new quality. We now had to define our ideas on a general process spanning ten or twelve years. What would happen after the initial phase of economic and monetary union? What powers did the Community's institutions require? Quite rapid decisions might prove necessary in the monetary sphere. The national central banks would therefore have to be grouped into some form of European central banking organization.

Pompidou said that, like me, he was presupposing a period of ten to twelve years and concurred with the German demand for parallel co-operation in economic and monetary policy. He hoped that national currencies would be automatically linked after an initial phase of roughly three years, a concomitant of this process being support for weak currencies. I interjected that we wanted an agreement on future procedure before the initial phase ended, and that this entailed the formulation of political objectives.

The President said he did not oppose the transfer of powers to the Community provided the Community was not equated with the Commission. The joint body composed of central bank presidents should be strengthened and in some measure subordinated to the Council of Ministers. We both favoured a precautionary or safety-clause during the initial phase, in case a national currency became effectively devalued and the government in question was unwilling to take the necessary remedial measures. We both assumed, therefore, that the creation of a monetary union would take at least a decade and be dependent on the steady growth of economic integration.

The President had spoken at a recent press conference of appointing Ministers for Europe. Though interested, I drew attention to the problems that would confront a co-ordinative minister without powers of his own. The President had also mentioned that Ministers for Europe might some day bear European as opposed to national responsibility. I found it hard to envisage this transition.

Pompidou replied that he had no wish to be dogmatic and that these ideas had referred to the distant future. Some day there would be a European government – perhaps initially composed of one member representing the interests of each nation – which would possess powers conferred on it by the national governments. In the final phase, there would undoubtedly be a European parliament as well. The federative structure of the Federal Republic might possibly serve as a model in this respect. 'But these are all things which I myself – you too, perhaps – will not necessarily live to see.' The President wanted to emphasize two points: we must advance along the road to European union, but he wanted to do so cautiously and flexibly. The Federal Republic might well be even more devoted to flexibility than France because its fundamental and justifiable aim was national unity.

We again discussed the question of Ministers for Europe in summer 1972. I had given thought to two models and was open to either solution: co-ordinating Ministers for Europe without administrative machines of their own, or permanent members of the Council of Ministers with national cabinet rank. Pompidou replied, somewhat more guardedly than before, that his suggestion posed internal problems such as the overlapping of Foreign Ministers' responsibilities. We must, he said, revert to the question after British entry – or certainly next year. It would not be a bad idea for governments to incorporate a new form of Permanent Representative. Early the following year Pompidou said that the appointment of Ministers for Europe was probably premature. It might perhaps be easier to set up a body of State Secretaries to co-operate with the Permanent Representatives at Brussels in handling current business under Foreign Office supervision.

I noted that the President's forecast for 1971 was thoroughly optimistic: 'It is clear that, if marked by a Berlin settlement, the ratification of your treaties, the beginning of economic and monetary union and the admission of Great Britain and others to the European Community, this year will hardly have been a year of immobility.'

When we met in July 1971, I took the President up on one of his earlier remarks and tried to lay even stronger emphasis on integration as a political objective. Without effacing national identities, we should aim at the creation of a rationally organized European government 'which can make decisions in areas of common policy and is subject to parliamentary control'. This was not disputed, nor was my description of the relations between our two governments. Not that we exchanged letters every other day, these had become extremely easy and natural, and had proved to be an *entente élémentaire*. (This conversation took place while we were cruising down the Rhine from Mainz to Koblenz in the motor vessel *Loreley*. I did not know when I suggested the trip that 5 July was Pompidou's sixtieth birthday. He wanted as little fuss made of it as possible.)

Two months previously, at the beginning of May, we had decided to float the German mark after being inundated with DM40,000 million in foreign currency in a short space of time. This cautious prophylactic measure involved me in an argument on two fronts. It had to be explained to the Opposition at home that we were dealing with a crisis affecting the dollar and the international monetary system, not our own currency. Our European partners, in their turn, had to be assured that we were not treating them unfairly. The French were fiercely critical. Pompidou, who was convinced that we had deliberately floated as a prelude to revaluation, expressed great concern on behalf of the French economy and the European agricultural market. I explained that floating the mark was not intended as a long-term policy. Where exchange rates were concerned, we wanted a greater external fluctuation range (Pompidou: 'Like the Americans . . .') and a smaller internal one. The French thought it essential to control movements of capital.

Our two Economic Affairs Ministers, Schiller and Giscard d'Estaing, who did not get on too well for all their *politesse*, disputed among themselves and in our presence. Pompidou was most insistent. How could we possibly dispense with restrictions on capital movements? There was, for instance, the question of the Arab oil producers. We must surely be able to control such an abundance of capital or we might one day find ourselves at the mercy of some unpredictable head of state.

The monetary problem continued to dog us. It received further discussion when I visited Paris at the beginning of December 1971, outside the consultative cycle. (Having meanwhile failed to evolve a common formula at Brussels, we had simply agreed to 'tie in' different procedures while awaiting a reform of the international monetary system.) Pompidou and I were eager to compare notes after our meetings with Brezhnev. Apart from that, we were both scheduled – like the British Prime Minister – to have talks with President Nixon: Pompidou in mid-December on the island of Terceira in the Azores, Heath a week later in Bermuda, and I myself at the end of the month in Florida. Pompidou had opposed the idea of announcing these meetings in a joint communiqué on the – in my view – rather overstated grounds that we ought not to look like 'satellites'.

He did, in fact, refer with some sarcasm to the 'US poker game over devaluation' and made it clear that France would stay with Britain and Italy. He appreciated what the American alliance meant, just as I did, but he could not on principle accept that Europe should finance America's military, political and economic activities out of its own deficits – and that was just what we were being asked to do. I conveyed my impression that Nixon, too, was seeking an accommodation. Then I took Pompidou fully into my confidence and informed him of the guide-lines Schiller had taken to the Club of Ten conference held in Rome a short time before.

In Paris in February 1972 we were confronted by the results of the monetary conference that had taken place in Washington in December. First privately and then in the presence of our Foreign and Economic Affairs Ministers, Pompidou voiced his dissatisfaction at the attitude since adopted by the Americans. We ought, he said, to resume work on economic and monetary union. We could not manage without instruments for the control of short-term capital movements. He wanted to tell me – 'before Schiller comes' – that he did not believe in the feasibility of 'total' economic liberalism. This invariably meant that the strongest triumphed. It was pointless to court death for the sake of liberalism's rosy illusions.

I had asked that thought be given to whether political co-operation, which was only pursued as an itinerant business shuttling between capitals, might be reinforced by the establishment of a small administrative secretariat. Pompidou agreed that a 'lightweight' secretariat was worth considering and suggested that our projected State Secretaries' committee might devote itself to the problem. Our next meeting failed to yield agreement on whether the secretariat should be based in Paris or in Brussels. No disharmony resulted from this difference of opinion.

P.P.–R

As Pompidou remarked after our consultations, there was genuinely no reason to speak of clouds in the Franco-German sky.

At the Bonn consultations early in July 1972, the President seemed understandably disappointed by the results of his referendum in April. It could hardly have rejoiced his heart that fewer than 60 per cent of French citizens went to the polls to vote on the enlargement of the European Community. After a 7 per cent deduction for blank or spoiled ballot papers, those in favour amounted to only 36 per cent of the total electorate and 68 per cent of actual voters.

Pompidou was also dissatisfied with preparations for the 'summit' which I had taken the precaution of suggesting early in 1971 and which was now scheduled for the autumn. Information reaching him from the Benelux countries implied a revision of the Rome treaties. France was not dogmatic, but she wanted no such amendments. Having recourse to the treaty provision whereby the Community could be assigned new functions was another matter. Pompidou did not want the Commission upgraded, nor did he at present wish to discuss direct elections to the European Parliament. We could talk about the appointment of State Secretaries for Europe. It would be realistic to concentrate on economic and monetary union, but the British had called another temporary halt to this by floating the pound. In view of the new dollar crisis, we should agree to throw our ideological or theological ideas overboard. Under present circumstances, it would be better to postpone the summit by a few months.

Replying, I said I had never believed that Europe could take shape on the drawing-boards of constitutional lawyers; its development would be promoted by the solution of real, practical problems. In my opinion, the enlargement of the Community was sufficient justification for a summit in itself, though I would not object to a postponement.

After reverting to the subject of institutions, Pompidou declared that we were not far apart. But there were proposals which, for all their sincerity, made him suspect that some people cherished vain illusions. There were also inordinate proposals obviously designed to cast France in the villain's role. He did not mind this in itself, but we had to be clear on whether we wanted to create Europe at all – he sometimes doubted it. Nevertheless, substantial progress had been made during our own period of co-operation. The Hague conference had been held, agreement had been reached on the problem of agriculture, Britain's membership was on the cards, and a joint European approach had been hammered out – after a fashion, but still – at the monetary conference in Washington. A preliminary step, albeit more symbolic than real, had resulted in the monetary field from the narrowing of fluctuation ranges.

He sometimes had the impression that, even if their motives differed, France and Germany were the only two countries with a genuine desire to progress along the road to Europe.

Like Mediterranean problems, the Western and Eastern components of our foreign policy were regularly discussed with our West European partners and the French President in particular. At our very first consultation in January 1970, the latter spoke of his anxiety lest the two super-powers agree on the demilitarization or neutralization of Western Europe. He also foresaw a danger of unequal reductions in American and Russian forces. By July 1970, when we next met in Bonn, his fears had crystallized: the conference on security and co-operation in Europe would and should take place, but he had grave misgivings about MBFR and thought it might accelerate an American withdrawal. Apart from the material content of what was to be negotiated, I regarded both schemes – CSCE (Conference on Security and Co-operation in Europe) and MBFR – as a new means of linking North America with Europe.

Despite the candour and cordiality of our relations, French suspicions were easily kindled. My American trip in spring 1970, during which I emphasized the future ties between Europe and the United States, seemed to arouse fears in Paris that it might be a manœuvre designed to mobilize US support for British entry negotiations. The genuineness of my desire to promote the European Community to the status of a partner on equal terms with the United States found only gradual acceptance. This was the very point on which Pompidou posed four questions in January 1971. While not rejecting my proposal for necessary consultations between the European Community and the United States, he opposed their institutionalization. The Americans must not, he said, be led to believe that they could exercise a right of supervision over the European Community.

At our meeting in July 1971 I compared my previous month's trip to America with my visit to Washington fourteen months before. The US–EEC relationship had also been discussed then, but American interest in the subject was rather theoretical. Things had now changed. Many leading Americans had grasped that the Europeans were engaged in an earnest endeavour, not only to enlarge the Community but to develop and deepen it.

Pompidou replied that we had similar interests but different points of departure. The Western Alliance was indispensable, certainly, but its decisions were taken outside Europe. That was why he urged the Europeans to acquire greater weight. The danger of total integration was that the Russians and Americans might agree to neutralize us all.

This, quite clearly, was Pompidou's nightmare. While remaining thoroughly loyal to the Alliance, France had wanted to preserve her individuality. This was not vanity but an expression of individual freedom and of the country's determination to confront the United States as a partner in its own right. Besides, the fact that the French had withdrawn from NATO but not from the Alliance obliged the United States to pay more attention to European interests.

Pompidou again referred to the potential danger of a Russo-American get-together. If this came about, it would testify to Europe's impotence. France had reorganized her defences after the Algerian war and built up her nuclear armaments at great national expense. She was not prepared to carry out enforced reductions.

In December 1971, after my visit to Brezhnev, I placed German-American relations in a suitably wider context. It was not US-German relations that concerned me now, but a European policy co-ordinated with and directed towards the United States. Our interests prescribed that the withdrawal of US forces be delayed. This necessitated good relations inside the Alliance and an avoidance of economic friction as well. I was not among those who overestimated the current US crisis. The United States still possessed great reserves of untapped energy. Many dominant political sentiments and groups would disappear, facilitating the country's transition to a phase in which it ceased to think itself capable of ruling the entire world – for nobody could do that any longer. I also wanted to get the following remark off my chest: whenever Americans, for instance at a NATO Council meeting, spoke of financial reliefs, it never occurred to the French representatives, either, to do more than glance at the Germans and nod approvingly. (I forbore to mention my recollection of the horror that had dawned on French faces during my Foreign Ministry days when someone asked what people would say if we, too, withdrew from the integrated defence system and requested the Americans to vacate the Federal Republic!)

In summer 1972, with reference to renewed controversy over the monetary problem, the French President declared that the concerted floating currency system was leading to a sort of Yalta between the United States and Europe. The result would be a monetary partition of the world in America's favour. I suggested that we might sit down with Nixon or ask him by some other means what the Americans themselves were prepared to do to defend the dollar. Pompidou agreed, but opined that Nixon would not want a conference before the Presidential election. Once again: the Alliance must not be destroyed but US tutelage could not be permitted. Patently wavering in his assessment of the danger of isolationism, the French President declared that the Americans could not, in any case, turn their backs on Europe unless they were afflicted with complete clouding of consciousness and prepared to run an inordinate risk.

At the Paris summit we agreed, after some argument, on the formula 'constructive (transatlantic) dialogue'. I must, however, make it clear that my French partner's profoundly sceptical attitude had remained unaltered during our talks in 1973. Pompidou declared in January that Europe was not simply an outpost of the United States. Equally, détente would be impossible if people in the West asked themselves every five minutes if the Soviet Union were about to descend on us. In June 1973 he added that the Americans should demonstrate that their interests were linked with the continuing existence of freedom in Europe. The US Government sensed this, but public opinion in the United States made isolationism seem possible, and isolationism meant Soviet supremacy.

In November 1973, after the Middle East war, Pompidou described his misgivings thus. Events had shown that, were a serious crisis to arise some day, the American President would resort to the use of American military strength without prior consultation. If he had enough time and were not too worried, he might perhaps say a word for courtesy's sake, but he alone would decide. (Brezhnev never thought of asking Bulgaria either!) This was precisely what France had always realized, hence de Gaulle's withdrawal from NATO integration. Relations with America ought to be extremely close, but Pompidou was still opposed to any institutionalization of US-EEC relations. The Americans might by this means try to insinuate themselves into the Community as a form of censor. (It was only an apparent contradiction that we – like the British – had simultaneously gained the impression that France was preparing to draw somewhat closer to NATO.)

Where our *Ostpolitik* endeavours were concerned, we could count on the solidarity of all our West European allies. From the first day of my Chancellorship onwards, Pompidou left me in no doubt that he intended to help me overcome any difficult problems. He confirmed this at our consultations in January 1970, when talks with the Soviet Union had just opened. Despite all the obstacles to my efforts, which were being undertaken in our joint interests, he urged me not to give up. The French had repeatedly emphasized when conversing with the Russians that they had great faith in the German Federal Republic and in my government, and that they regarded German revanchism, so called, as a pure fiction. In July 1970 the President underlined his 'moral and political support' and stressed the importance of Four-Power rights in Berlin.

My account of the *Ostpolitik* controversy back home betrayed an excessive faith in the Opposition's common sense. I told Pompidou that our political warfare would no doubt become even fiercer in the short term. As soon as the treaties were signed, however, or probably by the end of the year, the situation would resemble that which had ensued on the signing of the hotly disputed non-proliferation treaty. Our citizens would discover that Soviet tanks were not drawn up outside the Palais Schaumburg. We would then reapply ourselves to less spectacular foreign policy assignments. By the year's end, inter-party controversy would be once more focused on domestic issues.

In January 1971 Pompidou described the Moscow and Warsaw treaties as proof that I had chosen the path of realism. We were thus moving parallel to French government policy. France unreservedly supported my efforts to deal with the consequences of the last war and promote genuine security in Europe. I thanked the President for having actively and expressly backed this policy – 'for which France has in some respects pointed the way' – in all its phases.

Pompidou spoke of a race between West and East. The Western economic and social system was incontestably superior. It was nonetheless likely that the East – because of the Czech crisis, conflicts in Poland and internal difficulties in the Soviet Union itself – would intensify and rigidify its ideology still further. The progress of the East would then become even more laborious. But there might later come a day when the East took the road to liberalization. This would make it possible to raise a number of issues. We must not represent ourselves to the East as a bloc. Like me, he was well aware that communist references to co-operation were aimed at driving a wedge between Western Europe and America. On the other hand, the East must be given to understand that the West, and the European Community, was amenable to genuine co-operation.

I said that we knew too little about the opinion-forming process which was at work inside the Soviet leadership. Relapses could not be ruled out. As I saw it, the Kremlin had decided after the Czech crisis that its own camp would be easier to discipline politically if individual countries were granted opportunities for economic, technical and cultural co-operation with the West. However, the Soviet Union wanted to participate and not let go of the reins.

In February 1972 Pompidou declared that a substantial East–West rapprochement in Europe was inevitable. We could not ignore one another, nor were we doing so. The process was already under way economically but would also develop in the human, cultural and even political domains. To him, the great question seemed to be which of us would submit to 'corruption' by the other. He believed in freedom, which was anyway more appealing than totalitarianism. It had, however, to be recognized that a totalitarian system could take swift and ruthless action in cases where a liberal system required more time. That was why the Europeans had to be extremely wary and present a firm front, thereby facilitating contacts and promoting détente in the best possible way.

In July of the same year Pompidou said he was not of the opinion that CSCE should encompass the establishment of a 'permanent body', but he advocated firm dates for ministerial meetings or the like. As to MBFR, he surmised that if Nixon were re-elected he might regard these negotiations as a diverting pastime and ensure that they were spun out. France did not oppose 'stabilizing measures' designed, say, to render troop movements more easily detectable. Although his government favoured détente, the Russians should not be led into temptation.

I said we should watch to see whether the Americans betrayed an interest in something over and above SALT after Nixon's trip to Moscow. I was thinking principally of CSCE. MBFR, too, would bind the Americans to Europe, though negotiations would doubtless drag on for years.

In January 1973 Pompidou reported on his talks with Brezhnev at Minsk ten days before. The European Security Conference theme had occupied more than half their time. They had also discussed the possibility of talks on cultural and related matters. In contrast to six months earlier, Pompidou speculated that it might after all be wise to establish a permanent institution after Helsinki; this might diminish the risk of aggressive moves. Brezhnev had reacted favourably to proposals for confidence-building measures such as the reciprocal observation of military manœuvres. The Russians favoured French participation in MBFR. France would not be represented at Vienna on 31 January but was taking an interest in the subject. It might be useful for her to participate in the discussions at a later stage. However, Pompidou instinctively sensed the possibility of becoming enmeshed in dangerous machinery.

Brezhnev had said that, in any case, the initial value of force reductions could only be symbolic. Even so modest an objective would probably require a hundred meetings. The General Secretary had also told Pompidou that it was wrong to assume that the Soviet Union planned to neutralize Central Europe and Germany in particular. This did not accord with Soviet ideas. Brezhnev regarded the Common Market as a fact of life, Pompidou said, though he had not made himself very clear on the subject. Pompidou went on to welcome the SALT agreement for its effects on détente but expressed his abiding opposition to a US–Soviet condominium. Brezhnev had spoken of his confidence in me and declared his readiness to discuss important matters 'with Nixon and Brandt'. He was extremely mistrustful of Britain.

It was stated – in the presence of Premier Pierre Messmer – that we were now at one on the subject of MBFR. During my last talks with Pompidou in the summer and late autumn of 1973, his concern over the future course of Soviet policy became more explicit.

I have already commented on the difficulties of mounting the October 1972 summit conference in Paris. The effects of the programme agreed there remained disappointing, perhaps because we reached too far into the future. This does not, however, preclude the implementation of our plans on a different time-scale.

Pompidou's attitude during the prelude to the conference was vacillating, hesitant and moody. I never quite discovered why the French delayed their invitation to the summit conference until autumn. (Did they hope to barter it for an acceptance of Paris as the head-quarters of the Political Secretariat?) Foreign Minister Schumann, who visited Bonn at the end of August, had asked us *inter alia* if it might not be better to wait until after the Dutch elections and our own. I found this altogether incomprehensible, given that some sort of election was always impending in a nine-member Community. The Community's enlargement certainly justified a meeting between heads of government. However, I let it be known that we were not '*demandeurs*' and could tolerate a postponement if need be.

On 26 August I noted: 'It still isn't clear whether a Paris conference will come off in October.' On 9 September: 'Pompidou arrived for a private talk. I still can't quite decide whether or not he wants to postpone the Paris summit scheduled for 19–20 October. I stressed that we could put up with a postponement from the German angle, but that it would entail substantial disadvantages from that of Europe.' I neither urged nor insisted. We both agreed that progress towards economic and monetary union should not, for practical reasons, be hurried.

Heath and I had separately informed Paris that we considered a postponement unwise. After my conversation with Pompidou in Bavaria I telephoned the Prime Minister, who had visited me there some days earlier, and conveyed my impression that the summit would take place after all. An invitation for 19 and 20 October arrived from Paris shortly afterwards.

Speaking after the conference opened, I said it was an event of historic importance that nine nations numbering 250 million people should now be united in the enlarged Community. For our own people and many others, it was important to know that this union served to safeguard and consolidate peace. 'It may be useful to reaffirm the objectives of European unification. I am in favour, but I do not think this conference is expected to produce pipe-dreams. What we are rightly expected to produce are realistic decisions affecting the months ahead and the next few years.'

Internally, I said, this meant further progress towards economic and monetary integration in defiance of all attendant difficulties. It meant establishing a fund for monetary co-operation. But it was also necessary, in view of our common task, for this conference to give a sign and make practical decisions aimed at checking the growth of inflation. I strongly emphasized that joint efforts must be made to restore greater price stability. Failure to do so might rock the social and political, and not merely the economic, foundations of the Community.

Externally, however, we should have to discuss not only our relations with our major partners in the industrialized world, notably the United States, but opportunities for co-operation with Eastern Europe and partnership with the developing countries. In all these matters, it was important that the Community should display a readiness to accept worldwide responsibility.

The subject of social progress having been included in the agenda at my suggestion, I had prepared a memorandum on which I now proceeded to enlarge. I was concerned, I said, that people should realize what the Community meant and could mean to their conditions of life and employment. 'Social justice must not remain an abstract concept, nor must social progress be misconstrued as a mere appendage of economic growth. If we develop a European view of social policy, many of our countries' citizens will more readily identify themselves with the Community.'

Meanwhile, the Council's decision-making powers must be enhanced by investing it with a certain permanency and tightening up its procedures. Ministers or State Secretaries for Europe could relieve Foreign and Economic Affairs Ministers of some of their work and facilitate internal co-ordination. The European parliament must have its powers strengthened.

On foreign relations, I said that the enlarged Community must not make its presence felt in the world by means of economic weight alone. It should enlist that presence in the service of broad political objectives. However, the Community and its member-countries would be able to contribute to the world's store of common sense and stability, peace and prosperity, only if it were capable of presenting a common front based on shared and carefully considered positions. I urged that we should resolve to initiate an organic dialogue, beginning with our principal partner, the United States. Community institutions should be charged with conducting a regular exchange of views at the highest level. 'Western Europe and America need one another as confident and equal partners.' Both parties had lately been over-concerned with matters relating to their own short-term interests.

I thought it unwarrantable and improper that the French draft for a final communiqué should make no mention whatever of our relations with the United States and Canada. This led to an open dispute at the conference table. I could only construe the absence of any allusion to America as a snub, and ostentatiously declined to suggest any amendments. My point was taken, and the joint communiqué finally assumed a form acceptable to me in that it spoke of a 'constructive dialogue'. One peculiar feature of current US policy – unless I was being fed with false information – was that the Americans carefully notified the French Government that they had not asked me to take up the cudgels on behalf of a European-American dialogue (which they had not!).

In conclusion, I was able to state: 'We have seen to it that a constructive dialogue will be initiated with America, together with other important trading partners – Japan and Canada, to name but two.' A readiness for neighbourly relations with the countries of Eastern Europe was also expressed. On behalf of the Community and its member-countries, the heads of government made an offer of co-operation based on a common trading policy. They also resolved to act in concert at the projected conference on security and co-operation.

Where crucial economic and financial questions were concerned, there unfortunately seemed no possibility of progressing beyond joint declarations to effective joint decisions on a policy of stabilization. On the other hand, my government was expected – mainly by the British, Italians and Irish – to make a decisive contribution to the financing of the new Regional Fund. Although Pompidou and I had agreed in July on a 'cautious entry', I had in Paris to adopt an extremely reserved attitude rather than incur accusations from Opposition spokesmen at home that I was on the verge of giving away good German money. Our partners also expected us to make greater contributions in favour of joint aid to the developing countries – another point which we were unable to concede.

Our 'iron rule' of parallelism between monetary and economic measures had nonetheless been reaffirmed. In resolving to set up the European Monetary Co-operation Fund (before 1 April of the following year), we had taken care not to create a new source of inflation – nor the 'extraction plant' for German currency reserves to which our critics made irresponsible allusions at home. The Paris resolutions expressed the Community's intention of embarking on new activities in regional and industrial, scientific and technological, environmental protection and energy policy. For the first time, social adjustment had been placed on a par with economic decisions.

References to the efficiency of Community institutions remained nebulous. Only an exchange of views took place regarding the Council of Ministers. No agreement was reached on appointing Ministers or State Secretaries for Europe. Controversy reigned over direct elections to the European Parliament. The Dutch and the Italians were foremost among those in favour, Pompidou and Heath were both against. All in all, it was hard to contradict the Danish premier when he asked why anyone should think it suddenly possible for the Nine to resolve what the Six had disagreed on for so many years. I myself concentrated, as I have already mentioned, on securing wider powers for the Strasbourg assembly, but I only succeeded to a modest extent.

Many members of the public may be unaware that issues debated on the periphery of such conferences sometimes carry as much weight as the items on the agenda itself. Lunch on the first day of the Paris conference was an 'intimate' affair – there were ten of us including Premier Pierre Messmer – at which we animatedly discussed the oil crisis, which all of us knew to be imminent but none knew how to avert.

These occasions also provide scope for many 'one-to-one' discussions, nor are the conferences themselves as tedious as the texts of official communiqués might lead one to suppose. This time in Paris I was the centre of cordial – indeed, jovial – attention. My predominantly non-socialist colleagues inferred from their ambassadors' reports that the outcome of the Bundestag elections was no longer in doubt, and they did not seem displeased. At table I came under fire. Was I a genuine socialist, or did I really feel part of the conservative majority? Although I was on good personal terms with everyone there, I had no wish to be branded an ex-socialist. This applied to Messmer, if anyone – or, if one wanted to delve back further, to Pompidou himself, who once confided to me that he had felt attracted to the Young Socialists prior to 1933 and that his father had been a socialist.

I stated at a Federal press conference that our decision to enlarge the Community, taken at The Hague in December 1969, had already stood the test: the three new member-countries had been an enlivening factor in Paris. 'To view things in broad perspective, the most significant result of the summit conference is that our heads of state and government have undertaken to establish a European union by the end of this decade . . . This union has become a long-term project for West Europeans, and to that I attach great importance.'

My visit to Paris in January 1973 coincided with the tenth anniversary of the Franco-German treaty of friendship. Accompanied by seven Federal ministers and the premier of Baden-Württemberg, who was then responsible for cultural affairs, I expressed our gratitude for 'privileged co-operation'. Our French hosts did not omit to provide a stylish setting for the festivities, and Pompidou invested me with the Grand Cross of the Legion of Honour. He called my vote of confidence in the November elections 'a valuable pledge for the future'.

At this meeting, Pompidou said we had no cause to complain of inadequate progress in bilateral relations. The economic enlacement of our two countries was, in fact, far advanced, and their governments had greatly encouraged this process. Many of our citizens had come to know and respect each other, almost as if the tribulations of the past had never been. Youth activities had been broadly successful, and numerous town-twinnings bore witness to active neighbourly relations. Pompidou's sole complaint – and not a groundless one – was that the French language had a hard time holding its own in our schools. The President declared it a bad thing to grant English monopoly status. He also found it rather incongruous that German and French ministers should communicate in English and preferred them to master each other's languages. We ought also, he said, to encourage greater variety in language teaching outside our two countries.

Not for the first time, Paris pressed for greater co-operation in the sphere of arms procurement. My own view was that the wrong course had been set in earlier years – certainly, French attention had concentrated rather one-sidedly on the financial easing of France's own projects. The same applied to aviation and space travel. Strong national interests also came into play when preference was given to American partners in the field of nuclear energy or when the French colour television system, rather than the German, was pushed through with massive government backing but limited success.

My visit to Paris in November 1973 was meant to introduce a new rhythm into our meetings – autumn in Paris, spring in Bonn – because we did not see why we should invariably assemble in the French capital under grey skies and beside the Rhine in the oppressive heat of summer. For all that, we never had any time to spend on our respective cities, countryside and people. Only once – during the anniversary consultations in Paris – did Scheel and I manage, without supervision and ceremony, to dine with our wives at a first-class bistro.

Many of Pompidou's pronouncements at our last two meetings – as well as a presidential conference in Copenhagen in December – had a testamentary flavour. He believed, for example, that 'this Franco-German entente is indispensable, not only to Europe but to the equilibrium of the world'. On the afternoon of 22 June, when we were alone, he asked:

How do you see Germany's future in the light of what is happening? Don't think me indiscreet, but much depends on this from France's point of view. My question doesn't refer to the sort of German future you would *like*. If the GDR ceased to be communist and reunification followed, France would applaud, but this is surely improbable. Recognizing the attitude of the United States and the Soviet Union, and viewing matters in the light of your policy and your relations with the countries of the East, how do you visualize Germany's future *then*? That's the question as I see it. I am asking you to interpret a policy which must necessarily be more complex than the French.

Replying, I said that politically authoritative figures in the Federal Republic, both inside and outside the ruling coalition, realized that Germany's problems could not be solved in isolation. We could hope for an improvement in the state of affairs created by partition only if relations between the two parts of Germany became easier. However hard we found it, and in the hope that future generations would not disown us, we had to give peace-keeping in Europe precedence over the nation-state concept. If we wished to help the nation, especially in its spiritual dimension, we had to help its human components. Although our Constitution pledged us to national unity it also pledged us to Europe, and we needed Europe for at least three reasons: first, as a factor in the organization of peace; secondly, because it afforded a greater opportunity to make life easier for people by means of communication; and, thirdly, because it could become a species of greater fatherland even for those who deliberately took their stand on the soil of German history.

None of us could have detailed knowledge of the political future, but France could rely on the existence of Federal German leaders who would not be diverted from their European course even if certain temptations were placed in their way – which could not be ruled out. In saying this, I was also making a sober assessment of those politicians in the Opposition camp who regarded themselves as an alternative government. One day, perhaps, a reunited Germany might take its place within the framework of a greater Europe in which the question could be differently put. One could not anticipate the workings of history, but the President need have no fear that the Federal Republic would pursue a see-saw policy even if it were exposed to the temptations I had hinted at.

Pompidou replied:

I must tell you in all sincerity that the leaders of France, and I myself in particular, have always been among those who have best understood the need for your *Ostpolitik*, and who sense the real nature of the German national drama. I want to emphasize this, even though there are memories that might have prompted me to feel concern. You have tried, with some success, to banish such memories. Since you have referred to a constant factor in Germany's new policy, I would draw your attention to two fixed magnitudes in that of France. One is that France could not fail to be extremely alarmed by the neutralization of Central Europe – even if unarmed – and all that might conduce to it. Secondly, you need not fear that there is no alternative to the present French majority – excluding the communists – which would guarantee a continuum in foreign policy . . . Relative strengths have changed and political relationships have been transformed. America's vast superiority over the Soviet Union, the Cold War, universal fear of a united Germany which once defied the entire world – all this has vanished. I realize that MBFR serves the US leadership as an instrument, but the projected reductions should not relate to national [European] forces. [Nixon had told him at Reykjavik a few months earlier to urge me not to earmark any German forces for reduction on the grounds that these were a sustaining element in the defence of Europe.] Brezhnev's visit illustrated to me yet again that it is one of the Soviet Union's aims – a Russian foreign policy objective which has now been pursued with admirable perseverance for almost a decade – to accomplish the neutralization of Central Europe. The Soviet Union has a policy which it pursues with extreme consistency. The army plays a very important role. The members of the political leadership are exchangeable.

I said that, to judge by my talks with Brezhnev and Nixon, no major progress in MBFR would be possible. (Nixon had told me that he was not interested in having one 'good' German division set off against one Czech or Polish division.) The formula 'security equals defence plus détente' had, I said, been approved by a large majority at my last party conference in Hanover. MBFR could not be restricted to the two German states. On the other hand, it should not be conveyed that the Germans' sole function in the Alliance was to provide the infantry, either because their allies needed them or because there was a wish to tie up their economic potential. Furthermore, the Americans would ultimately be guided by what they deemed their own best interests, not by what we told them. We should have no alternative to NATO in the foreseeable future. I did, however, agree that no 'European finality' would be feasible unless it incorporated defence. I required answers to the following questions. First, how were we to interpret French strategic thinking and the operational plans based thereon? Secondly, what areas of Germany were covered by French nuclear weapons, and did they by any chance include that part of the country which maintained close links with France? One of my first duties as Foreign Minister at the end of 1966 had been to conclude an agreement on the stationing of French troops in Germany. This was inconsistent with the quality of our relations in other respects.

After making a provisionally adequate response to my question about operational planning, Pompidou said:

> European wars like those of the past are inconceivable. The probability is that there will be peace in Europe while relations between the Soviet Union and China remain as they are. One cannot, however, rule out the hypothesis that political upheavals – in Yugoslavia, for example – or a communist take-over in Italy or even France might prompt a Soviet attempt to encroach on Western Europe. This is a working hypothesis, albeit not a very likely one. In such an eventuality, France would stand by her allies. She would not remain aloof. France has taken up a specific position because it was thought necessary to kindle French patriotism and abolish straightforward subservience to American decisions. But France will not abandon solidarity with her allies . . . It is clear that, from the strategic aspect, Europe's defence cannot be guaranteed by conventional means alone. This applies as much to France as it does to the United States. Europe cannot be effectively defended except with American nuclear weapons. As the years go by, and to the extent that progress is made in tactical weapons, talks must be held between the Americans and ourselves.

Neither the Federal Republic nor France could accept, Pompidou went on, that their armoured divisions should be annihilated, that the

Russians should suddenly appear on the Rhine and the Americans then decide to use atomic weapons. We should then be liberated but – unfortunately – dead.

Pompidou reaffirmed that he was not convinced of the survival of economic liberalism.

Certainly I don't consider the Soviet system a good one, but some measure of central planning is essential. The future course of the European economy will necessarily be a middle road between the Soviet system and theoretical economic liberalism. Large firms will have to back these endeavours. The same applies to multinational concerns. They will have to make a start too, and doubtless they are already coming to see that their interests must not invariably be viewed from the standpoint of their American parent companies.

When I objected that experience favoured the preservation of as much competition as possible, Pompidou said that the French intended to make their planning increasingly supple and turn it into more of a guidance system. He was a supporter of the market economy, but it should be remembered that the weak required protection against total dependence on the strong. (Where oil was concerned, we had to organize ourselves so as to resist certain operations by the producing countries. Concessions should be made to the raw materials producers or they would succumb to communism.)

On the European Security Conference, Pompidou said that the Russians had suggested holding it in Paris so as to lead him into temptation. He had greeted their proposals coolly and did not intend to go to Helsinki in person. He had told Heath that he was quite as opposed to performing a French cancan at Helsinki as a *pas de neuf* with Nixon. As for Nixon's proposal for a summit with the Nine: 'I'm not going to rush to pay homage to Nixon. Even allowing for present power relationships, I've no intention of behaving towards Nixon like a vassal towards Caesar.'

I shall discuss this allusion in the chapter that follows. In April, Henry Kissinger had delivered a speech on US relations with Europe and canvassed the idea of a 'new Atlantic Charter' which was, for rather obscure reasons, to embrace Japan as well. The impression I formed in Washington was that European observers had read too much into this speech. Nixon, whose knowledge of its substance was only superficial, had concentrated on bilateral issues when I tried to discuss the broader complex of European problems. He did, however, make a definite reference to his intention of visiting several European capitals and NATO headquarters in the autumn.

According to Pompidou, Nixon had told him at Reykjavik that what was involved was a new alliance, not the reaffirmation of old principles. 'I told him I had no intention of rocking the Alliance. I also told him that there were no profound difficulties or real points of friction between Europe and the United States.' Commercial negotiations with the United States were going to be long drawn out. The Senate would have to be given something and concessions demanded in return.

Where monetary problems are concerned, the United States puts me in mind of a singer who repeats the same refrain for years and suddenly notices that it has lost its appeal. Given tact and patience, however, we shall deal with this subject as well. I asked Nixon how one was really supposed to regard the 'Year of Europe' – as the beatification or subjugation of Europe? The Americans are engaged in turning a corner – but they're taking it very wide, as American cars do.

Pompidou took a pessimistic view of the Middle East situation subsequent to the October War (of which more will be said).

French policy is not directed against Israel. However, it has to be appreciated that Israel's existence is dependent on external relations, not only with her immediate neighbours but with the entire Arab world. We are faced with a contradiction which has to be accepted and lived with: on the one hand, we need the aid and protection of the United States – the protection of Europe being wholly in the US interest; on the other, there is a realization that the course of developments compels us to possess something that is not solely dependent on the Alliance and its aid.

The French President and I agreed that no transition to the second phase of economic and monetary union would be possible by January 1974, but that we should plan for greater monetary support without pooling our reserves. Pompidou's main insistence was on settling the problem of gold. He could hardly have guessed that only a few months later – in January 1974 – he would be sending Giscard to me to announce France's withdrawal from the West European monetary association known as 'the Snake'. It was important that we should maintain this form of co-operation with our Benelux neighbours and Austria, Sweden and Norway. By summer 1975, as everyone knows, France found herself in a position to rejoin the Snake at least temporarily, though the

P.P.–S

question of British and Italian membership had to remain pending.

Pompidou's verdict on détente policy during our last consultative meeting was that it should be pursued 'with both eyes open'. The power of the Soviet Union was still growing and the future did not look altogether rosy. Continued vigilance was essential. France's positive attitude towards the West had just been reaffirmed, as witness the co-operation of his officials in framing the statements that had been drawn up by the Nine and the fifteen members of the Alliance with a view to ensuring that the Kissinger initiative did not fall on barren ground.

However, the French Government is wholly opposed to Kissinger's proposals for a triangle or circle inclusive of Japan – though not opposed to supplementary joint declarations with Japan and Canada. I am convinced that relations with the United States should be extremely close, not only within the Alliance but in the commercial, economic and monetary sphere. The Americans may have tried to push the countries of Europe somewhat further than the latter wished. This may be attributable to a measure of insecurity prevailing in the United States, even if it conflicts with the assurance displayed by Kissinger.

Pompidou and I met once more at the Copenhagen conference in mid-December 1973, when he took an active and patient part in our deliberations in spite of failing health. We had seen the extent to which illness had affected his appearance when he visited Bonn in June. He and his wife did not hide their concern, though they naturally made no reference to the gravity of his condition – if, indeed, they realized it themselves. News of his death reached us at the beginning of April 1974. My tribute included the following words:

I think of Georges Pompidou with a sense of gratitude. He represented the French state and its great history to the full, but of himself he made little. He gave service and did his duty. To do this demands the iron self-control which was a distinguishing feature of his personality. To use a hackneyed but, in his case, fitting phrase: he died in harness. Historians of the future may question whether it was a good thing that he never felt able to yield to pain instead of resisting it so courageously. It does not behove us to judge. We can only admire his self-discipline.

I attended the memorial service in Notre Dame. My gaze fell on

Giscard d'Estaing and Chaban-Delmas, who – though temporarily united in mourning – were preparing to contest the succession with results that are now common knowledge.

The road to the Community's new summit conference in Copenhagen was paved with disappointments and setbacks. The EEC had not covered itself with glory when the Middle East conflict flared up again. The attitudes adopted by the Nine in their Brussels declarations hardly justified any claim to a balanced approach, and there was no question of their exerting any real influence on the dangerous situation. Europe displayed no perceptible solidarity in face of the oil crisis – short-term as regards supply and long-term as regards price – and this against a background of the monetary confusion and economic distortions that were barring the way to economic and monetary union. What was more, the Nixon-Kissinger 'Year of Europe' had never been co-ordinated with us, nor could it be described as a successful operation in other respects. As one who had always championed a well-ordered relationship between the European Community and the United States, I was very depressed by the squabbles between us and Washington.

Regrettable contradictions became apparent in US policy towards Europe. On the one hand, Washington had for years recommended the unification of Western Europe – indeed, promoted it – on the relevant grounds that it would become a stabilizing factor in international relations. On the other, it doubtless seemed easier in practice to deal with a number of small and medium-sized European countries rather than undertake a more definite adjustment to the West European factor.

During the months that followed Kissinger's April speech, I consistently recommended that the governments of our West European neighbours react to US policy in a way which would harmonize European and American interests to the fullest extent possible. By the time Kissinger visited Bonn in July there had been a substantial – and, if my memory serves me, not purely tactical – approximation of attitudes. In mid-September the nine Foreign Ministers approved a number of principles governing our reply to the Americans. Then came the Middle East war. Discussion of the subject was resumed at the December summit meeting, and six months later – without much drama – approval was given to the new texts, which related partly to the Alliance and partly to economic relations between the Community and the United States. (The Luxemburg resolution of June 1974 pledged the nine governments to consult the United States in all matters of common interest, either individually or jointly. The NATO heads of government, with Nixon participating, signed the new

Declaration on Atlantic Relations at a meeting in Brussels on 26 June.)

The Copenhagen conference of December 1973 undoubtedly suffered from the fact that it had to be organized by a government fresh from a severe defeat at the polls. Outwardly, the meeting was strongly coloured by the technological and journalistic adjuncts of a big international conference. No really confidential exchanges were possible except during dinner and an ensuing get-together at Christiansborg, where we frankly aired our concern about problems relating to energy and raw materials.

A special problem arose from the presence of several Arab ministers, who requested an interview with our Foreign Ministers. Our reception of them may have been over-constrained. In any case, I felt bound to insist that the Israeli Ambassador was likewise offered an interview by the Danish chairman. I only succeeded in overcoming stubborn French resistance by hinting that, if the worst came to the worst, I would invite the Israeli Ambassador to meet me independently.

Copenhagen yielded a well-phrased document on the European identity. This accorded with the French wish that our new agreements with the Americans should, as it were, be prefaced by a European statement of personal particulars. This document attempted to outline the international role and responsibilities of the union-to-be. Its claims may have been too remote from reality for it to gain the attention its careful phrasing deserved.

Copenhagen also witnessed some interesting exchanges of view on the burning question of energy. Encouraging pronouncements were embodied in the communiqué, too, but there was no breakthrough to a common policy. Such was the impact of the oil crisis, however, that it bred a new willingness to conclude long-term agreements on deliveries to the consumer countries and guaranteed returns to the producers. Although no detailed statements resulted, it became clear that resistance to the regulation of trade in raw materials – of which Bonn was a prime exponent – would not endure for much longer.

The Copenhagen participants limited themselves to cosmetic resolutions on economic and monetary union. A second phase, termed 'consolidatory', was ordained, but the Paris time-table could not in fact be fulfilled because economic circumstances varied between one Community member and the next. Economic and monetary union was becoming a longer-term objective.

Thanks to the restrictive attitude of my financial experts towards the establishment of a regional fund, I found myself in a rather embarrassing position at Copenhagen. Deliberately addressing myself to our own government as well as others, I set the 'ante' for admission to European regional policy so low that those present could not have taken me seriously. At the summit conference in Paris a year later, a genuine decision was taken on this matter.

(The December 1974 conference also reached agreement on corrective mechanisms for the financing of the Community budget and on direct elections to the European Parliament in 1978. In March 1975 the heads of government held their first-ever meeting in Dublin under the designation 'European Council', having agreed to confer thrice yearly in this capacity. It was intended to relax the unanimity rule governing the Council at Brussels and widen the powers of the Commission. In June 1975 the British referendum yielded a clear majority.)

The road to Europe was not blocked, but progress remained slow and arduous.

12

Washington

America during my years as Chancellor was the land of Richard M. Nixon, a Republican President who governed despite Democratic majorities in both houses of Congress and despite the powerful and, so it sometimes appeared, dominating influence of strong personalities such as Henry Kissinger and James Schlesinger, who undoubtedly left their mark on foreign and defence policy.

Although I did not observe Nixon and Kissinger together often enough to be able to pronounce with certainty on their mode of co-operation, it was not my impression that the President functioned as the puppet of his senior foreign policy adviser. Nixon's authority could be not only seen but sensed, and he had no need to emphasize it unduly. He was well-informed about events, persons and developments in the world at large. His judgements did not match Kissinger's in every detail, but their strong general similarity was unmistakable. Even if the Harvard professor, with his instinctive grasp of the necessary and opportune, may sometimes have regarded the President as his 'instrument', Nixon nevertheless contrived to become master, as it were, of the ideas with which his confidant supplied him. He certainly never dispensed with personal evaluations. Only during our last encounters, when the pressure of the Watergate affair was endangering the functional efficiency of his entire administration, did Nixon's sense of reality seem to have suffered. He delved all the more doggedly into the foreign policy problems in which he saw his true mission and enduring source of achievement. Ideological bias had ceased to play any appreciable part in his decisions or his analysis of international relations. True, he never for a moment disguised the fact that he still regarded the Soviet super-power – notwithstanding a desire to advance 'from confrontation to co-operation' – as the main adversary to be held in check. But his aim had ceased to be an imaginary 'victory' over the arch-enemy and become a rational, balanced system which additionally embodied an accommodation between the United States and the vast Chinese dominions of Mao Tse-tung. Tension plus balance between the 'big Three' – the United States, the Soviet Union and China – were the basis of the equilibrium which Henry Kissinger expanded into the 'five fingers' system in which Western Europe and Japan were to fulfil an equilibrating function of their own.

Whereas we in the Federal Republic were saddled with conservatives who overwhelmingly lacked the courage to face facts and break taboos, both Liberals and Social Democrats were impressed by Nixon's relatively free and flexible foreign policy as manifested by his visits to Moscow and Peking. He never let scruples stand in his way. Even so, it was hard to associate Nixon the amiable host with the man who transformed the White House into a stronghold for ruthless practitioners of power and an operational base for arbitrary zealots. Whether chatting informally or debating with clarity and precision, the President was always faintly inhibited. He seldom seemed at ease or entirely relaxed. A hint of restlessness and insecurity lingered, perhaps because he had never quite come to terms with the straitened circumstances of his early life. He was doubtless aware that I had not been born with a silver spoon in my mouth either. This may have prompted him to inject a certain camaraderie into our relationship which he occasionally overdid. He was only too fond of pointing out that we had each entered two races (I for the Chancellorship, he for the Presidency and Governorship) before clearing the final hurdle.

Nixon had a keen sense of timing when trying to be funny. He sometimes reminded one a little too forcibly of an experienced solo entertainer, as, for example, when he arranged variety programmes for soirées at the White House. His entrances were skilful if a trifle over-staged, like the evolutions of his White House guards, who seemed to have borrowed their uniforms from a provincial production of *The Merry Widow*. The President was an obvious striver after style.

Nixon's insecurity may also have accounted for the imbalance of his domestic power politics, which were in remarkable contrast to the reasoned nature of his major foreign policy objectives. To wind up the Vietnam War required courage, even if the President was naturally at pains to avoid representing the transformation of the 'old' Cold War champion into the 'new' exponent of restraint in foreign policy as a dramatic conversion of Saul into Paul. The American withdrawal from South-East Asia was, in fact, covered by means of operations involving a drastic use of force (one need only cite the 'Christmas bombings' or the campaign against Cambodia). But the basic common sense discernible in the strategy underlying his foreign policy, though not always in its implementation and methods, seemed to fail as an element of power-control and self-control at home. Whether blindly or – in the end – with his eyes wide open, Nixon allowed the United States to drift into the most dangerous constitutional crisis in its history, steadfastly refusing to avert disaster with the aid of a ruthless candour which might well have saved him at an early stage in the Watergate affair. It is ironical that he should eventually have fallen prey to the monitoring devices which he himself had installed in the White House so as to preserve every utterance and every incident for 'history' – or so he claimed.

I feel unable to pass any 'definitive' judgement on the incumbency of the 37th President of the United States. To do so I should have to be more impartial than anyone could be after several years of generally businesslike and sometimes close co-operation. It would also be rather tactless of me to deliver a verdict on something which American experts will undoubtedly continue to debate for years to come, not uninfluenced by the ebb and flow of public opinion, so final judgement will have to be deferred.

As a modest personal contribution, let me say that my own picture of Richard Milhous Nixon has undergone considerable fluctuations. I first had a chance to observe the then Vice-President, who was less than a year my senior, while visiting the States in 1954. This was during the McCarthy era, and I shared the horror it aroused in many Americans whom I respected, including some from deep in the traditional Republican ranks. When I returned four years later as Mayor of Berlin, Nixon was again Vice-President under Eisenhower. He proved himself a pleasant, sympathetic and helpful partner, though we did not discuss any matters relating to the substance of democratic society.

I preserve a vivid memory of the day in November 1963 when I met Nixon in the Washington church from which President Kennedy was borne to his final resting-place. After losing to Kennedy by a short head and failing to win the gubernatorial contest in his home state of California the previous year, Nixon had bidden farewell to politics – for good, or so it seemed. He looked profoundly shocked and quite devoid of any lingering political ambitions. Nobody could have guessed that circumstances within the Republic Party would contribute to his re-nomination in 1968. He narrowly defeated Hubert Humphrey, a good friend of mine but one whose ability to make a good president I then regarded with some doubt.

In November 1972, during the time we worked together, Nixon won one of the most sweeping electoral victories in US history, though he did so against a Democratic opponent who failed to command support among large sections of his own party. Our years in harness left me convinced of Nixon's talent and energy, and none of the slight reservations to which I have already alluded could detract from this.

Even in spring 1973, I was no more certain than most other people that the budding Watergate affair would develop into a scandal of the first magnitude. This became clearer by the end of the year. Although I had never been impressed by the domestic achievements of the Nixon Administration, it was not for me to judge them like an American. To me, Nixon was not just another partner in the field of foreign policy but, in virtue of my country's special interests, the most important partner of all and the one whose opposition could have nullified our policy of compromise, normalization and active peace-keeping. We did, in fact, discover a broad area of common ground because Nixon himself had an interest in overcoming US immobility. My memory of this endures despite Vietnam (and what the student protest movement, transmitted by American universities, meant to us in Germany and Europe). It endures despite the burden imposed on us by US policy when the international monetary system collapsed and despite Nixon's agonizingly protracted refusal to resign, which poisoned the atmosphere until he finally departed at the beginning of August 1974 under circumstances of which some are public knowledge but others may still be cloaked in secrecy.

Henry Kissinger's great gifts cannot fail to evoke admiration. That the son of an immigrant family should, by dint of talent, industry and skill, have assumed responsibility for the foreign policy of the United States in one of the country's highest offices remains a major achievement and a tribute to the free society which gave this member of a minority group his chance. Unlike several of my friends, I only met Kissinger fleetingly during his academic years. I, too, was fascinated by his exceptional intelligence, his subtle grasp of international dynamics and the vigour with which he managed to convert acquired knowledge into practical politics. His historical and strategic works had given a convincing demonstration of his intellect. I was impressed by his habit of approaching current problems by way of historical experience. Although this practice has never been alien to me, it presents dangers of which Kissinger himself is doubtless aware. The world in the latter half of the twentieth century can never correspond to the 'concert of powers' which determined the politics and diplomacy of the nineteenth. On the other hand, the security adviser and Secretary of State showed himself capable of introducing totally novel and unconventional methods into the diplomacy of our time. One has only to think of the quasi-oriental perseverance with which he conducted negotiations for a Vietnam cease-fire with his opposite number Le Duc Tho, or the shuttle conferences with which he 'imposed' an armistice in the Middle East. Swiftly as the basis of the South-East Asian equilibrium disintegrated, and precarious as the situation between Israel and its Arab neighbours remained, these were impressive ventures and still are. Kissinger's conception of détente, which he sought to endow with an overriding strategic framework by means of the SALT agreements, has undergone repeated tests. The balance between the super-powers can never be immutably fixed by a series of agreements and must be continually re-established. But these endeavours are essential to the control of destructive forces capable of blowing our civilizations out of existence. They are also the framework with which our practical détente policy in Europe can never dispense.

The word Europe provides a clue to the shadows which occasionally flitted across my relations with Henry Kissinger. I could not escape the impression that he was reluctant to pay clear enough regard to the existence of the European Community and its slow and laborious evolution – as if he, in particular, found it hard to grasp the transformation that was overtaking the continental home of his fathers and forefathers. He may sometimes have viewed the old continent with the disdain of the new Roman for Hellenic petty states which devoured each other in their mutual ill-will, machinations and jealousies. But it was precisely this 'Greek fate' which the European Community was seeking to avoid. The laboriousness and irrationality of its procedures undoubtedly frayed the nerves and tried the patience of all its partners, Henry Kissinger included, but he did not always contrive to be helpful and understanding. Many of his reactions seemed arrogant or intolerant, though this could hardly have been intentional. Perhaps he became mentally as well as physically overtaxed as the years went by.

Our meetings were stimulating, productive and, in a few important instances, characterized by extreme mutual trust. Contact between the Palais Schaumburg and the White House became closer in my time than it had ever been. Together, we helped to ensure that Atlantico-European policy was always translated into a common design even if the interests of all parties failed to achieve a perfect dovetail (not an invariable disadvantage). Even when I felt myself insufficiently understood as a European, this was the predominant consideration governing my discussions with President Nixon and his senior aides.

Early in 1970 Bonn played host to one of those German-US gatherings which are usually characterized by the presence of more American dignitaries than German. On this occasion the guests included, apart from John McCloy and George Ball, a number of leading Congressmen. Welcoming them, I outlined the common themes of the years to come. 'Everyone present should know that we shall never abandon the view that friendship between Germany and America is essential to us. Close and trustful co-operation must be pursued, and not only in the political sphere and in defence.' Conscious of the burden that had devolved on the American nation from the stationing of its soldiers on European soil for the past twenty-five years, we had endeavoured largely to offset this charge on the American balance of payments. We stood by the obligations we had undertaken, and we expected our allies to do likewise.

I further pointed out that our two countries were on the threshold of important negotiations with the countries of the Eastern bloc. 'Objectively speaking, the time is ripe for a transition from confrontation to co-operation.'

This echoed the phrases with which Henry Kissinger had, on Nixon's behalf, summarized the American interest in modifying East-West relations. On 18 February 1970 Nixon presented Congress with a 'State of the World' report which referred to a strategy for peace. It also contained the assertion that America could no more detach itself from Europe than it could from Alaska. The US role in the world – and thus, to some extent, in the Alliance – had substantially changed since Kennedy's day. Growing involvement in Vietnam was consuming America's resources, moral as well as material, and there was a widespread feeling that the country had overreached itself internationally. The government seemed temporarily unable to cope with its domestic problems. Though latent at first, economic difficulties led in 1971 to a lifting of the free convertibility of the dollar into gold – a step that would have been unthinkable a few years earlier.

Despite this, America's status as the Western super-power remained intact. So did my conviction that, for all its problems, the country possessed almost inexhaustible resources and a capacity for regeneration. At all events, nothing overrode the need to solve our European problems – especially those affecting the East-West relationship – in close accord with Washington. Nixon's report to Congress in February affirmed America's intention to support the continuing development of the European Community. I was nonetheless aware that, where the Community was concerned, we had to reckon with a somewhat ambivalent attitude. America's chief fear was that its own commercial interests might be prejudiced by the Common Market and its enlargement. I resolved to make this the central theme of my talks in Washington.

I began my first visit to America as Chancellor – in April 1970 – by inspecting some German soldiers who were being trained at Fort Bliss in Texas. My trip to the Mexican border was sadly overshadowed by the kidnapping of our ambassador to Guatemala, Count Spreti. This was a particular blow to me because we had both been elected to the first Bundestag in 1949 and had remained in personal touch thereafter, especially during Spreti's tour in Cuba. Having already discussed possible ways of helping him while passing through Washington, I addressed an urgent appeal to his captors, but in vain. Spreti was found murdered. What was to be done about international terrorism? What protection could be afforded to diplomats serving abroad? These were problems which acquired grim topicality in several of my conversations on this trip.

My Washington programme was prefaced by three restful days at Camp David, the Presidential retreat in Virginia which had originated under Roosevelt as a kind of labour corps camp. Nixon put the place at my disposal, probably at the suggestion of Ambassador Rush. I was excellently looked after, and seized the opportunity to watch some wide-screen Westerns in the evenings. Preparations for the forthcoming political talks were made at Camp David by Egon Bahr, myself and Henry Kissinger, at that time the President's chief security adviser. Kissinger's interest in our *Ostpolitik* was lively but not untinged with scepticism. I gained the impression – one which occasionally recurred in later years – that he would rather have taken personal charge of the delicate complex of East-West problems in its entirety.

My meeting with Nixon on 10 and 11 April was the first since his visit to Bonn and Berlin early in the preceding year. We were on easy terms, having known each other for over fifteen years. I had also established a friendly relationship with Secretary of State William Rogers, as with his predecessor Dean Rusk, and respected his acumen.

Foreign Minister Scheel had arrived in Washington the night before. Defence Minister Helmut Schmidt and Finance Minister Alex Möller were holding simultaneous talks with their opposite numbers in the American capital.

Ceremonial banquets are customarily followed by after-dinner speeches. In the case of gatherings with a political background, these addresses, which are usually brief, give one an opportunity to strike important 'atmospheric' notes. They do not have to adopt as states-manly a tone as an official speech, nor – of course – do they have to be as businesslike, outspoken and detailed as actual talks with foreign partners. After-dinner speeches can thus be of great assistance in explaining unfamiliar views to those present, who are usually representative of various social sectors.

On this occasion I referred to the dictum that America could no more detach itself from Europe than it could from Alaska. Europe, I said, would no more be able to detach itself from America than it could from itself. There were voices that accused the Germans of being willing to plunge into a course of 'Realpolitik' in a questionable sense. They implied that we tried to follow a policy of self-interest in disregard of the moral values which must also guide international policy.

I am certainly not thinking in terms of that kind of 'Realpolitik' when I speak of the necessity to accept realities. Freedom, democracy and self-determination are values which we would never renounce. Not only has their significance been borne out by our experience; they also define our moral position in world politics.

Nixon's guests at this dinner included a number of senior officials and military figures who had been concerned with Germany after the war. In his own speech, the President joked about his premature phone-call to Kissinger on election night the previous October, claiming that he had got the wrong number. He also flirted with the German names of a substantial proportion of his White House aides and cited his German mother-in-law as a further example of our many and various ties.

We began our talks in the Oval Room on 10 April and continued them next morning. Nixon opened by stating that agreement on every detail was less important than the certain knowledge that we were linked by common interests and objectives. Proceeding on this assumption, we could learn from one another by frankly speaking our minds. He therefore wanted to ask, right away, what my principal objections were to a substantial reduction of the American military presence in Europe. I drew attention to the politico-psychological factors involved, and, above all, to the fact that the essays in détente which we both considered necessary must be founded on an effective alliance.

Nixon replied that he was fundamentally opposed to withdrawing troops from Europe. However, he had to tell me in all honesty that he was subject to considerable domestic political pressure on this point. I quoted his February report to Congress and spoke in favour of NATO Secretary-General Brosio's proposal for a discussion of strategic and fundamental issues within the framework of the Alliance. Bilateral problems relating to offset payments must be resolved well before the present agreement expired. Neither of us would benefit from the creation of a vacuum or the need to negotiate in haste. Nixon agreed with me that it would be unrealistic – if only from the aspect of inter-Allied balance – to expect the Bundeswehr to expand in the event of more than marginal changes in the US presence. I added that we would persevere in our efforts at qualitative improvement but could not compensate for the withdrawal of American divisions.

I had referred before my departure to the question of future relations between the Community and the United States. Having naturally received reports of this, Nixon asked me to comment further. Nothing had altered America's interest in British membership, mainly for political reasons. How did I visualize closer ties with the United States? I based my reply on the Hague conference and its resolution in favour of the enlargement principle, but also on the stimulus to political co-operation which this promised to impart. In order to obviate conflicts of interest between the enlarged EEC and the United States, or at least to resolve them in an objective manner, we should aim to set up a liaison committee. I was not, however, authorized to speak on the Community's behalf. We would have to allow for the likelihood of French reservations and should for that reason confine ourselves to planning *ad hoc* talks between Brussels and Washington. Nixon concurred with these remarks and intimated that he was anxious for a further improvement in relations with France. He spoke favourably of what he called Pompidou's 'economic orientation'. The President was particularly interested to know what insights we had gained from our talks with the Russians. Was he correct in surmising that no real progress had yet been made? I said I supposed that the Soviet leaders wanted to improve their relations with the United States and Western Europe and had presumably grasped that this would be difficult to achieve without regard to the Federal Republic. It was still uncertain whether we would be able to engage in actual negotiations after our exploratory talks in Moscow. We would remain in close touch with Washington, as with London and Paris.

Nixon gave an account of American views on the SALT discussions which would shortly be opening in Vienna. The situation had changed fundamentally since the Cuban crisis. There had then been a strategic nuclear weapons ratio of ten to one in America's favour, but relative parity now prevailed. We could rely on the United States not to agree to anything that would jeopardize NATO security interests. For the rest, it was possible that partial agreements would be concluded instead of a single all-embracing accord.

Turning to our *Ostpolitik*, the President stated that he would quite understand if we came to the conclusion that the Oder-Neisse line should be recognized; it had, after all, become an accomplished fact. He would also welcome the securing of humanitarian concessions towards Germans still resident in Poland. As to the GDR, did I think it conceivable, from what I had seen at Erfurt, that the East Berlin government might – if the occasion arose – take a decision without reference to Moscow? On Berlin: he regarded this as a point on which no concessions were possible. Like us, he was of the opinion that what mattered most, apart from the 'freedom of West Berlin', was integrity of access.

Our discussion of the Middle East crisis yielded little that was new. Nixon stressed that America would not leave Israel in the lurch but would strive, all difficulties notwithstanding, to secure better relations with the Arab countries. How could we favourably influence the situation in the Mediterranean area? Did I not agree with him that the time had come, thirty years after the Civil War, to introduce Spain into the process of Western co-operation? I expressed myself in favour of such an 'introduction' but pointed out that, in Europe, psychological factors relating to Franco Spain could not be ignored. We ought where possible to support France in her Mediterranean role, Italy being hampered by political problems at home. We also wanted to expand our co-operation with the Maghrib states. Referring to the trials then in progress, I urgently requested Nixon to exert a moderating influence on the government in Athens. He agreed to do so 'without publicity'.

On Vietnam, Nixon said that he would stick to his declared policy but that the Russians were being unhelpful. He attached great importance to relations with Japan. Prospects of improving relations with the People's Republic of China should not be wholly discounted.

Addressing the National Press Club in Washington on 10 April, I stated that my talks with President Nixon were devoid of tension and sensation and sustained by trust and common responsibility.

In a few weeks twenty-five years will have passed since the end of World War II. Europe lay in ruins. Germany was at the same time vanquished and liberated. It remains a moral act of high eminence that we Germans – in the Western zones – were not debarred from the effects of the American people's willingness to help. In particular America's action to save West Berlin during the Blockade is unforgotten. A little later, we were offered the chance of comprehensive co-operation. However little a sense of gratefulness may usually persist among nations, the people of the Federal Republic and of West Berlin have not forgotten all this, nor will they ever forget it. My numerous conversations at home – as well as public opinion polls – show that close relations with the United States are considered as number one priority in foreign affairs and that the presence of US forces in our country continues to be regarded as vital. This has nothing to do with indolence nor with any attempt to escape our own responsibility.

Because many people in the United States feared that the European Community might disrupt US commercial interests, I quoted trade figures and tariff rates in an endeavour to make it clear that nobody in Europe had any thought of incapsulation. Our present state of development confirmed this, even in agriculture.

I took advantage of the occasion to point out, yet again, that American involvement in Central Europe was also a prerequisite of realistic negotiations on a reciprocal and balanced reduction of forces and an effective system of arms limitation.

I rounded off my Washington visit with an excursion to Cape Kennedy. During my first trip there five years before, I had been lectured on the marvels of space technology by specialists of German origin. This time my wife and I witnessed the lift-off of Apollo 13. We were also able to have some memorable conversations with astronauts during the flight there, on which we were accompanied by Vice-President Agnew.

When I revisited Washington in the early summer of 1971, I could proceed on a number of assumptions: any doubts about our *Ostpolitik* hitherto raised by Washington's German experts could be regarded as largely dispelled; negotiations on Berlin had reached a critical stage; MBFR seemed (in 1971!) to be acquiring topicality; and, finally, relations between the United States and Europe were receiving the lively attention I had hoped for. On the debit side, adverse affects were accruing from the weakness of the dollar.

I never encountered what I have called 'doubts' about our *Ostpolitik* in conversation with Nixon and Kissinger, far less with Secretary of State Rogers or my old friends in the Senate Foreign Relations Committee. It was, however, clear that men like Clay, McCloy, Acheson and, last but not least, the veteran trade union leader George Meany, were filled with concern and transmitted their objections to the President. Dean Acheson referred after one such meeting to 'an insane race to Moscow'. George Ball, who had been one of our critics, was among the first to recant. There were signs that substantial reservations persisted in the Defence and State Departments. Many people even alleged, though without being able to prove it, that Henry Kissinger voiced different shades of meaning in our absence than in our presence.

The State Department spokesman stated more than once, however, that the Brandt government's policy enjoyed the unqualified support of the US Government. Kissinger said the same to Horst Ehmke when he visited Washington in December 1970. Ehmke reported that the tide of opposition that had flowed in autumn 1970 was now ebbing. An assiduous Opposition lobby, mainly from the CSU, played many an old and unmelodious tune in Washington. Advantage was taken of the widespread lack of foreign policy experience in both houses of Congress. Newspapers of the Springer group and the *Bayern-Kurier* joined in with a will, carefully exploiting American naiveties in this respect. However, when Barzel visited Washington a year later, presumably in the hope of returning laden with anti-*Ostpolitik* ammunition, he was disappointed. Ehmke had been specially instructed to oppose any postponement of the Berlin negotiations. Having been suspended for two ten-week periods in summer and December 1970, they made good progress in spring 1971.

Several more references will be made to preparations for the MBFR talks. At this stage, my main concern was to register our fears of inordinate US-Soviet bilateralism. However, I also considered it advisable not to waste the Russians' newly awakened interest in this subject. (I could not foresee that, five years later, discussion would still be confined to the taking of a first 'symbolic' step.) As for talks on the CSCE, or CSE as it was then called, our partners in Washington viewed them with surprising indifference. Even later on, they persisted in regarding the conference as a legitimate concession to the Russians – legitimate because it appeared to have little significance – without sufficiently discerning the great opportunity that might stem from a novel link with Europe which neither derived from legal rights acquired in the last war nor reposed solely on the North Atlantic Pact.

The EEC-US theme was another matter. In 1970 I had encountered lukewarm or, at best, academic interest. Things had changed by 1971. Keen attention was bestowed on the subject I had raised at the very inception of my Chancellorship: close co-ordination with a view to abolishing or limiting conflicts of interest. The countries of Western Europe were guilty of a sin of omission in failing to react more swiftly and positively to America's favourable response. Their failure was attributable mainly to French objections but also to the fact that the Americans demanded a good deal of their partners over the dollar crisis, a problem which they fundamentally expected others to solve for them or cope with its consequences unaided. We had already been embarrassed by a massive influx of speculative funds at the end of 1968 and in spring 1969. In 1971 the weakness of the dollar signalled a renewed and avalanche-like descent upon the mark. We decided to free our exchange-rate, effectively supported the dollar, and braved the annoyance of our European partners.

My trip to America in June 1971 began with an informative and colourful weekend in Jamaica. From there I flew to New Haven, Connecticut, to collect an honorary degree. At Yale, as elsewhere, only relics of the radical student movement could be detected.

On 15 June, after flying on to Washington, I spoke at the Woodrow Wilson International Center in response to a personal request from Hubert Humphrey. Our American friends, I said, should be able to subscribe to the following sober statement: the Alliance had gained strength, its internal co-operation had grown closer, America's European partners were engaged in fulfilling a billion-dollar programme designed to reinforce their defensive endeavours, and something new – something of practical and fundamental significance – had begun.

Allow me to recall a few facts that are sometimes forgotten. Ninety per cent of the ground forces in Europe and seventy-five per cent of the air forces are provided by the European members of the Alliance . . . Let me add, however, that only a strong, united Western Europe can in the long run take over that kind of responsibility in world affairs which will effectively relieve the United States and thus become an adequate partner. Unfortunately, I cannot help gaining the impression that because of their many other problems the Americans hardly notice that what is at stake in these very weeks and months is a breakthrough in the process of enlarging the European Community . . . We are intensifying political co-ordination so that the countries of Western Europe will be able more and more to speak with one voice in international affairs. We in Germany belong to the vanguard of those who insist that the European Community, rather than isolate itself, must be outward-looking . . .

Our policy, I went on, was logically embedded in the common policy of the Western Alliance.

It starts from the reality of the situation. It expresses our renunciation of force in relation to Eastern Europe after having done the same in our relations with the West as early as 1955. It is the logical complement of our agreements with the West. Moreover, it sets the Germans a task which no one else can fulfil on their behalf. Those who feared that the Alliance would suffer as a result, that it might even end up in a reversal of alliances, and that the Soviet Union would receive advantages which would extend its influence as far as the Rhine, were mistaken and should be glad to be able to admit their mistake.

We could not, I said, have looked on idly while efforts at détente grew up around Germany and Berlin and we remained a barrier which others had to scale or a stone for détente to stumble over.

No, we have instead made this particularly difficult point the test of the goodwill of both sides. There has been the courage to tackle the most difficult, the most delicate, the most emotional problem and the one most susceptible to crisis there is in Europe: Berlin . . . What is called German 'Ostpolitik' . . . enhances the prospect of removing confrontations and achieving co-operation between East and West.

During our discussion on 15 June Nixon, too, showed a far greater interest in the Europe-USA theme than he had done fourteen months earlier. I stated that the Europeans were reinforcing their responsibilities within the Alliance and hoped that the American people appreciated their efforts. What might only a year ago have seemed a mental exercise was now on the verge of fulfilment; British accession could only be halted by the British themselves. Improbable as it might seem, Heath would get his majority. The Community of Ten (including Norway) would be even more accessible to international trade than the Six. After years of stagnation, political co-operation, too, was developing, though not along the lines of the 1950s. What mattered now was to establish organic links between the Community and the United States, economically as well as in the political sphere.

Nixon eagerly supported this.

Individual countries have their own national identity. I don't even know if supranationality would be a good thing. Gone are the days when the United States dominated or virtually dictated. The future of Europe will be decided in and by Europe. I am following developments with great interest. Some people are worried about European unity, especially in the economic sector. I don't share this view. I think the new Europe can have a stabilizing effect on international relations. These worries are in line with nineteenth-century thinking. But I won't have an easy time at home. Some people are asking why we should support the world's third-largest economic power. Take away your other commitments and we may soon be able to call you the premier economic power.

I emphasized that the United States would have to pay no economic price whatsoever. US trade with the Community had shown a greater increase than with other parts of the world. To repeat: the enlarged Community would be even more internationally accessible.

We exchanged views on France. I spoke of my good working relationship with Pompidou, and we both expressed the hope that it would be possible to restore closer French links with the military framework of the Alliance by practical means. Nixon said that his relations with Pompidou were also good. The French must not be made to feel isolated, but Pompidou's freedom to disregard traditional Gaullist policy was only relative.

Little needed to be said about our *Ostpolitik*, which met with palpably greater approval than it had the year before. Thanks to the NATO ministerial conference recently held in Lisbon, we felt assured of adequate co-ordination and support. The President was all the more interested in knowing whether the Berlin negotiations would prove successful. Our views coincided perfectly on this point. Nixon opined that the present phase would lead to success provided there were no unexpected volte-face on the Soviet side. He attached no particular importance to the fact that the Russians were persisting in their public allusions to West Berlin as a 'separate political entity'. As he saw it, they meant to go two-thirds of the way to meet us. They had made substantial concessions regarding access routes. All that remained to be settled was external representation and the question of a Soviet office in West Berlin. I pointed out that we had already been obliged to live with sundry Soviet offices during my years in Berlin, and that it was easier from the security aspect to supervise the legal tip of an iceberg. It would be psychologically beneficial if the West Berliners could obtain visas in their own part of the city. Nixon found this interesting. He also took careful note of my remark that the emerging Berlin settlement contained much more substance than the points discussed at Geneva in 1959 and Kennedy's three 'essentials' in 1961.

Nixon: 'My aim is to strengthen the German position. We want an agreement – you want one too. You must carry on, but for tactical reasons it mustn't look as if we're forcing the pace. The United States is ready to take a tough line on the question of a Federal presence. Berlin is still a test case.' If tensions were reduced, he went on, it would be possible to create the prerequisites for a reduction of forces as well.

That was a logical connection, but it did not have to be called a package deal.

On MBFR, our talks did not yield appreciably more than an agreement that the West's internal exchange of ideas should be encouraged and that, as a preliminary step, it might be worth discussing a symbolic reduction of some kind. I said that what we needed was bilateral reconnaissance followed by multilateral action. The matter could not be left to the United States and the Soviet Union alone. While concurring with this principle, Nixon insisted that the biggest performer should have the biggest say. The UN principle did not apply here, but he was not at any stage thinking solely of bilateral negotiations.

It emerged from my exchange with Rogers that he applied the idea of a potential and preliminary 'symbolic' step to both the superpowers. Amplifying this on the evening of 16 June, he said that Ambassador Dobrynin had told him the same afternoon that his government approved the idea of holding troop reduction talks *before* a European Conference and agreed that these talks would have to encompass national as well as allied forces. Although happy about the CSCE procedure agreed in Lisbon, Rogers made no secret of the fact that he pinned few hopes on such a conference. He further emphasized that he considered it highly undesirable to strengthen the special EEC-US relationship in isolation from the OECD. Discussion also turned – peripherally with Nixon and in somewhat greater detail with Rogers – to the need for suitable arrangements between the enlarged EEC and the remaining EFTA countries. Where agreements with non-European countries were concerned, I gave an assurance that we would make a special effort to avoid damaging American interests.

On the situation in the Senate, Nixon predicted that the 'Mansfield movement' would revive. The White House had won its case by arguing that others – the Europeans – were doing their share and that MBFR stood a chance. A spirit of solidarity was the main requirement. His administration was being accused of not doing enough to distribute the burdens of the Alliance. I agreed that, in very general terms, what mattered was to impress upon the Senate and the American public that we Europeans were fulfilling our commitments. Nixon and Kissinger both assured me that criticism of 'the Europeans' did not extend to the Federal Republic.

On SALT, Nixon said that, contrary to outward appearances, there was a connection between ABM (defensive or anti-ballistic missiles) and offensive weapons. Official ABM negotiations would open in July, and it was hoped to reach agreement by the end of the year. ABM could help Berlin and vice versa. Nixon made only a brief reference to the offset theme. He expressed the hope that talks between our experts would be constructively resumed in Bonn at the end of June. He found it more important that the Europeans should display a general readiness to co-operate, militarily and commercially.

I stressed, in regard to the offset question, that our military purchases in the United States would be treated as a contribution. It was not, however, true that we had a definite obligation to buy a supplementary aircraft from America – a step that would certainly earn us French disfavour. To increase our contribution out of the Federal budget would be difficult and, in terms of principle, dubious.

Negotiations on the agreement covering the two-year period to mid-1973 were not completed until December 1971. As against DM1200 million earmarked for purchases of US arms and equipment, mainly Phantom fighter-bombers, less than DM200 million were allocated to the modernization of barracks and other installations. We also purchased US Treasury Bonds to the value of DM600 million. I paved the way for the next agreement, which ran until mid-1975, by discussing it with Treasury Secretary George Schultz in Bonn during October 1973. Schultz and Helmut Schmidt negotiated this agreement at the beginning of 1974. Although associated with lower expenditure, it satisfied the Americans.

However, Nixon was not thinking solely of the offset complex when he said that balance of payments problems should not attain such proportions that they overshadowed questions of security. I was able to state with a clear conscience that the decision to float the mark had not been directed against the dollar, and that it was not meant to be a long-term measure. Nobody could guarantee a reversion to our former course, but we needed the Community's approval. The dollar influx had been directed against the dollar and was hampering our fight for stability. Nixon replied:

Criticism from various quarters was levelled at the process rather than the measure taken. We have an interest in cooling the situation and not creating an impression of major crisis. The mark and the dollar – and the pound, too – are more important today than other currencies. We must keep in close touch. Our relations are so important to the entire free world that nothing must come between us.

Nixon's line of reasoning became clear when he roughly outlined the course of future developments.

Europe is going to take time, but the Germans will be playing a pretty big part in the world for the rest of this century. They are strong – economically, apart from anything else. Without making adverse remarks about others, nobody looking fifteen or twenty years ahead can allow eight hundred million people to remain isolated. The United States must take a hand so that China can play a normal role in the world. The Soviet Union is worried about China – so is Japan. Every country looks after its own interests. There's a lot to be said for the hand-and-five-fingers metaphor. Things may change later on, but in our own generation the relations between these five should be governed by the principle of live-and-let-live. Japan is a difficult problem. The Japanese sell their transistors and keep their cars rolling in. They only spend between one and two per cent on defence. As far as hard work and energy go, the Japanese are like the Germans. They may put on a little fat as time goes by . . .

We discussed Vietnam at table. Nixon presented a detailed account of his continuing efforts to carry out a planned withdrawal – which he still thought feasible. He barely touched on the Middle East. Rogers, who commented on the subject at greater length, said that Washington was doubtful whether the treaty between the Soviet Union and Egypt had materially affected the situation. In any case, the Americans would continue to seek a first step towards a peace settlement on the assumption that success was attainable. We also discussed the problem of the Pakistani refugees. I was asked if we could help to facilitate their return. Our main concern was to avoid any action that might be thought hostile to Pakistan.

The high-spot of my ensuing visit to New York was a speech I gave at the invitation of the American Council on Germany. This organization regularly convened at the Waldorf-Astoria Hotel to celebrate 17 June. A large audience had assembled, consisting of old friends and new. Mayor Lindsay welcomed us, McCloy gave a speech and General Clay also put in an appearance. The old war-horses did not seem dissatisfied with what I had to say. Addressing the old guard direct, I took them up on their suggestion that our current policy – 'the policy of the Alliance, of the West Europeans, and of the Federal Government' – had become too remote from the fruits of our common experience in the past. Major developments had undoubtedly taken place in the preceding decade-and-a-half, but certain basic elements had remained unchanged.

In a certain respect, I went on, the German Federal Republic was making up for lost time by normalizing relations with the countries of

Eastern Europe as its allies had already done. At the same time, we recognized that certain social systems defied fusion. We were aware that democracy and communism were separated by an indelible line . . .

> And finally that, no matter how much it hurts, the division of the German nation has become surmountable only in so far as the division of Europe can successfully be surmounted . . . It is no use assailing walls when they are held together by the cement of world politics. Protests and lamentations become embarrassing if they end up in self-pity or resignation. Removing the unnecessary and inhuman consequences of the division – this is the challenge we have to face . . . Whatever becomes of Germany as a whole depends on future developments between East and West and between the parts of Europe, as much as on the future will of the German people . . .
>
> It was against our wish, but it is a reality, that the Germans today live in two States. However, this does not decrease their responsibility for peace in Europe. And therefore this day is for the German Chancellor the day on which to affirm our responsibility to do all we possibly can to enable the nations of Europe to move closer to each other and to live together side by side – among and with them the German people.

Nixon wanted to see Pompidou, Heath and myself at the end of 1971, before visiting Peking and Moscow. He also wanted to discuss a number of disquieting monetary problems. A monetary crisis had arisen at the beginning of May 1971, and on 10 May we floated the D-Mark. Other European countries followed suit by either revaluing or barring all international access to their home foreign exchange markets. In mid-August – in an abrupt and unilateral move believed to have been inspired by Nixon's Texan Treasury Secretary, John B. Connally – the Americans had announced an emergency programme, imposed a ten per cent import surcharge and terminated the Bretton Woods monetary system by abolishing the convertibility of dollars into gold. Speculation against the US dollar assumed unprecedented proportions. The European foreign exchange markets were closed again and did not reopen until 23 August, after a one-week interval. However, all the leading industrial countries were at that time in favour of a return to fixed parities. The idea of currency realignment gained ground. Despite US reluctance, a preliminary conference in Rome was followed on 18 December by a Washington meeting of the Club of Ten at which it was agreed that the US Government should recommend Congress to devalue the dollar by 7·9 per cent. At the same time,

Belgium and Holland undertook to revalue their currencies against gold by 2·8 per cent. The Federal Republic revalued by 4·6 and Japan by 7·7 per cent.

It was thought at the time that correct long-term parities had been established. In fact, they only survived until spring 1973, though the US State Department's annual report for 1972 stated that the Germans had evinced an understanding of the dollar problem and the aims of the new US economic policy.

Ambassador Rush asked me – after Pompidou and Heath had requested meetings in the Azores and Bermuda – whether I would consider it injurious to my prestige to visit Nixon in Florida between Christmas and the New Year. Not regarding the matter in that light, I decided to combine the meeting with a family holiday. Matthias accompanied me on these New Year's excursions, and Ninja and Jarle arrived from Norway. I had once stayed at a pleasant hotel outside Sarasota in 1965. We received an equally cordial welcome this time. The Gulf of Mexico afforded ample opportunities for fishing, and I found it most informative to spend two full weeks among Americans outside New York and Washington. We were very impressed by their open-minded and helpful attitude.

Walter Scheel flew on to Miami. I followed him next morning and had several hours' conversation with Nixon at Key Biscayne in the two succeeding days. His minute-taker was General Haig, then Kissinger's deputy at the White House and later military head of NATO. Kissinger had 'flu, so I was only able to speak to him on the telephone via Nixon's personal link with Washington. I attended these private talks accompanied by Ulrich Sahm, who became our ambassador in Moscow shortly afterwards. Parallel discussions were held by our Foreign Minister and the Secretary of State.

Nixon declared that his forthcoming visits to China and Russia would be vitally important, not only to America but to us and our policy. 'I attach particular value to close consultation in the coming year. The summit meeting with Brezhnev has been under discussion for some time. After the success of the Berlin negotiations, the right time has come.' The connection became clear: no Moscow treaty, no Berlin agreement; no Berlin agreement, no break-through in US-Soviet relations.

The meeting will not succeed in solving all outstanding problems. What matters is that we should define those areas of difference in which agreement seems possible. Under no circumstances will I permit the meeting to have results detrimental to the unity and cohesion of the Alliance. My meetings with you, Pompidou and Heath are intended to lay the foundations for talks with the Russians. The same applies to my forthcoming meeting with the Japanese premier in respect of my visit to China. I have no wish to convey to my opponents – not enemies – that a condominium is to be established at super-power level. I should regard that as a betrayal of my friends.

Nixon several times reverted to the importance of consultations, but I had to agree with Pompidou when we subsequently compared impressions and he remarked that, in high-level politics, the will to consult was not enough in itself. The President continued:

The United States has certain interests connected with the world's various current problems, like the Soviet Union and China. The Russians know that. The future of Germany and its position in the Alliance are always in the forefront of American deliberations. The preservation of the strength of the Alliance and the integrity of the Federal Republic are preconditions of the striving for détente.

He then asked my impression of the Soviet leaders, notably Brezhnev, whom he had briefly met on one occasion but never talked to. His question was matched by Brezhnev's keen curiosity about himself. The Soviet leader had told me in summer 1970, using even more formal language, that he desired better relations with Western Europe and the United States. In the Crimea – only three months previously – he had asked whether Nixon really wanted peace and whether he felt, as he himself did, that the burdens of arms expenditure were too heavy.

I told Nixon that it would pay him to adopt an open-minded approach and assume that Brezhnev's interests favoured peace-keeping and increased co-operation. Conversely, I had tried to impress upon Brezhnev that he ought not to suspect Nixon of all kinds of sinister ulterior motives. However alien he might appear, the leader of the Western super-power had a certain interest in paving the way for reductions in tension. I also endeavoured through other and more indirect channels to steer the President and the General Secretary towards a position in which prejudices would be dispelled and joint responsibilities more clearly recognized.

I reaffirmed during my talk with Nixon that no major misunderstanding should be allowed to arise between the United States and the German Federal Republic or the European members of the Alliance in general. We might have reached a stage at which we, too, could exert an influence on the Soviet Union. It was quite possible that the Soviet leaders wanted not only more economic co-operation but less arms expenditure in the years to come. We must, of course, be wary. We did not know how much longer the Russians would continue to respect the Western interests and positions which we could not abandon. It was also debatable how much influence a co-operative phase would have on the countries of Eastern and South-East Europe. We could not produce any fundamental change in the East European power structure, nor could we offer any guarantees against its transformation. A growing exchange between West and East would undoubtedly stimulate more positive forces. I had gained the impression that the Soviet leaders were not altogether happy about their intervention in Czechoslovakia. I also thought it noteworthy that the Polish crisis at the end of 1970 had been treated as an internal problem. There had been no talk of 'German interference' or 'counter-revolutionary elements'.

As for our relations with the Soviet Union, there had been a definite improvement during the eighteen months since the Moscow treaty. Propaganda furnished one indication of this, and an important one, because anti-German slogans had hitherto been a major aid to cohesion in the communist camp. Nixon also expressed interest in the relations between the Soviet Union and the GDR. How should Ulbricht's replacement by Honecker be interpreted? Germany was what really counted with the Russians in Europe. On the one hand, the Federal Republic needed the Soviet Union because of Berlin and its relations with the GDR. On the other, the Russians needed the Federal Republic because, without it, Europe would be a 'lame duck'. For all that, he sometimes wondered why the Russians were now adopting quite such an accommodating attitude towards the Federal Republic.

I replied that the switch from Ulbricht to Honecker had certainly not been made without Soviet acquiescence. While rarely straying from the Moscow line, Ulbricht had built up his personal prestige over the years. As to Nixon's second question, the Soviet leaders doubtless hoped that well-ordered relations with the Federal Republic would help them to secure quasi-recognition of the *status quo*. This they wanted for the sake of the GDR and other members of their bloc. Furthermore, the Russians genuinely wanted more contact, primarily in their own interests but also, perhaps, because the events of 1968 had persuaded them that the requisite discipline would be more readily upheld if bloc members were given some scope for non-political exchanges with the West. But they wanted to share in these themselves, partly to get a slice of the cake, as they saw it, and partly because they would thus be enabled to keep developments under control. After all, their desire for better relations with the United States was doubtless illumined by the knowledge that these would be greatly hampered by an inimical attitude towards the Federal Republic.

The President said that, despite his contemptuous remarks, Brezhnev's policy seemed to be greatly influenced by the problem of China. China and its 750 million inhabitants were a fact, and the country was developing a nuclear capacity which could become significant 'in twenty years or so' (far less, as it turned out!). The Chinese were threatening Soviet hegemony in the communist camp and building up a potential in the Middle East, Latin America and other parts of the world. War was remote but conflict probable. Even if the Soviet Union meant to extend its influence, the presence of an enemy in the East dictated a need for peace in the West.

Nixon then inquired about our trade with the countries of Eastern Europe. His own Secretary of Commerce, who had been very cordially received in the Soviet Union, had conducted lengthy discussions with Kosygin and believed that prospects for co-operation were good. Credit terms, most-favoured-nation clauses and similar matters would, however, require Congressional approval, and the Russians had been bluntly informed that this would be withheld for as long as they pursued an obdurate policy in the Middle East. Progress in the political sphere would result in a more accommodating attitude.

I summarized the growth of our trade with Eastern Europe and the Soviet Union. Nixon agreed when I said that we ought – without interfering – to help Yugoslavia solve her problems. I also said that Brezhnev had been at pains to convey, with reference to the Middle East as well, that he was not only uninterested in fomenting new crises but anxious to avert them in US-Soviet relations. The Russians would confine themselves to giving the Arabs defensive weapons, whereas the Americans – he claimed – were supplying the Israelis with offensive weapons.

Nixon said that the Russians genuinely had no desire for confrontation and were trying to cool the situation. After all, they had a heavy financial burden to bear. Cuba was costing them 1·5 million dollars a day and Egypt 750 million a year. The present Soviet leaders might feel, without abandoning their basic objectives, that it was time to concentrate more on the internal development of their country. If so, they would probably have to cut down on some of their exte rnl commitments – as the US Government was doing. Finally, even Moscow had to take account of the broad mass of the population. The Soviet Union might be a nuclear power and possess worldwide influence, but this did not help its inhabitants. I could not but agree. I, too, regarded the desire of Soviet workers for a better standard of living as a major determinant of Kremlin policy. Nixon said that, if this were so, it would accord with the interests of Western countries. The promotion of trade and the production of consumer goods might lessen the tendency towards expansion. We must remain in close touch for all these reasons. In any event, he had no intention of striking any bilateral bargain with Moscow which might weaken the Alliance.

We then turned to the treaties and the Berlin agreement. The Russians had not liked it when we coupled ratification with the latter. Now they had set up a reverse package-deal of their own, which I considered unpolitic. Nixon commented that the Russians were playing a stubborn game by reversing the Berlin package-deal, but the West would probably have acted little differently. He also said that the diplomats entrusted with the Berlin negotiations deserved a big pat on the back. Close co-operation with the Federal Republic, he went on, had set a good example for the future. I outlined our time-table and the constitutional problems involved in ratifying the Moscow and Warsaw treaties. Nixon was anxious that the third reading should be completed before his visit to Moscow.

We also discussed the admission of both German states to the United Nations. I favoured 1973 rather than 1972, even if some of our partners in the Alliance were urging greater speed. We wanted to normalize our relations with the GDR before tackling the question of UN membership, and it was important that the Four Powers – or certainly the Three – should reinforce their legal status.

Nixon replied that no one who wished the Federal Republic success in its policy – a policy pursued with one foot firmly planted in the West – ought to anticipate what should primarily be a German decision. On this point, there ensued a passage in our dialogue which I found hard to follow. Was Nixon debating in a formalistically polite manner, or had he – with an eye to our next elections – been advised not to commit himself and missed the point? I reproduce his argumentation below.

Nixon: 'The United States' position is to back the Berlin agreement. However, we don't want to exert any influence which might be disadvantageous to the Federal Government. In particular, we don't want to convey that we are backing the Federal Government.'

Brandt: 'The Federal Government has repeatedly emphasized that the treaties have been evolved in close consultation with the Three Powers and NATO. The decision itself must naturally be taken and upheld by ourselves.'

Nixon: 'If difficulties arise from the American attitude as I just explained it, please let me know via Rush, Rogers or Kissinger. It's the best way of ensuring that the decision is taken by the Federal Republic as an independent power. The United States will respect that decision with benevolent neutrality.'

Brandt: 'The United States, together with Britain and France, must always safeguard its rights in any case, where residual responsibilities for Berlin and Germany as a whole are involved.'

Nixon: 'The United States wants to leave the Germans complete freedom of action, not tell them what they should or shouldn't do.'

I reverted to this subject next morning. Undoubtedly, we both agreed that there must be no outside interference in the treaty dispute at Bonn. It was nonetheless important to stand by NATO's public declaration that the treaties had been worked out in close consultation with the Three Powers and the Alliance. The issue at stake was our contribution to the general policy of the Alliance as expressed by the words 'defence and détente'.

Nixon concurred. We had indeed discussed the treaties with our allies, he said, and the Alliance had raised no objection. It was a basic fact that the decision rested with the Federal Republic. Whatever our decision, the United States would accept and not oppose it. Asked by Nixon if this was an apt definition, General Alexander Haig gave a more precise one: the US Government had always expressed support for normalization, which had now occurred; to reaffirm that support could not have any adverse effect on the internal situation. Nixon duly reaffirmed that normalization was the objective favoured by the US Government. It was for the Germans to decide on the means whereby this objective was attained.

A joint statement released at the end of our meeting noted that 'close partnership between America and Europe has successfully withstood difficult tests and has demonstrated its importance for their common future'. We welcomed the solidarity and close co-ordination between the three Western Powers, the Federal Republic and the other NATO allies throughout the negotiations on Berlin as well as the implementing agreement with the GDR, 'which are important elements of the common Western policy'.

In addition to MBFR and CSCE, we naturally touched on the problems of SALT. Nixon said that negotiations presented extreme difficulty because their subject-matter had a crucial bearing on American and Soviet security, which the test-ban and non-proliferation treaties did not. The key to the problem was that the Russians wanted to restrict the number of American anti-ballistic missiles (ABM) whereas the United States wanted to limit Soviet intercontinental ballistic missiles (ICBM). Talks were progressing, and he estimated that the Russians might be ready to reach a point at which agreement would become possible. Even if agreement were reached on anti-ballistic and intercontinental missiles, a number of other questions in the field of arms limitation would remain to be solved. He had, however, declined to negotiate on weapons of significance to the security of Europe.

When I inquired the state of negotiations on missile-carrying submarines, the President said that the Russians were still far behind in this field. They were only prepared to negotiate the limitation of weapons or weapons systems in respect of which they themselves had attained an advanced position. American progress in the field of submarine-launched missiles was conspicuous. The Soviet attitude to MIRV (Multiple Independently Targeted Re-entry Vehicle), which had temporarily aroused so much public interest in the West, was typical. The Russians were unwilling to negotiate on these because they still had none of their own. In regard to offensive weapons, they were only prepared to discuss absolute numbers. The Americans were trying to make progress in all sectors because the cause of world peace would not be served by a continuing increase in armaments. The Russians having now attained parity, neither of the so-called superpowers would permit the other to gain a lead. This meant either that the arms race would have to be continued or that a sensible arrangement must be reached. A lot depended on negotiating procedure. After all, a good Berlin settlement had eventually been concluded by this means.

As far as MBFR and US troops in Europe were concerned, Nixon said, the Federal Republic's attitude was very reasonable. Its bargaining power would be considerably reduced if the present balance were altered. The American attitude to MBFR was dependent on whether an acceptable formula could be found. Of the immense number of studies submitted, none contained a serviceable formula covering quotas and elements of comparison in force reductions. There was also the internal 'Mansfield problem' to be dealt with. A unilateral reduction of US forces in Europe would harden the Soviet attitude instead of making it more conciliatory. The British shared this view, and so – despite their 'interesting' relationship to NATO – did the French. Paris felt that any formula endangered security and that it would be better to concentrate on principles before discussing unit strengths and associated problems. The US Government wanted American public opinion to preserve its awareness of America's firm links with the Alliance.

It was to be hoped, Nixon went on, that US forces would not have to remain in Europe indefinitely. On the other hand, the Alliance must not be jeopardized and a united front must be maintained. He appreciated the fact that additional contributions had been approved at NATO's last ministerial meeting; this would make things simpler for him at home. It had emerged from talks with the Russians that MBFR was not their primary concern. Differences of opinion would exist in the world for as long as there were communists. What mattered was to reduce the chances of confrontation, and that was the real reason for his trips abroad.

I then reverted to our previous discussion of an institutional link between the EEC and the United States. This applied to economic matters, defence being already handled by NATO. The US mission to the Community and the EEC mission in Washington were adequate to deal with current business. In addition, however, senior representatives (on the EEC side, drawn from the Council and Commission) should meet once or twice a year to explore means of limiting common problems.

Nixon replied that some Americans had misgivings about supporting an enlarged EEC. The business community, in particular, thought that it would prejudice American interests, that the EEC was tending to be even more self-contained than before and that the result would be economic confrontation. This would be a tragedy, because it would inevitably pose political problems as well. Competition was a good thing but conflict was intolerable. My idea was extremely valuable. Not all the members of the Community were as outward-looking as the Federal Republic. The Americans must be assured that the Community would not adopt a protectionist attitude towards them. The Japanese must be brought in too. It was important that they should not be isolated economically because this might react on Japan's relations with the Soviet Union. They ought therefore to be included in my proposed group.

I said that we maintained good relations with Japan and would be glad to examine prospects for closer co-operation inside international bodies. I still failed to understand American worries about the Community. I had also discussed the question of an organic link with Pompidou. He took a cautious view and expressed fears that the British were aiming at a special form of membership which would reinforce American influence on the Community. He further speculated that détente might be made more difficult by unduly close ties between the EEC and the United States. In his opinion, it would be easier if the Soviet Union were confronted by two groups which, though militarily allied, were economically separate.

Nixon commented that the Russians were realists. The better Western co-operation became, the readier they would be for détente. The West had so much economically in common that co-operation could only be beneficial to both parties. I mentioned the special problem of associations. In my view, the EEC ought not to deal with ex-colonial territories *en bloc* but conclude suitable agreements in each case. Black Africa and the Mediterranean were another matter. The EEC had contributed to stability in those areas, especially as the United States had been prevented from doing much by its many other commitments. Confirming this, Nixon said that no political vacuum should be left there.

Dining in private, Nixon reverted to the subject of an institutional link and insisted that Japan should be included. America would take care of the country's nuclear defence, but a sense of economic isolation might encourage extremist elements there. I pointed out that Japan collaborated with the Club of Ten in the OECD. To establish a triangular relationship – as Kissinger publicly proposed in spring 1973 – struck me as over-complicated. It went without saying that the United States and the EEC maintained good relations with Japan, but the first requirement was to regulate those prevailing between the EEC and the United States. Nixon agreed that we ought to concentrate on this point and stressed that Canada should not be overlooked. But the Japanese must not feel that they had been left out in the cold, nor should they be exclusively under American influence. The Federal Republic's position was important – that was why he urged me to give the matter further thought. His démarche towards China, so necessary in other respects, had hit the Japanese hard. They must not be propelled in the wrong direction.

Scheel interposed that the Federal Republic was already the focus of Japanese activities in Europe. I recalled that, irrespective of the role of the Chinese People's Republic, the Japanese were worried about developments relating to Taiwan. Its expulsion from the United Nations had come as a blow to them. They would be strongly influenced by an assurance that Taiwan was not to be abandoned. Nixon declared that there was no question of its abandonment. Ambassador Rush supported my view that the cardinal problem was that of American-European relations. Nixon said that the initiative must come from Europe. Scheel commented that we could form a committee manned by representatives from the United States, Canada, the Commission and the EEC member-countries, and set up a meeting between leading economic experts from both sides.

Our talks also served to provide information about Vietnam, the Middle East and other difficult areas. On Vietnam, Nixon said that the withdrawal would be continued after the New Year. The South Vietnamese training programme was proving remarkably successful. It was now impossible (!) for North Vietnam to overrun the South. American losses in the preceding week had dwindled to one fatal casualty. North Vietnam no longer had the strength to conduct offensive operations. South Vietnam now possessed one of the finest armies in Asia.

The current air raids on North Vietnam did not have the significance ascribed to them in the press, being directed against the installation of new supply depots. These raids had a prophylactic function and were designed to prevent the North Vietnamese from launching any effective attacks in two or three months' time. The United States was still aiming at a complete withdrawal. Even if only symbolic, however, some US forces would continue to be stationed in Vietnam for as long as American prisoners remained in North Vietnamese hands.

It had to be recognized that the Russians and the Chinese both felt compelled to support North Vietnam. Both would like to off-load this burden but neither could do so without incurring propagandist accusations of having betrayed the sacred cause. He had conveyed to the Russians that it would be difficult to grant them most-favoured-nation treatment or co-operate with them in the Middle East, Europe and SALT, as long as they maintained their present role in Indo-China. He was convinced that South Vietnam would survive in the long term, and the same probably went for Cambodia. Laos, where the North Vietnamese were present in considerably greater strength, presented a more doubtful picture. If the Americans withdrew from these areas it would be an acknowledgement of the fact that neither side could gain a decisive advantage or win an outright victory. At all events, the position in Vietnam was very much better than at the time of our last meeting in June 1971.

On China, Nixon said that, since his election, efforts to establish direct contact had been pursued for two years after the United States had intimated via Pakistan that it was willing to talk. Then had come Kissinger's celebrated visit. No 'recognition' (establishment of full diplomatic relations) would result from his own visit. He did not intend to sever relations with Taiwan, but it was important to find means of avoiding future confrontations, for example in Korea and Vietnam. The general shape of future relations, which was equally important, depended on the role which China meant to assume. China and the United States were separated by a wide gulf. The Chinese were very much 'more communist' than the Russians. They were also tough negotiators. It was very noteworthy, however, that they no longer regarded America as their principal foe; Russia, Japan and India took precedence. The Chinese feared encirclement. It was part of their official dogma that the Americans must leave Asia, but they might not mean this literally. Amplifying, General Haig said that events in the Indian subcontinent had profoundly shocked the Chinese. Their Pakistani allies had been mauled by the Indians with Soviet backing. In that respect, the Americans represented a stabilizing factor which had enabled Pakistan to survive. The Chinese were making immense preparations to defend themselves in the event of a nuclear war. The Russians had stationed a substantial number of divisions in the Far East.

After we had touched on the position of Australia and New Zealand, Nixon turned to the complex problems posed by Southern Asia. He had, he said, been accused of adopting an unrealistic policy because of US aid to Pakistan. His attitude was based on a direct relationship with the Middle East. If the Russians had felt they enjoyed a free hand, the result might have been an Indian attack on West Pakistan. The Russians might have thought they possessed freedom of action in the Middle East as well as India. As it was, having once humiliated Pakistan's Chinese backers, they decided to exert a moderating influence. If the Russians had allowed India to overpower West Pakistan as well, it would have had a pernicious effect on the entire Moslem world. The Chinese would then have felt that their southern border, too, was in jeopardy; and that was the real heart of the matter.

On the Middle East, negotiations were still being pursued by Secretary of State Rogers and his deputy responsible for that area, but without success. He had assured Mrs Meir that he would not permit any change in the balance of power. It would be dangerous if the Russians made aerial defence installations available to the Arabs. The process could not continue indefinitely, because the Russians were supplying war material in quantity and the Americans had to maintain a balance. It was hard to persuade the Russians to restrain Egypt sufficiently to induce the Israelis to negotiate. Israel was important to him, and not only because of the Jewish vote in New York. It could not be allowed to succumb to direct aggression.

I reported on our resumption of relations with Egypt and the Sudan. Nixon said it would be good if the Egyptians realized that they were not solely dependent on the Soviet Union. In a marginal reference to Iran, we agreed that the Shah required co-operation and that relations should be cultivated.

On Latin America, brief allusions to Brazil and Argentina were followed by a discussion of Cuba. Nixon stated that Castro's influence in Latin America had declined because of communism's failure in his own country, but that the continent was in a state of considerable turmoil. The United States would oppose Cuba's readmission to the Organization of American States as long as Castro persisted in fomenting unrest among his neighbours. If its own interests were affected, the United States would have to defend itself. However, we were living in a foreign policy era in which large countries had to recognize their own limitations.

More philosophically, Nixon said that we had to see the world as it was. To assess problems from a purely ideological standpoint would not get us far. What Brandt was now doing did not imply that he judged shortcomings and disadvantages differently than in the days when he had delivered his celebrated speeches as Governing Mayor of Berlin. Brandt was trying to introduce a change in Central Europe; he – Nixon – was making the same endeavour in Asia. The alternative, which was simply to dig in and be as intransigent as the communists, was not acceptable to him. That was a downhill road. We had to deal with the real world even if we did not like its present condition. In *Present at the Creation*, Acheson had written that we had inherited a dangerous world. We were trying to build a new world, but ours would never be perfect either. All we could do, very gradually, was to make it a little less dangerous, 'a little happier than it was before we came'.

I was back in the United States at the beginning of June 1972, visiting Harvard. My government wanted to mark the 25th anniversary of the launching of the Marshall Plan with something more than just a friendly word of remembrance. On 5 June 1972, therefore, I found myself standing on the spot where George Marshall – recently appointed Secretary of State by Truman – had proclaimed US support for the European Recovery Plan (ERP) that more commonly bears his name. I myself announced that the Federal Government had, with parliamentary approval, resolved to make resources available for a Marshall Memorial Fund (DM150 million spread over ten years). This sum was to provide backing for American-European studies and research projects.

I said in my address that history seldom gave us an opportunity to refer to strokes of good fortune. However, what had taken place in that very hall a quarter of a century before could justly be accounted one of the happy dispensations of the present century, which had not often been illumined by the light of reason.

I had referred to the problems of the Alliance some days earlier, when the NATO ministers assembled for their spring meeting in Bonn, Joseph Luns having succeeded Manlio Brosio as Secretary-General. Recalling that the Alliance had been based on the twofold concept of defence and détente since the Harmel Report in 1967, I said:

The politico-military equilibrium which we owe to the Alliance has rendered this policy of détente not only possible but necessary. In this way, NATO is becoming a prime mover in the era of negotiations. It is certainly not easy to maintain a balance between defence and détente. With most of our fellow-citizens in the various countries of the Alliance, détente is understandably more popular than the other component. Yet both components are inseparably linked.

During the same month – May 1972 – President Nixon had visited Moscow and concluded the first SALT agreement. He and Brezhnev issued a joint statement of intent relating to general principles of détente and coexistence.

We were careful to ensure that our defence policy dovetailed perfectly into the plans of the Alliance. We also bore in mind that agreement on strategic nuclear potential required a doubly careful equilibration of the weapons systems referred to as 'conventional' or 'tactical'. I had drawn attention to this in a speech to the NATO Nuclear Planning Group at Mittenwald in May 1971 – designedly, because I was just about to address a meeting of the Socialist International in Helsinki and planned to re-emphasize the connection between defence and détente on that occasion too.

The Nuclear Planning Group had acquired formal status in 1966, and the Federal Republic was one of its four permanent members. The doctrine of a flexible response to potential attacks had been adopted without German opposition at the NATO ministerial meeting in May 1967. At the same time, great care was taken to guard against any diminution of the West's deterrent potential. US forces in Europe were reduced from 366,000 to just on 300,000 between 1966 and 1968, but certain units transferred to Kansas and Idaho in the latter year were earmarked as a permanent operational reserve capable of being flown at once to Europe in the event of a crisis. Several Atlantic exercises demonstrated the feasibility of their rapid deployment.

In NATO as a whole, defence expenditure slightly decreased between 1960 and 1970, partly as a result of inflation. All the Western armies suffered from the fact that pay and other current outgoings claimed 60 per cent of their funds as opposed to a reputed 25 per cent for the Warsaw Pact forces. In addition, France withdrew from the integrated defence system in 1966 and the Canadian contribution was appreciably reduced. The Alliance was also weakened by the dispute between Greece and Turkey and the situation in Portugal. Finally, the Dutch and the Danes did not altogether resist the temptation to lighten their defence burdens by taking unilateral action. This meant that, apart from US forces and, to a limited extent, the French nuclear strike potential, it was the Federal Republic which principally sustained the policy of détente as an element in European security by fulfilling its defence obligations to the letter.

At Nixon's express request, I visited Washington for more talks early in May 1973. He had been re-elected in November, gaining a clear-cut victory over his Democratic challenger Senator George McGovern, but the dark clouds of Watergate soon started to gather. Even before the internal crisis became dominant, Nixon and Kissinger encountered strong Senatorial opposition to their foreign policy. In March Senator Mansfield persuaded the Democratic majority to vote in favour of halving US forces in Europe. There followed a series of disconcerting votes in the Senate, and it was not until October that a committee of both houses voted to annul the Mansfield resolution (of September). Senator Henry Jackson later steered a reverse course, partly by coupling trade concessions with demands on behalf of Soviet Jews and intellectuals.

In April Henry Kissinger startled us – still in his capacity as security adviser, for he was not to become Secretary of State until August – with a public interpretation of Nixon's 'Year of Europe' dictum. Speaking in New York, he called for a new Atlantic Charter inclusive of Japan and described European interests as 'regional'. My invitation to Washington made no mention of any such initiative. I took it that Nixon's main purpose was to exchange views in advance of our meetings with Brezhnev a few weeks later. I myself was keenly interested in the transatlantic dialogue. This being so, I suppressed my fears that Kissinger had over-closely commingled the themes of defence, trade, currency and diplomacy and was not doing justice to the expanding European Community, even though it had to be conceded that the Community's worldwide role as an economic factor was not matched by any supra-regional commitment (or potential) in the field of security.

Conferring with Nixon at the White House on 1 May 1973, I was forced to conclude that the President had only a superficial knowledge of what Kissinger had set in motion. Despite his New York speech and

'Year of Europe' slogan, not to mention our earlier conversations and correspondence, Nixon discussing problems of US-European relations did not receive on the wave-length I used for transmission. All who were acquainted with the subject realized this at dinner, when I was mainly plied with German-American courtesies although everyone knew that I thought it desirable to say more.

I noted in my own after-dinner speech that Nixon had been re-elected by a large majority, and that he had contrived to exert a lasting influence on international affairs. The Vietnam cease-fire had brought the world closer to peace. We shared the Americans' joy at the return of their prisoners of war. We also shared their hope that the guns would at last fall silent in the tormented countries of South-East Asia. I was as little entitled as Heath and Andreotti, who had visited the White House before me, or as Pompidou, whom Nixon would be meeting in Iceland in a few weeks' time, to speak on behalf of the European Community, but none of us met the American President solely as a representative of his own country. 'The declared aim on this and the other side of the Atlantic has been, and – I am confident – is, equal partnership. We realize that this requires Europe to assume a large amount of responsibility – as regards both regional self-responsibility and the share in world-responsibility.'

We had to join in a quest for solutions to problems that devolved on us precisely because peace was no longer in such jeopardy. I was confident that we would successfully organize the peace of Europe by establishing the world equilibrium which the President had described. This could mean the fulfilment of Kissinger's dictum that power was capable of transformation into an instrument of self-control. 'Yet we should not deceive ourselves: organized peace will not be a period of social immobility.' I called for courage to face the reality of tomorrow.

The night after my arrival, Nixon had delivered a televised address announcing the dismissal of his senior political aides, renewing his promise of a ruthless inquiry into the Watergate affair and – rather emotionally – accepting responsibility for what had happened. I watched the broadcast with some uneasiness on one of the guest-house television sets. My after-dinner speech duly contained an assurance that we did not take our hospitality for granted, particularly at this time, 'because we know that you, Mr President, [have] had to settle problems of a domestic nature.' I had made a slightly less diplomatic allusion to the subject at the start of our private discussion, but Nixon brushed it aside, saying that he had no serious worries. When Kissinger joined us with Egon Bahr, the President told him of my remarks and repeated his assurance that 'our German friends' need not believe in the existence of any real problems. Kissinger seemed less certain. Far from disagreeing when Bahr told him that he would have advised his own boss to have spoken on television for half as long, he said: 'If only the President had asked me!'

I naturally sought to discover what lay behind Kissinger's New York speech. Nixon told me, seconded after a while by 'Henry', that it should be regarded as the basis for an open discussion, and that he was not absolutely set on the 'New Atlantic Charter' label. My impression grew that Kissinger's speech had been somewhat hurriedly drafted, partly in order to divert attention from the political crisis at home by means of a new and resounding slogan. The President seemed to be toying with the idea that it might be a good thing if his projected tour of Europe yielded an impressive document signed in concert with the political leaders of America's partners in the Alliance.

Nixon went on to speak of the potential growth of a détente euphoria which would foster tendencies towards isolationism or unilateral disarmament in the United States. In negotiating with the East, we must never lose sight of reality. He was convinced that the Soviet Union did not want war but might still – or again – be tempted to drive a wedge between Europe and America. He showed interest when I alluded to changes in the Soviet Union's attitude during the previous two years, as evidenced by its recognition of America as a permanent partner in MBFR, CSCE, and the open-ended Berlin Agreement.

On the complex of problems in the Middle East, Nixon said that, however much the Americans strove to maintain contact with all concerned, he saw no real chance of success in face of the attitude adopted by both sides. At the same time, more was going on than could be made public. He also expressed concern at the growing importance of the oil factor.

When Brezhnev visited Bonn at the end of May, shortly before a scheduled visit to Washington, he was naturally interested in knowing how to evaluate the storm that was gathering round Nixon's person. In June 1973 Nixon and Brezhnev concluded their important agreements eschewing the use of nuclear weapons and establishing consultative machinery designed to prevent the escalation of local conflicts. Kissinger had initiated me into these plans earlier than most. He visited me in September 1972, before flying on to Moscow. I noted at the time: 'Contact with the White House is good. We are discussing matters which presuppose re-election in both cases.'

Nixon and Brezhnev also agreed that CSCE should be brought to a successful conclusion with all speed, probably by means of a conference at the highest level. They interpreted MBFR as 'negotiations on the mutual reduction of forces and armaments and associated measures in Central Europe'. In July 1974 Nixon and Brezhnev held a third summit conference in Moscow but made little progress in regard to strategic weapons. (The next interim SALT agreement was concluded by Brezhnev and Ford at Vladivostok in November 1974.)

What affected us even more directly was that the dialogue between the United States and its European allies threatened to take a most unwelcome turn in summer 1973. Nixon described the EEC members' efforts to develop a common position as 'ganging up'. I tried during one of Kissinger's Bonn visits to steer our exchange of views back to the subjects that really mattered: a reaffirmation of the Alliance and relations between the European Community and the United States. Instructions were given for the preparation of draft statements on both themes, but I cannot pretend that they made much of an impact.

At the end of September 1973 I revisited America to address the General Assembly of the United Nations, to which we and the GDR now belonged. On the same day, 26 September, I met Secretary of State Kissinger. He informed me that his talks with the Danish Foreign Minister K. B. Andersen – the presiding chairman of the Nine – had taken place in a constructive atmosphere. His talks with Michel Jobert, the French Foreign Minister, had also gone well.

Kissinger did, however, wax sarcastic about the meticulous pedantry displayed by hordes of European civil servants when preparing the 'solemn' declarations mentioned above. He had welcomed European unification at a press conference the same day. As in the summer, he stressed the importance of avoiding any impression that a nagging controversy had arisen in the relations between the EEC and the United States. It must remain clear that both sides were eager for a constructive dialogue. He welcomed our assurances – which I thought went without saying – that we had no intention of holding any bilateral talks. His government was most anxious to remain in close touch with the Federal Republic. How could our dialogue be pursued?

From New York I flew on to Chicago and from there to Denver, Colorado. Having hoped to spend a few stimulating but restful days at Aspen, I was compelled to leave after a few hours because President Nixon wanted to see me. It turned out that his only real purpose – though this possessed importance in itself – was to discuss the ways and means of his forthcoming trip to Europe. A certain measure of activity in foreign policy was always welcome to him during these months of steadily mounting crisis. Also present on Nixon's side were

Henry Kissinger and General Brent Scowcroft (later Ford's security adviser); on mine, Ambassador von Staden and a senior member of the Foreign Office.

I opened the discussion by stating that the Atlantic dialogue had, after all, made progress since May. The decision when to visit Europe naturally rested with the President alone; he would be welcome at any time. Replying, Nixon congratulated me on the German response to his Atlantic initiative, which he termed an 'opportunity'. By announcing a 'Year of Europe', the United States had not meant to propel Europeans in an unwanted direction. The President went on to stress the special responsibility of the larger countries concerned. The timing of meetings between political leaders ought partly to be determined by a knowledge of what they would lead to. Substance was needed, not symbolism, hence the importance of preparation – in which no dominant role was claimed by the American side. It was particularly important during a period of détente to promote the co-operative discussion of problems that had exercised the members of the Alliance for years. However welcome, the period of détente harboured a danger that the Alliance would be precipitately weakened. The Soviet Union was continuing to reinforce its military potential. It was probable that no country had a greater interest in the successful outcome of our Atlantic dialogue than the Federal Republic.

While agreeing that the President's trip to Europe should possess more than formal significance, I said that symbolism also played a role. The President would be meeting Brezhnev in 1974. I was due to meet him in the latter half of the year. So – probably earlier still – was Pompidou. A meeting between the General Secretary and Prime Minister Heath was also on the cards. That was why, if only as a demonstration, the Atlantic summit conference should be held in good time.

Nixon conceded that, in this particular case, symbolism implied substance as well. Depending on the current state of progress, he intended to fix his itinerary when Kissinger returned from Europe in mid-October. He welcomed the fact that the proposal for a meeting of the Alliance had come from me.

Commenting on the Canadian draft for a declaration by the Alliance, I recommended that we should concentrate on security matters and exclude ideological factors as far as possible, or there would only be distasteful arguments over the internal situation in several NATO countries. Kissinger agreed, and Nixon said that 'ideological' elements should be mainly confined to the joint US-EEC declaration.

Kissinger again aired his ideas on Japan and the possibility of a very broad declaration to be signed by ourselves and the Japanese. (When I discussed this with Premier Tanaka, he showed no particular interest in any such '*chapeau*'.) Nixon then reverted to the idea that the Atlantic dialogue should not smack of confrontation. It would, he said, be unacceptable to the United States if the Nine adopted immutable positions and appointed a spokesman who had no authority to negotiate.

To the President's satisfaction, I stated that we had always entertained the possibility of bilateral exchanges parallel or additional to multilateral talks. I hoped, however, that Europe would more and more frequently speak with a single voice as time went by, even if this unison sometimes posed problems of its own. We had to proceed in a commonsense manner.

Nixon said that we should have to allow for a growing danger of isolationism in the United States. Although a realistic view was taken of the Common Market, it was economically regarded as a competitor. We could not ignore the political implications of this.

Kissinger added that there were 'strong feelings' in Congress on these matters. That was why the 'Year of Europe' possessed such significance. Above all, we must demonstrate our solidarity. There would be some fierce battles with Congress, but the President had instructed the Administration to do its utmost. Nixon said that one or two members of Congress were beginning to see the dangers inherent in a 'Fortress America' doctrine. This was one option at a period when the United States no longer possessed overwhelming nuclear superiority. Congress was a real problem, hence the importance of Kissinger's allusion to the 'Year of Europe'. Kissinger said that the older Democrats supported government policy whereas many of the younger entertained an attitude towards Europe similar to that which they had hitherto reserved for Vietnam. According to Nixon, the situation in the House of Representatives was better than in the Senate. A generous offset settlement would be extremely helpful. I trusted that there was an appreciation on the American side of how helpful the Federal Republic had been in regard to the monetary problem.

Nixon concluded by referring to what he called my statesmanlike achievements and reaffirmed his desire to work with me as closely as possible. Developments in America would have precluded this even if I had not resigned in May 1974. Nevertheless, my working relationship with Nixon coincided with a generally harmonious phase in German-American relations. To put it another way, the 'rightward' swing in the United States and the 'leftward' swing in the Federal Republic had no adverse effect on Western co-operation. More clearly than their respective Oppositions, both parties recognized the need for worldwide efforts to reduce tension.

For all that, autumn 1973 and the new Middle East war imposed strains which might have had grave repercussions. Like the rest of the Allies, we in Bonn were startled by the decision to place American military units (primarily, one assumes, nuclear strike forces) in a state of readiness throughout the world. I do not know if this step will ever be fully elucidated. Washington had evidently received reports that sizeable Soviet units were likely to be flown to Egypt. (Near-confrontation was subsequently dispelled by indirect contacts.)

This hazardous US-Soviet crisis occurred at the end of October. In the days beforehand, during the cease-fire decreed by the Security Council, our Foreign Office learnt by chance that two Israeli ships were taking on American military supplies at Bremerhaven. A third freighter, which was waiting in the roads, had to sail for England unladen because of the stir the incident caused. I was not merely dismayed that nobody had seen fit to inform us (the US Embassy was not over-communicative even when confronted with the report from Bremerhaven). What I failed to understand was why, if the shipments were considered so vital, they had not been put aboard vessels flying the US flag. It seemed unfair to me that such manifold doubts should be cast on our official expressions of non-partisanship, the more so because I had made it clear that this even-handed attitude should not be equated with indifference.

We knew what was at stake in the Middle East and were aware of American efforts to end the renewed fighting as speedily as possible. What we could not accept was an initial reluctance to tell us the truth (evinced by American uneasiness) when we detected some arms deliveries from an unspecified source. Washington began by reacting fiercely to our inquiries. It was even intimated to our representatives that the Federal Republic enjoyed only limited sovereignty in American eyes, and that the United States reserved the right to take any steps which seemed proper and necessary in the interests of international security. Nixon regretted this in an exchange of letters, accepting our point of view and undertaking to consult us on any future occasion. Our own reaction was extremely restrained in comparison with the outrage expressed by Adenauer when German bases were utilized for the Lebanon operation in 1958.

In January 1973 a cease-fire had at last been arranged in war-torn Vietnam. It soon turned out that the Americans cherished substantial illusions about the durability of such agreements. The actual end of the war two years later presented a different picture from the one we had been promised.

The Americans had again mounted heavy air raids on targets in North Vietnam over Christmas 1972. There were grave misgivings about this, even among America's most loyal allies. Nixon, who had by summer 1972 reduced US forces in Vietnam to one-tenth of their strength three years earlier and lived in hopes of winding the affair up smoothly, was very indignant at European protests and told Heath that, under prevailing circumstances, he would not visit Europe in the next six months.

At the end of March 1975, when I visited Washington just a year after my resignation and met Kissinger and the new President, Gerald Ford, I witnessed the official reaction to South Vietnam's rapid military and political collapse. One could not help feeling that the political leadership had been appallingly misled by the Pentagon's misjudgement of the situation. It was dismaying to sense the trauma inflicted on a world power by defeat in a costly regional war. Against this bleak background, President and Congress were wrangling over the possibility and expediency of further aid. Ford warned publicly against repercussions on Europe and said that Kissinger's scope for negotiation in the Middle East had already been impaired. I advised the President not to burden himself with additional misgivings about American credibility in Europe, but Kissinger stated – publicly as well as privately – that a constitutional conflict between the White House and Congress would preclude the fulfilment of America's international responsibilities. Speaking in my presence, he urged Senators and Representatives to brace themselves for another major effort; if collapse came notwithstanding, it must not be attributable to America's failure to help. His appeal was lost on the members of Congress: they were willing to render humanitarian assistance but nothing more.

I could, of course, glean only a vague idea of what the American people felt about the abandonment of Vietnam because most of the people I talked to were insufficiently representative. One of the major disadvantages of brief trips abroad – even when the visitor no longer holds office – is that most of his time is spent with members of the establishment. I nonetheless sensed or, rather, was confirmed in my belief, that the Americans would find the strength to overcome their Vietnam trauma just as they had surmounted their Presidential crisis. My sole task was to help in a minor way to ensure that its repercussions on Europe were not misinterpreted. The vast majority of Europeans had come to the conclusion, even if most of them conveyed it in diplomatic language, that the ill-starred venture must finally be brought to an end. Like me, however, many Europeans had faith in the United States' reserves of material and, above all, moral strength.

Not for the first time, I expressed sympathy with the hard-pressed inhabitants of 'Indo-China' as a whole. We had no reason to greet the political and military developments there with either jubilation or dejection. We could only regret that the Paris agreements which brought about the withdrawal of American troops had not been more successful in preserving peace. It was nonetheless clear to me and my political associates that the struggle in Vietnam represented something more than a conflict between a communist and a non-communist social system. Over thirty years old, it had always possessed the additional attributes of a war of national independence. Furthermore, the withdrawal of French colonial authority had been succeeded by a clash between the interests of three world powers. If glorification tends to bypass reality, so does execration. None of the participants was innocent of aggression, breaches of good faith and acts of gratuitous violence, but that is not the whole story. The nature of the American commitment was bound to cause moral and political qualms, even among America's best friends.

I do not, however, wish to imply that I would always have presented the matter in this light throughout the years. Vietnam was a subject about which I simply knew too little. I may even have preferred ignorance because enlightenment would have brought me into conflict with US policy, on which I was heavily dependent not only as Mayor of Berlin but in subsequent years. I was faced with a threat to my fellow-citizens' existence – with dire injustice on our very doorstep. Our survival depended on trustful collaboration with the American Protecting Power – that much I realized. My dilemma consisted in the fact that it seemed 'irresponsible', as it were, to develop an overtly critical attitude towards our most important guarantor. Instances of this type of mental block may well be a good deal commoner than is generally supposed.

It should be remembered that the primary significance of Indo-China in the 1950s was a partial collapse of French colonial rule. Paris failed in its attempt to urge a major military commitment on the Americans. Dien Bien Phu fell early in 1954, during my first visit to the States. Its surrender had been preceded by a dramatic French appeal to Washington – even accompanied by a request for the use of nuclear weapons.

By 1954 the Americans were already bearing the financial brunt of the war in Indo-China. Although they were not subscribers to the Geneva Agreement of that year, Eisenhower assured President Diem that the United States would support the government of South Vietnam in order to 'resist subversion and aggression by military means'. For his part, Diem renegued on the Geneva plan for all-Vietnamese elections in

1956. A year later the civil war was in full swing. General de Gaulle was speaking from more experience than most when he subsequently dissociated himself from US policy in Vietnam. Although one could not escape the impression that he was settling old scores with the Americans, it was quite consistent that de Gaulle should have asserted the impossibility of winning a purely military contest against national socio-revolutionary movements.

At the beginning of the 1960s I hardly realized that – albeit by very limited degrees – the Kennedy Administration was risking embroilment in a struggle on Indo-Chinese soil which was destined to be misinterpreted as an extension of the East-West conflict. To me it appeared that the war had really unfolded during Lyndon Johnson's Presidency. In March 1975 I heard Secretary of State Kissinger declare that, questionable or even mistaken as it had been from the outset, the commitment had originated under Kennedy. Though doubtless not technically inaccurate, this is a biased view because Kennedy's dispositions could always have been revised.

There were 2000 US 'military advisers' in Vietnam when Kennedy became President. 400 specialists were sent there for training purposes in May 1962. At the end of 1961 there had been 2500 US soldiers in Indo-China. After an on-the-spot reconnaissance in Saigon, two of the President's aides recommended that 10,000 men be dispatched, primarily equipped with helicopters. Americans in Vietnam numbered 11,000 at the beginning of 1963 and 17,000 at the end of that year. Kennedy realized, and stated, that the political aspect was more important than the military – 'We cannot fight their war' were his exact words. In late autumn 1963 President Diem and his brother-in-law, the chief of police, were murdered. The situation deteriorated.

Why under Kennedy – or upon the transition to Johnson – was no decision made in favour of a political solution rather than military intervention, which was almost bound to grow? I believe the crucial factor to have been that Washington recognized *one* major communist peril, suspected connivance between Moscow and Peking, and mistook the nature of the communist movements which were fighting for national independence on the one hand, and, on the other, for the replacement of decrepit feudal régimes. Added to this, the head of the Pentagon thought victory could be predicted by computer. The other side of the coin was that the Americans – but by no means they alone – identified themselves with brittle social systems and seemed to classify all that was non-communist under the glamorous heading of 'the free world'. The domino theory never managed to convince me entirely because of its seductive simplicity. I recall a conversation I had with the Indian Ambassador B. K. Nehru in Vienna at the beginning of 1964. He was convinced that Ho Chi Minh would steer a course largely independent of Moscow and Peking – possibly 'Titoism on another level'. Ho Chi Minh had sought contact with the Americans immediately after his country was liberated from the Japanese, but his letters to the US Presidents probably remained unanswered. It is quite possible that his successors will float free from both the leading communist powers and essay an independent course appropriate to the entire South-East Asian area.

I forbore to strike any critical attitudes even when the war spread so alarmingly, contenting myself with references to the unspeakable sufferings of those involved. I also rejected critical inquiries levelled at myself because I felt that our process of national rehabilitation was still far short of the stage at which we could play the world's conscience or claim the role of moral arbiter. This is still true, though it should not be employed as an excuse. Finally, I was irritated by anti-American prejudice, especially where Vietnam campaigns were communist-directed.

The picture had already begun to change before the student revolts, in which a leading role was played by emotional and in many cases conscientious objections to the war in Vietnam. I remember arriving home after a trip to the States in spring 1965 and being taken vehemently to task by my sons – Peter was then sixteen and Lars fourteen – because my remarks to the press in Washington, as recorded, did not express dissociation from air raids and other abominations. I and Fritz Erler had been with President Johnson at the White House when he received some reports of the fighting and commented on them aloud. The effect was unconvincing – rather too lofty and abstracted – but we refused to be detached from US policy and urged in general terms that peace should be sought by negotiation. Our scope for contributing to this end was exceptionally limited.

In February 1966 I attended a New York function at which President Johnson spoke. Thousands of demonstrators had gathered in the streets outside the Waldorf-Astoria Hotel, and the President – with whom I drove to the airport accompanied by Bobby Kennedy and Chief Justice Warren – had to be protected by large numbers of police. The veteran American Socialist, Norman Thomas, took exception to my having attended a gathering at which Johnson upheld his policy. I respected Thomas for his integrity and his indestructible faith in the future, so I answered him at some length. Although we Germans were not tutors in international relations, I wrote, it certainly did not behove us to be straightforward fellow-travellers – 'not a satellite which

With President Pompidou
at the Elysée

Walking with Indira Gandhi
in the garden of Gymnich
castle on the Lower Rhine

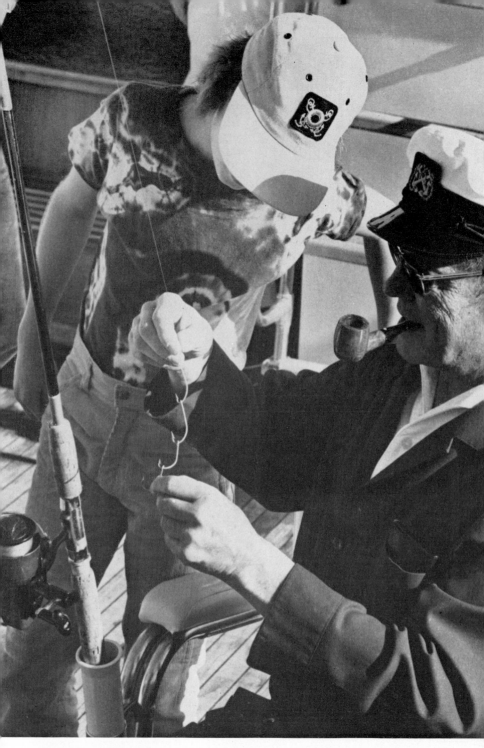

Fishing off the Florida coast with my son, summer 1971

concurs in everything the leading Western Power thinks right'. In the same letter, I attacked 'oversimplified and unfounded comparisons between Vietnam and Berlin'. It might be, I reflected, that the people of the United States were only at this stage becoming fully aware (and flinching from the discovery) of how burdensome it was to be a world power, and that it also entailed, with regrettable frequency, the need to choose a lesser evil. At the same time, no one who shared my hopes of a substantive détente between East and West could lose sight of the fact that 'events in Vietnam will determine whether the theory of the American paper tiger and the possibility of limited vicarious wars against a helpless nuclear power will continue to prevail'. Nothing had altered my impression that President Johnson was striving for peace on supportable terms. 'I am advising my friends in Germany to refrain from superficial and extreme pronouncements.'

This brief visit to America had, however, made it clearer to me that we in Germany nourished a wholly inadequate conception of what Vietnam conveyed to the American mind. Discussion of the war was more profound and impassioned than any public controversy since World War II. The current Vietnam debate was infinitely fiercer in the United States than any comparable debate in Europe, and many Americans saw this as a sign of strength.

As Foreign Minister, I had to refrain from giving the Americans advice in public. On the other hand, we declined to shoulder an impossible commitment or venture into a grey zone by declaring our 'moral support' as previous Federal administrations had done. Even before entering government, our party had stated at its Dortmund conference in 1966 that the Federal Republic must not render direct or indirect military assistance in Vietnam. Considerable disquiet arose in my party executive at the beginning of 1968, after the massive air raids on North Vietnam, and we issued a balanced statement pointing out that peace could only be attained if both sides wanted it. I also undertook to explain our misgivings in a private letter to Secretary of State Dean Rusk. He responded with some annoyance, insisting – in our view irrelevantly – that Vietnam was inseparable from the credibility of the American commitment in Europe.

In spring 1968 the SPD conference at Nuremberg declared that our faith in the guarantee afforded by the Alliance would not be affected if the United States released itself from its involvement in Vietnam. By rejecting the parallels between Vietnam and Germany, we tried to make it easier for our chief ally to embark on the arduous but ineluctable process of self-extrication. Writing as Foreign Minister in 1968, I put it thus:

P.P.–X

Were the United States to forgo a military solution, it would not affect our faith in the US guarantee, without which there can be no security for Europe, the Federal Republic and Berlin. The undeclared war in South-East Asia is impeding the further reduction of tensions between East and West. It harbours the risk of extension. For that reason, peace in Vietnam is also in the immediate interests of Europe and Germany.

The extent of the American commitment in Vietnam can be gauged from the numbers of US troops stationed there, which mushroomed during Johnson's time: 14,000 in 1963, 267,000 at the end of 1966, half a million by mid-1968. The figures at first continued to rise when Nixon assumed office, reaching 540,000 in mid-1969. Before the cease-fire agreement was signed in January 1973, Nixon had – in mid-1972 – reduced American strength in Vietnam to 50,000. There was no doubt that the President and Kissinger had determined to end the war and bring their soldiers home – with honour, as the saying went.

A foundation was laid by the Paris agreements of January 1973, but the authorities in Washington could hardly have failed to realize that South Vietnam, too, would sooner or later be ruled by a communist régime. Everything indicated that the Saigon government's defeat was attributable, not to insufficient aid from outside, but to the absence of a credible policy tailored to the interests of its people.

Our task now was to help our American allies extricate themselves from their ill-starred commitment, adopt a sympathetic attitude towards American self-scrutiny, and persevere in our cautious but steadfast quest for détente. Addressing the Bundestag in May 1975, I said: 'Our American friends are in trouble, and it is precisely when friends have problems that one stands by them.' Nobody should be disconcerted by the inward stirrings of America, I went on. 'The ruthless and sometimes agonizing self-inquiry to which the Americans are subjecting themselves is not a sign of weakness. I, for one, am confident that the United States will emerge with renewed inner strength from the process in which it is currently engaged . . .'

13

Moscow

My visit to Moscow on the conclusion of the treaty between our two countries in August 1970 was unplanned. Foreign Minister Scheel had been conducting final negotiations there with State Secretaries Bahr and Frank. Although on holiday at the time, I was of course kept regularly informed of their progress. Prompted by talks with the Russians, Walter Scheel eventually telephoned me to suggest that I should also come to Moscow for the signing.

In his capacity as Chairman of the Council of Ministers, Alexei Kosygin met me at the airport and escorted me to the 'Residence' in the Lenin Hills. This villa, where my wife and I stayed for a second time in July 1975, was one of the houses allocated to Politburo members in Khrushchev's time. When we had left the University behind us and reached the road in which the 'Residence' stands, Kosygin stopped the car. We got out, and the Premier showed me the capital from the spot where Napoleon had caught a last glimpse of Moscow in flames. His historical reminiscences, especially those of more recent date, made a stronger impact on me than the city itself, though I found the Kremlin imposing. The planning of the modern quarter is certainly a source of Muscovite pride, but cannot compare with the handsome architectural consistency of Leningrad, the former capital.

During the drive from the airport, conversation quickly turned to economic matters. Kosygin gave an account of harvest prospects. This appeared to be a major preoccupation of his, as it doubtless was of other Soviet leaders. Had I not already known it, my first half-hour with the Chairman of the Council of Ministers of the USSR would clearly have conveyed that I was talking to the head of the biggest industrial monolith in the world. I told Kosygin that opinion polls conducted among the citizens of the Federal Republic indicated a substantial majority in favour of our treaty policy. He listened with interest, then declared that a similar poll in the Soviet Union would have yielded 99 per cent in favour. I gathered that he was being entirely serious, just as I gained the impression on other occasions that the Soviet leaders failed to understand why their electoral support, which invariably exceeds 90 per cent, is regarded in the West as spurious. What we find mystifying, they seem to take for granted. As Brezhnev remarked next day, there was no other country in the world where 99.99 per cent of the electorate went to the polls and voted almost exclusively for communist and non-party candidates!

Alexei N. Kosygin was born in Leningrad, then St Petersburg, in 1904. The son of a factory worker, he attended the city's engineering school and became its mayor at the age of 34. His great test came when Leningrad was besieged by the Germans, and it is still widely considered miraculous that so many of the inhabitants escaped starvation and death during the crucial winter of 1941-2. Kosygin, whose ascetic demeanour may well owe something to this experience, has held numerous administrative posts over the years – as head of various ministries and the Planning Commission, as premier of the RSFSR, the largest of the 16 Soviet Republics, as deputy head of the Soviet Government proper, and finally, in August 1964, as Chairman of the Council of Ministers after Khruschev's fall.

He joined the leadership of the Soviet Communist Party as a Politburo candidate in 1946 and became a full member two years later. He was down-graded after Stalin's death but regained membership of the Politburo in 1960 and joined the inner circle – with Brezhnev, Podgorny and Suslov – in 1964. Soviet foreign policy was closely associated with Kosygin's name during the latter half of the 1960s, as when he met President Johnson at Glassboro or tried to reach an accommodation with Peking. From 1970 onwards, however, control increasingly passed to Brezhnev.

One could tell that Kosygin was a man who drove himself hard. His face bore the imprint of strain and exertion. The deeply etched features testified to long experience – bitter too, undoubtedly – of a political life which may often have developed into a fight for survival. They also conveyed a hint of resignation. My impression of Kosygin, especially when compared with the unclouded optimism displayed by Leonid Brezhnev at our meetings in 1970 and 1971, was of a sceptical if not pessimistic man.

On the night of 11 August, Scheel and I held an informal preliminary discussion with our companions at the residence of the Federal German Ambassador. There was no need to retire to the Embassy's (allegedly) soundproof booth. My attention having been drawn to the possibility of bugging devices, I addressed several injunctions to an imaginary eavesdropper to pin his ears back.

The first item on our programme for 12 August was a wreath-laying ceremony at the Tomb of the Unknown Soldier, with background music provided by a movement from a Rachmaninov piano concerto. After that the delegations met in Kosygin's office for a discussion lasting just over two hours. Foreign Minister Gromyko and Ambassadors Tsarapkin and Falin were present on the Soviet side; my own team comprised Foreign Minister Scheel, State Secretaries Frank, Bahr and Ahlers, and Ambassador Allardt.

Kosygin began by expressing his profound satisfaction that I had travelled to Moscow for this great ceremonial act, to which the Soviet leadership and the entire world attached major importance. He hoped that this day would prove to be of historic significance to our relations.

I thanked the Soviet premier for his cordial welcome. 'We too feel,' I said, 'that the treaty is of very great importance and may introduce a new element. Important as the treaty is, however, what we make of it will be more so. It can constitute something more than the basis of our bilateral relations. Without trying to efface our differences, we can in many areas join forces for the purpose of ushering the affairs of Europe towards an organized peace.' I then invited Kosygin to submit his views on European security and the development of bilateral relations.

Kosygin outlined the direction of Soviet policy. European security was, he said, the key to world peace. Both world wars had broken out in Europe. The Soviet people desired to enter upon détente in Europe with firmness and resolution. Relations between the Soviet Union and the German Federal Republic were the central problem of détente in Europe. 'We intend to make every possible contribution to détente and prevent another war in Europe. This entails that the results of World War II should not be simply left in the air but embodied in treaties. The alternative is war, but war is lunacy.' War was no longer an instrument of policy, Kosygin went on. Disputes had formerly been settled by violent means. Today we had to travel new roads of the kind that had been discovered in the treaty to be signed that day. This not only possessed great importance but indicated the nature of the forces now in power. There were others, however. Anyone who wanted war and an arms race stood to lose by this treaty. There were wide variations in its assessment by the international press, but most public voices held that it might help to promote a substantial reduction of tension and arms expenditure. 'All the phenomena that play upon national sentiment and incite chauvinism in the Federal Republic seem to lack conviction. We are firmly resolved to defend the treaty. Opposition to it will gain little popular support.'

Kosygin did, for all that, strike a surprising note in his response to my inquiry about bilateral relations. 'We are worried about the forces of revanchism, about fascist ideas, about the NPD conferences – about that party's attempt to persuade young people that they belong to a great race whose right it is to conquer other nations. These phenomena are primarily your concern, of course, but it makes us wary when the NPD is sanctioned and the Communist Party driven under ground.' I might think, he continued, that all these things were trivial, but Hitler had also started off in a beer cellar. If the United States spawned a party which hung up pictures of Hitler, that too should be combated, however small it was. Developments in the Federal Republic were now greeted with greater confidence. 'We welcome the policy you are conducting . . . We do not, of course, mean this treaty to detach you from your allies. We have no such intention, nor would it be realistic, but we wish to place our relations on a new footing.' The same afternoon, Brezhnev also remarked that the Soviet people were extremely sensitive to any sign of revanchism and neo-Nazism.

Kosygin went on to state that great openings existed for co-operation in the fields of science, industry and technology. He spoke of the Five-Year Plan for 1971–5 and a long-term plan for the coming two decades. Soviet mineral resources were so vast – here he gave detailed figures – that they could satisfy the requirements of Europe as a whole. He took it that we were interested in exporting capital equipment, chemical products and consumer goods. 'It used to be claimed that we would not buy any consumer goods from the West. This can be said no longer, because we are doing so on a large scale.' Kosygin proposed that we should jointly develop a programme of economic co-operation, initially for five years and later for twenty. He also mentioned individual projects such as a new Soviet method of conducting electrical power over long distances. There would soon be an integrated grid system covering the entire Soviet Union. The development and manufacture of large generators might be one field in which we could co-operate.

He emphasized the Soviet Union's good commercial relations with Japan and stated that there were 'almost no' economic links with the United States. The Soviet Union was interested in developing its economic links with the Federal Republic, both by treaty and by co-operation between individual concerns. 'Interesting areas must be found for both sides. Neither we nor you are charitable institutions, so co-operation must benefit both parties. We do not expect you to supply manna from heaven. Good bases for co-operation exist, and in this way we can improve our relations.' The same applied to cultural matters.

I replied that anyone who thought in terms of the past mistakenly believed that co-operation between countries of unequal size automatically implied a gain for the larger and a loss for the smaller. 'There have been many grounds for mistrust in our relationship. If we eliminate this mistrust, build up confidence and organize practical co-operation, both parties will benefit.' I then raised a number of separate economic questions – infra-structural projects as well – and expressed the hope that we would succeed in developing machinery suited to our respective circumstances. I was nevertheless bound to point out that, as part of the EEC, we should no longer be as independent in future. The enlarged EEC would, however, be outward-looking. What might at first sight seem detrimental to bilateral relations would become beneficial if it enabled us to contribute to realistic links between the EEC and Comecon.

On the other hand, I had to point out that there were many people in my country who claimed that our new-found co-operation suffered from an element of uncertainty. They believed that the Soviet Union would one day revive the question of reparations for war damage. 'This uncertainty could sap the energy we require. It would not only make my life easier but facilitate our common task if you would inform me, today or tomorrow, that I can go home and declare the problem settled.' The Chairman could take it that the German people desired to tread the path of peace. 'We too have undergone dire experiences, and they were not in vain. We must not only eliminate tensions but organize peace as well. Practical co-operation is one aspect of this. We must also devise a means of reducing armaments and military concentrations in Europe. We are under no illusion that this can be done quickly, but minor steps have great importance in this respect too. We are loyal members of our alliance, and you do well to recognize the fact. We are working for détente within the framework of our alliance, and it is good that others in your alliance are doing likewise. The projected European Conference will be successful to the extent that problems deriving from the past are solved in advance. This has a bearing on our relations with other countries in the Warsaw Pact, but above all with the GDR. We need a working-level on which to conclude agreements with the GDR. I say this not as a request but in order to clarify our position. If you do not regard what I have told you as altogether irrelevant, I should welcome its inclusion in your own deliberations.'

In regard to Berlin, I asked that recognition be given to our vital

interest in a reasonable settlement. I described the links between West
Berlin and the Federal Republic and said that the people of West Berlin
desired their retention. 'I am alive to the dangers of subjectivism in
politics, but I spent too long in Berlin and am too deeply committed to
be able to forget those years of my life. I am also Chairman of the SPD,
which incorporates a Berlin *Land* association. And another thing: hearing me invoke my years in Berlin, you may perhaps say that I was not
always wise and did not always make entirely wise statements. If that
were held against me, I should have to reply that nobody did me any
favours either.' The international situation had been different in those
days. Today's reality was that West Berlin could not remain a Cold War
crux if we wanted détente. I could envisage forms of existence which
would enable West Berlin to play a constructive role in the relations
between the two German states and in Europe generally.

The signing of the treaty took place in the Saint Catherine Room soon
after lunch. One of those present defined the setting as 'Tsarist grandeur
plus air-conditioning'. Brezhnev turned up unannounced, together with
such other members of the Politburo as were in Moscow, and greeted
me with conspicuous affability. My four-hour conversation with him
took place in his office in another part of the Kremlin.

Kosygin presided over the official banquet in my honour. Brezhnev
did not attend it but joined us for drinks beforehand. He had told me
that he was not feeling well and had been in hospital. Kosygin declared
in his after-dinner speech that this was a memorable day in the relations
between our two countries. The ceremonial act performed by both
governments should not be viewed in isolation. It was only one of a
series of efforts being made by various governments to improve the
situation and construct a firm foundation for the security of Europe. All
this was well understood by political and social circles in Europe, and
not in Europe alone. The treaty was dictated by life itself. It accorded
with the long-term interests of peace.

After dinner we drove at our hosts' suggestion to the television
tower and spent an hour together in the restaurant there. Little was
said about politics. We stopped en route and walked a little way down
Kalinin Avenue to have a look at one of Moscow's principal modern
thoroughfares.

I naturally saw little of the city and its inhabitants during this brief
visit. In general, Moscow impressed me as being 'more European' than
I had expected. I was struck by a certain contrast in dress, though this
was less noticeable when I revisited the capital five years later. Most
of the older women wore rural dress, whereas the young people were
clearly influenced by Western fashions. Apart from this, the Moscow

street scene is strongly coloured by the many nationalities that converge on the city from all parts of the Soviet Union.

Certain difficulties had arisen over the transmission of a short address which I had promised to deliver for German television. The Russians were acquainted with its text and had presumably taken exception to a passage dealing with 13 August and the Wall. I let it be known, off the record, that I would make arrangements to fly home if the transmission did not take place. This seemed to do the trick, but the occasion was deemed important enough for the minister in charge of broadcasting to turn up at the studio. The text of what I told my fellow-countrymen on the evening of 12 August 1970 was as follows:

The signing of the treaty between the Soviet Union and the Federal Republic of Germany is an important moment in our post-war history. Twenty-five years after the capitulation of the German Reich which Hitler destroyed, and fifteen years after Konrad Adenauer agreed to establish diplomatic relations here in Moscow, it is time to rebuild our relations with the East on an unqualified renunciation of the use of force, proceeding from the political situation as it now exists in Europe . . . This treaty in no way impairs the Federal Republic's firm attachment to the Western Alliance and its freedom of association within it. Our staunch partnership with America remains intact, as does our reconciliation with France. We also preserve our enduring determination to link more and more European countries more and more closely with the aim of political integration. The treaty endangers nothing and no one. It is intended to open up the way ahead. If it does, it will benefit peace, Europe, and each one of us.

I had a second talk with Kosygin on the morning of 13 August, this time for an hour-and-a-half. Invited to speak first, I began by making the following statement: 'The treaty, whose importance no one should underestimate, is not just a treaty concluded by one political party or two coalition partners or even a government; it is backed by the majority of the German people.'

I went on to say that, after looking through my notes, I wanted to add a response to one of Brezhnev's remarks and would like it brought to his attention. The General Secretary had intimated there were grounds for fearing that we might misinterpret the treaty and that, if so, the Soviet Union would have to amend its position. I made it clear that we had no intention of construing the treaty otherwise than as it had been negotiated.

Thirdly, I wished to amplify my previous remarks on the subject of Berlin. We had no wish to exert pressure on anyone, far less blackmail them. 'We are concerned to point out frankly that, from the political aspect, things will fare better if West Berlin ceases to be a bone of contention and acquires a role in peaceful co-operation. If we succeed in this, both of us will have gained.'

Fourthly, I raised humanitarian problems such as the reuniting of families and the repatriation of persons who had been German nationals at the outbreak of war.

Replying to my first point, Kosygin agreed that both sides had concluded the treaty on behalf of their entire peoples. 'It requires explanation, which is not easy. Some of your people will understand, but certain sections will cling to their own view. Things are simpler here . . . We are convinced that the treaty will be very well received in the Soviet Union and that ratification will not present us with any problems. I therefore note that we have common views on the assessment of the treaty.'

Secondly, the General Secretary had informed him of our conversation. He was satisfied with my statement and would convey it to Brezhnev.

As to point three, the general situation in West Berlin and the Soviet attitude to it were quite clear. We could say nothing new at this juncture. The three Western Powers were keeping us fully informed. 'We can give you additional information as well – you are very familiar with the Berlin situation.' Now that the treaty had been signed we could discuss all manner of political issues, this one included.

Finally, the two Red Cross societies should continue to work on the problem of divided families. He would brief himself and get in touch with me later.

Reverting to my previous day's inquiry about reparations, Kosygin said he could not go into it today. 'I had no time to take advice. I will do so and then give you an answer.' The matter remained unresolved in Moscow, but I was informed next year in the Crimea that, from the Soviet point of view, 'the problem is not outstanding'. It was explained that the Moscow treaty had established a relationship which rendered it politically impossible to make any such claims on the Federal Republic. Bahr informed the Russians on my behalf that we would make public use of this formulation at some future date.

As regards the institutional framework for practical co-operation, I said that we would submit our views in due course. 'It doesn't have to be a *grande commission*.' Kosygin: 'Its form is of no fundamental importance to us. We're all for less fuss and more success.' While he was reading out his communiqué – which embodied an acceptance of our invitation to pay a return visit – he remarked: 'Your friends will be pleased. We didn't lay any underwater obstacles, although we could have done. Something could have been said about Vietnam.'

My reply: 'Just as you gentlemen thought of our friends when drafting your text, so we thought of your friends when drafting ours.' I thanked Kosygin for my friendly reception in Moscow and for the calm, frank and objective way in which he had facilitated my brief mission. Kosygin conveyed greetings from his comrades, notably Brezhnev, and wished all success to our 'noble activity on behalf of the peoples' welfare'.

Addressing a crowded international press conference that midday at the Intourist hotel, I said:

The foreign response to the conclusion of this treaty was more than once mentioned and evaluated in the course of our discussions. On the subject of this foreign response, permit me to say that I am slightly alarmed by the superlatives audible in some quarters. Whenever I hear talk of 'historic significance', I can only say, as a well-trained Berliner, *'Ham Sie's nich ne Nummer kleener?'* [Don't you have a smaller size?] It already means something to ourselves and others that this treaty can provide a new foundation. At no stage in the talks – and this is a piece of political evaluation in itself – did we encounter even a glimmer of the idea that we had met to play others off against each other or to detach ourselves, either or both of us, from those with whom we co-operate. Without my asking, I was told on very good authority: 'We have considered this matter carefully. We do not want the improvement in our relations to be purchased at the expense of your relations with others. That would have been impossible anyway, but it is important that it should cut both ways.

We noticed while driving back to the airport that small German and Russian flags were flying from the poles along our route – an outward token of our newly established relationship. Kosygin, who was again accompanying me, inquired after various European Social Democrats whom he had met in an official capacity. Many, he said, were back in opposition. 'Take Krag – he isn't in charge any more.' We also discussed whether occasional private contacts between the authorities in Bonn and Moscow might be of benefit. One such link was established between myself and Brezhnev, and proved advantageous to both parties. Instrumentally speaking, this afforded us the same scope for liaison as we had with other major partners. It would have been hard to conceive of this a year earlier.

The preamble of the treaty which Walter Scheel and I signed with Alexei Kosygin and Andrei Gromyko acknowledged the purposes and principles of the UN Charter. The heart of the treaty comprised two articles relating to the renunciation of force and the inviolability of frontiers. Both parties declared that they would in future settle their disputes exclusively by peaceful means. Also in the renunciation-of-force category came a mutual undertaking to refrain from violating any existing European frontiers – 'including the Oder-Neisse line which forms the western frontier of the People's Republic of Poland and the frontier between the Federal Republic of Germany and the German Democratic Republic' – or making any territorial claims. Article 4 reaffirmed the validity of all existing bilateral or multilateral treaties or arrangements, in other words, did not exclude those between the Federal Republic of Germany and its allies in the West.

The goal of German unity by means of self-determination was not affected by the treaty. In a so-called Letter on German Unity whose receipt the Soviet Government acknowledged, and whose text it communicated to the Foreign Policy Committee of the Supreme Soviet, Foreign Minister Scheel stated that 'this Treaty does not conflict with the political objective of the Federal Republic of Germany to work for a state of peace in Europe in which the German nation will recover its unity in free self-determination'. Our attitude to this question was further clarified by several other references and statements. Egon Bahr noted:

> Firstly, as long as the Four Powers' rights exist, the Federal Republic of Germany cannot avail itself of those rights; it cannot undertake the legal recognition of frontiers on German soil even if it wished to. There is no peace treaty, and that exercises an effect. Secondly, the unaltered goal of the Federal Republic of Germany, as embodied in the Basic Law and consonant with our belief, continues to be national unity and free self-determination. Reconciliation with the peoples of the West can be followed by reconciliation with those of the East only if the German people are not precluded from the goal of unity. Otherwise, new mistrust would be substituted for old.

Both sides set forth their views. It was urgently submitted on our side that détente in Europe was impossible without some improvement of the situation in and concerning Berlin. We added that the treaty could not become effective in default of a satisfactory Berlin settlement. The Soviet Government concurred with our view that an agreement to respect the territorial integrity of all European countries as defined by their existing frontiers did not diminish the sovereign right of any country to adjust its frontiers with the consent of other countries. This further implied that European integration could not be affected by the treaty.

The aforementioned statements of intent related to: (a) the equivalent force of treaties with the Soviet Union and with other members of the Warsaw Pact; (b) the Federal Republic's willingness to conclude a treaty with the GDR based on equality, non-discrimination and independence, and having the same binding force as those with third countries; (c) support for the accession of both German states to the United Nations 'in the course of the détente in Europe', that is to say, temporally dependent on the conclusion of a treaty-based settlement with the GDR; (d) co-operation with the CSSR in settling issues connected with the invalidation of the Munich Agreement; (e) further development of bilateral Soviet-German relations; and (f) support for the plan to hold a conference on European security. Thus, Bonn and Moscow were in agreement that the treaty of 12 August 1970 and the agreements we were striving to reach with Poland, Czechoslovakia and the GDR would constitute an integrated whole. The communiqué of 13 August voiced the expectation 'that the treaty would help to strengthen security in Europe, to solve problems existing there, and to establish peaceful co-operation among all European States, irrespective of the difference in their social systems'.

Another practical result of the treaty negotiations was that relations between the Federal Republic and the Soviet Union were divested of any reference to the 'enemy state' articles of the UN Charter. In concluding the treaty, the Soviet Union modified its twenty-year-old attitude towards Bonn. What it recognized was the peaceable character of the German Federal Republic.

Egon Bahr said later that the duration of the Moscow talks had greatly disappointed him. He had at first thought that one or two thorough discussions would reveal 'whether it's on or not, whether the scheme will work or not'. This had been a mistake. He had initially found it hard to tell whether the Russians were at all prepared to discuss a fundamental change in relations.

The current popular impression was that it was all taking a dreadfully long time. Actually, I felt the same way . . . Anyone who talks to the Russians is well advised to take plenty of time. Once I grasped this, I took an unlimited amount of time because I felt that few things could be more important to us than to establish proper, decent and, if possible, normal or even good relations with a neighbour who, though not on our immediate doorstep, is one of the two most powerful countries in the world . . . And if the Soviet Foreign Minister had time for this, to the great interest and, in part, suspicion of others, we had to have even more time than he did.

To begin with, Bahr went on, there was mistrust on both sides.

After all, we both had past experience of each other. I discovered, secondly, that our way of thinking was unfamiliar to the Russians. That is to say, we had to go to the lengths of discussing individual words and explaining what was meant by them . . . How, for instance, to interpret our acceptance of the GDR as a state but our refusal to recognize it in terms of international law? This is hard enough for Germans – how much more so for Russians? In other words, it turned out that we could not discuss one important topic without discussing the entire scheme of things.

My four-hour conversation with Leonid Brezhnev on the afternoon of 12 August 1970 was carefully noted by the world at large. Few non-communist visitors from abroad had yet been granted a lengthy interview with the General Secretary. He made a rather wary impression and spent considerable periods of time referring to his written material, whole passages of which he read aloud. But this was clearly the stage at which Brezhnev had resolved – and been empowered – to take personal charge of important aspects of Soviet policy towards the West. At the time, he and Kosygin struck me as the Kremlin's '1a' and '1b'. A year later Brezhnev's definite and undisputed supremacy could not escape the eye or ear. He was also a master of his material.

To me he seemed a man who had been altogether moulded by his position and advancement within the ranks of Party officialdom – not that he personified the hidebound type of Party Secretary. His personal appearance testified to the cultivation of a well-groomed exterior. To my surprise, his stature did not fully correspond to the proportions that photographs seemed to convey. Far from being a 'monumental figure', he made an almost dainty impression despite his bulk – lively of gesture and expression, vivacious and quasi-Mediterranean in his movements when he warmed to a conversation. (He hails from the industrial region of the Ukraine, where various national influences coincide.) Unlike Kosygin, who seemed on the frigid side, Brezhnev could be impulsive and even boisterous. He betrayed occasional surges of feeling and – if one will – the 'Russian soul' that does not flinch from shedding a quick tear. Recollections of World War II, with which he was abidingly preoccupied, moved him to strong and spontaneous displays of emotion. Though unforthcoming on the subject of cultural interests, he displayed a noticeable attachment to Russian history. He would laugh whole-heartedly in the presence of others and even indulged in little flights of irony. None of this detracted from the salient impression of a man whose sweeping self-assurance waxed from meeting to meeting – certainly from 1970 (Moscow) to 1971 (Oreanda) and 1973 (when he visited me in Bonn). Brezhnev's propensity for making full and trenchant statements of position seemed to grow as his authority became ever more manifestly undisputed. In 1975 (Moscow), when slightly subdued by illness and perhaps by other considerations as well, the Soviet leader failed to disguise the concern that underlay his cheerful manner.

Leonid Ilyich Brezhnev, a smelter's son, was born in 1906 and worked his way up to become an engineer – a source of pride to which he often refers. He held various local and regional Party posts from an early age and served in the Armed Forces Political Administration during the war. He became Secretary of the Central Committee in Stalin's time but was later ousted. Under Khrushchev, who knew him from the Ukraine and may have looked upon him as his successor, he regained the second rung of the leadership, first as reappointed Secretary of the Central Committee and a candidate, then as a full member of the Party Presidium, as the Politburo was then called. Between 1960 and 1964 he held the post of nominal head of state, becoming First Secretary after Khrushchev fell from power. His appointment as General Secretary followed two years later, and his increasing hold on the reins of power has been detectable since 1970.

There are, however, many signs that his position inside the Politburo, or actual government of the Soviet Union, has been far from undisputed over the years, and that he has had to fight hard to maintain it. Given the circumstances of his country and its power structures, he has generally tried to pursue a middle course – as, for instance, in the economic field, where he tentatively decided to encourage the production of consumer goods without antagonizing the military. Khrushchev had introduced some degree of cultural relaxation. Although Brezhnev reversed this trend, one gained the impression that he would have preferred to compromise with intellectual critics but lacked the breadth of vision to do so. In the Soviet sphere of influence his name is associated with the brutal disciplining of Czechoslovakia in 1968. In other contexts he has shown himself responsive to the sectional interests of his treaty partners. Where East-West policy is concerned, his decision in favour of reducing tension has certainly not been prompted by altruistic motives or an abandonment of super-power aspirations but is sustained by a fervent and credible desire for peace. I think I managed to satisfy myself of this.

The first thing to emerge from our discussions was his interest in economic matters. It was also obvious that he had begun his career as a technologist (he was a metallurgical engineer). His experience of the West was very limited in 1970, but he soon staked his entire reputation on a policy of détente. In autumn 1971 I told President Pompidou of my belief that, for personal reasons connected with internal and power politics, Brezhnev was seeking better relations with Western Europe and the United States. Although it doubtless failed to eliminate them, the trust he showed me in the course of our own relationship certainly mitigated some of his prejudices against 'the Germans' – in fact he conveyed as much to Pompidou. As was only natural, however, our first meeting remained a cautious and tentative affair. Each of us was quietly taking the other's measure.

Many of my fellow-countrymen could not grasp that, as General Secretary, Brezhnev was senior to the Chairman of the Council of Ministers. I was asked in what capacity we had conferred – for instance, as Chairman of the SPD and leader of the Soviet Communist Party? Even when Brezhnev visited Bonn in 1973, the gentlemen in charge of protocol found the set-up too mystifying to unravel. The General Secretary was obliged to forgo a gun-salute on arrival although he had long ago been greeted in Paris with all the honours befitting a head of state: it was a triumph for the German tendency to go by the book.

Brezhnev began by explaining the Politburo's working methods and the practice of 'collective leadership'. He said that a lot of ridiculous nonsense was written about these matters in the Western press, which also stooped to calumny. In fifty years, nobody had managed to shake the Soviet people's faith in the Party. Western observers had a poor understanding of Russian psychology and the peculiarities of political life since the Revolution. The Great Patriotic War and the post-war period had left people and Party even more united. I was not, of course, told where the Soviet leaders found all the time they devoted to conversations with visitors from abroad, nor how the country was governed when its overlord departed on lengthy foreign tours, nor how an ageing political executive proposed to surmount the generation-gap.

The General Secretary declared that we should speak frankly rather than stick to diplomatic procedure. I led off by saying what a great experience my visit to Moscow was. Differences of opinion should not

With my wife in Leningrad, July 1975

Tête-à-tête with the Shah, Tehran 1972

With Mr Brezhnev in Moscow, 1975

Three-cornered conversation with Henry Kissinger and Helmut Schmidt

be overlooked, even at a time like this, but I was nonetheless convinced that we had common interests in a number of important areas. I regarded the treaty that had just been signed as a terminal act, but even more so as a point of departure for all that we could jointly undertake, not only in the field of bilateral co-operation but in helping to promote peace in Europe. I would say quite candidly when our views diverged, both now and later, but I suspected that much could be done in concert despite our differences of opinion.

I had brought a small present which struck me as appropriate to 'Lenin Year', the centenary of the birth of the Soviet Union's founder: a postcard written in German by Comrade Ulyanov to a German Social Democrat in Breslau before World War I. Brezhnev was delighted, and said that 'this document' would be greatly prized by the Party and country. (We also obliged Ambassador Tsarapkin with one or two contributions to Lenin Year. The Federal archives sent him a copy of a short film sequence showing Lenin immediately after the Revolution – one which the Russians themselves did not possess.)

Brezhnev then launched into a lengthy dissertation which claimed nearer two hours than one. He described the treaty, whose signing he had been glad to witness, as an act of great political importance. It could create the prerequisites for an entirely novel development of the relations between our two countries. The treaty also underpinned the idea of security in Europe and the world. He welcomed this opportunity to become mutually acquainted. Each of us had read the other's speeches, of course, but the study of another's policies or speeches was no substitute for meetings in person. Personal contact enabled one to form a better appraisal of other countries' problems.

The importance of the treaty would be proportionate to the determination with which our countries fulfilled its provisions. Both sides had worked hard to conclude the treaty, thereby creating the conditions under which mutual understanding could be enhanced and bilateral co-operation in all fields intensified. Political determination was of paramount importance. On it would depend how the conditions established by the treaty were utilized. This political resolve and determination existed on the Soviet side.

A change for the better is not a simple or easy matter. The past weighs heavily between our countries and our peoples. The Soviet people lost twenty million of its number in the war unleashed by Hitler. It is impossible to erase such a past from people's memories. Many millions of Germans also lost their lives in that war. In the post-war years, relations between our countries were generally worse than cool and sometimes strained. But I mention that only in passing. What I want to say is this: Soviet policy towards the Federal Republic of Germany is dominated not by recollections of the past but by concern for the peaceful future of our peoples. If what is intended is moral and political rapprochement between our peoples and countries, as opposed to the mere development of commercial relations, both sides face a difficult task. Memories of World War II live on, and the question is whether the Soviet people can rest assured that our foreign policy is laying new foundations.

And again:

The Party and State will take very active steps to demonstrate the utility of the measures deriving from the treaty and foster an attitude of public goodwill towards the Federal Republic. This will be done not only in speeches and at conferences but with the aid of press, radio and television. We are living at a time when the population of both countries consists largely of young people who have no recollection of the war. Therein lies the importance of how you, and we, educate our younger generation and our peoples. Irrespective of any controversies, we should be capable of teaching them to respect each other.

Brezhnev then spoke of how post-war Germany had contained elements which pursued an unrealistic policy and did not accept the situation in Europe as it stood. These elements had 'sometimes gained the upper hand'. Since I became Chancellor, there had been signs that we meant to abandon the unrealistic policy of the past, and there had been a prompt response to my initiative on the Soviet side. The General Secretary proceeded to enlarge on three subjects which he termed cardinal issues.

It had, in the first place, been clear to him for many years that the more independent a partner's foreign policy, the better the development of relations. 'When de Gaulle asserted his independence in foreign policy, for example, it enabled our relations to develop constructively in all areas.' It had been wholly abnormal that the Federal Republic's position *vis-à-vis* the Soviet Union and other communist countries had until lately been such as to preclude it from taking fundamental decisions. The Soviet Union advocated that the Federal Republic should assume a place in the world commensurate with its economic and technological status, and that it should use its influence in the attainment of security and co-operation in Europe.

There were forces which hoped to profit from tension between our countries. If we jointly strove to improve the European situation, nobody in the world could oppose our united resolve. 'I should like to emphasize that we have no intention of pursuing a policy whereby the Federal Republic develops its relations with us at the expense of its relations with other countries, particularly the USA, because the USA is probably your most important partner in foreign policy. We neither had nor have any such insidious plans, and I consider this an important factor.'

Secondly, the treaty had been signed at a time when the two blocs were in confrontation. The Soviet Union – and here he was alluding to what had since 1968 been called the Brezhnev Doctrine – had defended the 'socialist community of states' and would continue to do so without intending a threat to anyone. The alleged communist danger from the East was a propagandist slogan. The road to our treaty's future fulfilment ran via the Federal Republic's relations with the members of the Warsaw Pact, and especially with the GDR. Much was talked about nationhood, national unity and special relationships. In a certain sense, he regarded the genesis of the GDR as a product of World War II and believed that it accorded with the popular will. It was impossible to depart from these facts. Friendship and co-operation were incompatible with revanchism and aggressive intentions, whomsoever they were directed against.

Thirdly, there were great opportunities for co-operation between our countries. The Americans had committed themselves in Europe and, to an appreciable extent, in the Federal Republic as well. Were we really dependent on this? 'I can well recall pictures of Russians and Germans fraternizing in World War I. From the purely human standpoint, our peoples have a disposition towards friendship. I am sure that we shall achieve such a friendship. However fanciful it may sound, I am convinced that this policy is of great significance.'

Brezhnev then referred to an interview given by Foreign Minister Scheel a few days earlier in which he had spoken of the connection between the Moscow treaty and a favourable Berlin settlement. What did this mean?

West Berlin was a complicated matter, and one on which the Four Powers were currently engaged. He would not exclude the possibility that universally acceptable compromises might be found with the goodwill of all Four Powers. If Herr Scheel had made his statement with my approval 'for propaganda purposes', that was one thing. If it genuinely represented the Federal Government's position, how should it be construed? It would surely imply that we reserved a right of veto for the USA. Notwithstanding all my political difficulties at home, I would be falling back on the defensive if I handed the USA this trump card.

Later in our talk I drew attention to what Foreign Minister Scheel had told his colleague Gromyko on the subject of Berlin. Brezhnev: 'So you don't posit any connection between the ratification of the treaty and the West Berlin question? After all, the latter may drag on, not being solely dependent on us.' I replied that my Foreign Minister had been alluding to a practical connection, not a legal nexus. 'But the politico-psychological situation in the Federal Republic is such that we expect wider approval of the treaty if there is progress on Berlin.' Brezhnev: 'I think we should ratify the treaty as soon as possible.' Brandt: 'The Federal Republic considers itself politically bound by the treaty from this day forth and will act in accordance therewith. We reserve no right of veto, even for our best friends. Study our point of view, which is a reasonable one, and use your influence to ensure that West Berlin does not become a bone of contention but is able to play a constructive role, however modest, in co-operation.' Brezhnev: 'Your remarks about ratification puzzle me a little. Any delay might substantially diminish the treaty's political importance. To temporize would delay the solution of other problems, including that of West Berlin. Please bear that in mind.'

My response to Brezhnev's dissertation opened with an assessment of the treaty. The important thing was to develop and exploit it in a manner compatible with our common interests and those of other European peoples. I referred to three of Brezhnev's speeches which I had carefully studied (one marking the Lenin celebrations, one during the election campaign early in June, and one – on agricultural matters – to the Plenum of the Central Committee). I had inferred from them that, notwithstanding the anxieties to which he had also referred, the General Secretary was prepared to co-operate with the Federal Republic. (Brezhnev: 'Yes, that's correct.') Secondly, he had, on the subject of peaceful coexistence, alluded to President Nixon's dictum that we must pass from the era of confrontation to that of negotiation. Thirdly, he had stated in his June speech on the relationship between communists and social democrats that, while there could be no effacement of ideological issues (a view with which I fully concurred), those charged with political responsibility could, without sacrificing their ideological positions, explore practical opportunities relating to peace and the interests of our peoples. I agreed with this too. As to the results of the treaty, we should obviate setbacks and disappointments by not undertaking too many things at once. I was in favour of patience and solid planning. In implementing the treaty, we had a lead weight attached to each leg. The first was that the war had left many open wounds; the other dated from the post-war period, dominated as it had been by the Cold War, into which Germany had been drawn to a special extent.

I shall not recount our extremely wide-ranging discussion of the origins of the Cold War. It may be taken for granted that the attendant circumstances were less straightforward than they originally appeared to many people, myself included. In the light of subsequent knowledge and experience, however, I see no reason to amend my view that, although questionable decisions were taken in the West and, thus, in Washington, responsibility for the growing rift should definitely be attributed to the Soviet foreign policy associated with Stalin's name.

It was here, during our talk in August 1970, that Brezhnev interrupted me: 'The Cold War spirit was not a Russian invention. It emanated from the West, from Dulles and Adenauer, although the latter also took some positive steps. I can very well understand your attitude to Nazi Germany, but in this instance we are talking about the policy of *Germany*.'

I explained that I did not want to debate the 1950s at this juncture, except to state that those who had taken over one-third of Germany had brought two-thirds of it into greater conflict with themselves than was necessary. Brezhnev could take it, I said, that my government's foreign policy was founded on the experiences of the past – that we aimed to safeguard peace and preserve our own interests. The Federal Government supported the policy of détente in company with its treaty partners as well. Certain reactions to our treaty, for instance in some sections of the French and British press, should be met with a patient attempt to demonstrate the falsity of the assumption that it had been concluded at others' expense. I had encountered no objections to our foreign policy in conversation with President Nixon.

I explained our position in the European Community, which would soon be expanding. This would be beneficial to international trade. Looking to the future, there was also the question of relations between the Community and the CMEA [Council for Mutual Economic Assistance, or Comecon]. (Brezhnev, later: 'We are against self-contained blocs, but we are realists: the EEC exists. Possible co-operation with the CMEA can be discussed at expert level. The results could be very interesting.') On the other hand, I continued, we also belonged to NATO, which was irreplaceable – given the prevailing world situation – but in and with which we were striving for international détente.

On the plan for a European security conference, I said that I concurred with many of the suggested items for an agenda, but that the Federal Republic must reserve its position. Besides, I was convinced that we ought not to evade one crucial issue, to wit, the attempt to reduce armaments and armed forces in Central Europe, however slowly. At the most recent NATO meeting in Rome (in May), the Federal Government and its allies had evolved sundry ideas for a mutual and balanced reduction of forces. It was unlikely that any solution would be found at a preliminary conference. We had to think not only of the members of both alliances but also of the non-aligned countries, even though the latter were not directly involved in the problems of mutual reduction. I was under no illusions, especially in the military domain, but favourable results might flow from minor steps of an initially symbolic nature. Reverting to this later on, Brezhnev said that it was 'not a cardinal decision' despite its importance. The Soviet proposals for complete disarmament still stood.

Turning to the Soviet Union's allies, I declared that there was every prospect, now that our treaty had been signed, of reaching a relatively quick settlement with Poland. (Brezhnev: 'Yes, I think so.') As for the CSSR, we were ready to resolve the outstanding problem that arose from the past. If we had not made any approach to Prague, it was because we felt that the Czechs still had problems of their own. For that reason, we would rather await a sign from them that they were ready to negotiate. Brezhnev said that the foundations had been laid.

For reasons which he could doubtless only partly appreciate, I continued, the GDR presented special problems. These would none the less have to be overcome. However one regarded our national problem, a number of matters remained to be settled between the GDR and the Federal Republic which were not comparable with those existing in the relations between other states. Human and psychological factors played a major role. Our treaty's provision in regard to the inviolability of frontiers applied to the GDR as well. For all the peculiarities of the situation, we aimed to reach a contractual settlement with the GDR which would be as binding as our treaties with other countries. We had striven to discover what basis would be suitable. We wanted any treaty to embody terms such as territorial integrity and inviolability of frontiers. What mattered most of all, however, was that serious discussions should actually take place. They ought to be held at expert level – at working level. The Moscow treaty would never have materialized in any other way. I was making no demands, simply stating my position. If Brezhnev did not consider it irrelevant, I thought he could exert a favourable influence. In this context, I drew the General Secretary's attention to some SED literature in which I had been described as an exponent of imperialism. People must learn to be more discriminating in their judgements and arguments.

On Berlin, I had rejoiced to hear Brezhnev state that it would be possible to find a solution acceptable to all. This problem being a Four-Power responsibility, it had been logical not to make it an official matter for negotiation between us. Brezhnev said that he 'unofficially' considered an acceptable solution possible. The fact still remained that the territory of West Berlin did not belong to the Federal Republic. A Federal political presence 'in the strict sense' was out of place. Where West Berlin was concerned, although we did not occupy the legal positions *vis-à-vis* the Soviet Union on which the Western Powers were able to take their stand, we did have vital interests. (Brezhnev: 'I see that.') I explained the nature of the ties between the Federation and West Berlin and pointed out that I bore an additional responsibility for Berlin as chairman of my party. We needed a solution that would not disrupt economic links. We needed a simplified arrangement in regard to corridors. This ought also to be feasible from the GDR's point of view. Both of us should be interested in ensuring that West Berlin ceased to be a Cold War island and took its place in the context of internal German and European co-operation. The question of the Federation's political presence should be viewed in concrete terms. Given that West Berlin had the same currency and largely the same laws, this fact ought to find expression in the official sphere. The Federation did not 'govern' West Berlin, but scope for close co-operation with it had to be provided in accordance with the inhabitants' wishes.

Brezhnev repeated his assurance that the Soviet Union was ready to join in wide-ranging economic ventures. He also wanted to make it clear that the Soviet Union naturally aspired to good relations with the USA – 'good in the true sense of the word'.

Finally, Brezhnev asked why the KPD was still banned whereas the neo-Nazis were not. There was no time for a proper reply because Kosygin and his banquet were waiting. I might have added that much time would be needed to explore all the subjects we had broached. This applied *inter alia* to the allegations of revanchism and our relations with the United States. The wish to continue our discussion was expressed on both sides. A special little communiqué stated that it had taken place 'in an objective atmosphere and with candour'.

One of my strongest impressions was of the extent to which Brezhnev – and certainly not Brezhnev alone – overestimated the German Federal Republic. Whether deliberately or no, he appeared uncertain in his evaluation of developments in the West. What, for example, was he to make of Nixon? I knew him – did I think he really wanted peace? One novel feature was the rudiment of an undogmatic attitude towards West European unification: acceptance of the EEC as a fact allied with continuing mistrust of political fusion. Speaking to the press in Bonn, I said that the Russians had been urged to acknowledge that the existing and expanding Common Market was part of that actual situation on which all assumptions should be based. I also thought I detected some curiosity on Brezhnev's part about the phenomenon of West European social democracy, almost as if he felt it not quite sufficient to fall back on the Bolshevik-Menshevik formula.

It may be assumed that the Soviet leaders were unprepared for the fact that the West would be shaken by a major economic crisis, and that they were gambling on the benefits that might accrue from economic co-operation. I thought it probable that their reasoning was as follows: given that the revolutionary movement in Europe would gain no successes in the foreseeable future, and that revolutionary developments were only to be expected in developing countries, the logical course was to develop the best possible relations with the West under the auspices of peaceful coexistence. We noticed appreciable changes even in direct relation to the treaty. These included a reduction in polemics, a more accommodating attitude towards the Berlin negotiations, an expansion of trade and some measure of relaxation on the scientific and cultural plane.

Was there opposition within the Soviet leadership? Misgivings in Moscow would not have been surprising and were probably voiced as well. For example: Berlin could no longer be used as a lever, or not as it had been in the past; if the anti-German card were removed from the inter-communist pack, the 'struggle against the Federal Republic' would cease to serve as cement for the Eastern bloc; the consolidation of the GDR might, under certain circumstances, be reimperilled; Poland would become somewhat less dependent. Besides, why not wait for the Americans to withdraw instead of granting them concessions in Berlin? In any case, why take on renewed obligations there? Or, one stage further: why not let the USA and Canada become parties to an all-European conference? However, anyone who made a negative response to these questions would have had to be prepared for the situation to deteriorate.

While it is certain that the treaty was overwhelmingly accepted by the inhabitants of the Soviet Union as an augury of peaceful progress, there were some unexpected reactions as well. In areas that had suffered particularly badly in the war, notably White Russia, there were reports of hoarding. The reason? Last time, a treaty was swiftly followed by invasion . . . After talking to Marshal Grechko, one of my

Scandinavian friends told me of a special problem. The treaty called for comprehensive reindoctrination inside the Soviet armed forces because the 'enemy image' no longer applied. From autumn 1970 onwards, the Red Army was in fact provided with new training aids which refrained from anathematizing the Federal Republic. This was no small matter. I know from experience in other contexts that it is far from easy to wean an army from its traditional conception of the foe.

The Soviet leaders considered that their own renunciation of force carried greater weight than ours. Be that as it may, both sides had to make considerable efforts on the treaty's behalf. I have often wondered whether the opportunity has been thoroughly exploited by both sides, and I fear that the answer must be no. Opposition in the Federal Republic turned out to be greater than was justified by public opinion. The dispute over ratification dragged on. Uncertainty arose on the Soviet side as to whether the treaty would come into force at all. The grand design was so circumscribed that it forfeited much of its potential effectiveness.

Addressing the Bundestag in mid-September, after the summer recess, I said: 'The Federal Government believes that the time had come to re-establish our relationship with the Soviet Union and Eastern Europe, and to normalize it as far as possible. In concluding this treaty, the Federal Government stood by what it had undertaken in its policy statement.' The treaty had given nothing away. It was based on the situation as it actually stood. It stipulated that existing frontiers were inviolable and that all outstanding questions must be settled peacefully.

In December 1970 we signed the Warsaw treaty. In April 1971, at the 24th Congress of the CPSU – 'Brezhnev's Congress', as it was christened – Brezhnev delivered a speech in which he advocated détente and co-operation. Early in September the Four Powers concluded the Berlin Agreement. At that juncture I was asked if I would visit Brezhnev in the Crimea for a few days in the middle of the month – unofficially, without protocol or delegations. The invitation was not mysteriously smuggled through to me, as the current rumour ran, but delivered in a wholly normal fashion by the Soviet Ambassador.

Suspicious voices inquired what a personal invitation might really signify. Speculative and futile references to a 'meeting of party leaders' revived, almost as if there were a steadfast refusal to acknowledge the structure of the Soviet hierarchy. A few of our senior civil servants were also greatly exercised. One objector wondered if I ought to accept an invitation to a place near Yalta, where Stalin, Roosevelt and Churchill had sealed the fate of our defeated country at the beginning of

1945. Many seemed annoyed that no provision would be made for a press escort, as on official visits, though numerous journalists found their way there just the same. Finally, no undue demands were made on the departmental sense of propriety. My only companions apart from Egon Bahr were a Foreign Office expert and an interpreter-cum-minute-taker.

But there was one other focus of suspicion which had to be taken more seriously. Brezhnev was no doubt anxious to speak to me before his visit to France in October, and the impression seemed to have been conveyed to Paris and elsewhere that the Oreanda meeting was an initiative of my own. This, as I have already indicated, was a mis-understanding which I managed to dispel when I visited Pompidou in Paris late that autumn, outside our normal consultative cycle. Petty manœuvres designed to arouse suspicion had to be taken for granted – as they still have. Press reports from Washington alleged official resent-ment that the Administration had been informed of my Oreanda trip but not consulted. No such complaints were made to me direct. There were also those in the West who claimed secret service confirmation of their absurd rumours to the effect that secret agreements had been reached at Oreanda. There were no secret agreements.

We took off from Bonn in a military aircraft and landed at Simferopol late on the afternoon of 16 September. (The crew got a friendly reception. It was the first time, and rated as something of a sensation, that uniformed members of our armed forces had set foot in the Crimea.) Brezhnev was waiting for me at the airfield – without a delegation, so as to underline the personal nature of the meeting – and had been chatting to some journalists in an almost American fashion before we landed. He urged the photographers not to miss the touch-down of our Bundeswehr machine on the grounds that it would make a historic picture. Our relations had been poor for long enough, he said – nobody must spoil them now. This was an optimistic variation on Egon Bahr's phrase. Referring to the GDR, Bahr sometimes commented that we had been on no kind of terms for long enough – at least we were now on bad ones . . .

Brezhnev proposed a little refreshment before the ninety-minute drive to Oreanda, where we were to have dinner. Our light snack in Simferopol's equivalent of a VIP lounge developed into a lengthy dose of hospitality accompanied by informal conversation. It is possible that the Russians were testing their visitors' capacity for drink. If so, I passed with flying colours. Brezhnev being the only senior Party representative there, I was doubly impressed by the free-and-easy way in which local and regional officials took part in the conversation. There was no hint of subservience in their attitude to the General Secretary. After I had led off with some political pleasantries, the Russians contributed several entertaining anecdotes whose conformity to the Party line was dubious. I had told them – to their great amusement – that the difference between capitalism and communism was that capitalism was the exploitation of man by man whereas communism was the exact opposite. Brezhnev capped this with enormous relish by describing a visit he had paid to a collective farm in the Caucasus. He had told his audience of the benefits that would flow from the next Five-Year Plan. There would be milk every day for the children and plenty of meat all round on Sundays. Everybody would be able to buy one pair of shoes and the womenfolk two dress-lengths annually. 'Interjection from an old peasant-woman at the back of the hall: Could she ask a question? "Have I understood you correctly, *Gospodin* General Secretary? You mean it's going to be more or less like it was under Little Father Tsar?" ' The Russians enjoyed the joke as much as I did – Brezhnev most of all.

We considered it futile to engage in mutual indoctrination, but both sides knew what was really at stake even when talk turned to the weather. I was much struck by some unprejudiced allusions to war-time events in the Crimea. One regional Party official, originally a doctor, described how he had helped everyone he could when the situation became fluid – 'everyone including our own people, Red Army men or German stragglers'. He would never have phrased it like that a few years earlier. While still at table and before conversation drifted away from politics, I remarked that we were over our initial difficulties. Brezhnev expressed some misgivings and said that we could only claim to have got the beginning of the beginning behind us. He did, however, agree with me when I said that the experiences of the past year had shown that, so far from having been achieved at others' expense, improved relations between our countries had generally conduced – in the face of great mistrust – to a lessening of tension.

On the drive from Simferopol to the Black Sea – it was well past midnight – my host told me that he attached exceptional importance to our meeting and predicted that it would go down 'in European history'. He would also have to discuss some distasteful subjects with me, but what mattered was our 'general orientation', and he hoped that we would succeed in finding a common denominator. Developments in Europe would largely depend on how relations shaped between the Soviet Union on the one hand and the Federal Republic and France on the other. He appreciated the significance of the Brandt government and was prepared to move in its direction. This went for the other

Warsaw Pact countries as well; he had recently met their senior representatives at the place where I would be staying as his guest. I distinctly sensed during our drive that Brezhnev was oppressed by the dangers of a nuclear war, nor have I forgotten that he showed sympathy for Germany's fate. But that, he said, was Hitler's responsibility, not his or mine.

My own concern during this warm-up for the talks of the next two days was to make it clear that I proposed to discuss bilateral relations, and that inter-party contacts were not at issue. I also made it clear to my host that our treaty policy was encountering substantial opposition and that many people were bracing themselves for what they pessimistically called a 'Year of Metternich'.

The General Secretary had the use of a spacious and comfortable estate beside the Black Sea. My stay was an enjoyable one, and we even found time to bathe. (The fact that Brezhnev and I waded into the sea together was long cited in certain quarters as an abandonment of principle of my part!) However, the Russians' hospitality is only matched by their disinclination to abide by a prearranged time-table. We had agreed to talk 'in the mornings'. This turned out to mean late in the morning, and I assumed that we would adjourn for a meal after a couple of hours. Instead, there was a round of talks lasting four hours followed by a lengthy boat-ride, followed by an informal supper. Little mention was made of politics during the meal or the sea-trip that preceded it. We spent most of the time discoursing on a rather personal level, not only about the country and its inhabitants but about the very different experiences we had undergone as members of the same generation. We also swapped numerous anecdotes and stories. On the second morning we met for a further session lasting two-and-a-quarter hours. Counting our conversation on the return drive to the airport, we talked for a good sixteen hours in all.

This undoubtedly enabled me to become better acquainted with Brezhnev than had been possible in Moscow in 1970. There were two respects in which I sensed that a change had occurred in my opposite number. First, his status as the dominant member of the Soviet leadership could hardly have been more manifest and he made no attempt to disguise it. Secondly, he showed greater self-assurance when discussing international affairs and leaned far less heavily on the written briefs which had – as is the custom in all countries – been prepared for him on this occasion too.

Like our aides in their parallel talks, we naturally began by discussing bilateral relations, a subject to which we reverted at a later stage. These had developed tolerably well since the summer of 1970. There was more trade and less recrimination, and political contact had acquired greater substance. Although the treaty had yet to be ratified, its effects were beginning to be felt.

Quite understandably, Brezhnev's interest centred on one particular point. When would the Federal Republic ratify? I carefully explained that we were hurrying the process along as best we could and expressed my belief that it would be successfully concluded – albeit with only a small majority – in the coming spring. Brezhnev thought this all very slow. There was no opposition in his country, but the Soviet people were displaying a certain guarded expectancy. It had not escaped them that the treaty remained unratified despite all the talk in high places. Although no direct inquiries had been made, the Soviet leaders knew that these matters were being discussed. On the return drive from Oreanda, Brezhnev – who also appeared to be worried by economic problems – asked me 'just between ourselves' if the treaty would really be ratified. I said I was certain of it. That meant a great deal to him, Brezhnev replied, because failure to ratify would be a setback whose effects might linger for decades. He was clearly impressed when I added that I had harnessed the fate of my government to the outcome of our treaty policy.

He had earlier stated in regard to the ratification problem that, without making any demands, he was counting on the simultaneous ratification of the Warsaw treaty. I confirmed this and emphasized the special status of German-Polish relations. I mentioned on the same occasion that it had been impossible for me to accept an invitation from the Polish Government to fly on to Warsaw for talks after my Oreanda visit. I hoped my refusal would not be misinterpreted. Brezhnev proposed to telephone Gierek next day and inform him of our conversation.

We spoke of the still outstanding treaty with the CSSR. Brezhnev had discussed the problems of the Sudeten Germans with Husak – problems which partially escaped him, of course – and the Czech Party leader had responded in a co-operative vein.

On the GDR, Brezhnev said that he was naturally averse to our making any superfluous demands. He did, however, listen carefully when I expounded our scheme for special arrangements (primary consideration was then being given to the Traffic Treaty). I also made it clear that heed must be paid to special German factors such as ties of kinship. We had to aim at a future in which there could be no recurrence of the events which I termed consequences of the Cold War, nor of the sort of tragedies that could still be observed on the frontiers.

Where bilateral issues were concerned we were unanimous that economic relations – not excluding Berlin – should be developed. We resolved to set up a Mixed Commission. Further agreements and an exchange of delegations were also discussed. Brezhnev again referred – like Kosygin a year earlier – to his country's vast mineral resources (apart from oil and natural gas). He recommended 'high-yield' technological co-operation, among other things in the construction of nuclear reactors. Passing references were made to Comecon and the EEC – a subject which was no longer virgin territory as it had been in 1970.

Not quite so incidental was the Soviet recognition of our desire, where the settlement of humanitarian problems was concerned, to increase exit visa quotas. Brezhnev inquired in passing if it was true that 'Herr Bachmann's party' (the DKP) was legally active in the Federal Republic. (This was his way of evading the DKP issue, which clearly annoyed him.) I confirmed that the DKP was legally active and could run for office like any other party. It was not well disposed towards me personally, but that I could hardly expect. Some people wanted to ban it, but I did not share their view. (This minor point was to play a major role in the post-Oreanda controversy. I mentioned it when briefing the Opposition immediately on my return home. The rumour was then circulated that, by confirming the legal existence of their party, I had signified my goodwill towards the West German communists.)

One of the main issues at Oreanda was, of course, the Berlin question. I stated that the Quadripartite Agreement, which had been signed two weeks earlier, would have a great bearing on the European political climate. All parties had contributed to it, whether present at the negotiating table or not. The Soviet contribution and that of the General Secretary were well known to me. Brezhnev declared that the Soviet side had gone to great lengths to avoid impeding the treaty's ratification. During our talk last year he had made bigger demands and been less flexible. The Soviet negotiators had adopted a lower limit which public opinion and the Party, too, regarded as a threshold. They had allowed themselves to be guided by the principle of flexibility so as to resolve complex problems and modify the bilateral and European climate. Replying, I expressed surprise that any controversy should have arisen. I believed, quite candidly and without exaggeration, that ratification of our treaty with the Soviet Union could not be introduced until the problems associated with the Berlin Agreement had been resolved, as I hoped they would be within a few months at most. Brezhnev said he had no knowledge of any outstanding problems. I told him that I was referring to the technical supplements to the

Quadripartite Agreement, which the Federal Government and the Berlin Senate would have to negotiate with the GDR. Brezhnev replied that, in any case, the Berlin Agreement could only come into force after the treaty had been ratified, and that it was important to be clear on this point of detail.

From being a detail, of course, this constituted a package-deal in reverse and one of which I was bound to take note. Formally, it was a matter for the Four Powers. Politically, I considered this nexus incorrect and said so. I also pointed out that, although I had not come to make complaints about anyone, I could not forbear to mention the troubles we had had with the GDR during the past fortnight. These were largely connected with the argument over a few words in the German translation of the Quadripartite Agreement. I had been all the more depressed by this dispute because I had had grounds for supposing that an agreement had been reached on the German text.

Brezhnev, who had clearly been afraid that this subject would crop up, professed surprise that I had raised it. He was compelled to state, with some embitterment, that the Soviet side had been most accommodating. The text had been faithfully recorded in the signatories' three languages, after which an attempt had been made 'from among your associates' to distort several points with the aid of the German translation and thereby delay further negotiations from the Bonn end. His government would not meddle in the translation question, but he did wonder how it was possible for a translation to render individual words differently from the way in which they had been laid down in official texts (a question which may still be asked). I reverted to this next day. Would the practical effects of the Berlin Agreement really have to wait until the Final Protocol had been signed – was their timing dependent on the treaty's ratification? Would it not be advisable, for humanitarian as well as broad political reasons, to implement practical improvements in advance? Brezhnev insisted that the Final Protocol would not come into force until our treaty had been ratified. He then added soothingly that the agreement of 3 September was already having beneficial effects. I replied that the Soviet proviso would have to be discussed with the Western Powers. I was afraid that, apart from anything else, it would retard the development of a favourable attitude towards the European Security Conference.

As for the dispute over the German translation, I made it clear that we would abide by the signatories' official texts. There could be no question of my associates' having distorted the text of the agreement. Summarizing what had actually happened, I said that two five-man teams – two civil servants and three interpreters from each of the

German states – had spent hours going over the text of the agreement together. Nineteen discrepancies had been discovered in the two German translations submitted. Seventeen of these had been resolved. I had been telephoned from Berlin in regard to the two remaining points on the morning of 3 September. After making some recommendations I had been informed that agreement had been reached – not, it was true, on an official document, but on a semi-official working text. It offended me to be told that no further action had been taken since the message alleging agreement. This was an impossible mode of procedure, especially as the two German teams had been joined in their deliberations by American and Soviet embassy counsellors who were expert linguists. The US Ambassador had thereupon stated that he had signed the agreement in the belief that the two German sides had resolved their differences over the translation. Brezhnev thanked me, but added that his thanks committed him to nothing. He reiterated that there would be no Soviet involvement in the matter of the German translation. He had made no demands and would make none in this connection.

A more important feature of the Oreanda meeting was our exchange of views on the themes that were later to preoccupy the conferences in Helsinki, Geneva and Helsinki (CSCE), as well as the consultations in Vienna (MBFR). As to the Conference on Security and Co-operation in Europe, I was able to inform Brezhnev that NATO could be expected to give the go-ahead and that we could ready ourselves for a preliminary conference in 1972. Brezhnev, who wanted preparations to be completed quickly, expressed no further objection to the idea that an all-European conference should include the United States and Canada. I considered this point to be of fundamental importance because it meant that, after the Berlin Agreement, America would be involved in all-European agreements of wider scope without relying solely on rights of conquest secured in World War II.

On the subject of arms limitation in Europe, I submitted that we should not stop short at invocations of the general disarmament theme. What mattered was a balanced reduction of armaments and armed forces in Central Europe – balanced so as not to disturb the global equilibrium. I made no secret of what I had also told Nixon a few months earlier, namely, that the MBFR theme could not be restricted to negotiations between the United States and the Soviet Union and must involve the countries of Europe as well.

At this stage, Brezhnev drew no real distinction between the terms of reference that were subsequently assigned to the conferences in Helsinki and Vienna. He addressed a number of questions, not only to me but also – I felt – to himself. Should reductions (initially) be confined to troops stationed on foreign soil? Should they be based on percentages or units? (The term 'balanced' meant nothing to him, or so he said; we agreed that neither side should be 'disadvantaged'.) At all events, he continued, it was important that arms and troops should be reduced, not only politically but in order to save resources for productive purposes. Our communiqué adhered to this line.

I further submitted that progress would undoubtedly be gradual, that consideration could certainly not be limited to troops on foreign soil, and that areas of reduction – here Brezhnev agreed – could not embrace the two German states alone. I had been asked early that summer why the Russians had taken so long to respond to the Reykjavik initiative. I replied that one indisputable factor had been the Czech crisis, which was nearer its climax in June 1969 than we could have guessed. Apart from anything else, it had led to an increase in Soviet military strength in Central Europe. But NATO, too, had taken some time to put our initiative into concrete form. The United States had been rather cautious at first. Since then, ideas in Washington and Bonn might be termed synchronized.

At 'his' 24th Congress Brezhnev spoke of 'reducing armed forces and armaments in areas where military confrontations are particularly dangerous, above all in Central Europe'. There was an unmistakable connection here with the Moscow treaty. In the general 'without disadvantages' formula which we had devised at Oreanda as a substitute for 'balanced', the Russians for the first time expressed a readiness to discuss the reduction of armed forces separately from the broad CSCE context – in other words, operatively. Another noteworthy feature was that both sides entertained the possibility of not limiting reductions to troops stationed on foreign soil.

Conversation also turned to other countries. Brezhnev was at pains to convey that his forthcoming visit to France was unconnected with any anti-German tendency. I took the opportunity to explain the central role which Germany and France would have to play in the process of European unification. Brezhnev was interested in my impressions of America and Nixon. The US President had told me in June that his China initiative would not affect America's predominant interest in an accommodation with the Soviet Union. Brezhnev said that Rogers and Kissinger had almost daily emphasized the importance attached by Washington to relations with Moscow. I was able to convey my own impression that Nixon wanted negotiations on MBFR. The Pentagon might have its doubts, but so – undoubtedly – did military circles in other countries too.

P.P.–Z

Brezhnev, who did not dispute this, said that the Soviet Union was ready to normalize relations with the United States, expand trade 'without discrimination' and initiate substantial exchanges 'including space technology'. A businesslike relationship with the Americans had developed over the Berlin Agreement. Naturally, some outstanding problems remained. The Soviet Union was supporting socialist Vietnam and dangerous situations had arisen in the Middle East, but the Soviet Union had not become involved in a war anywhere. Unlike the USA (I am merely reproducing Brezhnev's argument), the Soviet Union was not supplying any country with offensive weapons. He was not suspicious of Nixon's forthcoming visit to China. The Soviet Union was trying, constructively and objectively, to improve political and economic relations with America on a basis of greater trust so as 'jointly to take historic steps for the accomplishment of peaceful coexistence'.

China occupied a special place in our discussions. Having given notice that I would raise the topic, I reminded Brezhnev of this on the first day. Would he care to impart his views? This was a difficult subject, Brezhnev said; he would give it some thought before tomorrow morning. When he still failed to broach the matter, I did so myself. I knew the map, I said: I was no adventurer, but I certainly refused to be toyed with. Our relations were of great importance and I did not want anyone to impair them. On the other hand, my policy statement had called for normal relations with all countries desirous of them. This naturally included the People's Republic of China. To me, normal relations did not signify sometimes normal with this one, sometimes normal with that. However, there were right-wing as well as left-wing Maoists who sought to disrupt our policy with allusions to a 'Chinese gambit'. If the question of normal relations with China presented itself in the next few years (as it did in 1972), we should inform the Soviet Union in good time. (I had given the same undertaking to Japan and India as well as the United States.)

Brezhnev did not seem displeased to note that we had not as yet considered exchanging ambassadors. He then spoke for nearly an hour, beginning with a calm and objective review of Sino-Soviet relations. The Soviet Union was ready at all times to improve these, but little progress had been made in trade – discounting a few kopeks – during the last few years. His historical, philosophical and psychological exegeses were more detailed. To put them in a nut-shell, the Chinese were hard to fathom. Their thought-processes, mental disposition and mode of behaviour were virtually incomprehensible to a European. A basic feature of China's nationalistic and chauvinistic policy was its divisiveness. Brezhnev proceeded to inveigh against Maoist and anti-Soviet activities in France, Italy, India, Algeria and Latin America, as well as objectionable developments in other parts of the Third World.

He had already told me, he said, that he was not opposed to relations between China and other countries. Nixon would have a hard time of it if he went to China. It was not known, either, what line China would take in the United Nations; the UN would discover that in due course. China was a poor country with a hard-working population, but it would take decades to lift its economic potential and cultural level. There was no immediate military threat from that quarter. (Describing his last conversation with Brezhnev in January 1973, Pompidou told me that the General Secretary had made his first unprompted reference to China. There was considerable friction between the Party and the army in Peking, he said, and it was to be hoped that Mao's departure would herald a more favourable development in Chinese policy.)

Speaking at Bonn airport on my return from the Crimea, I said that most but not all of my sixteen-and-a-half hours with Brezhnev had been devoted to politics. The frankness of our talks, which were conducted in a spirit of complete loyalty to our respective allies, had shown that progress was possible since the signing of the treaty. On the subject of practical results, I emphasized that direct bilateral relations were to be improved and extended wherever common interests made this possible. I also underlined the connection with other Eastern treaties, confirmed that our treaty with Poland would be ratified at roughly the same time as the Moscow treaty, and stressed the importance of the Berlin Agreement. On CSCE and MBFR, I said that it was our common aim to achieve greater security by avoiding confrontation, but that we had only been able to 'touch on' this difficult subject. If, during the return trip, I had asked myself what the truly novel aspect of the situation was, the answer must be this: 'The Federal Republic of Germany and the Soviet Union are making progress in their mutual relations, just as other countries are. We know where points of agreement, convergence and difference lie. We are thus on the way to treating each other naturally and normally.'

Domestic political controversy over the Moscow and Warsaw treaties, and later over the Basic Treaty with the GDR, grew fiercer than I had expected. I sometimes wondered if it would have been possible to discuss these matters more fully with the Opposition. Gerhard Schröder, who had visited Moscow at the beginning of 1971, took a very moderate line there and informed me in his subsequent report that he and a number of his colleagues would not put any obstacles in the way of ratification. Although we could hardly have kept the Opposition better informed than we did, I doubt if even closer consultations would have made any difference. There were those within the CDU/CSU – numerous then and still more numerous in later years – who had no wish to be taken into our confidence at all, or, if they had, converted the information they were given into vicious public diatribes. The battle over the treaties had become a struggle to overthrow my government.

At the beginning of February 1972, the CDU/CSU-led *Länder* in the Bundesrat delivered an unfavourable verdict on the treaties by one vote. The treaty provisions received their first reading in the Bundestag between 23 and 25 February. In an allusion to Oreanda, I commented during the ratification debate that I had lately been accused of bargaining with General Secretary Brezhnev for the restoration of German unity in return for German neutralization. This was a brazen and ridiculous canard, and those who spread it with no attempt to check its accuracy should realize that they were participating in a propaganda campaign. A fundamental source of tension would, it was true, have been removed by the existence of a Germany that was undivided, democratically governed in compliance with the Basic Law, and unattached to either military bloc.

But we have long accepted the situation that arose from the course of post-war developments and was laid down in our treaties with the West and the GDR's treaties with the East. It follows from the course of post-war developments that there can be progress towards German unity only to the extent that general East-West relations fundamentally improve . . . Even today, I reject it as intolerable to approve the division of Germany after the event. That would be an affront to our dignity, our history and our interests. Nobody can expect it of us. But the acceptance of a given state of affairs in the desire to improve it is something crucially different from inaction accompanied by imploring statements . . . We all know the difficulties of the road to détente and the depth of the world's conflicts. We also know that the wind may veer again and that fresh conflicts may arise. I am against embellishment, against effacing and adulterating divergent beliefs and attitudes. Euphoria cannot be too strongly warned against, today no less than one and two years ago. But it is truly absurd to suppose that the leaders of the Western Alliance, with the President of the United States in the van, would pursue and support a policy which deliberately caused a weakening of the Western Alliance. The West naturally allows for the Soviet Union's desire to consolidate its power base. If the West as a whole and our relations with it were weakened, our Allies would notice this and say so, because they are not stupid; they are certainly not all more stupid than the Opposition in the German Bundestag . . . Today, we can still be among the pace-makers of a new policy; tomorrow, we should at best be numbered among the stragglers.

Our chances could not be improved by craftily adopting the view that German *Ostpolitik* should be preceded by a *Fernostpolitik* [Far East policy]:

So far from calling this realistic, anyone who knows his atlas will necessarily fear that it may lead us astray. The Federal Republic of Germany is a European country. Our fate is being decided here in Europe, in company with that of our allies, in relation to the countries of Eastern Europe and the Soviet Union. I would advise against illusory attempts to gamble on miracles of any kind. We must solve our problems here, unaided by any secret weapons. China is not one such.

Immediately after the ratification debate, our small government majority began to waver. It was against this all too turbulent background – the Opposition having failed to secure a vote of no confidence – that preparations were made for the ratification debate on 10 May. The vote had to be postponed for a week until 17 May. In the interim, representatives of all three parliamentary groups strove to hammer out a joint resolution designed to safeguard German 'legal positions' and make it possible for the Opposition – or large sections of it – to vote in favour. These efforts strained my capacity for acceptance to the limit and brought some grotesque consequences in their train. The Soviet Ambassador, who was called in as a kind of expert adviser on what might have the desired effect in Moscow, found himself inadvertently involved in inter-party negotiations at a Venusberg meeting. He confirmed in response to a question from Rainer Barzel that the obligations and rights of both parties were only derivable from the text of the treaty itself. I drew attention to this in the Bundestag when the resolution was being legally evaluated. It was at least of some benefit that Gromyko distributed the Letter on German Unity to members of his foreign policy committee and referred to the document in his speech. Having been reported in *Pravda* and on Soviet television, it could not be left unmentioned in the GDR.

Although the joint resolution materialized, it proved abortive.

Opposition leader Rainer Barzel pleaded for qualified approval but could not prevail over the CSU and the right wing of his own party. Strauss advocated outright rejection. Thanks to an eventual compromise between CDU and CSU, the Opposition abstained. The Moscow treaty was adopted by 248 votes to nil, with 238 abstentions; the Warsaw treaty – contrary to expectations that it would receive greater support – by 248 to 17, with 230 abstentions.

Because it was then considered diplomatically proper and had been agreed with the Russians, I had invited Kosygin to pay a return visit when the treaty was signed in Moscow. At Oreanda, I extended this invitation to Brezhnev and Podgorny, but it was Brezhnev himself who wanted to come. Although careful preparations were made for his visit in May 1973, the rather hectic and edgy atmosphere conveyed that our Russian guests felt they were entering hazardous waters.

(Shortly before, during the second week of May, the Bundestag had approved our Basic Treaty with the GDR, for which several Opposition members voted. Accession to the UN was approved by a large majority, roughly half the Opposition being in favour of the bill.)

Security measures were extremely tight – much to my displeasure, because I was not eager for Brezhnev to feel hemmed in by police from morn till night and wherever he went. Unfortunately, the world is full of madmen. Terrorists of extreme right- and left-wing persuasion might well have tried to vent their hatred on the Soviet Union's leading citizen, and the international reactions and repercussions did not bear thinking of. The nationalists had threatened anti-Soviet demonstrations, so it was provisionally decided to house Brezhnev in the Hotel Petersberg. There was no great technical difficulty in sealing off this old and spacious but not very stylish establishment overlooking the Rhine, where Chamberlain had once stayed as Hitler's guest. The building had long been closed to the public, so it had to be reopened and done up specially for the occasion. The view from the Petersberg is the finest Bonn has to offer, and Brezhnev enjoyed it. (I suppose it is in keeping with the inverted snobbery of a *nouveau riche* country not to maintain a guest-house where large foreign delegations can be suitably accommodated!)

Considerations of security precluded Brezhnev from visiting a Soviet cultural exhibition in Dortmund, where Maoists had given prior warning of demonstrations. The Russians also voiced extreme misgivings about a helicopter trip along the Rhine Valley to the Bergisches Land, where Premier Kühn was to give our visitors lunch. The flight took place none the less, and it probably afforded Brezhnev his most important single glimpse of the German countryside. He saw Bonn, Cologne and Leverkusen, at least from the air, and was struck by their neat and tidy appearance. What also impressed and surprised him was the integration of industrial and rural areas, which seemed to coalesce.

We had some intensive discussions despite Brezhnev's occasional symptoms of strain and nervousness. I had met him at the airport, where I felt it unnatural that the leader of the Soviet Union should inspect a guard of honour mounted by a free German state. Although nearly three decades had elapsed since the end of World War II, I knew how fresh that dire period still remained in his memory.

From the airport we drove to the Petersberg for an informal meal and a preliminary two-hour talk which consisted largely of a monologue by Brezhnev. He came straight to the point. Time was the best aid to an accurate assessment of what we had achieved and what was in progress. He thought that our two nations and we ourselves had yet to acquire a full grasp of the importance and magnitude of our joint policy. In Moscow and Oreanda he had spoken to me of the Soviet people's great trauma. Perhaps he had begun by adopting too harsh a tone, but he had expressed himself more mildly later on. We had taken decisions for the sake of our cause, and we must take more decisions so as to breathe life into our treaty.

He and his colleagues set great store by what we had initiated with our new *Ostpolitik*. The Soviet Government had tried to be helpful, but he did not know how successful it had been. An important re-thinking process was now under way. We had previously discussed our mutual relations. Although these had been of the utmost importance, their scope was relatively limited. Since then, there had been a plenary session of the Central Committee. Party policy and his personal role had met with unanimous and conspicuous approval. In addressing the Plenum, he had devoted due attention to relations with the Federal Republic. His report had been transmitted to all republics and regions, where it had been read, discussed and understood. Consequently, he possessed a favourable mandate.

What now mattered was to endow our common task with fresh substance. The Federal Republic had its own ties and arrangements. If these militated against good relations with the Soviet Union, they might result in some measure of deterioration and distrust. It was not, of course, his intention that the Federal Republic should become a military ally of the Soviet Union, but the Soviet Government wanted us an ally against a recurrence of the past and a good partner in matters transcending bilateral relations. And that brought him to the subject of an all-European conference. Although it was a problem which might at first sight seem difficult, history had shown that even the most complicated problems could be solved by dint of patience. He had been through the World War, and found the memory of it particularly distressing. He could muster enough courage for any feat of heroism, but memories of the past forbade him to speak calmly. That was why we must both perform a 'heroic deed' so that the new relations between our countries filled their inhabitants with conviction and restored their sense of trust. At the same time, the Soviet Government never lost sight of the Federal Republic's importance in Europe. Soviet policy was honest. The resolutions of the 24th Congress of the CPSU were founded on the principles of peaceful coexistence. He had not invented these. They derived from Lenin, and the latter had taken his stand on Marx and Engels.

We now had a practical task. His visit to the Federal Republic accorded with the wishes of the Party, the Central Committee, the government 'and the whole Soviet people'. We must give a clear indication of our resolve to continue what had been started in 1970. We must transmit impulses. Coming after the Moscow treaty, our treaty with Poland had been noted with satisfaction. He now believed the time was ripe to 'get rid of the damned Munich Agreement'. Husak had twice confirmed to him that he was ready to approach us himself. After that, the way would be clear to relations with the other socialist countries. This was a new political situation for Europe. Both German states would soon be members of the United Nations. Concurrently with the new political situation, a new era of economic co-operation was unfolding.

There had been an appreciable increase in the trade between our two countries. (In fact, our trade with the East had grown threefold between 1970 and 1975.) He supposed that prejudices, doubts and misgivings still existed on our side, even now. Soviet ministries and institutions, too, had not always measured up to their tasks, and he had sharply criticized this at the last Plenum of the Central Committee. He and his colleagues favoured bold and sincere co-operation on a grand scale, with targets set for decades ahead. For example, we could jointly develop ultra-modern methods of processing wood, copper, natural gas, petroleum and aluminium. The Soviet Government was in favour of co-operation beneficial to both sides. Industrialists in the Federal Republic had begun to think in these terms, but for the moment only tentatively. As a metallurgical engineer, he had urged that the steelworks at Kursk should be built on direct reduction lines.

No country in the world had as much natural gas and coal as the

Soviet Union. Something could surely be done on the basis of these raw materials and then offset. To be honest, the Soviet Union needed co-operation on equipment. It was like building a house: first you paid out, then you lived in your own home. He was in favour of 30-, 40- or 50-year agreements. No country in the world had such an abundance of wood as the Soviet Union. Couldn't we give joint consideration to a large-scale cellulose project? None of this implied that he was thinking of competing with the USA or the EEC. All industrial nations, not to mention the countries of the Third World, needed energy. Shouldn't it be possible to evolve some form of co-operation in the field of equipment for nuclear power stations and then approach third markets? There was a worldwide demand for chemical fertilizers, too. Our systems differed, of course, but allowance could be made for that. Orders could be issued in the Soviet Union. It was different with us, but our businessmen would also start thinking along different lines if a stimulus were imparted by their leaders. His ideas probably went a little further than we could embody in the texts to be agreed during the next few days. Nevertheless, he wanted to stress that his Party and nation were prepared for an even bolder perspective. We had for too long thought in terms such as 'I'll sell you a jacket for ten ties'. A different approach must be adopted today, even if the results were not apparent for five years. In economic matters, the Soviet Union opposed a bloc policy and favoured co-operation with every country on a basis of equal rights. He might not have a very precise knowledge of our administrative machinery, but it would only complicate matters if the Soviet Union had to approach Brussels in order to buy something from Krupp. For all that, the Soviet Union did not shut its eyes to the fact that the EEC existed. He had already mentioned it in his speeches, and we would explore the subject more fully during his visit.

I confirmed that we had taken note of Brezhnev's pronouncements in the past two years. Relations between the Soviet Union and Great Britain not being especially good, I wanted him to know that Heath, in particular, had often emphasized during our talks that Brezhnev's statements merited a favourable response from the Community.

Brezhnev said it was known that the Soviet side had begun by stating its basic attitude, which still stood today. It was against groupings of all kinds. Never mind about principles, Moscow had told itself; the EEC exists and that is that. He had stated that he acknowledged the existence of the Common Market as a reality. However, the Soviet Government was still unclear as to how the EEC would affect the external relations of individual member-states. I replied that questions of historical development were also concerned here, and that a great deal depended on what could be jointly arranged in Europe between East and West. Brezhnev agreed. It might be a good thing to explore opportunities for some kind of economic co-operation between the EEC and CMEA [Comecon].

Political relations still dominated the foreground. The Soviet Union was not looking for new allies, military allies least of all. No fresh mistrust should be aroused. We needed a common language; we needed harmony in bilateral relations and international policy so as to make progress in peaceful co-operation. That was why the convening of the CSCE was so important. Nixon and Kissinger had assured him of their concurrence. It was essential to issue a declaration designed to set people's minds at rest and reassure their political leaders. We could then devote ourselves to peaceful topics without being afraid that something would happen in the next few days. There had never been such a thing in the whole of history, hence the significance of the position adopted by Federal Germany and the Soviet Union.

Brezhnev then reverted to the link between a security conference and force reductions. He recalled that I had spoken at Oreanda of reducing national as well as foreign troops. The Soviet Union said yes to force reductions in Europe – whether by three, five, ten or fifteen per cent was a matter for the military to explore.

Our further talks confirmed my impression that Brezhnev rejected any link between CSCE and MBFR, which at that time conflicted with one of NATO's established lines of approach. In the case of Vienna (MBFR) he advocated 'open-ended negotiations' in the belief that something sensible could be achieved by undertaking a number of minor reductions over the years. He would be discussing the further limitation of strategic weapons with Nixon in the coming month. This brought him to relations with France and – beyond what had already been said – with the United States.

On France, Brezhnev said that relations were quite normal and good foundations existed. The only point at issue was France's refusal to take part in exploratory talks on force reductions. He had told Pompidou on the subject of confidence-building measures that the Soviet Union had no objection to announcing major troop movements or admitting foreign observers to manoeuvres. It did not hold manoeuvres in order to camouflage preparations for war.

Where the USA was concerned, his recent talks with Kissinger had been generally productive. Mainly devoted to ways of evolving measures calculated to reduce the risk of nuclear war, they had also dealt with the exceptionally acute problems of the Middle East, where some very specific factors had to be taken into account. 'Israel is being obstinate. There is also the problem of Zionism, the Arab temperament and the fact that this is a difficult part of the world.' Economically, the past year had yielded an accord on most-favoured-nation treatment. Nixon had certain difficulties to contend with (many people were currently making a lot of fuss about the Jackson amendment), but the US President had assured him that consent would be given.

I replied only briefly to these remarks, which occupied nearly two hours. From my point of view, there was no objection to the statement that more and more life should be breathed into the Moscow treaty. Far from forgetting the past, I said, we must accept its lessons for the future. There would be no reluctance to do so on our side. We also agreed that the treaty had exerted a favourable influence on our relations with third countries and their relations with each other, sometimes beyond the confines of Europe. Considerable scope existed for economic co-operation, which should be viewed on a long-term basis, but we must not overlook the obstacles in our path. Under present circumstances, we were not interested in greatly expanding our export trade (so my advisers assured me). I did, on the other hand, stress our keen interest in oil, gas and electricity link-ups, as well as in other raw materials. The Iran triangle project – natural gas from Iran to the Soviet Union and from there to us – was also discussed (and in 1975 embodied in an agreement). Brezhnev mentioned the Americans' interest in exports of liquefied natural gas via Murmansk. Premier Tanaka had also expressed interest on behalf of Japan.

On Monday afternoon we signed a joint declaration in the Petersberg and had another private discussion, after which came the Soviet dinner. Brezhnev had asked me if I was opposed to his inviting Strauss, who had expressed a desire to be present. I offered no objection. He had also remarked that he would like to see a delegation from the DKP. I replied that this was up to him. While driving into the city, Brezhnev noticed that among the benevolently waving citizens lining the Autobahn feed-road was a DKP group armed with flags and placards. Rather surprised and amused, he remarked that we certainly had a 'system' of our own.

In previous conversations, the General Secretary had often recalled an episode from the first day of the war. As secretary of the Dnepropetrovsk regional committee, he had then been responsible for halting consignments of wheat and other goods bound for Germany. Consignments of wheat . . . Surely that testified to Soviet goodwill! He only mentioned this to show what friendly sentiments the Soviet people had entertained and how unsuspecting their leaders had been. The Soviet press had been full of pictures exemplifying German-Soviet co-operation, and everyone had thought that all was in order; in reality, it had all been a sham. Brezhnev recounted this and other things without mentioning Hitler or the 1939 pact. He referred to good co-operation with German firms during the pre- and inter-war years. Many of his colleagues had been trained by concerns like Krupp and Mannesmann. German experts had visited the Soviet Union and been cordially received. German troops had been stationed in his home town during World War I, yet relations had been good for a period between the wars. For example, German engineers worked at the factory where he and his father, brothers and other relatives had been employed. The German experts had been welcome both socially and at work – in fact, relations between the Soviet Union and Germany had been good. In his after-dinner speech at the banquet I gave for him at the Palais Schaumburg, Brezhnev said: 'It seems logical that the restoration of relations between our countries should have been undertaken by representatives of the generation which experienced the horrors of the war that is past.'

Helmut Schmidt picked up the same thread at dinner on the Venusberg. He recalled his mixed emotions as a young German officer on the Eastern front: resolute by day, filled with dire forebodings by night. He would never have thought it possible that such a terrible war could be followed by a dialogue between Germans and the leader of the Soviet Union. Brezhnev was deeply moved by the reminiscences of the then Finance and former Defence Minister. He responded with some highly emotional toasts. Our Russian hosts also became moist-eyed when, during my speech at their return dinner, I quoted from a letter written to his parents by a German soldier who did not survive our invasion of the Soviet Union: 'I know that our armies will once more leave this country in a wretched procession. Nothing will remain but sorrow and destruction – hatred too, perhaps. Yet there is nothing I desire more fervently than one day to greet these people in peace and friendship.'

Brezhnev also spoke of my impending visit to the Soviet Union. Apart from this, he thought that more frequent personal exchanges might be of value. Older people were already set in their beliefs. We must think of the generations to come. Federal President Heinemann, on whom the General Secretary paid a courtesy call, earnestly stressed (by prior arrangement with me) the importance of humanitarian measures such as the reuniting of families. Brezhnev assured the President that he would do his best to ensure favourable consideration of this matter, but said that the settlement of such questions could only be impeded by a public scrutiny of statistics. (For some time, repatriations totalled roughly 500 a month. The figures declined during the early months of 1975, and I revived the subject during my visit to Moscow in July of that year.)

The Berlin theme was delegated to Gromyko and Bahr. Talking to me after dinner the first night, Gromyko had professed a belief that the West Germans and West Berliners wanted to manœuvre and place their own interpretation on the Quadripartite Agreement. I said he was wrong. We had no intention of pursuing old policies with new treaties. After long and laborious discussions – and a hint from me that no communiqué would be issued without a reference to Berlin – the Foreign Minister and the Minister without Portfolio eventually devised the formula 'strict observance and full application'. Our joint statement ran: 'Willy Brandt and L. I. Brezhnev are agreed that strict observance and full application of this agreement are an essential pre-requisite of lasting détente in Central Europe and of the improvement of relations between the states concerned, especially between the Federal Republic of Germany and the Soviet Union.'

I added in conversation with Brezhnev that the Berlin passage in our joint declaration must be borne out in practice. The successful development of our relations depended to a large extent on whether both parties refrained from a biased and restrictive interpretation of the Berlin Agreement. I had the impression, later confirmed, that Brezhnev wanted to get this bone of contention out of the way. Unfortunately, he failed. The ensuing series of squabbles related to Berlin but poisoned the general atmosphere between the two countries.

While strolling in the grounds of the Hotel Petersberg during our private discussion on Monday evening, Brezhnev jocularly and obliquely inquired whether I was planning a visit to Mao. I replied that my immediate schedule did not include any such trip, and pointed out that Foreign Minister Scheel had visited Peking the previous autumn. We both considered it beneficial that diplomatic relations had been established between us and the People's Republic of China. In fact, no trip to China was scheduled at this stage, nor had any invitation been received. This arrived later, and we agreed on a date in autumn 1974.

The Federal Chancellor's projected state visit to the Soviet Union in 1974 was undertaken by my successor. Brezhnev informed me immediately after I resigned that the invitation to me and my wife still stood, regardless of my official capacity.

14

Erfurt, Kassel and Berlin

I had announced in my policy statement of October 1969 that we would engage in negotiations with the Soviet Union and propose talks with the People's Republic of Poland. Both processes were initiated without delay. Following up proposals advanced by the Grand Coalition government, I had made the Council of Ministers of the GDR an offer of non-discriminatory negotiations aimed at achieving treaty-based co-operation. East Berlin responded with a draft model treaty in December 1969 and a proposal for talks in February 1970. Apart from this, we had recommended the Western Powers to pursue their Berlin talks with the Soviet Union as vigorously as possible. These were continued as formal discussions at the end of March.

The motives underlying our *Ostpolitik* were not only clear but understood and approved by our allies. We construed this policy as a patient attempt to improve relations between countries with different or conflicting political systems because therein lay the sole chance of preserving peace. We laboured under no illusions. Experience had taught us that agreements with communist countries neither could nor should gloss over conflicts of principle. We none the less wanted to evolve modes of communication which would enable us to hammer out our differences in a more civilized and objective manner, and without endangering peace. Talking to Harold Wilson early in 1970, I defined the political landscape in which we proposed to essay a preliminary dialogue with East Berlin. We had, I said, inferred from the Warsaw Pact summit conference at the beginning of December 1969 that the governments of the East European countries had agreed not to impose any prior conditions on negotiations with us. Our analysis of Soviet interests suggested that Moscow harboured no illusions about the durability of the Atlantic Alliance. Kosygin had told Bahr that it was accepted that one part of Europe was organized by the Western and the other by the Eastern defensive alliance. It was also possible that relations with China wielded an indirect influence. Apart from this, both the Russians and the Poles were displaying a perceptible interest in better trade relations and closer technological co-operation. Moscow was doubtless averse to our talking to the Poles first. The Russians' more receptive attitude might also be a consequence of the Czech crisis; from their angle, better relations with the Federal Republic might conduce to stabilization in their own camp.

My government policy statement declared that the problems arising from World War II – and, as I deliberately added, from our national betrayal by the Hitler régime – could only find their ultimate solution in a European peace settlement. The Germans had as great a right to self-determination as any other people. The object of our practical political endeavours, under given circumstances, was to preserve national unity by deconstricting the relationship between the two parts of Germany. It was important to peace in Europe and East-West relations to progress from a regular *modus vivendi* to co-operation. Our willingness to reach agreements on the renunciation of the use or threat of force applied to the GDR as well.

Such was the background against which we offered to negotiate with the GDR Government on equal terms. We insisted, however, that the Federal Republic and the GDR could not be regarded as foreign countries and that there was no question of our legally recognizing the latter. The Opposition took particular exception to the opening words of this passage from our policy statement: 'Even if there exist two states in Germany, they cannot be foreign countries to each other; their mutual relations can only be of a special nature.' By saying this – so ran the accusation that was to dog us for years – we had substituted the two-state theory for the claim to sole representation.

I countered these charges by asserting that we had simply been forced to acknowledge the development of a two-state reality. There could be no question of our having come to terms with the partitioning of Germany. What we had done, on the basis of the experience which I myself had gained as Foreign Minister, was to draw a few conclusions which no one had been willing to draw until now. In the first place, we recognized that the division of Germany was a consequence, not a cause, of the division of Europe and that we could not expect our national problem to be solved in isolation. Secondly, we had associated ourselves with a verdict that had been current even before the Grand Coalition, namely, that it was unrealistic to make improved East-West relations dependent on the reunification of Germany. It had proved equally unrealistic to try and normalize our relations with Eastern

Europe without acknowledging the GDR's status and adjusting our relations with it on a basis of non-discrimination and equal rights. Its progress towards full international recognition could not, in any case, have been delayed indefinitely.

Contributing to the debate on our policy statement at the end of October 1969, I said that we had no wish to prevent the inhabitants of the GDR from participating in international trade and cultural exchanges. We did, however, posit a connection between internal German arrangements and the GDR's international relations. The former could not but affect the latter. I stated on another occasion that a renunciation-of-force treaty with the GDR would naturally be binding in terms of international law. We were concerned to preserve national cohesion and keep the door ajar to a European peace settlement without relapsing into narrow-minded nationalism.

National components would have their place even in a European peace settlement, but the road to German self-determination within such a peace settlement would be a long and arduous one. The length and difficulty of this road should not deter us 'from achieving at the present stage in our history, if it be possible, a regular *modus vivendi* between the two states in Germany'. Patriotism called for a recognition of what existed and repeated attempts to discover what was possible. It called for the courage to face facts.

I could tell that the Opposition had not fundamentally set its face against talks with East Berlin, nor against the European orientation of our internal German policy.

What matters here, at bottom, is that a European peace settlement, if it one day comes into being, should leave the door open for the Germans – and the fact that this may take generations rather than years compels one to add the proviso: if they so desire – to coexist and organize their coexistence otherwise than developments have so far enforced upon them . . . What our fathers have lost will not be regained by any amount of fine rhetoric or polished legal argument.

It was reported to me after this speech that students in East Berlin had distributed leaflets stating that it was a 'national duty' to study the Federal Chancellor's proposals.

On 17 December 1969, before I could submit this preliminary report on the state of the nation to the Bundestag, Walter Ulbricht had written to Federal President Heinemann and by this means transmitted the text of a draft treaty. East Berlin knew it to be unacceptable, but the GDR leaders had taken their own kind of initiative and were temporarily off the hook *vis-à-vis* the Soviet Union. On 22 January I wrote to Willi Stoph, Chairman of the Council of Ministers of the GDR, and proposed that we institute negotiations on an exchange of declarations renouncing the use of force. 'These negotiations, to be conducted in accordance with the principle of non-discrimination, should offer scope for a wide-ranging exchange of views on the settlement of all questions outstanding between our two states, among them those connected with mutual relations based on equal rights.' This entailed that each side must be free to submit such considerations, proposals, principles and draft schemes as it thought fit. At the same time, it was my government's wish, 'in the course of negotiations on practical problems, to arrive at settlements capable of making life easier for the inhabitants of a divided Germany'. The Federal Minister for Internal German Affairs would be available for a preliminary discussion at which the sequence and course of negotiations could be arranged.

Stoph replied on 11 February that the principle of equality and non-discrimination, which I had emphasized, 'naturally' entailed 'that the GDR and FRG recognize and respect each other for what they are, namely, sovereign subjects of international law with equal rights'. He regretted that I had not gone into the proposal embodied in Ulbricht's communication to Federal President Heinemann and stressed the importance of East Berlin's draft treaty. The two of us should enter into direct negotiations. What were ultimately involved were 'problems of peace or war, guarantees of security for the creative endeavours of people in the GDR and FRG'. On 13 February I delivered a lecture in Copenhagen. In it I inserted a remark to the effect that Stoph's letter – which had arrived the day before – would be studied with an open mind. However: 'Herr Stoph informed me in his letter of yesterday that we ought to meet during the present month because war and peace were at stake. I cannot agree. We shall have to see one another, not because it is a matter of war or peace, but because it can only be a matter of peace.'

Asked if I would be willing to meet Ulbricht or Stoph shortly after forming my government, I had replied: 'Why not? We don't necessarily have to start with a so-called summit, but I wouldn't dodge one.' Didn't the prestige requirements of the other side prescribe such a meeting? 'They can have one if they want, but they must also know from political experience that such a meeting requires preparation.'

The crucial point was how the East Berlin authorities interpreted their interests and whether, in contrast to 1967-8, they were anxious for something more than trade. I answered Stoph by telex on 18 February. I was willing to meet him in order to get negotiations moving, but it seemed inexpedient to go into details at this stage. 'I cannot accept any preconditions. Incipient normalization of the relations between the two states in Germany will mean a joint contribution to détente and security in Europe. I think it time to discard divisions and seek links. If we succeed, we should also find it possible to reach contractual agreements.'

Stoph had proposed a meeting on 19 or 26 February 'at the Council of Ministers Building in Berlin, the capital of the GDR'. I suggested that officials from each side should meet to discuss practical arrangements and fix the date of our first encounter – not later than the second or third week of March. I would work on the assumption that our second meeting would take place in Bonn. I further informed Stoph that I would be accompanied by the Federal Minister for Internal German Affairs, Egon Franke, among other advisers. Stoph had mentioned that his Foreign Minister, Otto Winzer, would be taking part. The significance of this contrast in choices was obvious.

On 20 February we nominated the officials who would be handling the technical preparations – on my side Dr Ulrich Sahm, who had joined me from the Foreign Office to take over the foreign policy section of the Federal Chancellery and later became our ambassador in Moscow. Agreement on the first meeting with Stoph proved to be harder than we could have foreseen. The GDR did not wish me to travel by train and stop in West Berlin, coming or going. It was suggested that I should come by air and land in Schönefeld, not West Berlin.

On 8 March I wrote to Stoph that the preliminary talks had disclosed potential threats to the exchange of views desired by both sides. 'I therefore suggest that our delegations be instructed jointly to examine the possibility of finding a new basis for the programme and procedure of our first meeting – and, if necessary, a different venue.' On 12 March we were able to announce that the meeting would take place at Erfurt on 19 March 1970. All the signs were that Moscow had helped things along.

Speaking on television before I left by special train, I said that I was going to Erfurt with good intentions but no illusions. 'As I see it, there is no purpose in politics unless they benefit people and peace . . . I shall do my best to establish preliminary contacts, to be followed by others . . . We must never lay ourselves open to the charge of having failed to try every means of improving the situation in Germany.' I pointed out in an interview that the fact that Stoph and I were now meeting was an almost extreme expression of the special nature of our relations, not to say non-relations. At the very least, it was my aim 'to preserve intact the willingness for a second meeting which has been reaffirmed during the preparatory talks'. I could take it that the establishment of these relations was agreeable to Moscow.

It was after midnight when I halted the special train at a siding short of the frontier. Many people gathered to wish us *bon voyage* when we resumed our journey early in the morning. One group of youngsters loudly demanded recognition for the GDR. Waving figures lined the track and station platforms or appeared at windows as we glided by. On this day, many Federal German citizens seemed possessed by a lively sense of solidarity which tended to be latent at other times. At the frontier I was greeted with all due ceremony by a GDR official. My eyes roved pensively over the late winter landscape. Members of the People's Police had cordoned off the villages and townships along the track, but I received waves of welcome from lone figures and large groups including an entire factory work force. There were raised arms, outstretched hands and open windows all along the route. Some people looked subdued, others were enthusiastic and waved tablecloths or sheets. I was deeply moved to read the names of towns which had played so important a part in the history of the German labour movement and, more especially, in that of social democracy.

'In recent days,' I said in a subsequent television address, 'it has been inquired of our common history what Erfurt – where Luther presented his doctoral dissertation – has already meant to the Germans. It was here, on 2 October 1808, that Napoleon said to Goethe: "Politics is destiny!" It was also here in Erfurt, on 20 March 1850, that a final attempt was made – after the Revolution of 1848 – to unite Germany in a peaceful and democratic manner.' Apart from this, it was logical for a Social Democrat to ponder on the role which the Erfurt Programme of 1891 had played in the rise of the German labour movement. Whatever place one assigned that programme in the history of ideas, how much misfortune the German people, Europe and the entire world would have been spared if the desire for democracy and peace had prevailed in time!

The train pulled into Erfurt at 9.30 a.m. Premier Stoph's welcome was polite but a trifle constrained. I heard chants of 'Willy!' They could have been directed at either of us. Then came confirmation: my full name. It was only later that I heard what happened in the station forecourt during my arrival. Apparently, thousands of people risked life and limb by bursting through the flimsy barriers. We covered the fifty yards between the station and the Erfurter Hof Hotel before order temporarily broke down altogether. After a few minutes Conrad Ahlers came to my room, where I was freshening up, to tell me that the crowd was chanting 'Willy Brandt to the window!' with growing insistence.

I hesitated, then went to the window and looked down at the excited and expectant people who had claimed the right to hold this spontaneous demonstration. For a moment, they had felt sufficiently free to show their feelings. It was certainly no perfervid national or nationalistic emotion that flowed to meet me. I reminded myself that this was not the first time I had visited a Germany deprived of freedom. Then, I could not help feeling an enemy in my native land. Here it was different. I was moved, but I had to consider the fate of these people: I would be back in Bonn next day, they would not . . . I made a gesture urging restraint, and my point was taken. The crowd fell silent. Turning away with a heavy heart, I noticed that many of my aides had tears in their eyes. I was afraid of kindling hopes that could not be fulfilled, so I adopted a suitably low-key manner. (The authorities later sent in People's Police reinforcements and squads of loyal factory workers who chanted Stoph's name and demanded 'recognition'.)

At 10 a.m. the delegations repaired to the conference chamber, where the customary refreshments were awaiting. My own party comprised Federal Minister Franke, Parliamentary State Secretary (and FDP member of the Bundestag) Wolfram Dorn, Conrad Ahlers, Dr Ulrich Sahm of the Chancellery and Jürgen Weichert from the Ministry of Internal German Affairs. Stoph was accompanied by Foreign Minister Winzer, State Secretary to the Council of Ministers Dr Michael Kohl (later plenipotentiary in Bonn), Günther Kordt (State Secretary at the Foreign Ministry), and Drs Gerhard Schüssler and Hans Voll of the civil service.

In his preliminary statement, which lasted almost an hour, Stoph described our meeting as 'an event of political significance'. One could hardly dispute his contention that our two governments bore 'a major responsibility for ensuring that war never again originated on German soil'. The rest of what he said was unproductive. He wasted time on needless tirades, expounded the alleged infallibility of communist ideas and focused all his arguments on recognition as understood by the GDR authorities. It may help to convey some impression of the conflict between our views if I compare what we said about a few essential issues.

I began by recalling in my own statement that twenty-five years had elapsed since National Socialist tyranny had ended in the collapse of the German Reich.

Whatever else may divide us, that event forms a bond between all who sit round this table. The world was filled with horror at the outrages committed in the name of Germany and at the destruction that was wrought. We are all liable for what happened, wherever fate may have placed us. This liability, for which we were rightly held responsible by the world, is one of the sources of the present situation in Germany. But historical argument will get us nowhere now. Many may think it tragic that the path of the German nation divided, and that it could not be trodden in political unity after 1945, but we cannot undo this. That is why I began by saying that the situation prescribes a quest for areas in which it is possible to achieve progress on behalf of peace and people in Germany . . . The fact that we are facing each other across this table does not make demands on the intellect alone – there is an emotional resonance as well. Both sides are aware, too, that our meeting is an object of great attention far beyond the borders of Germany.

Stoph: 'Everyone knows that we have not met here to settle questions of second- or third-rate importance. What is at stake is the overriding question of how to bring about a change in the relations between the GDR and FRG in the interests of European security and of a peaceful life for the people of our countries.'

Brandt: 'Efforts to promote peaceful relations in the world will be credible and convincing only if we create peace between ourselves and on behalf of our citizens. Formal documents are not in themselves sufficient to normalize relations. People on both sides must get something out of normalization . . . We must make a start sometime if we are serious about normalization and if treaties are not to remain an empty shell.'

Stoph: 'Anyone who has grasped that legal recognition of the GDR cannot be evaded should have the political wisdom to say so immediately and in due form.'

Brandt: 'I am presupposing that our relations will have to be established on a basis of non-discrimination and equal rights. Both the states in Germany must make it their aim to achieve a specially close relationship, even though it would initially be a step forward to establish relations of any kind. In my view, neither the concept of legal recognition nor the concept of non-interference in internal affairs has any bearing on the establishment of relations between the Federal Republic and the GDR based on equal rights.'

Stoph: 'We cannot help being concerned and filled with grave misgivings by the fact that representatives of the Federal Republic make public references to détente and a regular *modus vivendi* while simultaneously continuing to develop and perfect dangerous military plans directed against the GDR and other socialist countries.'

Brandt: 'Détente instead of tension, the securing of peace instead of military confrontation – those are the aims of my government, and I know that I am supported in them by responsible circles in the Federal Republic of Germany. We are not pursuing an aggressive defence policy. We are a loyal member of the alliance to which we belong, just as you are.'

Stoph: 'Germany was not split by us – the Federal Republic and the Western Powers bear sole responsibility for that. It is therefore baseless to speak of or try to preserve the unity of a nation which was selfishly abandoned by the ruling circles of the Federal Republic and has not existed for two decades.'

Brandt: 'For all the constructive achievements on both sides, German policy after 1945 was largely a function of the policy pursued by the powers who had defeated Germany and occupied it. Since then, the East-West power confrontation has dominated the German situation and kept Europe divided. We cannot simply unmake this division, but we can do our best to mitigate its consequences and actively contribute to a process aimed at filling in the trenches that separate us in Germany.'

Stoph: 'If the policy of the present Federal Government is also based – as you yourself have stated – on the Paris treaties, the formula of internal German relations can only be designed to extend the Federal Republic's imperialist system of authority to the GDR and incorporate the GDR in the NATO pact . . . The formula of special internal German relations embodies the old claim to tutelary rights over the GDR . . . Apart from this, the relations between any two states are inevitably of a special nature as compared with their relations with other states. For example, the Federal Republic's relations with the Republic of Austria or Switzerland possess special characteristics and are thereby differentiated from the Federal Republic's relations with, say, the French Republic.'

Brandt: 'Instead of "internal German" we could equally talk of "inter-German" relations – relations between the two states in Germany . . . We claim no rights of tutelage, nor do we assign the GDR a status inferior to that which we claim for ourselves. In speaking of a special inter-state relationship, we are taking account of the special conditions prevailing in Germany, which the GDR also presupposes after its own fashion.'

Stoph: 'The FRG's widespread thesis that Four-Power responsibility extends to the GDR and its capital, Berlin, is untenable.'

Brandt: 'In view of the victorious powers' agreements on Germany dating from the post-1944 years, agreements between our two states can neither affect nor replace the existing rights of the Four Powers ... If I draw attention to the Four-Power agreements and our own arrangements with the Three Powers, it is largely because of Berlin. I must ask you to take this statement very seriously ... One cannot expect a recognition of realities on one side and a unilateral alteration of the given situation on the other.'

Stoph: 'The citizens of the GDR have been "relieved" of over one hundred thousand million marks [by way of the open frontier up to 13 August 1961]. We expect the FRG to settle all its debts to the GDR and meet its indemnification liabilities.'

Brandt: 'We do not in any way dispute that the GDR has had to bear heavy burdens resulting from the war. I must, on the other hand, point out that the Federal Republic assumed sole responsibility for making good losses inflicted on Jewish fellow-citizens by the German Reich. The extent of the post-war charges on both parts of Germany could be ascertained by joint study. I am assuming, of course, that the GDR does not hold the Federal Republic responsible for the consequences of a social policy which ultimately conduced to the emigration of numerous inhabitants of the GDR.'

Stoph: 'The safeguarding of our national frontier in 1961 [the Wall] was a humanitarian act.'

Brandt: 'My government regards efforts at normalization and détente in Central Europe as inseparably linked with détente and with normalizing the situation in and concerning Berlin ... As I see it, genuine normalization must help to overcome internal German frontier entanglements and walls.'

Stoph: 'The two sovereign states, GDR and FRG, cannot be amalgamated because opposing social systems are incapable of amalgamation ... As socialists, we are naturally interested – who would deny it? – in the victory of socialism in all countries including the Federal Republic, which would make possible a future amalgamation founded on democracy and socialism.'

Brandt: 'I know that I am free from the nationalistic ideas of bygone days. But I am fairly certain that national components will not forfeit their importance, even in the process of European and international fusion ... A policy which attempted to gainsay or disregard this fundament of national existence would be doomed to failure. One must proceed upon the basis of this reality just as much as on the fact that Germany contains within its actual 1970 frontiers two states which have to live side by side. We therefore possess common features that are not shared by other states. Even the arguments we conduct differ in character from those between foreign peoples. They relate to the unity of our nation.'

Stoph: 'There can be no talk of normal relations as long as your government, too, persists in discriminating against and damaging the GDR at international level . . . Kindly take note that the GDR and its allies will not fail to respond to attempts by the government of the FRG to prevent the GDR from developing its international relations and to exert continuing pressure on third countries.'

Brandt: 'For my part, I already made it clear in my policy statement of 28 October 1969 that the Federal Government intended to co-operate more fully in the UN and other international organizations. I also said that, like that of our friends, our own attitude to the GDR's international relations was largely dependent on the attitude of the government of the GDR itself.'

Stoph: 'To renounce the use of force without this elementary pre-requisite [mutual recognition under international law] would be futile – it would be an empty shell. I must stress that I do not mean mere informal acknowledgement; I mean unqualified legal recognition of national borders and territorial integrity.'

Brandt: 'The Federal Government regards peace as the greatest good. We are certainly agreed that no new war must originate on German soil. The two German states have neither the right nor the ability to employ force or the threat of force in pursuing the objectives set them by their constitutions. A peaceful and united Germany can never be established by war or civil war.'

Stoph: 'The GDR's draft treaty provides that both states should dispense with nuclear weapons of any kind, refrain from manufacturing, stationing or storing chemical and biological weapons on their territory, and undertake to promote disarmament negotiations.'

Brandt: 'We Germans should set an example in our efforts to promote disarmament and arms limitation. By signing the nuclear non-pro-liferation treaty, the Federal Government reaffirmed its desire to contribute to the maintenance of world peace. As for B- and C-weapons, the Federal Republic undertook to refrain from their manufacture as long ago as 1954.'

I also touched on some practical matters which did not fit into Stoph's prearranged scheme of things. His response to my com-paratively detailed remarks on West Berlin was that this topic had considerably hampered preparations for our meeting and could not be discussed now. He stated that West Berlin did not belong to the Federation and was an independent political entity in the middle of the GDR. This was not the view of the GDR alone; it was shared by the Soviet Union and the socialist camp and had been confirmed in principle by the three Western Powers. The GDR had proposed in its draft treaty that relations with West Berlin should be regulated on the basis of this status. Reverting to the dictum that no new war should originate on German soil, Stoph returned again and again to the subject of legal recognition and maintained that both sides should apply to join the United Nations. Didn't the Federal Government's policy merely betray a change in tactics? Would I care to outline our long-term political objectives?

Prepared for this question, I stated that our aims were to dispel confrontation in Europe, conclude a lasting peace, achieve détente between East and West, and consolidate relations between the two parts of Germany. Problems arising from World War II could only be conclusively resolved within a European peace settlement. It was one of the peculiarities of the relationship between the two German states that both constitutions (including that of the GDR, from which all reference to German unity was not eliminated until 1975) were tailored to the unity of the nation and assumed that partition would not be a permanent state of affairs. Both states maintained treaties with one or more signatories of the Quadripartite Agreement, which contained special clauses relating to Germany as a whole. I had little need to make special mention of family ties or our common heritage. Like the Federal Government, the government of the GDR did not – to judge by public speeches and pronouncements – regard its fellow in such a way as to warrant treating it like a foreign country. We did not presume to claim sole representation, but we did consider it our legitimate task to watch over the interests of the entire German nation just as the GDR claimed the right to be mindful of its future.

The essential thing, I went on, was to essay an agreement on practical issues and progress from there to the assumption that a number of individual matters ought to be specially resolved to our common advantage. Our concern was to regularize relations, improve communication and reduce discriminatory measures. We wanted to achieve a genuine change, not a merely formal one. My proposal to appoint representatives and provide them with permanent working facilities in both seats of government met with no response.

My introductory declaration of principle was reproduced verbatim in *Neues Deutschland*, the SED's central mouthpiece, alongside Stoph's own statement. I was later told that this was one of the few editions of the paper to be sold out within hours. For the first time in many years, the citizens of the GDR had an opportunity to read in their own press how German affairs were viewed and dealt with by a Chancellor of the Federal Republic.

Stoph and I had two private discussions in Erfurt – private in the strict sense, since we needed no interpreter. 'We both speak German,' as Stoph said. He showed an interest in commercial matters and betrayed some readiness to co-operate in the field of postal services and telecommunications.

He had, incidentally, read what I had said about him in a newspaper interview the day before, and inferred from it that I thought him 'obdurate'. (I had actually called him a politician with 'very firmly moulded, rigid views' and predicted that he would be a tough negotiator). He tried – not over-successfully – to correct this impression with a few disarming gestures and phrases.

Our second talk took place late that evening. Stoph surprised me by asking whether we could not agree on an immediate joint application for membership of the United Nations and embody the announcement in a communiqué. This was impossible, as Stoph must have been well aware, so the communiqué remained a meagre document. It simply recorded the participation of both sides and the acceptance of my invitation to a second round of talks on 21 May. The venue was to be Kassel, which the GDR authorities found more acceptable than Bonn (given that we ourselves had not gone to East Berlin). Having satisfied myself by telephone that the relevant departments were agreeable to this, I offered no objection.

On the afternoon of 19 March Otto Winzer accompanied me to Buchenwald, where I laid a wreath at the memorial. Many people lined the route, especially when we drove through the outskirts of Weimar. Winzer, an elderly man, was quite an agreeable companion. Rooted in the traditions of the Berlin labour movement, he was self-assured but unbombastic and ever so faintly resigned in manner (though transparently proud that he had come straight to Erfurt from Algiers, where he had arranged to establish diplomatic relations).

A number of party and factory delegations had been transported to Buchenwald by bus, evidently to offset the impression created by my spontaneous welcome at Erfurt. Our conducted tour of the erstwhile horror camp placed rather too exclusive an emphasis on the communist victims of the Nazi régime. Like so many others, Ernst Thälmann had been murdered there, but I did not forget the Social Democrat, Liberal, Christian and Jewish prisoners and their sufferings. Rudolf Breitscheid was among those who met a frightful end in Buchenwald. Despite current controversies, I felt that we should not only preserve our respect for the victims but proclaim our resolve to do everything possible to avoid a repetition of the horrors of the past.

I did not regret having suggested the visit to Buchenwald, nor was I unduly annoyed that my refusal of 'military honours', which had been agreed at the preparatory talks, was flouted to the extent that a contingent of the People's Army carried the wreaths and a military band played both national anthems. It touched me all the more that so many thousands of Erfurt citizens again turned out, unasked, to line the streets on my return journey. I was only sorry that we did not have time to visit Weimar itself. I should have liked to see more than the outskirts of the city which had lent its name to the first experimental founding of a free German republic. Seldom had the historical continuity under whose banner we serve been as vividly apparent to me as it was in that German heartland.

Taking leave of Stoph was a bleak performance made faintly agonizing by the minutes he spent politely waiting on the platform until the train pulled out. There was little more to say – for the moment – and I did not feel that I had drawn any closer to the man in human terms. Exhausted, I tried to sum up the day's events and conversations. It had been a day of overwhelming displays of sympathy by GDR citizens, a day of subdued hope, of satisfaction at a venture and an initiative that could not have been left untried.

The report which Stoph presented to the People's Chamber was even more restrained than mine, although he too confirmed that our meeting had been 'useful'. He regretted that I had 'yet again' avoided taking up a clear stand on the basic and omnidecisive issue of peace or war. Fundamentally, he said, our policy was not so different from that of previous Federal Governments.

This did not augur well for the second exchange of views in Kassel, which was further impeded by problems of an awkward nature. It may be asked why I engaged in these talks at all during the early months of my Chancellorship, given that success was unlikely under prevailing circumstances. Some may wonder, after the event, whether it would not have been better to conclude our talks with the Soviet Union first. The answer is that my primary concern was to weaken East Berlin's unfavourable influence on Moscow and simultaneously demonstrate that there were important areas in which, pursuant to our policy, we wanted to reach accommodations with individual members of the Warsaw Pact. This applied particularly to our relations with the GDR, which required easing partly because of the inter-German amplifications of a Four-Power agreement on Berlin. Our policy called for an all-round initiative, not least towards the GDR.

I did not, however, leave all ideological demarcation to the other side.

Our readiness for regularized co-operation between the two states in Germany by no means implied that we were hoisting the white flag in our battle of principle. Addressing the SPD conference at Saarbrücken in mid-May 1970, I said: 'The fact that we are prepared to regard the GDR as a state with equal rights does not, of course, mean that we would or could regard it as a state similar to our own.' People 'over there' were always talking about contrasting economic and social systems, but more important still was the contrast in our political systems. 'In the twenty-year existence of the Federal Republic, German social democracy has proved that our own state's social system can be developed and modified by democratic means in favour of more social justice, and we shall continue to prove this by our actions. So far, the Socialist Unity Party has failed to demonstrate that its state is capable of change in the direction of greater freedom.'

The Kassel meeting on 21 May 1970 was heavily overshadowed. Extreme right-wing groups, mainly of NPD complexion, had mobilized their supporters. So had the communists. It was a gathering of diehards and sectarians, but the activitists on both sides – no more than a few thousand in each case – were numerous and obstreperous enough to create hours of pandemonium in the environs of our meeting-place. It was small comfort that our country's freedom of speech and association should have been demonstrated in so dramatic a manner. Our guests from East Berlin were flatly unsympathetic. Their comment: 'It wouldn't have happened with us.' All they saw was an abuse of the liberties on which most citizens of the Federal Republic so justly pride themselves. They noted that the police – who had likewise lost control for a few hours in Erfurt – were unequal to the situation in Kassel. They also noted that, so far from being confined to the GDR, the hatred of the neo-Nazis, old and young, extended to their Social Democrat Federal Chancellor and the policy for which he stood. One of the organized chants ran '*Volksverräter Hand in Hand – Willi Stoph und Willy Brandt!*' [National traitors hand in hand – Willi Stoph and Willy Brandt]; another urged '*Brandt an die Wand!*' [Brandt to the wall]. As one reporter put it: 'Reds marched against Brownshirts, the *Internationale* vied with the first verse of *Deutschland über alles*, red flags were levelled at black.' Most of Kassel's inhabitants steered clear of these pernicious goings-on, but a whiff of 'Weimar' and its street battles hung in the air.

Shouts from portable loud-hailers and the roar of the demonstrators carried to the little station of Kassel-Wilhelmshöhe, where I met the premier of the GDR. Our cars came under attack as we drove to the scene of the talks. Many placards were reiterations of the dire threats that had poured in by post and telephone. Shortly after we arrived at the Schloss-Hotel, three youths hauled down the GDR flag and tore it to shreds. Extreme right-wingers had penetrated the grounds armed with forged press cards. I formally apologized for these incidents before the afternoon session began.

The planned wreath-laying at the memorial for the victims of fascism had to be postponed after lunch because the chief of police reported that he could not guarantee the safety of our guests although 2000 policemen had been deployed in the centre of the city. The wreath-laying finally took place that evening. One reporter described his impressions from the side-lines of the conference as follows:

> The official convoy suddenly moved off, heading down into the city from the Schloss-Hotel. Was Stoph going to make an abrupt departure after all? Glued to the television screens in the press centre, many eyes watched spell-bound to see which route the column would take. It drove down Wilhelmshöher Allee but did not turn off at the station. It continued to head for the city centre – for the memorial. The demonstrators had started to leave the city long before. There were only a few hundred people left at the memorial. They broke into subdued applause and then stood motionless as that which it had been impossible to do earlier was finally done. Willy Brandt stood at Willi Stoph's side, and Stoph did not disguise his appreciation of the gesture.

The city showed its better side during the drive back to the hotel and later on the way to the station. We received friendly waves from pavements and windows. Left to themselves again, the citizens of Kassel showed that they wanted nothing to do with imported rioters.

These incidents provided Stoph with an opportunity to begin by straying from the real theme of our discussion – not that he needed any excuse. He had come equipped with a list of complaints and was determined to get them off his chest. Scarcely had I opened the morning session – the delegations were the same as in Erfurt – when he interrupted me and started to read a prepared statement. It referred to 'a whole system of laws, judgements and other official acts whereby novernment bodies and courts of the FRG claim, contrary to intergational law, to exercise rights and competences in regard to the GDR and its citizens beyond the national borders of the Federal Republic'. This charge, which was not wholly unfounded but presented in a grossly exaggerated form, had already been served on us in an exchange of letters at the beginning of May. I had pointed out to Stoph that each state had laws which would be considered discriminatory by the other. I now handed him an expert study in which our Minister of Justice refuted the charge of 'juridical aggression', and stressed that the Minister of Justice and his colleagues in the *Länder* were at pains to prevent any wrongful application of our penal code. I also had reason to point out to the other side 'that the suspicions and imputations to which my government is almost daily exposed can neither serve a purpose nor wean us from our belief, nor are they likely to exert a favourable influence on public opinion on our side'. The proposals I made for further negotiations stated: 'Both sides shall seek to ascertain the areas in which conflicts occur between the legislation of both states; they shall use their influence to eliminate such conflicts so as to avoid detriment to the citizens of both states in Germany. In so doing, they shall work on the principle that the sovereign authority of each side is limited to its state territory.'

Stoph had called upon us to ensure that the GDR delegation's sojourn in the Federal Republic would be free from any form of discrimination, and I had replied that our guests would enjoy the same rights and treatment as I and my companions had been accorded in Erfurt. Stoph now felt obliged to state that the Federal Government had failed to curb neo-Nazi elements and even to put a stop to outright threats of murder. I pointed out that the different circumstances prevailing in our two states extended to freedom of speech and association. The fact still remained 'as our guests here, you enjoy the protection and respect of the Federal Government'.

However many references were made to discrimination, I went on, one should not ignore the advantages that had accrued to the GDR from the Federal Republic's attitude in many spheres, for instance that of trade. (I was primarily alluding to the GDR's indirect participation in the Common Market, which other members of the Warsaw Pact regarded with envy.) I was also bound to mention that the government of the GDR had repeatedly sought to obstruct our efforts to improve relations with the countries of Eastern Europe. I could not believe that a demand for formal recognition was all the government of the GDR had to put forward.

On Berlin, I said we welcomed the initiation of talks between the Four Powers. My government took the view that progress towards normalizing the situation in and concerning Berlin would also have an important bearing on the future course of negotiations between our two governments. The Four Powers' endeavours should not be disrupted. The two German governments would, however, have to make definite arrangements as soon as the Four-Power negotiations reached a definite conclusion.

The heart of my statement consisted of twenty points in which we had summarized our ideas on 'principles and contractual elements for the establishment of relations based on equal rights'. I had got the cabinet to discuss and approve these twenty points. Point 1 called for a general treaty between the Federal Republic of Germany and the GDR. Point 3 related to human rights and the principle of non-discrimination, Point 4 to the renunciation of force, Point 5 to internal sovereignty, Points 7, 8, and 9 to the safeguarding of peace, questions of security, and participation in efforts at disarmament.

Point 10 reaffirmed the existence of two states comprising a single nation, Point 11 our common obligation to respect the rights of the victorious powers in World War II, and Point 12 Four-Power responsibility for Berlin. The practical points included an expansion of tourist traffic aimed at freedom of movement, efforts to solve the problems of divided families, co-operation on the frontier and in postal services. They also covered exchanges of information, science, culture, environmental matters, sport and trade. Point 19 proposed an exchange of 'plenipotentiaries', and Point 20 a settlement relating to our membership of international bodies (the United Nations) on the basis of the treaty to be concluded.

Though not until eighteen months after the Kassel meeting, all the essential ingredients of this twenty-point programme were included in the settlements ultimately reached with the GDR. As to the manner in which our relations were to be adjusted, I pointed out in Kassel that the arrangements to be concluded 'should incorporate a treaty forming the basis on which the relations between our two states are regulated'. I also revived my Erfurt proposal that we should appoint representatives and conclude preliminary agreements.

This did not match the plans with which the GDR delegation had come to Kassel. Baldly stated, what Stoph told me was that negotiations must be limited to the GDR's draft treaty and concluded on that basis with the utmost speed.

Stoph's lengthy statement, which abounded in polemics, took no account of our approach to non-recognition of German partition, to the continuing validity of Four-Power rights, or to the future of our nation. He submitted that we wanted to perpetuate the basic questions of war or peace and were playing a dishonest game if we created the impression that outstanding problems could be resolved by small stages. We were not prepared clearly to acknowledge the consequences of the defeat of Hitler-fascism and jettison the ballast of a revanchist policy. My speeches, which had been studied with close attention, betrayed 'nothing aimed at the disclosure of a genuine change, at real and fundamental reform, at final ascendency over a calamitous past'. Our reaffirmation of the Atlantic Alliance, my recent visit to Washington and the role of Federal armed forces also came under attack. Stoph renewed his complaint that we were obstructing the GDR's development of its international relations. (The fact was that we had asked the relevant countries to await the outcome of our efforts *vis-à-vis* the GDR.) On the subject of trade, Stoph presumed to assert that the Federal Republic had not only benefited most but harmed the GDR by meddling in its economic relations with third countries. The morning session in Kassel was followed by a private discussion in the open air (presumably because Stoph thought it might be recorded on tape indoors). Despite the acerbity of his official statements, he was very interested in reaching a practical understanding to the effect that our trade relations would not suffer. Apart from this, his confidence seemed slightly shaken by the talks which Egon Bahr was having in Moscow. He bitterly reproached us for having tried to get the GDR seated at a side-table at a recent meeting of the ECE (the UN Economic Commission for Europe) in Geneva. Actually, our representatives had been trying to promote an interim solution in the belief that it had also been accepted by the GDR representatives.

Another private conversation that afternoon was partly devoted to the events of that morning, which Stoph characterized as a 'murderous campaign'. I informed him of our legal position and our intentions. We later agreed to perform the wreath-laying ceremony despite the objections raised on security grounds. Stoph said he would much appreciate it if this joint gesture could be retained in the programme. We also agreed not to sever contact even though our differing positions precluded us from entering into treaty negotiations. 'Pause for thought' was the term devised to cover this.

Addressing the delegations when they reassembled that afternoon, I regretted that Stoph had taken such a contentious line. In spite of our conflicting views – on the national question, on political realities and the substance of a treaty settlement – I tried to define the area where our points of departure coincided. I duly reinvoked the statement that a war must never again originate on German soil. Renunciation of force would have to be one of our contractual provisions, as the Russians themselves had stressed during our exchange of views with Moscow. The Federal Government's favourable attitude towards the reinforcement of security in Europe must be known to all, and it also extended to the painstaking preparations for a European security conference. There could surely be no objection to both sides proclaiming a desire to base their relations on a respect for frontiers and territorial integrity.

As regards relations with third countries and international organizations, we regarded it as conducive to efforts to devise suitable types of relationship between our two states if a friendly country refrained from anything that might hamper those efforts. 'You, too, expect your friends to back your policy. If our joint endeavours are aimed at mutual understanding, our relations with the countries round us will eventually become clarified too.'

On trade, I said that arguments over advantages or disadvantages were superfluous. It was unprofitable to proceed on the present basis of internal German trade. 'The Federal Government will persevere in its efforts to promote the special economic relations between itself and the GDR, and any contractual settlement between our two states should confirm existing agreements, instructions and arrangements.'

Even if treaty negotiations were still impracticable, we should in any case consider resuming our exchange of views at the proper time. Both proposals – our own treaty components and East Berlin's draft – should be examined in concert to see whether they could be developed into 'agreements which are in keeping with the situation, and in which, should the occasion arise, the application of principles of international law to the relations between our states may receive formal expression'. The GDR side, too, should review its position. In due course, we should get in touch with a view to resuming the discussions between our governments. 'Meanwhile, we must not be deterred from tackling solutions to problems wherever possible. This includes any form of progress, be it ever so small.' Addressing myself to Stoph direct, I said:

Do you under present circumstances believe, Herr *Vorsitzender*, that any treaty between our two states is practicable, and can be approved and accepted by the alliances in Europe and the countries outside those alliances, which does not declare and affirm that the existing Four-Power agreements on Germany and Berlin will be respected? Again, what under present circumstances would a treaty be worth which failed to guarantee that our projected arrangements would not affect the obligations which we have respectively undertaken *vis-à-vis* France, Great Britain, the United States and the Soviet Union, and which repose on the special rights and obligations of those powers in respect of Germany and Berlin? Where in your proposed treaty is there any discernible readiness for practical co-operation and the development of relations to the common benefit of the citizens of our states – of the Germans on whose behalf it is our duty to act?

If it were possible to answer the questions about material content, I went on, I was convinced that it would also be possible, in the course of time, to solve 'the question which you refer to as legal recognition of the GDR'.

Stoph remained adamant. The principles I had advanced could only be construed as 'a veiled but unequivocal refusal to establish relations based on equal rights under international law'. He went to great lengths to substantiate the 'socialist state of the German nation' thesis, extolling development in the GDR and painting a blacker-than-black picture of conditions in the Federal Republic. He also placed an unfavourable construction on the 'pause for thought' formula, suggesting that we doubtless needed time to come up with some better ideas (his own brand of humour). Finally, he revived his proposal that we should apply for UN membership at once. I had allegedly told him at Erfurt that the USA was against it, and that that was why we could not make a decision.

The meeting broke up without a communiqué. On 25 May the East Berlin Council of Ministers declared its readiness to resume discussions, but only on condition that we gave evidence of 'a realistic attitude'.

Addressing a Federal press conference on the morrow of the Kassel meeting, I said I had told Herr Stoph that, notwithstanding all our differences, the statements we had made embodied several points of contact.

To render them productive does, however, presuppose that the other side contributes slightly more goodwill and slightly fewer juridical formulas. The Federal Government has not surrendered to wishful thinking. For all that, I should like to deliver yet another warning against false hopes. The road to contractual settlements between the two German states will be long and arduous. Time does not automatically work in favour of common sense and peace. We must bestir ourselves.

I told the Bundestag a few days later that, although Kassel had yielded wholly unsatisfactory results, the fact of the meeting was an advance compared with the years when the two German states had stood back to back. It would be wise to proceed methodically, as in our negotiations with the Soviet Union. We had undoubtedly come up against 'the limits of German reality', as one commentator had put it, yet I received many moving letters from the GDR after the Erfurt and Kassel meetings which showed how many hopes were riding on our policy. Despite everything, the experimental dialogue between Germany and Germany was not in vain. At the end of October 1970, or five months after Kassel, our exchange of views with the GDR was resumed at junior ministerial level. Its preliminary outcome was the December 1971 Transit Agreement which, like an agreement between the Berlin Senate and the GDR, formed part of the Quadripartite Agreement on Berlin. Subsequent results were the Traffic Treaty of May 1972 and, finally, the Basic Treaty of December 1972.

At the end of October 1970 we duly agreed with the government of the GDR 'to conduct through official channels an exchange of views on questions whose settlement would benefit détente in Europe and are of interest to both states'. Thanks to the GDR's inflexible attitude, these talks between Egon Bahr and Michael Kohl were slow to get under way and began by concentrating on traffic questions.

Meanwhile, at the end of March 1970, the Four Powers had initiated talks on Berlin which were closely connected with the overall pattern of our policy towards the East and the GDR. We insisted that any Berlin settlement should embrace open-ended arrangements between East and West designed as far as humanly possible to safeguard West Berlin against interference and thereby afford scope for the city's peaceful future development. 'Berlin, that symbol of Cold War controversy, must become a symbol of acknowledged co-existence and co-operation in the midst of a peacefully collaborating Europe.'

Matters were made no easier by the interdependences that emerged. For instance, our relationship to the Western Powers had to be preserved intact and employed as a constructive influence on the Berlin negotiations. But the Three had also to maintain their own rights in Berlin and, with differing emphases, to uphold their own interests. Another factor was the changing relationship between the United States and the Soviet Union. Compared with the substance – and the currently debated risks – of the détente talks, West Berlin's problems were bound to assume lesser significance in the eyes of many participants. Above all, there was a connection with the Moscow treaty of August 1970. It is clear, on the one hand, that the conclusion of this treaty was a substantial aid to negotiations between the Four Powers. On the other, the Federal Government had stated in June that unless Berlin were safeguarded (by the Quadripartite Agreement) its treaty with the Soviet Union could not be put into effect. Although I warned against allowing this statement to become a 'political straitjacket', Bonn's politico-diplomatic thinking has a fatal tendency, even when there is no need, to exalt an objective connection into a legal nexus. Many people are surprised when others follow their example, as when the Soviet Union declared in 1971 that the Berlin Agreement would not come into force until the Moscow treaty had been ratified.

As I have already said, President Nixon took advantage of his visit to Berlin on 27 February 1969 to sound a new note by stating that the situation there was unsatisfactory. This was meant to be universally interpreted as a summons to negotiate. Addressing members of the Siemens work force, the US President said: 'When we say we reject any unilateral change in the *status quo* in Berlin, it does not mean we regard the *status quo* as satisfactory . . . Let us – all of us – look upon the situation in Berlin as a summons to negotiate, as a call to end the tensions of a bygone period, there and throughout the world.'

At the NATO Council meeting in Washington in April 1969, the Foreign Ministers resolved at my suggestion to consider the possibility of official Three-Power soundings in Moscow with a view to improving the Berlin situation. On 6 July 1969 the Western heads of mission in Moscow submitted to the Soviet Government that the Federal Government was ready to conduct discussions with the GDR on traffic problems and improvements in the Berlin situation, particularly in regard to access. They also pointed to the Federal Government's readiness to compromise over Soviet complaints about certain Federal activities in Berlin. Addressing the Supreme Soviet on 10 July, Foreign Minister Gromyko thereupon stated that the Soviet Government was fundamentally interested in an exchange of views with its 'war-time allies' on the future avoidance of 'complications over West Berlin'. The Soviet Government reaffirmed its readiness to talk in a reply dated 12 September 1969. After a further preparatory exchange of notes, the Four-Power talks on Berlin finally opened at ambassadorial level on 26 March 1970, in the offices of the Allied Control Commission.

The ambassadorial discussions were very closely co-ordinated by representatives of the three Western Powers and the Federal Government, with the Berlin Senate participating. (The Opposition was regularly consulted too.) I said of this co-operation that it 'acquired almost unprecedented intensity'. Co-ordination was effected in the 'Bonn Group of Four' (a team of diplomatic counsellors) and through Egon Bahr's regular consultations with the three ambassadors, in which his 'direct line' to Henry Kissinger proved of value. The Western Powers' preliminary approach to talks had been laid down in the days of the Grand Coalition. On 5 August 1969 Chancellor Kiesinger had approved the outcome of consultations on the substance of the Three-Power démarche to be undertaken in Moscow.

Gromyko had tried to sound out our ideas by raising the Berlin theme with Bahr in February 1970. This was a step forward, considering that Moscow had long declined all discussion of Berlin problems with Bonn. Our side stressed its interest in any Berlin settlements which were concluded by the 'competent' Three Powers. The Three Powers expressed fears that we might weaken their negotiating position. Once they had agreed to enter into negotiations on Berlin with the Soviet Union, Gromyko dropped the subject *vis-à-vis* Bahr.

The four ambassadors' preliminary meetings, which were mainly devoted to an account of their varying legal positions, at first suggested that practical progress would be impossible. The Soviet side laid emphasis on inordinate demands for a reduction of the Federal presence and described Western proposals for the external representation of West Berlin as out of the question. The ambassadors talked on and on, clearly waiting for the outcome of our Moscow negotiations. If these failed, their own efforts were likely to be just as unproductive. There was no real movement until the Moscow treaty had been signed. Although the Russians expressly rejected any formal link between treaty ratification and a Berlin settlement, they did in practice gear themselves increasingly to an objective connection between the two. On 25 September 1970 the two sides exchanged papers for the first time, but their positions were still far apart. Early in October, diplomatic counsellors acting in an expert capacity began to make joint preparations for ambassadorial meetings. They drafted the first joint paper, an informal list of the points which both sides wanted to embody in a settlement. At the same time, they began to develop common ideas on the possible structure of a settlement. Pursuant to a Western proposal, three stages were envisaged: Four-Power agreements, German implementation agreements and, thirdly, a final quadripartite protocol.

All concerned were aware that the Western side had numerous requirements but could make few concessions if the objective of genuine improvement were to be attained. There were fears that a full statement of Western requirements would overtax the Soviet readiness to give ground and thus cause negotiations to break down. For that reason, the West at first concentrated on securing unimpeded access routes.

The real or 'hard' negotiating phase opened with an exchange of papers on 5 February and 26 March 1971. These papers betrayed certain similarities of form and content but diverged in their basic politico-legal approach. Rather than become bogged down in insoluble conflicts, the two sides agreed to bracket off irreconcilable statements of principle and concentrate on practical arrangements which did not affect the legal positions of either party. In this manner, they managed by the end of May to construct a joint outline sprinkled with brackets and footnotes. The pace of negotiation accelerated during the summer until the last remaining problem was resolved and agreement reached on the Quadripartite Agreement and Final Protocol, which were signed – or, where the Final Protocol was concerned, initialled – on 3 September 1971.

I was closely in touch with the Berlin negotiations throughout these months, not only via my expert advisers but also thanks to numerous conversations with the three Western ambassadors: Jean Sauvagnargues (later Foreign Minister), Sir Roger Jackling and Kenneth Rush, who as a professor of law and president of Union Carbide had gained valuable experience outside the confines of classical diplomacy. But for the American's drive and energy, the Berlin Agreement might never have come into being. Rush enjoyed Nixon's confidence and was able to contact his security adviser, Henry Kissinger, without running the gauntlet of the State Department.

The Quadripartite Agreement heralded improvements for West Berlin and its inhabitants in five respects: traffic between Federal territory and Berlin, visits to East Berlin and the GDR, external representation and consular facilities in the Soviet Union, inclusion in the Federation's international activities, and Federal links.

In the first two areas, beneficial effects were soon felt. Traffic to and from Berlin assumed forms which were essentially free from the interference and obstruction of previous years. Opportunities to visit East Berlin went far beyond what we had achieved in the passes agreements; visits to the GDR by West Berlin citizens had for many years been quite impossible. West Berlin's external representation and consular facilities and its participation in the international activities of the Federation did, it is true, continue to be a source of friction and controversy. The Russians, who sometimes placed a more than restrictive interpretation on the Agreement, were occasionally supplied with pretexts for so doing.

We insisted that an attempt be made to produce a common German translation of the official English, French and Russian texts. In default of this endeavour, which delayed things yet again, there would later have been more 'grounds' for conflicting interpretations. On one important point, no agreement was reached. The GDR insisted on describing the contacts between West Berlin and the Federal Republic as *Verbindungen* ['links', rather in the sense of 'communications'], whereas we called them *Bindungen* ['ties'].

On one aspect of 'representation abroad' and consular services, I managed to elicit a favourable response by means of direct personal intervention. My summer 1971 vacation was not, for once, spent in Norway but on the island of Sylt, where my colleagues could contact me more easily. I was going over the latest results of the Four-Power negotiations with Egon Bahr and Mayor Klaus Schütz. It appeared that the Russians were disinclined to restore the West Berliners' right to hold Federal passports, and the representatives of the Western Powers did not seem to attach any particular importance to this point. However, I still nursed a bitter recollection of the day during my own mayoral term when it was decreed that West Berliners could no longer visit the countries of Eastern Europe on a Federal passport. Without more ado, I wrote a personal letter to Brezhnev. The upshot was that West Berliners could travel to the Soviet Union using a Federal passport, though the latter had to be stamped 'Issued pursuant to the Quadripartite Agreement of 3 September 1971'.

Apart from authorizing the establishment of a Soviet Consulate-General in the Western sectors of Berlin, the Western Powers made most of their concessions in regard to the so-called Federal presence. Plenary sessions of the Bundestag, Bundesrat and Bundesversammlung [Federal Assembly for Presidential elections] could no longer be held in Berlin.

In a televised address on 3 September 1971, I said:

Many of you will question the true significance of the agreement which was signed in Berlin today. Well, I believe its true significance lies in the fact that, from now on, there will be no Berlin crises. This would mean a great deal, after so many years of uncertainty . . . What will the future position be? In the first place, the status of Berlin remains unaltered. Thus, the Western Powers' supreme responsibility for West Berlin still stands. Secondly, West Berlin's association with our Federal Republic will no longer be disputed. There is also the agreement on unobstructed access routes. West Berlin will still be represented abroad by the Federal Government, but in future in the East as well. The people of West Berlin will be able to visit the GDR and the Eastern part of the city. Last but not least, you will be able to live and work in safety. That is a good deal. Nevertheless, who of us would not wish that even more could have been done! That Germans could move about freely – that there were no frontiers or shots fired along them. However, no one could seriously have expected the Wall to vanish at this stage in history. It was a limited but very important task.

Thanking Nixon, Pompidou, Heath and Kosygin for the work their four ambassadors had performed, I described the agreement as 'an important step on the road to détente in Europe'.

First of all, agreements had to be concluded between the Germans themselves. Our transit agreement with the GDR related to traffic by road, rail and water. Air traffic was excluded, as in the Quadripartite Agreement, because it was covered by agreements between the victorious powers. Compensation for road-use tolls and visa fees was fixed in the form of an annual lump sum, and a commission was set up to resolve difficulties and differences of opinion arising from the application or interpretation of the Agreement. The Berlin Senate and the GDR approved regulations covering travel between West and East Berlin and between West Berlin and the GDR: visits could be made on one or more occasions in the year, but were not to exceed a total of thirty days. Applications did not have to be made solely for family reasons but could be granted on 'compassionate, family, religious, cultural and touristic grounds'.

The German agreements were signed in Bonn on 17 December and in Berlin on 20 December 1971. The Western Powers were now ready to sign the Final Protocol. The Soviet Union waited until the Bundestag had approved the Moscow treaty in May 1972. On 3 June 1972 the Final Quadripartite Protocol was signed in Berlin by Foreign Ministers Schumann, Gromyko, Douglas-Home and Rogers. The results were reflected in some striking statistics: during 1970, some 3·5 million people had travelled to West Berlin overland; by 1975 that figure had more than doubled. In the same year, West Berliners paid more than 3 million visits to East Berlin and the GDR. It was also possible to telephone again from one part of the city to the other.

The number of visitors from Federal territory to the GDR doubled in the course of five years to more than 3 million. In 1975, over 400,000 people took advantage of the newly established 'minor frontier traffic' facilities between the Federal Republic and the GDR. Visits from the GDR by 'persons of pensionable age' rose from 1 to 1·3 million. A substantial number of GDR citizens were granted travel permits for 'pressing family reasons'. The number of telephone lines between the two German states rose from 34 to over 700. Gift parcel traffic services became easier.

The figures I have quoted were not, however, attributable solely to the

Quadripartite Agreement. They also derived from agreements between the two German states. The adjustment of our relations with the GDR was an extremely laborious business.

On 3 September 1971, simultaneously with the conclusion of the Quadripartite Agreement, the Federal cabinet took note of reports on the exchange of views that had been conducted with representatives of the GDR since the agreement of end-October 1970 'on questions whose settlement would benefit détente in the centre of Europe'. This exchange of views had at first related to questions of general traffic between the Federal Republic and the GDR. Egon Bahr was now authorized to join GDR representatives in negotiations 'initially directed towards the preparation of an agreement between the two states on improving traffic and creating conditions advantageous to those who participate therein'.

Bahr and his tenacious opposite number, Michael Kohl, now had, subsequent to the German amplifications of the Quadripartite Agreement and the Traffic Treaty, to negotiate other partial treaties or – as it turned out – the 'Basic Treaty'. In addition, they naturally discussed other matters of which one government wished to apprise the other. Bahr's partner was very constrained at first, and the atmosphere was icy in patches. When negotiating in Bonn, Kohl seemed to feel that he was on alien and enemy soil, but Bahr never got the impression that he was being 'hoodwinked' by him. Their relations became somewhat easier as time went by.

Meanwhile, Ulbricht had been replaced as Party leader. He was old and ailing, but political analyses suggest that a major reason for his departure was his hard line towards the Federal Republic. The decision to replace him seems to have been taken during the 24th Congress of the CPSU in March 1971. Erich Honecker became First Secretary of the SED at the beginning of May. Though stripped of influence, Ulbricht remained Chairman of the Council of State until his death. Stoph succeeded him in this post in 1973.

We could not tell whether the change of leadership portended a change in policy. It was none the less fair to assume that the Russians were tired of Ulbricht's pigheadedness and expected Honecker – whether rightly or wrongly remains an open question – to be rather more amenable to their new policy towards the West. In November 1971 Brezhnev visited East Berlin after I had been his guest in the Crimea and he himself had paid a state visit to Paris. It is likely that he prompted the GDR leaders to take a few initiatives in the matter of inter-German agreements – at any rate, that had been my suggestion to him. In April 1972 I gained the impression that Honecker had, during his visit to Moscow, shown greater flexibility in certain areas relating to the settlement of our practical problems.

Speaking in Sofia a short while before (we knew that he wished to convey something to us there), Honecker had made a statement on the subject of a basic treaty without actually using the term. In so doing, he referred to some of the points I had raised with Stoph in 1970. We also had to accept that between 30 and 35 countries would be recognizing the GDR in the months ahead.

I have already mentioned that telephone and teleprinter links had improved since 1970. This was especially important to the people of Berlin, who had been quite unable to telephone from one part of the city to the other, even by way of the Federal Republic, for eighteen years. It also carried some weight that the GDR authorities were now prepared to allow former refugees to benefit from the easing of travel restrictions. At Easter 1972 West Berliners were once more able to visit the Eastern part of the city even though the arrangements forming part of the Quadripartite Agreement were not yet officially in force.

The Traffic Treaty between the Federal Republic and the GDR was signed on 26 May 1972. It was concluded 'in an endeavour to promote détente in Europe and develop such normal good-neighbourly relations between the two states as are customary between independent states'. The preamble also spoke of 'sovereign territories'. Although the nature of the treaty was absolutely plain, the Opposition had not withheld its approval shortly before the autumn 1972 elections. This made its subsequent attitude all the harder to understand: in May 1973 the CDU/CSU rejected the Basic Treaty.

I could not tell in summer 1972 whether negotiations on the Basic Treaty would take two months or twelve. On 26 August I noted: 'It is, of course, particularly important how our *Ostpolitik* progresses after the treaties have been ratified. Some pessimists believe the Russians will now back off and take no great interest in the treaty we have to negotiate with the GDR. Egon Bahr takes a more favourable view. Still, the Basic Treaty with the GDR will give us a lot more trouble yet.' On 8 September I noted: 'Bahr turned up this afternoon [at the Starnberger See] and briefed me on a detailed but unreported discussion between himself and Honecker in East Berlin the day before. It looks as if most of the major questions relating to a Basic Treaty can be satisfactorily resolved according to circumstances.' On 28 September: 'Egon Bahr reports from East Berlin that the Basic Treaty can, after all, be effected before the end of October.'

The Basic Treaty – or, more precisely, the Treaty on the Bases of

Relations between the Federal Republic of Germany and the German Democratic Republic – was actually initialled by Michael Kohl and Egon Bahr, who had previously been occupied in Moscow, on 8 November. The two negotiators signed it in East Berlin on 21 December. The Bundestag elections had been held in the interim. The GDR amnestied a sizeable number of prisoners in connection with the initialling, and several hundred were released into the Federal Republic. The initialling also helped to reunite a large number of families. It had been suggested that I myself might sign the treaty, but I declined because East Berlin was unaccommodating over dates.

The preamble of the Basic Treaty embodied a renunciation of the use of force. It also stated that, 'proceeding from the historical facts and without prejudice to the differing concepts of the Federal Republic of Germany and the German Democratic Republic', the two states had agreed 'to create preconditions for co-operation' between them.

In Article 9 the two states agreed that any bilateral and multilateral international treaties and agreements previously concluded by or concerning them would remain unaffected. As in the Moscow treaty, the other party was given a letter in which the Federal Government stated 'that this Treaty does not conflict with the political objective of the Federal Republic of Germany to work for a state of peace in Europe in which the German nation will recover its unity in free self-determination'.

Under Article 4, both states accepted that neither could internationally represent the other or act in its name. Article 6 affirmed the principle that each of the two states' sovereign power was confined to its own state territory and that each respected the other's independence and sovereignty in internal and external affairs.

Article 8 laid it down that 'permanent representative missions' should be exchanged. (These were set up on 2 May 1974 and their two heads, Günter Gaus and Michael Kohl, accredited on 20 June 1974, Gaus by the Foreign Ministry of the GDR and Kohl by the Federal Chancellery, in conformity with the differing legal interpretations of the two parties.)

It was stipulated in an exchange of letters that the rights and responsibilities of the Four Powers and 'the corresponding relevant quadripartite agreements, decisions and practices' could not be affected by the treaty. A joint declaration further agreed on the form of West Berlin's co-representation and the representation of West Berlin's interests by the permanent representative of the German Federal Republic. Yet another exchange of letters recorded that both states would initiate the necessary measures to seek membership of the United Nations Organization and to advise each other of the date of their applications.

It was agreed in a supplementary protocol to set up a commission to examine the demarcation of the border and assist in resolving problems relating to its location. The same document laid it down that trade between the two states should be developed on the basis of existing agreements.

The treaty itself (Article 7) spoke of a readiness to settle practical and humanitarian problems in the course of normalizing relations. Various special areas were more closely defined in the supplementary protocol. In another exchange of letters, the GDR held out the prospect of solving 'problems arising from the separation of families', also of easing travel restrictions and the passage of non-commercial goods traffic.

Numerous though they were, these major and minor steps did not directly bring us closer to the goal of German unity. 'Germany and German,' I said in my report on the state of the nation in February 1972, 'are terms to which we adhere and which others can scarcely evade.' East Berlin had considered it desirable to draw an even sharper political and ideological line between itself and the German Federal Republic. We had not only to accept this but, on our side, to persevere in drawing a clear line of demarcation.

Meanwhile, attempts were being made in the GDR to reinforce its identity by a vigorous and sometimes grotesque debate on the concept of 'nationhood'. The SED and its leaders had originally adhered to the traditional picture of Germany and its existence as a nation. Like the Constitution of the GDR, official spokesmen avowed that reunification was the ultimate goal, though propaganda swiftly added that it must be attained under communist auspices. East German reunification policy displayed expansionist features or withdrew to a neutralist position depending on current Soviet requirements.

Allusions to national unity became rarer during the late 1960s and finally ceased altogether. Instead, the GDR Government (or, more precisely, the SED's executive team) somewhat laboriously tried to restrict the concept of nationhood to their own part-state, which was now defined as 'the Socialist State of the German Nation'. Eventually, even this formula was modified by Honecker into 'the Socialist German National State'. East Berlin was at pains to equate nationhood with the GDR. Unlike the similar treaties of 1955 and 1964, the Treaty of Friendship and Mutual Assistance which the Soviet Union and the GDR concluded in October 1975 omitted all reference to reunification.

As for us, we clung to historical reality. I was well aware that, throughout its phases of historical development, Germany had never entirely corresponded to the 'classical nation-state'. On the death of those eager hopes of reunification that flourished immediately after the war, it became clear to me that there could be no return to a nation-state on the 19th-century pattern. I nevertheless remained convinced that the nation would live on, even under differing political systems, because nationhood is a matter of awareness and resolve. Although the identity of nation and state had been destroyed, its existence in Germany had in any case been brief. Germany had always existed as a 'cultural nation', and it was as a 'cultural nation' that it would retain its identity, whatever might be the chances that, in the course of an all-European process, the two states would some day evolve forms of coexistence amounting to more than inter-state relations. To keep 'cultural nationhood' as intact as possible in everyday life: to me, this has always been an objective which should not preclude the western part of Germany from seeking a wider political home in the European community of the West.

15

Warsaw and other Landmarks

In December 1970 I flew to Warsaw to sign our treaty with the People's Republic of Poland. My feelings at this time were those of someone who felt obliged to mount a historical test-bed on behalf of his fellow-countrymen. My journey to the Polish capital was fraught with the remembrance of murders by the million. Here, more than in any other phase of our treaty policy, we found that stirrings of sentiment and the dictates of reason provided mutual reinforcement. Stark statistics cannot convey the horrors to which the Poles were subjected between the invasion of September 1939 and the terrible culmination of their national nightmare. The Polish people lost six million dead, a figure which included almost the whole of the Jewish population. Polish soil witnessed the mass annihilation of Jewish men, women and children. Approximately four million people were murdered at Auschwitz alone. In 1944 the Warsaw Ghetto rose and waged a fight to the death of which the world took little more notice than it did of the Polish capital's insurrection a few months later.

I landed in Warsaw on the afternoon of 6 December and was welcomed with military honours. One journalist reported that 'the faces of the Poles, many of whom had been detained in concentration camps for years, betrayed violent agitation when the German national anthem was played . . .' My next morning's programme allowed for two wreath-laying ceremonies to be performed before the treaty was signed. The first was at the Tomb of the Unknown Soldier, where I inscribed the visitors' book as follows: 'In memory of the dead of the Second World War and of the victims of violence and betrayal, in the hope of an enduring peace and of solidarity between the nations of Europe.'

I went down on my knees before the memorial to those who died in the Warsaw Ghetto. Despite malicious comments in the Federal Republic, I was not ashamed to have done so. This gesture, which attracted worldwide attention, was not 'planned', though I had certainly debated earlier that morning how best to convey the special nature of this act of remembrance at the Ghetto monument. I discussed it with no one. Oppressed by memories of Germany's recent history, I simply did what people do when words fail them. My thoughts dwelt not only on the millions who had been murdered but also on the fact that, Auschwitz notwithstanding, fanaticism and the suppression of human rights persisted. My gesture was intelligible to those willing to understand it, and they included many in Germany and elsewhere. The tears in the eyes of my delegation were a tribute to the dead. As one reporter put it: 'Then he knelt, he who has no need to, on behalf of all who ought to kneel but don't – because they dare not, or cannot, or cannot venture so to do.' That was what it was: an attempt, through the expression of fellowship, to build a bridge to the history of our nation and its victims.

My Polish hosts seemed rather disconcerted that December morning. Nothing was said at lunch or dinner, and I concluded that the Poles, too, had yet to assimilate this chapter in their history. In the car next morning, however, Premier Cyrankiewicz took me by the arm and told me that many people had been deeply affected by my gesture. His wife had telephoned a woman friend in Vienna the previous night, and both of them had wept bitterly.

Speaking on television the same evening, I said:

The purpose of the Warsaw treaty is to write finis to the sufferings and sacrifices of a grievous past. It is meant to build a bridge between our two states and nations. It is meant to open up a road that will enable divided families to be reunited and frontiers to separate fewer families than before. Even so, the signing of this treaty had to be preceded by an earnest examination of conscience.

We had to proceed on the basis of what existed – of what had come into being on Poland's western frontier as elsewhere. Nobody had enforced this realization upon us. What mattered was to demonstrate our maturity and have the courage to face reality.

It [the treaty] surrenders nothing that was not gambled away long ago – gambled away not by us who bear and have borne political responsibility in the Federal Republic of Germany, but by a criminal régime . . . Our Polish fellow-negotiators are aware of what I want, with all due clarity, to reiterate to you at home: this treaty does not imply that we recognize injustice or justify acts of violence, nor does it imply that we are legitimizing expulsions after the event.

Great suffering had been inflicted on our own people too, and especially on our East German compatriots. Among those who had paid most dearly for the war, he who had lost his home came second only to him who had lost his life or family.

We grieve for what we have lost, and our sorrow will be respected by the sorely tried Polish people . . . Names like Auschwitz will haunt both our nations for a long time to come, reminding them that hell on earth is possible. We have experienced it, but that very experience compels us to tackle the tasks of the future with determination. Evasion of reality breeds dangerous illusions. Approval of this treaty, of reconciliation and peace, means the acceptance of German history as a whole. A lucid view of history precludes any claims that cannot be fulfilled. It also precludes those 'secret reservations' against which Immanuel Kant, the East Prussian, warned in his treatise *Perpetual Peace*. We must focus our gaze on the future and acknowledge morality to be a political force. We must break the chains of injustice. By so doing, we shall be pursuing a policy based on reason, not renunciation.

Speaking in Bonn as soon as the treaty was initialled by our Foreign Ministers at the end of November, I had already addressed a special word to the expellees, begging them to look to the future rather than dwell in bitterness.

None of us found it easy to accept the loss of one-quarter of Germany's territory as it was before Hitlerite expansion pushed our frontiers back – territory which had meant much to Prusso-German history and German culture. And yet it accorded with a simple truth when we said that nobody can give away what he no longer possesses. Nobody can dispose of that which has already been disposed of by history. (As a woman expellee from East Prussia wrote: 'The treaty with Poland lays a wreath on Prussia's grave, but the grave has existed for many years.')

As neighbours, the Germans and the Poles had travelled a long and arduous road through history, and the years between 1939 and 1945 were its darkest stretch, but the two nations' cultures had also undergone a lengthy process of interaction and cross-fertilization. The Germans and Poles should be able to draw on this without casting the bitter lessons of history to the winds.

In the Moscow treaty, of which the Warsaw treaty was an amplification, we had accepted the Oder-Neisse line as Poland's western frontier. Even the Federal Governments that preceded my own had solemnly renounced the use of force against all existing frontiers including those of the GDR. Nevertheless, many of our German contemporaries accused us of being the first to crystallize what they refused to accept as an accomplished fact and would rather have continued to ignore. Distressing though many Germans found it, this was the point on which the Poles, and not merely their government, required clarification.

It is true that the Potsdam Agreement between the victorious powers in summer 1945 had postponed any formal decision on Germany's eastern frontier until after the conclusion of a peace treaty. The area east of the Oder and Neisse were placed under Polish administration, with the exception of northern East Prussia, which the Soviet Union annexed. A quarter of a century later, the following state of affairs prevailed. No peace treaty had been concluded; instead, the Four Powers had reached an accommodation based on two separate German states. Most Germans had fled or been expelled from Germany's erstwhile eastern province - Poland's new western territories - shortly after the war. Polish settlers, many of them from the east of pre-war Poland, which had since become Russian, moved into these Germans' homes and installed themselves in their towns and villages (the number of Poles born in our former territories since 1945 already exceeded that of the post-war migrants). At the same time, by a remarkable process of integration which should perhaps be regarded as the true 'German miracle', refugees and expellees from East Germany were assimilated into the Federal Republic and - a fact which is often forgotten - into the GDR. Although I myself had hoped that it might be possible to modify the Oder-Neisse frontier, at least in places, chances of this dwindled as the end of the war became more remote. Ever since the 1950s, well-disposed Western politicians had been recommending the abandonment of all opposition to the new line of demarcation in the East. No government in the entire world was prepared to commit itself on behalf of German claims in this matter.

The Federal Government could only speak for the German Federal Republic, not for the Four Powers nor for some all-German sovereign state of the future. It was none the less necessary to resist demagogy and wishful thinking without taking refuge behind any legal reservations that might be desirable on other counts. We had to state, loud and clear, that this consequence of World War II must be accepted if we were serious in our endeavours to obtain a European peace settlement and the German-Polish reconciliation which formed one of its basic constituents.

My policy statement of October 1969 affirmed that the Federal Government would contact the government of the People's Republic of Poland with a proposal to initiate discussions 'in response to Wladyslaw Gomulka's remarks of 17 May 1969'. Shortly before Christmas, the Polish Government responded with a note expressing its willingness to join in the discussion we had proposed. Gomulka stated in his New Year speech that an official exchange of views between Bonn and Warsaw would commence in the next few months.

Our own appointed negotiator was State Secretary Duckwitz. His Polish opposite number was the Deputy Foreign Minister, Josef Winiewicz, a diplomat of the old school and a patriot in the service of the new régime. The preliminary talks opened in Warsaw at the beginning of February and dragged on for five more rounds, two of them in Bonn.

During the third round, which took place in Warsaw during the second half of April, a misunderstanding arose on our side. Since this led to my one and only clash with Scheel, it deserves a mention. I had given Duckwitz a letter designed to secure him an interview with Gomulka. Being on the point of travelling to Oslo, I forgot to notify the Foreign Minister. In Warsaw, a newspaperman noted that Duckwitz – who doubtless assumed that Scheel had been informed – handed over a letter from the Federal Chancellor. His report gave rise to some fantastic speculations and provoked talk of secret contacts. Scheel angrily telephoned Oslo while I was discussing EEC matters with members of the government there. We cleared up the misunderstanding back in Bonn, where the wholly straightforward substance of my letter to Gomulka spoke for itself and rebutted the imputation that I had meant to go behind the Foreign Minister's back. It was bad organization, nothing more, but it unfortunately cast a shadow over Scheel's relations with his State Secretary, who was soon to retire in any case.

It became apparent during the discussions with Winiewicz that Polish preconditions – for example, concerning our relations with the GDR – had been dropped. However, the talks also disclosed how hard it was to find a formula on the frontier question which would reduce the legal and politico-psychological requirements of both sides to a common denominator. Renunciation of force had been an essential item in Bahr's programme for the preliminary negotiations in Moscow, and this formula was echoed by the Moscow treaty itself. We and the Poles could not negotiate this key item in our treaty from scratch. We had presupposed this sequence of events, which actually stemmed from the circumstances of the Warsaw Pact. The Poles would doubtless have preferred us to conclude a treaty with them first, but they knew that they had to yield precedence, both in time and content, to the senior power. I too would have welcomed it if we had been able to bring the German-Polish treaty forward, and said so in conversation with Gomulka. I also explained to my Western colleagues, more than once, that I ascribed special moral status to a settlement with Poland.

Where people of German stock still resident in Poland were concerned, we felt it our duty to enable as many as possible to settle in the Federal Republic. By the beginning of October – negotiations had since been taken over by State Secretary Paul Frank – we were far enough along the road to agreement on this problem and others for the Foreign Ministers to embark on formalization. Foreign Minister Scheel and a team of senior Foreign Office officials travelled to Warsaw for nine days of talks between 2 and 13 November, so it could hardly be said that the negotiations were concluded in haste and without expert diplomatic advice. It was quite clear that the courage to tackle problems went hand in hand with an ability to explore their complexities in the requisite depth. Critics of the Warsaw treaty took no account of this. On 9 November, having seen the Polish premier while negotiations were still in progress, Scheel flew back to Bonn to report. He also brought me an invitation to visit Warsaw at the close of negotiations, although diplomatic relations were not to be established until the treaty had been ratified.

The Warsaw treaty was neither a pure renunciation-of-force agreement nor a straightforward boundary treaty. Its true significance was better expressed by its official designation: 'Treaty on the Bases of the Normalization of Relations'. It thus paid primary regard to what had arisen between the two countries as a consequence, in the more immediate and the wider sense, of World War II.

The western border of Poland was described as a reality. The treaty further stated that both parties would always settle their disputes by peaceful means and were desirous of undertaking further steps towards the complete normalization and comprehensive development of their mutual relations.

As in the case of our treaties with the USSR, GDR and CSSR, it was important to us to establish that the new treaty did nothing to impair the validity of previously concluded treaties or international agreements affecting either party. We had to make it clear that bilateral arrangements were no substitute for a peace settlement embracing Germany in its entirety, and that Four-Power rights in and responsibilities for Germany as a whole continued to exist intact. The Federal Government further clarified the position by exchanging notes with the three Western Allies between the initialling and signing.

Not as part of the treaty, but as an outcome of negotiations, agreement was reached on the future treatment of problems arising from the status of ethnic Germans remaining in Poland. Although they could not see their way clear to settling these questions by treaty, the Poles did not dispute the need to resolve them on a practical basis in the interests of normalizing relations. Agreement took the form of a unilateral 'Statement' from the Polish Government on the measures it proposed to take. The Red Cross Societies were to deal with applications for resettlement. The Poles assured us that the figures indicated by their records ('some tens of thousands of people', interpreted to our cabinet as a circumlocution for 60,000–100,000) did not represent an upper resettlement limit; furthermore, the conclusion of the treaty would facilitate visits by relatives in both countries. Although nothing was said about this in the Statement, we expressed the wish that cultural restrictions on German-speaking inhabitants of Poland should be eased.

By agreement between the German and Polish Red Cross Societies, approximately a quarter of a million people had left Poland between 1955 and 1959. The Polish Government declared in its Statement that it could not allow its favourable attitude in this matter to be abused 'for the emigration of Polish nationals for employment purposes'. Even among persons of indisputable German ethnic origin and those of mixed parentage, there had in past years been a dominant sense of belonging to Poland. Despite this, persons 'of indisputable German ethnic origin' in either of the two states would be permitted to leave and 'be reunited with near relatives in the Federal Republic of Germany or the German Democratic Republic'. The Polish Government would issue the appropriate instructions so that applications submitted to the German Red Cross could be examined. Co-operation between the two Red Cross Societies would be facilitated and no obstacles placed in the way of visits by members of families.

I pressed for an open-minded approach to the treatment of these humanitarian questions when discussing them with Premier Cyrankiewicz in Warsaw. In studying the Polish Statement, I said, my cabinet and I had assumed that no arbitrary limit would be imposed.

The premier was sympathetic but asked me not to underestimate

Poland's own difficulties. His country had proved its goodwill in past years. The persons concerned lived mainly in Silesia and were employed in industry there. It was not easy to replace them with suitable 'cadres'. Many people eager to 'swim away too' suddenly discovered a 'distant aunt' elsewhere. In contrast to earlier times, Poland needed man-power and had no wish to become a land of émigrés, nor did it want the Federal Republic to serve as a staging-post for immigrants to America. I pointed out that better visiting facilities might be a help to many people. Cyrankiewicz agreed, but recalled some dubious experiences recorded in earlier years: for instance, visitors from the Federal Republic had inspected their former homes or farms and then told the new occupants to keep everything spick and span until they handed them back . . .

The results of the assistance promised by the Statement were unsatisfactory. Although some 60,000 people were resettled, the operation became a source of controversy and unrest. The Polish Government had underestimated the resistance of local and regional authorities. On the German side, people found it hard to understand why the rulers of a communist state should represent any departure from their territory as a 'concession'. Apart from this, the figures quoted by one side often differed widely from those accepted by the other. Applications and information reaching the German Red Cross pointed to a total of 90,000–100,000 cases justifying resettlement on family grounds. It was also estimated that 180,000 persons wished to settle in the Federal Republic without such family ties, or 270,000–280,000 in all. The same figure was quoted five years later, when doubts arose over its accuracy. What is a German? – that was the real question, and answering it was bound to pose problems. Plenty of families were split down the middle, and many well-informed sources, particularly in the Church, pointed out that resettlement had in some cases led to fresh separations. No simple solution was possible, nor is it now, but the prerequisites for continuing adjustment were finally secured on the side-lines of the Helsinki Conference in summer 1975.

On 3 December 1970 the Federal Cabinet resolved in favour of signing the treaty. I expressed the (vain) hope that the ratification debate would be preceded by the creation of a political climate in which the treaty could be evaluated without regard to party boundaries and free from political emotions. Bundestag members of all parties visited Poland in 1970 and thereafter. Many CDU/CSU politicians intimated that, where this particular treaty was concerned, their approval would not be withheld. In the event, the CDU/CSU-led *Länder* in the Bundesrat voted against the Warsaw treaty just as they had done against the Moscow treaty. As I have already mentioned, the Bundestag approved both treaties in May 1972, the vote in favour being 248 in each case. 17 members voted against the Warsaw treaty while the bulk of the Opposition – 230 – abstained. The road to ratification was an arduous one, and its Warsaw milestone merits description.

Premier Josef Cyrankiewicz and Foreign Minister Jedrychowsky were there to greet us when we landed in Warsaw on 6 December. That evening our Polish hosts gave a small dinner at the Netolin Palace. The burdens of the past, future relations and developments in Europe were all discussed with due gravity, but the atmosphere made it possible to talk more frankly than I had dared to hope. Gomulka, whom I had not met before, gave notice that he intended to raise the subject of compensation next day. I recommended that the process of rapprochement be viewed in terms of at least ten years, not one or two.

On the morning of 7 December, after the wreath-laying ceremonies and before the treaty was signed at the Namiestnikowski Palace, I called on the premier at his office accompanied by Walter Scheel and the leader of our trade mission. Josef Cyrankiewicz, who hailed from the old Socialist Party, had suffered badly under the Nazis. An impressive-looking man, he might from a distance have been mistaken for the actor Erich von Stroheim and did not seem at pains to conceal a faint aura of Austro-Hungarian traditionalism.

Cyrankiewicz opened the conversation by stating that, although the past could not, of course, be erased, the Polish Government was also looking to the future. This, he said, was the best way to make progress. Both sides must take the road that led to normal relations. Extensive co-operation between our two peoples would gradually succeed in dispelling the complexes and healing the deep wounds which still afflicted the Poles and, though not in equal measure, the Germans. In regard to the relations between their countries and peoples, both governments should jointly undertake a sort of psychoanalytical cure. Its primary function, as in the case of analysis, would be to unearth the root of the trouble. After that, talk and therapy could commence. He envisaged this therapy first and foremost as an effective and many-sided process of co-operation whose outcome must be a growing exchange of personnel and views. He was confident that time would exert a remedial effect.

I emphasized how very important it was that young people from both nations should become better acquainted – hence the fact that my delegation included representatives from five youth organizations. I also stressed the importance of work done by the historians of both countries. Valuable results had been obtained in recent years, especially in the difficult field of school textbooks (which were being objectivized and divested of nationalistic elements by a German-Polish committee modelled on the Franco-German prototype).

Cyrankiewicz agreed, but added that we must not expect or undertake more than could, with the best will in the world, be accomplished. Speaking at the lunch given for me by the Polish Government, he declared that it was the moral duty of our own generation, which had lived through World War II, not to bequeath the younger generation anything capable of provoking renewed conflict. The tragic cycle of war, misery and injustice which had so far bedevilled the history of German-Polish relations must be broken and the abyss between the Polish and the German people bridged. There was an awareness of the fact that 'in the name of the Federal Republic of Germany, the treaty has been signed by a man who, at the very outset of fascism's assumption of power, grasped the boundless misfortune which would flow from it for the German nation, for the nations of Europe, and for peace in the world'. I responded as follows:

In signing the treaty, we have undertaken to terminate something and signal a beginning at the same time . . . I know that we cannot by today's act fill the chasm that has so brutally been torn open. I also know that understanding and reconciliation cannot be decreed by politicians but must mature in the hearts of people on both sides . . . My government accepts the consequences of history. Conscience and insight have led us to conclusions without which we should not have come here, but no one can expect me to shoulder more, from the political, legal and moral aspect, than is consistent with insight and conviction . . .

On the evening of the same day I played host at the Wilanow Palace, my temporary residence by courtesy of the Polish Government. Like so many other historic Polish buildings, this gem of Baroque architecture had been admirably restored. There could have been no more splendid setting, nor one that better recalled the German-Polish ties of bygone days. We dined in the banqueting-hall of Augustus the Strong of Saxony, who had also been King of Poland. I said in my after-dinner speech that when two nations had lived in such close contact as ours, and had done so through all the vicissitudes of history, they should not shrink from taking up the common elements in their cultural heritage and fructifying them in their future relations.

In looking ahead, I would ask that we acknowledge the things achieved by members of both nations before the onset of barbarism. They live on primarily in the spiritual domain, and they live on in what you have painstakingly reconstructed with a respect for history. If we summon up the courage, the strength and the humility to say yes, nothing of spiritual substance will be lost and our two nations may end by gaining something . . . There is only one way: our frontiers must bring less division and less sorrow.

I went on to recall my conversations with Charles de Gaulle, who had referred not only to Germany and France but to Germany and Poland. 'We agreed that the nations of Europe would, in their identity, discover a grand perspective for our continent . . . I know that there are only European, not isolated, answers to our national problems. That is another reason for my presence here.'

Cyrankiewicz affirmed, as Gomulka had done at Zabrze (Hindenburg) a few days earlier, that the present atmosphere should be regarded as heralding a climate conducive to co-operation between our countries. There might come a time when 7 December 1970 was accounted a historic date.

Wladyslaw Gomulka, the Party leader, attended all these functions. He looked like a strict but amiable schoolmaster, and it was hard to credit him with the toughness he had shown when directing communist resistance to the Nazi occupation, spending years in prison (during the post-war Stalinist period), standing up to Khrushchev in October 1956, and – last but not least – stifling intellectual activity in the years following the 'October spring'. Gomulka had been responsible, with Cyrankiewicz, for the socialist-communist merger at the end of 1946. Originally a Galician artisan, he joined the left-wing youth movement and engaged in revolutionary trade union activities at an early age. This earned him several lengthy prison terms but spared him the fate of those Polish communists who were liquidated while in exile in Moscow. He became leader of his illegal party during the war and was a member of the provisional Lublin government when it ended. In 1948 he swam against the tide and was charged with 'right-wing deviations' (overemphasizing national characteristics and defending Tito). After spending the years 1951–5 in prison without trial, he was readmitted to the Party and resumed its leadership during the crisis of October 1966. He then stood up to the Moscow authorities, who were toying with the idea of intervention, and either sanctioned or positively encouraged a series of 'liberalizing' measures. Although most of these were revoked and his dependence on the Soviet authorities became exceptionally close in the years that followed,

I suspect that Gomulka has been too harshly judged. Certainly, his economic difficulties had assumed proportions of which I was quite unaware during my official visit.

Gomulka sat next me at every Warsaw function, so we were able to exchange views on a wide range of topics. After the Wilanow dinner he chatted easily to journalists in a way which the German correspondents found sensational and described as such. ('In Warsaw during the past twenty-four hours,' one newspaperman reported, 'Germans and Poles have drawn closer in human terms than they have ever done at any other meeting between German politicians and our former adversaries in war.') Nobody suspected that the boss of the People's Republic had only three more weeks in office. The man who had been arrested as a 'Titoist' in 1948 – who had armed the citizens of Warsaw in defiance of pressure from Khrushchev in 1956 – ordered striking workers to be fired on at Gdynia in 1970.

Table-talk apart, Gomulka and I had a chance to converse at length on the afternoon of 7 December. It was not, I must add, an exchange of views in the real sense. The First Secretary of the Polish United Workers' Party spoke for two hours; my response to his remarks took an hour. After these monologues, little time remained for dialogue.

The First Secretary impressed me during this encounter as an elderly man who, though unable to conceal his spiritual wounds entirely, was striving for a businesslike settlement in the interests – as he saw them – of his country. Applying himself first to the problems of ratification, he said that some circles in the Federal Republic were debating whether to approve the Warsaw treaty and leave our treaty with the Russians in abeyance. Nobody who entertained such ideas should ignore the facts, and one of them was that both our countries belonged to political and military alliances. All preparations for further moves must be made on this basis. Any attempt to detach Poland from the Warsaw Pact alliance, let alone drive a wedge between Poland and the Soviet Union, was doomed to failure – just as neither Poland nor the Soviet Union had any intention of weakening our links with our Western partners. In any case, the Moscow treaty had been concluded first. The Polish Government assumed that both treaties would be ratified simultaneously or in quick succession.

Continuing, Gomulka said that to make ratification dependent on West Berlin might delay it for a long time – at worst, for years. The United States might block the quadripartite talks. What would the Federal Republic do then? (He remarked in passing that the Federal Republic probably wielded more influence over its allies and had greater scope for independent initiatives than Poland, which was 'a comparatively weak country' in relation to its partners.) Would I care to state my views on the Berlin question? It was conceivable that the GDR would in due course submit proposals, possibly through the Soviet Union, which the Federal Republic could define as satisfactory. (It was reasonable to assume that Gomulka's remarks had been influenced by consultations with Ulbricht. A Party leaders' conference had recently been held in East Berlin, where the Poles had obtained the go-ahead for an establishment of diplomatic relations between us – once the treaty had been ratified – irrespective of the progress of our negotiations with the GDR.) Our relations with Prague, Gomulka went on, should be relatively easy to adjust; those between the two German states undoubtedly presented greater difficulty. Normalization would have to be based on the Moscow statement of intent. It worried the Warsaw Pact countries that the Federal Republic had so far declined to conclude a transit treaty with the GDR, which desired a reasonable accommodation. Any notions of isolating the GDR in the course of certain political undertakings were erroneous and unrealistic; no Warsaw Pact country would permit the GDR to be isolated. Would it not be possible, before the Moscow and Warsaw treaties were ratified, for both German states to agree on a joint declaration that they aspired to membership of the United Nations? He could not grasp the difference between formal recognition in terms of international law and recognition of statehood. It meant nothing to him, not being a lawyer, but he did not think that formal recognition would exert a decisive influence either. Although he was not entitled to speak for the GDR, he could well imagine that progress would be made if we first concluded a transit treaty and then prepared to reach further agreements.

On German-Polish relations, ratification must be accompanied and succeeded by further advances towards normality. He agreed that this would be a lengthy process. Poland had an Opposition too. It was not as vocal in the press as that of Western countries but transmitted its views through other channels. He foresaw substantial opportunities for co-operation, primarily economic. Unofficial discussions with our firms, industrial organizations and chambers of commerce might be conducive to the development of effective methods. We should also devote special attention to joint projects in third countries.

Gomulka then turned to the knotty problem of compensation, saying that it had not been fully discussed during the treaty negotiations. Where reparations were concerned, Poland's 1953 renunciation still held good. He was reluctant to go into the compensation issue because the time might not yet be ripe, but he did wish to make a suggestion without expecting an immediate reply. He had told me last night that roughly ten million Poles would be entitled to compensation if the West German restitution laws were applied. Working on this basis, experts had arrived at a figure of DM180,000 million. Well, experts were there to do sums, whereas what mattered was a political solution. He was neither serving notice that ten million cases would be documented nor pressing for a lump-sum indemnity, which would only cause contention over the sums due to individual claimants. Instead, he was toying with the idea of declaring the compensation problem settled if we saw our way clear to granting Poland a substantial ten-year credit (interest-free or at two per cent maximum, but repayable annually). This would enable Poland to press ahead with its economic development and promote a manifold exchange of experts at the same time. He also saw it as a prophylactic measure, being anxious to conclude agreements on long-term economic co-operation before the EEC became integrated still further. If I found his proposal unacceptable – and he repeated that it was only an idea – would I kindly regard it as never submitted? The subject in question would then have to remain open.

This confidential exposé presumably accounts for subsequent Polish statements to the effect that Gomulka intended in 1970 to propose settling the 'humanitarian complex' by means of extensive trade credits, and that others had dissuaded him. The Polish Government had, in fact, confirmed during the treaty talks that Poland had formally renounced reparations in 1953. Gomulka commented that the 1953 declaration had referred to 'Germany as a whole' and that his government adhered to it. On the periphery of the negotiations, the Poles said they assumed that it would be possible to discuss compensation for injuries sustained by Polish concentration camp inmates and labour conscripts. (Thanks to the agreement reached by Federal Chancellor Schmidt and First Secretary Gierek at Helsinki in summer 1975, this subject required no further discussion.)

I did not find it hard to answer the political questions posed by Gomulka. I hoped that the treaties would be approved by a large majority but was determined, if need be, to get them ratified by a small one. I did not myself espouse the idea of giving precedence to the Warsaw treaty, which had been advanced by well-meaning Polish journalists. We certainly had no intention of splitting the Eastern bloc. I set forth our attitude to Berlin, the GDR and the outstanding treaty with Czechoslovakia but also conveyed some hints on how to assess the European Community, the Western Alliance and force reductions as an element in European security. We were naturally interested in economic co-operation, but government credits and subsidized interest rates presented a difficult problem, as our relations with the

Soviet Union had already shown.

I left Gomulka in no doubt that a solution of the kind he envisaged would present us with grave difficulties. Any form of compensation, indirect included, would have to be legally viewed in relation to the London Debt Agreement. There would be fears of a chain reaction in the Federal Republic. Besides, a major psychological factor operated in the special case of Poland. The Poles had suffered terribly, but large tracts of German territory had been transferred to them after the war. Our refugees and expellees had been forced to abandon property of incalculable value. I told Gomulka that to raise his proposal might provoke distasteful arguments. I would, however, discuss it privately with a few of my colleagues in Bonn.

It should be remembered in this connection that the Federal Republic's restitution agreements were restricted to Western countries and the Jewish domain including the state of Israel. An exception was made for victims of medical experiments, who in Poland received DM140 million. While Foreign Minister, I had helped to overcome bureaucratic resistance and bring about a settlement with the aid of the Red Cross. The subsequent agreement on compensation for German social security contributions paid by Polish conscript workers did not come up for discussion during the treaty negotiations but was mooted while I still held the Chancellorship. I did find it reasonable - irrespective of the scale on which Gomulka was thinking - that we should render indirect aid conducive to the development of economic relations. Polish wishes apart, our policy was handicapped by the dogma that inhibited the relevant Bonn departments from emulating the practice of other countries and giving consideration in certain instances to credits with government-backed interest rates.

On the afternoon of 8 December I held a press conference at the Hotel Europejski. Cyrankiewicz had asked if I would be agreeable to his taking part, and I welcomed the idea. (One reporter described this first joint appearance by the heads of government of one NATO and one Warsaw Pact country as a 'world première'.) I said that I and my companions had been deeply moved by our stay in Warsaw, and that I deduced from newspaper reports that people at home in the Federal Republic had been gripped by the same emotion. The Polish premier told correspondents: 'I agree with Willy Brandt's remarks. You can take it that what the Federal Chancellor has said goes for me too.' He went on to say that, although life might now become easier for both countries, the road to complete normalization would be difficult and necessitate the overcoming of many prejudices. 'If the treaty finds support among the bulk of society in the Federal Republic of Germany, it will be our joint victory over the past.'

Although I had seen little of Warsaw when we flew back to Bonn on the evening of 8 December, it was enough to convince me of the Poles' immense achievements in the field of reconstruction. What had arisen on the ruins of old Warsaw was a city in which, disregarding a few Stalinist monstrosities, the spirit of history seemed to have been resurrected.

Each of the two principal German religious communities had helped, psychologically, to prepare for the treaty. Writing on my return to Bishop Dietzfelbinger, president of the Council of the Evangelical Church in Germany, I said: 'It is my dearest wish that all Germans should join in the quest for reconciliation. I thank you, in particular, for having once more underlined the role of the expellees, from whom the greatest sacrifice is demanded but whose contribution will also prove to be decisive.' I wrote to Cardinal Döpfner, chairman of the German Bishops' Conference, as follows: 'You voice my innermost thoughts when you say that reconciliation between peoples cannot be effected by politicians alone but necessitates a contribution from individuals and groups in each nation. This is precisely what I meant when I said [in Warsaw] that understanding, or indeed reconciliation, cannot be decreed by politicians but must mature in the hearts of people on both sides.'

I had, however, been mistaken in assuming that the prejudice-laden tide of opposition would soon recede. On the contrary, it gained new strength. My one consolation was that the bulk of the expellees, like other victims of the war, declined to be mobilized for purposes of hostile protest. Many letters bore this out. I also took to heart some advice given me by a woman whose own fate it had been to suffer expulsion: she solicited my sympathy for those who levelled hurtful remarks at me because these sprang from the kind of sorrow that blinded people to a long-disguised reality. I was particularly impressed by a message from a group comprising some of the best-known names in the old East German aristocracy. With it came a small sculpture entitled *The Warning* which has stood in my study ever since.

A few weeks after our visit, internal difficulties precipitated a change in the Polish leadership. The government came to grief over food shortages, a problem which it tried to surmount by raising prices. Strikes and demonstrations resulted. The danger was spotlighted by a show of force, and unrest threatened to spread throughout the country. Under these circumstances, the government team resolved that Edward Gierek, who had won his spurs in the province of Katowice, should be appointed to lead the Party. Gomulka was pensioned off and Cyran-kiewicz took over as chairman of the Council of State for a transitional period. This time, nobody adopted the time-honoured expedient of blaming the crisis on the German Federal Republic.

The new leadership was quick to approve the existing line in foreign policy. The Warsaw treaty received a special mention. Nevertheless, it made at least an atmospheric difference that co-operation pursuant to the treaty no longer depended on the men with whom it had been laboriously negotiated. Gierek, who was doubtless better acquainted than most with conditions in Silesia (his forebears came from the environs of Breslau and had moved to Upper Silesia), could be expected to take the economic and administrative problems of resettlement very seriously and favour a restrictive interpretation of the Polish 'State-ment'.

For their part, the Poles may have been disappointed by the dilatory treatment accorded the Warsaw treaty in the Federal Republic. They were not alone. I myself was dismayed by the blinkered and acrimonious debate that ensued at home. As in the case of the Moscow treaty, it exposed us to the risk of killing off the positive moves whereby we hoped to surmount the past and dispel a petty, legalistic attitude. Major initiatives in the sphere of economic co-operation could not be followed up. Political exchanges of views between the two governments remained predominantly routine. It would have been important to convey to Warsaw that we recognized it as an independent decision-making centre. Above all, we should have avoided making the Poles feel that they were being treated like an appendage of a greater power. In making these critical remarks, I realize that some of them are levelled at myself. I should have taken it for granted that my own policy would only be implemented in part. An understanding on the material content of outstanding questions could have been achieved earlier than summer 1975 had those involved shown a greater readiness to co-operate.

Gierek and I never met, though the possibility was mooted on several occasions. When I visited Brezhnev in the Crimea during September 1971, the Poles asked whether I could fly home via Warsaw. As I have already mentioned, other commitments rendered this impossible. In autumn 1972 we inquired whether Gierek could stop off in Bonn on his way home from a visit to France, but Warsaw felt that the occasion was inadequate from the protocol aspect. I did not fully realize at the time that such a visit would have been regarded as some-thing unique in the annals of German-Polish relations. When Brezhnev visited Bonn in May 1973, he mentioned that Gierek had expressed a wish to visit the Federal Republic after him. I replied that we would be happy to welcome him after the summer recess. This suggestion, too, came to nothing because the agreement reached by our Foreign Ministers at the end of 1973 (on a credit, on compensation for social security contributions, and on resettlement) was not of long duration.

During the final weeks of my Chancellorship, efforts were made on the Polish side to resume a dialogue 'at party level'. Ryszcard Frelek, the Party Secretariat member responsible for external affairs, brought me a long message from Gierek in April 1974. I was only able to acknowledge it by word of mouth, not answer it in detail.

It is hard to explain why our treaty with Czechoslovakia was not concluded until three years after the signing of the Warsaw treaty in December 1970. By the time it eventually was, our treaties with the Soviet Union and the People's Republic of Poland had been ratified, the Berlin Agreement and the inter-state Basic Treaty were in force, the two German states had become members of the United Nations, and East and West had consulted at Foreign Minister level in Helsinki. What delayed the development of relations between Bonn and Prague?

I must frankly confess that, after the Moscow-Warsaw-Berlin package, we concentrated less on Prague than on our basic relationship with the GDR, which came higher in our scale of interests. It emerged after the elections late in 1972 that the difficulties besetting our relations with Czechoslovakia were not material, but reposed solely in the emotionally charged problem of the 1938 Munich Agreement. On the other hand, there is no doubt that the inflexibility of the Prague negotiators stemmed partly from the difficulties of the government and the party that sustained it. Even though several years had passed since August 1968, these had still to be surmounted.

It is unlikely that the Soviet Government urged Prague to postpone the establishment of normal relations with the Federal Republic. Brezhnev conveyed the opposite impression – not, of course, that this implies that Prague was encouraged to negotiate in haste. In August 1970 Brezhnev told me he thought that the ground for negotiations with Czechoslovakia had been 'prepared'. Gomulka said in December that he saw no insuperable obstacles where Prague was concerned. Brezhnev also discussed Sudeten German problems – which he confessed he only partly understood – with the Czechoslovak Party leader, Gustav Husak, before I visited Oreanda in September 1971. At Bonn in May 1973 he told me he thought the time was ripe 'to get rid of the damned Munich Agreement' and that Husak had twice stated his willingness to meet us half-way.

There can be no doubt that East Berlin supported the opposing faction in the Czechoslovak leadership – partly, one presumes, from a wish to show the Russians that the rulers of the GDR also had a say. It was one of their *idées fixes* that the Berlin settlement had been reached at their expense. This was a devious way of demonstrating that they were not devoid of influence in the Eastern bloc and perfectly capable of rocking the boat.

The existence of such wheels within wheels became clear after Foreign Minister Scheel and his Slovak opposite number, Bohuslav Chnoupek, had initialled the treaty in Bonn in June 1973. Despite this, the Prague signing had to be deferred for months. The reason was the so-called West Berlin clause on which, in conformity with the Quadripartite Agreement, we were obliged to insist. Debate centred on the partial question of how the German Federal Republic could represent the interests of West Berlin and guarantee its citizens inter-jurisdictional assistance. This point was briefly raised when I met Gromyko in New York at the end of September and we sat next to each other at a dinner given by UN Secretary-General Waldheim. The Soviet Foreign Minister thought we ought to settle the matter. Agreement on guaranteeing interjurisdictional assistance in regard to West Berlin courts was not reached until Scheel visited Moscow at the end of October and negotiated a compromise formula which Prague accepted too: it was agreed to resolve each problem as it arose, employing the normal channels for interjurisdictional assistance.

It was not until 11 December that Scheel and I could fly to Prague to sign the 'Treaty on Mutual Relations'. Our opposite numbers were the Czech premier, Dr Lubomir Strougal, and Foreign Minister Chnoupek. It was cold and dank when we landed in Prague, but the depressing atmosphere could not be attributed to the weather alone: the feel of the place was generally unpleasant. I have seldom seen such an array of security men, many in plain clothes, as I did on the drive from the airport to the city. Solely for my protection? If so, against whom? I did not go down from the castle where I was lodged into the city of which I preserved such agreeable memories from my earlier visits, but I did pay tribute to the victims of persecution and war by laying a wreath at the foot of the equestrian statue of John Ziska, the one-eyed Hussite general who had defeated the forces of Emperor Sigismund. I abandoned my intention of meeting a group of Prague intellectuals because I might only have got them into trouble.

It was regrettable that our visit threatened to become so super-ficially routine a proceeding. The history and antecedents of the meeting deserved attention and commitment, bearing in mind the common German-Slav heritage in Bohemia, the twin tragedies of occupation and expulsion, and our new joint venture into the realm of good-neighbourly relations. Memories of 1968 – of blighted hopes and hardened attitudes – could not, of course, be suppressed, but we had to demonstrate that the road to détente should be pursued still further.

The treaty itself, which had been negotiated by State Secretary Paul Frank and Deputy Foreign Minister Jiri Götz, referred in its preamble to the determination of both parties 'to put an end, once and for all, to the disastrous past . . . above all in connection with the Second World War, which inflicted immeasurable sufferings on the European peoples'. It also stated that 'the Munich Agreement of 29 September 1938 was imposed on the Czechoslovak Republic by the National Socialist régime under the threat of force', though the preamble acknowledged that 'a new generation has grown up, which is entitled to a secure and peaceful future'.

The crucial article stated that both countries considered the Munich Agreement null and void 'under the terms of this treaty in regard to their mutual relations'. This was the compromise formula between *ex tunc* and *nunc* over which international lawyers had contended for so long – and not for the mere joy of learned hair-splitting. The next article supplied three important interpretations of this. First, the treaty did not affect the legal consequences arising with regard to private persons and legal entities from the laws applied in the period 30 September 1938 to 9 May 1945. Excepted from this were the consequences of measures which both contracting parties considered null and void by reason of their incompatibility with the basic principles of justice. Secondly, the treaty did not affect the citizenship of persons alive or dead where it derived from the legal system of either party to the treaty. Thirdly, the treaty and its declarations on the Munich Agreement did not constitute a legal basis for material claims by the CSSR (and its natural and juristic persons).

These legal formulas related to practical problems. After the Munich Agreement and the incorporation of the Sudeten territories in the 'Reich', numerous opponents of Hitler were arrested. Sudeten German *Reichsangehörige* [second-class Reich citizens] were later – whether pro-Hitler or not – conscripted into the Wehrmacht. More than three million Germans had been expelled from their native land. We could not allow it to be inferred from a treaty concluded with ourselves that the Czechoslovak authorities were entitled to regard these Germans as traitors after the event – something which might have had dire practical consequences.

At dinner in the Castle, Premier Strougal testified to his government's genuine desire to make a fresh start despite 'historical experiences . . . which cannot be erased from the memory of our citizens'. He spoke of the 'friendly atmosphere' in which our meeting had taken place. I replied that 'the common foundation on which further development can build should not now be restricted by one-sided interpretations. I say this advisedly, because my government regards the treaty as another major element in our endeavours for a lasting system of peace'. I recalled that this was not my first visit to Prague.

Between my first visit at the end of 1936 and that of today lie several decades which have changed the face of Europe. They have left their mark on us all. Nobody can escape his past, his history. Only he who faces it will be able to convert it into something positive and constructive. This does not apply to the darkness of the 'thirties . . . Deep-rooted mistrust cannot be eradicated overnight. It is continually stirring – for how much longer, no one can tell. This renders our joint task doubly important.

Prague, I went on, was not a city which left the visitor unmoved.

It confers a special awareness of our European commitment – the burden and, at the same time, the positive obligation laid upon us by a history which displays so many links and associations . . . Few cities have been as privileged and few have suffered as greatly or seen as much light and shadow. The same can be said, in a figurative sense, about the relations between our peoples . . . We should be blind to the truth were we not to venture to speak of that which is associated with a common history.

Next day I gave a lunch at the Czernin Palace, where I again recalled the shared experiences of our peoples. There was a widespread recognition today that the tragedies of our own century were, among other things, an endeavour to evade the obligations of European destiny and European responsibility.

You will forgive me if personal recollections obtrude at such moments. They do not date solely from the time when refugees from the German Reich sought refuge in your country, hoping to continue the struggle until able to return home. I am also thinking of those who, during the years after the war and that which followed it, have striven for reconciliation and co-operation. And a special salute is due to those who are intellectually active on both sides of the border and who would, I know, welcome closer mutual contact . . .

Replying, Strougal agreed that his country had more than once been a point of intersection between the historical currents which had created 'towering billows' in the development of our continent.

You referred to the disgraceful Munich *Diktat*, which heralded the darkest years in our eventful common history – years in which our peoples were threatened with physical annihilation. Lidice's crown of thorns, which symbolizes the sufferings of our people under the Nazi yoke, has become an enduring memento, and not for the peoples of Czechoslovakia alone . . .

Speaking on television from the 'Golden City', in which one encounters – compressed into a few square miles – so many relics of the grandeur and misery by which Europe has been fashioned, I once more addressed a special word to the Germans who had lost their homes in Czechoslovakia. In signing the treaty, I had been conscious of the sum of suffering represented by what had actually preceded it – 'of the suffering inflicted on Czechs and Slovaks by the brutality of self-styled supermen. Of the suffering of the Germans who have had to pay a terrible price for the injustice of Nazism . . .' I repeated what I had said in Moscow and Warsaw: the treaty did not sanction wrongs already committed, nor did it imply that we were legitimizing expulsions after the event. But 'yesterday's guilt, which no words can banish, will not be strong enough to deter our peoples from venturing upon reconciliation'.

The treaty itself, like the parallel agreements, affirmed the renunciation of force and the inviolability of common frontiers. An agreement to exchange ambassadors was also concluded on the day of signing. Apart from exchanging letters with Berlin, the Foreign Ministers laid down procedures for dealing with humanitarian problems such as emigration requests and travel facilities. The Czechs submitted a letter stating their position in regard to criminal prosecution (no statutory time-limit on war crimes and crimes against humanity, for which their law provides the death penalty).

Before the signing I had a talk with Dr Gustav Husak, Dubček's successor as First Secretary (who additionally assumed the Presidency in spring 1975). The then head of state, General Ludvik Svoboda, received us briefly but with great cordiality. Although unable to contribute much to the discussion, the old and ailing President was clearly glad to have assisted at the birth of the treaty. In 1972, when negotiations were lagging, he had spoken of 'good-neighbourship' with the German Federal Republic. Many of his compatriots thought he had been too accommodating towards interventionist and communistically 'conservative' circles in his own country, not only at the Kremlin in August 1968 but thereafter. However, no objective account can overlook the fact that he performed his statesmanly duties with a courage which extended to personal commitment on behalf of individual victims of persecution. He certainly thought in military rather than political terms, nor should one forget that he commanded the Czechoslovak units on the Soviet side during World War II. This may have bred a special sense of loyalty.

I found Gustav Husak an agreeable person to talk to. One could tell that he had suffered a great deal (he had, after all, spent nine years in prison). He also conveyed a hint of resignation. Even from Bonn, I had got the feeling that he wanted to help his country along as Kádár had managed to do in Hungary during the difficult post-1956 years. He was undoubtedly distressed by the opposition and mistrust of many of his fellow-countrymen. I well remember that his response to my plea for mercy on behalf of several convicted Germans was far from stereotyped and inflexible. He would see what he could do, he said – 'I know myself what it means to be in prison'.

The premier's critical compatriots regarded him as the intellectual superior of the group that conducted the fateful negotiations in Moscow during August 1968. Husak bore a considerable responsibility for the agreements reached there. He solicited acceptance of the Kremlin's demands, first at the Slovak Party Congress and then in the Prague Central Committee. His critics accused him of ambition and excessive deference to Moscow. Husak himself may rather have felt that he was making the best of a given set of galling circumstances, on the principle that someone had to do the job. I recognize the dubious nature of this attitude.

Once the Prague treaty was signed, the trade missions in Budapest and Sofia could finally – still in December 1973 – be converted into embassies. No special treaties were required in the case of Hungary and Bulgaria.

We still maintained no official contacts with Albania. Even if we had been very eager to establish such relations, it is doubtful whether the Chinese themselves could have helped to bring them about.

Our relations with the People's Republic of China had been regularized during a visit by Foreign Minister Scheel in October 1972. We agreed to exchange ambassadors and shortly afterwards reinforced our already appreciable economic links with a trade agreement.

This accorded with our interests. I harboured no anti-Chinese prejudices. On the contrary, I regretted the fact that China had been virtually ignored by previous Federal Governments and that we had conformed far more than necessary to the guide-lines issued by Washington. As Foreign Minister, I had advocated China's inclusion in schemes for international co-operation. On the other hand, I had always been opposed to the visionaries who thought we could promote or even replace our *Ostpolitik* with a Far East policy, heedless of the extent to which they overestimated the political capabilities of the German Federal Republic. One sometimes felt that they were painfully converting themselves into the instruments of an unrealistic Machiavellism of which no one could be sure that it had ever existed in the form they dreamed of. When Franz Josef Strauss styled himself a friend of Mao, it was not fortuitous that he should have been showered with applause by those whose conception of a 'strong' German policy had been a Far East alliance – except that China now took the place of Japan. They saw the key to all politics in the same old foolish formula which decrees that my enemy's enemy and my neighbour's neighbour must be my friend. (In this connection, I liked to recall a little anecdote of war-time vintage. A German father gave his twelve-year-old son a globe for Christmas and pointed out the relative positions of Germany, Russia and America. 'But Daddy,' the boy exclaimed, 'doesn't the Führer know?')

Hostility towards the Chinese people and its communist leaders had always been alien to me, little though I sympathized with the excesses of the 'cultural revolution' and incomprehensible as I found the attitude of those who extolled in Peking what they condemned in Europe. I clung to the realistic view that China could not replace the Soviet Union as a collaborator in the tasks we had been assigned in Europe and Germany. I also felt that the Federal Republic should not be involved in an unnecessary clash with the United States, Japan and India.

The situation had, of course, changed by 1971–2. I have already mentioned that Nixon gave me notice of a new US policy towards China in 1970, and that Brezhnev hinted to me in 1971 that he would prefer us not to concern ourselves with Peking. I pointed out in my address when accepting the Nobel Peace Prize at the end of 1971 that mighty China was, apart from all else, a developing country and a nuclear power combined. I also said on the same occasion that the People's Republic's admission to the organized community of nations did not, in my view, portend a transition to tripolarity because 'there are more centres of political power than two or three'. Addressing a UNICEF conference three years later, I paid tribute to the truly remarkable achievements of the Chinese, who, unlike wide areas of the developing world, had succeeded by their own efforts in conquering the threat of starvation. I now propose to recount how our approach to the China problem was modified, primarily by our main allies.

When I visited Nixon in spring 1970 he told me that, apart from the US-Chinese ambassadorial discussions in Warsaw, the two countries maintained 'a few other contacts as well'. He also said that chances of establishing better relations should not be altogether discounted, though there could be no question of abandoning Taiwan. The President fully concurred when I said that, in view of our current interests, we did not wish the Russians to gain the impression that we intended to make trouble for them by way of Peking. In June 1971 Nixon said he was unconcerned whether China entered the UN at once or in the next six months. I commented that, in the US President's place, I too would be striving for an accommodation with China, but that our own primary concern was to reach one with the Soviet Union. I was also bound to state that China was trying to 'dally' with East Berlin. Nixon replied that he entirely understood the priorities governing German diplomacy, and that America would likewise have far more to do with the Soviet Union than China. Following this talk in Washington, I told a press conference that – as I had long ago pointed out when Foreign Minister – China not only should but would assume its rightful place in international politics. This would naturally entail the appropriate practical and formal consequences for the German Federal Republic as well. Everything depended on timing – and clearly, Peking was in no hurry either.

In summer 1971 Kissinger embarked on his first sensational trip to China, of which we were notified. Nixon's spectacular visit followed in February 1972. Shortly before, during our discussions in Florida, I had again informed the President of our desire to normalize relations with Peking as soon as the time was ripe. In view of our impending accession to the United Nations, we had to consider Communist China's role as a permanent member of the Security Council. Nixon undertook to bear this point in mind during his Peking visit. The People's Republic of China had been admitted to the United Nations at the end of 1971, but I was greatly concerned at the ruthless way in which Taiwan had been shown the door. Where would things end if the world organization began to breach the principle of universality in so arbitrary a manner?

Relations with China were naturally a matter for consultation between us and our West European partners. They accepted that we needed better relations with the Soviet Union before we could tackle our relationship with China. In December 1971 I drew Pompidou's attention to the blatant way in which the Chinese were trying to intrigue with the GDR, partly against us and partly against the Soviet Union, *inter alia* by arguing that Moscow had let its East German allies down over the Berlin Agreement. Being interested in the European Community, however, they would eventually have to come back to us. Reverting to the subject early in 1972, I said that a country which aspired to good relations with the European Community must logically be bound to maintain normal relations with its member-states. No doubt this hint was passed on and duly taken.

The subject of China cropped up in many other conversations, especially with visitors from Asia and Africa. I have already mentioned Brezhnev, but Tito's views were also of interest. Sometimes Peking's favourite target for attacks on 'revisionism', the Yugoslavs passed through phases in which they genuinely feared that the Chinese leaders were flirting with the idea of a major war. There were also subsequent periods when Belgrade gladly accepted conciliatory gestures from Peking. I was informed that West European communists sometimes wondered if they had been too uncritical in accepting Big (Soviet) Brother's verdict on China. They displayed a growing reluctance to take part in wholesale condemnations of the Peking 'heresy'.

I had one more exhaustive discussion on China with Pompidou at the end of 1973. The French President had sought to gather first-hand impressions during his state visit to Peking. He also said that reports reaching him from there had for some time been almost exclusively concerned with the Soviet threat. This, he surmised, was partly attributable to personal feuds and jealousies at the highest level. In addition, the Chinese leaders showed themselves particularly allergic to anything that might reinforce a US-Soviet condominium. Viewed from the Chinese standpoint, the American super-power was showing a tendency to retreat whereas the Russian super-power was expanding still further. For this reason, Peking had recently developed some sympathy for the Americans. The Russians were an object of fear, but Pompidou also believed that this attitude served a useful secondary purpose in that it reinforced internal Chinese unity. Mao looked old and ill, but his mind was still alert. Chou En-lai, who held the reins of government, made a youthful impression. One sensed his firm determination not to rush things; he was permeated by the idea that China had time to spare. The younger politicians in the leadership spoke of

Mao and Chou with respect, but one sensed that it was based on their past achievements.

I told the French President that the Chinese had inquired when they might welcome me to their country, but that a visit would hardly be feasible before autumn 1974. Preparations were in progress when I resigned the Chancellorship in May of that year. My successor actually made the visit in autumn 1975 (and brought me greetings from Chairman Mao).

In September 1973 the Federal Republic of Germany and the GDR were admitted to the United Nations Organization. We had gained support for our view that the two German states could only become UN members if they did so simultaneously and if all-German status under international law were expressly preserved – additional confirmation of the special German position. I regretted the fact that, despite our co-operation with special UN agencies and the not inconsiderable aid we had given to individual programmes, the Federal Republic had adopted a somewhat wary attitude towards the UN because of fears that influences might arise there to threaten 'inviolable' positions in our policy towards Germany. There then ensued a period which warranted genuine concern that those who branded the Federal Republic 'imperialist' might muster a majority – whatever its motives – to oppose our accession. Unfortunately, this danger was not universally apparent. By the time the question of membership finally arose in connection with our Eastern treaties, the UN was on the threshold of a turmoil which threatened its continued existence.

During the world parliament's early post-war years, Washington could command a majority of countries – or rather, of votes – if it came to the pinch. Dominance then appeared to pass to the Soviet bloc. What really dominated after the influx of more and more young countries was a rather diffuse majority whose decisions were often based on protest and prone to numerous contradictions. I thus felt rather sceptical about the international assembly's practical utility and capacity for effective action in the foreseeable future. I realized at the same time that it did fulfil a useful function as a point of reshipment for ideas, information and views, that it had proved its worth by keeping the peace in a series of crises, and that a number of its specialized agencies were performing valuable work. It is probably not too late for the realization to dawn that co-operation between fluctuating numbers of countries tends to be more fruitful than a negative use of rigid majorities, which are apt to turn into veto-machines or demand the impossible of the minority. A world parliament which observed the law of the united front would condemn itself to paralysis.

Walter Scheel had travelled to New York for the Federal Republic's accession to the United Nations, which our German policy had made possible. Addressing the General Assembly on 26 September 1973, I said that I spoke as a German and a European. 'More precisely, my people inhabit two states but have not ceased to regard themselves as a nation. At the same time, although our part of Europe has yet to become much more than an economic community, it will grow into a European Union during the present decade.' I added that I had not come to use the United Nations as a wailing wall for German problems or make demands which could not in any case be fulfilled there. We had come to assume joint international responsibility on the basis of our beliefs and to the limit of our abilities. Despite their differing social systems and political structures, and bound as they were by treaty and conviction to differing alliances, the two German states had resolved to initiate a policy of peaceful neighbourliness, of coexistence and – we hoped – of co-operation. 'We shall therefore endeavour to spell out peaceful coexistence in German. Given the thoroughness sometimes ascribed to our national character, I cannot promise that this will always be easy.'

We had been encouraged by the bilateral renunciation of force on which our treaties were founded to embark on a second and multi-lateral phase in European diplomacy. On the basis of what had come about, there must be a genuine change in the relations between European states. The process to which I alluded might some day be regarded as a significant experiment in how countries could learn to curb conflicts and eliminate violence. 'Were we actually to succeed by dint of confidence-building measures in reducing that vast waste of resources which is the product of mistrust between opposing systems, we should have set a historic example.' I spoke of the relationship between the two nuclear super-powers. Neither of them was replaceable in terms of its responsibility, and neither could divest itself of that responsibility. 'That is how our world now finds its equilibrium. But it cannot dispense, in maintaining that difficult balance, with the specific weight of the People's Republic of China, Japan and the European Community. Within this system, the inexchangeable role of Latin America, the African states, the Indian subcontinent and our other partners in Asia is taking effect.'

I was not preaching an existence devoid of conflict and tension; that I regarded as a bloodless illusion.

I am speaking of the fruitless and negative conflicts which daily confirm that man in fear of man is capable of self-destruction. Hardship is conflict. Where hunger reigns, no lasting peace is possible. Where abject poverty reigns, justice is absent. Where the simplest necessities remain daily at risk, there can be no talk of security. There must be no resignation in the face of poverty. There is such a thing as violence by toleration, intimidation by sloth, menacement by passivity, murder by inaction. That is a frontier at which we must not stop short, because it can be the frontier between survival and destruction.

There was a growing awareness of the limitations of our globe. We must not unrestrainedly deplete its resources and continue to poison its biological cycles. Population growth must be kept within justifiable bounds. Nutritional planning was called for on a world scale. 'It makes no difference, morally speaking, whether a human being is condemned to die of starvation by war or indifference. We must make up our minds to break with ritualized traditions: he who wants to banish war must banish hunger too.'

Solidarity, I declared, was the basic requirement of world society and the prerequisite of its survival. 'We condemn racism as an inhuman sentiment and as a source of the most terrible crimes; our own history has become our bitterest experience in this respect.' I affirmed the universality of human rights. A policy based on peace, solidarity and the renunciation of force was indivisible. The good-neighbourly system must prevail over unbridled nationalism – 'perhaps our most dubious legacy from the history of Europe'. The human capacity for reason had made the United Nations possible; the human propensity for unreason made it necessary. Reason would have triumphed if, one day, all countries and regions lived and worked together in a world community governed by the principles of the United Nations. 'I shall not live to see that day, but I should like to help it dawn.'

During the same autumn – 1973 – the European Conference at Helsinki passed through its initial phase 'at Foreign Minister level' and consultations on mutual and balanced force reductions got under way in Vienna. Both these projects have been discussed at various stages in this book, so my personal commitment to them must be obvious. Our bilateral treaties played a big part in their antecedents. The conference itself was delayed by our insistence that relations with the GDR be settled first. The manifold difficulties besetting negotiations in Geneva, especially during the inter-officialdom phase, cannot be recounted here, but they were sometimes attended by a grotesque lack of realism . . .

Since then, the third phase of 'Helsinki' has been completed, leaving behind an aftermath of unease. 'Vienna' still seems to be an ever-receding horizon.

Senior officials had gathered in the Finnish capital in November 1972, followed in July 1973 by the Foreign Ministers of thirty-three European countries (down to the smallest but excluding Albania). Also represented were the United States and Canada. The choice of venue had long been a bone of contention. In May, President Kekkonen had asked me through Rafael Paasio, chairman of the Finnish Social Democrats and erstwhile premier, not to pass Helsinki over. Finland was quite acceptable to me. The Foreign Ministers' speeches were succeeded by expert consultations in Geneva. It was this second phase that took so long. The concluding conference between heads of state and government – the third phase – took place at the end of July 1975. Helsinki's 'Act III' cannot be examined in detail here. I only regret that the initial response to it was so cool. Regardless of all the differences between their political systems and all the compromises whose aid they enlisted, the participating governments finally concurred in some declarations and recommendations which were remarkable compared with the state of Europe in 1945 and the climacterics of the Cold War. There were the inevitable *status quo* passages, pronouncements on non-aggression and the inviolability of frontiers, and tentative moves towards confidence-building measures in the military sphere. There was a large and extensible list of economic and scientifico-technical items. There was also a 'Basket Three' – only filled after long and laborious discussion – devoted to cultural and humanitarian matters and contacts on a personal level. I have reason to believe that the East European leaders did not make things easy for themselves by approving the latter section. Having undoubtedly checked to see what their systems could tolerate, they must have been surprised that the West so largely ignored their own considerations and so often yielded to the illusion that all agreements would be promptly and unreservedly implemented – that the leaders of the Eastern bloc would ultimately decide, in view of the outcome of the conference, to abolish communism at the very least!

Unfortunately, not everyone grasped what it meant that North America's association with Europe had been reaffirmed in a novel way, and not merely by invoking rights of conquest and NATO treaties. The original aim of communist strategy in pressing for this conference had doubtless been quite different, namely, the separation of Europe from America. Far too little note was also taken of the fact that the European Community, so far from being weakened by the CSCE, was strengthened by it. The Community not only proved its worth during the political consultations but, within the limits of its competence, presented itself to the world as a whole composed of many parts.

I cannot, for all that, suppress the bleak realization that Helsinki has become the (rather apathetic) end of an epoch. Neither the Soviet Union nor the West was as prepared for a new phase in their relations as it could and should have been. However, the book has not simply been closed. The results of the conference are to be periodically reviewed, for the first time at a meeting of government representatives in Belgrade in 1977. I have continued to advocate this review and re-examination of results since resigning the Chancellorship, and I hope that it will prove valuable.

In November 1972, interested NATO members proposed to the other side that exploratory talks be held on a mutual and balanced reduction of armed forces. These opened in Vienna during the first half of 1973. Actual negotiations between twelve NATO countries and seven members of the Warsaw Pact began on 30 October. The aim of the NATO negotiators was, and still is, to stabilize the relative strengths of land forces in Central Europe and, if possible, to limit the number of troops and quantity of armaments. The land forces deployed by the participants on both sides in Central Europe are to be roughly equalized. It is intended to achieve this goal by means of equivalent maximum personnel strengths and other stabilizing measures. The principle of balance entails that military and geographical conditions favourable to the Warsaw Pact shall be offset by agreed limitations on troop strengths and offensive capabilities.

The worst that can be said about the Vienna negotiations is that they have failed to prevent the continued growth of armaments, more particularly on the Warsaw Pact side; their best feature is that they have not ground to a halt. They will undoubtedly be of long duration and can only lead, in the first instance, to modest and 'symbolic' progress. Even if the talks yield no swift and spectacular results, however, their very existence is important. MBFR remains a proving-ground for détente.

16

A Change of Direction?

At the end of 1971 I was awarded the Nobel Peace Prize. In February 1972 I became a freeman of my native city, Lübeck. At the end of the year my name was identified with a major success at the polls. A year later I was facing grave difficulties and my capacity for leadership had come under fire. I shall endeavour to recount the changes that occurred in this brief space of time.

The news that the Nobel Committee of the Norwegian Storting [Parliament] had awarded me the Nobel Peace Prize for 1971 reached my office in the parliament building on 20 October. Conny Ahlers brought me the Oslo agency report. Hot on its heels came a telegram from the committee chairwoman and President of the Lagting [Upper House], Aase Lionäs, whom I had known well ever since my years in exile. I did not interrupt my work – I was writing a foreword to a volume of parliamentary speeches by Helmut Schmidt – and many observers concluded from my apparent indifference that I had prior knowledge of the Oslo decision. This was not so. It had merely occurred to me that I might have been short-listed after reading a press report the day before, but I kept the idea to myself. I heard later that the five-member committee had unanimously chosen me from among 39 nominees. I myself had supported a proposal to honour Jean Monnet. After receiving the award I confessed to being embarrassed and made no use of my prize-winner's right of recommendation.

The public reaction was overwhelming. The Bundestag offered its congratulations, my party colleagues being slightly more pleased than the rest. That evening a torchlight procession of young people – not the first or last – appeared outside my house. One of the visitors who dropped in at a late hour was a delighted CDU/CSU ex-colleague from the Grand Coalition cabinet. He showed greater generosity of spirit than those of his colleagues who broadcast the absurd allegation that the Peace Prize had been awarded by a group from the Socialist International. Telegrams and letters poured in from all over the world, from heads of state and schoolchildren, from happy and tormented souls, from a relative of Anne Frank, from victims of war. Many people wrote to tell me that they had regained their pride in Germany. One woman, whose fate had been a harsh one, reminded me of the story of the Red Indian boy who turns to his father after watching a Western and asks 'Do we *never* win?'

Speaking in Oslo, I disclaimed any belief that I had 'won' on behalf of those who were prompted to ask themselves the same question. 'The young man who was once persecuted, driven to Norway and deprived of citizenship, is not now speaking solely on behalf of European peace in general but also, and more especially, for those from whom the past has exacted a heavy toll.' I saluted former members of the Resistance in every land and addressed a word to those of my committed fellow-citizens who took an active interest in people imprisoned for their beliefs or persecuted in other ways. What the bestowal of the prize also meant to me, more than anything else, was a chance to affirm before the world that 'Germany has become reconciled with itself; it has returned to itself just as this exile has been privileged to rediscover the peaceful and humane characteristics of his native land.'

I naturally debated whether I was worthy of the award. That decision must be left to others, but I had long been aware of the problems besetting the choice of prize-winners, especially for services to peace and, in another way, to literature. Whatever the facts of the matter, I was certain of one thing: I could only accept the prize on behalf of many others, and I had above all to include the companions who had rendered me such vital assistance in the foregoing years. That was why I invited Egon Bahr and Walter Scheel to accompany me to Oslo in December. Some of my companions in exile were able to attend the ceremony. Also represented was my native city of Lübeck, where there had been an inter-party dispute over whether to make me a freeman late in 1970 (Berlin came to a decision with less fuss). I asked to be kept out of the Lübeck controversy, being reminded – without intending any comparison – of Thomas Mann, who was not made a freeman until three months before his death in 1955, and then only after many impassioned debates in the House of Burgesses. (Many Lübeckers were incensed by his attitude while in exile, and some of the older ones had never forgiven him for *Buddenbrooks*.)

The Oslo award also reminded me that I had been of some service in getting the 1936 Peace Prize awarded to Carl von Ussietzky. The honouring of this prisoner of the Third Reich was a plain indictment of his Nazi persecutors and tormentors. (Ussietzky was the third and I the fourth German recipient of the Peace Prize, our predecessors being Gustav Stresemann and the pacifist Ludwig Quidde.) In its citation, the Oslo committee expressed a wish to pay tribute to the initiatives I had made towards détente while Foreign Minister and Federal Chancellor. It was aptly stated that I considered West European unification to be an integrative component of a peace plan for Europe as a whole. The committee regarded 'this overall commitment' as a substantial contribution to the strengthening of opportunities for peaceful development, not only in Europe but throughout the world.

My wife and Lars flew with me to Oslo. My daughter Ninja and her husband Jarle joined us from Trondheim and my wife's relations from Hamar. Gerhard Ritzel, our ambassador in Oslo, who had run my office at the Foreign Ministry and Chancellery (and later took over the embassy in Prague), organized a dinner for the Nobel Committee. My friends from the trade unions and Oslo City Council held receptions. I myself played host to a sizeable gathering of people with whom I had been associated in good times and bad. The Norwegian Juvenile Book League, a conservative association, held a torchlight procession outside my hotel. Before the prize-giving ceremony I called on the King, who was confined to the University Hospital. Crown Prince Harald gave a banquet at the palace. All in all, those wintry Norwegian days developed into a gruelling round of festivities which would have taxed a less exhausted man than myself.

My speech of acknowledgement on 10 December was delivered in the well-remembered university auditorium where I had matriculated in 1934. I welcomed the fact that I had been privileged, after the ineffaceable horrors of the past, to bring the name of my country and the desire for peace into accord – indeed, to reduce the words 'Germany' and 'peace' to a common denominator. I recalled that Nobel was supposed to have said, when drawing up his will, that he would leave nothing to men of action because it might tempt them to desist from their labours. Instead, he wanted to help 'dreamers who find it hard to prevail in life'. It was not for me to judge whether the Nobel Committee had made an apt choice, but I served notice that I could not afford to cherish political dreams and had no wish to stop work yet. (I also recalled in an after-dinner speech the same evening that Alfred Nobel in his latter years had described himself as 'a kind of social democrat, but with sundry reservations'. Nobel did in fact subscribe to some modern views on social policy, though his closest associate, Ragnar Sohlman, emphasized that Nobel had been anything but a social democrat in thought, word or deed: 'He was not a democrat at all.')

I said that, if I were credited with having helped to pave the way for a sense of reality in Germany, one of my greatest hopes in life would have been fulfilled. Lecturing on 11 December, I amplified this statement as follows: 'A good German cannot be a nationalist; a good German knows that he cannot forgo his European destiny. Through Europe, Germany is returning home to itself and to the constructive forces in its history. Our Europe, born of the experience of suffering and failure, is the binding commandment of reason.'

Active coexistence should be sustained neither by fear nor by blind faith, but we must also reject the 'fanciful principle' that countries of diverse social and economic composition could not live together without grave conflicts arising. The solution of common problems implied the development of links and bonds through a meaningful process of international co-operation which transcended the frontiers between blocs.

It implies the transformation of conflict. It implies the removal of real or imaginary barriers by taking peaceful risks on each side. It implies the creation of confidence by practical settlements that work. This confidence may then provide the new basis on which old and unsolved problems become soluble. This opportunity may be Europe's opportunity in a world of which it has been demonstrated that it cannot be ruled from Washington, Moscow or Peking alone.

Europe had proved its vitality after the last war; its future still lay ahead of it. It would unite in the West – above and beyond the Economic Community – in such a manner as to be able to assume a share of international responsibility, independent of the USA yet firmly attached to it. There were also opportunities for all-European co-operation and peace-keeping – 'perhaps for something like a European peace partnership; if I were not aware of the practical and theoretical obstacles that have still to be surmounted, I would go so far as to talk of a European peace league'.

It was important to me to state the principle of coexistence – a coexistence worthy of mankind – *vis-à-vis* the champions of orthodoxy on both sides.

Ideologies, their prophets and believers, are for ever disregarding the basic ethical precepts of coexistence because they aspire to improve humanity, preserve doctrinal purity or prevail over other doctrines. No lasting peace can be established between such forces. It is part of a peace policy to impress upon them that neither states nor ideologies are ends in themselves, but that their function is to serve the individual and his purposive self-fulfilment.

Absolute claims were a threat to mankind. Anyone who believed himself to be in possession of the whole truth, anyone who wanted his own conception of paradise here and now, was only too apt to destroy the ground on which a system worthy of mankind could arise. Apart from a humanitarian tendency, the European democratic tradition, too, contained a doctrinaire tendency that led to tyranny and transformed liberation into servitude.

Young people often expect me to utter an unqualified yes, a straight-forward no, but it has become impossible for me to believe in a single truth – in *the* truth. So I say to my young friends and any others who care to listen: there are more truths than one. That is why I believe in diversity and also in doubt. It is productive. It calls what exists into question. It can be strong enough to dissolve petrified injustice. Doubt has proved its worth in opposition. It is tough enough to withstand defeat and bring a victor to his senses . . . As a democratic socialist, I focus my thoughts and activities on change. I have no wish to remodel man because forcing him into a system destroys him, but I do believe in changing the human condition . . .

Nobody suspected at the beginning of 1972 that my government was heading for serious trouble, nor did anyone guess that elections would have to be brought forward to help overcome a parliamentary stalemate. When the Bundestag gave the Eastern treaties their first reading at the end of February, I felt certain that our coalition's slender majority – albeit reduced by the defection of three FDP members the previous autumn – would hold firm. Gomulka had asked me in December 1971 about the attitude of a colleague in our parliamentary group who was chairman of the Silesian Association [of refugees and expellees]. I had replied in all sincerity that he would sooner resign his seat than break faith with me. Gossip had it that a well-known parliamentarian intended to abstain because he could no longer support our foreign policy. Other and more sinister rumours predicted that an attempt would be made to 'entice' members away from the coalition. The first hints of this had appeared in the press as early as autumn 1969.

In April, immediately after the Landtag elections in Baden-Württemberg, which gave the CDU an absolute majority, the CDU/CSU leaders resolved to try and bring the government down with a 'constructive vote of no confidence'. Provided for by the Basic Law, this instrument is designed to obviate negative alliances and stipulates that the Federal Chancellor cannot be voted out of office unless another candidate succeeds in mustering a Bundestag majority by secret ballot. Its success in the south-west regional elections had given the Opposition a one-vote majority in the Bundesrat (Berlin being excluded by reason of its status). Expectations of a change in the composition of the Bundestag, too, encouraged the belief that one or two coalition members would vote for Rainer Barzel.

On 26 April the motion of no confidence was proposed by Kurt Georg Kiesinger. My predecessor accused me of jeopardizing the 'grand design of German national restoration' on the grounds that I had pursued a policy which barred the path to that objective by consolidating or recognizing the European *status quo*. He went on to defend the renegades and characterize his motion as the repudiation of a 'socialist Germany'. I defended myself by listing what I regarded as our not inconsiderable achievements and stressed that, although I did not think it dishonourable to change parties, I questioned whether seats should be arbitrarily filched. 'If the proposers of the motion have received pledges from members who do not belong to their parliamentary group, why don't the latter at least stand up – what have they to fear?' Barzel and his friends were striving to assume a bitter responsibility because they would only attain it with the aid of a handful of members 'of whom one would be entitled to say that they had battered their consciences past recognition'.

In the course of this heated debate, Walter Scheel warned against working high-flown words to death when the points at issue were quite straightforward. 'The safeguarding of one's own political future is not a question of conscience,' he declared, and proceeded to counter-attack the Opposition fiercely. 'You want to take over the government without winning a Bundestag election . . .' After two decades, he said, the 1969 change of government had been long overdue. The social-liberal government had achieved more with its slender majority than others with a large majority had either failed or been unwilling to accomplish: '. . . to lead our nation through the taboo-barrier, to wean it from illusions, to tell it harsh truths and thereby permanently to secure the residue of national substance which it had lost after losing two world wars. We have cleared away the rubble and bloodied our fingers in the process.' As for the new government to which the Opposition aspired, it would bear 'the stigma of treachery' from its hour of birth onwards. 'Our nation does not deserve a government inimical to loyalty and good faith.'

The following day's vote upset the Opposition's calculations. Barzel received 247 votes instead of the 249 he needed. Scheel and I had both accepted the possibility of defeat. I had a personal word with two members of our own parliamentary group who were soon to change sides, also with two or three colleagues who still belonged to the FDP. In at least one case I sensed the moral dilemma of the man involved (and affected), who betrayed concern for his livelihood and family. Since the ballot was secret, it will never be known how the voting went. My conjecture that 'corruption' had been at work during the run-up to the vote could not be definitely substantiated, but the whole affair left an unpleasant aftertaste.

I was profoundly impressed by the remarkable degree of support I received during those weeks in spring 1972. It related to the substance of our policy – treaties with the East and reform – and was focused on the person of the Federal Chancellor. On the evening of 26 April, Bonn witnessed a protest rally by youth organizations whose more usual attitude towards the government was one of critical detachment. Spontaneous demonstrations were reported in many places. There were stirrings of unrest in factories, mainly but not exclusively in the industrial areas of the Rhine and Ruhr. There were also brief withdrawals of labour accompanied by signs that my parliamentary defeat would provoke opposition on a massive scale. It was my duty to restrain this mood and solicit respect for the decisions of the Bundestag 'whether they suit one or not'. My political opponents were ill-advised to try and dismiss this surge of indignation as 'pressure from the streets'. The huge May Day rally in Dortmund's Westfalenpark made it clear to me that people not only wanted to demonstrate their emotional attachment but were prepared to fight for the essence of democracy.

In the Bundestag, however, the Opposition followed up its abortive attempt to unseat me with a not unskilful counter-move. On 28 April the Union parties again mustered 247 votes, this time against the Chancellery budget. Only 247 members voted in favour, so the budget was rejected. At the Bungalow the same evening I summoned a meeting of leading representatives of the coalition and Opposition (Wehner, Schiller, Schmidt and Ehmke from my own party; Scheel, Genscher and Mischnick from the Free Democrats; Barzel, Schröder, Strauss and Stücklen from the CDU/CSU). We discussed possible means of preventing the parliamentary stalemate from leading to political paralysis. I reported on our deliberations to the Bundestag next day. Sentiment was not yet predominantly in favour of new elections. A substantial number of Opposition members accepted that the treaties could not be left in abeyance. Rainer Barzel and I had several private talks at this period. We were both alive to our share of overall responsibility but had no chance to resolve the crisis jointly. Where foreign policy was concerned, my opponent shouldered a greater burden than his parliamentary supporters were ready to share.

Objectively speaking, it behoved us to prepare for early elections to the Bundestag, regardless of the fact that those who drafted our Basic Law had purposely made it hard to dissolve parliament. (If the Federal Chancellor requests a vote of confidence under Article 68 and fails to secure a favourable response, he can recommend the Federal President to call new Bundestag elections – unless the Bundestag has elected a new Chancellor in the interim.) The CDU/CSU were at first unwilling to commit themselves, rightly fearing public reaction to the dispute over the 'vote-switchers'. They also wanted to leave scope for a repetition of their abortive April experiment. The Free Democrats were averse to holding new elections at short notice because a campaign would have overtaxed their weak party organization. From my own point of view, it was urgently desirable to ratify the treaties without delay so that the Berlin Agreement could come into force.

This was also in the interests of US-Soviet relations. Nixon was anxious to persuade his Soviet opposite numbers to bring the Quadripartite Agreement into force as soon as possible because he regarded it as a basis for further progress. A loose agreement on timing with Washington envisaged that the treaties would complete their passage through parliament by the beginning of May. This meant that, even if the Bundesrat objected to them the second time round, the ratification procedure would be completed by mid-June. We almost managed to keep to this time-table. The first Bundestag debate took place on 10 May and the vote on 17 May. Reintroduction proved unnecessary because the Bundesrat did not demur.

These were hectic weeks. We negotiated – and agreed to support – an all-party resolution on the assumption that it would enable the Opposition to vote for the ratification bills, though its wording came very close to the limits of what I could accept. Barzel's own supposition that the treaties could be rendered acceptable to his parliamentary associates turned out to be mistaken. When Strauss advocated their rejection, the Union resolved to abstain. Both treaties obtained only 248 votes, as I have already said. The Union-controlled *Länder* in the Bundesrat also adopted the abstention line. (For Barzel, who went into the election campaign in a weakened condition, this was a foretaste of the state of affairs that arose in summer 1973, when the Opposition again declined to follow his lead over the decision to enter the United

Nations and he relinquished the chairmanship to Professor Carstens.)

So we had pushed the treaties through but lost our majority in the Bundestag. The inescapable consequence was that we had to seek a fresh mandate. Addressing my party executive in Berlin at the end of June, I announced – by agreement with Scheel – that we would aim for new elections in November.

My request for a vote of confidence under Article 68 of the Basic Law was laid before the Bundestag on 20 September and rejected – according to plan – two days later. To make doubly sure, I and a number of my colleagues abstained. Before the vote, I declared that it should really be sought, not in parliament, but from the sovereign electors of the country. Those who had switched their allegiance were fulfilling a veto function. 'The electors can decide whether to confirm that veto or, in accordance with my expectations, set it aside.'

The Federal President dissolved the Bundestag and set new elections for 19 November. It was an open race. Our wave of support had ebbed since spring. If elections had been held that summer, opinion polls suggested that the CDU/CSU would have won by a short head. What had changed? It was not foreign policy that had caused sentiment to waver. Our settlements with the countries of Eastern Europe were controversial but not unpopular. The fact that European unification was proceeding at a snail's pace was nothing new, unfortunately, nor could my government be blamed for the obstacles in its path. (The Norwegian vote against membership of the European Community played little part in our domestic debate, especially as the Danish referendum had turned out favourably, and the anti-European attitude so widespread in the Labour Party was correctly interpreted as more of a British than a social democratic phenomenon.)

No, it was a combination of domestic issues that suddenly cast doubt on our electoral prospects: prices, problems of internal security, doubts about the cohesion of my party. The Opposition quite naturally seized upon the subject of rising prices. They refused to concede that our spell of extreme (some might say exemplary) stability was already at an end in 1968–9 and that the Federal Republic had done well to hold its own since the change of government. The effects of the world monetary crisis, including an abnormal influx of foreign currency, had been successfully parried in 1970–1 and 1972. We had saved our people from having to pay for the economic upswing of 1971 with a high unemployment rate. Thanks to our policies, employed persons and pensioners had all enjoyed an increase in real income. Businessmen, too, had no cause for complaint even if many of them declined to acknowledge their favourable position. Our reforms had far from unleashed the uncontrollable spate of public expenditure to which Opposition propaganda referred. Although results had in many instances fallen short of our forecasts, the public finances were not overstrained. The tax burden was slightly less than in 1969, opportunities for credit financing were being cautiously exploited.

Be that as it may, Karl Schiller's resignation as Minister of Economic Affairs and Finance early in July seemed to bear out the Opposition's charges. Soon after I accepted his resignation he left our party and collaborated with Professor Erhard on an advertising campaign which sought to create the erroneous impression that our market economy system was in danger. An extremely talented but egocentric man, Schiller had joined me in Berlin a decade earlier as Senator in charge of economic affairs. His grounds for resigning – a limited measure of control over foreign currency movements – were trivial. The fact was that he had managed to alienate nearly all his cabinet colleagues. My mistake lay in appointing him Minister of Finance as well as Minister of Economic Affairs when Alex Möller resigned in 1971. Helmut Schmidt took over his posts until the elections and Georg Leber moved to the Ministry of Defence.

I do not cast stones at comrades of long standing, even when they disappoint me, but I was relieved when the fuss that greeted Professor Schiller's departure in Bonn was far from universally regarded as a crisis. I did not share the pessimism of those who considered the election lost because of a switch by 'Schiller voters', though the state of my party caused me some concern. The Opposition adopted a facile Reds-under-the-bed line. The facts were quite different and far more complex.

German social democracy was engaged in the most difficult remodelling process in its hundred and more years of existence. Its membership was being restratified by a process of sociological change corresponding to the growth of the so-called *Dienstleistungsgesellschaft* [performance-based society]. Its internal climate was also being modified by an influx of young and restless recruits. Within a single decade transformation and expansion had accounted for the remarkable fact that only one-third of the membership was 'old' while two-thirds were new recruits, very many of them academics, students and white-collar workers. The successful assimilation of this greatly altered body of support was not a foregone conclusion. Many feared – and others hoped – that a substantial left-wing socialist group would diverge from the mainstream of the party. While opposing any form of compromise with communist factions, I just as fervently resisted those who sought to differentiate – artificially, in my view – between social democracy and democratic socialism. These terms I have always regarded as synonymous. Personal experience and post-war developments in other European countries bade me do my utmost to prevent the SPD's strength from being sapped. I succeeded despite difficulties which were not all engendered by 'radical' groups. Party unity would doubtless have been tested even more severely but for the discipline imposed by our exiguous and ultimately non-existent majority. It none the less required a great effort to preserve our sense of the possible without losing sight of fundamental values and long-term programmes of reform. Critics inside the party, not all of them drawn from its younger wing, had to be reminded that factional strife within our own ranks should not be allowed to weaken us in our hard-fought and vital war of words with the Opposition. After a conversation on the morning of the day when terrorists struck during the Olympic Games, I noted: 'The party has always contained currents and bodies of opinion throughout its history – naturally, but what worries me is the extent to which energy is being squandered on internal disputes when the real essential is to prepare for this most important of Bundestag election campaigns.' Some of my party colleagues seemed more preoccupied with apportioning blame for defeat in the elections than with the more important task of winning them. Looking back, I said with some bitterness: 'In summer and early autumn, many of our comrades were polishing up their arguments for a different outcome and the rolling of heads to follow.'

Apart from these troubles and the debate on prices, our main worry was internal security. If reports of general alarm were to be believed, our citizens felt threatened, especially in the major cities. Outrages committed by terrorist groups had, in fact, provoked an understandable mood of apprehension – which was precisely what their perpetrators intended. (Attacks on me and my family were also planned, and our youngest son Matthias had to receive police protection for years.) My government, which combated this campaign with vigour and determination, strengthened the effectiveness of the Federal Crime Bureau. The nucleus of the Baader-Meinhof group was arrested before the summer recess. My appeal to sympathizers not to shield criminals through a false sense of solidarity had the desired effect, but public indignation was not so swiftly allayed. Confused ideas about the feasibility of total protection went the rounds.

This only intensified the shock-effect of the Munich attack on 5 September, which claimed the lives of eleven Israeli athletes and cast a dark shadow over the carefully organized Olympic Games. Alerted in Bonn that morning, I flew to Munich at noon after a cabinet meeting. There was little I could do on the spot. The Bavarian authorities were in charge, backed up by the Federal Minister of the Interior and Federal police. All concerned were at full stretch, and it is only too easy to be dogmatic, after the event, about how such situations could have been better handled. That evening, when the drama was nearing its climax, a Foreign Office representative suggested that something might be gained from a direct approach to the Egyptians, with whom we had recently resumed diplomatic relations. Having succeeded with great difficulty in reaching Premier Aziz Sidky by telephone, I tried to impress upon him that it was in our common interest to resolve the problem without further loss of life. I asked whether the aircraft which the terrorists had demanded for themselves and their hostages could land in Cairo. Couldn't they be separated from their prisoners at the Egyptian capital? Sidky would not entertain the idea. In vain did I point out that further grave damage would be inflicted on the Arab cause. I was flatly informed that Cairo wanted nothing to do with 'those people'.

Some people alleged that I also telephoned Golda Meir, but this is not so. We kept in touch with the Israeli Government through other channels. They dispatched a security expert and urgently advised us not to yield to the terrorists' demands. I drove back to my quarters that night firmly convinced that the hostages had been freed on the runway at Fürstenfeldbruck. This was what the authorities had told me and what the government press officer proclaimed in public. I was only acquainted with the truth after a couple of hours' sleep. All the hostages, one German policeman and several of the terrorists had been killed. Hans-Dietrich Genscher, the Federal Minister of the Interior, tendered his resignation next morning, but I had no grounds for accepting it. Both he and Mayor Vogel had vainly offered to take the hostages' place. I was moved to learn that my son Peter had made a similar offer.

My disappointment at the time was intense, first because the Olympics on which we had expended so much loving care would not go down in history as a happy occasion – indeed, I was afraid that our international reputation would be blighted for many years – and secondly because our counter-measures had proved so abortive. Some critics referred, not without reason, to their 'downright amateurism'.

Instead of letting disappointment get us down, however, we strove to learn from this grievous experience. It pointed to the need for police reorganization, for the establishment of a special anti-terrorist unit, and for numerous measures designed to promote co-operation in the fight against terrorism and the taking of hostages. The time was not yet

ripe, but new attitudes were taking shape – in the Arab world as elsewhere. One lesson of Munich, if any were needed, was that pacifism
must cease when confronted by terrorism. Something else I learned
was that an even greater effort should have been made to play for
time.

No such course was possible when, on 29 October, a Lufthansa
plane was hijacked over Yugoslavia in a follow-up to the Munich
attack. The passengers and crew were threatened with annihilation
unless we released the three Palestinian survivors of the Fürstenfeldbruck massacre. Like the Bavarian government, I then saw no alternative
but to yield to this ultimatum and avoid further senseless bloodshed.
This shattering experience confirmed my belief that international
measures to combat the epidemic of terrorism are urgently required.
Even if such a programme fails to receive the support of all countries,
the rest should not be dissuaded from doing what is necessary. Governments which aid terrorists must be taught that connivance does not
pay. All responsible governments must do their utmost to ensure that
terrorist activities are vigorously resisted by constitutional means.
Experience has also shown, however, that nobody should act as if he
has an ideal solution. Each case must be individually assessed because
what is feasible and proper in one instance may be wholly inappropriate
in another. The Federal Republic likewise failed to gain complete
mastery over terrorism on its own soil, but it was not unsuccessful.

The Opposition's exaggerated tirades against our alleged neglect of
internal security fell on empty air. All they did, if anything, was
heighten the public sense of insecurity. We also repulsed an attempt to
discredit our efforts at reform. Although it was the product of barely
three years' work, our interim balance of achievement spoke for itself.
Social security had been reinforced and its benefits extended in respect
of war victims and the disabled. We had made it our new and avowed
task to humanize working conditions. Our society was being modern-
ized in the spheres of education and research, by environmental protection, urban assistance legislation and other essential changes. The
industrial relations code had been amended as a further step on the
road to greater co-determination. We could also demonstrate that we
were sincere in our demand for more democracy. Larger numbers of
young people and women were playing an active part in political and
public life. Artists and intellectuals felt strengthened in their political
commitment. Although the electoral strategists of the Opposition
undoubtedly mobilized the fear of 'socialism', we launched a counter-
offensive. We not only defined the fundamental line that divides social
democracy from communism and state socialism but detailed what had

actually been achieved under the auspices of democratic socialism in more than a century.

Willi Daume, President of the German Athletics Federation, had supervised the organization of the Olympic Games from a house in Feldafing, not far from Munich. This he made available to me during the Olympics, and here I received a number of distinguished visitors including Heath, Pompidou and Kissinger, the Austrian Federal President Franz Jonas, Prime Minister Lynch of Ireland, and presidential adviser Mohammed Heikal of Egypt. In Munich itself I met the Soviet delegation, the UN Secretary-General and other notables. The projected European summit claimed my attention almost daily during these weeks. Other focal points were the progress of our *Ostpolitik* endeavours and, above all, our chances of concluding a Basic Treaty with the GDR. I did not intend to let this become a bone of party-political contention. Critics of my government found it hard to dispute that we were successfully representing German interests abroad. Speaking at Oberhausen in mid-September, when the campaign proper opened, I said: 'The foreign policy co-ordinated with our allies can be pursued only by those who have championed and implemented it in the face of great opposition – not by those whose tactical subterfuges have proved them unfit to govern.'

Autumn came, and still our prospects remained uncertain. However, the pre-election party conference at Dortmund in mid-October, which was a splendidly spirited occasion, encouraged me and my colleagues to believe that we and our coalition partners would obtain a clear vote of confidence from the electorate if only the party and its helpers braced themselves for a supreme effort. My friend Holger Börner had organized an effective campaign 'from scratch', and we received some magnificent demonstrations of support. I won approval by declaring that those who wished to live in safety tomorrow must fight for reforms today, and we did not hesitate to kindle our compatriots' pride in their own native land and ours. In terms of politicization, the election campaign was a high-water mark in German post-war history – yet another indication that it paid to venture more democracy.

It turned out on the night of 19 November that my party had won 45·9 per cent of the votes in a record 91 per cent poll. This was a good 3 per cent more than in 1969. For the first time, our 230 seats made us the strongest single group in the Bundestag.

The Free Democrats under their outstanding secretary-general Karl-Hermann Flach, who was already a dying man, increased their share of the poll from 5.8 to 8.4 per cent and their number of seats from

30 to 42. The government majority in parliament, which had amounted to only 12 seats in 1969, rose to 48. Electoral analyses showed that the FDP had profited from the second votes of potential SPD voters – a fact to which I had little objection under current circumstances. It also emerged that a clear preponderance of young electors had voted for social democracy and the coalition. Our share of women's votes, especially among the young, showed a substantial increase. Certain losses in 'senior' professional groups were balanced by gains among skilled workers, and CDU/CSU inroads into the ranks of the unskilled had been offset. We found it significant that our support among Catholic workers had increased.

The foreign response to our election triumph was overwhelming. Palme and Heath telephoned the same night. Teddy Kennedy and some of his colleagues, who were visiting Bonn for a conference of NATO parliamentarians, actually attended our election party. Nixon, Brezhnev and Pompidou sent messages of congratulation. Letters and telegrams arrived from West European heads of government, from Tito, Ceauşescu and Gierek, and from African and Asian leaders. Among the personal messages from all parts of the world were many from the countries of Eastern Europe. I received numerous tokens of international solidarity that autumn, and not for the last time. Friends in America made a presentation which I esteemed a signal honour: the Reinhold Niebuhr Award, bestowed in memory of a great and socially committed theologian.

My foreign engagements for 1973 took me to Yugoslavia in the spring, Israel in June, the United Nations and Washington in September. I also attended several European meetings of a more than routine nature, and our pre-Christmas summit of the Nine in Copenhagen took place in the shadow of the oil crisis. I had signed our treaty with Czechoslovakia a few days before. My trip to America at the end of September had been docked by a few days because I thought I would be able to settle differences within the party leadership by returning to Bonn. A few days later, on 6 October, the new Middle East war broke out, and nobody could tell what demands it would make on Germany and Europe as a whole.

Confidence in my government was badly shaken by the uncertainty brought to Europe's doorstep by the war and the threat of an oil embargo (which produced an explosion in oil prices). In November 1973, twelve months after the Bundestag elections, opinion polls recorded considerable dissatisfaction with the performance of the government team in Bonn. Opinion research institutes had already registered a substantial change in the political climate during the summer. Although this was not a 'conservative swing', as many precipitately claimed and others unthinkingly repeated, acceptance of reforms seemed definitely on the wane. Calls for law and order were much applauded, and the desire to extend social benefits was more pronounced than the readiness to pay for them. Nevertheless, the black-and-white artists refused to acknowledge that a clear majority continued to support our foreign policy and register definite approval of the Federal Chancellor's efforts. I could also take comfort from the thought that Adenauer himself had sustained major reverses after his sweeping electoral triumphs in 1953 and 1957.

But the uncertainties of 1973 were not confined to the Federal Republic. In Britain, Heath was moving inexorably towards defeat at the polls. In Denmark and Norway, the traditional party system was showing signs of dissolution. In France, after Pompidou's death the following spring, Giscard d'Estaing – not the Gaullist candidate – gained a slender victory over Mitterand, the candidate of the 'Left'. The new economic facts of life – fashionably termed 'dislocations' – were beginning to take shape. Anxious inquiries about the ability of the parliamentary system to cope with this new set of problems were becoming more and more frequent. The democratic system was once more in danger of being undermined by demagogy and insecurity. The real interrelationships and decision-making processes became obscured, to the benefit of authoritarian tendencies. Although convinced of liberal democracy's powers of survival, I do not disguise my belief that the crisis affecting constitutional democratic systems will endure, and that these will have to be fundamentally reformed if they are to preserve their essential nature in a rapidly changing world.

In our own case, apart from some important material circumstances to which the initial response was instinctive and emotional, three decisive factors were at work. First, our programme for the new legislative period was not clarified quickly enough because of inadequacies on my own part and that of my party and government. Secondly, there was the querulous pessimism of those members of the public and groups of civil servants who like to think they constitute 'industry'. Last of all, a very critical tone was adopted by organs of public opinion whose attitude had hitherto ranged from the objective to the well-disposed.

My second Chancellorship was dogged by misfortune from the very outset. Immediately after the gruelling election campaign I had to go into hospital and have my larynx treated. Some people interpreted my absence as a sign of weakness and duly exploited it. Another disadvantage was that I changed my inner circle of associates more drastically than I should have done. The new team had plenty of individual talent but lacked a sense of the duty to co-operate. Unfairly, criticism sometimes centred on my friend Klaus Harpprecht, who was responsible for preparing my speeches and published utterances.

It is probable that I showed insufficient vigour in combating those who foolishly proceeded to squander our success at the polls. Writing from hospital to our newly elected group in the Bundestag, I said that we must not overdraw our account. References to the historic significance of the social-liberal alliance would become farcical if we failed to think a few years ahead. On 10 December, immediately before the new Federal Government was appointed, I warned the SPD executive against arrogance and involuntary self-destruction. Our victory had not been a foregone conclusion. We could now say, with some pride, that we had won despite smear tactics and treachery, and that we had resisted defeat by big money and mud-slinging hypocrites. At the same time, success had been achieved despite petty-minded wrangling in our own ranks. I urgently advised my party colleagues to resist the perils of self-destruction, adding: 'It would be better if I were not elected Federal Chancellor in the coming week than if I were to be elected on false premisses.'

As for the counterblast from 'industry', the general level of political nous prevailing among our entrepreneurs had never been over-impressive and was in many cases barely distinguishable from that of any agitated petit bourgeois. A few months before the greatest steel boom German industry had ever enjoyed in peace-time, I heard it seriously stated by a senior executive of undoubted competence – and one who had just assumed additional responsibilities outside his special field – that he had never met such a hopeless situation in four decades of professional experience. It must have required a remarkable displacement process to be able to make such an erroneous comparison – embracing, as it did, not only the war and Nazism but the days of the Great Depression. Such statements did not diminish my respect for the achievements of the German business community; I have always acknowledged that not every politician would make a good businessman.

In fact, the Federal Republic compared favourably not only with the past but with current conditions in most other countries. The gross national product had risen by 3 per cent in 1971 and 3.4 per cent in 1972, while 1973 showed a growth of no less than 5.3 per cent. Industrial peace was being preserved by good relations with the unions and an improved social security network. Prices had risen appreciably, but far less than in almost all comparable countries. The Mark was consolidating its status as one of the hardest currencies in the world. A recrudescence of the international monetary crisis in spring 1973 had been checked. The February stability programme was followed by a second one in May. The Mark had to be revalued upwards by another 5.5 per cent at the end of June.

Some sections of what may be termed the property-owning middle class allowed themselves to be persuaded that a radical change in the economic system was in progress. They took fright at their own crude conception of 'socialism' and deluded themselves into believing that a policy aimed at greater social justice might 'take something away' from them. It made little difference that I and my political associates were committed by sentiment and conviction to the protection of property, that we did not aspire to a command economy, and that we conceded the right of all major sectors of the economy – whether private, mixed or public – to an appropriate level of investment. On the other hand, I made no secret of my belief that the growth of social democracy must necessarily entail a suppression of those privileges which militate against the common good, and that it is equally inevitable that the proportion of the national product devoted to social purposes should be carefully increased. My respect for economists, and their predictive abilities in particular, has never been unbounded. I was correctly quoted by those who publicized my assertion that, compared to economics, I regarded foreign policy as an exact science. I more than once felt that expert knowledge of economic and financial matters had let me down, especially when experts rejected overnight what they had yesterday proclaimed to be an irrefutable fact.

I did not shirk new lines of inquiry. My government policy statement of January 1973 pointed out that increased production does not automatically connote greater personal freedom – that the quality of life signifies more than living standards and demands a new conception of the common good. I also pointed out that modern social policy no longer concentrates on eliminating the fear of material hardship and social decline. 'It strives for greater justice and aims to ensure that more true freedom prevails in our society.' Although there were no Landtag elections in 1973, I and my colleagues failed to exploit this interlude resolutely enough to secure parliamentary enactment of the realistic reforms which both coalition partners should have supported. Certain elements in both parties were in danger of misinterpreting their mandate. Cabinet solidarity left something to be desired and the sectional interests of the various departments should have been more firmly held in check.

The government did not always succeed in imposing its authority on sectional groups, a fact which impaired public confidence. Our partial impotence *vis-à-vis* small and specialized key-groups such as air traffic controllers had a demoralizing effect. There was no simple solution, but the extremely careful decisions required took too long to make. During the winter of 1973–4 we were confronted not by a small group of interested parties but by representatives of the numerous and powerful public employees' organizations. The question was whether, against a background of fundamental changes in the world economy, wages and salaries should be raised to the extent demanded by the organizations concerned. I emphasized, not only to them but in parliament, that there was no longer any scope for two-figure increases and that union negotiators should temporarily concentrate on safeguarding their members' real income. President Heinemann backed me with vigour and authority. Others were lukewarm or exerted counterpressure, only to feign innocence after the event. I shall not readily forget the callous way in which certain union representatives brushed my valid warnings aside. I debated the advisability of resigning as a public demonstration of my feelings, but the lesson was soon brought home in another way.

All in all, the authority of our democratic state was sorely tried. Many citizens held their own government responsible for the oil crisis because the true facts were hard to fathom. Hostile comment in the press was a partial reflection of the mood in 'industry'. Even journalists who were thoroughly sympathetic to us opined that a little adversity was good for a government armed with a solid majority. Our 'left-wing' or 'left-wing liberal' supporters were disappointed because their conception of the practicable far exceeded the possible. Those who had misunderstood our *Ostpolitik* and ignored my warnings against self-delusion were surprised at the continued existence of countries where writers, for example, were subjected to persecution. Others declined to acknowledge the cost explosion – in particular, that part of it which was attributable to labour costs in education and public health – and thought that the voting of additional funds was simply a matter of good intentions. But despite all these shortcomings, some of which stemmed from excessive rivalry between the *Länder* and the Federation, definite progress had been made towards better educational opportunities.

The edifice which I had come to personify was not the work of our enemies, nor even of our opponents, but of criticism levelled by overzealous friends. It was a monument that seemed to invite vandalism. By the time my sixtieth birthday came in December 1973, I sensed that the air in which I had to operate had become thinner. My public standing with the supporters of the social-liberal coalition was not seriously impaired, but the cliché that my policy had failed was surreptitiously broadcast by some who must have known that they were talking irresponsibly or essaying a self-fulfilling prophecy. I have no cause for complaint in other respects. The cast-iron assertion that 'toughness' is what matters has never appealed to me – it seldom does people any good. Patience is a better guarantee of long-term success than the tub-thumping so often and so loudly recommended over glasses of champagne and beer alike. But it is equally true that one who values objective compromise and team-work must ultimately recognize that the political leader who fails to defend himself in time is doomed to defeat.

The SPD party conference at Hanover in April 1973 displayed a notable measure of solidarity, both despite and because of some spirited debates. Early in March 1974 my party was heavily defeated in the local elections at Hamburg. Although there were local as well as national reasons for this reverse, it was largely blamed on 'Bonn'. Victory has many fathers but defeat is an orphan. In fact, the April opinion polls showed – and the ensuing regional elections confirmed – that there was no question of an irreversible downward trend. It could not, however, be denied that my party had temporarily lost some of the support bestowed on it in the Bundestag elections. No serious investigation of causes could overlook my own mistakes and weaknesses. In many people's minds, expectations of success had become transmuted into an obsession with success which no government, far less a coalition, could hope to satisfy in full. Exaggerated demands and verbal excesses contributed to this weakness, but the decisive factor was the economic pressure to which the Federal Republic had been increasingly exposed since the end of 1973.

We coped quite well with the problems engendered by the oil and oil-price crisis during the winter of 1973–4. Our energy programme had already been introduced in September. Early in November we guided an energy-conservation law over the parliamentary hurdles in a record three days. Our prudent attempts to save petrol and fuel oil were initially supported with sympathetic and often touching enthusiasm, though some of our opponents waxed hysterical. A thoroughly German and grotesque debate on the (internationally accepted) imposition of speed-limits got bogged down in a jurisdictional morass. This issue kindled some ugly emotions.

It was later asserted, quite wrongly, that we had been unaware of the dangers bearing down on us, notably in the field of international energy policy. Neither I nor my colleagues were blind to these problems, but I cannot deny that the product of all our deliberations and discussions was meagre. It was disappointing that our partners in the European Community failed to evolve a co-ordinated approach, far less a joint policy. The Americans' attitude was not very helpful either. Their desire for a co-ordinated approach was not matched by any readiness to show solidarity in time of crisis.

It took some while for the energy crisis to be seen not only as a near-disaster but also, at least fleetingly, as the profound upheaval which it genuinely was. That it coincided with other worldwide economic factors was largely fortuitous but greatly augmented its effect. Abrupt increases in the price of oil – which had long been underpriced – and other raw materials were synchronous with growing disruption of the international monetary system, worldwide inflation, an incipient trade crisis and rising unemployment. In reality, we too had reached a watershed in the relationship between world population and world food supplies. Though often exaggerated, questions about the finite extent of natural resources were posed so forcibly that they could no longer be ignored. I did not shut my eyes to these developments, nor did I gloss them over, but public receptivity was at first rather limited.

Day-to-day work continued, as did high-level politics. I still drew an undiminished response in Europe and the world at large. Of this I could have assured myself (had it mattered to me) when I visited Algeria and Egypt at Easter 1974, when I travelled to Paris for Pompidou's funeral, when Gierek sent me his personal representative or the Portuguese socialist leader Mario Soares appeared at the Palais Schaumburg early in May.

My party's internal difficulties were surmountable, and we proceeded to tackle them. I observed the public response at home early in April – and again at the beginning of May – during the pre-election campaign in Lower Saxony. My meetings were packed, and I was enthusiastically applauded when I called for an end to the 'spoiling' of Germany. The work of government needed tightening up, and the days prior to my resignation were spent in reconstructing my cabinet. Our coalition with the Free Democrats remained intact and co-operation with the new ministers had proved its worth.

Some degree of uncertainty did arise when it was announced that my excellent partnership with Walter Scheel, who had decided to stand for the Federal Presidency, would be ceasing in its present form. My friends and I had originally assumed that the Federal Republic's supreme office would continue to be held by a Social Democrat between 1974 and 1979, either by Gustav Heinemann, re-elected for a second term, or by one of my cabinet colleagues. Heinemann declined to stand for personal reasons to which no one could have taken exception. It came as a surprise when Scheel announced in the course of a four-man discussion (with the parliamentary chairmen Wehner and Mischnick) that he intended to stand unless I myself did. The Foreign Minister informed me during the return flight from Prague on 12 December that his colleagues were prepared to nominate him. My party and its parliamentary group unanimously decided to support his candidacy, but the picture was soon to change.

On the morning of 24 April 1974, when I returned from Cairo, I was greeted with the news that one of my Chancellery advisers had been arrested as a spy. This was a severe blow, though it did not immediately occur to me that considerations of personal responsibility would force me to resign. I continued with my work. The same evening I negotiated with our coalition partners on the subject of land legislation. Next day I participated in the Bundestag debate on the reform of Paragraph 218. There followed speeches in Saarbrücken and Hamburg, a visit to Heligoland and election meetings in Ostfriesland. I conferred with the Minister of Finance on the problems presented by the new budget, supervised other aspects of cabinet work and attended a private meeting with trade union leaders. Throughout these days, my decision to resign matured without undue haste. It was finally taken on 6 May.

I must disappoint those readers who have been expecting new disclosures about the 'Guillaume Affair'. This was dealt with by the competent court and a parliamentary committee of inquiry. I have nothing to add here to what I said there, speaking to the best of my knowledge and belief. There is no doubt that I took advice which, looking back, I should not have taken. I was right to shoulder the political responsibility. What is more, I have been confirmed in what I surmised at the beginning of May 1974, namely, that I could not have soldiered on with an easy mind.

It is a source of personal satisfaction that I was at once able to set about the task of serving my party and easing the burdens of my successor at the Federal Chancellery. The shock of my resignation stimulated an insight into many political exigencies. The opportunity so happily afforded by my relinquishment of the Chancellorship also made it easier for me to perform my duties as chairman of the German Social Democrats. I have not found it unduly hard to cope with the change it signified to be free from responsibility, in the sense of public office, for the first time in twenty years. I am still at work on the same elements of the same policy.

17

Crises and Opportunities

In June 1973 I became the first German Federal Chancellor to visit Israel. In April 1974 I visited the Presidents of Algeria and Egypt. Between these two dates, the Middle East was shaken by a new and violent eruption of hostilities. The Yom Kippur War affected us more than most. Not only were we striving for peace in our immediate European vicinity, but we felt a fateful – the word is justified here – involvement in the future of the Jewish state.

As a young socialist, I had taken a sceptical view of Zionist ideas and the Zionist controversy which divided my Jewish friends into two camps. I was afraid that the return to a Jewish nation would mean a retreat from problems that ought to have been surmounted by a process of social and cultural integration – and by social tolerance towards minorities. The Third Reich and its crimes had, however, driven me to conclude that those Jewish survivors who had the will to start a new national life in Israel should not be deprived of the opportunity. Immediately after the war, this seemed to be a largely uncontroversial issue – even the Soviet Union voted for the United Nations resolution sanctioning the establishment of the new state. Israel's arduous thirty years of existence need not be recounted here, but I was never indifferent to its fate. I and my political associates also supported compensation payments, although we were well aware that they could never atone for millions of murders and all the wrongs that had been done.

My wife and I were welcomed as friends when we paid a brief visit to Israel in autumn 1960. At Tel Aviv I addressed a meeting of the International Association of Municipalities in my capacity as president of the German *Städtetag* [Conference of German Cities]. A crowded two-day programme beginning in Jerusalem brought us face to face with relics of the history which is so overwhelmingly perceptible in this part of the world, and also with the constructive achievements to

which Israel could already point after so brief a span of national existence. A helicopter took us to the Negev and the Dead Sea, to Beer-
sheba and various agricultural settlements. We gained a vivid impression of the Israelis' will to succeed and of their remarkable ability
to make the desert bloom. In Jerusalem we dined with Golda Meir,
then Foreign Minister. I talked to Ben-Gurion and Finance Minister
Levi Eshkol, who was destined to succeed the first head of government.
I also met the legendary Moshe Dayan.

Ben-Gurion impressed one by his simple line of argument, which
was unashamedly biased. In the belief that he could rely on Adenauer's
pledges, he was currently expecting the Federal Republic to provide
economic aid on a scale which I considered unrealistic. When I met
him again at Bonn in 1967, on the occasion of Adenauer's funeral, only
two questions interested him: West European unification and China.
In June 1973 the old man set off by car to meet me at Herzlia. His
health was failing so badly that he had to receive medical attention on
the way. He no longer talked politics but sought to convey that his
thoughts were now centred on the Prophets.

David Ben-Gurion was 87 when he died at the end of that year. In
him the youthful state of Israel lost a man who was probably its
strongest and possibly its most idiosyncratic figure. It was he who had
proclaimed national independence in May 1948 and become premier and
minister of defence after previously commanding the Haganah, or
military self-defence organization. Originally of lower-middle-class
Polish-Jewish stock, he had come a long way since joining the
Zionist-socialist movement in the country of his birth. He emigrated to
Palestine at the age of 20, worked on the land for five years, studied in
Istanbul, engaged in politics and journalism, and served as a corporal
in the Jewish Legion under Allenby during World War I.

His career was exceptional in another respect. The founder of the
Labour Party (Mapai) ended his days under no party colours after
trying his luck with a break-away group (Rafi). He first retired to the
kibbutz which he had founded – and which we visited in 1960 – at the
end of 1953, when the new state seemed to have consolidated its
position. He was recalled in 1955, and it was not until eight years later
that he left office for good. His conciliatory attitude towards the German Federal Republic was disputed by many of his fellow-countrymen,
and his prestige took an even harder knock when the super-powers
compelled Israel to withdraw late in 1956, after the Suez campaign.
There was, incidentally, a wide gulf between Ben-Gurion's moderate
exhortations to seek peace with Israel's Arab neighbours and his long-

term visions of a 'Greater' Israel based on historical precedents.

By 1965 German policy towards the countries of the Middle East had entered a critical phase. Egypt and other Arab countries broke off diplomatic relations with the Federal Republic on the grounds that it had become involved in secret arms deliveries to Israel. I deplored the obscure features of the situation and would have given priority to an attempt to normalize relations – a point on which the Israelis had so far failed to make up their minds – if only by establishing a consulate-general. A conversation with President Nasser in 1963 led me to assume that there would not have been any undue objection to this on the Arab side. Nasser mentioned the name of an Israeli officer (he had since become a diplomat) who had faced him across no-man's-land in 1948, and added that he would like to talk to him. I passed on this hint to the Israelis but have no idea if contact was ever established.

An exchange of ambassadors with Israel followed the severance of diplomatic relations, which considerably strained our traditional links with the Arab world. Morocco, Tunisia and Libya did not take part in this move, and Jordan resumed relations in 1967. Relations were also re-established with the Republic of Yemen shortly afterwards. As Foreign Minister, I negotiated in spring 1967 with Abdel Khalek Hassuna, the Secretary-General of the Arab League, with a view to improving relations between the Federal Republic and the members of his organization. We failed. All that remained was an aid programme for Palestinian refugees which supplemented our existing support for the programmes of the UN.

When the Six-Day War broke out in June 1967, I and many of my fellow-countrymen feared for the survival of the Jewish state and its inhabitants. Israel's lightning victory posed new and disturbing questions which continued to haunt me in the years that followed. Was everything possible being done to bring about a settlement in the disputed area? Was it over-confident of us to assume that time would work in Israel's favour? Could American support be relied on indefinitely? My feeling that some avenues had been left unexplored was confirmed, *inter alia* by discussions with Nahum Goldmann, the unique 'stateless statesman' who had for years been President of the World Jewish Congress. I recall that the Israeli Government declined Tito's offer to mediate in a dialogue with the Cairo authorities during my first term as Chancellor.

Visiting Morocco early in 1968, I was struck by King Hassan's expressions of anxiety about probable developments in the next few years. As he saw it, the Six-Day War had produced two grave consequences: a rapid growth of Palestinian extremism and the undisputed presence of the Soviet Navy in the Mediterranean (of which I received a vivid demonstration in spring 1969, when I spent hours watching ships pass through the Bosphorus from a hotel window in Istanbul). My discussion with the Moroccan king made it clear that the deliberate shelving of the refugee problem had been transformed into a highly political issue by the PLO (Palestine Liberation Organization) and its constituent organization Al Fatah, founded in 1965 and led by Yasser Arafat.

The Israeli Government defended itself against the charge or supposition that it had wasted opportunities to negotiate. Golda Meir told me of her visit to Bucharest in 1972. After paying an official visit to Egypt, Ceauşescu had sent his Deputy Foreign Minister to Israel. Apparently, Sadat had declared his willingness to talk to an Israeli representative, possibly the Premier herself, but nothing more had happened. (Even during our own talks in 1967, Ceauşescu had stressed that Rumania was striving to proceed with care and deliberation in all matters relevant to the Middle East conflict. He hoped for a permanent peace settlement and would resist any solution that might threaten Israel's survival.)

While Foreign Minister I maintained good relations with my opposite number Abba Eban, a man of great charm and outstanding intellect, whom I met several times in New York and elsewhere. He visited us in Bonn after I became Chancellor – the first Israeli Foreign Minister ever to set foot on German soil in an official capacity. Eban repeatedly emphasized that he had no fear whatsoever that our *Ostpolitik* might embarrass Israel because – so many people argued – the Russians would acquire greater room for manœuvre in the Middle East if the European 'seams' between East and West were normalized. He also betrayed no misgivings about our efforts to re-establish normal relations with the Arab countries. It became considerably harder to exchange views with our Israeli friends when the six members of the existing European Community tried to define their attitude to Middle East issues in spring 1971. I was not persuaded of the wisdom of tackling the problem at that stage in our joint political endeavours and on the basis of the French text of UN Resolution 242 (which called for a withdrawal from *the* occupied territories, whereas the English text referred to 'occupied territories' without the definite article and thus left the possibility and nature of any compromises open). I could not, however, agree with Golda Meir's contention that the European Community had absolutely no right to concern itself with the delicate problems of the Middle East. I politely pointed out to her that we would claim such a right in respect of an even bigger country, to wit, the United States. This was at Helsinki in May 1971. Mrs Meir's prevailing attitude struck me as a mixture of defiance and despair: the Israelis stood alone – they had no friends left and would, if need be, fight to the last man.

Her language had somewhat moderated when we met in Vienna a year later. We had become quite well acquainted at international social democratic conferences over the years. I observed many over-reactions on her part, sometimes triggered by false information, but I also had first-hand experience of her will-power and sensitivity. After emigrating from Russia to America as a child, Golda Meir had for decades fulfilled a central function in the Palestinian labour movement and the new state of Israel. The secret of her success may have been that, like Jean Monnet, she always performed variations on the same theme. Her speeches proclaimed the right to exist and will to live of the Jewish people, for whose benefit she played the role of the 'iron grandmother' without fully disclosing her warmth of character.

Golda Meir, née Mabowitsch, had been a schoolteacher in America. She worked as a teacher and librarian in Milwaukee, Chicago and New York before emigrating to Palestine with her husband, a Denver Zionist named Morris Meyerson, at the age of 23. Early days on a kibbutz were succeeded by posts at trade union headquarters, in the women's movement and the Jewish Agency. Here Golda Meir applied her stubborn streak – which she once demonstrated by maintaining a 100-hour hunger strike – to the task of helping Jews in distress to emigrate from Europe. She joined the provisional government in 1948, spent a year in Moscow as Israel's first accredited envoy, and followed up seven years as Minister of Labour with almost ten years as foreign minister. Her retirement for health reasons did not betoken any renunciation of politics. Early in 1969, after the sudden death of Premier Eshkol, she became head of government.

She remained in office until spring 1974, when her labour bloc sustained heavy losses in the post-Yom Kippur elections. The opening phase of the war had brought down a storm of criticism on the premier and her Minister of Defence. Israel succumbed to a certain sense of isolation which led, in turn, to a mood of impotence and frustration. In Golda Meir, as we shall see below, this mood expressed itself in bitter criticism of the foreign friends from whom she had expected too much.

Her attitude was no tactical device. It was based on conviction, even if it took insufficient account of changing international factors. My own line of argument was clear and consistent. Speaking in Cologne at the beginning of 1971, I declared that Israel represented a grandiose attempt to provide a largely homeless people with a secure homeland. Nothing could change this – not even the anti-Israeli slogans mouthed by extremist groups. It was cruel that the birth of such a country should demand fresh sacrifices and renewed suffering.

> Who would gloss this over? Who would deny the misery of the Palestinian Arabs? But we are not entitled to play the arrogant international moralist. Instead, we must recognize where this causal nexus of suffering and injustices has its origin: here in the heart of Europe . . . We believe ourselves to be fulfilling our country's task and special responsibility when we do our best, with due moderation, to promote the desire for a peaceful settlement in the Middle East field of tension. It would be presumptuous to say much more on the subject. We are none the less convinced that our steadfast peace policy in Europe can become an element in worldwide détente. Relaxation is as transmissible as tension. Dissension can be infectious, but so can the desire for peace.

Despite its geographical remoteness, I went on, Israel had become a close neighbour of ours. Our economic and technological exchanges had become more intensive and better balanced. Our cultural ties had drawn tighter. We had acquired the courage to rediscover our common heritage, accept it with less prejudice and examine new developments with sympathy or at least with attention. Respect for the other party counselled us to be patient, calm and moderate. Even in circumstances as difficult as the present, a frank statement of each side's interests provided the firmest basis on which to reconcile and harmonize them.

I had told the Yugoslav press agency the year before that, despite our belief that Israel's right of survival should not be disputed, we were striving to be fair to the legitimate interests of all parties and improve our relations with the Arab countries at the same time. Our government unanimously supported the UN Security Council resolution of 22 November 1967. We hoped that a just and lasting settlement designed to eliminate conflict could be found by means of negotiation. We were gratified to note that senior representatives of the Arab world no longer questioned Israel's right to exist and accepted that the Israelis, too, were anxious to dwell within guaranteed frontiers.

The extent of the prejudices to be surmounted became apparent in 1972, when my acceptance of an official invitation to Israel aroused public controversy there over whether the Federal Chancellor should be received at all. The ensuing demonstrations were minor affairs which neither surprised nor upset us.

I flew to Tel Aviv on 7 June accompanied by several good friends. They included Walter Hesselbach, board chairman of the *Bank für Gemeinwirtschaft*, Günter Grass (who had insisted on being allowed to draw Golda Meir), Werner Nachmann, chairman of the Central Jewish Council in Germany, and Klaus Harpprecht and his wife Renate (Lasker), whose arm is still tattooed with an Auschwitz number. The Israeli premier welcomed us at Lod Airport. She referred to my conduct 'in mankind's darkest hour' and paid tribute to me for having initiated developments conducive to peace in my capacity as Federal Chancellor. Replying, I said that she had invited me as the responsible representative of a new epoch in German governmental status. 'In other words, you are offsetting the power of the past with the requirements of the present and, thus, with the demands imposed by a bold and humane attitude. I believe mankind would be lost without such bold initiatives.'

Conscious that it was no matter of course for the Jewish state to welcome a German head of government, I can honestly say that this visit to Israel was one of the most momentous experiences in my political career. Shortly after arriving in Jerusalem I laid a wreath at Yad Vashem, the place sacred to the memory of the victims of Nazism, and read Psalm 103, verses 8–16, at a brief memorial service there.

Mrs Meir and I opened our political discussions in private while State Secretary Frank conversed with Israeli government officials. That evening we were invited to dine in the main hall of the Knesset. During her after-dinner speech Mrs Meir expressed the hope that my visit would help to bring our peoples closer – 'in friendship and sincerity. Not glossing anything over, but openly and straightforwardly, in the knowledge of what has happened in the past but with courage and hope, resolved to show the whole of humanity the way to a better future.' Two nights later, when I returned her hospitality at the Hotel David, she exclaimed: 'You recently said that anyone who wants to attain peace, understanding and a measure of agreement must be prepared to compromise . . . Quite so. We're prepared to compromise on each and every point with the sole exception of our survival and our right to live in this country and this part of the world.'

We continued our political discussions on a team basis and completed them over coffee at the premier's home late the following day. I was able to inform a press conference of our common belief that co-operation had developed favourably in a wide variety of areas and that increased exchanges and co-operation accorded with our joint interests. (It was hardly surprising that our resources fell short of some of the schemes advanced.) Secondly, we had discussed international relations in general, including our attempt to reduce tension between East and West. Thirdly:

> We naturally devoted particular attention to the Middle East conflict and the problems of this area. I appreciate the frank manner in which Israeli considerations have been laid before me. As regards the Federal Government, it has neither the intention nor the authority to overreach itself by taking sides, whether invited to or not. We have not been appointed to play the role of mediator, nor are we in a position to do so, but the German interest is plain: it calls for a peaceful solution negotiable by and acceptable to those directly concerned. Apart from this we hope that the Secretary-General of the United Nations and those governments which have a special commitment will succeed in creating a framework for meaningful discussions and negotiations between those immediately involved.

In the fourth place, we had talked about the European Community, its prospects and its relations with this area. The German Federal Chancellor could not speak for the Community but he was able to express his views as a European. We had also discussed Israel's interests in relation to the European Community. Many Israeli ideas tallied with our own, and we would bear them in mind when the enlarged Community proceeded to adjust its Mediterranean policy in a comprehensive and balanced manner. Finally, I was able to announce that the premier had accepted my invitation to pay an official visit to the Federal Republic. (This pledge was fulfilled in summer 1975 by her successor, Itzhak Rabin.)

Although the Israelis had expressly emphasized their willingness to compromise during the inter-delegation talks, they also betrayed grave errors of judgement. They cited regional stability as a point in their favour, arguing that the truce had already lasted three years. (It was not destined to last much longer: war broke out again only four months later.) King Hussein had considerably reinforced his position in Jordan, they said, and the same applied to other 'conservative' Arab countries. The Palestinians' radius of action was diminishing and the refugee problem gradually losing its importance, at least as a social and humanitarian problem.

Abba Eban told us quite candidly that the Middle East pronouncements of the European Community would continue to be noted with concern. On past experience, the Israelis could not but fear that a joint EEC attitude would in no way be balanced because of French influence. They would therefore prefer the members of the Community to dispense with a common line and maintain their independent positions. As for EEC economic policy in the Mediterranean, Israel welcomed the idea of a 'global solution' in the form of a free trade zone encompassing the whole area.

On the subject of peace moves, Golda Meir stated that her country had not only accepted the Jarring Mission at the Security Council's request but declared its willingness to enter into indirect negotiations. We could also let the Egyptians know (which I did) that Israel was prepared to talk: they had only to name the time, the place and the people. Independently of this, the Italians had been asked to inform President Bourguiba that the Israelis reacted favourably to his recent hints of a readiness to talk. It is probable that there were also direct contacts between the Israeli Government and King Hussein.

I pointed out that, despite many disappointments, the United Nations seemed a suitable framework for the introduction of peace moves. A preliminary dialogue between the parties to the conflict might commence there and subsequently lead to direct negotiations. The UN framework would additionally involve the two super-powers. They ought likewise to concern themselves with the Mediterranean situation, if only because of a common interest in ridding their relations of seriously disruptive factors. In this context, we found it interesting to contemplate the idea of reinforcing the Jarring Mission with an advisory group provided, say, by the two super-powers, the two other principal victors of World War II, and perhaps other countries as well. (I quoted similar suggestions advanced by Heath, Brezhnev and Tito.) I pointed out that the oil problem would influence developments in general and the American attitude in particular, and that the law of numerical superiority would ultimately work to Israel's detriment.

My brief for the Jerusalem talks actually consisted of a single sheet of paper on which I had graphically expressed my evaluation of the major East-West factors with lines and arrows. One of my main arguments was based on what I had recently been told in Washington. This could be summed up in one bald sentence: Jewish influence on American policy would not in the long run outweigh the American interest in oil. The Egyptians had intimated to me that they were prepared to make sacrifices and pay regard to the security of Israel. It might be better to begin by discussing the future of the Middle East – peace-keeping and economic co-operation – and temporarily shelve the territorial problems. The only rational solution being a political one, I wanted to encourage Mrs Meir to explore it. Although she was not deaf to such suggestions, the premier's past disappointments readily prompted her to relapse into profound pessimism. Viewed objectively, she said, all these ideas about the need to involve third parties in peace moves were correct. However, the Israelis' problem was that they ultimately and invariably stood alone. They could not cede the decision on matters affecting their own survival to others. It might seem presumptuous for a small country like Israel to believe that its views were always correct, 'but this is genuinely the case'.

I had no doubt, even so, that the desire for a settlement was strong in Israel too. It still preys on my mind that I and others failed to impress even more cogently on both sides that it was high time to translate that desire into political action. Apart from Golda Meir's more general remarks – and her challenge to Cairo – what particularly struck me was the endeavour made by her deputy and Foreign Minister, Yigal Allon, to adopt a discriminating attitude towards Israel's Arab neighbours. It also encouraged me that a man like Moshe Dayan could say, off the record, that if he had to choose between politically secure and militarily semi-secure frontiers he would pick the former.

From Jerusalem I flew by helicopter to the Sea of Galilee, where I was a guest of the Allons at Kibbutz Ginossar, founded early in the Nazi era by Jews from Germany and Austria. At a cheerful Sabbath lunch in the communal dining-room I met members of a group which had invited me to debates in Sweden during the war. It was the first time for years that many of them had consented to use the German language.

In Jerusalem next day I had a demonstration of the immediate proximity of three of the world's major religions: I visited the Church of the Holy Sepulchre, the Dome of the Rock, the El Aqsa Mosque and the Wailing Wall. I was welcomed by Christian, Mohammedan and Jewish dignitaries. Many Arabs attended the reception given for me by Mayor Teddy Kollek at his city hall. That evening I played host to numerous old friends and new acquaintances at Herzlia. We witnessed some touching – indeed, moving – scenes. Despite or, rather, because of all the human warmth, it saddened me to meet so many Israelis who had once been fellow-Germans – people whom our nation had wantonly discarded but for whose survival one could not fail to give thanks.

The last day of my stay was almost my last day on earth. I was due to visit the historic mountain-top fortress of Masada (of which I was later given a memorable account by Yigael Yadin, the celebrated archaeologist and one-time chief of staff). After touching down, our helicopter was caught by a gust of wind and narrowly escaped plunging into a precipice. I commented that Israel was a country where miracles were to be expected. It was not the only disaster to which I almost succumbed during my time in office.

The Israeli ambassador, Asher Ben Nathan, who had previously completed a tour in Bonn and was now serving in Paris, happened to be attending a function given by President Pompidou that day. Pompidou asked him why better care had not been taken of the Federal Chancellor. 'What do you expect, *Monsieur le Président?*' the ambassador quipped. 'A French helicopter plus an Arab wind . . . Fortunately, there's a great Jewish god!' (The helicopter actually came from America, not France, and the wind from the Mediterranean, not Arabia. I won't argue about the great Jewish god.)

The Israeli authorities were still highly perturbed when I reached Revohot, where I was the first foreigner to receive an honorary degree from the Weizmann Institute. I later said that this trip to Israel had been the most exacting I had undertaken as Chancellor. However, the Israeli leaders made my mission as easy as they could. Their desire for a settlement was more apparent than I had expected. The Arab governments reacted calmly to my visit, noting that I steered clear of occupied territory. I had signified my willingness to act as a transmitter of viewpoints but declined to undertake the functions of an intermediary because this would have exceeded my country's competence. When I spoke to Pompidou he gloomily observed that Israel's minimum demands would never be accepted, even by Arab moderates, and that the influence of the extremists was growing. Apparently, King Feisal had referred during his recent Paris visit to the 'oil weapon'.

Fighting broke out again on 6 October 1973, while I was staying at Chequers with the British Prime Minister. Named after the most important Jewish fast-day, on which it was launched, the Yom Kippur War temporarily put paid to those manifold peace-seeking endeavours which I have already described as insufficiently determined. The risk of a wider confrontation could not be excluded. After sustaining heavy casualties, the Israelis fought back desperately and gained some major successes. The need for a negotiated settlement became even more obvious than before.

Golda Meir later reproached herself bitterly for having listened to her intelligence advisers, who had ruled out the possibility of an attack on that day in October, and for having consequently failed to mobilize until the assault was in progress. The Americans, too, were harshly criticized for ignoring danger signals and taking too long to organize an air-lift. After the cease-fire Mrs Meir telephoned me and requested a meeting with other social democratic party leaders. I applied myself to the problem, and a meeting took place in London on 11 November under the chairmanship of Harold Wilson. Golda Meir presented a harrowing account of the course of events. 'When I got through,' she writes in her autobiography, 'the chairman asked if anybody wanted to speak. But nobody did. Then someone behind me – I didn't want to turn my head and look at him because I didn't want to embarrass him – said, very clearly: "Of course they can't talk. Their throats are choked with oil." And although there was a discussion, there wasn't really any more to say. It had all been said by that man whose face I never saw.'

My own recollection of the matter is different. True, nobody wanted to make an immediate response. The chairman, who was obviously reluctant to speak first, called an adjournment. It was then agreed that I should take the floor. We were all exceedingly dismayed by the accusing, pessimistic and inflexible tone of Mrs Meir's remarks. I could sympathize with Israeli disappointment, which extended to the attitude of European governments as well. The Community had adopted a cautious approach rather than risk military involvement. The governments of the Nine issued statements on 13 October and 6 November. Although I was not entirely happy with some of their wording, the Israeli premier placed a needlessly unfavourable interpretation on them. I tried to point out their more positive aspects and urged her to acknowledge them. I also cited evidence of German solidarity, of which she was doubtless aware. For the rest, I advised her to be more active in engaging the interests of the great powers on Israel's behalf and to bear in mind that the European Community could fulfil a conciliatory function. This, I said, would be all the more effective if the ties between Israel and the United States were subjected to less strain. Mrs Meir had difficulty in coming to terms with the changed situation. Her profound dejection persisted, as I noticed at dinner that night.

It is true that the Europeans cut a far from impressive figure during the war that heralded the oil crisis. Various governments allowed themselves to be played off against each other by countries determined to use oil as a weapon. They cannot, however, be blamed for taking their immediate worries as seriously as the fate of their citizens demanded. Within the limits imposed by our national interests and the extremely precarious international situation – indeed, by the balance between war and peace – we did not stand aloof. American supply arrangements did not break down through any fault of ours, but I have already pointed out that we expressly protested against the use of our territory without notification, let alone consultation, as if NATO did not exist. I refer in particular to the use of Israeli vessels for shipping

US war material for the ostensible reason that ships flying the American flag were not available. This might easily have been seen as a (renewed) attempt to involve us in an involuntary commitment whose consequences we could not foresee. I conveyed our complaint to Nixon, who promised that nothing of the kind would recur: in future, we would be consulted.

Even at this stage, I still have no full conception of what happened on the night of 24–25 October, when Washington issued a worldwide military alert. Many people insinuated at the time that its object was to divert attention from political problems at home. I think they were wrong. It is fair to assume that the stand-to ordered by Kissinger and secret service chief William Colby on the President's authority was attributable to a false evaluation of intelligence reports. The UN Security Council had ordered a cease-fire on 22 October, but fighting continued until 24 October. Because Israeli counter-attacks were becoming a serious threat during this phase, Sadat had called for joint intervention by the United States and the Soviet Union. The Russians notified us that they were considering joint military action to safeguard the cease-fire – a piece of intelligence which might equally have been construed as psychological pressure. The Americans seem to have mistaken Soviet military preparations for a sign that Russian paratroops were about to go into action on the Egyptian side. A sharply worded message from Brezhnev may further have contributed to this misconception. At all events, nothing came of Brezhnev's and Nixon's spring 1973 agreement to consult in time of crisis. US bases in Britain were also affected by the worldwide alert. When I spoke to Heath in mid-November he confirmed that London had not been informed. It was thought that certain Soviet activities had prompted the mobilization of individual US units 'situated in the vicinity'. Heath and I exchanged views on the lively developments in progress during those weeks. We realized that a great deal depended on Sadat's standing and influence. I knew that he had striven to exert a moderating influence on Libya over the oil question. In fact, no further action had ensued on Gaddafi's oil ultimatum. Saudi Arabia seemed implacable, but I had received an extremely reasonable communication from King Hussein.

Pompidou told me at the end of November that this was the first time genuine uncertainty had prevailed over the possibility of massive US intervention. Israel's existence had been at stake. Proposals which had always been rejected were now receiving consideration. He was not optimistic, but there might still be a chance of effecting an agreement between Israel and Egypt. Syria and Jordan must be induced to join in. In his view, this could not be managed without the UN Security

Council. It was also conceivable that other Arab countries would refuse to recognize an agreement. Sadat would then be subjected to pressure, for example by students and the army. That might lead to a fresh outbreak of hostilities, hence the importance of enlisting the Security Council. The President naturally set store by this because it would entail French participation.

Nahum Goldmann's analysis was as follows. Politically speaking, the Arabs had won the Yom Kippur War. They were compelling Israel and the super-powers to seek a political solution of the conflict. Israel had to acknowledge that time and numbers were working against its policy. The problem was more psychological than territorial and political. Nasser had told Dag Hammarskjöld in his day that the major problem was Israel's division of the Arab world, not the partition of Palestine.

Thanks to his admirable diplomatic activity after October 1973, Henry Kissinger managed to consolidate and crystallize the fragile cease-fire in a series of three-cornered talks. In so doing, he was able to build on the Egyptian-Israeli agreement which his predecessor, William Rogers, had effected a month before Nasser's death in 1970. Face to face for the first time, Egyptian and Jordanian representatives conferred with Israeli envoys at Geneva in December 1973. The armistice agreement was eventually signed at 'Kilometre 101', that now celebrated landmark on the Cairo-Suez road. The disengagement agreement with Syria followed on 5 June 1974.

Golda Meir resigned the day before, as she had forecast that spring. Visiting Cairo shortly after the announcement, I heard Sadat quote Kissinger in support of some almost friendly remarks about her putative successor, Rabin.

The situation in the Mediterranean, the Middle East conflict and the problem of oil supplies, which was fraught with mounting uncertainty, were topics that dominated many of the discussions I had as Chancellor with representatives from the East as well as Western politicians: with European heads of government, with Nixon and Brezhnev, with Persian and Arab ministers, with friends from Austria and Norway. I talked to Presidents Suharto and Senghor about new oil finds and to Premier Tanaka of Japan about the exploitation of solar energy. The visit which my wife and I made to Iran early in 1972 left a deep impression on me. Conversations with the Shah and his advisers not only gave me an insight into the problems of the major oil-producing countries but conveyed some of the contradictions between cultural antiquity and 20th-century civilization, rapid modernization and a stringent exercise of political authority.

In January 1970 President Pompidou remarked that the Federal Republic, like all the countries of Western Europe, could play a useful role in the Mediterranean area. Couldn't aid for the Maghrib countries be co-ordinated by Germany and France? The French were on good terms with the Maghrib states and must pay due consideration to their country's long-standing cultural presence, not only there but in the Mohammedan republics of Black Africa. The French approach to the Middle East conflict was consonant with a policy of practical common sense. The sale of more than a hundred Mirage fighters to Libya and an embargo on arms for Israel were being debated with some vehemence at this time. Pompidou defended the arms sales by asserting that 'the Russians would have supplied them otherwise'. The Libyans had undertaken not to lease or resell the aircraft, he said, so the balance of power was unchanged.

I was bound to point out that, discounting the Maghrib, we had still to resume normal relations with most of the Arab countries. We would naturally welcome increased trade. On the other hand, we were also anxious to contribute, in so far as our resources allowed, to a balanced policy conducive to peace in the Middle East. We acknowledged the Arabs' legitimate rights – indeed, there was a tradition of good German-Arab relations – but we had, particularly in view of very recent history, to come out strongly in favour of Israel's survival.

Pompidou wondered whether a Palestinian buffer-state would materialize and thus spell the political extinction of King Hussein. Arafat, he said, was leaning more and more towards Moscow. He also enjoyed growing support in countries like Morocco and Algeria, which were more afraid of Egypt than Israel. France wanted to guarantee Europe's presence in the Mediterranean area – preferably in concert with us – if only to prevent other powers from usurping our place there. The Maghrib countries approved of this. The Russians had once glimpsed America's vulnerable 'belly' in Cuba. The Mediterranean area must not become a European equivalent. (This was a variant of Churchill's 'soft under-belly' formula.)

In July 1970 we were preoccupied with the latest meeting of the oil-producing countries in Algiers. No agreement had been reached there because some of the participants were opposed to what they then considered the 'brutal' demands of Libya. (So the consumer-countries were not yet faced with a producers' united front. As late as summer 1973, we still found it hard to drum up sufficient interest in discussions on the subject of oil.) Pompidou told me in summer 1970 that France's concern was to draw all the Mediterranean countries – and, fundamentally, the whole of Africa – closer to Europe. We must harness them to Europe or they would become the cat's-paw of Russo-Chinese rivalry. Peace in the Middle East could not be attained under American or Russian auspices. Although he did not believe there would be war between the two super-powers, this area contained all the makings of a world war from which our only ultimate protection was the atom-bomb.

In January 1971, when Algeria was engaged in nationalizing its oil industry, the French President declared that solidarity among the consumer-countries, but especially those of Europe, was essential. The Americans might be tempted to supply themselves from their own and other readily available sources, leaving Europe to fend for itself. We must speed up the production of nuclear energy so as not to be wholly dependent on oil. On the Middle East, Pompidou expressed greater confidence at this stage. Egypt appeared to be more peaceably inclined since Nasser's death. The United States seemed prepared to exert some degree of pressure on Israel. The Soviet Union had presumably realized that an extension of the conflict might lead to confrontation with the United States. What was needed, once again, was a reinforced European presence in the Mediterranean area and a co-ordinated Franco-German policy. We wondered who in Israel would be capable of implementing a policy of withdrawal. Pompidou averred that it would take a politician of de Gaulle's calibre – one who possessed the stature and courage to evacuate indefensible positions as the General had done when winding up the Algerian War.

I often discussed the problem of energy supplies with the British Prime Minister as well. In April 1971, Heath said that our best policy might be to participate in the development of Alaska, and that oil searches in the North Sea had not been as productive as the British had hoped. (This impression was destined to change. Within a couple of years Britain had become a potential candidate for membership of OPEC, the organization of oil-producing countries, as Harold Wilson remarked on a subsequent occasion – only half in jest.) If the Arabs were agreed on one thing, Heath said, it was that the West should be subjected to permanent blackmail. Our problem was how to prevent this. The State Secretary at our Ministry of Economic Affairs, who had accompanied me to London, reported that the price increases ensuing on negotiations in Teheran and Tripoli were already having a serious effect on our economy. In the interests of our own security we should have to get away from a liberal oil policy. (We also informed our partners of efforts to procure more natural gas from the Soviet Union and of our plan to involve a German oil company in dealings with Iran.

On the Middle East, Heath said that Ambassador Jarring should be encouraged to step up his efforts on behalf of the Security Council. The Americans should make their influence more strongly felt at the same time. Israel would soon have to modify its attitude because Sadat would not be able to maintain his readiness to reach an agreement for more than a limited period. A year later, in April 1972, the Prime Minister stated in London that the Soviet Union had reinforced its position in the Middle East. The treaty with Iraq gave it a stronger military power-base than its previous agreements with Egypt. He did not see how the Russians could be checked in this area. My own impression was that things might take a turn for the better in Egypt, and that it no longer seemed impossible to bring about an agreement. Heath thought it unlikely that the Israelis would be prepared to accept any sort of compromise in an American election year.

Commenting on the oil question at the beginning of March 1973, Heath said that the Americans had suddenly woken up to this problem, though they had yet to decide on a course of action. Their demand for energy would have increased considerably by 1975. The United States would exploit new sources of supply such as oil shale and nuclear energy. At an evening get-together late in May, when Heath was again visiting us, Walter Scheel reported on his Middle East trip and said that the Americans would not be submitting any new plans because of previous rebuffs. The Soviet Union was now in favour of a lasting settlement. The Egyptians had no alternative because the Russians would not supply them with any offensive weapons. For all that, direct negotiations with Israel were their overriding fear. Scheel thought that talks might be held under the aegis of the United Nations but that a new Jarring Mission would have little prospect of success. I mentioned a letter I had recently received from Tito in which he advocated that the Four Powers – in other words, France and Britain as well – should assume a decisive role.

Heath said it had always been taken for granted that the Soviet Union and the United States would become embroiled in an Egyptian-Israeli conflict. Last time, however, the Soviet Union had steered clear. Energy supplies for the Western world were his main worry. A situation might arise in which the Arab countries would refuse to supply the Americans with any more oil while they continued to support Israel. The United States might then be compelled to use force – or the Europeans would have to go shares with them. Ten years ago it had

still been his belief that the Arab countries would never agree on anything, but we were now entirely dependent on their goodwill in the
matter of oil supplies. Nobody could tell what price they would demand
for oil in 1975.

On the same occasion, Helmut Schmidt stressed the importance of
forming an oil consumers' counterpart to OPEC. Large oil concerns
should be brought under state control. An oil crisis might be just
around the corner, and Western countries were unprepared for one.
Heath thought it essential that the European Community should evolve
a common energy policy. The Arab countries must be restrained from
using their economic power for political ends. In his view, Israel's
withdrawal from the occupied territories was inevitable. The countries
of the West could then confront the Arabs with their own demands.
Not even the Americans would support Israel to the bitter end. As long
as the Israelis believed the West to be exclusively afraid of war, they
would do nothing. If they became aware how greatly America and
Europe were preoccupied with the oil crisis, they would change their
tune. I said I would try to clarify these issues during my visit to Israel.

When I talked to Pompidou in November 1973, after the Yom
Kippur War, he said that all European countries were faced with the
long-term need to undertake geographical and technological diversifica-
tion in respect of oil supplies. De Gaulle had predicted that the Arabs
would one day use oil as a weapon, and he himself had been much dismayed when King Feisal dropped a hint to that effect. France's attitude
consisted in taking no decision that might damage her own prospects.
He could not forbear to point out that France had long ago drawn her
partners' attention to the oil problem. 'France has defended her own
rather *dirigiste* system. Others have prided themselves on practising
a free market system in this area too. I take the view that the moves
undertaken by France *vis-à-vis* the Arabs offer every prospect of
benefiting the other countries of Europe as well.' Pompidou recalled
our conversation on board the *Loreley* in 1971. 'It was then a question
of controlling movements of capital. I did not think of oil at that time.'
He had no wish to start a verbal war over oil with the Dutch, who were
afraid of being particularly hard hit by selective embargoes and opposed
independent action by the French. The Dutch, he said, had never been
paragons of solidarity. 'Perhaps you could help by convincing them
that present-day France is no longer the France of Louis XIV. Anyone would think they were afraid of a French invasion.'

I gave an account of our energy conservation law and stressed
that we must not allow the European Community to fall apart over
this issue. European solidarity must be more than verbal. I solicited

Pompidou's continued understanding of German-Israeli relations and said that the Nine should not be more pontifical than the Popes of the Arab world. Certain frontier modifications were reasonable. We must encourage any Arab initiative that might lead to closer co-operation with Europe. The American action in October had been unhelpful and engendered discord. This had since been overcome, though one still heard the odd unpleasant remark. Washington now realized that its autumn 1973 behaviour would not do.

The Middle East situation also received special attention during my talks with President Tito in spring 1973, when elements of a compromise emerged which later formed part of the objective under-lying Kissinger's dogged negotiations. The Yugoslav President, who scented danger, considered the situation extremely precarious and likely to produce a fresh outbreak of hostilities at almost any moment. Even at that stage, he said that hopes of a peaceful settlement appeared to have been abandoned in Egypt and elsewhere in the Arab world. Like me, he believed that all depended on the two super-powers, but especially on the Soviet Union. The Egyptian President had visited him two months before. 'My discussion with Sadat interested me all the more because I had previously received reports that he might be prepared for concessions now that Soviet experts had been withdrawn from Egypt. I was not over-inclined to believe these reports because I know the way the Egyptians' minds work.' Sadat was insisting that the Israelis should withdraw 50 to 60 kilometres from the Suez Canal, which could then be reopened. Given guarantees from the United Nations or the super-powers and the withdrawal of Israeli forces, further solutions could be considered in respect of the Gulf of Aqaba, Sharm el Sheikh and the Gaza Strip. The question of what troops should be stationed where – whether provided by the UN or the super-powers – was open to discussion. 'But Israel refuses to make any concessions on this point. Above all, it wants to keep the Gaza Strip and Sharm el Sheikh. The Canal Zone and Cairo would be threatened from there. The Arabs cannot agree to this under any circumstances.' Tito went on:

The Arabs would probably agree to a UN force but they want to have Arab troops there too. Israel will not hear of this and refuses to comply with Resolution 242. The internal situation in Egypt does not permit Sadat to yield, but things cannot remain in this icebound condition for long. The younger generation in Egypt is becoming particularly impatient. There are 800,000 men under arms. The army is excellently equipped and trained. Under these circumstances, one cannot simply wait and see how things turn out. The Arabs may only be using the reports I mentioned to exert pressure for the moment, but the gravity of the situation should not be underrated.

He had told George Kennan the day before that it was high time to do something. It might well be impossible to contain a new conflict in this area. Sixty-five per cent of the world's oil supplies were concentrated there, and their disruption would probably cause the conflict to spread. He was extremely worried about the tense situation in the Middle East and feared the worst.

I pointed out that our room for manœuvre was even more limited than that of other European countries. We had always enjoyed good relations with the Arabs but owed Israel a special duty to maintain a balance. Millions of Jews had perished at German hands. The state of Israel was a reality, and one to which we could not remain indifferent. It became clear during a talk the same evening that Tito's approach to the Jewish problem was partly coloured by his war-time experiences. He said he had watched the first Jews being exterminated from his hide-out in Belgrade, but could not understand why they had meekly allowed themselves to be killed.

On the Palestinian problem, Tito quoted Sadat to the effect that it might be solved by the creation of a West Jordanian buffer-state. The Palestinians' representatives did not accept this, however, and other Arab countries were pressing Egypt to settle the matter by force of arms. Libya was making funds available. Morocco also favoured a military solution in default of any other, and was even prepared to supply troops. Syria was against UN Resolution 242 and in favour of a military solution, as was Iraq. Nobody knew exactly what the Saudis wanted, but they were lending Egypt financial support. 'You will soon be meeting Nixon. Please inform him what a grave view I take of the situation. It is essential that an attempt be made to resolve this question peacefully. It cannot be postponed any longer. The super-powers must take some action, particularly the United States.'

I pointed out in this connection – not for the first time – that it might help if the Soviet Union resumed relations with Israel. Tito, who had noted that the Soviet Union's relations with Egypt and other Arab countries were deteriorating, replied that Egypt was hypersensitive. 'If the Jews were now allowed to emigrate from Russia to Israel without repayment of school fees, and if Israel were additionally recognized by the Soviet Union [he meant a resumption of diplomatic relations], this would mean a complete break between Egypt and the Soviet Union.' Like me, he had several times spoken to Nahum Goldmann and told him that the present situation might possibly drag on for another five, ten or even fifteen years, but what then? Would the United States continue to maintain a presence in the Mediterranean? Wouldn't the Israelis do better to withdraw from the occupied territories and aim for ultimate co-operation with the Arab countries? Goldmann had conveyed this to the Israeli leaders and been rebuked for his pains.

Neither the Americans nor the Russians wanted war in the Middle East, I said. What did Israel want? Could it be that, there too, a militant group considered another war inevitable? 'Do you think there is a growing disposition among the Arabs to risk war even without Soviet support?' Tito replied: 'The Arabs are preparing for total war. It is no longer just a question of the Suez Canal. They are ready to annihilate Israel and have the means to do so. Besides, the Arabs far outnumber the Israelis and have large areas at their disposal. There will be no repetition of June 1967 in the event of war. Egyptian weapons will not fall into Israeli hands again.'

When I visited Belgrade as Tito's guest in summer 1975, he still thought it essential that the United States and the Soviet Union should co-operate on the Middle East question. His attitude to Israel seemed considerably more cautious. Yugoslavia opposed discrimination against Israel in UNESCO and was resisting attempts to oust the Jewish state from the United Nations.

The Middle East conflict came up for renewed discussion when I visited Leonid Brezhnev in July 1975. Though clearly dissatisfied with Egyptian policy and certain other developments in the Arab camp, he also pointed out that the Soviet Government had often spoken of guarantees 'for Israel and all countries'. Israel could not retain the occupied territories. The Soviet view of the extremely complex Palestinian problem had not altered. For all Kissinger's shuttle diplomacy, the Americans had likewise failed to achieve a settlement. Only the day before, a US Senator had requested his help in solving the Middle East dispute. Soviet help would certainly be forthcoming, but certain matters must be worked out before the Geneva conference convened or all would be sound and fury. The countries in the Middle East field of tension would have to learn to compromise: one side must withdraw a little and the other move up to the old frontiers – that would restore the situation. (Gromyko put it in tougher language.) A settlement between Israel and Syria, Egypt and Iraq would be far more complicated than, say, the situation in Southern Europe. If the Federal

Republic could assist in the Middle East, Moscow would certainly raise no objection.

My knowledge of the Arab world no longer derived solely from books or conversations of a more or less fortuitous nature. Even as Mayor of Berlin I had an opportunity to get to know some of the Arab countries, and other contacts followed later. In autumn 1963 I accepted an invitation from the Governor of Cairo and met President Nasser, who expounded his policy in surprisingly moderate language. In Algeria I visited – shortly before his overthrow – the rugged-looking chairman of the Revolutionary Council, Ben Bella, who showed an interest in developments inside Germany. I had visited Tunisia as a tourist early the year before and talked with President Bourguiba and members of his government. I had also met other prominent Algerians who told me of the impending peace settlement with France, which was finally concluded at Evian in spring 1962 and wrote finis to the last French colonial war.

Tunisia I revisited during spring 1968 in the company of the Federal President and late in 1969 with my family. Morocco and its king I visited as Foreign Minister at the beginning of 1968. I only managed one intermediate stop and some rather modest discussions in Libya at the end of 1971. King Hussein of Jordan I had met in London years before. Hussein had visited Berlin and Bonn. He had also invited me to his country at a time when diplomatic relations were severed, leaving me free to combine my visit with a brief excursion to Israel. Visitors from Syria and other countries had conversed with me, first in Berlin and later in Bonn.

Our relations with the Arab countries began to return to normal during my Chancellorship. Diplomatic relations were resumed with Algeria and the Sudan in December 1971, with Lebanon in March 1972, and with Egypt in June. I was visited during the Olympic Games by the editor and presidential adviser Mohammed Hassanein Heikal, whom I had already met and knew to be an exceptionally well-informed person. He conveyed the impression that influential figures in the Arab world, and not in Egypt alone, were interested in a peace settlement which would guarantee the existence of Israel, and that Egypt would additionally welcome a European-Arab dialogue. Heikal later fell from grace. In 1973 Sadat sent me his adviser Hafiz Ismael for an informative discussion, and there were many others whose hints and suggestions helped to prepare me for my Easter trip to Algiers and Cairo in 1974.

Houari Boumedienne greeted me in Algiers on the afternoon of

19 April. I was accompanied by Federal Minister Bahr, State Secretaries Frank and von Wechmar, and my son Lars. The President struck me as a precise and austere man, but not as a fanatical zealot. He spoke frankly, as when he pointed out that an Algerian nationalist could hardly have failed to welcome Hitler's victories over the colonial powers – a remark that echoed pronouncements made by numerous Indian politicians. Algeria had made substantial strides in the ten years since my first brief visit to the country. Its régime was displaying tendencies towards what might be described as puritanical Arab socialism.

My reception in Algeria was impressive. The young country, which in many ways reflects the drive and cool discernment of its leader, Boumedienne, combines austerity with oriental charm. I was housed in the former summer residence of the French governors, now the Palais du Peuple, a snow-white Moorish confection of domes and arches hemmed in by numerous palm- and cedar-trees. Situated close to the Mediterranean and surrounded by gardens, the palace was guarded by black-uniformed Berbers in white cloaks. This was where my first talk with Boumedienne took place. I had not expected mutual understanding to be easy, having heard that the head of government was rather tense and withdrawn, so the real man came as a doubly pleasant surprise.

Boumedienne greeted me with a smile. It proved quite possible to converse in a relaxed manner, and the atmosphere soon showed traces of a cordiality for which I had been unprepared. Our talk was not overburdened even by a prior circumstance of which the press, in particular, had made much. Like other Arabs, Algerian citizens had been temporarily subjected to entry restrictions after the Munich massacre. Boumedienne found these offensive, especially as Algerians had not been involved in terrorist acts, but said that the problem could be overcome. Although I was depressed by his gestures and words of hostility towards Israel, I found that he respected our special relationship and practised a certain measure of self-restraint. I got the feeling that Algeria would not stand in the way of a reasonable settlement.

Our first discussion at the Palais du Peuple was also attended by five members of the Algerian Government including Foreign Minister Bouteflika. The Tunisian Foreign Minister, Bourguiba Jr, had introduced him to me at his home before diplomatic relations were restored, and he had since paid several visits to Bonn. Boumedienne had just returned from New York, where a special session of the UN had been convened at his request. I asked him to give me an account of it.

His reply was succinct but extremely civil. He had taken the initiative for a number of reasons, he said, though the idea stemmed principally from the summit conference of the 77 non-aligned countries held in Algiers in 1973. An imbalance existed in the relations between the industrialized and developing countries. Non-aligned and Third World countries regarded the structure of international relations, especially in the economic sphere, as inequitable. This sentiment had found a practical outlet in the energy crisis, sparked off by an unnatural situation in the Middle East. The oil crisis was only one aspect of a very much wider range of international tensions. It had none the less awakened a universal realization that the time had come to act. The United States was proposing to convene an oil conference and France wanted discussions on a broader scale, but Algeria considered it more logical and useful to discuss the raw materials situation in a UN context. Nations possessing raw materials must be enabled to retain control over them and use them for the development of their own countries; the problem of international indebtedness needed readjustment; the world economic system must be re-established on a new and more equitable basis in the interests of the developing and industrial countries alike; and, finally, a comprehensive dialogue must be started with a view to reducing confrontation.

In New York, Boumedienne went on, he had gained the impression that many countries were receptive to these ideas, though Secretary of State Kissinger's speech had conveyed a desire to retain the existing system. What mattered in the Algerian view was to take account of the interests of mankind as a whole. This entailed a comprehensive re-adjustment of the raw materials situation, not merely that sector of it – however admittedly important – which related to oil. He had consequently proposed the drafting of a special programme for the least developed countries and hoped that it would become operative in the near future. This depended on the response of the economically powerful countries. In his view, we must give practical effect to all-embracing human solidarity and reduce the gap between the affluent and impoverished countries. It would naturally be impossible for a three-week special session to resolve every associated problem such as the fight against inflation, a balance between the prices of raw materials and manufactured goods, the granting of credits to oil-producing and underdeveloped countries and the readjustment of international relations. There was every possibility, however, that these problems would be seriously debated for the first time and the way paved for better co-operation.

Replying, I pointed out that most large-scale objectives of this kind could only be attained by the piecemeal solution of their constituent problems. That was why, shortly after the UN special session, we should be discussing immediate practical steps at various levels, both bilaterally and by way of a European-Arab dialogue. This dialogue would have various points of departure including the said special programme for particularly disadvantaged developing countries, the restructuring of the raw materials markets (special consideration being paid to the interests of the producer-countries), the reform of the world monetary system, and a maximally balanced relationship between the prices of raw materials and manufactured goods. What mattered was to attain a sufficient degree of confidence in international relations. Now that the injustices of the colonial era had been abolished, we must prevent the growth of a new and pernicious disequilibrium in favour of those who produced raw materials, notably oil. Equilibrium in international relations called for practical initiatives and could certainly not be created by schematic measures. In this connection, I ventured to point out that, although the Germans might be classified as affluent today, they had started from scratch in 1945 and worked hard for their prosperity. Our controversial participation in the Washington energy conference (controversial especially in the Arab world) had been dictated by our national interests; we had always advocated subsequent negotiations with the oil-producing and economically weak countries. Wealthy countries should be sensible of their duty to lend greater assistance to countries hitherto at a disadvantage, but there still remained the difficult problem of how to readjust relations without atomizing the monetary and commercial system.

Boumedienne stressed that he appreciated Germany's positive contribution in this matter. Algeria too wanted a continuing dialogue, not confrontation, but it also wanted a comprehensive settlement which could only be reached within a framework transcending the Washington energy conference. He was bound to re-emphasize that efforts towards solidarity in the worldwide community of nations were providing a major impulse here. Political determination alone could solve the problem. His own country, too, was a prisoner of the world economic system, but we must eliminate monopoly positions – that of the dollar, for example – and at last do something to prevent the rich from growing ever richer and the poor ever poorer. The age of imperialism and exploitation must be finally laid to rest.

Before turning to our specifically national problems, Boumedienne and I spoke of the European-Arab dialogue which I had advocated in the European Community and which we had sometimes been obliged to defend fiercely against the suspicions of the State Department. I argued that the Mediterranean had always been a link, not a dividing-line, between the European and the Arab world. The geographical and historical ties between the two areas were in themselves an adequate basis for such co-operation. In the present post-colonial era, and in view of the European need for oil, this co-operation was becoming positively vital.

Speaking quite freely, Boumedienne said that Algeria opposed the division of the world into spheres of interest controlled by America and Russia. That was why the requisite balance must be based on Europe's relative independence of the super-powers – yet another argument in favour of increased co-operation between Europe, the Arab world and the African continent in general. Being situated at the point of intersection between Europe, the Arab world and Africa, Algeria was predestined for such co-operation. It also opposed super-power predominance, or even rivalry, in the Mediterranean area.

Boumedienne presented his interpretation of the Middle East dispute at a private meeting next day. None of our current endeavours could be deemed successful unless peace and security became permanent, he said. This entailed two things: an Israeli withdrawal from all occupied territories including Jerusalem, and a regard for the interests of the Palestinians. The Israelis now had no reason to fear that anyone intended to wipe their country off the map. The Arabs wanted peace on the basis of neutrality, or at least of balance. They did not, however, want what might be termed a *Pax Americana* because it would be unlikely to pay sufficient consideration to Arab interests. They would not accept a new form of imperialism as the price of peace. This was yet another reason for wanting a greater rapprochement with Europe. The super-powers were in direct confrontation in the Arab area. Confrontation would become more intense if the balance were upset, and the Arabs had no wish to be its victims. Peace in the Middle East was a matter which affected the entire Mediterranean area and thus had a direct bearing on Europe. This was a lesson taught by World War II, and one which Algeria had taken to heart. Boumedienne added, however, that I might have heard other Arab representatives give vent to differences of emphasis in their attitude to these matters.

I replied that the Federal Republic's attitude took account of the UN resolutions and the supplementary declarations of the Nine. I agreed with him that regard for the interests of the Palestinians must constitute an element in any peace settlement. On the other hand, we Germans must always be mindful of how the state of Israel came into being and could not forget the moral obligations imposed on us by the Hitler period. We were relieved that the existence of the Israeli state was no longer disputed by the Arab peoples. I fully sympathized with Algeria's efforts to avoid new forms of dependence.

Boumedienne remarked that Sadat lost no opportunity to emphasize his friendly relations with Kissinger. I suggested that the Russians might be less disturbed by Sadat's admiration for Kissinger than by a sense of having been unmasked. This could create problems for the Soviet leadership. It was my impression that Nixon did not view relations between Europe and the Arab world with any real misgivings, but one never knew if he was sufficiently well-informed about individual aspects. Although I could appreciate the Americans' disinclination to see their peace efforts in the Middle East endangered by European initiatives, the Europeans could not accept any stipulations over and above this.

Boumedienne enlarged on the subject as he saw it. Excessive Egyptian dependence on America was not, he said, conducive to solving the dispute but would tend to complicate it. The Arab countries needed a balanced policy. Discord in the Arab camp would only cloud the issue. He had told Kissinger that the Americans should make every effort not to foment dissension among the Arabs. (He added, jocularly, that Kissinger's slogan seemed to be: Russia supplies the weapons and Europe the declarations, but America the solution to the Middle East dispute.)

Boumedienne showed keen interest in my view of European affairs. I had said that Europe was an important factor economically but had not quite grown up politically. This contrast between economic strength and political limitations was particularly glaring in the case of the Federal Republic. Although the Federal Republic looked like a pocket handkerchief on the map, it had developed into a major mercantile power with bigger currency reserves than the United States. This accounted for our ability to pay out DM20,000–30,000 million more for the same quantity of raw materials this year than last year and still withstand price competition, at least for the time being.

I explained our interest in Europe's growing independence but denied that this development connoted any renunciation of the Western Alliance. We would preserve our loyal attachment to the United States and simultaneously strive for better East-West co-operation without engendering any new client relationships. Boumedienne said it would be a good thing if America accepted European unity – he had told Nixon so. Algeria and the United States had no political problems, and the two countries co-operated economically in conformity with their own interests. He had, however, been unconvinced by Nixon's comments on the European-Arab dialogue.

During our discussion of bilateral matters, Boumedienne acknowledged that the Federal Republic had become his country's strongest trading partner. He said that Algeria was seeking exemplary and mutually advantageous co-operation with us. He was particularly concerned that Germany should assist in the industrialization of Algeria and co-operate with it in third countries. I urged him to take an understanding view of our restraint in the matter of arms exports and stressed our interest in bigger deliveries of natural gas, the participation of German firms in gas liquefication, and better-defined investment regulations. The Federal Republic did, in fact, meet eleven to twelve per cent of its demand for oil (and, a few years later, a similar proportion of its natural gas requirements) from Algerian sources. Boumedienne said Algeria wanted to be more than just a supplier of raw materials, on the principle that industrialization was better than money alone. In four or five years' time it would possess large capital reserves. I noted this with satisfaction and made it clear how dangerously our currencies could be affected by roving capital.

I came away from my visit to Boumedienne much impressed by his lucid intellect and convinced that he was fully qualified to speak for the 'Group of 77'. Concentrated in his slight frame is a creative and formative urge which may make it easier for the North African and Arab nations to find their way into our technological and industrial age. Eight years after a military coup brought him to power, there was virtually no challenge to his authority. Apart from enjoying his generous hospitality, I had embarked on a practical understanding with him. Before flying on to Cairo during the afternoon of 21 April 1974, I declared that the European-Arab dialogue had begun and would be continued at my next port of call.

When we landed at Cairo airport on Easter Sunday 1974 after a direct flight from Algiers, we were told that the Egyptian capital had been swept by a severe sandstorm that morning. We could still feel the oppressive *khamsin*, or hot desert wind, which I had previously encountered in Israel. Vice-President Shafei escorted me to my temporary quarters in the Tahra Palace. The passers-by waved to us with typical Egyptian gaiety and lack of constraint. One reporter noted that the authorities had not lined the streets with 'rejoicing masses' as they did during Walter Ulbricht's state visit in 1965.

Late that same afternoon, President Anwar el Sadat greeted me at his apartment and introduced his family. Both then and later, in front of the press, he demonstrated his knowledge of German. He had learnt our language during the war, when the British interned him for a considerable period. At Abdin Palace, his official residence, Sadat somewhat ironically observed that King Farouk had once lived – if not actually worked – within its walls. The Egyptian President was always quick to smile or laugh. Extremely courteous in manner, he proved to be an alert and intelligent conversationalist whose flexibility and sporadic flashes of cunning did not detract from his sincerity, realism and emotional restraint. I had to accept the fact that his public and semi-public utterances – especially his after-dinner speeches – sometimes strained the limits imposed on us by our conception of impartiality. It was clear to me that, for the benefit of his political rivals in the Arab world and doubtless of elements in his own country, Sadat had to employ all the gestures and verbal displays typical of a 'policy of strength' in advocating a line which was fundamentally moderate and directed towards peace and compromise. His liking for our country seemed to be determined by genuine respect and not solely by memories of the fight against British colonial rule.

I strove to place our dialogue in a realistic historical perspective. Responding to Sadat's address at the state banquet, I said that our countries had long been joined by ties of a historical, economic and cultural nature.

In our first private discussion, Sadat acquainted me with his assessment of the Middle East situation. There was, he said, a danger of escalation on Syria's Golan front. This must be avoided at all costs because disengagement between Syria and Israel was a precondition of the Geneva conference. He had worked out a comprehensive plan with Kissinger which embodied separate steps and phases leading to a final settlement. The peculiarities of the Syrian Government gave the Russians room for manœuvre. This they were seeking to exploit with redoubled vigour because they were faced with a complete change in the situation in Egypt and had lost ground there in the previous six months. Egypt was the gateway to the Middle East, so the Russians were very annoyed at their loss of influence. Foreign Minister Gromyko had wanted to join Kissinger on his visits to Cairo and Damascus, but this had not been thought expedient. The importance of Soviet co-operation and aid had diminished considerably.

Continuing, Sadat said that if it proved possible to implement the plan he had worked out with Kissinger – including the Geneva negotiations – this would represent the first peace-making opportunity in 26 years. Israel's internal problems were only a minor snag because Kissinger would easily cope with them. He had managed to convince King Hussein that a Palestinian delegation must be admitted to Geneva as soon as the Palestinians had agreed on some form of joint representation. Only Egypt, Syria and Jordan would be represented to begin with. It had to be accepted that Israel would start by keeping the Palestinians out.

I said that the European Community was prepared to assume a supplementary role in securing peace in the Middle East. Economically, closer co-operation could begin at once. Politically, it would be wiser for Europe not to take on too much before its unifying process was more advanced. It was inexpedient to confuse matters and complicate solutions which others had already initiated. Sadat sympathized with these views and told me that he had discussed the matter with Kissinger in the same light. Economic co-operation could be developed in the interim, however, especially as Egypt was very interested in European technology. This might help to avert any future disputes or embargoes, as in the case of oil. I took the opportunity to thank Sadat for his moderating influence in the oil question. We discussed the projected European-Arab conference, and Sadat asked what Europe and the Federal Republic proposed to do in respect of the Middle East. After a long period of neglect, it was time to act.

The Egyptian President summarized the present state of leadership in the Arab camp. Complete agreement reigned between the Egyptian Government and King Feisal. The same applied to President Boumedienne, though he had to take account of one or two potential dissenters in his Revolutionary Council. Contact between Egypt, Saudi Arabia and Algeria – a sort of Arab Axis – was the decisive factor. Sadat was reserved about the Syrian President and the Sudanese head of government and extremely critical of the Libyan head of state. The Russians, he said, were trying to substitute Libya and the Sudan for the position they had lost in Egypt. He had his sources of intelligence and would not permit foreign bastions to be erected there. As for the Maghrib, President Bourguiba was a sick man. He had nearly been hoodwinked by Libya, but Boumedienne had stepped in and – in consultation with Cairo – made it quite clear where Algeria's interests lay. The situation in Morocco would stabilize itself. In view of Arab-Berber antagonism, King Hassan was a living guarantee of national unity. Algeria remained the most important country in the Maghrib and an important factor in the Arab world at large. Besides, the United States would scarcely tolerate a political upheaval in the Maghrib, and particularly in Morocco – America's transatlantic neighbour, so to speak.

The Soviet Union, Sadat went on, had already delayed his arms consignments for six months on the pretext that the matter was being studied. True, the Russians were annoyed and had felt left out in the cold since November 1973 because of his joint initiatives with Kissinger, but non-delivery of replacement weapons was a violation of existing agreements. He had duly announced to parliament, only the weekend before, that he was contemplating an arms switch designed to eliminate Egypt's dependence on Soviet supplies. Kissinger would also discuss this question with Gromyko at their forthcoming meeting in Geneva.

The course of this preliminary discussion showed how many hopes Sadat pinned on the US Secretary of State – 'our mutual friend Henry'. Egon Bahr, too, formed the impression during his own talks that Egyptian policy was in danger of relying almost too exclusively on the Americans' ability to settle everything. We found ourselves in the curious position of having to remind our Egyptian opposite numbers, with due discretion, that no peace settlement in the Middle East could be achieved in defiance of the other super-power. I had already made the same point in Israel.

The understanding between Sadat and Kissinger had a side-effect for which I was not wholly unprepared. I had twice discussed my trips to Algiers and Cairo with the US Secretary of State, and Kissinger had tried in his own talks with Boumedienne and Sadat to create what he considered the right climate for my visits. A few days before leaving Bonn I received a letter from Washington which implied that my trip to Egypt would serve little purpose unless I went armed with a substantial offer of financial aid. Encouraged by hints of a rather too precipitate nature, Sadat did in fact assume that I had a sizeable present in my luggage. He smilingly remarked at the end of our first meeting that we had had a good talk – tomorrow he would see what I had in my wallet. All I could have offered him were some rather modest and quite unsensational proposals. In view of the patently false hopes entertained by my host, I and my companions agreed that evening that it would be more sensible not to mention any figures at this stage – a decision to which I adhered.

Sadat's references to Kissinger were just as numerous on the second day. He said he had told the Secretary of State before my visit that he wanted to accomplish many things 'with Kissinger through Brandt'. When I asked what he meant, he replied that he was thinking of the technological sphere or, more precisely, of the fact that many of the measures agreed with Kissinger might be more promptly implemented with my help. All we did for the moment was emphasize the new quality of our relations and stake out terms of reference for the economic and technical co-operation which our departmental aides later put into concrete form.

Sadat repeated that he was having problems with the Soviet Union

which dated from before Nasser's death. There was clear evidence of
conspiratorial activities directed against his person. Though won with
Soviet weapons, his victory in the latest war had really been a gain for
America. Strong reservations about the Soviet Union had long existed
in the Arab world, if only for religious reasons. Kissinger had wrought
a genuine miracle in the past six months: he had completely transformed
the situation, so relations with the Soviet Union were bound to remain
strained in the foreseeable future. Against this background, he hoped
that Saudi Arabia and the Federal Republic would provide him with
what he needed to cope with the future.

I at once drew attention to the Federal Republic's special position and
attitude, which did not permit us to supply arms. Acknowledging this,
Sadat went on to assure me that he would do his best to avoid a crisis
with the Soviet Union. The Soviet attitude was a reaction to the fact
that Moscow saw its position in the Middle East being undermined
by Kissinger. President Assad of Syria, too, was more independent than
many supposed. In his own view, Kissinger was a grand strategist and
a man of visionary power. Referring to the Watergate crisis, which was
then approaching its climax, he added that we should both use all our
influence to ensure that Kissinger remained in office even if Nixon
stepped down. If Kissinger left office prematurely, it would have an
extremely detrimental effect on his part of the world.

Sadat hoped that, having assumed a major responsibility in pursuing
our *Ostpolitik*, my government was now prepared to undertake a
similar responsibility by addressing itself to the Arab countries. He was
convinced that my line towards the East was the best one possible and
would have a beneficial effect on the prospects for German reunification. I set forth the basic outlines of my foreign policy and stressed
that it could not be Europe's intention to obstruct American endeavours
in the Middle East. We wanted to expand our economic and technical
relations, develop our exchange of views and prepare ourselves to
assume greater political responsibility on a joint basis. I also said that
co-operation with Egypt might serve as a bridge between Europe and
large tracts of Africa.

It was not lost on me that President Sadat had a natural gift for
engaging the interests of others, including partners of our own calibre
as well as the super-powers. I took his more extravagant statements
cum grano, as when he exaggerated his friendship with America or
sharply inveighed against the Soviet Union. I was far from inclined to
ignore the continuity of self-interest underlying his swift tactical moves.
'*Geduld macht glücklich*' [patience brings happiness], he declared at a
press conference with some German newspapermen, translating one of

his native proverbs into our own tongue. What made me optimistic was the remarkable degree of circumspection which all his verbal strongman acts failed to hide. This was founded on a down-to-earth approach which I also encountered in Secretary-General Mahmoud Riad of the Arab League. At its Cairo headquarters I met representatives of all the Arab countries and was able to forge some useful contacts in the course of practical discussions.

On the third day of my stay in Egypt I was invited to visit the devastated port of Suez. The few citizens who still inhabited the ruins gave me a friendly reception. I was less concerned with whose captured weapons I was shown on this occasion than with the human lives that had been lost in battle. I crossed the Suez Canal without undue qualms and listened to Egyptian officers describing the conquest of the celebrated Bar Lev Line, whose fortifications had been hosed away with the aid of German pumps. Accounts of the fighting interested me less than the officer-types I now had a chance to observe. I noticed some degree of resemblance to the Israeli soldiers whom I had met on my visit to 'the other side'. Both countries seemed to have produced a generation of brisk and businesslike young men whose attitude was coloured by their first-hand experience of modern technology.

The fact that common features might one day become stronger than points of difference did not in itself preclude the possibility of strife. I recalled how many terrible wars and crises the nations of Europe had had to undergo before they resolved to discard the bonds of enmity. I none the less sensed that Israelis and Arabs of the new generation might gain the opportunity to decide in favour of mutual understanding. The dictates of reason had never seemed clearer to me than they did during those hours in the disputed desert whose wide expanses were an invitation to lucidity and simplicity of thought.

Even though the foregoing pages contain several allusions to a European-Arab dialogue, it should be realized that this had yet to be associated with any definite political plan. What, in that case, did it imply? In the first place, a recognition by the West Europeans that they would be unable to evade joint responsibility for an adjacent area; secondly, an interest on the part of the Arab leaders in reducing their dependence on the super-powers; and, thirdly, common economic interests. Discounting a variety of separate agreements, what was involved here was a free trade area on the southern margin of the European Community. Even as Foreign Minister, I had advocated a Community Mediterranean policy based on transitional arrangements for the Maghrib countries and separate trade agreements with the rest. Here, too, lay a chance of leading Israel out of its isolation and placing its technological and scientific resources at the service of an entire region.

Here as in other fields, however, the European Community was advancing too slowly. The sum of outstanding problems remained fairly constant. No one could be certain that endeavours towards a lasting peace in the Middle East would, or would not, be frustrated by another war. Anyone could see that the struggle for Arab unity was being hampered by a potent conflict of interests, and who was ready to predict what would become of the presence and influence of the Americans and Russians in the Mediterranean area, even a decade ahead?

In practical terms, what will become of Italy, and what effect will its political regroupings have, not only on the Mediterranean area but on the communities of the West? Will developments in the Iberian Peninsula give birth to a new and lasting democracy, or will it become a source of fresh uncertainty? Will Yugoslavia's national unity remain intact, and will it succeed in asserting its non-alignment? Quite apart from the Middle East conflict, the Eastern Mediterranean presents an abundance of unresolved and disquieting problems.

I was genuinely delighted when the Greek Colonels' régime reached the end of its tether in summer 1974. The new government sent me an invitation shortly afterwards, but I was unable to take it up until a year later. I received a splendid welcome in Athens, which I had visited as Mayor of Berlin in autumn 1960. This time I was received by the newly elected President, not the King. Konstantin Karamanlis had been head of government before, but there was a profound difference. His years in exile had left their mark, and it was a freer wind that smote the visitor's cheek. In 1960 I had been greeted by the then deputy premier, Panayotis Kanellopoulos, who later headed the government overthrown by the military coup in 1967. He now held no government post, but he still preserved the natural dignity that had sustained him as a central figure in the liberal resistance movement. I had also met old Georgios Papandreou at the German Embassy – perforce, since the leader of the Centre Union was not invited to any official functions. I now received a visit from his son Andreas but was not over-impressed by his radical socialist ideas. I felt politically close to the social democratic leaders of the new Centre Union, some of whom had lived in the Federal Republic during the years of dictatorship. The former Mayor of Athens, who was back in office, conferred hononary citizenship on me.

The services ascribed to me included a simple act of omission. On touching down at Athens airport in spring 1969, on my way back from Turkey, I had declined to leave the aircraft rather than be welcomed by the régime. Although I considered it inappropriate for us to sit in political judgement, even on Greece, I had made no secret of my belief that dictatorships did not belong in the community of European nations. Greek membership of the Council of Europe had to be suspended, certain economic undertakings withdrawn and deliveries of military equipment restricted to the minimum prescribed by NATO agreements. At the same time, I and my colleagues tried with some success to intervene on behalf of those who were being persecuted and lend their families a measure of support. Although I received more gratitude than I deserved, I do not deny that my encouragement of humanitarian assistance went beyond what others deemed to be the bounds of legality. As in the case of other countries, I preferred to dispense with public protests and swallow the criticism of those who shared my hopes whenever I could render practical assistance by discreet means.

What touched me most of all during my talks in summer 1975 was the extent to which not only Karamanlis – who solicited my friendship – but Professor Mangakis and other friends from the Centre Union evinced concern about their country's links with Europe. They regarded these links as a brake on antidemocratic temptations. Democracy in Greece would be more secure, so the argument ran, if everyone were aware of the disadvantages associated with severance from the European Community. Although I could make no promises on behalf of the government of my country or the Community, I realized that a formula for close association must be swiftly devised if the dangers of disappointment were to be avoided. A speech of thanks for my honorary degree at the Academy of Political Sciences provided me with an opportunity to present my own view of the relationship between democracy and European integration.

Karamanlis adopted a far more moderate tone towards the Cyprus problem than most of the Greek politicians I met. A wide degree of separation between the island's Greek and Turkish ethnic groups seemed to be taken for granted. The passage of time was not assisting the Greeks' understandable efforts to obtain a fairer line of demarcation than that produced by Turkish intervention in 1974. I had sensed a readiness to compromise when talking to Turkish representatives, but my occasional contacts with Cypriot politicians had done nothing to curb their antagonisms. It was depressing that Europe could not muster the wisdom or determination to strive for a fair compromise with those directly and indirectly concerned, thereby paving the way for a solution which would stand the test of time.

The European Community came close to failure over a very much simpler island problem – that of Malta. I had urged when Foreign Minister that Malta should not be simply left to itself and to random foreign influences when it cut adrift from Britain. As Federal Chancellor, I was able to help Premier Dom Mintoff with some of his more pressing problems.

It was not merely the dispute over Cyprus that kept alive the traditional Graeco-Turkish feud and imposed such a heavy and enduring strain on NATO. One had to accept that interests in the Aegean would give rise to other major controversies. The question, once again, was how the Europeans could exert a moderating and regulating influence. American activities were seldom attended by success. As for the Russians, nothing could be expected from them but a resolute pursuit of their own interests. In this connection, the Greek premier had told me – then in confidence – that he wanted to promote regional co-operation with Bulgaria, Rumania, Yugoslavia and Turkey. A modest start was made at the turn of 1975–6.

I had been somewhat favourably predisposed towards Turkey by Ernst Reuter, who helped to train a whole generation of senior civil servants while in exile there. I was also able to form some personal impressions of the great country on the edge of Europe when visiting it as Foreign Minister in spring 1969. They were strong impressions from the cultural aspect and not discouraging from that of modernization. The Turkish predilection for everything German would have shamed me had I not been prepared for it. I did not, however, find it easy to form a solid assessment of the Turkish political situation. One could not ignore the powerful influence of the military, who – as in many developing countries – saw themselves cast in a civilizing role. The Foreign Minister and Premier, both then and later, were Ihsan Sabri Caglayangil and Süleyman Demirel of the Justice Party. In recent years, Bülent Ecevit and his Republican People's Party had sought contact with the social democratic parties of Europe. We exchanged visits, and I found that he enjoyed strong support among those of his compatriots who were working in our country.

Only outnumbered by the Turkish contingent of migrant workers in the Federal Republic were the Yugoslavs, whose efficiency was much esteemed there. German-Yugoslav relations also benefited from a brisk tourist trade. In summer 1975 Tito sent an aircraft to Athens so that I could stop off in Belgrade and pursue my exchange of views with him and his colleagues. I found the 84-year-old President brimming with energy and far from decrepit, but I was not alone in wondering if his successors would be capable of holding their heterogenous country together. (Some sceptics regard Yugoslavia as one of the major threats to the European balance of power and, thus, to peace. Many of the régime's internal disciplinary measures should undoubtedly be viewed in this context.) At all events, the relationship between Belgrade and Moscow was of special interest.

In 1973 the President had said that the Western press often interpreted Yugoslavia's recent line as one of convergence with the Soviet Union. This was not so, nor was it seen as such by the Kremlin. 'We made it clear to the Russians that they must take us as we are, in other words, as a non-aligned country. Brezhnev fully concurred with this. Since then, our relations have been developing well.' Brezhnev did, in fact, intimate during our earliest meetings that he was concerned to maintain sound contacts with Tito. In May 1973 he said that, although relations with Yugoslavia had been temporarily marred by 'theoretical difficulties', they were now better. His personal relationship with Tito had always been 'splendid' and characterized by mutual respect. Tito's entourage had not been 'good' for a certain period, but Tito had realized this and taken a firmer grip on things.

On the internal situation in his country, Tito remarked that many difficulties had formerly been experienced with technocrats who tried to assert their claims to authority over the rights of the workers. It had later been necessary to subdue sporadic outbursts of nationalism and quell certain Cominform elements left over from the past. 'We have greatly strengthened the League of Communists,' Tito said. 'We have a great deal to do in our country. For instance, there is the question of the nations or republics. Many people believed that this would lead to disintegration, but the contrary is true. It is sometimes difficult to preserve unity in a country as nationally heterogeneous as Yugoslavia. What matters most is the solidarity of the League of Communists. This is the only force that can guarantee cohesion. That is why the principle of democratic centralism must be imposed despite opposition from individual republics.'

It was clear that the LCY – together with the army – was regarded as the country's essential binding agent. 1975 brought renewed evidence of this in the rigorous suppression of attempts, which were certainly not of domestic origin alone, to build up a rival communist party.

In the Iberian Peninsula, the surge of emancipation and internal transformation was swifter than most interested or expert observers had predicted. In Spain the Franco régime was dying on its feet, but it remained uncertain, even after the dictator's death, whether an entirely peaceful transition to modern constitutionalism would be feasible. Portugal witnessed the overthrow of Salazar's decades-long dictatorship, which had been perpetuated in a somewhat milder form by Professor Marcelo Caetano. The two neighbouring countries, which had turned their backs on each other for centuries, became a great new source of hope for European democracy.

Mario Soares came to see me on 3 May 1974 – the last foreign visitor of my Chancellorship. I knew him only slightly, though he had founded his Socialist Party two years earlier at Bad Münstereifel (the pretty little town near Bonn where I am writing this book). We had also been able to help him a little during his exile in Paris. He now came on behalf of the new President, Antonio de Spínola, who appointed him Foreign Minister shortly afterwards. His first but unrewarding task was to carry out decolonization. His real achievement consisted in transforming the idea of a party into a living reality beneficial to the Portuguese people. This he did with great courage, an incorruptible commitment to freedom and the gifts of a great public speaker.

As everyone knows, it was a military group, the Armed Forces Movement, which assumed power on 25 April 1974. Rebellion was ultimately triggered by the miseries of colonial warfare, in which many young officers had been influenced by contact with the liberation movements. The backward state of the Portuguese motherland, with its 40 per cent illiteracy, cried out for reform. As to the manner of reform, opinions soon diverged widely, not only among the military but among the new parties constituting the revolutionary government. Portuguese colonial policy had caused me much concern as Foreign Minister and Chancellor. Although we insisted when supplying arms within the framework of the Alliance that all such equipment must remain in Portugal, it was inevitable that the African liberation movements should mistrust us. Our own attitude to them was unduly reserved. The Soviet commitment in Angola might never have happened if the West had evolved a consistent policy towards Africa. I also recall the stupidity we encountered in Lisbon in autumn 1970, when, after consultation with Kenneth Kaunda, we sounded out the possibility that Portugal's possessions might be granted a change of status over the next ten to fifteen years. The Portuguese Government reacted negatively – so much so that a full transmission of their reply would have left the Zambian President with little more than a verbal kick in the pants.

I visited Lisbon in October 1974 feeling 'not like a schoolmaster', as the press aptly pointed out. My purpose was to gather information and lend all possible support to our young Portuguese affiliate. Though still in the throes of structural development, the PSP championed its conception of 'socialism in freedom' with great vigour. The revolution's early enthusiasm had evaporated. Spínola had been ousted on the grounds that he was too right-wing, and younger officers were calling the tune. Several of them made an outstanding impression while others appeared confused and some were falling under the sway of radical splinter-groups. The Portuguese Communist Party, whose influence seemed to be growing, could call on the framework of an illegal organization. It dominated Intersindical, the trade union federation, controlled a substantial section of the media and received considerable foreign backing.

Nobody knew what form the country's economic future would take. Major firms and banks had been nationalized and the big landowners were to be cut down to size by land reform, but little scope existed for a fresh economic effort. Many experts had deserted the country and prospects for increased co-operation with outsiders were lacking. My own view was that the European Community's hour had struck, but Brussels and the individual European governments failed to gird themselves for swift and constructive action. The Lisbon authorities were so preoccupied with other matters that they had little time for these practical tasks. There was widespread foreign uncertainty over what would become of Portugal. The same applied to its membership of the Atlantic Alliance, which the military rulers never disputed. Had communist influence prevailed, this would certainly have lapsed or become extremely problematic. The Communist Party's participation in government was perplexing enough in itself.

The Portuguese displayed an admirable capacity for preventing the escalation of violence. There was much talk and little shooting, but the political situation became increasingly unstable. As wielders of political authority, the officers presented a picture of great confusion. The democratic parties devoted most of their time to mutual strife. The communist leaders were doubly purposeful by comparison. In the spring, late summer and autumn of 1975 it looked as if they would take over the country completely. I urged the mobilization of a counter-force, not only out of solidarity with our Portuguese political allies but for the sake of European development as a whole. There followed a relief operation whose full story cannot yet be written. It was the product of secret collaboration between a handful of social democratic party leaders. We opened no new offices and shunned publicity. Instead, we strove to lend concrete political and moral support and combat the defeatism that was gaining a hold on influential circles in the West.

Many people were on the verge of writing Portugal off. I fiercely opposed this tendency, citing my own experience of life in support of the principle that few situations are hopeless provided one refuses to accept them. Without shouting it from the rooftops, we exploited numerous international contacts in an effort to secure a fair chance for Portuguese democracy. Also under this heading came the talks I had in Washington in spring 1975, first with Kissinger at the German Embassy and next day with President Ford at the White House. I was given an attentive hearing, and my judgement was confirmed when the results of the election to the Constituent National Assembly were published in April: the PSP emerged as the strongest party with 38 per cent of the poll, while the PCP had to be satisfied with 12 per cent. The Socialists also began to gain ground in trade union elections.

I publicly stated in Washington that the birth-pangs of Portugal's revolutionary upheaval after long years of dictatorship would have been eased by a more helpful attitude on the part of the Western democracies. An injudicious approach to developments on the south-west coast of our continent might have an extremely adverse effect, not only on Spain but on East-West relations. I drew Brezhnev's attention to these related factors and sources of concern when I visited Moscow in July 1975. He said that he did not know Portugal and its present crop of politicians. He had not met Alvaro Cunhal either, but approved of the communist leader's attitude. What worried him was that Portugal might put a brake on the CSCE. I pointed out that further friction would be inevitable if the communists joined forces with military elements in an attempt to nullify the election results and their consequences. Soares was not anti-Soviet, I said, nor was he opposed to a coalition government, but he refused to be done down and we would not leave him in the lurch. Portugal must find its own way without foreign interference. Wherever advice could be given, it should favour moderation.

Later in our discussion, Brezhnev remarked that the nature and pace of developments ought primarily to be a matter for the Portuguese. Soviet policy was founded on the principle of non-interference, but certain NATO countries had yet to abandon their efforts to meddle in Portugal's internal affairs. Although he still had insufficient documentation on the subject, he profoundly regretted the fact that many representatives of the international social democratic movement, not excluding the SPD, were attacking the Portuguese Communist Party and other forces of the Left. This could not be beneficial and was evidence of excessive partiality. Both sides harboured conflicting sympathies founded on different ideological platforms. It should none the less be their common endeavour to promote victory over fascist and anti-democratic elements by all available means; the right-wing forces of the past had yet to lay down their arms.

It was my impression that the Portuguese complex of problems was handled in Moscow by that part of the apparat which bore responsibility for co-operation with communist parties abroad (and that backing for the PCP was largely transmitted via the SED, in other words, East Berlin). The authorities in Moscow – as elsewhere – seemed to be in danger of misconstruing the Americans' obscure reactions and the uncertain attitude of the West Europeans. American intervention – of which I was naturally no advocate – would have been vehemently criticized but received with greater comprehension. The absence of any authoritative declaration (in the sense of an Atlantic Doctrine) may have prompted the Russians to believe that they could acquire something akin to a European Cuba. This was not, however, the impression conveyed by Brezhnev himself, who seemed intensely concerned that the policy of détente and co-operation should not fail.

I rejected the General Secretary's imputations of a 'pro-right-wing attitude'. On the contrary, I said, the danger was that an extreme left-wing movement might – as in Chile – provoke a reactionary counter-coup. Besides, there was no doubt that the Portuguese Communist Party had received incomparably greater support via its international links than the Portuguese Socialist Party, with its modest initial backing. If we wanted to prevent a return to fascism and avert a Chilean situation, nothing must be done to overturn the election results. Adverse repercussions on Southern Europe and Europe in general would otherwise become inevitable.

Before leaving Moscow, I reverted to this subject during a second interview with Brezhnev. He asked what both sides ought to do. I replied that I had no specific proposals to submit but thought the communists should be told to respect the country's electoral verdict and refrain from excessive pressure. It is probable that sundry pieces of advice were, in fact, transmitted to the Portuguese communist leaders. The Italian and Spanish communists had already expressed their firm dissociation.

But the situation remained fraught with danger. Civil war could no longer be ruled out and talk of a Lisbon commune went the rounds. Excesses of anti-communist vandalism were committed in the north. Right-wing groups in the interior and nests of resistance abroad tinkered with schemes for intervention – even for partition. Some measure of clarity was restored when an attempted left-wing coup failed in November. The decision seemed to have gone in favour of constitutional democracy. Impulses towards thoroughgoing social reform were bound to wane, but much now depended on how the

Portuguese Government tackled its grave economic problems. The high-level Committee for Friendship and Solidarity whose establishment I proposed at a meeting of social democratic party leaders in Stockholm in summer 1975, and whose chairmanship I was obliged to assume when Harold Wilson invited us to inaugurate it in London at the beginning of September, has striven to achieve something in this field.

Mario Soares seemed much relieved when he visited Bonn in mid-December. We and our Portuguese friends had been undeterred by defeatist forebodings. Those who were disposed to write off Portugal as a part of Europe and the Western community had been proved wrong. The Portuguese had made a major break-through to a better future. The solving of their economic problems was now of paramount importance, and there was still time to recognize this as a European task. I also saw it as a chance to prove whether and how Europe could assimilate democratic socialist developments.

Late in 1975 we were faced with a changed situation in Spain as well. The transition to the post-Franco era represented a break in historical continuity, but the country was only at the start of an arduous journey during which decisions would have to be taken about its internal structure and close ties with Europe. The statements of intent made by the new ministers responsible to King Juan Carlos, who had visited us in Bonn as successor-designate, were received with widespread and favourable interest. It had at the same time to be pointed out that, where friends of Spain were concerned, scope for increased co-operation depended on the creation of firm prerequisites for the growth of democratic institutions. Not regarding it as interference to draw attention to factors with an important bearing on Spain's peaceful domestic development and relations with Europe, I backed the demands of the Spanish opposition: the release of political prisoners, the repeal of the 'anti-terrorist' laws, freedom of the press and association, freedom of organization for trade unions and political parties.

I was among those who fully appreciated that more could be expected from a process of gradual transformation than from an abrupt change. It takes time to dissolve the incrustations of a decades-old dictatorship and lay the foundations of a new political and social existence. Although it could benefit no one to reopen the half-healed wounds inflicted by a brutal civil war, it was equally clear that the process of transformation would not follow a successful course if structural changes were too long delayed. Political and trade union forces had to enjoy freedom of organization and activity. The future of the Spanish people and their future relations with democratic Europe, its countries and communities, would be largely dependent on this. Spain's prime need of the moment was to be offered a practical democratic alternative. It was my natural duty to support our Spanish socialist friends.

During the latter years of the Franco régime, the long-established Socialist Workers' Party had moved its headquarters back to Spain from exile. Though still subjected to harassment, it acquired semi-legal status. I first met its Secretary, Felipe Gonzales, a young lawyer from Seville, when he visited Lisbon in autumn 1974. Some months later he contrived to attend a party leaders' conference in Berlin. We managed with some difficulty to get him to our party conference in Mannheim at the end of 1975, and our sedulous maintenance of a correct relationship with the authorities enabled us to intervene successfully in a number of cases. Through friendly observers in Madrid and elsewhere, I satisfied myself of the ramified and constructive nature of the opposition forces. There seemed every likelihood that a major role would be played by democratic socialists and that they would command considerably more support than the communists, however well organized. I also formed the impression that anarcho-syndicalism would not re-emerge as a mass movement, though some of its emancipatory tradition seemed to live on in those who called for a federal structure and greater regional autonomy.

When the Civil War began in summer 1936 and was swiftly characterized by intervention on a massive scale, many of us saw it as the prelude to a second world war. We were right, but few of us who so passionately espoused the cause of Spanish democracy and its legitimate government could have imagined that the Caudillo would rule for nearly forty years. His régime became the trauma of the European Left. For myself, I can say that, although the impressions I formed during the early months of 1937 had never become fainter or less vivid, I had eschewed the prejudices that might have been associated with them. What remained was my attachment to the noble nation of which Bismarck said that its rulers had done their utmost to destroy it over the centuries but failed; what remained was my memory of countless human sacrifices coupled with the hope that the horrors of the past need never be repeated.

Industrially, Spain had made considerable strides. Of this I saw evidence in Malaga at the beginning of 1969 and in the Canaries late in 1972. Culturally and socially as well, Spain was far better equipped for association with the development of Western Europe than its neighbour on the Atlantic seaboard. I can wish the inhabitants of this inalienably European peninsula nothing better than a secure and democratic future.

18

Outlook

By the end of 1976 the German Social Democrats will have been in government for a decade. I believe the effects to have been beneficial, and not only by national standards. The Federal Republic of Germany has made considerable gains in economic strength and political influence during these years, so far without acquiring any liabilities. Bonn's liberal-socialist coalition enjoys the confidence of the outside world; the Federal Republic's great resources – military included – arouse no fear and cause no disquiet. Much depends, of course, on whether Germany's major potential continues to be handled judiciously and with a sense of collective responsibility.

No ruling party, least of all one that has jointly held office for years, is immune from signs of wear and tear. The problems devolving on my own party from a change in generations and shifting social structures have been discussed elsewhere. It has never occurred to me to take them lightly. I have learnt that no one engaged in the struggle between democratic forces should ever be too sure of his opinions. Measured against current requirements, the Social Democrats, too, have far from always done justice to their historic responsibilities. But I would hasten to add this: just as the German Social Democrats have proved themselves a force for freedom and justice in Europe, so the forces of liberal socialism will have to prove their mettle as a whole, not only against conservative political groupings but also, and increasingly, as an alternative to communism.

It is a readily verifiable fact that wherever in Europe the broad working masses are represented by democratic socialists – in Germany by the Social Democrats – communist movements wield no appreciable influence. Although party patterns in other parts of the world are not strictly comparable, liberal socialism's worldwide mission remains the same.

For quite a while now, a ubiquitous and sometimes rather heated debate has centred on whether the policy of détente – a purposeful and realistic attempt to reduce tension – has failed. The quick answer is that nothing has occurred to change the fundamental interest of all countries in averting a third world war and a nuclear holocaust. Détente has never been a question of fashion. What matters is to reduce tensions, not eliminate them. My own concern has always been, and will ever be, to modify the basic circumstances of the East-West conflict in such a way as to diminish tension, develop effective forms of co-operation and increase the chances of peace.

It was not always clearly enough recognized that East-West détente derived its real impetus from technological progress. Both sides were enjoined to prevent a third world war by the theoretical ability of the super-powers to annihilate each other several times over. Renunciation of force in the attainment of unilateral objectives was based on the realization that, certainly in Europe, North America and the Soviet Union, the inter-bloc use of military force would be suicidal. The fact remains that rivalries persist. Neither side has abandoned its objectives and each thinks it knows the better course for mankind to adopt.

I and my political associates have always appreciated that détente is a process subject to setbacks but devoid of an acceptable alternative. We are now convinced that it has benefited East-West relations in Europe, that is to say, in the area where agreements have been reached in accordance with that process. Why should anyone have subscribed to the miraculous belief that détente would apply to the very areas for which no agreements existed? The world is suffering, not from a surfeit of détente, but from the fact that too few areas have as yet been covered by peace-keeping agreements. It was clear that the super-powers had come to no arrangement about crises in Africa. It was equally clear that they had not come to terms on the subject of naval armaments. This being so, nothing could prevent the Soviet Union from acquiring the status of an imperial power. The fact still remained that we were dealing with a changed set of international circumstances.

During the Cold War, strong and almost lethal tensions prevailed between East and West. It was a state of affairs in which almost all the ingredients of a real war were present apart from the sound of guns and the sight of blood. We played a major role in helping to overcome the Cold War and introduce a period of détente – one which we hope will be more than episodic. As things stood, our principal contribution had to be what I once described as a painful recognition of realities. The Russians too, have shared in this process. I refer not only to their laborious acceptance of West European integration. Above all, they have acknowledged the continuing American presence in Europe – politically, militarily and centrally. This was a significant change of tack.

Although the image of twin columns supporting the Atlantic partnership is accurate, it should not tempt one to conclude that there is a finite division of labour between the partners on either side of the Atlantic, nor that their range of functions coincides at certain points only. The tentative integration of the countries of Western Europe is being matched by an appreciable degree of American integration with Europe. This has occurred imperceptibly and almost as a matter of course. It need not weaken the process of convergence into a European Union. It need not endanger the development of what may be termed a European personality. It corresponds to natural interdependences and interrelationships whose essence is reciprocity.

I urged, perhaps a little too impatiently, that the United States should be quick to recognize the potential unity of its European partner and take it seriously. This had, and still has, nothing to do with my realization that the United States and Western Europe – even in its present form – have identical interests in vital areas, notably that of security. It would none the less be unrealistic and contrary to historical experience to expect an invariable identity of view to prevail between them. If the United States is to acquire a stronger partner in a united Western Europe, it cannot dispute that partner's right to adopt positions of its own.

The development of weapons systems has created a situation in which no effective system of defence for Western Europe and North America is conceivable except as a whole. The detachment of America from this system would jeopardize its own security. For Europe, it would spell an inevitable and central loss of security. This does not destroy the need to take serious note of security considerations in foreign policy debates between members of the European Community and, where circumstances permit, to promote their discussion.

Although I do not doubt the United States' capacity for regeneration, it does not absolve us Europeans from taking our own affairs in hand. None of the many disappointments that have beset convinced Europeans in recent years can detract from the historical need for close association. It is true that the European Community has been put to its sternest test, not only by worldwide economic developments but also by incapacity on the part of individual governments. It is equally true that proposals for differentiated integration – though without detriment to relevant Community interests – have been cast to the winds. Relations with neighbouring countries in the north and south, some of whom behave in a more 'European' way than the members of the Community itself, have often been denied the requisite attention.

At the beginning of December 1975, when the governments of the Nine resolved – in default of agreement on very much else – that the European Parliament should be directly elected by 1978, I took it as a summons. The reader will recall that I considered the powers of the European Parliament to be more important than its mode of election. Realizing that direct elections could lend fresh momentum to the process of European unification, I did not hesitate to take the governments at their word and announce my candidacy. It received due attention, but whether or when direct elections will become a European reality I would not, at the time of writing, venture to judge. The danger is that yet another sudden blaze of hope will be swiftly extinguished. For all that, we have no alternative to Europe.

In my view, the Community should be more than a framework of economic interests. Europe's place in the world will not be properly filled until it articulates a coherent political resolve and acts on it. This entails a governmental structure – suitably controlled – for areas of joint responsibility. The EEC must become capable of action in foreign policy; irrespective of what I have said about our links with America, it will not be able to exclude considerations of security policy. But the projected European Union will be nothing but a cloud-castle unless it acquires economic and monetary foundations commensurate with its democratic and social substance. The Europe for which we are working must be an example to the world of the rule of reason over productive factors, the rule of justice over the egoisms of power, and the rule of humanity over the disease of intolerance.

I have repeatedly pointed out, as I did on my last visit to the Soviet Union, that the European Community should be seen not only as an economic marriage of convenience but as a factor conducive to peace and security. It poses a threat to no one. The classic case of Franco-German co-operation has illustrated what positive forces can be mobilized for the permanent establishment of peace on our continent. To repeat: the policy of European unification and the policy of détente should be construed as two great parallel and interdependent undertakings.

Expectations of European unity cannot console one against West European disappointments. It has become clear that progress in European East-West relations will also remain limited in the foreseeable future. Trade has developed reasonably well. Practical relaxations have been negotiated for the inhabitants of both parts of Germany and Berlin in particular, but many other opportunities for co-operation have yet to be grasped. The illusionists who believed that international conferences would in future decree the abolition of communism have indeed been disappointed; so have those who imagined that agreement would be possible on matters irreconcilable with the interests of the governments concerned.

It was no small thing to have established the renunciation-of-force principle in our bilateral treaties, which in turn reacted on the Helsinki Conference and other related factors. This did not affect our claim to self-determination and national unity. It was simply that the Federal Republic's pledge to its Western partners to refrain from the use of force in pursuing given objectives had been conjoined with corresponding legal obligations towards the East. To put it another way, we had to accept the *status quo* territorially in order to dislodge it politically.

I have not disguised my faith in the regenerative powers of the United States. I have also presupposed that Soviet society, with its relative conservatism and sometimes hidebound appearance, will be equal to the new demands of international politics. Having no first-hand experience of China, I cannot judge which way the world's most populous country will turn. It is deeply engrossed in vast schemes for social development, however, and there are no signs that it is straying from the path of international moderation which its leaders have so far pursued.

I have not been surprised by the continuing process of differentiation in the Soviet camp (not that this renders it any less 'dangerous') or by the fact that the GDR has, despite everything, remained a peculiarly uncomfortable bedfellow. I was, however, distressed that the adjustment of our relations with Poland should have called forth spectral arguments reminiscent of the 1950s. It became clear that we, too, found it hard to break the bonds of the past and abandon rigid and reputedly impregnable positions.

It is an inescapable fact that confidence cannot grow unless progress is made towards reducing armed forces and armaments in Central Europe. The conferences at Helsinki and Vienna have shown that the policy of co-operation remains difficult, that it is far from always destined to make progress and must take repeated setbacks in its stride. There is certainly an abundance of contradictions: partial compromise and continuing rivalry, détente and armaments, spectacular joint ventures in space and growing worldwide confrontation on the high seas, increased trade between industrialized countries and with raw materials producers *vis-à-vis* inadequate steps to combat hunger in many parts of the world, professions of faith in peaceful coexistence and a reluctance to engage in intellectual debate . . . The ordinary citizen finds it hard to pick his way through this maze of conflicting tendencies, and the practising politician fares little differently. Such is the world in which we live, however, and the odds are that it will grow more complex still.

The dictum that East-West relations are already largely overshadowed by the exacerbation of the North-South conflict is gradually becoming a commonplace. Our species of democracy and liberal society is increasingly threatened by the growing gulf between affluence and poverty, between industrial wealth and stagnant underdevelopment, between technological advances and dwindling hopes of progress, between surfeited societies and stark hunger. There is a new and no longer silent majority in the world – a majority of undernourished nations. They face a minority of what they consider prosperous countries – a minority powerful enough to have influenced the fate of almost every human being in the farthest corners of the earth, yet not powerful enough to provide for a future free from fear and afford the majority of the world's inhabitants a life in which at least the simplest of daily needs can be satisfied.

An adjustment of interests is essential. The problems involved here will remain paramount, at least until the end of the millenium. Classical notions of hegemony are no longer up for debate. The world's leaders will be those who respond to the global needs of humanity with relevant and realistic ideas and can put those ideas into practice by dint of their economic and political muscle. This is another urgent reason for trust and partnership between Europe and America, but it will also require the consent and co-operation of the Soviet Union and the industrialized countries of Eastern Europe.

By the time I completed this manuscript, some corner of the world had witnessed the birth of the child who took the world's population past the four-thousand-million mark. Between 1800 and 1930, mankind doubled its numbers from one to two thousand million. The third thousand million came in thirty, the fourth in fifteen years. Before the end of the present century, the world's population will comprise six thousand million human beings. Who would deny that many of our current problems pale into insignificance beside this challenge? The imposition of curbs on the population explosion is becoming mankind's most pressing and important task.

The developing countries are calling for a new world economic system. Two-thirds of humanity are refusing to accept a seven per cent share of the world's industrial output. It is no longer a question of whether majority participation in the world's wealth can be prevented; the question is whether this development can be controlled or will be accomplished by force. For the moment, neither side can impose its economic system on the other. The new economic world order will consequently be a juxtaposition of diverse economic systems. The incipient dialogue between the industrial and the developing countries has brought a widespread realization that we require a fundamentally new approach towards the South as well. Both sides are capable of mutual injury but neither can defeat the other. Here too, therefore, it is necessary to achieve détente. Here too, only a limited reconciliation of interests will be possible. Rivalries will persist and setbacks continue to occur, but no reasonable alternative to détente can be discerned, least of all in this field.

If we are to master our material problems, we shall also have to determine the human image and ethical substructure on which our political decisions must be based. Every country will have to define the contribution it proposes to make to the development of a new world economic framework. Needless to say, nothing can be achieved unless decisive efforts are made in the developing countries as well.

At the end of 1974 I stressed my solidarity with UNICEF when it declared a state of emergency for children and documented the chronic malnutrition from which hundreds of millions were suffering. For many children, protein and vitamin deficiency spelt an untimely death or irreparable effects on growth. I defined the pernicious cycle as follows: poverty breeds malnutrition, malnutrition breeds suscepti-bility to disease, disease breeds apathy and a diminished capacity for work. The socially deleterious effects of such a vicious circle are obvious: family planning is impossible and communities decay, giving rise to more poverty, more starvation, more apathy.

The peace we seek cannot simply be equated with the proscription of war. It must be a peace rooted in interdependence and nourished by common interests: a peace that will help us human beings to bear con-jointly the burdens we still unfairly divide – a peace associated with hopes for a worthy mode of survival. For the sake of such a peace, the use of force must be opposed and negotiation encouraged. This is why it pays us to curb any revolutionary squandering of energy and pro-mote those peaceful reforms which are the essence of social democracy.

In more than one part of the world, people have begun to accept that peace must take precedence over ideology. I stated in my Peace Prize speech – and subsequently in Moscow and Washington, Cairo and Jerusalem – that there is no single truth. This realization, to which I myself found difficulty in adjusting, accords with the stratified and complex nature of our modern world. Its existence is governed by a plurality of opinions, ideals, doctrines and social systems: in the house of peace there must be many mansions.

The essential requirement is that world peace should be construed as a vital necessity in the technological age. Worldwide problems entail a quest for global solutions. It would, at the same time, be wrong if aid to developing countries and conservation of natural resources, the secure coexistence of differing political systems and vigorous measures against terrorism were to be regarded and treated as competing tasks instead of different dimensions of the same global domestic policy. It is not the Eastern bloc that has prevented the West from solving its own problems, settling the question of raw materials or evolving a policy towards Africa. In the same way, no one but the Americans themselves can prevent Washington from recognizing the existence of a democratic socialist alternative.

It seems to me that all parts of the world are breeding more and more movements dedicated to an equitable social structure and peace without domination by a ruling power. This may well produce a front opposed to interventionism and in favour of independent social democracy. In my view, the social democrats of Western Europe should prepare to develop their international co-operation along these lines. The traditional framework of the Socialist International has proved insufficiently flexible to cope with such important tasks.

But what of the future of democracy in general? How can it prevail in an age when economic and social problems of the greatest magnitude are disrupting the internal cohesion of countries everywhere, and when worldwide economic and political developments harbour dangers whose consequences could be catastrophic? The complexity of social problems, impotence in the face of difficult international conditions, the manipulability of public opinion and a growing inability to monitor bureaucratic and legislative activities – these and many other factors present us with a palpable and far from academic challenge. How can democracy survive when so many countries totter from superabundance, via depression, to recession? When international affairs hover with crippling uncertainty between détente and disaster? When we continue to dwell under the threat of war – not of nuclear war, perhaps, but of the so-called limited wars which are scarcely less agonizing to their victims than nuclear war itself? To me, the fight for democracy has never meant simply advocating an abstract system but working towards a system that will bring abstract principles to life.

Democracy is a means and an end in one. It cannot be restricted to the narrow political sphere but must encompass all the relevant areas of economic and social existence. Democracy is more than a list of rules for a game. In the words of the German Social Democratic programme, it should be regarded as our overall political system and way of life 'because it alone is an expression of regard for the dignity of man and his individual responsibility'.

Great efforts are needed to reinforce the democracies in such a way as to render them proof against these novel challenges. The democratic state must have its capacity for action strengthened. It requires the sort of authority which reposes on conviction and consensus, which is conferred by election and appointment, which is accountable and revocable – an authority which must also legitimate itself in terms of moral worth and spiritual integrity.

The organizational structures of parliamentary democracy will not be exempt from change or adaptation to new requirements. I cannot, however, subscribe to the pessimistic theory that the spirit of democracy is in retreat; despite everything, it has resumed its advance. Although the number of non-democratically governed countries has risen alarmingly in recent years, we must not close our eyes to the fact that democracy has also gained some notable successes – for example, the overthrow of the Portuguese, Spanish and Greek dictatorships.

Our brand of democracy is not for export. All previous experience suggests that it is associated with a certain level of economic and educational development, but this does not alter my belief that democracy is the form of government best equipped to deal with our appointed tasks. Democracy has proved itself the most flexible and vital form of human structure capable of doing justice to the opportunities and problems of our civilization. We may well be nearing the most crucial test of the democratic way of life. I am confident that we shall successfully withstand it.

That is why I say we need more democracy, not less, in the sense of individual and collective responsibility. We need more civil rights, not less. We need more co-determination, not less. We need more social justice, not less. We need more self-accountable freedom, not a diminution of freedom which may culminate in its abolition.

INDEX

Index

Compiled by Douglas Matthews

Abrassimov, Pyotr, 103–10, 155, 192, 195

Abusch, Alexander, 96

Acheson, Dean, 23, 288; *Present at the Creation*, 308

Adenauer, Konrad, and Berlin crisis, 17, 24, 30, 36, 57, 66; on W. Berlin referendum, 22–3; in 1961 election, 24, 26, 42–3, 48; and relations with USSR, 26–7, 29, 65–6, 68, 111, 166, 329, 341; Kennedy and, 36; and Allied presence in Berlin, 39; defers retirement, 42–3; leads 1961 government, 43, 45–6; and FDP, 43–4; rejects all-party government, 45; character and position, 48–50, 54–5, 68–9; political history, 50–4; and de Gaulle, 52, 57, 64, 68, 117, 121, 124, 144; and German re-unification, 54, 64–7; renounces Chancellorship, 54, 60–1, 138; relations with WB, 55–6, 61, 64–5; on Eastern bloc, 56–7; on Britain, 58; and *Spiegel* affair, 59; achievements, 60, 63, 68–9; honorary citizenship of Berlin, 61, 68; on Bundestag, 64; and *Ostpolitik*, 64, 68; visits USA, 66–7; and Kennedy, 68, 72, 75; death, 69; and Ben Gurion, 85, 452; and US-Soviet negotiations, 88; and WB's invitation from Khrushchev, 102; bans KPD, 107; and Franco-German treaty, 121–2; and Erhard, 144–5; and Britain's EEC application, 159; secures release of POWs, 220; and European integration, 244; and 1958 Lebanon operation, 316; reverses, 444

Adzhubei, Alexei I., 41, 103

Agnew, Spiro, 288

Ahlers, Conrad, 325, 371–2, 429

Albania, 179, 219, 420, 427

Algeria, 449, 451, 465–6, 472–6, 478, 480–1

Allardt, Helmut, 325

Allied Control Commission, 28

Allon, Yigal, 460

American-British-Dutch-Australian Command (ABDA), 201

American Council, 295

Americans for Democratic Action (ADA), 81–2

Amrehn, Franz, 103

Anderson, K. B., 313

Andreotti, Giulio, 311

Angola, 488

Arafat, Yasser, 454, 465

Aragon, Louis, 218

Assad, Hafis al-, 482

Atlantic Alliance, de Gaulle and, 120, 125; WB supports, 150, 156, 384; W. German adherence to, 154, 236; and European Security Conference, 187; and US interest in Europe, 260; Nixon on, 298, 314; Russian attitude to, 366; and Portugal, 489; *see also* North Atlantic Treaty Organization
Augstein, Rudolf, 58
August the Strong, King of Saxony, 407
Austria, 132–3, 164, 241–2
Averoff, Evangelos, 173

Baader-Meinhof group, 439
Bachmann, Kurt, 350
Backlund, Sven, 104–5, 107–9
Bahr, Egon, and proposed German settlement, 100–1; on Soviet suspicions, 108; at Abrassimov meeting, 109; negotiates trade missions with Czechs, 170; at Gromyko meeting, 190–1, 194; meets Berlinguer, 221; at Nixon meetings, 284, 311–12; in Moscow Treaty negotiations, 323, 325, 332–4, 384; at Crimea meeting with Brezhnev, 346; negotiates on Berlin, 365, 388–9, 391; and Kosygin's views on defensive alliances, 366; treaty negotiations with E. Germany, 387, 393–5; and Warsaw Treaty negotiations, 403; and WB's Nobel Prize, 430; visits Algeria, 473; visits Egypt, 481
Ball, George, 81, 283, 288
Barzel, Rainer, 102, 146, 235, 289, 357–8, 434–7
Basic Treaty *see under* East Germany
Baudouin, King of the Belgians, 92
Bauer, Leo, 220–2
Bebel, August, 165
Bech, Josef, 58
Belgium, 297
Belgrade Conference, 428
Ben Bella, Ahmed, 472
Ben Gurion, David, 85, 452

Bensberg Circle, 182
Beria, Lavrenti, 28–9, 104
Berkeley, California, 200–1
Berlin, status, 14; 1963 passes agreement, 14; crossing points, 15–16, 35; 1958 ultimatum, 20, 24–5, 66, 77–9; negotiations and proposals on, 88–9, 101; *see also* Berlin, East; Berlin, West
Berlin Blockade (1948), 14, 20–1, 34, 287
Berlin, East, and East Germany, 14–16, 25; WB visits, 17; Russians in, 35; escapes from, 40; pass agreements, 96–8; Soviet intervention in, 217; treaty negotiations with, 366, 368–9; visits to, under Quadripartite Agreement, 390, 392, 394
Berlin Task Force, Washington, 25
Berlin Wall, building of, 13–20, 27; justifications for, 23–4; effects, 25, 94–5, 98; Western reactions to, 25–7, 30–40; escapes and deaths at, 37, 40–1; and Western weakness, 57; pass agreements, 96–8; and E. German strength, 184; as frontier, 375; and Quadripartite Agreement, 392
Berlin, West, *Land* status, 14, 37; Senate, 14; Chamber of Deputies, 16; post-war reconstruction, 17; as escape haven, 20; free-city, 21, 24; Allied presence, 16, 21–4, 39–40; relations with W. Germany, 21, 328, 343, 390–1; referendum, 22–3, 39; US garrison in, 31–3, 35, 77; threatened E. German attack on, 38; access routes, 39, 67, 79, 88, 96, 100, 155, 343, 388; Adenauer and, 55, 61, 66, 68; Kennedy visits, 71–3, 77; Eisenhower on, 78; Robert Kennedy visits, 86–7; pass agreements, 96–8; Quadripartite Agreement on, 98, 101, 155, 312, 345, 350–2, 354, 365, 387–93, 415, 423, 436; and proposed Russian settlement, 100–1, 106; and cultural

Berlin, West [*cont'd*]
exchanges with USSR, 106; WB's mayoral duties and government, 139–40, 142, 148; elections, 139–40; Gromyko on, 192–3; Free University, 201; Federal Assembly convened in, 225–7; Pompidou on Four-Power rights in, 261; Nixon on, 287, 292, 297–8, 301–21; and détente, 291; Russian office in, 292; and Moscow Treaty, 328–30, 332, 339–40; Brezhnev on, 339–40, 342, 350; discussed at Erfurt meeting, 375–7, 379; citizens' passports, 391; and Warsaw Treaty, 409–11; clause on in Czech Treaty, 416

Berlinguer, Enrico, 221

Bermuda Conference *see* Nassau Agreement

Bernhard, Prince of the Netherlands, 91

Bismarck, Prince Otto von, and German liberalism, 43, 228; political régime, 50; popular concessions, 55; foreign policy, 152–3; dictum on politics, 162; on Chancellorship, 225; and German unification, 241–2; on Spain, 493

Blumenthal, Roy, 85

Bohlen, Charles, 32–3, 83

Böll, Heinrich, 179

Börner, Holger, 442

Boumedienne, Houari, 472–8, 480–1

Bourguiba, Habib, 459, 472, 480

Brandt, Lars, 128, 142, 174, 201, 320, 431, 473

Brandt, Matthias, 36, 297, 439

Brandt, Ninja, 297, 431

Brandt, Peter, 38, 142, 201, 320, 440

Brandt, Rut, 142, 288, 431, 451, 464

Brandt, Willy, nominated for Chancellor in 1960, 13, 47, 138; visits to USA, 36, 39, 75, 80–6, 88, 91, 122, 152, 155, 157, 259, 284, 288, 290, 295, 297, 308, 313, 317, 320–1, 443; personal attacks on, 47–8; Harvard lectures on co-existence,

84–5, 88, 98–9; GDR spy surveillance of, 95; honorary degrees, 108, 248; as Foreign Minister, 128, 130, 135, 143, 146–8, 151–65; as Party chairman, 138–9, 142, 146, 165, 229, 328; mayoral duties, 139–40, 142, 148; declines candidacy for Chancellorship (1965), 142; as Vice-Chancellor, 143, 145; health, 146, 444; attacked over European Security Conference, 187; elected Federal Chancellor, 223–5; work as Chancellor, 228–38, 444; Légion d'Honneur, 268; Nobel Peace Prize, 421, 429–30, 500; resigns Chancellorship, 424, 450; freedom of Lübeck, 429–30; receives Reinhold Niebuhr award, 443; helicopter escape, 461; candidacy for European Parliament, 497

Breitscheid, Rudolf, 378

Brentano, Heinrich von, 17–18, 26, 31, 64, 67

Brezhnev, Leonid, and de Gaulle, 131; and Czech Treaty, 179, 415; and European Security Conference, 187; on mutual force reduction, 188, 263, 270, 353; and Czech crisis, 210, 213–14, 217, 335; 'doctrine', 217, 339; attacks SPD, 221; talks with WB, 257, 260, 264, 310, 324–5, 328–9, 334–56, 414, 464, 471, 490–1; Pompidou meets, 257, 263, 355, 362; and Central European neutralization, 270; meetings with Nixon, 297–8, 309, 312–14; fear of China, 300; on Middle East, 300, 362–3, 459, 463–4, 471; and Watergate, 312; nuclear weapons agreement, 312; meeting with Heath, 314; on Soviet elections, 324; and WB's 1970 visit to Moscow, 329–31, 334; supremacy, 334, 336, 348; personality, 334–5, 347; health, 335; career, 335–6; policy of détente, 336, 345, 491; visits W. Germany, 336–7, 358–64, 414; on

Brezhnev, Leonid [cont'd]
  Moscow Treaty, 337–9; on cold war, 340–1; on disarmament, 342; on Nixon, 343; at 24th Party Congress, 345, 353; at Oreanda, 346–52, 356, 414; on technical co-operation, 350, 360–1, 364; on relations with USA, 353–4; on China, 354–5, 423; approves W. Berlin passports, 391; and inter-German agreements, 393; and Gierek's visit to Bonn, 414; congratulates WB on 1972 election, 443; on Yugoslavia, 487; and Portugal, 490–1
Briand, Aristide, 190
Brosio, Manlio, 188, 285, 309
Brown, George, 159, 161–3
Bucharest Declaration (1966), 170–1
Buchenwald, 378–9
Budapest see Hungary
Bulgaria, 111, 486
Bundy, McGeorge, 38, 72

Caetano, Marcelo, 488
Caglayangil, Ihsan Sabri, 486
Cambodia, 149–50, 178, 279, 306
Canada, 266, 305, 314, 427
Carstens, Karl, 105, 437
Castro, Fidel, 86, 308
Catholic Centre Party, 50–1, 62, 228
Ceauşescu, Nicolae, 174–5, 214, 443, 454
Central Intelligence Agency (CIA), 18
Černik, Oldrich, 213–14
Chaban-Delmas, Jacques, 275
Chamberlain, Neville, 358
Chile, 491
China, Soviet differences with, 108, 127, 131, 174, 179, 194, 222, 295, 300, 367, 423; de Gaulle and, 127; relations with USA, 127; nuclear weapons, 177, 307; supports Albania, 178, 420; and Czech invasion, 219; Nixon's policy towards, 279, 287, 295, 297, 305, 307, 353, 421–2; Nixon's visit to,

298, 306, 354–5, 422; supports N. Vietnam, 306, 319; Kissinger visits, 306, 422; defence, 307; Brezhnev on, 354–5, 423; W. German relations with, 354, 365, 420–24; relations with E. Europe, 422–3; and UN, 355, 422; and EEC, 423; outlook for, 498
Chnoupek, Bohuslav, 416
Chou En-lai, 423–4
Christian Democratic Union/Christian Social Union (CDU/CSU), 1961 election victory, 40, 42, 46; absorbs FDP right wing, 44; forms 1961 coalition government, 45; Adenauer and post-war development of, 52–3, 61–2; and Grand Coalition, 59, 145–6, 148–9; conservatism, 62–3; and SED talks, 112; and Franco-German treaty, 121; and Berlin government, 139–40; and Ostpolitik, 184; in 1969 election, 223–4; in opposition, 235; hostility to E. European treaties, 356–8, 394, 405–6, 435–6; success in 1972 Landtag elections, 433; and 1972 Bundestag elections, 436–7, 443
Christian Social Union (CSU), 40, 42, 45–6, 59, 62–3, 289; see also Christian Democratic Union
Churchill, Sir Winston S., 28–9, 69, 137, 244, 345, 465
Clay, Lucius D., 32, 34–6, 57, 84, 288, 295
Club of Ten, 257
Cohn-Bendit, Daniel, 204
Colby, William, 463
Comecon (CMEA; Council for Mutual Economic Assistance), 327, 341, 350, 362
Communist Party of the Soviet Union, 109; 24th Congress, 345, 353, 360, 393
Conference on Security and Co-operation in Europe, and US presence, 77; and US-Europe relations, 259; Pompidou on, 263;

Conference on Security and Co-operation in Europe [*cont'd*]
US views on, 289, 293, 302; Soviet attitude to, 312; Brezhnev on, 352-3, 355, 362, 490; and EEC, 427; Portugal and, 490
Connally, John B., 296
Couve de Murville, Maurice, 116-17, 127-30, 136, 159, 162, 203-4
Croatian Ustaše, 176
Cuba, 1962 missile crisis, 38, 86, 89-90, 167-8, 191, 465; Soviet financial aid for, 300; Nixon on, 308
Cunhal, Alvaro, 490
Cyprus, 155, 219, 485-6
Cyrankiewicz, Josef, 210, 399, 404-8, 412, 414
Czechoslovakia (CSSR), 1968 revolution, 30, 168, 170, 184, 189, 190, 196, 198, 207-18, 262, 367; frontiers, 126; de Gaulle on, 132; and West German Declarations, 133-4; and *Ostpolitik*, 166, 183-4, 193; trade missions negotiated, 170, 209; relations with E. Germany, 172; Tito on, 177, 179; W. German treaty with, 179, 349, 403, 411, 415-20; Russians invade, 214-17, 299, 335; international reactions to crisis, 218-20, 262; and Munich Agreement, 333, 342; Sudeten Germans in, 415, 417; 1968 negotiations with USSR, 420

Daume, Willi, 442
Dayan, Moshe, 460
Debré, Michel, 136, 215, 249
Defferre, Gaston, 122
Demirel, Süleyman, 486
Denmark, 164-5, 276, 437, 444
Devraigne, Pierre, 114
Diem, Ngo Dinh, 318-19
Dietzfelbinger, Hermann, 413
Djilas, Milovan, 179
Dobrynin, Anatoly F., 293
Döpfner, Julius, 413
Döring, Wolfgang, 45

Dorn, Wolfram, 372
Douglas-Home, Sir Alec (Lord Home), 392
Dubček, Alexander, 177, 208, 210-14, 216-18, 419
Duckwitz, Georg Ferdinand, 157, 194, 402
Dulles, Eleanor, 78-9
Dulles, John Foster, 57, 78-80, 94, 126, 341
Dutschke, Rudi, 201

East Germany (German Democratic Republic), control of E. Berlin, 14-16, 25, 97; and Berlin Wall, 18, 24-5, 37, 40, 95, 184; opposes free-city status for Berlin, 22; flight from, 24; separate treaty with USSR, 24, 100; 1953 unrest, 27, 29; recognition of, 35-6, 171, 183-4, 186, 367-8, 372-3, 376, 386, 394; troop concentrations, 38; control of Berlin access routes, 39, 343; West Berlin attitude to, 41; and Hallstein doctrine, 65; and absorption of Berlin, 66; and pass agreements, 96-8; and proposed Soviet Berlin settlement, 100-1; W. German relations with, 111, 169, 192-3, 195-6, 218, 301-2, 327, 346, 498; economic developments in, 112; and W. German declarations, 133; and *Ostpolitik*, 167, 169-70, 184-7; mutual assistance pacts with E. Europe, 172; strength in Eastern bloc, 184; and Czech reforms, 209-10, 212-13, 215; intervention in Czechoslovakia, 216; intransigence on Berlin, 226; Pompidou on, 269; Nixon's interest in, 287, 299; and admission to UN, 301, 358, 360, 376-8, 383, 386, 396, 410, 424; and Moscow Treaty, 332-4, 339, 342, 356; Basic Treaty with W. Germany, 332-3, 355, 358, 366-9, 370-85, 387, 393-6, 415, 425, 442; Brezhnev on,

East Germany (German Demo-cratic Republic) [cont'd]
349; and Berlin Quadripartite Agreement, 351, 388, 390–2; WB visits, 370–9; transit and traffic treaties, 387, 392, 394; W. German visitors to, 392; amnesties of prisoners in, 395; W. German representative mission in, 395; and nationhood, 396; 1975 Soviet treaty of friendship with, 396; migrations, 401; and Warsaw Treaty, 410–11; and Czech leader-ship, 416; China and, 422–3
Eban, Abba, 454, 458
Ebert, Friedrich, 185
Ecevit, Bülent, 486
Eckart, Felix von, 56–7
Egypt, Soviet aid for, 300, 307; and Olympic murders, 440; WB visits, 449, 451, 472, 478, 481, 483; breaks off diplomatic relations with W. Germany, 453; and Israel, 459; and Yom Kippur war, 463–4, 483; and Nasser's death, 466; and Middle East settlement, 467, 469, 471, 476, 479–81; USSR and, 469–71, 479–80; and Palestinians, 470; resumes diplomatic relations, 472; dependence on USA, 477
Ehmke, Horst, 289, 435
Ehrenburg, Ilya, 171
Einstein, Albert, 171
Eisenhower, Dwight D., 34, 77–8, 80, 83, 100, 120, 280, 318
elections see under West Germany
Elizabeth II, Queen, 118, 250–1
Erfurt, 370–9
Erhard, Ludwig, Adenauer ob-structs, 42; downfall, 44, 143–5; 1961 position, 46; and 'German miracle', 63; and Khrushchev's proposed visit, 103; and de Gaulle's European proposals, 124, 130; peace notes to E. Europe, 126; and China, 127; succeeds Adenauer, 138; in 1965 election, 141; foreign policy, 144; visits

USA, 144; political ideas, 144–5; and Britain's EEC application, 159; relations with USSR, 166; and 1972 election, 438
Erlander, Tage, 75
Erler, Fritz, 44, 113, 320
Ertl, Josef, 228
Eshkol, Levi, 452, 455
Euratom, 163, 245
European Coal and Steel Com-munity, 245
European Conference, Helsinki, 426–8, 498
European Economic Community, British entry, 58, 88, 120, 125–6, 128, 135, 157–63, 236–7, 245–56, 259; W. German membership, 68; Kennedy and, 81; de Gaulle on, 125–6; W. Germany opposes expansion of, 129; organization and procedure, 158; enlargement, 160, 162–5, 245–6, 258, 264, 267, 496–7; Irish membership, 163; and Yugoslav trade, 176; co-ordination and unification, 239, 244; 1969 Hague summit, 245–7; reserve fund, 247; economic and monetary policy, 254–6, 260, 266, 273, 276–7; Representatives, 255–6, 265, 267; and USA, 259–61, 265–6, 275–6, 283, 286, 288–305, 313–15; Brezh-nev accepts, 263, 344, 361; 1972 Paris summit, 264–8; and E. Europe, 265–6; regional fund, 266, 276; direct election, 267, 277, 497; 1973 Copenhagen summit, 274–6; and Middle East, 275, 454, 458–9, 462, 480, 484; financing of, 277; European Council, 277; Kissinger and, 282, 313; special associations, 305; and Comecon, 327, 341, 350, 362; Russia and, 344, 361; E. German participa-tion, 382; China and, 423; Norway rejects, 437; and energy crisis, 468; and Arab world, 475, 483–4; and Greece, 485; and Malta, 486; and Portugal, 488; political role, 496–7

European Free Trade Association (EFTA), 125, 128, 246, 293
European Monetary Co-operation Fund, 266
European Security Conference, 187–8, 195, 272, 341, 351
Evangelical Church in Germany (EKD), 181, 413

Falin, Valentin, 194, 325
Farouk I, King of Egypt, 479
Faure, Edgar, 203
Fechter, Peter, 37–8
Federer, Georg F., 84
Feisal, King of Saudi Arabia, 461, 468, 480
Fiduciary Authority for Inter-zonal Trade, 56, 96
Finland, 187
Fischer, Ernst, 218
Flach, Karl-Hermann, 442
Fock, Jenö, 210
Focke, Katharina, 245
Ford, Gerald, 313–14, 317, 490
Foreign Policy Association, New York, 122
Four-Power Foreign Ministers' Conference (1959), 25
France, and German reunification, 28; 1963 treaty with W. Germany, 57, 68, 111, 120–1, 135, 268; and great-power status, 81; frontier settlements, 99; WB's familiarity with, 114; and NATO, 120, 125, 128, 260–1, 310; relations with W. Germany, 124, 129–35, 144, 149, 157, 163, 246, 258–9, 271, 497; defence policy, 125, 271; détente policy, 126, 167; foreign policy, 126–8, 130; troops in W. Germany, 128–9, 271; relations with USA, 133, 271, 286; 1969 referendum, 136; and EEC, 158–60, 162, 258–9; 1968 disorders, 198, 200–5; and Czechoslovakia, 213, 215–16; Communist Party in, 213, 222; and nationalism, 240–42; Prussian War, 242; and German

rivalry, 242–3; and European defence, 244; and Britain's EEC application, 245, 249, 253–4; withdraws from 'snake', 252, 273; and defence forces, 259–60, 271–2; and Indo-China, 318; relations with USSR, 362; and inter-German treaty, 385; and Middle East, 454, 465; and Yom Kippur war, 464; and Mediterranean, 465; and oil crisis, 468, 474; peace in Algeria, 472
Franco, General Francisco, 487, 492–3
Frank, Anne, 430
Frank, Paul, 323, 325, 403, 417, 457, 473
Franke, Egon, 221, 370, 372
Free Democratic Party (FDP), 1961 election results, 42; in 1961 government, 43, 45; party history, 43–4, 228; proposed alliance, 44–5; and Franco-German alliance, 121; in Berlin government, 140; and Grand Coalition, 145, 206; in 1969 government, 224, 227–9; party desertions, 228; and no-confidence debate, 435; in 1972 elections, 442–3; in 1972 coalition, 449
Frelek, Ryszcard, 415

Gaddafi, Muammar al, 463, 480
Gaitskell, Hugh, 161
Galluzzi, Carlo, 221
Gasperi, Alcide de, 51, 244
Gaulle, Charles de, and Adenauer, 52, 57, 64, 68, 117, 120, 124; proposes joint nuclear force with Britain, 68; death, 69, 137; at Adenauer funeral, 69; Kennedy and, 74, 81; on East-West relations, 99, 115, 119, 121, 123, 126–33; Soviet proposals to, on Germany, 102; WB's meetings with, 114, 117–19, 130–6; authority, 115; attitudes, 115–16; on Berlin, 117–19, 121; 1962 state visit to

Gaulle, Charles de [*cont'd*]
Germany, 117–18; and Atlantic Alliance, 120, 122–3, 125, 128; on relations with W. Germany, 120–22, 124–6, 129–33, 144; on Europe, 120, 123–6; 1964 visit to Bonn, 122, 124, 136; on USA, 124–5, 132; on 'German question', 126–7, 130–31; détente policy, 130–5; on Wilson's EEC application, 134, 159, 162; dislike of English language, 135; and 1969 referendum, 136; resignation, 136–7; relations with USSR, 144, 338; at 1967 Rome EEC summit, 158; and May 1968 disorders, 203–5; and US Vietnam policy, 319; on Poland, 408; on Arab oil, 468
Gaus, Günter, 395
Geneva Conference (1959), 117
Genscher, Hans-Dietrich, 435, 440
German Bishops' Conference, 413
German Communist Party (KPD), 17, 107, 343, 350, 363
German Democratic Party (DDP), 62
German Foreign Policy Association, 123
German National People's Party (DNVP), 51, 62
German People's Party (DVP), 61
Germany (reunification of), 27–9, 35–6, 41, 54, 64, 237; Globke plan, 66; US and, 79, 88–9, 168; Abrassimov on, 106; SPD and, 110; de Gaulle and, 126–7, 130–3; USSR refuses, 133, 168; and *Ostpolitik*, 167; and Moscow Treaty, 332, 357; Gromyko letter on, 357; and inter-German treaty negotiations, 367; and self-determination, 368; *see also* East Germany; West Germany
Gerstenmaier, Eugen, 44–5
Gheorghiu-Dej, Gheorghe, 174
Gierek, Edward, 349, 411, 413–15, 443, 449
Giscard d'Estaing, Valéry, 135, 256, 273, 275, 444
Globke, Hans, 62, 66–7, 100, 102
Goethe, J. W. von, 240, 371
Goldmann, Nahum, 453, 464, 471
Gollwitzer, Helmut, 227
Gomulka, Wladyslaw, 182–3, 210, 402–3, 406, 408–12, 414–15, 433
Gonzales, Felipe, 493
Goodwin, Richard, 72
Götz, Jiri, 417
Grass, Günter, 227, 457
Great Britain, and EEC membership, 58, 88, 120, 125–6, 128, 157–63, 236–7, 245–56, 259, 277, 437; nuclear arms, 67; and European unity, 81, 244; conflict with Iceland, 155; WB's relations with, 161; student unrest in, 201; nationalism in, 240–41; and German rivalry, 242; floats pound, 258; Brezhnev mistrusts, 264, 361; and 'snake', 274; and inter-German treaty, 385; 1973 elections, 444; and N. Sea oil, 466
Greece, 30, 164, 484–6, 502
Grechko, Andrei A., 344
Grewe, Wilhelm, 45, 67
Grey, Sir Edward, 243
Gromyko, Andrei A., meeting with Rusk, 67; on E. German treaty, 89; on German settlement, 100, 357; de Gaulle on, 134; on talks with W. Germany, 190; meetings with WB, 190–7; career, 190–1; Moscow Treaty negotiations, 325, 332, 334; and Berlin Quadripartite Agreement, 340, 365, 388–9, 392; and W. Berlin representation, 416; on Middle East, 471, 479; and arms to Egypt, 481
Guillaume, Günther, 450

Haakon VII, King of Norway, 251
Haekkerup, Per, 161
Haig, Alexander, 297, 302, 307
Haile Selassie, Emperor of Ethiopia, 176
Hallstein, Walter, 158; 'doctrine',

Halstein, Walter [cont'd]
65, 170, 182
Hamlett, Barksdale, 83
Hammarskjöld, Dag, 464
Harald, Crown Prince of Norway, 431
Harpprecht, Klaus, 445, 457
Harpprecht-Lasker, Renate, 457
Harvard University, 84–5, 88, 98–9
Hassan II, King of Morocco, 453–4, 472, 480
Hassuna, Abdel Khalek, 453
Healey, Denis, 161
Heath, Edward, and Britain's EEC applications, 159, 248–52, 254; 1970 election victory, 162, 249; relations with WB, 249, 251–2, 442; meetings with Nixon, 257, 296–8, 311; at 1972 EEC summit, 264; opposes EEC direct elections, 267; and European Security Conference, 272; meeting with Brezhnev, 314; and Nixon's cancelled European visit, 317; and Soviet relations, 361; and Berlin Agreement, 392; congratulates WB on 1972 victory, 443; 1973 defeat, 444; and Middle East, 459, 467; and 1973 war alert, 463; on energy supplies, 466–8
Heikal, Mohammed Hassanein, 442, 472
Heine, Heinrich, 60
Heinemann, Gustav, 175, 226–7, 364, 368–9, 447, 449
Helsinki see European Conference
Hemingway, Ernest, 70
Herder, Johann, 241
Herrnstadt Group, 28
Hesselbach, Walter, 457
Heuss, Theodor, 42, 138, 185
Hindenburg, Paul von Beneckendorff, 51
Hitler, Adolf, dictatorship, 51; conquests, 133; de Gaulle on, 134; and effects of War, 141, 237; and German foreign policy, 152–3; and Poland, 181–2; as national saviour, 243; NPD and, 326; and 1939 Russian Pact, 364; and Czechoslovakia, 417
Ho Chi Minh, 320
Holland, 297, 468
Honecker, Erich, 299, 393–4, 396
Humphrey, Hubert H., 75, 82, 92, 280, 290
Hungary, 30, 111, 207, 209, 212, 217–19, 242
Husak, Gustav, 214, 349, 360, 415, 419–20
Hussein II, King of Jordan, 458–9, 463, 465, 472, 479
Hynd, John B., 161

Iceland, 155
India, 307
Indo-China, 318–19; see also Vietnam
Iran, 464, 466–7; see also Reza Pahlavi, Mohammed, Shah of
Iraq, 467, 470–1
Ireland, Republic of, 163–4
Ismael, Hafiz, 472
Israel, W. German relations with, 181, 452–3, 456–9, 469–70, 476; Pompidou on, 273; French hostility to, 276; Nixon supports, 287, 307; US aid for, 300; and Yom Kippur war, 316, 451, 461–4; Brezhnev on obstinacy, 362–3; W. German restitution to, 412, 451; Olympic Games tragedy, 440; WB visits, 451–2, 456–7, 460–1; 1967 6-Day war, 453; international position, 454–60; EEC and, 458–9, 484; US influence on, 466–8; and Middle East settlement, 467–71, 476, 481; Soviet relations with, 466, 470–1; conflict with Syria, 479
Italy, 164, 200–1, 205, 212, 216, 219–22, 274, 484

Jackling, Sir Roger William, 390
Jackson, Henry, 310
Japan, student unrest in, 201; Communist Party in, 222; EEC and, 266, 304–5; and Nixon-Kissinger

Japan [cont'd]
  policy, 272, 274, 279, 287, 310,
  314–15; concern over China, 295,
  297, 305; revalues yen, 297;
  relations with USSR, 304, 326;
  and OECD, 305; wartime alliance,
  421
Jarring, Gunnar, 459, 467
Javits, Jacob, 84
Jedrychowsky, Stefan, 406
Jefferson, Thomas, 240
Jenkins, Roy, 248
Jobert, Michel, 313
John XXIII, Pope, 92
Johnson, Lyndon B., visit to Berlin,
  31–4; at Adenauer funeral, 69;
  involvement in SE Asia, 74, 83,
  319–22; and Germany, 80; succeeds
  Kennedy, 92–3; and European
  unity, 124; and Erhard's China
  policy, 127; and Erhard govern-
  ment, 144; and détente, 167; meets
  Kosygin, 324
Jonas, Franz, 442
Jong, Piet de, 245
Jordan, 453, 458, 463–4, 480
Juan Carlos, King of Spain, 492
Juliana, Queen of the Netherlands,
  246

Kádár, Janos, 210, 214, 420
Kanellopoulos, Panayotis, 484
Kant, Immanuel, 400
Karamanlis, Konstantin, 484–5
Kassel, 378–87
Kaunda, Kenneth, 488
Kekkonen, Urho, 427
Kennan, George F., 33, 75, 178, 470
Kennedy, Edward, 87, 443
Kennedy, Ethel, 86
Kennedy, Jacqueline, 73, 92
Kennedy, John Fitzgerald, and
  Berlin Wall crisis, 15–16, 24–5, 30–
  6, 40, 94; and Khrushchev threats,
  19–21; 1961 Vienna meeting with
  Khrushchev, 20, 23, 100; 1961
  speech on Berlin, 22–3; WB's
  meetings and relations with, 31,

36, 70, 74, 80–1, 88, 102; relations
  with W. Germany, 39, 75, 80–1,
  88; and German reunification, 41,
  88; relations with Adenauer, 66–8;
  visit to Germany, 68, 73–5; death,
  69, 91, 280; political attitudes,
  70–1, 76, 83; 1963 visit to Berlin,
  71–3, 77, 118; on Europe, 74–6,
  81; speech on world peace, 75–6;
  and Bermuda Agreement, 81, 120;
  strain, 84; and Cuba crisis, 86–7,
  89–90; correspondence with
  Khrushchev, 88; popularity and
  achievements, 92–3; on East-West
  relations, 99; and USSR's proposed German settlement, 101;
  compassion, 222; and W. Berlin
  proposals, 292; and Vietnam, 319
Kennedy, Robert, 86–7, 92–3, 222,
  320
Kennedy, Rose, 73
Khrushchev, Nikita S., and Berlin
  crisis, 16, 26, 37, 40, 94; confrontation threats, 19; 1958 ultimatum, 20, 24–5, 66, 77–9; 1961
  Vienna meeting with Kennedy,
  20–1, 23, 100; proposals on Germany, 22; and Kennedy's Berlin
  speech, 23; and Adenauer, 26–7,
  65; denounces Beria, 29; proposed
  visit to Germany, 68; threatens to
  bury West, 73; and peaceful
  coexistence, 85; correspondence
  with Kennedy, 88; and Cuba crisis,
  90, 103; and Berlin settlement,
  101; invitations to WB, 101–3,
  140; downfall, 103–4, 324, 335;
  and Gromyko, 191; and Brezhnev,
  335; Gomulka resists, 408–9
Kiesinger, Kurt Georg, Abrassimov
  on suspicions of, 109; relations
  with France, 128–9; de Gaulle on,
  130; leads Grand Coalition, 143,
  145–6, 148–9, 166; relations with
  WB, 148–9; and Britain's EEC
  membership, 159; and E. Europe,
  166–7, 172; and Rumania, 173; and
  Yugoslav compensations, 177; and

Kiesinger, Kurt Georg [cont'd]
SPD's Polish policy 183; on E. Germany, 185; and Czechoslovakia, 217; 1967 visit to Italy, 220; in 1969 elections, 223–4; and Berlin as Federal Assembly venue, 226; and Berlin Four-Power talks, 389; moves 1972 vote of no-confidence, 434
King, Martin Luther, 82
Kissinger, Henry, military plans, 19; in Kennedy circle, 72; advocates negotiation, 156; and 'offset' problem, 157; respect for Gromyko, 191; proposes 'new Atlantic Charter', 272, 274–5, 310, 312; and 'Year of Europe', 275, 310, 315; influence on Nixon, 278; 'five-finger' system, 279; as Secretary of State, 281–2; and EEC, 282, 293, 305, 313; on East-West relations, 283–4, 288–9; 'flu, 297; and Nixon's German policy, 302; visit to China, 306, 422; Senate opposition to, 310; on power and self-control, 311; and Watergate, 311–12; co-operation with, 312; and Nixon talks with WB, 314; and Vietnam, 317, 319, 322; on CSCE, 362; talks with Brezhnev, 362; and Berlin Quadripartite talks, 388, 390; WB meets, 442; 1973 war alert, 463; and Yom Kippur war, 464; and Middle East settlement, 469, 471, 479, 482; and oil crisis, 474; Sadat and, 477, 481; and Portugal, 490
Kohl, Michael, 372, 387, 393, 395
Kollek, Teddy, 460
Kordt, Günther, 372
Korea, North, 222
Kosygin, Alexei, 1966 visit to Paris, 129, 131; de Gaulle on, 134; and Czechoslovakia, 210–11; and Nixon policy, 300; Moscow Treaty talks with WB, 323–32, 343; career and character, 324, 334; on European détente, 325–6; invited to W.

Germany, 358; on defensive alliances, 366–7; and Berlin Quadripartite Agreement, 392
Kotikov, Alexander G., 14
Krag, Jens Otto, 46, 332
Kreisky, Bruno, 100–2
Kroll, Hans, 102
Krone, Heinrich, 66, 68
Kühn, Heinz, 358

Lama, Luciano, 221
Lange, Halvard, 155
Laos, 83, 306
Lebanon, 472
Leber, George, 72, 439
Le Duc Tho, 282
Leichter, Otto, 190, 194
Lenin, V. I., 337, 340
Leopold, Kurt, 57
Libya, 453, 463, 465, 470, 480
Lightner, Allan, 35, 89–90
Lincoln, Abraham, 94
Lindsay, John V., 295
Lionäs, Aase, 429
Lodge, Henry Cabot, 87
London Debt Agreement, 177, 412
Longo, Luigi, 219–21
Louis XIV, King of France, 468
Lübke, Heinrich, 69
Luns, Joseph, 309
Luxembourg, 158, 219
Lynch, Jack, 442

McCarthy, Joseph, 34, 280
McCloy, John, 18–19, 23, 57, 157, 283, 295
McGovern, George, 310
Macmillan, Harold, 67, 80, 120, 248
McNamara, Robert, 19, 38, 83
Malraux, André, 118
Malta, 486
Manescu, Corneliu, 173
Mangakis, Georg, 485
Mann, Thomas, 430
Mansfield, Mike, 293, 303, 310
Mao Tse-tung, 105, 355, 421, 423–4
Marshall, George C., 63, 308
Masaryk, Jan, 207

Massu, Jacques, 136, 204
Maurer, Ion Gheorghe, 175
Meany, George, 72, 288
Meir, Golda, 307, 440, 452, 454–62, 464
Mende, Erich, 45, 228
Messmer, Pierre, 264, 267
Meyerson, Morris, 455
Mikoyan, Anastas I., 66
Mintoff, Dom, 486
Mischnick, Wolfgang, 435, 450
Mitterand, François, 122, 444
Möller, Alex, 47, 284, 439
Mollet, Guy, 118, 122
Monnet, Jean, 91, 118–19, 160, 244, 247, 249, 252, 429, 455
Morocco, 453, 470, 480
Moscow Treaty see under Union of Soviet Socialist Republics
Müller, Hermann, 223
Multilateral Force (MLF), 67
Munich Agreement (1938), 166, 170, 184, 192–3, 333, 360, 415, 417, 419
Mutually Balanced Force Reduction (MBFR), 188, 259, 263–4, 270–1, 288; talks on, 289; Nixon on, 293, 302–4, 353; Soviet-US participation, 312–13; Brezhnev on, 352, 355; and détente, 428

Nabokov, Nicolas, 82, 107–8
Nachmann, Werner, 457
Napoleon Bonaparte, 240–1, 371
Napoleon III, 241
Nassau Agreement, 81, 120
Nasser, Abdel Gamal, 453, 464, 466, 472, 482
Nathan, Asher Ben, 461
National Democratic Party (NPD), 132, 144, 224, 326, 380
National Press Club, Washington, 287
Nazi Party (National Socialists), 51, 243–4
Nehru, B. K., 32
Nenni, Pietro, 156, 164
Neues Deutschland, 112
New Zealand, 250

Nicholas I, Tsar of Russia, 36
Niebuhr, Reinhold, 443
Nikezič, Marko, 178
Nilsson, Torsten, 105
Nitze, Paul, 83, 86
Nixon, Richard M., Congress suspicion of, 93; de Gaulle on, 135; at 1969 NATO conference, 155–6; visit to Germany, 157, 194, 226, 284, 388; and détente, 167, 312, 340; and Middle East, 178, 307, 312, 464, 470; on W. Berlin, 194, 292, 388; and 1969 W. German elections, 223; meets Pompidou and WB, 257; and forces reduction, 263, 270, 293, 302–3; Brezhnev on, 264; Pompidou on, 272–3; and 'Year of Europe', 275, 310–11, 314; declaration on Atlantic relations, 275–6, 312, 314; Presidency, 278–81; and Watergate affair, 278, 280–1, 310–11, 482; foreign policy, 278–9, 282, 286–7, 295, 305–8, 310, 313; and China, 279, 287, 295, 297–8, 421–2; career, 280; peace strategy, 283; talks with WB, 284–7, 291–3, 297–306, 310, 313–15, 422; on NATO defence, 285–6; on Berlin, 287, 292, 297–8, 301; and EEC, 291, 304, 313, 477; and 'offset' agreements, 294; monetary policy, 294–6; and Vietnam withdrawal, 295, 306, 311, 317, 322; meetings with Brezhnev, 298, 309, 312–14, 363; visit to China, 298, 306, 354–5, 422; on German question, 301–2; on US forces in Europe, 304; 1972 re-election, 310; nuclear weapons agreement with Brezhnev, 312; 1973 visit to Europe, 314; Brezhnev's interest in, 343, 353–4, 363; on CSCE, 361; and Berlin Quadripartite Agreement, 392, 436; and WB's 1972 election success, 443; and US supplies to Israel, 463; and Yom Kippur war, 463; and Arab world, 477

Nobel Peace Prize, 421, 429–31, 500
Nobel, Alfred, 431
Nogueira, Franco, 178
North Atlantic Treaty Organization (NATO), 1961 Oslo meeting, 21; W. Germany and, 53, 78, 341–2; and US interest in Europe, 81, 260, 285–6; France and, 120, 125, 128, 260–1, 310; crisis in, 122; WB attends, 128, 154–6, 172, 186, 190, 304; HQ transferred to Belgium, 128, 154; conference procedures, 154–5; and *Ostpolitik*, 172, 292; and forces reductions, 177, 196, 310, 342, 353, 362, 428; and German question, 186; 'Reykjavik signal', 188; and Czechoslovakia, 215, 217; and communist plurality, 219; and defence forces, 271, 304; and Nixon-Kissinger Atlantic policy, 275–6, 314; and Berlin Agreement, 301–2, 388; Nuclear Planning Group, 309; defence expenditure, 309–10; and CSCE, 352; and Greece, 485; and Cyprus crisis, 486; and Portugal, 490; *see also* Atlantic Alliance
Northern Ireland, 164
Norway, 41, 162, 164–5, 291, 444, 497
Novotný, Antonin, 207, 213
Nuclear Non-Proliferation Treaty, 65, 157, 188–9, 193, 237, 376
Nuclear Test Ban Treaty, 68, 111

Oder-Neisse frontier line, 57, 111, 170, 180, 182–3, 287, 332, 401
O'Donnell, Kenneth, 72
Olaf V, King of Norway, 431
Ollenhauer, Erich, 44, 138
Olympic Games, Munich (1972), 439–42, 472
Oreanda (Crimea), 345–53, 356, 358–9, 414–15
Organization for Economic Co-operation and Development (OECD), 293, 305
Organization of Petroleum Exporting Countries (OPEC), 466, 468
Oslo, 21
Ossietzky, Carl von, 430–31
Ostpolitik, influenced by Berlin Wall crisis, 20; and SPD policy, 54, 221; Adenauer and, 64, 68; de Gaulle and, 123, 126; WB's proposals for, 126, 166–97; and 1968 Czech revolt, 215, 218; and Italian Communist Party, 221; and European monetary union, 254; Pompidou on, 261–2, 270; US attitude to, 284, 286–9, 292; and détente, 291; and China, 357, 421; Brezhnev welcomes, 359; and treaties, 366, 394; misunderstandings of, 447; and Israel, 454; and Arab world, 482
Oswald, Lee Harvey, 92
Oxford University, 248

Paasio, Rafael, 427
Pakistan, 307
Palestine Liberation Organization (PLO), 454
Palme, Olof, 443
Papandreou, Andreas, 484
Papandreou, Georgios, 484
Papen, Franz von, 51
Paris, 1968 disorders, 199, 202–4; *see also* France
Peter, Janos, 212
Philip, Duke of Edinburgh, 251
Pieck, Wilhelm G., 185
Podgorny, Nicolai, 131, 324, 358
Poland, 1956 unrest, 29, 208; German frontier settlements with, 99, 126, 166, 181–3, 332, 401–3; W. German mission in, 111; de Gaulle on, 126–7, 132; German attitude to, 128, 413; and *Ostpolitik*, 133–4, 166, 170, 179; relations with E. Germany, 172; W. German relations with, 181–3, 349, 400–2, 498; student protests in, 207, 210; and Czech crisis, 210, 213, 215; W. German trade with, 212, 367;

Poland, [cont'd]
nationalism in, 242; Germans resident in, 287, 403–5; 1970 crisis, 299; and Moscow Treaty, 332–3; 1970 Warsaw Treaty (with W. Germany), 345, 349, 355, 358, 360, 398–415; WB visits, 398–9; effects of War on, 398; emigration and resettlement, 404–5, 414; compensation claims, 410–12; leadership changes, 413–14
Polk, James, 72, 91
Pompidou, Georges, style, 115, 253; attends de Gaulle-WB consultations, 135; surrenders premiership over 1968 riots, 136, 203–4; and British EEC membership, 158, 237, 245, 249, 253–4, 256; on Soviet fears, 217–18; and EEC expansion, 245–6, 250, 258; and Heath, 249; WB's relations with, 252–3, 264, 274, 442; and de Gaulle, 253; and EEC policy, 254–6, 258, 264; and floating Deutschmark, 256; meets Brezhnev, 257, 263, 355, 362; and US monetary policy, 257, 260, 273; on defence policy, 259, 263, 271–2; on relations with USA, 259–61, 272–3, 304; supports Ostpolitik, 261–2; and USSR, 263–4, 274; opposes EEC direct elections, 267; on Franco-W. German relations, 268–70; on economic planning, 272; on Middle East, 273, 461; on monetary union, 273; death, 274, 444, 449; Nixon on, 286, 292; meetings with Nixon, 296–8, 311, 314; and Brezhnev's détente, 336; and Oreanda meeting, 346; and Berlin Quadripartite Agreement, 392; and China, 423–4; visits Peking, 423; on WB's 1972 election success, 443; and WB's helicopter escape, 461; on Yom Kippur war, 463; on Mediterranean, 465; on arms supply to Libya, 465; on oil crisis, 466, 468; and German-

Israeli relations, 469
Portugal, 178, 487–92, 502
Potsdam Agreement, 106, 401
Prague, 416, 418; see also Czechoslovakia
Price, Don, 85

Quidde, Ludwig, 431

Rabin, Itzhak, 458, 464
Rapacki, Adam, 182, 187
Rathenau, Walther, 151
Red Army, 345
Reuter, Ernst, 28, 41, 61, 64, 99, 182, 185, 486
Reuther, Victor, 81
Reuther, Walther, 75, 81
Reza Pahlavi, Mohammed, Shah of Iran, 201, 307, 464
Riad, Mahmoud, 483
Ritzel, Gerhard, 431
Robespierre, F. Maximilien J. I., 240
Rochet, Waldeck Emile, 213
Rockefeller, Nelson, 84
Rogers, William P., 237, 284, 288, 293, 302, 307, 392, 464
Roosevelt, Franklin D., 33, 82, 93, 137, 345
Rosenberg, Ludwig, 72
Rostropovich, Mstislav, 108–9
Ruby, Jack, 92
Rumania, trade missions in, 111; Schröder and, 126; de Gaulle and, 127, 136; diplomatic relations with, 170, 173–5; criticized by E. Europeans, 172; independent line, 173–4; WB visits, 174; student protests in, 207; and Czech revolt, 210–11, 213, 217, 219; and Greek co-operation, 486
Rush, Kenneth, 284, 297, 302, 305, 390
Rusk, Dean, and German unity, 36; and Berlin referendum, 39; meets Gromyko, 67; honorary Harvard degree, 75; WB meets, 82–4, 284; on Berlin access routes, 155; and Ostpolitik, 169; on nuclear non-

Rusk, Dean [*cont'd*]
proliferation, 188; and Vietnam
war, 221
Russia *see* Union of Soviet Socialist
Republics

Sadat, Anwar el, Tito and, 178, 469–
70; and Middle East settlement,
454, 469, 479–81; and Yom
Kippur war, 463–4; on Rabin,
464; on Palestinians, 470; and
relations with W. Germany, 472;
relations with Kissinger, 477,
481–2; WB meets, 478–9, 482–3;
difficulties with USSR, 481–2
Sahm, Ulrich, 297, 370, 372
Saint Andrews University, 108–9
Salinger, Pierre, 72–3
Salomon, Ernst von, 48
Saudi Arabia, 463, 480, 482
Sauvagnargues, Jean, 390
Scheel, Walter, and FDP, 43–5; and
1969 coalition, 224, 227–8; at 1969
EEC summit, 245; in Paris, 268;
talks in USA, 284, 297, 305; on
Japan, 305; negotiations for
Moscow Treaty, 323–5, 332, 339;
and Berlin settlement, 339–40,
416; visits China, 365, 420; clash
with Duckwitz in Poland, 402; in
Warsaw talks, 403; in Czech
negotiations, 416; attends UN
accession, 425; and WB's Nobel
Prize, 430; in 1972 no-confidence
debate, 434–5; and 1972 elections,
437; as Presidential candidate, 449–
50; on Middle East, 467
Schiebold, Werner, 95
Schiller, Karl, 135, 256–7, 435, 438
Schlesinger, Arthur M., Jr, 16, 25,
72, 75, 87, 278
Schmid, Carlo, 149
Schmidt, Helmut, visits Moscow,
107, 196; forgoes post in Grand
Coalition, 148; on non-proliferation, 196; talks in USA, 284; in US
arms negotiations, 294; at Brezhnev dinner, 364; parliamentary

speeches, 429; in 1972 political
crisis, 435; appointed Minister of
Economic Affairs & Finance, 439;
on oil crisis, 468
Schröder, Gerhard, and MLF, 68;
and US-Soviet negotiations, 88;
and WB's meeting with Abrassimov, 105; and nuclear test-ban
treaty, 111; and de Gaulle's Euro-
pean proposals, 124; contacts with
Rumania, 126; in Grand Coalition,
146; and border army manoeuvres,
209; as 1969 Presidential candidate,
226–7; on relations with USSR,
355; in 1972 political crisis, 435
Schultz, George, 294
Schumacher, Kurt, 52–4, 64
Schuman, Robert, 51, 244
Schumann, Maurice, 264, 392
Schüssler, Gerhard, 372
Schütz, Klaus, 47, 56, 91–2, 109, 172,
226, 391
Scowcroft, Brent, 314
Segre, Sergio, 221
Semyonov, Vladimir S., 28, 190
Senghor, Leopold, 204, 464
Servan-Schreiber, Jean-Jacques, 122
Shafei, Hussain al, 478
Shelest, Pyotr, 214
Shriver, Sargent, 81
Sidky, Aziz, 440
Šik, Ota, 208
Silesian Association, 433
Smirnov, Andrei A., 26, 66
Smrkovsky, Josef, 211, 213–14
Soares, Mario, 204, 449, 488, 490,
492
Sochi (Black Sea), 18
Social Democratic Party (SPD), in
1961 election, 42, 46–7; policies,
46–7; Adenauer's opposition to,
52–3; strength, 52, 110; and
national reunification, 53–4; and
EEC, 54; supports European
unity, 64; Soviet attitude to, 106–7;
proposed Russian Communist
Party talks with, 109; 1964 Con-
ference (Karlsruhe), 110–11, 140;

Social Democratic Party [*cont'd*]
1966 Conference (Dortmund), 111, 142, 182, 321; and Franco-German treaty, 121; WB as chairman of, 138–9, 142, 146, 165, 229, 328, 450; Berlin election successes, 139; in 1965 elections, 141–2, 144; in Grand Coalition, 145–8; Ulbricht's hostility to, 170; Nuremberg Conference (1968), 183, 186, 201, 210, 321; and relations with E. Germany, 185–6; and student protest, 205–6; Bad Godesberg Congress (1969), 206; and Czech crisis, 216; and Italian Communist Party, 220–1; 1969 election success and government, 223–4, 226, 228–9, 232; Saarbrücken Conference (1970), 234, 380; Hanover Conference (1973), 271, 448; in 1972 political crisis, 433–9; 1972 Conference (Dortmund), 442; 1972 election success, 442–3, 445; 1974 Hamburg election defeat, 448; internal difficulties, 449; attacks Portugal, 490; 1975 Conference (Mannheim), 493; as governing party, 494
Socialist Unity Party (SED), on closure of E. Berlin, 16; amalgamated with Communist Party, 17; and Herrnstadt Group, 28; internal dissent, 29; and pass agreements, 110; proposes public debate with SPD, 112–13; in W. Berlin elections, 140; and Czechoslovakia, 184; unpopularity, 184; 7th Conference (1967), 185; denounces social democratism, 219; attacks WB, 342; Honecker appointed First Secretary, 393; and nationhood, 396; and Portugal, 491
Sohlman, Ragnar, 431
Sorensen, Theodore C., 72, 89
Spaak, Paul Henri, 155
Spain, 125, 164, 205, 287, 487, 492–3, 502
Spiegel, Der, 58–9

Spínola, Antonio de, 488–9
Spreti, Karl, Count von, 284
Staden, Berndt von, 314
Stalin, Josef V., 28–9, 137, 345
Steinhoff, Johannes, 84
Stevenson, Adlai, 75, 82
Stewart, Michael, 237
Stikker, Dirk, 155
Stoph, Willi, 185, 210, 213, 369–87, 393
Strategic Arms Limitation Talks (SALT), 156, 263–4, 282, 286, 293, 302, 306, 309, 313
Strauss, Franz Josef, ambitions for Chancellorship, 42; and coalition, 45; 1961 attack on WB, 48; dismissed over *Spiegel* affair, 58–9; conservatism, 63; on Grand Coalition, 148; and Britain's EEC membership, 159; attacks European Security Conference, 187; on SPD and Italian CP, 220; meets Brezhnev, 363; claims friendship with Mao, 421; in 1972 political crisis, 435; opposes E. European treaties, 436
Stresemann, Gustav, 151–2, 190, 202, 431
Stroheim, Erich von, 406
Strougal, Lubomir, 416, 418–19
Stücklen, Richard, 435
Sudan, 472, 480
Suharto, T. N. J., 464
Suhr, Otto, 49
Sukarno, Ahmed, 117
Suslov, M. A., 324
Svoboda, Ludvik, 213–14, 419
Sweden, 104–5, 164, 205
Switzerland, 164
Syria, 463, 470–2, 479–80

Taiwan, 305–6, 422
Tanaka, Kakvei, 315, 363, 464
Taylor, Maxwell D., 19, 86, 125
Tepavač, Mirko, 178
Thälmann, Ernst, 378
Thomas, Norman, 320
Thompson, Llewellyn E., 33

Tillmanns, Robert, 56
Tito, Josip Broz, independence, 30,
217, 487; Adenauer on, 56; WB's
talks with, 176–80, 469–71, 486–7;
authority, 178; on Middle East,
178, 453, 459, 467, 469–71; and
Czech crisis, 212, 214; on invasion
of Czechoslovakia, 216; on China,
423; on WB's 1972 election
success, 443
Togliatti, Palmiro, 220
Truman, Harry S., 23, 162, 308
Tsarapkin, Semyon K., 108, 171–2,
190, 194, 325, 337
Tunisia, 453, 472
Turkey, 485–6

U-2 incident (1960), 100
U Thant, 75
Ukraine, 215
Ulbricht, Walter, denies intention to
build Wall, 18; and effect of Wall,
20, 24; dismissal calls, 29; and
Berlin access routes, 39; proposes
exchange of views, 112; and
Ostpolitik, 170; and Tsarapkin,
171; reputation, 184; intransigence,
185; and Czech crisis, 210, 213–14,
216; fear of contacts, 218; and
Bauer, 220; attacks Grand Coalition, 221; isolated stand, 221; and
Federal Assembly in Berlin, 226;
replaced, 299, 393; transmits draft
treaty to W. Germany, 368–9; and
Warsaw Treaty, 410; visits Egypt,
478
Union of Soviet Socialist Republics
(USSR), and E. German control of
Berlin, 14, 16, 25–6; threatens
separate E. German peace treaty,
19–23; authority in E. Berlin,
21–2; and Berlin status, 22, 27, 32;
peace conference proposal, 22;
and Berlin Wall, 24–5, 31–2, 40;
and German reunification, 28–9,
41, 106, 133; European policy, 30;
presence in E. Berlin, 35; W.
German relations with, 44, 133–4,

166, 179, 192–5, 237, 299, 325–7,
338–9, 344, 347, 359, 365; and
Cuba, 68, 86, 89–90; and peaceful
coexistence, 85–6; proposed German settlement, 100, 102; and
China, 108, 131, 174, 179, 194,
295, 354, 367, 423; de Gaulle on,
127, 130–4; nuclear weapons, 156;
and Ostpolitik, 166–72, 261–2; and
détente, 167–8; and renunciation
of force, 172–3, 345, 495; obstructs
Berlin traffic, 186; and European
Security Conference, 187; and
MBFR, 188, 193, 352, 362; and
nuclear non-proliferation treaty,
188, 193, 196; and Czech reforms,
210, 213, 215, 218–19; intervention
in Czechoslovakia, 214–16, 299;
and world communism, 222; protests at Federal Assembly in
Berlin, 225–6; and partition of
Europe, 244; Pompidou on relations with, 261; and reduction of
forces, 259, 289, 302–4; and
control of E. Europe, 262; and
central Europe neutralization, 270;
and Kissinger-Nixon policy, 278–
9, 297–301, 305; on separate W.
Berlin, 292; and E. Germany, 299;
foreign aid, 300; and EEC, 305,
344, 361; supports N. Vietnam,
306, 319, 354; in Middle East,
307, 316, 467, 471, 477, 479; and
1973 war alarm, 316; 1970 Moscow
Treaty with W. Germany, 323,
328–33, 337–40, 344–5, 349–51,
355–7, 363, 387–9, 392, 415; WB
visits, 323, 328–9, 345–53, 364–5,
414; Party role in, 336; war losses,
337; Brezhnev on resources and
technical co-operation, 350, 360–1,
364; W. German trade with, 360;
relations with Britain, 361; relations with France, 362; relations
with USA, 362–3, 387; supports
inter-German treaty, 370–1, 385,
394; and Berlin Quadripartite
Agreement, 388, 392; 1975 E.

Union of Soviet Socialist Republics [*cont'd*]
German Treaty, 396; and Yom Kippur war, 463; and Israel, 466, 470; and Egypt, 469–71, 480, 482; and Portugal, 490–1; as imperial power, 495; outlook for, 498

United Nations (UN), and Berlin problem, 31, 37, 85, 101; proposed move to Berlin, 88; and nuclear non-proliferation, 188, 196; 'enemy state articles', 190, 193–4, 333; W. German collaboration with, 236; German accession to, 301, 358, 360, 376–8, 383, 386, 396, 410, 415, 424–5; WB addresses, 313, 425–6; China and, 355, 422; Taiwan excluded, 422; and Israel, 450, 456, 458–9, 467, 469, 471; and Yom Kippur war, 463–4; and Palestinians, 470; and oil crisis, 475; and Middle East settlement, 476

United Nations Economic Commission for Europe, 384

United Nations Educational, Scientific and Cultural Organization (UNESCO), 202, 471

United Nations International Children's Emergency Fund (UNICEF), 422, 500

United States of America, and Berlin Wall crisis, 20, 31–2; presence in Berlin, 21–2; European policy, 29, 30, 76–7, 259–61, 272–3, 275; WB's visits to, 36, 39, 75, 80–6, 88, 91, 122, 152, 155, 157, 259, 284, 288, 290, 295, 297, 308, 310, 313, 317, 320–1, 443; and Cuba crisis, 38, 68, 86, 89–90; relations with W. Germany, 39, 75, 80, 121–4, 144, 149, 154, 157, 236–7, 260, 283, 285, 287–8, 298, 315; and access to Berlin, 67; in SE Asia, 74, 83, 167–8, 178, 200, 279, 283, 306, 316–22; and German unification, 79; de Gaulle and, 124–5,

132; defence policy, 125, 272, 496; and China, 127, 279, 306–7; and NATO, 156, 260; and détente, 167–8, 495; and nuclear non-proliferation treaty, 188; protest movements in, 200, 281; monetary policy, 257, 260, 273, 281, 283, 289, 294, 296–7; and reduction of forces, 259–60, 263, 270–1, 286, 289, 352; and British EEC entry, 259, 286; and French misgivings, 259–61, 271; and EEC, 259–61, 265–6, 275–6, 283, 286, 288–305, 314–15; military supplies to W. Germany, 294; and USSR, 299–300, 362–3, 387; forces in Europe, 309–10, 496; isolationism, 315; and 1973 war alert, 316, 463; and CSCE, 352, 362; and inter-German treaty, 385; at Helsinki European conference, 427; supplies Israel in Yom Kippur war, 462–3; influence on Israel, 466–9, 471; and energy crisis, 467–8, 474–5; and Middle East, 471, 476; and N. Africa, 480; and Portugal, 490–1; integration with Europe, 496; outlook for, 496, 498

Victoria, Queen of Great Britain, 250
Vienna, 20–1, 23
Vietnam, Rusk's attitude to, 83; US involvement in, 167–8, 283, 318–22; China and, 177, 306, 319; student protests over, 200–1, 281, 320; communism in, 222; end of war in, 279, 282, 311, 316–18; Nixon and, 279, 287, 295, 306, 311, 322; USSR supports north, 306, 319, 354
Vogel, Hans Jochen, 440
Voll, Hans, 372

Wagner, Robert F., Jr, 84
Waldheim, Kurt, 416
Warren, Earl, 92, 320
Warsaw, 413; *see also* Poland
Wechmar, Rüdiger von, 473

Wehner, Herbert, favours all-party government, 44; on Adenauer, 61; and SED debate, 113; and Grand Coalition, 145; and relations with E. Germany, 185; mishandled by protesters, 201; on Berlin as Federal Assembly venue, 226; in 1972 political crisis, 435; and Scheel's Presidential candidacy, 450

Weichert, Jürgen, 372

West Germany (German Federal Republic; FDR), [*for relations and treaties with other countries see under their names*] 1961 election, 13, 40, 42, 46–7; granted access to E. Germany, 14–15; separate Russian treaty threatened, 19–23; and W. Berlin, 21; flights to, from East, 24; Basic Law, 42, 184, 233, 332, 356, 434, 436–7; government of, 44; and European unity, 53, 76–7; strength, 59–60; membership of EEC, 68, 259; international relations, 76–7, 123–4; US presence in, 77; and Berlin pass agreements, 97; and Berlin Wall, 98; and Russia's proposed Berlin settlement, 101; bans KPD, 107; and E. Europe, 111, 126, 133, 166–7, 237–8, 327; 1965 elections, 124, 141–2, 144; and nuclear defence, 127; 1955 'general treaty', 128; French troops in, 128–9, 271; Grand Coalition, 129, 135, 143–50, 166–7, 170, 172, 188, 206, 224; 1966 recession, 143–4; *Ostpolitik*, 166–97, 295–6; renunciation-of-force declarations, 172; war reparations, 176–7, 180–1; and European Security Conference, 188; and arms control, 188–9, 193; 1969 elections, 194, 223–4; student protest movement in, 200–1, 204–6; and 1968 Czech crisis, 210, 212, 215–16; 1969 government, 226–38; social reforms and changes, 232–3, 439–40; DM revalued, 237, 297,

446; and EEC balance, 246; establishes European reserve fund, 247; DM floated, 256, 290, 294, 296; and EEC regional fund, 266; 1972 elections, 267–8, 429, 433, 436–7, 442–3; and German future, 269–70; defence forces, 270–1, 286; military purchases in USA, 294; trade with E. Europe, 300; accession to UN, 301, 358, 360, 376–7, 383, 386, 396, 410, 415, 424–5; and Middle East, 316, 451–9; Brezhnev overestimates, 343; trade with USSR, 360, 363–4; E. German representative mission established, 395; restitution laws, 411–12; 1972 Landtag elections, 433; 1972 no-confidence debate, 433–7; and international terrorism, 439–41; economic fortunes, 445–9; and oil crisis, 465–8, 474–5; currency reserves, 477; migrant workers in, 486

Western European Union, 39, 159, 245, 247, 497

Weyer, Willi, 228

Wilhelm I, German Emperor, 61

Wilhelm II, German Emperor, 250

Wilson, Harold, Kennedy sees as PM, 74; de Gaulle on EEC application, 134; and EEC entry, 159, 247–8; visits Berlin, 161; WB's relations with, 162–3, 366; election fortunes, 248; 1973 meeting with Golda Meir, 462; on N. Sea oil, 466; and 1975 socialist leaders' meeting, 492

Winiewicz, Josef, 402

Winzer, Otto, 370, 372, 378

Woodrow Wilson International Centre, 290

World Health Organization, 186

Yadin, Yigael, 460

Yalta Agreement, 131

Yemen, 453

Yugoslavia, position, 30; diplomatic relations with E. Germany, 56;

Yugoslavia [*cont'd*]
  W. Germany resumes relationships with, 170, 175; WB visits, 175–6; trade, 176; immigrant workers from, 176–7, 486; war compensations, 176–7, 180; party discipline, 178; Tito on, 179; persecuted writers in, 179; student protests in, 207; and Czech crisis, 209, 219; independence, 218, 487; communism in, 222; help for, 300; China and, 423; and Israel, 471; prospects, 484, 487; and Greek cooperation, 486; internal politics, 487

Zhivkov, 210

DATE DUE

FEB 2 1 1988

MAR 0 2 1988

APR 1 5 1988

HIGHSMITH 45-102

PRINTED IN U.S.A.